1 00 55

THE LEGAL STATUS OF THE TENANT FARMER IN THE SOUTHEAST

THE LEGAL STATUS
OF THE TENANT FARMER
IN THE SOUTHEAST

by

Charles S. Mangum, Jr.

Chapel Hill

THE UNIVERSITY OF NORTH CAROLINA PRESS

Printed in the United States of America

THE WILLIAM BYRD PRESS, INC.

Richmond, Virginia

This book is dedicated to my dearest Mother

Preface

WITH the completion of *The Legal Status of the Negro*, the next step in correlating the legal and social fields seemed to be the examination of farm tenancy law. This field promised excellent opportunity for further study along regional lines. It was realized at an early stage of the investigation into farm tenancy law that geographical limits must be set in respect to a study of this nature. The eleven states of the Southeast were chosen because they offered a region which was homogeneous in farming methods and social mores. Furthermore, the money crops of cotton and tobacco were very important in the agricultural economy of this section of the nation. The inclusion of Texas and Oklahoma would have meant that this treatise would have reached cumbersome proportions, both from the standpoint of material and geographical scope. Furthermore, mechanical implements and methods have reached the Southwest in greater abundance than in the earlier settled regions to the East.

In this study a thorough analysis of the statutes and appellate court decisions has been attempted with a view to obtaining a treatise which would be useful to lawyers, sociologists, agrarian economists, and agriculturists alike. An effort has been made to point up the phases of tenancy law which are peculiarly adapted to the problems to be met by the people of the rural areas of the states of the Southeast. The unsuitability of certain statutes and decisions to rural agricultural communities has been pointed out, and it is shown that the development of tenancy law from the time of the manorial system has favored the landowner at the expense of the tenant. An attempt has been made to deal fairly with the landlord, tenant or cropper, and the third persons who deal with them or are brought into controversies concerning them. It is hoped that the suggestions made with respect to changes in the statutes will be considered by state legislators with a view to the clarification and modernization of the law with respect to this very important segment of our population in the South.

Of inestimable help in the preparation of this treatise has been the interest and aid of the law and sociology faculties of the University of North Carolina, especially the work of Professors Maurice T. Van Hecke and Rupert B. Vance. The staff members of both the University of North Carolina Press and the University of North Carolina Law Library have been very helpful in making this volume possible. The work of Joel Denton, student assistant, and the advisory help of Arthur Raper and George Mitchell of the Southern Regional Council have facilitated the preparation and publication of the book. Much encouragement and aid of various kinds came from former President Frank P. Graham, Chancellor Robert B. House, Controller William D. Carmichael Jr., Claude E. Teague, J. Maryon Saunders, George M. Stephens, the late J. Frazier Glenn Jr., and numerous students of the law school.

CHARLES S. MANGUM JR.

Chapel Hill, N. C.
November, 1951

Contents

THE LEGAL STATUS OF THE TENANT FARMER
IN THE SOUTHEAST

Statement of the Farm Tenancy Problem and
Its Legal and Social Implications

W HILE the War Between the States and the accompanying emancipation of the slaves did not initiate the problem of farm tenancy in the South, they were responsible for the great growth of this type of land tenure in the years which followed. The landowners, who were land poor, had no way of cultivating the big plantations formerly tended by the Negroes. The freedmen, lured to the towns by their first taste of freedom and anxious to leave the scenes of their former enslavement, rushed in to the population centers and at first could not be persuaded to return to the land. "Scalawags" and "carpetbaggers," full of promises of "forty acres and a mule," made their appearance to get what they could from the distressing situation in which the landowners found themselves. Out of this set of circumstances came the so-called Black Codes, whose apprentice and vagrancy provisions forced the Negroes into circumstances little better than those from which they had just been released. These Black Codes, enacted by the white legislators who had just been deprived of their slaves, were played up in the Northern press. They were among the chief reasons why the radical element in Congress, led by Thaddeus Stevens and Charles Sumner, was able to obtain a majority of the votes and enact the Thirteenth, Fourteenth, and Fifteenth Amendments and the laws which implemented and carried out the purposes behind these fundamental changes in the Constitution.

When things finally began to become stabilized, it was realized by the more thoughtful among the state legislators that some system would have to be worked out to replace the slave economy which had been upset by the war and its aftermath. It was decided that it was not necessary to develop any special legislation with respect to the freedmen and other landless men, but that the situation could best be handled by a tenancy agreement between the landowner and those who were desirous of tilling the land, most of whom could not do anything else at all well. Uneducated and unaccustomed to providing a living for themselves, the Negroes were in need of the supervision which could be supplied only by the planters and by their former overseers, many of whom had turned "scalawag." Wage labor was tried for a short while, but it was found that the Negroes were inexperienced and unreliable wage hands. Many of them, suddenly relieved of the yoke of slavery, did not comprehend their responsibilities and were unequal to accepting the burden of making a living for themselves and for their women and children. Often they would go into the towns and stay for a week or more, leaving the crop to take care of itself. This failure of wage labor led directly to the establishment of the sharecropping system in the South.[1]

Of course the war had caused much confusion and dislocation in the cotton industry, the mainstay of prewar economy. The plantations and small farms were run down and extremely dilapidated. The landowners had no capital or credit with which to finance rehabilitation or improvements. Many of them were in such a terrible financial plight that they were unable to pay the high taxes assessed against them by the Reconstruction state governments. In many cases the land was forfeited and sold for a song to the highest bidder. Yet some of the planters held on to the land at the sacrifice of everything else they owned, feeling that it was the only solid thing in the chaotic situation which confronted them. Sentimentality overrode reason in many decisions to keep the plantation and attempts to make it a going concern. Cotton prices were high at the time, and cotton-raising seemed to offer the best opportunity to recoup the family fortune. There were a few who realized that the South could never take its proper place in the national scene without a more balanced economy, but their efforts were too scattered to have any effect on the majority of the planters. Agriculture, especially the growing and marketing of cotton, was all they knew. They had families who had been wealthy and were now poor, and one of the most difficult problems to face is an enforced reduction in the living standards of persons who have been wealthy for many years. They did not foresee the inevitable, the low price of cotton in relation to the prices of most of the commodities which were necessary in its production, such as capital, tools, fertilizer, and other supplies of various kinds. The only commodity which was plentiful was labor. Thus the prime

1. Zeichner, *The Legal Status of the Agricultural Laborer in the South,* 55 Pol. Sci. Q. 412, 419-20 (1940).

factor for the production of a cash crop like cotton was present in abundance. However, the difficult problem was to work out some method by which the laborers could be recompensed without the payment of wages in money, which was very scarce and hard to obtain. Therefore the device of payment for labor with a share of the crop was invoked and developed with various and diverse ramifications. There were few colored tenants who could pay cash rent at this time, and hence the sharecropping system was given its first great impetus.

FINANCE AND SUPPLY CREDIT TERMS

The large plantations of the prewar era resumed operations with free labor paid with a share of the crop, after deducting from the tenant's share the advances made by the landlord for the purpose of making the crop and for sustaining the tenant while the crop was being raised. The landlord would either supply the tenant or cropper from the plantation commissary or arrange for a certain amount of credit to be put at his disposal at the store of a supply merchant. This came to be known as "furnishing." The proprietors of smaller farms adopted the same method on a more limited scale, and this has come down to us in the present, although the plantation supply store is not used so much as it was in former times. Every farming community in the Southeastern states has its neighborhood supply store or is located within easy reach of a town where many of these stores are situated. The merchants are dependent upon the tenants for a large proportion of their business and cater to their preferences in buying goods from the wholesale dealers. Some states give the merchants an agricultural lien on the crop to secure these advances to the tenants. In certain instances the credit is extended to the landlord primarily, in others to the tenant with the landlord as surety, and in still others on the waiver of the landlord's lien for rent and/or supplies. There are all kinds of intermediate arrangements, many of them complicated.

The credit charges of the finance and supply business are very high. It is claimed that these charges must be high because the percentage of loss is great. While there is some truth in this, it is believed that there is a tendency for the merchant to exaggerate his losses and to make unjustifiable interest and carrying charges on that basis. High credit charges for both landlord and tenant increase the risk of an already precarious occupation. It has been said that this system is "a game played with borrowed stakes." [2] The loans made by the Farm Security Administration, its predecessors, and kindred agencies, did something to alleviate this condition, but they only scratched the surface of this great problem of agricultural finance. It is very easy to put the blame for the farming situation in the South upon the high cost of credit and the cupidity of the supply merchant, but, while these things undoubtedly are contributing factors, they cannot be blamed for everything. There are many other circumstances which must be taken into consideration in weighing the causes of Southern agricultural debilitation.

LACK OF CROP DIVERSIFICATION

One of these circumstances is the cash crop system, with its attendant evils and uncertainties. The emphasis is placed upon money crops like cotton, tobacco, and sugar cane, to the detriment of all concerned, especially the tenant. In the past the landlords made practically no effort to persuade the tenants to raise their own food and other articles which could be produced with little additional expense and labor. The average tenant did not have the initiative to plant food and feed crops and to adopt new agricultural methods. Vegetable gardens were few and not scientifically cultivated, and there were not usually many fruit trees on rented land. The farmers knew very little about improved methods of agriculture, such as crop diversification and rotation. When cotton or tobacco production is at its highest peak, prices are usually at a minimum. Therefore, the more the farmer grows, the less he gets per unit raised. If he has but one crop from which to maintain a decent livelihood and the price of the commodity is depressed, it is obvious that he will be at a great disadvantage. It would be profitable for him to produce several different crops unless all of the crops thus raised were selling at low prices, a thing less likely to occur with a variety of farm products.

The diversification of crops, however, is not as great a panacea as is thought by some agronomists, for it is tied in with the lack of scientific methods of farming generally. Improved methods must be used in all respects, and diversification is only one of many devices which have been urged for the betterment of farming conditions. There is a tendency for the prices of all farm products to rise and fall together, and a low price for one commodity often plays havoc with

2. T. J. Woofter, Jr., *Landlord and Tenant on the Cotton Plantation,* p. 49 (1936).

the price of another. Yet there is a great advantage to be gained in not concentrating on one crop alone. There might be a special demand for one of the many crops raised, and this would prove very advantageous to the farmer. The problem is to select the crop which is going to have the best price and to gauge correctly the physical and economic factors involved in the determination of that price. In the South, the average tenant farmer is not capable of making a decision of this kind, and hence the crop chosen is often not the right one. Furthermore, it is difficult to persuade the farmers, landlord and tenant, that it is to their interest to diversify the crops. The Southern farmer has raised cash crops like cotton, sugar, and tobacco for years and knows how to care for them. He resents any suggestion that the planting of cash crops alone is not sound agricultural practice. Some way must be found to give him a better understanding of the value of a well-balanced agriculture.

The farmer who has a crop of cotton or tobacco to sell is constantly troubled by the vicissitudes and vagaries of an unpredictable market. High prices in one year bring on a bumper crop, and this depresses prices for the succeeding year. The Southern farmer seems to be unable to grasp this simple demonstration of one of the most fundamental of economic laws. He is always led astray by the fancy that the high prices for the commodity will continue this time and that he will "make a killing." Although he knows that it has never occurred before, he is tempted by the thought that this time it is going to happen. This failure to observe and consider the workings of an economic law is psychological and hence difficult to overcome by the usual methods of enlightenment. Moreover, there are also the efforts of buyers and manufacturers to keep a good supply of the staple crops on hand and in this way to keep the prices from rising to a higher level. These efforts may to a certain extent be shortsighted on the part of the manufacturers, in that they fail to take into consideration the market for their own products which might be created by higher prices for farm products. It is unlikely, however, that such a problematical gain would deter the manufacturers from efforts to keep the prices down, even though they might be depressed below the cost of production and thus bring ruin to the growers.

CO-OPERATIVE UNIONS

The use of co-operatives for the marketing of crops is often opposed by buyers and manufacturers, who are interested in keeping the prices down. Some of these agencies fail because they do not have financial resources to withstand the opposition of the big interests. A new co-operative is often in too weak a position with its membership to get the full support it needs in order to win a battle against a powerful and resourceful antagonist. Farmers as a class are rugged individualists, and it is often difficult to keep the membership in line long enough for a thorough test of the efficacy of the co-operative device. Some members want to avoid the agreement when circumstances are such that an immediate gain is in prospect, leaving the co-operative organization in a terrible predicament. The farmer does not realize that, in so breaking his contract, he is often destroying the device by which the price of the commodity has been raised to the point where such a profit is possible. Co-operatives are, however, steadily increasing, to the substantial benefit of the farmers.

CROP LIENS FOR RENT AND SUPPLIES

It was realized at an early date that the landlord could easily be wronged by the failure of the tenant to live up to his obligations under the tenancy contract. The tenant could either mortgage or pledge the crop under various types of contracts and thus deprive the landlord of any means of redress. The personal responsibility of the tenant did the landlord no good, for the tenant was usually financially irresponsible. Oftentimes a tenant had very little property of any value whatsoever. In some states the landlord had the remedy of distress, the right to seize the goods of a tenant as a security for the payment of rent. This remedy, however, proved inadequate in that it allowed the tenant too much freedom in disposing of the property prior to the distress, so that the landlord was often left with nothing but an empty right. From this dilemma sprang the idea of giving the landlord a lien for rent and supplies on the crops raised on the rented premises.

While there are critics of the crop lien, it is noted that no workable and feasible substitute has been offered which fully protects the landlord from the machinations of unscrupulous tenants and others who would take advantage of the fact that the tenant has physical control of the crop and the land. It is probable that the abolition of this lien would be followed by a period of chaos such as the agricultural South has never known, at least since Reconstruction. Thus any reformer who wishes to abolish crop liens must devise some method by which a person who extends agricultural credit may be protected. The extent and incidence of the liens of the landlord, supply merchant, and farm laborer, the rights of purchasers from the tenant, and the claims of crop mortgagees and other creditors of both landlord and tenant make this subject the most controversial in the entire field of farm tenancy law.

REMEDIAL PROCEDURES

Both the landlord and the tenant have certain rights and privileges with respect to the leased premises and are permitted to bring separate actions for injuries to their respective interests. An act of trespass may constitute an injury to both and may be made the basis of separate and distinct tort actions. It is clear that the tenant has merely a particular estate carved out of the fee simple interest of the landowner.

Where the landlord wishes to evict a tenant who is holding over or has broken the lease contract, he has a simple remedy at hand. Though the form of action is different in various jurisdictions, the procedure conforms to a certain pattern in all the Southeastern states. Thus it makes little difference whether the proceeding to recover the possession of unlawfully withheld land is termed an action of unlawful detainer, summary ejectment, or just a plain possessory warrant.

LANGUAGE AND FORM OF LEASE

In the last hundred years, the real property law concerning the execution of lease contracts and the formalities needed to make them effective has been greatly liberalized. Lawyers and laymen alike are now confronted with fewer difficulties of a technical nature than those appearing under the earlier leases. The language of the lease has been simplified to a certain extent, and at present the average person, without technical legal knowledge, can usually understand the instrument he is executing. The requirement of the Statute of Frauds that certain leases must be in writing is helpful, in that long-term contracts are made more certain. Many controversies which would otherwise arise have been thereby avoided. The contract has been put down in black and white and cannot easily be varied by proof of prior or contemporaneous oral agreements. Deliberate efforts on the part of dishonest men to make false claims with respect to oral leases have thereby been reduced to a great extent, and the courts are no longer forced to depend upon the memories of the parties. There has not always been a nefarious motive behind every effort to escape the effect of some unprofitable transaction of this kind, but the memories of men have often been faulty and uncertain about business dealings which have taken place in the past.

For these reasons it has been proposed that all lease contracts be reduced to writing. Some persons object to a requirement of this kind and urge that farming operations are too uncertain to be carried on under a written agreement. It may be said that any long-term contract in any walk of life can be subject to the same objection. The Farm Security Administration has urged the adoption of model leasing agreements, but this agency has not been successful in getting the reform enacted into law in any one of the states in the Southeastern area.

BURDEN OF REPAIRS AND IMPROVEMENTS

The law of Louisiana in respect to farm tenancy bears the unmistakable influence of the Code Napoléon. Not only are the terminology and procedure in that former French possession different from those to be found in the other Southeastern states, but there are some phases of the problem, notably that concerning improvements, in which the substantive law is substantially different. Compensation may be obtained under the Civil Law for improvements made by a tenant.

The common law put the onus of repairing the leased premises on the lessee in the absence of special agreement. A somewhat similar situation existed in respect to improvements which were made by the tenant and were not exhausted at the termination of the lease contract. According to the common law rules such improvements, at least those which were not trade fixtures, became the property of the landlord at the termination of the lease. Of course it was possible to make a contract which would have avoided the effect of these rules in any given instance, but as a practical matter this was seldom done. In a large proportion of the cases the improvements had not even been thought of at the time of the execution of the contract and had been added as the need for them arose. This state of the law, when combined with the short-term lease, had a deleterious effect on farms run by tenants. A tenant would not repair a building or a fence when he did not know whether he was going

to be on that plantation the next year. He would make no permanent improvements on a farm when he did not know whether he
was going to be able to enjoy the profits from the investment. To a
large extent this state of affairs has continued down to the present
day.

It is contrary to human nature for a tenant to make improvements
when there is no reasonable certainty that he will receive the benefits, especially if he believes that they will redound to the advantage
of the landlord or a succeeding tenant. The landlord is protected in
case the tenant commits waste, and it seems only fair to give the
latter compensation where he has improved the property. Therefore
a change of the law in this respect is advocated by most of the students of the subject.

MISCELLANEOUS RIGHTS OF THE TENANT

The tenant is permitted to use the leased premises in any way
which is consistent with the rules of good husbandry, unless he
commits waste or is guilty of conduct which amounts to a nuisance.
He is entitled to a means of entrance to and exit from the premises
and to certain perquisites, such as water rights, the right to cut firewood, and other privileges.

At the termination of a lease contract the lessor is entitled to re-
enter and take over the premises. Where the date of the termination
is uncertain, a notice of some kind is usually required. These notices
are generally governed by statutory provisions which state the
time at which the notice of a termination is due in respect to various
types of tenancies, such as the tenancy from year to year and the
tenancy at will.

Certain statutes were enacted which made it a crime for an agricultural laborer or tenant, after leaving the employer or landlord
without his consent and before the contract was terminated, to
make another agreement with a third party without giving the latter
notice of the prior arrangement. Another type of statute made it a
criminal offense to enter into a farm labor or tenancy contract with
intent to defraud the landlord, and some of these acts added a provision which made the refusal of the laborer or tenant to perform the
contract presumptive or prima facie evidence of such an intention.
Out of these and kindred statutes arose questions of constitutional
law with respect to involuntary servitude and peonage.

RUNGS OF THE "AGRICULTURAL LADDER"

There is often a very thin line of distinction between the groups of farmers that make up the rungs of the "agricultural ladder," a term which is in common use and which denotes the successive steps which are usually to be taken in the climb toward the ownership of land in fee simple. The familiar steps in ascending this ladder are the following: farm laborer, sharecropper, share tenant, cash tenant, and owner. Of course there are numerous arrangements between landlord and cultivator which cannot be fitted into this picture, but these are the main classifications in the ascending scheme. There may be variations with respect to the main classifications, such as the ordinary contract for share-rent, where the tenant agrees to pay the landlord a fractional proportion of the crops, and "standing rent," where the tenant pays a specific amount of the crops, such as five hundred pounds of cotton, to the landlord as his share. During the last depression and the years of recovery it became increasingly difficult to ascend the agricultural ladder. Something must be done to make it less difficult for an industrious man to attain farm ownership within a reasonable time. This is one of the most important problems which faces a post-war America, and it throws out a challenge to our legislators and agricultural experts.

DISTINCTIONS BETWEEN TENANT AND CROPPER

The distinction between the relationships of landlord-tenant and landlord-cropper is also one which has caused a great amount of difficulty in the Southern courts. This matter is especially important since the tenant has title to the crops grown on the rented premises, whereas the cropper has no such property right. Sometimes it is difficult to ascertain from a given set of facts just what relationship there was an intent to create. Border line situations are continually arising, and the cases are not always reconcilable. If the landlord supplies the land only, the courts will in all probability rule that a tenancy relationship is created; if he supplies everything except the actual labor, this will constitute a cropper contract. Rarely does such a clearcut instance arise, however, for most of the cases are complicated by the fact that the landlord and tenant each supplies in whole or in part some of the other things which are needed for the effective use of the land, such as livestock, seed, fertilizer, tools, and farming machinery. Every case must be decided according to the intention of the parties as shown by the contract under consideration and by the facts surrounding its execution and performance.

WELFARE OF TENANTS AND CROPPERS

It has been found that the life of the tenant farmer or share-cropper in the Southeastern states is notoriously hard. His worldly possessions are few, and his diet is very inadequate. The families are usually large and number possibly eight or more. The children may prove to be a boon in later years, for they can help their father in his effort to raise bigger and better crops. In times of economic depression, however, the surplus population resulting from large families may back up on the farm and create a superabundant labor supply. The young people cannot make a decent living and are forced to continue residing with their parents, who are themselves that much more hard-pressed to make ends meet. The health of the tenant population deteriorates and morale declines.

The people are restless and desirous of a change of scene. Of course a change of landlord will do little good in most instances, and yet it is often difficult to persuade the depressed tenant that he cannot better his lot by getting a fresh start under another landlord. Sometimes the tenant has a real grievance, but in many cases his reason for moving is merely the desire to try anything that offers a reasonable opportunity for the betterment of his situation. There are also those instances in which the tenant moves in order to escape just debts which have accumulated against him, and he believes that, by removing from the neighborhood, he can escape paying them.

The tenant is also rather mobile in times of prosperity, but for a different reason. In this case he is the pursued and not the pursuer. The pull of other industries and occupations makes him sought after by all. There is a great deal of competition among the landlords, and the tenant can afford to wait and make up his mind concerning the offers he receives. In fact, the legislators have taken occasion to enact statutes making it a criminal offense for one landlord to entice a tenant away from the employment of another landlord.

Hence we see that, no matter whether the country is in a state of prosperity or depression, the tenant is continually changing his abode and moving around from farm to farm. This has a particularly bad effect with respect to the social, educational, and religious life of the tenant families, in that they do not stay in one place long enough to become integrated into the life of the communities in which they establish temporary homes. Of course there are a large number of tenant families who are satisfied to remain in the same place for years and settle down. Then there are those tenants who are too lazy or trifling to move and would rather eke out a bare existence on a poor piece of land than to take the trouble to find a more fertile spot. These families are usually either without hope or are afflicted with an apathy which is self-debasing. Illness and other misfortunes may force a tenant family to remain in the same community for years on a very meager income. Moreover, it may be that a tenant has become so attached to a worthy landlord that no one can persuade him to leave. Thus it is seen that there are forces which pull against one another in respect to the mobility of the Southern farm tenant.

As a general rule, the farm tenant is poorly housed, clothed, and fed. Oftentimes eight or ten persons, both male and female, live in a one- or two-room cabin without proper lighting and heating facilities. There are few screens, and sanitary conditions are often very bad. The furniture is rough, and there is very little of it. Of course there are some tenants who are adequately housed, but the average home is a poor thing to behold. The average tenant has only the poorest of clothing, for the money to buy more commodious apparel is not available. Overalls and untidy dresses are a common sight, and it is a rare thing for a tenant to boast a wardrobe of proper proportions. In good years the tenant may splurge and buy some cheap finery for his womenfolk and children or get himself a new suit, but ordinarily he cannot even afford these luxuries. The tenant's diet often lacks foods which are essential to his health. The traditional corn-bread, fatback, and molasses, although overemphasized in song and story, form a goodly portion of his fare. Pellagra and other dietary diseases are prevalent and create a very serious health problem. The alleged shiftlessness of Southern tenants, which is heard about from all sides, may be traceable to this lack of proper nutriment.

The dislocations among the tenants caused by the instability of tenure are a very serious matter. This is true from the social as well as from the economic viewpoint. Thus a child may be uprooted in the middle of a school term and forced to attend a strange school. Country churches are continually faced with the problems created by a changing membership. Moreover, successful organization for business and social enterprises is often hampered by the fact that the people are strangers to one another. Proper organization demands a thorough knowledge of the character and honesty of every member of the group.

The average white tenant is probably only a little better off than his colored brother. Of course the legal, economic, and social position of the Negro tenant is complicated by the race problem and its ramifications. This explains to a certain extent the tendency of some uninformed people to think of the Southern tenant farmer as a Negro. Another reason for this is that most of the tenants of song and story have been Negroes. Actually, a large percentage of them are white.

CONCLUSION

In general, it may be said that any effort to reform the tenancy laws should be addressed primarily to the state legislative bodies. The Federal government can do only certain things in this field of jurisprudence. Among the devices already tried by Congress have been the setting up of farm credit agencies and the Agricultural Adjustment Administration of the depression years. These efforts to benefit agriculture were brought to a fitting climax with the passage of the Bankhead-Jones Farm Tenancy Act of 1937.[3] Yet the major burden of carrying through any substantial reforms rests to a large extent on state legislators, who, if possible, must be made to see that certain revisions are necessary in order to remove this blot on the escutcheon of the New South.

3. U. S. Stat. at Large, Vol. 50, c. 517, p. 522 (1937).

II

Distinctions Between Tenancies, Cropping Contracts, and Other Relationships

A CONTRACT for the use of land by persons other than the owner or landlord is not always a tenancy within the legal meaning of that term. Laymen generally use the term "tenancy" rather loosely to include the cropping contract and other similar arrangements in respect to land used for agricultural purposes. The law concerning the distinctions and variations which have arisen in this field is somewhat confused, and there are numerous decisions which appear to be conflicting. There are, however, certain principles which seem to be followed throughout the cases, and these are the important things, no matter what may be the result of any particular controversy. Needless to say, divergencies from the expected result appear often. The types of contracts found are myriad and contain all kinds of provisions. Some of these provisions may be indicative of one relationship and some of another. When this is the case, the courts must decide the issue by an interpretation of the contract which makes the intention of the parties the controlling point in the scheme. Under such circumstances, prejudice, racial or otherwise, is likely to creep in and influence a jury's verdict or even the judgment of court officials. This does not mean, however, that such an attitude is universal among Southern court personnel. It is only that there are certain factors in the mores of the people which make prejudice a distinct threat to a just and fair administration of the law.

Much of the ambiguity arising in cases where the status is uncertain could be avoided if the tenancy and cropper contracts were put in writing. It is difficult to establish the terms of an oral contract. In fact the parties often make oral contracts without having a definite idea as to the kind of relationship created thereby. The parol evidence rule, a salutary rule in regard to most types of written agreements, may sometimes cause injustice in respect to written tenancy or cropping contracts by ruling out prior or contemporaneous oral agreements which the ignorant cultivator had overlooked at the time the instrument was reduced to writing or had thought it unnecessary to include. In theory, for the just application of the parol evidence rule, there should be two parties equal in intelligence. In practice, however, this is seldom the case, particularly in a great majority of the instances involving tenancy or cropping contracts. Nevertheless, there is a great deal to be said in favor of the rule, for it may protect a landlord, particularly one of the absentee variety, from the machinations of some dishonest tenant who is trying to take advantage of the fact that the members of the jury know him and are favorable to his cause.

What is the test to determine the distinction between a tenancy contract and an agreement creating a cropper relationship? What provisions of the contract and factors surrounding its execution are important in determining the relationship of the parties? The distinction between tenant and cropper has been succinctly stated in the Harrison case[1] from North Carolina: The tenant has an estate in the land for the term, and consequently he has a right of property in the crops. If the share of the produce which he is to deliver to the landlord is to be turned over to the latter as rent, it is the cultivator who divides off to the landlord the share due him, and until the division takes place the rights of property and possession in the whole are the cultivator's alone. The cropper, on the other hand, has no estate in the land; and although in a limited sense he has possession of the crops, it is only the possession of a servant and is in contemplation of law the possession of the landlord, who must divide off to the cropper his share after a settlement is reached.

In Alabama[2] and North Carolina[3] this distinction between tenant and cropper has been wiped away by statute. Previous to these changes in the law the courts of Alabama as well as that of North Carolina had recognized the distinction.[4]

Needless to say, the Harrison case[5] was decided with a view to the

1. Harrison & Son v. Ricks, 71 N. C. 7 (1874).

2. Ala. Code (1940) tit. 31, §23. See Jennings v. Walling, 250 Ala. 348, 34 So. (2d) 208 (1948).

3. N. C. Gen. Stat. (1943) §42-15.

4. See Ala. Code (1907) §§4742-43; Burgess v. Hyatt, 209 Ala. 472, 96 So. 222 (1923); Arrington v. State, 168 Ala. 143, 52 So. 928 (1910); Adams v. State, 159 Ala. 115, 48 So. 795 (1909); Courtney v. State, 10 Ala. App. 141, 65 So. 433 (1914); Neal v. Bellamy, 73 N. C. 384 (1875); Haywood v. Rogers, 73 N. C. 320 (1875); State v. Burwell, 63 N. C. 661 (1869); Denton v. Strickland, 48 N. C. 61 (1855).

5. Note 1, supra.

law as it was prior to the enactment of the North Carolina statute[6] which vested the possession of the crops in the landlord until all claims for rent and advances had been satisfied. It is clear that this act had the effect of abolishing the distinction between tenant and cropper in North Carolina.[7]

The history of the evolution of the Alabama law in respect to this matter is very interesting. Under the law as it was in the early years of the present century, a tenancy was set up if the cultivator supplied the labor and team and the landowner only the land, whereas the relationship was that of hirer and hireling if the landowner furnished both land and team and the cultivator only the labor.[8] Any contract in furtherance of which the parties raised crops by joint contributions of the means of farming seems to have created a sort of hybrid status called a tenancy in common, by which each party was given a lien on the crops for debts arising out of the joint venture.[9] Under this statute it was decided that where one party furnished the land and team and the other the labor, and in addition each party furnished one-half of the fertilizer, a tenancy in common was established and not a contract of hire.[10] In a somewhat similar case the court decided in favor of a tenancy in common, even though the agreement to share the expense of the fertilizer had not been made until after the entrance of the cultivator upon the land under the original contract.[11] However, in one situation it was held that a tenancy was established where the landowner had furnished the land and one-third of the fertilizer and the cultivator had supplied the labor, mules, farming implements, and the other two-thirds of the fertilizer, and had also agreed to deliver one-third of the corn crop as rent for the premises.[12] It was evidently felt that the tenancy in common should not be carried to absurd lengths, for every factor in the arrangement except the furnishing of a minor portion of the

6. N. C. Gen. Stat. (1943) §42-15.

7. Note (1942) 20 N. C. L. Rev. 216.

8. Ala. Code (1907) §§4742-43. For a tenancy, see Burgess v. Hyatt, 209 Ala. 472, 96 So. 222 (1923). For the hiring or cropper contract, see Arrington v. State, 168 Ala. 143, 52 So. 928 (1910); Adams v. State, 159 Ala. 115, 48 So. 795 (1909).

9. Ala. Code (1907) §§4792-93, later Ala. Code Ann. (Michie, 1928) §§8872-73, Ala. Code (1940) tit. 33, §§81-82.

10. Hendricks v. Clemmons, 147 Ala. 590, 41 So. 306 (1906).

11. Johnson v. McFry, 14 Ala. App. 170, 68 So. 716, 13 Ala. App. 619, 68 So. 718 (1915).

12. Kirkpatrick v. Harper, 119 Ala. 452, 24 So. 715 (1898).

fertilizer pointed clearly to an ordinary tenancy. Thus the fact that the owner had supplied something besides the land was not allowed to influence the decision unduly.

The exact limits of the various statutes were not known, and this led to efforts on the part of legislators to clear up the matter. Pursuant to these efforts the legislature in 1915 enacted an amendment to both the tenancy and contract of hire statutes stating that the relationships created under them should be the same whether or not the parties by contract, express or implied, had agreed to divide the expense of the fertilizer.[13] This left the tenancy in common applying to any case in which the joint contributions of the parties consisted of anything other than fertilizer. For example, there might be a situation in which the landowner furnished the farming machinery or tools and the cultivator the stock. The amended statutes seemed to have left the furnishing of the team as the important criterion for determining whether the cultivator would be considered a tenant or a mere laborer.

A few years later a case arose in which the landowner had furnished the teams as well as the land, and the cultivator refused to divide the crop or to recognize the landowner's title to it. According to the statutory rule this established the cultivator as a mere hireling. Although the laborer here was entitled to retain the produce until his lien was paid, he lost this right where, before a division, he assumed control over the crop to satisfy another debt against the will of the landowner. The landowner's title gave him the right to maintain the action of detinue to obtain possession of the crop.[14] The dissenting judge objected on the ground that the laborer's lien would thereby be so limited as to be of little practical value. Under the factual situation presented here it is doubtful if this criticism is justified.

In a later case the landowner was shown to have furnished the teams and the cultivator the labor, each supplying one-half of the fertilizer. The cultivator removed the crop without the landlord's consent. The court again decided in favor of a contract of hire, holding that the landowner, having the title, could maintain the action of detinue on the basis of his title.[15]

13. Ala. Gen. Acts 1915, Nos. 63, 89.
14. Crow v. Beck, 208 Ala. 444, 94 So. 580 (1922), clarifying a former opinion in 204 Ala. 295, 85 So. 489 (1920), and reviewing what is said in Williams v. Lay, 184 Ala. 54, 63 So. 466 (1913).
15. Stewart v. Young, 212 Ala. 426, 103 So. 44 (1925).

Such was the situation when the compilers of the 1923 Code took a hand in the matter. Without going before the legislature with respect to this specific subject, the Code Commission seems to have made a revolutionary change in farm tenancy and submitted this change along with the rest of the revision as a part of its work. In this way the change seems to have been approved without the usual opportunity for argument on the floor by the constitutionally authorized legislative body, a strange procedure to say the least.

The statute adopted[16] provides that where one party furnishes the land and the other the labor for farming operations, with stipulations for dividing the crops between them in certain proportions, the relationship of landlord and tenant will result, and the stated portion of the produce to which the landlord is entitled will be considered as rent. Furthermore, according to the express provisions of the statute, this is to be true whether the contract expressly or impliedly calls upon the landowner to furnish all or any part of the teams, feed, fertilizer, seed, or money for marketing expenses. It has been pointed out[17] that this statute does not specifically extend to instances in which joint labor is contributed, and hence it is suggested that there still may be room for the operation of the tenancy in common statute, which still remains on the books.[18] Moreover, since the Revision of 1923, the latter statute has been applied in a case involving an agreement to raise a potato crop, one party agreeing to furnish the seed potatoes and the other to procure the land, furnish the fertilizer, and advance the costs of cultivation, the advances to be paid out of the proceeds, and the remainder to be divided equally between the two.[19] It may also be added that as a general rule parties may be tenants in common with respect to crops without necessarily being tenants in common of the lands on which the produce was raised, it being perfectly possible for a landlord and tenant relationship to exist with respect to such lands.[20]

Since 1923 the cultivator has been held entitled to possession of the crop, subject to the landlord's lien for rent and advances.[21] It may be said that the revision has made the rights of the parties more

16. Ala. Code Ann. (Michie, 1928) §8807, now Ala. Code (1940) tit. 31, §23.
17. Stewart v. Young, 212 Ala. 426, 103 So. 44 (1925).
18. Ala. Code Ann. (1940) tit. 33, §§81-82.
19. Lufkin v. Daves, 220 Ala. 446, 125 So. 811 (1930).
20. 37 Am. Dec. 318; 16 R. C. L. 586.
21. Harris v. State, 25 Ala. App. 215, 143 So. 242 (1932); Heaton v. Slaten, 25 Ala. App. 81, 141 So. 267 (1932).

definite. The attorney and his client are no longer plagued by the former uncertainty with respect to the relationship created under any given crop-sharing contract. At present there is no cropper or employee relationship in this type of case in Alabama, and the possibility that a tenancy in common exists has been greatly reduced. All the evidence points to a decrease in the amount of litigation concerning crop-sharing agreements.

In its earlier form the Alabama statute concerning the hiring contract[22] contained a provision giving the employee a laborer's lien on the crops. While he had no exclusive possession of the lands or the crops, his possession was considered that of an agent for the purpose of the enterprise; and, since his laborer's lien had the same force and effect as the lien of the landlord, it carried no right of possession until his portion of the crops had been duly and rightfully received as wages in kind.[23]

In accordance with the former Alabama view, the Arkansas Court has held that a cropper relationship is established where the cultivator furnishes the labor alone.[24] There are numerous cases in which the Arkansas Court has ruled in favor of the relationship of cropper rather than that of tenant. This was the situation where one party had agreed to supply the land, tools, seed, and feed, and the other only the labor, which was to be done under the landowner's supervision.[25] There can be no doubt that a cropper relationship has been created where the contract specifically reserves title to the crop in the landlord until there has been a settlement of the cultivator's interest.[26]

In one instance it was shown that the plaintiff had contracted to cultivate the defendant's land and receive a part of the crop as compensation. According to the agreement the crop was to belong to the landlord until a division was made. The plaintiff occupied a house on the premises and had evidently been wrongfully discharged. The court decided that the plaintiff was a cropper and that he could maintain an action for damages to be measured by the value of the contract, the damages being entire and accruing on the day when the agreement was repudiated.[27]

22. Ala. Code (1907) §4743.
23. Stewart v. Young, 212 Ala. 426, 103 So. 44 (1925).
24. Hammock v. Creekmore, 48 Ark. 264, 3 S. W. 180 (1887).
25. Hardeman v. Arthurs, 144 Ark. 289, 222 S. W. 20 (1920).
26. Bourland v. McKnight, 79 Ark. 427, 96 S. W. 179 (1906).
27. Woodson v. McLaughlin, 150 Ark. 340, 234 S. W. 185 (1921).

Contracts in three other Arkansas cases were held to establish the cropper relationship. In an early case a landowner let a person have land to cultivate under an oral agreement. According to the contract the landowner was to furnish the land, teams, and farming equipment, and the crop was to belong to him. After the crop was raised the cultivator sold a portion of it to a third person. It was held that the cultivator was a laborer or cropper and had only a limited interest in the crop, amounting to an equitable right of division.[28] In another instance the landowner agreed to furnish a team and tools, and the crop was to be his property. He was to receive half of the crop and also enough of the cultivator's share to pay for the supplies which he had furnished, the remainder to be turned over to the cultivator upon the satisfaction of these debts. Here the cultivator was held to be a cropper.[29] Again, it was decided that a cropper relationship existed when a person cultivated lands under a contract by which the landowner agreed to furnish the lands, teams, and tools to make the crop, and the cultivator was to work the land and receive a specified portion of the produce.[30] All these cases show very clearly that in them the relationship was that of landlord and cropper.

On the other hand, there are Arkansas cases in which the court has decided that a tenancy existed. One such case was found where the landowner had agreed to furnish only the seed, electric power for irrigation, and an amount of money sufficient to cover reasonable expenditures, reserving a half-interest in the crop.[31] Again, a tenancy was said to exist where the parties agreed that the cultivator should furnish the labor necessary to make and gather the crops on the land in his possession; and that, when this was done, the crops should be divided into two equal portions. The court stated that in such instances the relationship would be determined upon a construction of the entire agreement, if in writing; or, if oral, from the language used by the parties and their actions in carrying out the various tasks of the farming project.[32] It was also held that a tenancy existed where the cultivator must furnish tools, team, and feed, and deliver one-half of the produce to the landowner.[33]

28. Hammock v. Creekmore, 48 Ark. 264, 3 S. W. 180 (1887).
29. Valentine v. Edwards, 112 Ark. 354, 166 S. W. 531 (1914).
30. Douglass v. Lamb, 157 Ark. 11, 247 S. W. 77 (1923).
31. Campbell v. Anderson, 189 Ark. 671, 74 S. W. (2d) 782 (1934).
32. Johnson v. Mantooth, 108 Ark. 36, 156 S. W. 448 (1913).
33. Barnhardt v. State, 169 Ark. 567, 275 S. W. 909 (1925).

A tenancy was held to be established under the following circumstances: A contract provided that the cultivator had "rented" the land and would put it all in cultivation during the year, raising such crops as might be approved by the landowner. The cultivator had agreed to take care of the place and not to permit the grounds to go to seed. The contract further provided that he should receive one-half of any crops he might raise, except the corn, which was all to go to the landlord at a certain rate per bushel. The landowner, in addition to furnishing the land, was to supply the seed and allow the cultivator to use the tools on the place. The landowner's share was to be delivered at a crib or other place designated to receive it, and the cultivator agreed to put it into the receptacle in good merchantable order. He consented not to "subrent" and not to sell, or try to sell, any of the crops until they were gathered and divided. Neither would he rent any more land nor undertake any other work without the landlord's consent. The contract also contained a provision stating that the land "now rented" would be "broke" in the fall and "crossbroke" in the spring. The court, in rendering a decision in favor of a tenancy relationship,[34] evidently believed that the provision for supervision of the choice of crops and the fact that the landlord had supplied seed and some tools did not override the evidence indicating that the intent was to create a tenancy.

Another Arkansas case is illustrative of the confusion in which the courts often find themselves as a result of inept terminology. In this instance a landowner made a contract providing that the cultivator should receive half of the crop in consideration for the labor performed in its production. It was further agreed that the cultivator's two sons should assist him and each receive a third of their father's half-share. The court declared that the contract operated to make the sons, as well as the father, "sharecroppers" of the landowner, and that the latter would be entitled to a lien for necessary supplies advanced to the father. Obviously something is wrong here, for the landlord cannot have a lien on his cropper's produce. He is endowed, under the correct theory of the cropper relationship, with a much more comprehensive right to the property, namely, the title. The court here probably used the word "share-croppers" hastily and without proper deliberation. It is supposed that the court meant that the father was a sharetenant, for in

34. Birmingham v. Rogers, 46 Ark. 254 (1885).

ordinary parlance a person in that category may sometimes be referred to as a "sharecropper." [35]

A Georgia court has said that the vital distinction between the relationships is whether the person making the crop does so as a laborer upon premises controlled by the landlord, or whether he performs the work for himself on lands in his possession or under his control.[36] Thus we see that in Georgia, at least, the control of premises is considered the most important criterion in deciding this matter.

Sometimes a cultivator may be specifically called a cropper in the contract or so denominated by his landlord. But where circumstances indicate that the cultivator has control or has furnished everything but the land, the appellation given him has been disregarded and a tenancy has been held to exist.[37] In another instance the contract called the cultivator a "tenant," but the control of the land was in the landowner, and this, added to the other circumstances of the case, made the court decide that a cropper relationship really existed.[38] The evidence in this case showed that the landlord, believing the cultivator was a tenant, had sued out a distress warrant and by other acts had indicated that he had been mistaken as to the relationship really existing. Since the testimony made it quite plain that the third party claiming under the cultivator knew his true status, the landowner was not estopped from proving that the fellow was merely a laborer. It has been said, however, that where a cultivator, in answering a landowner's distress warrant proceeding, had failed to question his alleged status as a tenant, such inaction is persuasive of the proposition that the cultivator had thought this relationship actually existed between the parties.[39] That a landowner is not entitled to a distress warrant against his cropper under such circumstances is proved by an earlier Georgia decision.[40]

Where the landowner furnishes the land only, the relationship is clearly a tenancy; [41] but where he furnishes the livestock, tools, farming implements, and fertilizer, or most of them, in addition

35. Cotton v. Chandler, 150 Ark. 368, 234 S. W. 165 (1921).
36. Souter v. Cravy, 29 Ga. App. 557, 116 S. E. 231 (1923).
37. Shepard v. State, 45 Ga. App. 519, 165 S. E. 320 (1932); Coleman v. Lawson, 29 Ga. App. 99, 114 S. E. 67 (1922).
38. Wilkins v. McMahan, 8 Ga. App. 182, 68 S. E. 941 (1910).
39. Souter v. Cravy, 29 Ga. App. 557, 116 S. E. 231 (1923).
40. Hancock v. Boggus, 111 Ga. 884, 36 S. E. 970 (1900).
41. Shepard v. State, 45 Ga. App. 519, 165 S. E. 320 (1932).

to the land, the relationship is that of employer and employee, and the cultivator is called a cropper.[42] A statement in the contract or in the negotiations that the landowner has "rented" the land may be indicative that the relationship created is a tenancy.[43] However, such a statement will not be allowed to influence a decision where the great weight of the evidence points to a cropper relationship.[44]

In an early case the cultivator agreed to a "standing rental" of sixteen hundred pounds of lint cotton. The court decided that the contract created a tenancy and that the landlord had no right to pick the cotton in the fields without the tenant's consent.[45] Another instance arose where the owner of land proposed to another person that he cultivate the premises and agreed to take therefor a certain sum of money or, in lieu of such payment, a stated portion of the crop. Neither proposition was accepted, but nevertheless the offeree entered upon the land and made a crop. The court decided that a tenancy had been created, and that, since no amount of compensation for the use of the land had been agreed upon, the law would imply an undertaking to pay such an amount of money as would be fair and reasonable.[46] Again, a landowner made two separate and distinct contracts with the same person, one including a third party, the other only the two. According to the first agreement the landlord promised to furnish the livestock and tools and the cultivators were to work the land under his supervision. This agreement also contained a provision that the crop should belong to the landlord until his share and all the advances were paid. The court held that this contract created a cropper relationship. The second agreement recited that the farmer should take over and work a crop set out by a former occupant, the cultivator agreeing to give the landlord half the produce and pay an additional sixty dollars, the other half to be security for the payment of the money. This agreement could easily be distinguished from the other and was said to establish a tenancy.[47]

When in Louisiana it is agreed that a person contracting with a

42. Borders v. Herrington, 45 Ga. App. 449, 165 S. E. 148 (1932); Kiker v. Jones, 20 Ga. App. 704, 93 S. E. 253 (1917); Garrick v. Jones, 2 Ga. App. 382, 58 S. E. 543 (1907).

43. Marshall v. Avera, 30 Ga. App. 79, 116 S. E. 662 (1923).

44. Kiker v. Jones, 20 Ga. App. 704, 93 S. E. 253 (1917).

45. Wadley v. Williams, 75 Ga. 272 (1886).

46. Taylor v. Coney, 101 Ga. 655, 28 S. E. 974 (1897).

47. Bryant v. Pugh, 86 Ga. 525, 12 S. E. 927 (1891).

landowner to make a crop is to receive a share of the produce in lieu of wages, it is held that a cropper relationship is established.[48] Nevertheless, in one case where no such provision was embodied in the contract, a Louisiana appellate court seems to have leaned over backwards in determining that a crop-sharing agreement established a tenancy rather than a cropping arrangement. In this instance the contract provided that the landowner should furnish the stock, farming implements, fertilizer, and some other supplies, and he actually furnished some money as well. There was no provision concerning wages and no clause giving the landlord supervision of the farming operations. The court emphasized the lack of the supervisory clause and held that a tenancy existed, although a great many factors pointed to a cropper status.[49] It may be that the court was influenced by the presence in the agreement of a void provision stating that the cultivator, when not working on his own crop, should remain on the plantation in readiness to perform such work as the landlord desired of him. Such a stipulation tended to show that he was not a mere laborer while working on his own crop. This provision was deemed invalid, however, perhaps because it would tie the cultivator too closely to the soil.

In another instance the decision of the appellate court in favor of a tenancy appears to have had more justification. The person cultivating the land had control over the premises, and there was no supervision by the landowner. He associated two men with him in the venture and agreed to divide with them his share of the crops in return for their aid in the process of cultivation. The landlord had nothing to do with making this arrangement. Here it is clear that a tenancy was established in the first instance by the original contract.[50]

In an early case a Mississippi farmer obtained land from another, for the use of which he agreed to give the landowner a certain portion of the crop to be raised thereon. The landlord, for his contribution, agreed to furnish necessary supplies. It was decided that this contract established a cropper relationship, making the parties tenants in common of the crop.[51] In a later case, however, the Mississippi Court decided in favor of a tenancy in a situation

---

48. Lalanne Bros. v. McKinney, 28 La. Ann. 642 (1876).
49. Jones v. Dowling, 12 La. App. 362, 125 So. 478 (1929).
50. Busby v. Childress, 187 So. 104 (La. App., 1939).
51. Batts v. Ratliff, 50 Miss. 561 (1874).

where the facts seem not to justify such a holding. In this instance the landowner furnished the land, team, feed for the team, and farming implements. The only thing furnished by the other party was the labor necessary to make and gather the crop, which was to be equally divided between the parties. It would be difficult to find a set of circumstances which point more clearly to a cropping agreement rather than a tenancy. Yet the court held that a tenancy was established.[52]

As has been seen, the enactment of the North Carolina statute [53] which vested the possession of the crop in the hands of the landowner wiped out the distinction between tenant and cropper for all practical purposes.[54] However, before this law went into effect, many cases had been decided in which the distinction was recognized and discussed.

In probably the most important of these controversies a farmer took a plot of ground for one year, the landowner agreeing to furnish and feed the teams, to supply the farming utensils, and to advance the cultivator bacon and corn. In consideration for this latter item he was to be recompensed out of the cultivator's share of the crop. The farmer agreed to furnish and pay for the labor and give the landowner half of the crop as rent. Here the court was faced with a difficult problem of balance. Some factors indicated that the parties had meant to create a tenancy, while others pointed to a cropper relationship. The contract provided that "rent" should be paid, and also that the cultivator should either furnish or pay for the necessary labor, both indicating that the parties had a tenancy in mind. In addition to these factors the agreement provided that the cultivator must turn over to the landlord the prescribed share of the produce, indicating that the former was entrusted with the division and payment. On the other hand the landowner had agreed to furnish the farming implements, teams, feed, and some food, factors which point to a cropper status. Apparently, the provision giving the cultivator the right to divide the crop into shares and deliver the landlord's portion to him had the most effect in bringing the court to a decision in favor of a tenancy status.[55]

In two other cases decided under the law as it was prior to the

52. Alexander v. Ziegler, 84 Miss. 560, 36 So. 536 (1904).
53. N. C. Gen. Stat. (1943) §42-15.
54. Note 3, supra.
55. Harrison & Son v. Ricks, 71 N. C. 7 (1874).

statutory change, however, the fact that the contracts provided for the delivery of the landlord's portion of the crop as "rent" did not prevent the North Carolina Court from holding that a cropper relationship existed. In one instance the contract provided that the cultivator might tend as much of the landlord's land as he could make ready for a crop with one horse during a one-year period. Two bales of cotton out of the first picking were to be delivered to the landlord, and no part of the crop would belong to the cultivator until the "rent" was paid. The court declared that the only clause of the contract which even "squints" at a tenancy was the clause concerning the payment of "rent." It stated that this provision should not be allowed to outweigh the other circumstances of the case, such as the omission to describe the land fully, the failure to designate the residence of the cultivator during the period covered by the agreement, and the fact that the contract provided that "no part of the crop is to be the property of the defendant (cultivator) until the two bales of cotton are received out of the first picking." [56] In the other case a farmer, in consideration of the use of a certain piece of land, had promised to pay to the landlord two bales of cotton and to keep the ditches cleaned out and the fences in repair; or, if he failed in respect to the latter portion of the agreement, to pay the landlord three bales instead of the two originally called for. With respect to both alternatives the contract provided that the cotton should be paid to the landlord as "rent." The landlord agreed to furnish advances, which, along with the so-called rent, were to be settled for before the farmer would be allowed to take any of the crop as his own. This agreement was also held to establish a cropper relationship rather than a tenancy.[57]

Of course the previously mentioned change in the law makes a discussion of this matter purely academic today, but the cases are important in that they discuss principles which at present govern decisions in the courts of a great majority of the Southeastern states.

There are several South Carolina cases in which the distinction between tenant and cropper was important. On the whole the law in that state differs but little from the view taken by the courts of the other states in the Southeast.

A South Carolina owner started an action to enforce a landlord's

56. Haywood v. Rogers, 73 N. C. 320 (1875).
57. Neal v. Bellamy, 73 N. C. 384 (1875).

lien on crops produced by a cultivator whose legal status was in much doubt. This type of remedy would not be appropriate if the cultivator was a cropper and not a tenant. It was held that the lower court had properly left the true status of the cultivator to the jury. If the jury should decide the issue in favor of a cropping agreement rather than a tenancy, then the lien would not exist and this type of action would not be maintainable.[58]

In one of its earlier expressions of opinion on this subject, the court ruled in favor of a tenancy where the contract gave the cultivator possession of the premises with authority to plant and cultivate a cotton crop at his own expense, with an added agreement to repair the fences and keep them in good condition.[59] Another contract provided that the landowner should have a lien on the crop for advances and that the cultivator should keep the place in repair, clear out all the ditches in the bottoms, clean off the bushes from the river and ditch banks, and give up possession at a certain time. The cultivator also agreed not to hire any of the landlord's "hands" during "crop time." Again there is a clear case in favor of a tenancy.[60]

However, there are other situations in which the court evidently felt that the agreement had created a cropper relationship. In one instance a farmer agreed to work for the landowner at a stated rate per day when he was not busy working his own crop on the land assigned him. It seems that it might have been argued, as the Louisiana court did in a previously mentioned case,[61] that this tended to prove that the cultivator was working for himself with respect to the crop which he tilled alone. However, the court decided that a cropper relationship was established.[62] It was declared that where the cropper had on his own volition ceased working the crop, he thereby broke his contract and would not be allowed to recover on a *quantum meruit* for the time which he had worked for the landlord according to the *per diem* clause in the agreement. In other words, he was held to have forfeited his rights under this clause because he had refused to carry out the other parts of the contract.

In other cases the decisions in favor of a cropper relationship

58. Prater v. Wilson, 55 S. C. 468, 33 S. E. 561 (1899).
59. Whaley v. Jacobson & Son, 21 S. C. 51 (1883).
60. Rakestraw v. Floyd, 54 S. C. 288, 32 S. E. 419 (1899).
61. Jones v. Dowling, supra Note 49.
62. Hardwick v. Page, 124 S. C. 111, 117 S. E. 204 (1923).

seem to have been clearly justified. Thus it was held that a person
was a cropper when he contracted with a landowner to prepare,
plant, cultivate, and gather a cotton crop as directed by the latter,
and to accept as his part of the produce certain cotton, corn, and
peas.[63] In another instance certain farmers agreed to "take in charge"
several parcels of land to be designated by the landowner. They
severally agreed to cultivate the plots according to his directions,
house the crop, and see that no portion of it was removed until
certain stated accounts, including advances on the crop, had been
deducted from the whole. The cultivators also agreed to behave
well and be respectful to the landlord and his family. The landowner
agreed to give them the entire surplus after the said deductions were
made. Under this arrangement it was clear that the cultivators were
not to pay the landlord and retain the balance, but the landlord was
given the privilege of paying himself out of the crops, after which
he would turn the balance over to the cultivators. Therefore it
seems that this contract established a cropper relationship, and it
was held that the cultivators could not give a valid lien on their
prospective crops for advances furnished by a third person.[64]

Certain facts in another case pointed to a tenancy agreement,
while others indicated that a cropper relationship was established.
Here the landowner agreed to permit the cultivator to "crop" the
land for a year, the latter consenting to furnish the stock, tools, and
seed. The landlord promised that after the crop was gathered he
would deliver two-thirds of the produce to the cultivator. The contract provided that all the crops should belong to the landlord until
all the indebtedness was paid. Apparently, the latter portions of this
agreement were held to outweigh the fact that the cultivator had
contracted to furnish the stock, tools, and seed, since the court
declared that a cropper relationship had been established.[65]

It has also been held that a tenant and a person working under
him as a sharecropper are not copartners in the undertaking. In this
instance another person making advances to the sharecropper was
declared to be entitled to recover from the original tenant the sharecropper's portion of the crop which had been appropriated by the
tenant.[66] In another instance a bank, the plaintiff, claimed a bale of

63. State v. Sanders, 110 S. C. 487, 96 S. E. 622 (1918).
64. McCutchen v. Crenshaw, 40 S. C. 511, 19 S. E. 140 (1894).
65. Lipscomb v. Johnson, 123 S. C. 44, 115 S. E. 753 (1923).
66. Watkins v. Coe, 141 S. C. 230, 139 S. E. 464 (1927).

cotton under a chattel mortgage given to it by the person who had produced the crop. The defendant landowner claimed that he had a right to the cotton as a part of the crop produced upon his land by a person whom he alleged to be a laborer and not a tenant. It was stated by the plaintiff that the defendant's right to the cotton was based upon a landlord's lien only. Under these circumstances the status of the cultivator was deemed important, and it was held to be erroneous for the court to fail to submit to the jury the issue as to whether he was a tenant or a cropper. The landlord claimed punitive damages, but the assessment was ruled not to be justified. The court declared that if the bank was mistaken in respect to its rights in the matter, it should beyond all doubt compensate the defendant for any loss which he had suffered, but that it would be shocking to the judicial conscience to penalize anyone for a lawful and orderly attempt to assert a right honestly and reasonably believed to exist.[67]

In what seems to be the only Tennessee case in which this matter is discussed to any great extent, there was an agreement on the part of a person who had promised to perform the necessary labor that he would take charge of and manage the premises for a share of the crops. The court said that this agreement did not constitute a lease and was only a contract for the payment of a portion of the crops for services rendered. It was further declared that if the contract stated that the specified crops should be divided, the owner and the occupant were not partners but tenants in common of the crops. Therefore either party might sell or mortgage his portion.[68] According to the treatment of this case by the appellate court, it would seem that the law of the cropper relationship was being applied here. However, the court in its opinion definitely calls it a tenancy. This is just another example of the confusion in which many of the judges often found themselves, especially in the early cases. They sometimes expressed themselves in rather loose language to describe this kind of relationship and occasionally employed terms which were not wholly accurate.

In one controversy which ended in violence, the Virginia court determined that a cropper relationship existed where the landlord contracted to give the cultivator the agreed portion of the crop

67. Bank of Pendleton v. Martin, 118 S. C. 74, 110 S. E. 76 (1921).
68. Mann v. Taylor, 52 Tenn. 267 (1871).

only after all claims for advances had been satisfied.[69] The court declared that the cultivator was not a tenant but a mere employee, and that therefore the ownership of the entire crop was in the landowner. The cropper had exceeded his rights by forcibly, and without the consent of the landowner, making an attempt to take possession of the crop. Therefore it was ruled that the landowner was justified in resistance to the forceful effort to remove the produce, in the course of which resistance the cropper was killed.

Hence it is seen that many controversies have arisen with respect to the distinction between tenant and cropper. The language of the courts has sometimes been confusing in the extreme, but many principles have developed which help the jurist in his effort to determine exactly what status has been established in a given instance. Sometimes it is very difficult to ascertain what was intended in the agreement made by the parties. Yet through all the cases a certain pattern runs which, if thoroughly analyzed, will help in the determination of the status of cultivators of land on shares.

AGRICULTURAL PARTNERSHIPS

At times a court will hold that an agricultural partnership has been created by an agreement between a landowner and someone wishing to manage and/or cultivate a farm. Although partnerships of this kind are comparatively few, it would not be proper to overlook the possibility that a crop-sharing contract can establish such a relationship. Hence the cases in which the courts have discussed the matter are important to a thorough knowledge of crop-sharing agreements. An analysis of the decisions shows that in respect to these matters the lines of distinction may sometimes be very thin.

However, a few general propositions may be stated, especially one which declares that an agricultural partnership exists where both the landowner and the cultivator are to share in the profits of the joint venture and are also liable for any losses which may occur.[70] The finding that there is a joint enterprise and that there has been no payment for either rent or labor as such may be an important factor in determining that a partnership exists.[71] A case

69. Parrish v. Commonwealth, 81 Va. 1 (1884).
70. Maynard v. Jackson, 159 Ga. 20, 124 S. E. 892 (1924); Reynolds Bros. v. Pool, 84 N. C. 37 (1881).
71. Green v. Hart, 27 Ky. Law Rep. 970, 87 S. W. 315 (1905); Lewis v. Wilkins, 62 N. C. 303 (1868); Moore v. Spruill, 35 N. C. 55 (1851).

arose in Louisiana which would seem to support this view. Here the court ruled that the fact that the contract required that rent be paid was a circumstance from which it could be inferred that a tenancy existed and that there was no partnership or joint venture.[72]

In a North Carolina case in which no third party was involved, it was stated that where one person furnishes the land, team, and its feed, and the other gives his time and attention to the crop and meets the expenses necessary to its cultivation, the gross profits to be equally divided between the two of them, a partnership was the natural result.[73] A few years later, however, a similar case arose in which the court explained that it had made these remarks with reference to a partnership *inter sese*, no third party being involved in that controversy. The language was not meant to be applicable with reference to a partnership of the usual kind, with joint and several liability for the debts of the firm to outsiders. The court ruled that in such a case a tenancy existed with respect to the rights of third parties.[74]

CONCLUSIONS

Thus it is seen that sometimes the courts find it difficult to determine the exact status of the farmer who is cultivating someone else's land. It might be well for other states to follow the lead of Alabama and North Carolina in simplifying the law by abolishing the distinction between the tenant and the cropper. These two states chose different methods of accomplishing this, but the practical results were the same. Any farmer under the usual forms of the crop-sharing agreement automatically became a tenant.

After all, any change in the law of farm tenancy which leads to simplification and the reduction of possible relationships ought to be welcome. It will still be possible for a landowner to hire day laborers or even more permanent farm workers on a daily, monthly, or yearly basis. In fact this would give him the opportunity to regulate the labor supply according to his needs, and he would not be obliged, as he is in many instances under the law as it is today in most of the Southern states, to support the laborers through a period when he does not need them. Of course this would be hard on some laborers, but they could avoid this difficulty by making

72. Blouin Co. v. Hebert, 134 La. 423, 64 So. 230 (1914).
73. Curtis v. Cash, 84 N. C. 41 (1881).
74. Day v. Stevens, 88 N. C. 83 (1883).

crop-sharing tenancy contracts under which they could be sure of obtaining the rights of lessees and would be relieved of the anxiety caused by the possibility that some court might declare them to be croppers with greatly reduced privileges. Hence it appears that the technical distinction between tenant and cropper can be altogether abolished without too many qualms.

III

The Making and Incidents of the Lease Contract

THE tenancy relationship grows out of the lease contract, which may be defined as a transfer of lands or tenements for a period of time, definite or indefinite, in return for rent or some other form of recompense. Proper definition of a term denoting a legal relationship is often a rather difficult task because of the number of other relationships which might be included. This is particularly true of an agricultural tenancy, since there are a number of relationships which are very much like a tenancy in their general make-up and characteristics, for example, the cropping contract, partnerships, and tenancies in common. The above definition, though not perfect, appears to be about as accurate as any short descriptive statement could be.

In commenting upon the relationship created by a letting of land the courts have sometimes been guilty of faulty definition. One example of this defective judicial effort is found where the term "tenant" was defined as denoting one in possession of realty by right, or one in occupancy or temporary possession of premises owned by another.[1] This statement is not sufficiently definite, for it is clear that it would include the cropper or farm laborer, the mere licensee, and perhaps others as well. Hence this effort at defining the term would need at least some additional qualification. In commenting upon the relationship created by a letting of land the Georgia Court remarked that "the relation of landlord and tenant exists where one person occupies the land of another in subordination of the other's title and with his consent, express or implied."[2] Even in Georgia, where the tenant, as distinguished from the holder of an "estate for years,"[3] is not regarded as having the usual estate in the land, it appears that this definition is too broad, since the cropper or licensee would assuredly be included in any reasonable interpretation of the language used.

1. Chastain v. Hall, 182 Ark. 920, 33 S. W. (2d) 45 (1930).
2. Hawkins v. Turner, 129 Ga. 497, 59 S. E. 225 (1907).
3. Infra Note 143.

THE NECESSITY FOR A LEASE CONTRACT
TO ESTABLISH TENANCY RELATIONSHIP

The tenancy relationship is created by the making of a lease contract which may be written or oral, subject to the differing provisions of the Statutes of Frauds in the several states. It is accomplished by negotiation between the parties and may be terminated either by contract or by operation of law. The common form of the lease is a letting of real estate by the owner to another person for a varying term of days, months, or years, usually the latter in agricultural tenancies. In other words, an estate for a certain period of time is carved out of the whole, leaving only a residuary interest technically known as the reversion, which is merely a future interest until the particular estate provided for in the lease is terminated. Of course there is the provision for a consideration known as rent, which may be paid in cash or other thing of value, according to the terms of the particular agreement. The landowner is known as the lessor or landlord and the holder of the term as the lessee or tenant. It has been said that in every contract of lease there must be a lessor, a lessee, and a thing demised; moreover, a lease without a lessor has been considered a nullity.[4] Another court enumerated as necessary the thing, the consent, and the price, which should be certain and determinate.[5] There must certainly be an agreement of the parties. Thus, where one person rented out land belonging to another, the latter could not recover against the supposed lessee on the contract for rent, unless an agency could be shown.[6] Sometimes a contract has every element of an effective lease but will be held to pass no interest because of the addition of certain words which tend to show that it was not intended to become a valid agreement until notes and papers were drawn up. Until this was done the instrument was meant to be only an executory agreement for a lease.[7]

The common law regards a lease for years as the grant of an estate and not a mere transfer of use and enjoyment of the thing leased, while under Civil Law a lease for years is regarded as a mere transfer of use and enjoyment of the property.[7-a]

4. Moore v. Brandenburg, 234 Ky. 400, 28 S. W. (2d) 477 (1930).
5. Jordan v. Mead, 19 La. Ann. 101 (1867).
6. Hardy v. Williams, 31 N. C. 177 (1848).
7. Harrison v. Parmer, 76 Ala. 157 (1884).
7-a. Rials v. Davis, 212 La. 161, 31 So. (2d) 726 (1947). See La. Rev. Civ. Code (1932) arts. 2674, 2710.

Sometimes it is necessary to establish the fact that a tenancy exists, or rather that a contract of lease has been entered into, in order that certain incidents of the relationship may be taken advantage of by the parties. This has been said to be essential in cases involving a distress warrant,[8] a notice to vacate the premises,[9] a landlord's lien,[10] and actions of forcible detainer,[11] summary ejectment,[12] and use and occupation.[13] It is commonly the duty of the person wishing to substantiate the existence of the lease contract to allege and prove everything necessary to the establishment of the tenancy relationship and the rights incident thereto.[14]

NEGOTIATION OF LEASE CONTRACT

The rules of law governing the negotiation of contracts in general control the preparation and perfecting of lease contracts. There must be an expression of mutual assent between the parties and a conformity with the rules surrounding the making of simple contracts, plus an observance of all technicalities respecting leases in particular.

It has been said that there can be no contract of lease without some agreement or stipulation in respect to the amount of rent to be paid.[15] Evidently the real meaning of this statement is that the stipulation for the consideration must be definite enough to satisfy the rules of law in respect to contractual certainty. There must be an agreement as to rent, and a mere statement made by a lessee to the lessor that he would rent for another year was held not to establish a tenancy relationship between the parties.[16]

There may be fraud in the negotiation of a lease contract. Thus in one instance a lease had been procured by the lessee's fraudulent representation that there was no encumbrance upon certain personal property mortgaged to secure the payment of the rent. Here it was held that the lessee might be enjoined from taking possession of and

8. Willingham v. Faircloth, 52 Ga. 126 (1874).
9. Miller v. White, 182 La. 837, 162 So. 638 (1935).
10. Ford v. Green, 121 N. C. 70, 28 S. E. 132 (1897).
11. Daily v. Rudy, 205 Ky. 658, 266 S. W. 347 (1924).
12. Hauser v. Morrison, 146 N. C. 248, 59 S. E. 693 (1907).
13. Littleton v. Wynn, 31 Ga. 583 (1860). But see Smith's Ex'rs. v. Houston, 16 Ala. 111 (1849).
14. See Winn v. State, 55 Ark. 360, 18 S. W. 375 (1892); Newton v. Farris, 191 Ky. 71, 229 S. W. 145 (1921).
15. McCain v. McCain Bros., 165 La. 884, 116 So. 221 (1928).
16. Field v. Newburn, 91 Miss. 861, 45 So. 573 (1908).

cultivating the land after having been notified that the contract was at an end, though the lessor had been negligent in failing to discover, by an examination of the records, that the property was encumbered with a prior lien.[17] In some cases the evidence will be insufficient to sustain the charge of fraud. This was the situation where an illiterate lessee, to whom the contract had been read slowly and carefully at the time of its execution before a notary, claimed that he had signed the instrument in ignorance of its true import.[18] Again, in a case involving an assignment of a lease, the original lessee made a statement in respect to the value of the term. The court declared that this was a matter of opinion and held that the statement, even if untrue, was not of such a nature as to invalidate the assignment.[19]

Sometimes cases involving negotiations for a lease contract will be decided on the basis of estoppel. In one instance copies of a new lease were signed in blank by a tenant after the expiration of an earlier term, but the contract was never completed as contemplated by the parties and no further settlement was made. The court declared that such an instrument could not be used as the basis of a new contract and that therefore it alone would constitute no defense to a possessory action. But, in this case, the landowner's agent had led the tenant to believe that he would be given a new lease, and on the strength of this representation the tenant had proceeded to sublet a portion of the land and plant a crop on the remainder. This conduct of the agent was held to estop the landowner from ejecting the tenant.[20]

Certain portions of the negotiations leading up to the final execution of the lease contract may be conducted by an agent. In one instance it appeared that the lease had been drawn up by the landlady's agent under instructions transmitted to him after she had a conversation with the prospective lessee in regard to its terms. The lease was sent to the lessee without any special accompanying statement describing its contents. The court declared that no fiduciary relationship had been shown and that the lessee had not signed the contract in reliance upon any fraudulent representation calculated to mislead him as to its contents. Under these circum-

17. Newcombe v. Ewing, 19 Ky. Law Rep. 821, 42 S. W. 105 (1897).
18. Lacaze v. Beeman, 178 So. 660 (La. App., 1938).
19. Lewis v. Brown, 145 Ark. 492, 224 S. W. 986 (1920).
20. Federal Land Bank v. Sanders, 167 So. 140 (La. App., 1936).

stances a lessee cannot, by the contention that he has no actual knowledge of the contents of the instrument, avoid liability where he has had the opportunity of examining the agreement. The lower court had excluded testimony in respect to a talk with the agent concerning the terms of the contract which had occurred prior to the conversation with the lessor. Also excluded was evidence that the lessee, in reliance upon this conversation with the principal, had signed the lease not knowing that it did not embody the terms agreed upon at this conference. It was held that the lower court had not acted erroneously in excluding this testimony.[21]

When a contract is made with an authorized agent of the landlord, it has the same effect as one made with the landlord himself.[22] The contract will bind the principal if the agent has apparent authority to make agreements of this kind.[23] It is held that a lease contract will be construed most strongly against the lessor if his agent or representative drew up the instrument.[24]

In one instance a tenant whose term was expiring drew up a lease for ten years and forwarded it to the landlady for her signature. The important portion of her reply was as follows: "I received the check also the contract, but Bubber has been so busy gathering his crop that he has not had time to go up. Will now soon. I am afraid to say what day for fear something might happen, so you go ahead and fix everything like you want it." The court declared that this letter was not an unequivocal approval and acceptance of the terms of the proffered instrument. Only the latter portion might be said to suggest an acceptance, and this suggestion is rebutted by the language clearly indicating an intention to send Bubber to do something which had to be done to complete the agreement.[25]

The usual rules of evidence govern in respect to lease contracts made with agents. In one instance involving a claim for rent it appeared that the defendant lessee had dealt with the lessor's agent, who had subsequently died. Applying the usual rule, the court stated that the lessee was not a competent witness with respect to statements and representations made by the deceased agent during the negotiations for the contract.[26]

21. Stewart v. Fleming, 105 Ark. 37, 150 S. W. 128 (1912).
22. Hallbrooks v. Rosser, 143 Ark. 559, 221 S. W. 483 (1920).
23. Taylor v. Crowe, 190 Ark. 71, 77 S. W. (2d) 54 (1935).
24. Lee Wilson & Co. v. Fleming, 203 Ark. 417, 156 S. W. (2d) 893 (1941).
25. Weeks v. Graham, 110 S. C. 150, 96 S. E. 399 (1918).
26. Burgess v. American Mortgage Co., 115 Ala. 468, 22 So. 282 (1897).

In another case a landowner prepared a written lease, describing the land and reserving certain portions thereof. However, the prospective tenant refused to sign the contract because it contained a stipulation requiring him to execute a chattel mortgage to secure the payment of the rent. No objections were made to the reservations contained in the instrument, and the parties finally agreed that a note for a stated amount of rent would be executed by the lessee. The unexecuted lease was ruled to be admissible for the purpose of showing that portions of the premises had been reserved, though the landowner had alleged in his pleading that no reservations were to be made.[27]

Sometimes parties will try to correct a written contract by making other arrangements of an amending nature. In one situation the contract stated that a certain amount of land was in cultivation, but the evidence showed that there had been a mistake of some two hundred acres. The tenants alleged that a subsequent as well as a contemporaneous agreement had been made to correct this mistake in acreage. Whether this amending agreement existed was clearly a jury question which had been decided in favor of the tenants. It was remarked by the court that the settlement of the acreage dispute furnished adequate consideration for the new agreement granting a refund in rent and reducing the amount of land which was supposed to be in cultivation.[28] In another instance a Georgia tenant tried to show that there had been a novation. The effort failed because it was brought out in the evidence that the supposed new contract was conditioned upon the proper cultivation of the crops, which stipulation had not been met by the tenant. Therefore, even if it could have been shown that there was an alteration in terms, there would have been no basis for an action on the new contract.[29]

CONTRACTS REQUIRED TO BE IN WRITING

According to the provisions of the Statute of Frauds, the details of which differ widely from state to state, a contract for the transfer of real estate must be in writing and is required to be signed by the person who is to be charged. With respect to leases, the statutes, if anything, vary to a greater extent than they do with respect to conveyances.

27. Simpson v. East, 124 Ala. 293, 27 So. 436 (1900).
28. Reisinger v. Dulaney, 168 Ark. 875, 271 S. W. 951 (1923).
29. Peterman v. Dunaway, 32 Ga. App. 171, 122 S. E. 727 (1924).

Most of the Southeastern states have statutes which provide that leases for a term longer than one year must be in writing. A memorandum will usually satisfy this requirement. The states having this one-year statute are Alabama,[30] Arkansas,[31] Georgia,[32] Kentucky,[33] Mississippi,[34] South Carolina,[35] Tennessee,[36] and Virginia.[37] In Florida the regular Statute of Frauds [38] requires written evidence for any lease of more than two years, but another act [39] seems to make a tenant at sufferance out of every occupant who holds under a parol lease. If this is the true meaning of this statute, and there seems to be no room for doubt about its future interpretation in this respect, then it goes a long way toward making parol leases impracticable in Florida. Written evidence is required in North Carolina for a lease of more than three years.[40] The Louisiana law seems to be that leases for any number of years are valid whether they be written or oral.[41] In fact it was held in an early case that an oral lease will prevail over a written one of later date.[42]

Certain cases have arisen in which the Statute of Frauds has been considered. In one instance an Arkansas landlord had brought an action of unlawful detainer, and the tenant filed a cross-action claiming that he had been evicted. The lower court instructed the jury that if the parties had contracted for the lease of the farm for the ensuing year, this would amount to a valid lease; but if the parties had previously made a parol lease for two years, then such lease would be void under the one-year Arkansas statute. It was held that this instruction was not objectionable on the ground that it was conflicting.[43] In Alabama a person was shown to have enjoyed the possession of a plot of land for one year under a five-year parol lease which was void under the Statute of Frauds. In this case the court

30. Ala. Code (1940) tit. 20, §3.
31. Ark. Dig. Stat. (Pope, 1937) §6059. Assignments of leases exceeding one year are included.
32. Ga. Code (1933) §61-102.
33. Ky. Rev. Stat. (1946) §§371.010.
34. Miss. Code Ann. (1942) §264.
35. S. C. Stat. 1946, No. 873, §§7, 8.
36. Tenn. Code Ann. (Williams, 1934) §7831.
37. Va. Code Ann. (Michie, 1936) §5561.
38. Fla. Stat. Ann. (1941) §689.01.
39. Fla. Comp. Gen. Laws Ann. (Skillman, 1931 Supp.) §5431.
40. N. C. Gen. Stat. (1943) §22-2.
41. La. Civ. Code Ann. (Dart, 1932) Art. 2683.
42. Rachel v. Pearsall, 8 Mart. (O. S.) 702 (La., 1820).
43. Smith v. Pearce, 174 Ark. 153, 294 S. W. 705 (1927).

held that the landowner might recover in an action sounding in quasi contract for the use and occupation of the premises during the period of time the occupant was in possession.[44]

It has been held that the Statute of Frauds applying to leases must be specially pleaded,[45] and that a party can take advantage of the invalidity of a contract under the statute only by answer to the complaint and not by a demurrer or objection to the evidence.[46] Furthermore, a question of invalidity cannot be raised by a stranger to the transaction.[47]

A lessee who has derived all the benefits arising from a contract which is inimical to the statute will not be permitted to avail himself of the defense that the lease is not in writing.[48] Although the lease is void under the statute, yet if the supposed tenant takes possession of the land and pays the rent stipulated by the agreement, this will impart validity to the lease, create a tenancy relationship between the parties, and as a result give the landowner a right to an attachment against the crops for advances made during the year.[49] An action for use and occupation of the premises seems to be a proper remedy in such a situation.[50] A similar result has been reached where a landowner has accepted the rent and the cultivators, having been put in possession under a former lease, have remained in possession under a renewal contract which was alleged to be void under the statute.[51] Furthermore, an action of use and occupation has been held to lie where a person is let into possession and enjoys the premises, either personally or by a subtenant, during the term stipulated for in a verbal rental agreement which was void because it was inimical to the statute.[52] In these situations it has been said that the landowner is entitled to recover a reasonable sum as rent from the occupant for the time he used the premises.[53] This is practically the same thing as saying that the Statute of Frauds applies

44. Hoye v. Goree, 4 Stew. & P. 170 (Ala. 1833).
45. Martin v. Blanchett, 77 Ala. 288 (1884).
46. Stephens v. Midyette, 161 N. C. 323, 77 S. E. 243 (1913).
47. Gafford v. Stearns, 51 Ala. 434 (1874); Jackson v. Coons, 285 Ky. 154, 147 S. W. (2d) 45 (1941).
48. Nelson v. Webb, 54 Ala. 436 (1875); Price v. Thompson, 4 Ga. App. 46, 60 S. E. 600 (1908).
49. Martin v. Blanchett, 77 Ala. 288 (1884).
50. Nelson v. Webb, 54 Ala. 436 (1875).
51. Dahm v. Barlow, 93 Ala. 120, 9 So. 598 (1891).
52. Bain v. McDonald, 111 Ala. 269, 20 So. 77 (1896).
53. Cannon v. Carr, 292 Ky. 793, 168 S. W. (2d) 21 (1943).

only to those contracts which are either wholly or partially exe-cutory.[54]

There is a definite split in the authorities in respect to the question of partial performance. The issue is whether or not the partial performance of a contract which is void under the Statute of Frauds will take the particular case out from under the statute. By far the greater number of the nation's courts hold that a part performance vitalizes the contract, and that it may therefore be enforced in spite of the fact that it is not in writing. However, a minority, which includes four of the Southeastern states,[55] have refused to adopt the doctrine of part performance and have denied relief where the parties have carried out a portion of the agreement. The majority view has been approved in agricultural cases in Alabama [56] and Arkansas,[57] while the Kentucky Court, which had formerly taken this view,[58] later refused to hold that a partially performed farm contract was enforceable.[59] In a case which arose before this reversal, the court used language which apparently entitled an unfortunate tenant to quasi-contractual relief.[60] This form of relief would no doubt prevail in all the states which take the minority view.

One of the provisions usually found in the Statute of Frauds is a clause which invalidates all parol contracts not performable within one year after being made. While most states have this provision, there are a few, like North Carolina, which do not have it. In some of the states of the Southeast it is held that a parol contract for a term of one year, to begin at a future date, is void under the statute, while in others such an agreement is valid. Usually the latter holding is influenced by the wording of statutes which provide that con-tracts creating the tenancy relationship "for any time not exceeding one year" may be by parol. This wording has been said to show an intention to validate all parol leases for one year, no matter when the term is to begin, be it *in praesenti* or *in futuro*. Those South-

---

54. Gafford v. Stearns, 51 Ala. 434 (1874).

55. Kentucky, Mississippi, North Carolina, and Tennessee. See 49 Am. Jur., Statute of Frauds, §425.

56. White v. Kinney, 211 Ala. 624, 101 So. 426 (1924). See also Dahm v. Barlow, 93 Ala. 120, 9 So. 598 (1891).

57. City Nat. Bank v. Fite, 186 Ark. 266, 53 S. W. (2d) 440 (1932); Newton v. Mathis, 140 Ark. 252, 215 S. W. 615 (1919); Storthz v. Watts, 125 Ark. 393, 188 S. W. 1166 (1916).

58. Commonwealth v. Jones, 31 Ky. Law Rep. 1148, 104 S. W. 782 (1907).

59. Gault v. Carpenter, 187 Ky. 25, 218 S. W. 254 (1920).

60. Thomas v. McManus, 23 Ky. Law Rep. 837, 64 S. W. 446 (1901).

eastern states holding such agreements to be void are Alabama [61] and Kentucky,[62] while those which seem to take an opposite view are Arkansas,[63] Georgia,[64] Mississippi,[65] South Carolina,[66] and Tennessee.[67]

This provision of the Statute of Frauds is not applicable to an oral lease of farm land for a period of one year from and after the date of the lease, the agreement being that the contract will run only to the same date in the next year and not to the end of that year.[68] In a recent case the Kentucky Court called for an adjustment of the equities where the contract violated this section of the statute. It was ruled in this instance that the female tenant and her husband were entitled to an equitable lien on the land for the sum paid by them for taxes and for the amount by which certain improvements had enhanced the vendible value of the property. However, the tenant was not permitted to recover an amount of money expended for ordinary repairs and upkeep. The landowner was also allowed a reasonable sum for the time the occupant had been on the premises.[69]

According to statutes in Arkansas [70] and Georgia [71] possession under a parol lease giving a term of more than the prescribed period of one year creates a tenancy at will.

61. Lane v. Henderson, 232 Ala. 122, 167 So. 270 (1936); Colvin v. Payne, 218 Ala. 341, 118 So. 578 (1928); White v. Kinney, 211 Ala. 624, 101 So. 426 (1924); Bain v. McDonald, 111 Ala. 269, 20 So. 77 (1896); Alabama Gold Life Ins. Co. v. Oliver, 82 Ala. 417, 2 So. 445 (1887); Martin v. Blanchett, 77 Ala. 288 (1884); Gafford v. Stearns, 51 Ala. 434 (1874).

62. Cannon v. Carr, 292 Ky. 793, 168 S. W. (2d) 21 (1943); Gault v. Carpenter, 187 Ky. 25, 218 S. W. 254 (1920); Jones v. Commonwealth, 31 Ky. Law Rep. 1148, 104 S. W. 782 (1907); Thomas v. McManus, 23 Ky. Law Rep. 837, 64 S. W. 446 (1901); Greenwood v. Strother, 91 Ky. 482, 16 S. W. 138 (1891).

63 Ark. statute interpreted in Anderson v. May, 57 Tenn. 84 (1872).

64. Roland v. Floyd, 53 Ga. App. 282, 185 S. E. 580 (1936); Ridgway v. Bryant, 8 Ga. App. 564, 70 S. E. 28 (1911); Gay v. Peake, 5 Ga. App. 583, 63 S. E. 650 (1909); Steininger v. Williams, 63 Ga. 475 (1879), overruling Atwood v. Norton, 31 Ga. 507 (1860), in which a contract of this kind had been declared void in accordance with the opposing view prior to the enactment of the more liberal statute.

65. McCroy v. Toney, 66 Miss. 233, 5 So. 392 (1889).

66. National Bank v. People's Grocery Co., 153 S. C. 118, 150 S. E. 478 (1929).

67. Hayes v. Arrington, 108 Tenn. 494, 68 S. W. 44 (1902).

68. Lane v. Henderson, 232 Ala. 122, 167 So. 270 (1936).

69. Cannon v. Carr, 292 Ky. 793, 168 S. W. (2d) 21 (1943).

70. Ark. Dig. Stat. (Pope, 1937) §6062.

71. Ga. Code (1933) §§61-102. See Price v. Thompson, 4 Ga. App. 46, 60 S. E. 800 (1908).

In one instance it has been held that a promissory note given for rent is, along with letters referring to the instrument, a sufficient memorandum in writing to satisfy a requirement of the Statute of Frauds that the lease contract must be in writing and signed by the "party to be charged." [72]

Sometimes it has been ruled that the agent negotiating a lease contract must have authority of the same quality and formality as that required by law for the signing and execution of the instrument itself.[73] However, an opposite view is taken in other jurisdictions.[74] Since in Louisiana leases for long periods may be either written or oral,[75] an agency to lease real estate in that state may be granted and/or proved by parol.[76]

RECORDATION

In most of the Southeastern states certain leases, for a greater or lesser duration as the several statutes provide, are required to be recorded. Of course, between the parties, lessor and lessee, the contract, though unrecorded, is effective in transferring the interest in the land. With respect to third persons, the effect of a failure to record a lease whose registration is required is well illustrated by what has been said in Louisiana. Here the courts have held that the possessor of realty under an unrecorded lease is invested with no rights whatsoever as against a third party purchaser of the property,[77] or a seizing attachment creditor.[78]

In Kentucky [79] and Virginia [80] recordation is required of all leases for a period of more than five years. The same applies to leases of more than three years in North Carolina [81] and Tennessee.[82] The South Carolina act [83] makes registration necessary for leases of more than a year, while in Florida the statute [84] reads "one year or more."

72. Alabama Gold Life Ins. Co. v. Oliver, 82 Ala. 417, 2 So. 445 (1887).
73. Hutchinson v. Platt, 119 Miss. 606, 81 So. 281 (1919).
74. Johnson v. Somers, 20 Tenn. 268 (1839).
75. La. Civ. Code Ann. (Dart, 1932) Art. 2683. Cf. Weatherly v. Johnson, 25 La. Ann. 229 (1873); Brown v. Martin & Crenshaw, 9 La. Ann. 504 (1854).
76. Hammonds v. Busbee, 170 La. 573, 128 So. 520 (1930).
77. Brown v. Matthews, 3 La. Ann. 198 (1848).
78. Flower v. Pearce, 45 La. Ann. 853, 13 So. 150 (1893).
79. Ky. Rev. Stat. (1946) §382.080.
80. Va. Code Ann. (Michie, 1936) §§5192-94.
81. N. C. Gen. Stat. (1943) §47-18.
82. Tenn. Code Ann. (Williams, 1934) §§7191, 7621.
83. S. C. Stat. (1946), No. 873, §48.
84. Fla. Stat. Ann. (1941) §395.01.

The law of Louisiana [85] provides for the registry of all contracts concerning immovables, and it has been held that leases of real estate are within the purview of this act.[86] In Mississippi it seems that any lease "for a term of years" is void if not recorded.[87] There seems to be no such requirement in either Arkansas or Georgia. In a case arising at the end of the last century, the Alabama Court held that a three-year lease of all timber on a certain tract was within the scope of an act requiring the recordation of conveyances.[88] In a more recent case, however, it was said that contracts for rent or the assignment thereof by the lessor need not be recorded.[89]

In a Virginia case the contract gave the occupant a lease for a period of two years and one month. An additional clause, however, gave the tenant an option providing for four successive renewals of the lease, each for a period of one year. This instrument was held to be a lease for more than five years under the aforementioned statute requiring the registration of such contracts. However, the court declared that the agreement for the original term was not void unless it was shown that the lessee had acted upon his options in such a manner as to extend the term to a total of more than five years.[90]

THE PAROL EVIDENCE RULE

The parol evidence rule, so called, is applicable to lease contracts as well as to other types of written agreements. It is not really a rule of evidence but a rule of substantive law. To be brief, the rule may be stated thus: Where a contract has been reduced to writing, a party to the instrument is not permitted to introduce evidence of any prior or contemporaneous oral agreement which would vary or contradict the terms of the written instrument. Some of the opinions add a statement that a written agreement cannot be added to by parol,[91] but this does not prevent the introduction of evidence of a separate and distinct oral agreement.[92] Also it has been declared

85. La. Civ. Code Ann. (Dart, 1932) Art. 2266.
86. Flower v. Pearce, 45 La. Ann. 853, 13 So. 150 (1893).
87. Miss. Code Ann. (1942) §868.
88. Milliken v. Faulk, 111 Ala. 658, 20 So. 594 (1896).
89. White v. First Nat. Bank of Opp, 236 Ala. 589, 183 So. 875 (1938).
90. Great A. & P. Tea Co. v. Cofer, 129 Va. 640, 106 S. E. 695 (1921).
91. Smith v. Green, 128 Ga. 90, 57 S. E. 98 (1907); Little v. Lary, 12 Ga. App. 754, 78 S. E. 470 (1913).
92. Bunn v. Wall, 180 N. C. 662, 104 S. E. 470 (1920).

that parol evidence may not be introduced where antecedent oral agreements have been merged into a writing in which all the difficulties were supposed to have been ironed out.[93] The general rule has been variously stated in the opinions of the state courts.[94]

The rule has been said not to be applicable where one of the parties is a stranger and not an original participant in the transaction.[95] But a sublessee having the right to possession under a separate contract with the lessee has been held not to be a stranger.[96] Yet parol evidence was not allowed to be presented in an instance where the landlord had aliened his interest in the land and transferred the rent note to another party.[97]

A peculiar question arose in Arkansas where a lessor was suing an assignee of the lease for rent. The latter introduced parol evidence that the lease was assigned as collateral security for a note signed by him in order to permit his assignor, the true holder of the lease, to obtain the money with which to purchase the lease from the original lessee. The court concluded that this testimony was not introduced to contradict or vary the terms of the written instrument but for the purpose of establishing the fact that such a contract existed and that the ultimate assignment had been made to secure a loan. Hence the evidence was admissible and was allowed to govern the decision.[98]

In one case a possessory action had been brought by the landlord's vendee against a tenant. The latter attempted to introduce evidence of a parol agreement made with the landlord's agent that he would be permitted to remain on the premises for a time after the termination of a written lease. The court applied the general rule and held that the parol agreement was inadmissible.[99]

If the written instrument appears to be a completed transaction in itself, it is clear that parol evidence should not be admitted. In a case of this kind parol evidence that the lessor had bargained for

93. Peters v. Pilcher, 211 Ala. 548, 100 So. 902 (1924); Vanhooser v. Gattis, 139 Ark. 390, 214 S. W. 44 (1919).

94. See Wilson v. State, 39 So. 776 (Ala., 1905); Coleman v. Siler, 74 Ala. 435 (1883); Parker v. Keenan, 181 Ark. 467, 26 S. W. (2d) 69 (1930); Smith v. Green, 128 Ga. 90, 57 S. E. 98 (1907); Little v. Lary, 12 Ga. App. 754, 78 S. E. 470 (1913).

95. Peters v. Pilcher, 211 Ala. 548, 100 So. 902 (1924); British & A. Mortgage Co. v. Cody, 135 Ala. 622, 33 So. 832 (1903).

96. Peters v. Pilcher, 211 Ala. 548, 100 So. 902 (1924).

97. Cobb v. Johnson, 126 Ga. 618, 55 S. E. 935 (1906).

98. Lansdell v. Woods, 127 Ark. 466, 192 S. W. 715 (1917).

99. Stewart v. Thrower, 212 N. C. 541, 193 S. E. 701 (1937).

the personal skill, judgment, and fidelity of a particular person was inadmissible.[100] Where a written contract is clear and unambiguous, parol evidence is held not to be admissible. In one instance a landlord was suing his tenant for rent alleged to be due, and the latter attempted to introduce evidence of a parol agreement by the landowner to put up fences. This was held to be inadmissible as an attempt to vary a complete and unambiguous written agreement.[101] In another case a landowner had entered into a written contract which stipulated that he would receive a certain amount of the produce from the tenant as rent. It also provided that the tenant would leave the seed from sixteen bales of cotton on the place at the expiration of the five-year term or when he left the premises. This was said to imply that the seed would become the property of the landlord at the termination of the tenant's interest. The landlord sold the land and indorsed upon the agreement a transfer of the "within contract" to the purchaser. During the continuance of the tenancy the purchaser declined to allow the former owner to seize certain cotton seed, with the assent of the tenant, as being the cotton seed referred to in the written contract. The former landowner sought to introduce parol evidence that there had been an agreement to dispose of the cotton seed other than as provided in the original agreement. The court was of the opinion that the contract was plain and unambiguous and therefore held that the parol evidence was inadmissible.[102]

It has been decided that where a written contract was in the form of a lease with an option to purchase the land at a named price, parol evidence that the transaction had been intended as a contract for the outright sale of the property cannot be successfully introduced.[103]

Parol evidence that a lessee had agreed to give notes *in praesenti* for the rents of succeeding years was held inadmissible where the lease was reduced to writing and contained no such agreement and there was no averment that owing to fraud, accident, or mistake the written contract did not fully express the concurrent intention of the parties.[104] In another instance a landlord whose tenant held under an oral lease accepted his rent note for a definite term. This

100. Charles v. Byrd, 29 S. C. 544, 8 S. E. 1 (1888).
101. Frazier v. Riley, 215 Ala. 517, 111 So. 10 (1926).
102. Cobb v. Johnson, 126 Ga. 618, 55 S. E. 935 (1906).
103. Smith v. Caldwell, 78 Ark. 333, 95 S. W. 467 (1906).
104. Pickett v. Ferguson, 45 Ark. 177 (1885).

note included various covenants which were not contained in the oral agreement. Here it was conclusively presumed that the writing superseded the oral agreement and contained the entire contract, there being no proof of fraud or mistake.[105] Where fraud or mistake is demonstrable, however, it may be shown by parol. In fact the Arkansas Court admitted evidence that there had been an obvious clerical mistake with respect to the date in a written lease.[106]

A written contract of lease may be amended by a subsequent agreement, which may be proved by the introduction of parol evidence. In one instance a written lease provided for the payment of money rent, but a subsequent oral agreement was entered into by the terms of which the landlord agreed to accept a portion of the crop in lieu of the sum of money stipulated in the lease. The written instrument also provided that if the rent was paid by the first day of November, the lessee would have an option to renew the lease for the next year on the same terms. The first of November passed without any effort being made to pay the rent in kind. In fact the crop was not even gathered by that date. In view of the change made by the subsequent oral agreement and the established custom of the neighborhood that crops were never gathered by the date set in the written agreement, it was held that an extension of the time of payment would be implied. The tenant's option for the following year was not destroyed by his failure to pay the rent in kind on the date specified in the written contract.[107] In a case where a landlord was trying to dispossess his tenant, the court applied the same principle of law. Here the written lease provided that the landlord might increase the rent at any time by giving the tenant proper notice, and it was shown that this notice had been given before the dispossessory proceedings were begun. The tenant introduced parol evidence of another contract, subsequent to the lease, whereby, in consideration of his making certain improvements on the premises, he was not to be disturbed for a period of one year, which term had not expired at the time the dispossessory action was brought. This evidence was held admissible, and the subsequent agreement prevented the landlord from dispossessing the tenant upon the latter's failure to pay an increased rent.[108]

105. Anthony Shoals Power Co. v. Fortson, 138 Ga. 460, 75 S. E. 606 (1912).
106. Spann v. Spann, 105 Ark. 697, 150 S. W. 409 (1912).
107. Parker v. Vaughn, 180 Ark. 890, 25 S. W. (2d) 19 (1930).
108. Bizzell v. Auto Tire & Equipment Co., 182 N. C. 98, 108 S. E. 439 (1921).

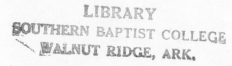

A landlord in a recent Louisiana case brought an action to cancel the lease and to dispossess his tenant on the ground that the latter had violated certain terms of the contract. Evidence was introduced tending to show that, after the signing of the lease, the tenant had made an independent agreement to purchase a mule from the landlord, an obligation that he did not fulfill. The court ruled that the evidence was not admissible in this action, since the breach of an independent agreement of this kind would not be the basis for a cancellation. It was further said that this was not an occasion for the application of the rule that parol evidence is admissible to prove subsequent oral agreements.[109]

In accordance with well-recognized principles of the law of contracts and evidence, one court declared that, in a suit on a written lease, parol evidence that the instrument was not to go into effect unless the lessee was able to rent certain adjoining lands had been properly admitted by the trial judge. The introduction of this evidence was permitted, not for the purpose of varying the terms of the written instrument, but in order to show the lessee's failure to fulfill the terms of a condition upon which the validity of the instrument was predicated. The court declared that parol evidence is admissible to prove that an instrument in writing has never become operative because of the failure of a condition precedent to its operation. In this particular instance it seems that the evidence was sufficient to show that, had the lessee tried a little harder, he might have obtained a suitable lease to adjoining lands at a just rental and thereby satisfied the condition. It was declared that a condition is deemed to be fulfilled where the fulfillment has been prevented by the action or inaction of the party in whose behalf it is to be performed. The lessee claimed that he had not obtained the lease to the adjoining lands because the alleged agent of the owners of the desired property did not truly represent the said owners. However, it was declared that the lessee had not sustained the burden of proving this. Therefore it was held that the condition should have been fulfilled, thus making the lease contract operative.[110]

Questions often arise as to whether the consideration clause in some formal instrument like a deed or a lease can be contradicted or varied by parol testimony. The general rule has been stated thus in a North Carolina case: "Although it is always competent to

109. Lillard v. Hulbert, 9 So. (2d) 852 (La. App., 1942).
110. Mire v. Haas, 174 So. 374 (La. App. 1937).

contradict the recital in the deed as to the amount paid, in an action involving the recovery of the purchase-money, or as to the measure of damages, in an action upon the covenants in the deed, it is not competent to contradict the acknowledgment of a consideration paid, in order to affect the validity of the deed in creating or passing a title to the estate thereby granted."[111] To the same effect is the Alabama Court's statement that the consideration clause in such a formal instrument is open to inquiry and explanation. According to what is said here, the true consideration may be shown by parol, except when it is different in character from that recited or expressed. In this instance rented lands were sold and conveyed by a deed which recited a money consideration only. In a subsequent action by the vendor against the lessee on the rent contract, it was said that the former landlord might show by parol that, according to the terms of the contract of sale, the note for the rent had been reserved and retained by him, along with the sum of money specified in the contract, as an additional part of the consideration for the transaction.[112] In a recent case from Georgia it was found that a statement of consideration regarding acreage in a rent note which had formed the basis for a distress warrant proceeding had been by way of recital only. With respect to the size of the property leased, the tenant had claimed that the true acreage was less than the amount of land represented as being in the tract. The appellate court decided that the lower tribunal had erroneously refused to permit a witness to testify that the landlord had represented to his tenant that there were one hundred acres in cultivation, the tenant having claimed that the tilled portion was only slightly more than seventy-six acres.[113]

On the other hand, the Alabama Court has ruled that it is not permissible to introduce parol evidence of an additional agreement to deliver a certain quantity of cotton seed, where there was a written obligation which clearly stated that the rent would be a specified number of cotton bales and made no mention of any other consideration. The landlord attempted to introduce oral evidence of a custom on his plantation to the effect that all the cotton seed raised on the premises were to be his property. This testimony was held to be inadmissible as tending to contradict the written instru-

111. Deaver v. Deaver, 137 N. C. 249, 49 S. E. 113 (1904).
112. Steed v. Hinson, 76 Ala. 298 (1884).
113. Rentz v. King, 66 Ga. App. 264, 17 S. E. (2d) 896 (1941).

ment and also for the reason that one man cannot establish a custom.[114]

It has been held in a case from Mississippi that where a landlord has conveyed leased premises without having reserved the rent in the deed, the rent passes to the grantee, and parol evidence is not admissible to show oral understandings and agreements which are contrary to the legal effect of the deed.[115]

ASSIGNMENT AND SUBLEASE

In certain instances a lessee may desire to transfer to another the property which he has rented from the owner. Sometimes it may be very difficult to determine just what type of situation is presented, an assignment or a sublease. The determination of this matter may make quite a lot of difference, for there is privity of contract and estate in the case of an assignment [116] but not in the case of a sublease.[117] Hence one may sue on the covenants of the original lease where there is an assignment [118] but not where there is a sublease.[119] When a subtenant agreed to pay the landlord a sum greater than the rent demanded by the original lease, then the tenancy relationship existed between landlord and subtenant and the larger sum was recoverable.[120] Here we have something very much akin to a novation. Moreover, an alleged assignee who clearly indicates that he does not intend to be bound by the terms of the lease contract is absolved from anything to which he has not assented.[121]

One of the criteria employed in ascertaining whether a given transfer amounts to an assignment or a sublease is the entirety of the term alienated. If the whole term was transferred, this would tend to show an assignment; whereas, if the transferee took only a

114. Powell v. Thompson, 80 Ala. 51 (1885).

115. O'Keefe v. McLemore, 125 Miss. 394, 87 So. 655 (1921).

116. Johnson v. Moxley, 216 Ala. 466, 113 So. 656 (1927), *rev'g*. 22 Ala. App. 1, 113 So. 651 (1926); Lansdell v. Woods, 127 Ark. 466, 192 S. W. 715 (1917); Cox v. Fenwick, 7 Ky. 538 (1817).

117. Robinson v. Lehman, Durr & Co., 72 Ala. 401 (1882); Ashley v. Young, 79 Miss. 129, 29 So. 822 (1901); Doty v. Heth, 52 Miss. 530 (1876); Krider v. Ramsay, 79 N. C. 354 (1878).

118. Johnson v. Moxley, 216 Ala. 466, 113 So. 656 (1927); Cox v. Fenwick, 7 Ky. 538 (1817).

119. Robinson v. Lehman, Durr & Co., 72 Ala. 401 (1882); Ashley v. Young, 79 Miss. 129, 29 So. 822 (1901).

120. Moore v. Collins, 36 Ga. App. 701, 138 S. E. 81 (1927).

121. Hamilton v. House, 6 Ala. App. 86, 60 So. 429 (1912).

portion of the term, this would indicate a sublease.[122] In fact, where the circumstances showed that the entire term had been transferred, the court held that this outweighed the reservation of rent by the original lessee and the form of the contract, which in the instant case seemed very much like a sublease.[123]

In an early North Carolina case [124] the original tenant, after subleasing the rented premises, surrendered the remainder of the term to the lessor, who made an effort to oust the sublessee. The case was brought in a justice's court, which at that time had no jurisdiction in cases of tort. Therefore an action on the order of trespass *quare clausum fregit*, the old common-law tort action respecting trespass to land, could not be maintained here. According to the principles stated above, the lessor could maintain no action *ex contractu* against the sublessee on the promise to pay rent. From what is said in the opinion, moreover, it would seem that, after the surrender, neither the lessor nor the original lessee could maintain an action for rent against the subtenant, there being no privity of contract in the case of the lessor, and no interest in the subject matter as far as the original lessee was concerned. The fallacy in this argument seems to lie in timing. The argument that the lessor cannot maintain the action appears to be timed before the surrender, while the contention that the lessee cannot sue is timed after the surrender. Since the interest of the lessee can well be said to have been transferred to the lessor by the surrender, why couldn't it be argued that the transferee or assignee of this interest could sue the sublessee on his promise to pay rent to the lessee? In other words, why isn't the surrender a transfer or assignment to the lessor of the original tenant's interest? The court also declared that the lessor could not maintain an action for use and occupation against the sublessee, since the relationship of landlord and tenant did not exist between them. Although there seems to be some authority for the strict application of this proposition,[125] an Alabama court has ruled that the action of use and occupation will lie against a defendant who either came into possession unlawfully or entered as a party to a contract,

122. Johnson v. Moxley, 216 Ala. 466, 113 So. 656 (1927); Crump v. Tolbert, 210 Ark. 920, 198 S. W. (2d) 518 (1946); Cox v. Fenwick, 7 Ky. 538 (1817); Krider v. Ramsay, 79 N. C. 354 (1878).
123. Johnson v. Moxley, *supra* Note 122.
124. Krider v. Ramsay, 79 N. C. 354 (1878).
125. Littleton v. Wynn, 31 Ga. 583 (1860).

express or implied, creating between the parties the technical relationship of landlord and tenant, or another relationship imparting
similar rights and duties.[126]

The Arkansas Court ruled [126-a] that a lease of land to a rice grower
for the production of rice, with the reservation of a fourth of the
crop to the lessor, and a provision obligating the lessee to put down
a rice well at a cost payable from the proceeds of a fourth of the
rest, was not assignable by the lessee to persons who were not rice
growers. This case presents a peculiar situation and hence could not
be used as a precedent for the proposition that a farming contract
is not assignable.

In one instance the right to sublease was duly recognized. The
proponent of parol evidence tried to develop a theory that a subtenant would be considered a stranger to the original contract
within the well-recognized exception to the rule permitting a party
in that category to introduce oral testimony. The court, however,
refused to accept this view of the matter and ruled that parol
evidence was not admissible to vary or contradict the terms of a
written instrument.[127] Where there are no covenants in a lease
contract interdicting a sublease, it is a general rule that there can be
no objection to the transfer of the premises to an undertenant.[128]
In another case the lessor attempted to collect the rent in an action
against a person taking possession of the land under a contract with
the lessee. A jury question arose as to the lessor's acceptance of this
third party in place of the original tenant. It was held that the trial
judge had correctly instructed the jury that the transferee was not
liable if the lessor had treated the original tenant as his lessee until
the rent became due and suit was commenced.[129] This appeared to
be a correct statement of the law, since the transferee could not be
held liable under these facts, and the lessor would not be allowed
to make inconsistent claims with respect to the responsibility of the
lessee and the person claiming under him.

An Arkansas statute [130] provides that a tenant who has sublet any

126. Hamilton v. House, 6 Ala. App. 86, 60 So. 429 (1912). See also Smith's
Ex'rs. v. Houston, 16 Ala. 111 (1849).

126-a. Crump v. Tolbert, 210 Ark. 920, 198 S. W. (2d) 518 (1946).

127. Peters v. Pilcher, 211 Ala. 548, 100 So. 902 (1924).

128. Peters v. Pilcher, 211 Ala. 548, 100 So. 902 (1924); Hamilton v. House,
6 Ala. App. 86, 60 So. 429 (1912); Weatherly v. Johnson, 25 La. Ann. 229
(1873); Krider v. Ramsay, 79 N. C. 354 (1878).

129. Hamilton v. House, 6 Ala. App. 86, 60 So. 429 (1912).

130. Ark. Dig. Stat. (Pope, 1937) §8850.

portion of the land may not, before a final settlement with the landlord, take or collect rent from the subtenant without first obtaining the written statement of the landlord directing the amount to be so paid. In a case arising under this statute it was held that recovery in a tenant's action against a subtenant for rent would be allowed where the tenant, without obtaining such written instructions, had made a final settlement with the landlord before the proceedings were instituted.[131] A Kentucky statute [132] provides that, without the landlord's consent in writing, every assignment or transfer of a tenant's interest by one who has a term of less than two years shall entail the forfeiture of the lease and entitle the landlord to begin possessory proceedings. Under this act a case arose where the lessee had a two-year lease under which he occupied the land for a short while and then orally assigned his interest to another. The court decided that the right of the lessor to have the lease forfeited depended upon the length of the original term and not on how long the lease had yet to run at the time of the assignment. Therefore, since the original tenant had a two-year term, which was clearly not within the statute, the oral assignment was effective and there was no forfeiture.[133]

The right to assign or sublet being generally recognized at common law, modern leases often contain a provision absolutely or conditionally restricting assignments and/or subleases. There are many types of these covenants and conditional clauses.

A typical provision is the one which makes written consent of the landlord obligatory in any valid transfer of the lessee's interest. In a case involving a covenant of this general type, the lessee attempted to show a waiver. The lessor had testified that he did not object to the cultivation of the land by certain Negro subtenants and that he would not remove them if he got possession. The fact that he did not want to move them would be no waiver of the lessee's covenant not to sublet the premises without the written consent of the lessor. The remark was said to indicate no acquiescence to the subletting and no intention to waive the provision requiring written consent.[134] In another instance the lessee had agreed neither to assign nor sublet the rented land. The lease was absolute for the first year and optional with the lessee for two addi-

131. King v. Wilkerson, 149 Ark. 670, 235 S. W. 803 (1921).
132. Ky. Rev. Stat. (1946) §383.180.
133. Grizzle v. Pennington, 77 Ky. 115 (1878).
134. Grantham v. Walker, 159 Ark. 351, 252 S. W. 13 (1923).

tional periods, one for four years and the other for five. The covenant was held to cover the whole period that the lease might run, and it was declared that a transfer of the lease to another during this term would constitute a breach. It was also said that acceptance of the rent after the breach would not be considered as a waiver of the covenant unless the lessor, at the time of accepting, had knowledge of all the facts in the case. It was further declared that knowledge that there had been a breach during the year for which the lessor had received rent could not be considered as a waiver for the full term of the contract but would be a waiver for that year alone. As a matter of law, the establishment of the defense of waiver would not entitle the lessee or his transferee to a reimbursment for expenses incurred in making permanent improvements upon the premises while they were in possssion.[135]

With respect to a somewhat similar contract it has been held that, in the absence of any evidence tending to show that the tenant has authority to act as his landlord's agent, the fact that the landlord has consented to a sublease will not render him liable for the tenant's breach of a subleasing agreement.[136]

A South Carolina statute [136-a] provides that a sublease by a tenant without the written consent of the landlord is a nullity in so far as the rights of the landlord are concerned, and that rent collected by a tenant from a subtenant shall be deemed to be held in trust by the said tenant for the benefit of the landlord until the payment of the landlord's claim for rent. It is a question whether this statute will prohibit an assignment.

That a provision not to assign may be strictly construed is indicated in an early North Carolina opinion. Here a condition in a lease provided that the instrument would be void if the lessee assigned his interest. According to the court's statement, the purpose of the lessor in requiring such a condition had been to compel the lessee to retain an interest in the premises, since he had particular faith in the latter's skill and honesty. He did not intend to limit the lessee's operations by excluding the aid of associates. Hence it was held that this condition would not be construed in such a manner as to prevent a subletting or the employment of others to help with the project.[137] That this decision would be followed today is indi-

135. Walker v. Wadley, 124 Ga. 275, 52 S. E. 904 (1905).
136. Purdon v. Brussells, 23 Ky. Law Rep. 1796, 66 S. W. 22 (1902).
136-a. S. C. Stat. 1946, No. 873, §45.
137. Hargrave v. King, 40 N. C. 430 (1848).

cated by a recent North Carolina decision that an assignment will not be construed as a violation of a covenant not to sublet.[138]

ABORTIVE CONVEYANCE OR SUBLEASE BY TENANT

What is the result where a tenant makes an abortive transfer of real estate in which he has only a lessee's interest? It has been said that an attempted conveyance by a tenant in possession can pass no greater interest than the tenant is lawfully entitled to under the lease contract.[139] As is said by one court, "a stream can rise no higher than its source." [140] A conveyance under such circumstances operates as a mere assignment of the lessee's interest in the property.[141]

Sometimes a lessee in possession under a contract which has only a short time to run will make an agreement in the form of a sublease with another party for a future term. In one case of this kind it was held that such a contract was not rendered invalid because the tenant had no agreement with the landlord for an additional term.[142]

THE GEORGIA "ESTATE FOR YEARS" AND ITS APPLICATION

A very strange quirk is found in Georgia, where there are two categories in which a contract concerning the letting of land may fall. There is the "estate for years," [143] which is an estate in the land, and the relationship of landlord and tenant, which confers no estate upon the occupant and clothes him with a mere right to use the land and claim the produce.[144] No adequate criterion is set up in the law to help in the comparison and distinguishing of these two concepts. Hence it is rather difficult to attempt any critical analysis of this oddity and its consequences.

A case arose where the evidence showed that a tract of land was rented for fifteen years. The contract provided that a failure to comply with a covenant for the payment of rent at a certain time should terminate the "lease." Later the occupant let another person have a part of the land. The agreement by which this transfer was

138. Rogers v. Hall, 227 N. C. 363, 42 S. E. (2d) 347 (1947).
139. Missouri Pac. R.R. Co. v. Bozeman, 178 Ark. 902, 12 S. W. (2d) 895 (1929); Fordson Coal Co. v. Wells, 245 Ky. 291, 53 S. W. (2d) 564 (1932).
140. Fordson Coal Co. v. Wells, 245 Ky. 291, 53 S. W. (2d) 564 (1932).
141. Missouri Pac. R. R. Co. v. Bozeman, 178 Ark. 902, 12 S. W. (2d) 895 (1929).
142. Watkins v. Haigwood, 41 Ga. App. 598, 153 S. E. 609 (1930).
143. Ga. Code (1933) §§85-801-06.
144. Ga. Code (1933) §61-101.

made specified that if for any reason the original tenant failed to comply with the terms of his contract with the landowner, the transferee should have the right to pay the rent stipulated in the original lease and should thenceforth succeed to his transferor's rights. Upon the failure of the original tenant to perform, the transferee went to court and procured a decree of specific performance compelling the transfer of the above-mentioned portion of the property to himself. He claimed that the landowner and the original tenant had conspired to defeat his rights by having a new lease made with the latter's nephew, who had threatened to take possession and dig up all the fruit trees which the transferee had planted. The court ruled that there had been a cancellation of the original contract. The transferee claimed that an estate for years had been established and that by virtue of the decree of specific performance he had succeeded to the original tenant's rights, subject, of course, to the payment of rent. The court refused to follow this view of the law, however, and held that the relationship of landlord and tenant had been established. The conclusion was reached that the cancellation would cut off the right of the transferee, or rather the subtenant, to retain possession of the property.[145] There is no reason given for the decision, the appellate court merely affirming what had been decided in the lower tribunal.

It would seem that even under a landlord-tenant relationship the decision is unfair to the transferee or subtenant. In fact, if this is any indication of the results obtainable under the Georgia statute, it is recommended that the state legislature be urged to adopt more reasonable rules in respect to the tenancy law. If this case were followed, no transferee of a term would be safe from such machinations as the conspiracy allegedly occurring here. It must be remembered, however, that it is not actually stated that the allegations were true. Even in the absence of fraud or conspiracy, it is clear that the rights of the transferee should be protected in a case of this sort.

RENEWAL OF LEASE CONTRACTS

Contracts for the renewal of leases may be express or implied. Most of the cases to be considered here will involve express covenants, but it may be said that implied renewals are sometimes very important also. Such is the case when it is ruled that a renewal is

145. Johnson v. Brice, 151 Ga. 472, 107 S. E. 338 (1921).

implied where there is a lease for one year and the tenant, after the term has expired and with the assent of both parties, remains in possession of the premises and continues to pay rent to the landlord according to the terms of the lease.[146]

In respect to a tenancy from term to term, where the right to hold for the succeeding term is dependent upon the faithful performance of the conditions of rental for the preceding period, a breach of the contract during this past period, unless it is waived, will forfeit the right to the succeeding term.[147] The court in this case was very particular to point out that a different result might be reached where there was an independent contract for a new lease.

A few cases have arisen concerning express provisions permitting the renewal or extension of farm leases. In one instance a landlord, upon sufficient consideration, rented certain premises to a tenant for a term of three years, the contract giving the tenant the privilege of extending the lease for five additional years. It was said that this privilege was not void for lack of mutuality, since it was an integral part of the contract and was supported by the general consideration.[148]

An Arkansas lessee was given the right to extend the term from year to year for one, two, three, or four years. This covenant was construed to give the lessee an option to extend the lease by merely holding over and paying rent, a formal renewal not being required.[149] Another lease gave a term of eight years and provided that the tenant should have a right to renew for a term of ten years. The court declared that the contract did not grant an eighteen-year term through an automatic extension, but provided for a ten-year extension at the lessee's option, if he had not forfeited that right in the meantime.[150]

In Kentucky a lease contract gave a seven-year term along with a renewal option for eight additional years. The instrument provided that certain buildings, to be erected by the lessee, should belong to the lessor at the end of the stated time. The court interpreted this contract as giving the lessor the buildings at the end of the seven-year term, unless the lessee elected to renew the lease for the addi-

146. Allen v. Montgomery, 25 Ga. App. 817, 105 S. E. 33 (1920).
147. Hallbrooks v. Rosser, 143 Ark. 559, 221 S. W. 483 (1920).
148. Kerr v. Black, 137 Ga. 832, 74 S. E. 535 (1912).
149. Keith v. McGregor, 163 Ark. 203, 259 S. W. 725 (1924).
150. Felder v. Hall Bros. Co., 151 Ark. 182, 235 S. W. 789 (1921).

tional term, in which case they would become the lessor's property at the end of that period.[151]

In one instance a distinction between a renewal and an extension of a lease contract seems to have been attempted. The distinction was important because of the possible application of the Statute of Frauds. Here the court decided that the agreement was one of extension, and that it gave the lessee the refusal of the property for the following two years at the same rental figure. It was further declared that, upon exercising his option to extend the arrangement, the lessee became entitled to an extended term of two additional years. Following this theory, the Statute of Frauds would not be applicable, and it would not be necessary for the lessee's acceptance of the option to be in writing.[152]

Sometimes a lease will provide that the contract is to be terminated at the end of the stipulated time unless it is renewed by written agreement. In a situation of this kind the written contract was not renewed, the lessor merely telling the lessee that he might stay on the land. There was no definite agreement in respect to terms or conditions. The court treated the occupant as a person holding under a void contract and held that he was responsible only for the usual and customary rental and not for that stipulated by the agreement for the past year.[153]

As a final consideration, it may be said that a contract can be drafted in such a manner that the length of the term may be curtailed instead of being extended. Thus it was held that the nature of a written lease for five years was changed by an addition in pencil to the effect that "the lessee is to have the farm for the term of five years so long as the lessor and lessee can agree." [154] Sometimes the two ideas are combined, as in the cases where an agreement provides for an option to continue the pact from term to term for so long as conditions remain satisfactory to both parties.[155]

COMPLIANCE AS PREREQUISITE TO PERFORMANCE

It is often necessary to comply with the terms of a lease contract before a party can claim that there should be a full performance by the other party. In such instances the covenants are said to be

151. Parsons v. Ball, 205 Ky. 793, 266 S. W. 649 (1924).
152. Neal v. Harris, 140 Ark. 619, 216 S. W. 6 (1919).
153. Mitchell v. Henderson, 193 Ark. 1041, 104 S. W. (2d) 799 (1937).
154. Gay v. Hardman, 276 Ky. 624, 124 S. W. (2d) 1048 (1939).
155. Lamew v. Townsend, 147 Ark. 282, 227 S. W. 593 (1921).

dependent as distinguished from those that are independent.[156] Thus in one instance it was decided that payment of the rent as it accrued was of the essence of the agreement. It was held that the lessees, who had failed to pay the rent for an entire year, were not entitled to hold possession for the succeeding year. They were not permitted to claim reimbursement for improvements made on the premises.[157] In another case the landlord, at the time of delivering possession of a farm under a lease, had left a few miscellaneous articles in some of the rooms of the farmhouse. He had also rented a portion of the house under a continuing contract with a construction foreman who was in possession at the time when the lessee arrived to take control. It was said that the articles could have been removed in a few minutes after the unexpected arrival of the lessee and that therefore their presence alone did not constitute a breach. But the renting of the rooms to the construction foreman with the definite understanding that he might remain until his job was completed was held to be a breach of the lessor's agreement to give possession.[158]

By way of contrast, cases may arise in which the courts rule that there has been a sufficient performance. In one instance a Louisiana tenant injured his foot and could not do the work necessary for proper husbandry. However, the plowing and planting were carried on by his two sons, who were capable of performing the task. It was also shown that the farming methods employed, though not in accord with the most modern practices, were not completely outmoded or inefficient. The court held that there was no such breach as would justify the landlord in his efforts to take possession of the premises.[159]

Generally speaking, a lease contract will not be annulled where a party has partially met his obligations under the agreement, unless the breach is a material one. Where a proceeding was initiated to cancel a lease and eject a tenant, the landlord based his claim on the ground that the tenant had violated the contract by failing to grow certain crops which he had agreed to raise. It was said that the tenant's breach was so material that an annulment was justified. These particular crops, including money crops, had not even been put in, and ample time had been given to sow them, the landlord having waited until April to begin proceedings. The court said that

156. Tiffany, *Landlord & Tenant*, §51, p. 342.
157. Smith v. Caldwell, 78 Ark. 333, 95 S. W. 467 (1906).
158. Adams v. Hambrick, 161 Ky. 797, 171 S. W. 398 (1914).
159. Hammond v. Lafferty, 192 So. 746 (La. App., 1939).

it was no defense that the tenant was not possessed of sufficient seed and farming implements, since the landlord had not obligated himself to furnish these articles. An agreement was alleged by the lessee that the landlord would dispose of his dairy cows during the summer, thus giving the tenant the use of the entire barn for his own cattle. This was disproved by the tenant's admission that he had contracted to milk the landlord's dairy cows during the summer for a smaller sum than he would charge for that same service in the winter. The court rendered a judgment cancelling the lease and awarding possession to the landlord.[160]

MANNER OF OCCUPATION

Sometimes the scope of a lease contract may be influenced by the manner of the tenant's occupation of the rented premises. Thus, in an early Kentucky case, it was held that a tenant to whom a landowner had rented a certain tract of land, without delineating any boundaries, was *ipso facto* in possession of the whole tract, and it made no difference whether or not the tenant really occupied the entire estate.[161] In another instance a rented farm had two dwellings. The landlord, after executing the lease, lived in one of the houses for a part of the time and for the remainder rented it to a third person, collecting the rent therefrom. The tenant acquiesced in this arrangement for some years, and the lease was renewed from year to year. Under these circumstances it was said that the parties had intended that the tenant should have the use of only one of the houses. This was held to be the case, notwithstanding the fact that the language used in the lease was broad enough, if liberally construed, to give the tenant the use of every building on the premises.[162] Although the court did not mention it, this seemed very much like an argument of estoppel or laches. It might well be contended that the tenant, by not objecting to the landowner's use of the house, had estopped himself from making a point of the matter at a later date.

A share tenant under a farming contract has a duty to cultivate the land, and the extent and manner of cultivation and the acreage allotted respectively to suitable crops is addressed to wisdom and good husbandry.[162-a]

160. Lillard v. Hulbert, 9 So. (2d) 852 (La. App., 1942).
161. Lee v. McDaniel, 8 Ky. 235 (1818).
162. Ely v. Myers, 177 Va. 323, 14 S. E. (2d) 298 (1941).
162-a. Sledge v. Potts, 202 Miss. 480, 32 So. (2d) 262 (1947).

ABATEMENT OR APPORTIONMENT OF RENT
IN CATASTROPHIC CIRCUMSTANCES

Ordinarily, in the absence of a specific covenant excusing the lessee from liability in case of catastrophic occurrences, there is no cancellation or abatement of rent where the premises are made unsuitable for the intended use by the happening of some natural phenomenon like a flood or a storm.[163] The courts evidently considered such occurrences as acts of God and said that they would excuse the non-performance of a duty created by law but not one created by contract. There is here no implied covenant that the premises shall be fit for the purpose for which they were leased, and a person who wishes to protect himself from such occurrences must include a provision to that effect in the lease contract. However, in an early South Carolina case where a farmhouse was made uninhabitable by a storm, it was held the rent should be apportioned according to the period of time it was occupied.[164]

Under a Louisiana statute a lessee of a predial (agricultural) estate is not permitted to claim an abatement of the rent for the reason that either the whole or a portion of the crop has been destroyed by accidents, unless they be of such an extraordinary nature that the mishaps could not have been foreseen by either party to the tenancy contract at the time of execution.[165] In fact it has been said in one case that to justify an abatement the occurrence must be a catastrophy such as the ravages of war over a countryside formerly at peace.[166] An overflow of a river like the Mississippi is not an event of such infrequent occurrence or extraordinary nature that it could not have been foreseen. Hence it has been held that no abatement of rent is authorized in a case of this sort.[167] Another necessary condition for the abatement required by this statute is that the

163. Rogers v. Rob Roy Plantation, 208 Ark. 429, 186 S. W. (2d) 661 (1945); Patout v. Bourriaque, 44 So. (2d) 238 (La. App. 1950); Bunting v. Orendorff, 152 Miss. 327, 120 So. 182 (1929).

164. Ripley v. Wightman, 4 McCord 447 (S. C., 1828).

165. Payne v. James, 45 La. Ann. 381, 12 So. 492 (1893).

166. Vinson v. Graves, 16 La. Ann. 162 (1861).

167. Payne v. James, 45 La. Ann. 381, 12 So. 492 (1893); Jackson v. Michie, 33 La. Ann. 723 (1881); Norman v. Lacroix, 148 So. 458 (La. App., 1933); Haygood v. McKenna, 11 La. App. 312, 123 So. 479 (1929). But see Viterbo v. Friedlander, 120 U. S. 707, 7 Sup. Ct. 962 (1887), in which the Federal Supreme Court decided that a serious overflow which made a farm practically untillable was an extraordinary event, and this in spite of the state court's contrary holding.

damage to the agricultural tenancy must amount to at least half of the crop.[168]

This construction of the statute has made it practically mandatory for any lessee who wishes to protect himself to have inserted in his lease contract a provision permitting an abatement of rent in the event of an overflow. The state court has held that such a provision is enforceable.[169]

In a case where a crop failed because of an overflow, the lessee argued that the payment for supplies advanced by the lessor was conditioned upon the production of a crop and its delivery to him. The court declared that the failure of a particular fund or crop out of which a debt is to be paid will not operate as a discharge of the obligation.[170]

TERMINATION OF LEASE

When is a tenancy terminated? How long does the relationship continue? What terminates the tenant's interest in the land? The answers to these questions will often be important in determining whether a tenancy has continued or ceased to exist. All sorts of situations arise in which it is necessary to determine the exact time the tenancy came to an end.

In one instance a tenant took possession under an agreement to pay a standing rent of one hundred pounds of seed cotton. An agent of the landlord, authorized to rent but not to sell, made an unauthorized contract with the tenant for the sale of the property. The contract stipulated that the tenant should remain in possession and continue to make payment in cotton as interest on the purchase price. The landlord had no knowledge of this transaction but did receive the purchase money. The court ruled that the tenancy relationship, when once shown to exist, presumably continued for so long as the tenant was in possession. Therefore the burden of proving that the tenancy had been terminated by a contract to purchase was upon the tenant, which burden he had not sustained. Since the landlord had no knowledge of the unauthorized and unratified contract, he was not bound thereby. Hence the tenancy relationship

168. See Miller v. Texas & P. Ry. Co., 148 La. 936, 88 So. 123 (1921); Haygood v. McKenna, 11 La. App. 312, 123 So. 479 (1929).
169. Norman v. Lacroix, 148 So. 458 (La. App., 1933).
170. Blouin Co. v. Hebert, 134 La. 423, 64 So. 230 (1914).

continued, thus estopping the tenant from denying his landlord's title in accordance with the familiar rule to that effect.[171]

In South Carolina a life tenant died in April, and soon afterwards his executor rented the land from the remainderman for a term of ten years. The executor refused to pay the rent at the end of the year, and the remainderman successfully distrained for the rent. It was alleged but not proved that the executor had made the contract in ignorance of his rights under certain statutes which extend the life tenant's estate until the crop for the current year is finished.[172] The contract was regarded as a lease for an entire term of ten years and not as a lease from year to year to extend for ten years. The court said that it was wholly immaterial that the life estate had not terminated at death, but was extended, by operation of law, until the crop was harvested. It was argued that this consideration might have induced the remainderman to grant more favorable terms in the transaction for the long-term lease.[173] This seems somewhat specious, in view of the probability that the remainderman was just as ignorant of the real situation as the executor.

It has been said that neither the death of the lessor [174] nor a conveyance by him [175] will terminate a lease contract, his interest passing with the property. The same is true with respect to the interest of the lessee. The Georgia Court has held that a landlord may, without being an intruder, enter the premises upon the death of his tenant and finish the cultivation of the crops, if the circumstances be such that an entry is reasonably necessary for that purpose.[175-a]

In one instance a Mississippi lessee died and his administrator abandoned the premises. The lessor rented the land for a sum smaller than that which the lessee had agreed to pay and notified the administrator that the estate would be responsible for the difference. It was held that an action would lie against the administrator, who was not relieved from liability for the amount of rent called for by the lease. Therefore he was judged to be responsible for the deficiency. The court remarked that the lessor might even have permitted the

171. Rhodes v. Downing, 13 Ala. App. 494, 68 So. 788 (1915).

172. S. C. Code Ann. (1932) §§8797-99.

173. Fraser v. Davie, 5 Rich. 59 (S. C., 1851).

174. Kelly v. Kelly, 250 Ala. 664, 35 So. (2d) 686 (1948); Lewis v. Wilkins, 62 N. C. 303 (1868).

175. Cobb v. Johnson, 126 Ga. 618, 55 S. E. 935 (1906). See S. C. Stat. 1946. No. 873, §45-A.

175-a. Riddle v. Hodge, 83 Ga. 173, 9 S. E. 786 (1889).

premises to remain vacant and in that case could have recovered a greater sum, but he was not compelled to take this course.[176]

A lease for one year may include an option to continue from year to year for so long as conditions remain satisfactory to both parties. The continuance of the tenancy after the expiration of the first year will be contingent upon the satisfaction of the parties and the failure of either of them to terminate the contract according to the mutually reserved right. Each is entitled to reasonable notice from the other of an intention to terminate, and what constitutes reasonable notice is a question for the jury to determine from all the facts of the particular case. Under these circumstances, where a tenancy from year to year is created and notice is given after the start of a new year, it does not take effect until the end of that year, such being the rule in respect to this periodic tenancy.[177] Statutes with respect to notice to terminate certain tenancies, such as the tenancy at will or from year to year, are confined to these tenancies and have no application to cases in which the contract names a specific time for termination.[178] Moreover, where a specific method has been named for a notice to end the relationship, that method must be followed.[179]

A North Carolina lessor sold the rented premises and the purchaser brought a possessory action against the lessee. Evidence was introduced that when the tenant signed the lease the landowner's agent orally agreed to allow him to remain in possession after the expiration date set in the written agreement until a fixed future date. It was held that this testimony had been properly excluded under the parol evidence rule. The tenant also introduced a letter sent by the landlord notifying him to quit the premises. It was shown that this communication had been written nearly two months after the sale and received a month after the lease expired. This letter was also held to have been properly excluded. There can be no doubt that the original landowner, after selling the property, had no right to extend the lease.[180]

A landowner may make a lease contract with his tenant for a

176. Alsup v. Banks, 68 Miss. 664, 9 So. 895 (1891).

177. Lamew v. Townsend, 147 Ark. 282, 227 S. W. 593 (1921).

178. Graham v. Cauthen, 175 Miss. 751, 168 So. 58 (1936); Biber v. Dillingham, 111 S. C. 502, 98 S. E. 798 (1919).

179. Biber v. Dillingham, 111 S. C. 502, 98 S. E. 798 (1919).

180. Stewart v. Thrower, 212 N. C. 541, 193 S. E. 701 (1937).

time certain, with the added proviso that the tenancy will terminate if the premises are sold during the term.[181] In a case where this was done the court declared there could be no unexpired term in the event of a sale. A provision in the lease giving remuneration for damages sustained by reason of the conveyance was held to relate only to compensation for amounts expended for permanent improvements and for taxes paid by the lessee, which were in excess of the true value of the land for the part of the term that had passed.[182] It has also been held that an agreement by a lessee to allow the lessor to cut his term short by a sale must be supported by a consideration.[183]

When a leasehold interest of the tenant and the immediate reversionary interest become vested in the same party, a merger results, and the incidents of the relationship, including rent, are extinguished.[184] A fusion has been held to take place where a lessor bought his lessee's interest or right of occupancy at a sale under execution of a judgment for rent. The court declared that this merger did not operate retroactively to destroy the landlord's lien on property which had been sold by the sheriff in partial satisfaction of the judgment.[185] In one case a guardian rented the land of his ward to another and took no security for the rent. The ward reached his maturity before the rent was due and conveyed the land in fee to the lessee. It was held that a merger had taken place and that the claim for rent was extinguished.[186]

What happens when land which is leased is condemned under the power of eminent domain? According to a Mississippi case [187] a lessee, as owner of the term, is entitled to notice and damages just as any other owner. Where the whole of the premises is condemned, the tenancy relationship is dissolved, and the present value of the property is apportioned according to the respective interests of the lessor and lessee. The rule of apportionment is to give the lessor the value of his reversionary interest and the rents reserved during the term, less an abatement for present payment; and to give the lessee the value of his term, less the rent reserved on the premises. The

181. Jones v. Shibley, 113 Ark. 598, 166 S. W. 937 (1914).
182. Miller v. Jenkins, 95 Ark. 144, 128 S. W. 856 (1910).
183. Sullivan v. Wilson Mercantile Co., 168 Ark. 262, 271 S. W. 30 (1925).
184. McCullen v. Mercer, 192 Miss. 547, 6 So. (2d) 465 (1942).
185. Ranson v. Voiron, 176 La. 718, 146 So. 681 (1933).
186. Mixon v. Coffield, 24 N. C. 301 (1842).
187. Board of Levee Comm'rs. v. Johnson, 66 Miss. 248, 6 So. 199 (1889).

condemnation of a portion of the land dissolves the relationship *pro tanto* and the rent is so apportioned.

TRANSFER OF REVERSIONARY INTEREST

The owner of a reversion can convey the whole or any portion of the leased premises, such right being incident to the right of property and necessary to the full enjoyment thereof. He may sell to as many persons as he desires, and in several portions at different times.[188] As a general rule rent may be said to follow the reversion,[189] and in the case of the sale of such an interest, whether voluntary [190] or involuntary under the authority conferred in a security deed,[191] by a sale ordered in a court of equity,[192] or through other modes of transfer, a rent claim maturing after the sale is collectible by the transferee. However, if the rent matured prior to an effective transfer, the transferee is not entitled to enforce the claim.[193]

In the case of a mortgage or security deed, even after default, the right to collect the rent does not pass until some action is taken to intercept it.[194] When the rent is supposed to go to the transferee, it should be his to the exclusion of the original owner.[195] In fact he is entitled to the rent regardless of how it is to be paid, whether in a stipulated share of the crops or in some other form like cash.[196] Therefore, if the specified rent be in a share of the crops and they have matured after the sale, the transferee is entitled to have the rent in specifics paid to him.[197] If the crops mature prior to the sale or transfer, however, the transferee cannot recover.[198]

188. Cheairs v. Coats, 77 Miss. 846, 28 So. 728 (1900).

189. Lewis v. Wilkins, 62 N. C. 303 (1868).

190. Cobb v. Johnson, 126 Ga. 618, 55 S. E. 935 (1906).

191. Chastain v. Gardner, 187 Ga. 462, 200 S. E. 786 (1939); Neal v. Hubbard, 53 Ga. App. 267, 185 S. E. 384 (1936); Edwards v. Askew, 51 Ga. App. 85, 179 S. E. 598 (1935); Paul v. Mutual Benefit Life Ins. Co., 50 Ga. App. 762, 178 S. E. 926 (1935).

192. See Hand v. Liles, 56 Ala. 143 (1876), where the sale was not confirmed until after the expiration of the lease and the lessee had remained in undisturbed possession of the premises during the entire term.

193. Edwards v. Askew, 51 Ga. App. 85, 179 S. E. 598 (1935); Jennings v. Shannon, 200 N. C. 1, 156 S. E. 89 (1930).

194. Lamar v. Johnson, 16 Ala. App. 648, 81 So. 140 (1919).

195. Chastain v. Gardner, 187 Ga. 462, 200 S. E. 786 (1939).

196. Paul v. Mutual Benefit Life Ins. Co., 50 Ga. App. 762, 178 S. E. 926 (1935).

197. Ball v. Citizens' Bank of Rome, 143 Ga. 55, 84 S. E. 122 (1915); Neal v. Hubbard, 53 Ga. App. 267, 185 S. E. 384 (1936).

198. Jennings v. Shannon, 200 N. C. 1, 156 S. E. 89 (1930).

In one situation a landowner entered into a contract with a tenant stipulating that the former should receive as rent one-fourth of all the cotton, corn, and fodder raised on the place, "and at the expiration of five years, or when the said (tenant) shall leave the place, he is to leave the seed out of 16 bales of cotton on the place." The landowner sold the plantation and indorsed on the agreement a transfer of "the within contract" to the purchaser. It was said that this transaction transferred to the purchaser any rights which the landowner had in respect to the seed out of the sixteen bales. While the lease was still in effect the purchaser declined to allow the former owner to take possession of certain cotton seed on the place, as being the seed referred to in the contract, even though the consent of the tenant had been obtained. It was held that the purchaser was in no way responsible for the conversion of the cotton seed.[199]

A landlord's transfer of the title to leased premises, without more, will not abrogate the rental agreement with the tenants, since ownership in one particular person is not necessary to the continued existence of the tenancy relationship.[200]

It has been said that the landlord, when he sells leased lands, may reserve a right to sue for damages to the property caused by the lessee before the conveyance.[201]

The doctrine that rent follows the reversion can be applied in favor of devisees of the future interest in leased property, as well where this interest is directed to be sold and the proceeds divided amongst them, as where it is specifically willed to them.[202]

It seems to be well established that the death of the lessor will not terminate the leasehold interest in the land.[203] Upon his death intestate, within the term specified by the rental contract, the lands descend to the heirs, encumbered with the right of possession previously disposed of by their ancestor. They are not entitled to the immediate possession and cannot, merely as heirs, collect the rent for the land.[204]

In a Georgia case it was held that the rent was personalty, and that the personal representative of the decedent had the right to

---

199. Cobb v. Johnson, 126 Ga. 618, 55 S. E. 935 (1906).
200. Mathews v. Priest, 165 So. 535 (La. App., 1936).
201. Payne v. James, 42 La. Ann. 230, 7 So. 457 (1890).
202. See Lewis v. Wilkins, 62 N. C. 303 (1868).
203. Kelly v. Kelly, 250 Ala. 664, 35 So. (2d) 686 (1948); Lewis v. Wilkins, 62 N. C. 303 (1868).
204. Autrey v. Autrey, 94 Ga. 579, 20 S. E. 431 (1894).

collect the money or other rent and distribute it to those who might be entitled to it under the law. The court also came to the following conclusions: If tenants occupy the premises under a contract made with the intestate himself, a conveyance by an heir to a purchaser, which is silent in respect to both rents and the time of taking possession, passes no title to rents to become due from tenants who are rightfully in possession for the year during which the intestate died. But if the tenants occupy under contracts made with the administrator, it is otherwise, unless creditors or the expenses of administration are unsatisfied. In other words, when the heir, as such, would be entitled to rent collected by the administrator, his vendee will succeed to his rights in respect to rents accruing after the ownership changed hands.[205] The decision in this case may be influenced by the peculiarities of the Georgia law, which, as has been stated above, differentiates between an estate for years [206] and the landlord and tenant relationship, which passes no estate and entitles the tenant to the use alone.[207]

SURRENDER BY TENANT

Sometimes it may be to the advantage of both the lessor and the lessee that a tenancy be abandoned. The technical name for the device for accomplishing this is a "surrender." It is necessary to the efficacy of a transaction of this kind that both parties shall accede and indicate their consent. The agreement to surrender, if unexecuted, must be supported by a sufficient consideration.[208] Where there is an agreement effecting the release of reciprocal obligations, each release furnishes the consideration for the other.[209]

A surrender is like any other contract in that there must be an offer and acceptance.[210] The acceptance may be either express or implied. If, after an offer on the part of the tenant to surrender, the landlord resumes possession or exerts a control over the premises which is inconsistent with the tenant's right of occupation, a cancellation or rescission of the lease contract is effected and the tenant discharged from liability for future rent.[211] However, in the absence

205. Autrey v. Autrey, 94 Ga. 579, 20 S. E. 431 (1894).
206. Ga. Code (1933) §§85-801-06.
207. Ga. Code (1933) §61-101.
208. Sullivan v. Wilson Mercantile Co., 168 Ark. 262, 271 S. W. 30 (1925).
209. Penney v. Burns, 226 Ala. 273, 146 So. 611 (1933).
210. Penney v. Burns, 226 Ala. 273, 146 So. 611 (1933).
211. Johnson v. Watkins, 26 Ga. App. 759, 107 S. E. 341 (1921); Gay v. Peake, 5 Ga. App. 583, 63 S. E. 650 (1909).

of other facts showing that such a move was contemplated and accepted, no surrender is to be implied from the mere taking of the keys to a rented house from the tenant or his agent.[212]

In one instance an offer was made to surrender, and the lessor made no reply but soon afterwards took charge of the premises. He thereupon induced a subtenant to take up the rent note which he had given the lessees and execute a new note with the lessor as payee. The lessor had given no notice that he was managing the farm for the lessees or that he expected them to make up any deficiency. The court held that there was an offer on the part of the lessees to surrender and an acceptance by the lessor.[213] Again, a lessee, after being in possession a short while, removed his laborers from the land and abandoned it. Thereupon the owner, without giving the tenant notice that he intended to enter or to hold him responsible for the rent, leased a portion of the premises to others and placed them in possession, thereafter receiving rent. It was held that this amounted to an offer to surrender and an acceptance, and any liability of the original lessee for future rent was denied.[214]

Suppose the tenant subleases the land and then surrenders all his rights under the original lease. In a North Carolina case it was held that the land might be recovered in a possessory action against the sublessee, even though the sublease had not expired at the commencement of the action.[215] The rights of the subtenant do not seem to be adequately protected here.

Generally speaking, no particular form is required for an effective surrender. Thus it has been said that a lessee may abandon a tenancy contract by words or equivalent acts.[216] In South Carolina, however, a statute requires a surrender to be in writing,[217] and an oral agreement to surrender the unexpired portion of a term has been held ineffective under this statute.[218] In this instance the surrender had been made by an administratrix, and it was said that abandonment of the lease would be violative of her duty to the estate.

The sale of a term for years in land may result in a surrender. In

212. Johnson v. Watkins, 26 Ga. App. 759, 107 S. E. 341 (1921).
213. Williamson v. Crossett, 62 Ark. 393, 36 S. W. 27 (1896).
214. Rucker v. Tabor, 127 Ga. 101, 56 S. E. 124 (1906).
215. Lange v. Evans, 209 N. C. 747, 184 S. E. 467 (1936).
216. Mizell v. Mercer, 165 Ark. 224, 263 S. W. 398 (1924).
217. S. C. Code Ann. (1932) §7043.
218. Charles v. Byrd, 29 S. C. 544, 8 S. E. 1 (1888).

one instance of this kind the lessee put the transferee in possession and told the lessor that thereafter he must look to the transferee for the rent. Thereupon the lessor cancelled the original lease and executed another with the transferee named as lessee. It was held that this amounted to a complete surrender of the original tenancy and the creation of a new one.[219]

When the surrender of a lease before its expiration is unconditionally accepted by the lessor, without any reservation whatsoever, he can claim no damages because of the diminished rental paid thereafter by a new tenant.[220] Neither may a lessee, after surrendering, maintain a suit in equity to restrain the landowner or any subsequent tenant from cultivating the land or removing the crop.[221]

A South Carolina lessor, before the planting of the crop, had agreed to pay a merchant's debt incurred by the lessee as a part of an arrangement whereby the latter agreed to surrender the premises. The merchant made an effort to enforce a lien, and it was held that his remedy, if any, was not a proceeding to enforce a lien upon crops raised by a subsequent tenant, but an action sounding in contract based upon the lessor's promise to pay the indebtedness.[222]

It has also been held that where a landlord moved in after a surrender and his ex-tenant had agreed to remain on the leased premises for a number of days, during which time he looked after the owner's cattle and fed them, it could not be said that a new tenancy had been established.[223]

The courts' treatment of the problems growing out of a surrender is usually entirely adequate. However, it might be well to note that something should be done to protect the interests of a sublessee, a thing not done in the North Carolina controversy mentioned above.

EFFECTS OF THE ABANDONMENT OF CULTIVATION

Sometimes a tenant or cropper may, without any legitimate excuse, decide to abandon the agricultural project. This may occur in any season and at any point along the road to a finished crop. The tenant may leave before the crop is very far advanced or he

---

219. Morgan v. McCollister, 110 Ala. 319, 20 So. 54 (1896).
220. Everett v. Williamson, 107 N. C. 204, 12 S. E. 187 (1890).
221. Monig's Adm'x v. Phillips, 16 Ky. Law Rep. 838, 29 S. W. 970 (1895).
222. Brock v. Haley Co., 88 S. C. 373, 70 S. E. 1011 (1911).
223. Tuten v. Towles, 34 Ga. App. 465, 129 S. E. 906 (1925).

may not make his move until later in the year when the crop has practically matured. The reasons for the abandonment are of course varied. Frequently it is trouble with the landlord and dissatisfaction with the prospects for a good crop. There may be other reasons, however, such as family difficulties or just a restless spirit. When the abandonment occurs, the landlord is faced with a rather awkward situation. Obviously he will wish to do everything he can to prevent a total loss. An action for breach of the contract will in most instances prove useless, as most of the tenants are financially irresponsible. One solution of this difficulty is for him to take over the property and finish the crop, charging the tenant for his expenses in so completing the tasks which the latter had promised to perform.

In a few of the Southeastern states statutes have been enacted which deal with situations of this kind, while in others courts have rendered decisions which delineate the rights of the parties where there has been an abandonment. While there are some local differences, the general theme of this legislation and judicial interpretation can be said to be the protection of the landlord against the delinquent or irresponsible tenant. The usual tenor of the statutes and decisions is to allow the landlord to go on the land and finish the crop, with the reserved right to sue for any damages which may have been caused by the tenant's failure to fulfill his obligations under the contract.

Thus in Alabama a landlord may recover the leased premises when a tenant has refused or failed to plant a crop without just excuse for the refusal or failure.[224] When the tenant has removed from the premises, leaving an immature crop, the landlord may enter and finish the cultivation, the cost to be paid from the proceeds along with the rent and advances.[225] A Kentucky statute [226] provides that "when a tenant enters or holds premises by virtue of a contract, in which it is stipulated that he is to labor for his landlord and he fails to begin such labor, or if, having begun, without good cause fails to comply with his contract, his right to the premises shall at once cease, and he shall abandon them without demand or notice." In Mississippi if a tenant deserts the premises and leaves them unoccupied or uncultivated, with the result that the remedy of distress

224. Ala. Code (1940) tit. 31, §24.
225. Ala. Code (1940) tit. 31, §13.
226. Carroll's Ky. Stat. Ann. (Baldwin, 1936) §2327.

will not satisfy the landlord's just claim, any justice of the peace may, upon the affidavit of the injured party and the successful outcome of the resultant hearing, put the landlord in possession of the abandoned farm.[227] Statutes in South Carolina [228] and Virginia [229] authorize the landlord to repossess the land when the tenant has abandoned it. The same is true under certain North Carolina laws [230] applying to some counties but not to others. In Arkansas an act dealing with croppers provides that if any laborer shall abandon his employer, he shall thereupon forfeit his wages, namely, the share of the crop due him under the cropping agreement.[231] This act has been applied in at least one case, the court ruling that the evidence of abandonment should have been submitted to the jury.[232]

Where an Arkansas tenant abandoned the crop and failed to carry out the terms of the lease, it was said that the landlord could not only collect the rent out of the crop, but also gather, gin, and bale the tenant's cotton. In addition he was permitted to take and retain, against the tenant or his mortgagee, remuneration for expenses incurred in preserving the cotton from waste and preparing it for market.[233] Thus it may be said that the Arkansas Court, without legislative sanction, has reached practically the same results as those which have been obtained in other jurisdictions where statutes have been enacted.

A Georgia tenant was shown to have abandoned a crop on leased premises. The landlord re-entered and cultivated the crop to maturity without obtaining the consent of the tenant. In this process the landlord incurred expenses which were alleged to exceed the value of the matured crop. Having credited the tenant with the value of the crop, he attempted to recover for the sum of the advances made both before and after the abandonment. The court, however, limited his recovery to the value of the advances made prior to the tenant's breach.[234]

In an instance where an Alabama tenant had been charged with allowing land to lie idle, it was said that proof of this would entitle

227. Miss. Code Ann. (1942) §959.
228. S. C. Stat. (1946), No. 873, §47.
229. Va. Code Ann. (Michie, 1936) §5518.
230. N. C. Gen. Stat. (1943) §42-27.
231. Ark. Dig. Stat. (Pope, 1937) §8842.
232. Crawford v. Slaten, 155 Ark. 283, 244 S. W. 32 (1922).
233. Fry & Co. v. Ford, 38 Ark. 246 (1881).
234. Douse v. Griffen, 37 Ga. App. 734, 141 S. E. 672 (1928).

the landlord to such a portion of the crop actually raised as his share would have amounted to if proper husbandry had been expended upon the project. The difficulty in computing this amount was not a fatal stumbling block in the way of a recovery.[235] It is interesting to note in this connection that a Louisiana statute [236] provides that where a tenant takes possession of land and fails or refuses to cultivate the premises or abandons the same, without a reasonable excuse, he shall be responsible to the landlord for damages to "an amount equal to the market value of the average crop that would have been grown on said land, or on like land located in the immediate vicinity."

Where there has been an abandonment, it seems to be proper, though not obligatory, for the landlord to allow a furnisher of supplies, in order to avoid loss, to enter and finish cultivating and gathering the tenant's crop. In the event that he does so, and after a proper rental has been paid, the crop must be turned over to the supplyman. Should he fail to avail himself of the opportunity thus offered, any right he may have to the crop is relinquished in favor of the landlord, and he cannot levy upon it afterwards as the property of the tenant. Where, in accordance with such a renunciation, the landlord finished the production of the abandoned crop, the advancer of the supplies was not allowed to claim any priority over the landlord. Perhaps if a surplus remained after the satisfaction of the claim for rent and the payment of the expenses incurred by the landlord in completing the work on the crop, the furnisher might maintain an action.[237]

The South Carolina court has held that where the abandonment was not due to illness or other extenuating circumstances, the tenant by his action forfeited all interest in the project.[238] A dissenting judge, however, was of the opinion that if the crop had been advanced by the cultivator's labor to a point where it would be of material value to the landlord, then the tiller of the soil should be given some form of compensation for his labor prior to the abandonment.

Often the abandonment of the project will not be complete.

235. Wheat v. Watson, 57 Ala. 581 (1877).
236. La. Gen. Stat. Ann. (Dart, 1932) §6604.
237. Wheat v. Watson, 57 Ala. 581 (1877); Thigpen v. Leigh, 93 N. C. 47 (1885).
238. Salley v. Cox, 94 S. C. 216, 77 S. E. 933 (1913).

There will be no desertion of the premises but only a failure to cultivate at all or to use proper methods of cultivation. It is clear that a difference of opinion over the proper methods to be employed would not justify the landlord in taking over the crop and evicting the tenant.[239] In Louisiana a tenant was shown to have abandoned a portion of a cotton crop, neglected the rent, and unnecessarily delayed the picking of the cotton. Under these circumstances the court held that the landlord could institute an immediate suit to recover his share of the crop and the advances made to the tenant.[240] Furthermore, courts in the same state have said that a landlord may discontinue the advancing of supplies agreed upon if the tenant either refuses to work the crop and care for livestock supplied under the agreement[241] or does not labor as assiduously as he might have done.[242] The doctrine last stated might lead to abuse by unscrupulous landlords. The Alabama court has held that damages caused by imperfect cultivation cannot be accurately ascertained by calculation or be the subject of an affidavit in support of a writ of attachment, and that they cannot justify the landlord's possession of the crop against the holder of a recorded chattel mortgage.[243]

It has been said that where a farmer abandoned the premises through the fault of his landlord before the crop was wholly gathered, there would be no credit to the landlord for the expense of harvesting the portion of the crop which had been gathered after the farmer's departure.[244] The decision would have been otherwise if there had been no fault on the part of the landlord and the farmer had broken his contract by leaving. If no abandonment has been actually shown, the landlord will not be entitled to his expenses in finishing the crop, and an appropriation will make him guilty of a conversion.[245]

Generally speaking, it may be said that the courts have made satisfactory disposal of the few abandonment cases which have arisen in our region and have rightly interpreted such statutes as have been enacted on this subject. It might be well, however, to

---

239. Heaton v. Slaten, 25 Ala. App. 81, 141 So. 267 (1932).
240. Dixon v. Alford, 143 So. 679 (La. App., 1932).
241. Harrison v. Goldberg, 133 La. 389, 63 So. 59 (1913).
242. Dixon v. Alford, 143 So. 679 (La. App., 1932).
243. Wilkinson v. Ketler, 59 Ala. 306 (1877).
244. Skelton v. Baker, 189 Ala. 512, 66 So. 695 (1914).
245. Heaton v. Slaten, 25 Ala. App. 81, 141 So. 267 (1932).

encourage legislators to pass more adequate laws concerning this matter. There are some states in which no statute at all has been enacted on this important subject. In these jurisdictions the courts are left to do what they can according to common-law rules, which are often inadequate to meet present needs.

FORFEITURE UPON EXPRESS OR IMPLIED CONDITIONS

Many leases have provisions which expressly declare that the tenant's interest is to be forfeited if certain conditions stated in the instrument are not met. Furthermore, conditions are often implied, and a failure to meet these implied terms authorizes a forfeiture just as readily as the breach of an express provision. A condition differs from a covenant in that a breach of the former will entail a forfeiture of the tenant's interest, while a breach of the usual covenant will not have such dire results. A good illustration of this difference is to be found in a Kentucky case. Here the lessee agreed to execute a rent note with personal security to be approved by the lessor's agent. There was no specific provision for a forfeiture should he fail to give the note or pay the rent. The court declared that clauses of the lease were not worded as conditions providing for a re-entry upon a breach, but only as covenants to meet the obligations for the rent. Therefore, a default in the payment of the agreed rental did not work a forfeiture of the term.[246]

Conditions may be implied from the circumstances of a particular case. In one instance an attorney purchased land at a foreclosure sale and agreed to permit the former owners to remain on the premises for a reasonable time. After taking possession the former owners brought suit to impose a trust on the land in their own favor. The court intimated that by so doing they had violated the implied terms of their agreement and had thereby forfeited their right of possession.[247]

Provisions which call for a forfeiture upon the failure of the lessee to live up to some stipulation in the agreement are clearly conditions. An instance of this may be seen where a lease provided that a non-compliance with a clause which obligated the lessee to make certain improvements by a specified time would entail a forfeiture.[248] In considering a clause authorizing a forfeiture for non-

246. Morgan v. Chamberlain, 156 Ky. 369, 160 S. W. 1066 (1913).
247. Griffin v. McKay, 199 Ark. 747, 135 S. W. (2d) 850 (1940).
248. Winn v. State, 55 Ark. 360, 18 S. E. 375 (1892).

payment of rent, the Arkansas court has declared that the lessor, in order to enforce the penalty, must bring himself strictly within its provisions.[249] It has also been said that a stipulated right to cancel a lease in case of a default in the payment of rent existed only in favor of the lessor and for his benefit.[250]

A provision for forfeiture for non-payment of rent or other reasons may be waived, and where the evidence on the point of waiver is conflicting, it is error to fail to submit the testimony to the jury.[251] Waiver may be express or implied but cannot be inferred from mere silence unless other circumstances exist, and once there has been a waiver it cannot be recalled.[252] Acceptance of rent after a breach of the condition will commonly be considered as a waiver of the right to have the lease forfeited.[253] This is true only where the lessor had full knowledge of the facts concerning the breach.[254] In accordance with this rule a lessor was held to have waived his right of re-entry where he had waited until after the beginning of the year to assert his right and knew that its assertion at that time would be prejudicial to the lessee.[255]

In one situation a lessee released to his landlord a portion of the demised premises for a consideration to be credited on the rent subsequently accruing. This was said to constitute an affirmance of the continuance of the tenancy at the time of the execution of the release, and therefore a prior breach of the terms of the lease contract was waived. In this case the landlord gave notice, pursuant to a requirement of the lease, of his intention to re-enter in ten days, alleging a violation of a condition in the lease to the effect that the lessee should not clear lands or cut and destroy timber. According to the contract, the lease was not to be automatically void upon the breach of the condition, but could only become so at the option of the lessor. Another provision made it possible for the lessor to object if the lessee failed to make certain repairs. In the possessory action the court pointed out that the lessor had brought the suit upon the theory that a forfeiture had resulted from a breach of the condition

249. Sells v. Brewer, 125 Ark. 108, 187 S. W. 907 (1916).
250. Penney v. Burns, 226 Ala. 273, 146 So. 611 (1933).
251. Sells v. Brewer, 125 Ark. 108, 187 S. W. 907 (1916).
252. Penney v. Burns, 226 Ala. 273, 146 So. 611 (1933).
253. Brooks v. Rodgers, 99 Ala. 433, 12 So. 61 (1892); Richburg v. Bartley, 44 N. C. 418 (1853).
254. Brooks v. Rodgers, 99 Ala. 433, 12 So. 61 (1892).
255. Penney v. Burns, 226 Ala. 273, 146 So. 611 (1933).

concerning the timber, and that upon the trial he had attempted to introduce evidence with respect to a breach of the provision concerning repairs. To allow him to do so would give the lessee no opportunity to prepare a defense concerning the violation of the latter provision, which the court treated as a covenant and not a condition. The lessor could no doubt sue and recover damages for the breach of this covenant, but such a remedy would entail the exercise of a right far different from the forfeiture which he was trying to enforce here. It would be manifestly unjust to permit the lessor, after notifying the lessee of the grounds upon which he based his claim of forfeiture and right of re-entry, to introduce evidence with respect to the breach of an entirely different provision, of which the lessee has been given no notice in the pleading.[256]

An Arkansas lease of a tract of land provided that the rent should be payable in advance on the first day of each month and that any default in the payment would bring about forfeiture. It was shown that the lessee had never paid the rent on the first day of the month but had always paid it before the end of the month. Though the rent did not inure to the sole benefit of the lessors, their continued acceptance of the late payment was said to constitute a waiver of the right to claim a forfeiture because of the lessee's failure to pay promptly. It seems that it is within the jurisdiction of a court of equity under these circumstances, even in the absence of fraud, mistake, or accident, to give the lessee relief, all arrears of rent having been either paid or tendered.[257]

DAMAGES FOR BREACH OF LEASE CONTRACT

Where the landowner has failed to fulfill his obligations under a lease contract, the general rule in respect to the measure of damages seems to be that the lessee will be allowed the difference between the amount of rent agreed upon and the rental value of the premises.[258] If there is no difference, then the lessee may recover only nominal

256. Brooks v. Rodgers, 99 Ala. 433, 12 So. 61 (1892).
257. Pierce v. Kennedy, 205 Ark. 419, 168 S. W. (2d) 1115 (1943).
258. Nelson v. Nelson, 249 Ala. 482, 31 So. (2d) 685 (1947); Tomlinson v. Williams, 210 Ark. 66, 194 S. W. (2d) 197 (1946); Howell v. Duty, 178 Ark. 1196, 10 S. W. (2d) 857 (1928); Sullivan v. Wilson Mercantile Co., 172 Ark. 914, 290 S. W. 938 (1927); Person v. Williams, 125 Ark. 174, 187 S. W. 1063 (1916); Thomas v. Croom, 102 Ark. 108, 143 S. W. 88 (1912); Miller v. Townley, 57 Ga. App. 645, 196 S. E. 80 (1938); Sheppard v. Warthen, 19 Ga. App. 677, 92 S. E. 39 (1917); Devers v. May, 124 Ky. 387, 99 S. W. 255 (1907).

damages.[259] It has been said that there can be no recovery in the absence of evidence with respect to the rent agreed upon.[260]

How is the value of the term to be calculated? In Georgia a lower court held that in cases where the landlord refused to perform, the proper measure of damages was the difference between the gross profits and the rent fixed by the agreement. The appellate court, however, declared that this proposition was erroneous in that it failed to take into account the cost of production, and emphasized that the scale of measurement used by the lower court would make it more advantageous for a landowner to break his contract at the beginning of the term than to perform his obligations under its provisions.[261] In three later decisions the principle of the appellate court was reiterated, the court evidently being of the opinion that the true value of the term is the difference between the value of the gross profits from the products of the farm and the cost of production, or in other words, the net gain.[262]

In Arkansas it has been said that the "rental value" is not the probable profits which might accrue to the tenant but may be more truly said to be a sum, ascertained by proof of the rent the premises would bring or by evidence of other facts, which would represent the fair value of the land for the term.[263]

In case of breach of contract by the landlord, the court may properly consider the market value of the crops, less the expense of raising and harvesting them; and also such sums as the tenant and the dependent members of the family could have earned in other employment.[263-a]

The law with respect to probable profits as a measure of damages in farm tenancy cases is in a rather confused state. In fact it may be said that, in some jurisdictions at least, the authorities cannot be reconciled. In some instances such an estimate seems to have been approved where sufficient data exists from which a definite calculation can be made, while in others it is declared that probable profits

259. Howell v. Duty, 178 Ark. 1196, 10 S. W. (2d) 857 (1928).

260. Person v. Williams, 125 Ark. 174, 187 S. W. 1063 (1916).

261. Palmer v. Ingram, 2 Ga. App. 200, 58 S. E. 362 (1907).

262. Shiver v. Burkett, 39 S. E. (2d) 431 (Ga. App., 1946); Miller v. Townley, 57 Ga. App. 645, 196 S. E. 80 (1938); Nicholson v. Williamson, 29 Ga. App. 692, 116 S. E. 321 (1923).

263. Sullivan v. Wilson Mercantile Co., 172 Ark. 914, 290 S. W. 938 (1927).

263-a. Nelson v. Nelson, 249 Ala. 482, 31 So. (2d) 685 (1947).

are much too conjectural to form the basis for a recovery. It is probable that the same principles will apply no matter who has broken the contract, the lessor or the lessee,[264] or whether the cultivator is considered a tenant or a cropper.[265]

In Georgia it seems that probable profits may serve as a proper guide for the computation of damages in tenancy cases,[266] and the same result seems to have been reached in controversies of this sort in Alabama [267] and Kentucky,[268] although there are instances in both jurisdictions where the courts seem to have refused to apply this measuring rod.[269] It has been said in a recent Tennessee case that loss of profits may form the basis of a claim for damages where farming operations are involved, the court recognizing a distinction between breaches of agricultural contracts and agreements in respect to urban business property.[270]

The opposing view that such a measure of damages is merely conjectural and therefore can form no basis for a recovery has found some support in Arkansas,[271] Florida,[272] Louisiana,[273] and Mississippi.[274] It has been said that the courts are slow to adopt the profit rule as a measure of damages and will not do so where a more certain and definite means of computation can be found.[275]

In Arkansas, however, there are at least some instances where probable profits seem to have been used as a measure of damages. In

264. See Miller v. Townley, 57 Ga. App. 645, 196 S. E. 80 (1938); Clifton v. Hester, 139 Miss. 524, 104 So. 609 (1925).

265. See Williamson v. Payne, 30 Ga. App. 652, 118 S. E. 598 (1923); Somers v. Musolf, 86 Ark. 97, 109 S. W. 1173 (1908).

266. Miller v. Townley, 57 Ga. App. 645, 196 S. E. 80 (1938); Williamson v. Payne, 30 Ga. App. 652, 118 S. E. 598 (1923).

267. Nelson v. Nelson, 249 Ala. 482, 31 So. (2d) 685 (1947); Wilson v. Stocks, 231 Ala. 58, 163 So. 606 (1935); Snodgrass v. Reynolds, 79 Ala. 452, 58 Am. Rep. 601 (1885).

268. Lawrence v. Fielder, 186 Ky. 324, 216 S. W. 1068 (1919).

269. See Dawson v. Haygood, 235 Ala. 648, 180 So. 705 (1938); Cundiff v. Cundiff, 18 Ky. Law Rep. 1059, 39 S. W. 433 (1897); Smith v. Phillips, 16 Ky. Law Rep. 615, 29 S. W. 358 (1895).

270. Fuqua v. Madewell, 25 Tenn. App. 140, 153 S. W. (2d) 133 (1941).

271. Brown v. Bradford, 175 Ark. 823, 1 S. W. (2d) 14 (1927); Johnson v. Inman, 134 Ark. 345, 203 S. W. 836 (1918); Person v. Williams, 125 Ark. 174, 187 S. W. 1063 (1916); Thomas v. Groom, 102 Ark. 108, 143 S. W. 88 (1912).

272. Rutig v. Lake Jem Land Co., 155 Fla. 420, 20 So. (2d) 497 (1945).

273. Florsheim v. Penn, 18 La. App. 375, 137 So. 749 (1931).

274. Clifton v. Hester, 139 Miss. 524, 104 So. 609 (1925).

275. Johnson v. Inman, 134 Ark. 345, 203 S. W. 836 (1918).

one of these cases the lessee broke the contract by planting only 35 acres out of 120 which he had agreed to plant in a certain crop.[276] In another instance prospective profits were allowed to form the basis for a claim against a landlord who had broken his contract with a cropper, the court allowing the owner to set off a sum representing the amount of money the cropper would have made in other employment had he made reasonable efforts to find work elsewhere.[277] Here the contract required the cropper to furnish the labor of his family, including that of two brothers. It was decided that the sum due the cropper could not be reduced by the amount the brothers had earned during the remainder of the unexpired term, but that he was only required to suffer a deduction for the cost of their services. The landlord could not require the cropper to continue to employ them, and hence their earnings in other occupations, to which they had transferred, could not be used to minimize the damages caused by the landlord's breach.

Even in jurisdictions where profits, when sufficiently definite, are considered a proper element in the measurement of damages, there must be enough data to give the jury a just, fair, and full estimate of the injury suffered by the complaining party.[278] In one instance an appellate court indicated its approval of evidence in respect to the kind of crop the land was capable of producing, the adaptability of the land to the crop planted, the average yield per acre of land where similar conditions had prevailed, and the market value of the prospective crops.[279] In another the court approved testimony of the different varieties of crops the tenants had planned to cultivate, the number of acres planted to each crop, the estimated yield and its value, and the extent of a reasonable production.[280]

It seems that it is proper, in estimating the value of land for rental purposes, to receive evidence of the rent brought by neighboring lands of a like quality, during the same period, and also testimony

276. Arkansas Rural Rehabilitation v. Longino, 192 Ark. 912, 95 S. W. (2d) 897 (1936).

277. Somers v. Muself, 86 Ark. 97, 109 S. W. 1173 (1908).

278. Wilson v. Stocks, 231 Ala. 58, 163 So. 606 (1935); Snodgrass v. Reynolds, 79 Ala. 452, 58 Am. Rep. 601 (1885); Miller v. Townley, 57 Ga. App. 645, 196 S. E. 80 (1938); Williamson v. Payne, 30 Ga. App. 652, 118 S. E. 598 (1923); Lawrence v. Fielder, 186 Ky. 324, 216 S. W. 1068 (1919). See also Gulley v. Raynor, 185 N. C. 96, 116 S. E. 171 (1923).

279. Farrow Mercantile Co. v. Riggins, 14 Ala. App. 529, 71 So. 963 (1916).

280. Shiver v. Burkett, 39 S. E. (2d) 431 (Ga. App., 1946).

that, during that time, many nearby plantations had been allowed to lie idle and that it was common practice in the vicinity for plantations to be rented once in every four or five years for no other consideration than an agreement by the tenant to make repairs.[281] Where similarity of conditions is not shown to exist, however, testimony with respect to the amount of money received for a crop raised on a neighboring tract during a past year is inadmissible.[282] It was also held that where a tenant had executed a rent note in which the amount to be paid the landlord was definitely fixed, it was proper to exclude evidence showing what the premises rented for in prior and subsequent years.[283]

In Kentucky recovery was denied where a share tenant instituted a suit for breach of a lease contract on the fifteenth of March, a month after the agreement was made and before a tobacco crop could have been planted or a plant bed prepared by burning the ground. The court seemed to be of the opinion that in the case of a share tenant there was no basis for an accurate estimate of damages prior to the maturing of the crop and suggested that the tenant should have waited until the crop was produced and ready for market, at which time the tenant's damages would have been better subject to calculation. An added remark was made that this delay in bringing suit would give the tribunal an opportunity to obtain additional information about weather conditions and seasonal changes, the character and quality of the crops actually grown on the land, and the market value of the produce. The court declared that a different rule should apply in the case of a cash tenant, the correct measure of damages in such a situation being the difference between the contract price and the actual value of the interest in the land.[284]

A Kentucky tenant introduced evidence of expenses incurred in relieving himself from a contract subletting a portion of the premises, in obtaining a residence for his family to move into, and in efforts to induce the landlord to carry out the terms of the contract. Additional testimony was brought forward showing the productiveness of the land, the adaptability of portions of the property to the

281. Royston v. Royston, 29 Ga. 82 (1859).
282. Doyle v. Whitley, 214 N. C. 814, 200 S. E. 888 (1939).
283. Simpson v. East, 124 Ala. 293, 27 So. 436 (1900).
284. Turpin v. Jones, 189 Ky. 635, 225 S. W. 465 (1920).

raising of certain crops, and the value of parts of the uncultivated lands for pasturage. The court held that all of these items were admissible on the issue of damages.[285]

In a rather unusual Georgia case the court appears to have adopted the view that in estimating the value of a lease it might consider labor, supplies, and fertilizer utilized in the preparation and cultivation of specified land. The court felt these allowances should be made even though such work and merchandise had been expended in the cultivation of a first crop subsequently destroyed by a hail storm, the destruction of which led to the making of a new contract, broken by the landlord. From the language used by the court, it would appear that a recovery could be had on these items, no matter to which crop they had been devoted.[286]

An Alabama lessee produced evidence showing that the property leased consisted of a meadow of about thirty acres sown in "Johnson grass," one crop of which was ready for mowing. With this as a background, it was ruled that the lessee could introduce testimony tending to prove the number of crops of this grass the land would produce in each year with normal seasons and the probable quantity and market value of each crop as it matured. It was said that this evidence was properly admitted, not as a basis for the recovery of profits as such, but as facts to be considered by the jury in estimating the value of the land for the term.[287]

A North Carolina landowner who was seeking to recover rent admitted that in violation of the lease contract he had ousted a tenant, seized a mule and some guano which he himself had supplied, and refused to furnish an agreed amount of fertilizer. In a cross-action for the breach the tenant set up the contract and introduced evidence showing the value of his services in preparing the land for cultivation. Here the court ruled that such testimony was admissible on the issue of damages.[288]

The Arkansas court dismissed as too remote a claim for a sum expended by a tenant to buy a rake needed in cultivating and harvesting a prospective crop of alfalfa on premises which he had not been permitted to use fully. A similar point was made with respect

285. Lawrence v. Fielder, 186 Ky. 324, 216 S. W. 1068 (1919).
286. Sheppard v. Warthen, 19 Ga. App. 677, 92 S. E. 39 (1917).
287. Snodgrass v. Reynolds, 79 Ala. 452, 58 Am. Rep. 601 (1885).
288. Seawell v. Person, 160 N. C. 291, 76 S. E. 2 (1912).

to a claim for a loss sustained in a deal for hogs and cattle purchased for pasturing on the land.[289]

The lessee may be the one who fails to carry out the agreement made by the parties. In one such situation it was held that a lessor who was entitled to receive a certain amount of cotton as rent would be permitted to recover the value of the product instead of the agreed number of units of the cotton itself.[290]

In a suit by a landlord to collect the rent, a tenant may recover, either in an action of his own or by way of a counterclaim, any special damages which he may have suffered as a result of the landlord's failure to fulfill his obligations under the lease contract.[291]

In one instance the lessor alleged that certain pecan trees on the leased premises had been injured by rabbits. The court declared that in the case of special damages of this sort it must be made to appear that at the time the contract was made the lessee expressly or impliedly consented to be bound in respect to extraordinary damages of the type alleged here to have been suffered. It was decided that there was not sufficient evidence to show that the lessee knew the predatory habits of rabbits with respect to pecan trees or that the lessee's failure to cultivate the land had caused the pecan grove to become infested with these marauding animals.[292] This case shows that damages which are a mere remote possibility at the time a contract is executed and which are not in the contemplation of the parties to the transaction will not be allowed.

CONCLUSION

The subject of lease contracts and their incidents has been discussed elsewhere in this treatise wherever some other problem has seemed to require a clarification or amplification of the material examined in the present chapter. In fact the entire treatise is replete with instances in which the principles herein reviewed are applied. However, a fundamental exposition of the general principles governing the lease contract through its various phases from execution to termination seemed to be an indispensable requirement for a thorough analysis of the problems which lie ahead.

289. Sullivan v. Wilson Mercantile Co., 172 Ark. 914, 290 S. W. 938 (1927).
290. Stansel v. Roberts, 35 La. Ann. 885 (1883).
291. Dawson v. Haygood, 235 Ala. 648, 180 So. 705 (1938); Devers v. May, 124 Ky. 387, 99 S. W. 255 (1907); Florsheim v. Penn, 18 La. App. 375, 137 So. 749 (1931).
292. Arkansas Rural Rehabilitation v. Longino, 192 Ark. 912, 95 S. W. (2d) 897 (1936).

IV

Shifting Relationships—Option Contracts

SOMETIMES it is desirable for the parties to a real estate transaction to draw up an agreement which will allow a change of relationships after some time has elapsed or upon the performance or non-performance of some condition. In such instances the happening of an event is usually made the point of this change. Again there may be an agreement under which either the landlord or the tenant has an option to decide whether a change shall be made. Many cases involving such changes in status have arisen in the courts of the Southeastern group of states.

Depending upon the type of contract involved, the tenancy may come into being immediately or in the future. The contract can be so worded that a tenancy will spring up out of an interest of another kind, as a sale or mortgage transaction. In these and other situations the tenancy usually comes into being by operation of law. Again, the transferee may be given an immediate interest for years with the privilege to convert his term into a more permanent estate in the land.

There are many and varied contracts in which a sale or mortgage transaction may be followed by a lease. The crux of such an agreement is the condition which is the focal point of interest in the real estate transaction. A discussion of a few of the variations to be found in the cases will be of interest here.

SALES TRANSACTIONS

An installment contract for the sale of land may provide that, upon the non-payment of any one installment of the purchase price when due, the relationship of landlord and tenant will automatically arise with all its consequences and incidents. Upon a default, therefore, the bargainor will immediately become the landlord and be invested with all the advantages incident to that status, including the right to rents and the landlord's lien on the occupant's crops.

86

Contracts of this type have been held to have such results in several of the Southeastern states.[1]

Sometimes a contract will be worded in such a manner that the bargainee may have the choice of becoming the purchaser of the land upon the annual delivery of a certain quantity of produce, or of becoming a tenant by delivering a smaller quantity. Under an agreement of this kind the Alabama Court declared that the bargainee had an option to become either purchaser or tenant, his status to be determined by the quantity of produce delivered at the time fixed for the payment of the first annual installment. Upon his failure to make the election, the other party might treat him as a purchaser or tenant at his pleasure. When an election was made, it was said to be irrevocable. The choice, when made by the bargainee or his personal representative, would depend for its effectiveness upon the actual performance of either one of the alternative propositions, and thereupon one relationship or the other must be created and the incidents of the status established. In this instance the court decided that a tenancy had been created by the acts of the parties. It was said that the incidents of this relationship, including the landlord's lien, would attach and relate back to the time when the contract containing the alternative was made. Therefore anyone who had notice that such an agreement existed would then have no claim to the crops superior to that of the bargainor, who would be in the position of a landlord.[2] The result of such a holding in a state like Mississippi, where a bona fide purchaser of the crop is not protected[3] as he is in Alabama, would be dangerous in the extreme, for supply merchants and others dealing with the bargainee would be put in a very precarious position. Hence it is unlikely that any such doctrine would be approved in any jurisdiction where an innocent purchaser of the crops is not protected. The doctrine of this case, permitting the retroactive establishment of the tenancy status, finds some support in a case from Arkansas.[4]

1. Madden v. Wheeler, 140 Ark. 55, 215 S. W. 699 (1919); Murphy v. Myer, 95 Ark. 32, 128 S. W. 359 (1910); Block v. Smith, 61 Ark. 266, 32 S. W. 1070 (1895); Reddick v. Hutchinson, 94 Ga. 675, 21 S. E. 712 (1894); Wilkins v. Fulcher, 9 Ga. App. 68, 70 S. E. 691 (1911); Moore v. Moore, 126 S. C. 226, 119 S. E. 248 (1923).
2. Collins v. Whigham, 58 Ala. 438 (1877).
3. See Ch. 18, Note 73.
4. Murphy v. Myer, 95 Ark. 32, 128 S. W. 359 (1910).

Contracts of this general type take many and varied forms. In one situation a landowner sold a tract of land for ten thousand dollars, payable in five annual installments of two thousand dollars each, the first to be due on January 1, 1879. The contract stipulated that the bargainee should pay one thousand dollars as rent for the year 1878, and that if the installment of the purchase price due at the beginning of the year 1879 was paid, then the rent for that year would be eight hundred dollars. This arrangement was to continue at the same ratio until all the installments were paid, or, in other words, for every one hundred dollars paid on the purchase price, it was provided that the rent should be reduced ten dollars. The amount remaining unpaid at the end of the five-year period would bear interest at ten per cent. When the whole sum was paid, the bargainee would be invested with a good title to the land. There having been some trouble in collecting the "rent" for the year 1880, the bargainor, claiming to be a landlord, sued out a writ of attachment on the crops for the amount due that year. The court declared that this arrangement amounted to a bond for title and was not to be considered as a lease, the stipulation for "rent" being manifestly an agreement for interest on the indebtedness. Since there was no tenancy relationship, it was held that the writ of attachment could not lawfully be executed.[5] In the course of its opinion the court made the following remark: "No doubt a vendor may, by contract, reserve a lien upon land and crops, its fruits, to secure the payment of purchase money and interest." There seems to be no rule of law which would prevent the making of such a contract, though an instrument of this kind is very unusual.

A Georgia landowner gave a bargainee a bond for title, and the latter went into possession, afterwards transferring to the owner certain contracts made with several croppers. The bargainee applied to a merchant for an arrangement by which the croppers could be furnished. The merchant agreed to supply their needs if the bargainor, the transferee of the contracts, would waive a certain amount of his claim against each cropper. It was held that the waivers signed by the bargainor did not have the effect of canceling the conveyance of the land, as the bargainee had transferred only his claims on the croppers' produce. The effect of the transfer of the contracts was merely to place the right to them in the transferee, and this carried the claims to the produce as necessary incidents thereof. The fact

5. Walters v. Meyer & Co., 39 Ark. 560 (1882).

that the transferee was also the original owner of the land did not cancel or rescind the real estate transaction, nor did this circumstance create a relationship of landlord and cropper between the bargainor and those cultivating the land under the bargainee. The bargainor was vested with no title to any of the crops and had nothing but the claims which had been transferred to him by the bargainee. Therefore the court ruled that the supply merchant had the better claim to the crops.[6]

In a pre-Civil-War case from Louisiana there was a contract for the sale of a plantation and slaves for a stipulated sum on long-term credit, the agreement reserving an annual rent. It was held that this contract would not be regarded as establishing a tenancy relationship purely on account of the provision for rent, that clause having been inserted for the purpose of disguising a stipulation for interest on the unpaid balance of the purchase price. The purchaser had subsequently executed an instrument which stated that he had "rented" from his named transferror "his plantation, whereon I now live, together with the negroes . . . and I engage to pay the taxes . . . and a certain sum clear and free of all expense," and that the transferror should have a privilege on the crops. It was held that this constituted only a harmless simulation of a tenancy relationship and that the true status was that of vendor and purchaser.[7]

Sometimes the contract is worded in such a way that there is a tenancy up to a specified time and upon the fulfillment of certain terms a more permanent estate is established. Thus in an early case[8] a landowner entered into an agreement in which it was stipulated that the other party should have the use of the land, for which he was to pay a certain sum yearly as rent. The annual payments were to be credited upon a note held by the landowner, and if in a given time the credits amounted to a sum sufficient to satisfy the note and interest, a deed to the property would be forthcoming. This contract was held to be a valid one and was said to create an immediate tenancy relationship, subject to change upon the fulfillment of the terms of the agreement.

A Georgia landowner put another in possession under a parol contract of sale, the price to be paid in installments, and the transfer to be conditioned upon the payment of the installments when

6. Scott & Co. v. Ward, 23 Ga. App. 416, 98 S. E. 412 (1919).
7. Bissell v. Erwin's Heirs, 10 La. 524 (1837).
8. Nobles v. McCarty, 61 Miss. 456 (1884).

they became due. If the transferee was unable to meet any payment, he agreed to pay as rent for the land, for each year it was occupied, a sum equal to ten per cent of the price set in the agreement, together with the taxes. The occupant failed for two years to make any payment to the landowner, either as purchase money or as rent. The court ruled that a tenancy relationship existed between the parties with respect to the second year's occupation. Therefore the issuance of a distress warrant was the proper procedure to enforce the claim for the sum which was due as rent, the warrant having priority over a general judgment of earlier date.[9] In a somewhat similar case from Arkansas there was an agreement for the sale of land for $3600.00, payable over a period of years. The cash payment was stated to be $300.00, and the yearly installments were $330.00 over a ten-year period. Each installment, when paid according to the terms of the contract, was to be applied upon the principal indebtedness. It was declared that under this arrangement a tenancy relationship was created and that the status of the parties would not be that of vendor and purchaser until the purchase price had been fully paid. Therefore the court held that the original landowner had a landlord's lien on the cotton grown upon the premises, enforceable against anyone with notice of the agreement.[10] Under this decision, which seems unjustifiable, a supplyman who did not understand the effect of an agreement of this sort would be in grave danger of advancing too much credit, since the landowner's claim would be superior to his.

In another case a landowner executed a bond for title and gave the purchaser possession. The bond provided that the conveyance would be made upon the payment of certain notes and interest, the latter to be considered as rent unless each note was paid at maturity. It was held that after default a tenancy existed, the provision for interest merely fixing the amount of rent to be charged. The court declared that the failure of the landowner to notify a person who had extended credit to the cultivator in reliance on the crops would not estop the former from subjecting them to his landlord's lien. This was true even though the bond for title was not recorded, since there seemed to be no duty on the part of the landowner to give the creditor notice that the tenancy relationship had arisen or to

9. Reddick v. Hutchinson, 94 Ga. 675, 21 S. E. 712 (1894).
10. Soloman v. Keesee, 156 Ark. 387, 246 S. W. 469 (1923).

warn him that he would be extending credit at his own risk.[11]

Sometimes the installment payments, when they are not considered in connection with the entire contract of purchase, are excessive as rent. In one instance of this kind the court ruled that the contract established a tenancy with an option to purchase. But upon default the landowner was allowed to recover only a reasonable rent, as the stated installments were tied in with the entire agreement of purchase.[12]

A Georgia court has said that a landowner may contract with his conditional vendee that if the terms of payment are not met, then the contract of sale may be rescinded and a tenancy relationship will spring into being automatically and retroactively for the year in which the default in payment occurred. In this instance the court declared that rescission of the contract of sale involved the duty of restitution, and that the landowner must account to the vendee for any payments made on the purchase price. He must also account to the vendee for the value of all improvements which the vendee may have put upon the premises. Any person who dealt with the vendee with full knowledge of the rights the landowner had reserved was in no position to object because the landowner, in his capacity as landlord, and by virtue of the ensuing rescission of the agreement, was attempting to enforce a landlord's lien upon the crops. The person dealing with the vendee here was assuredly charged with such knowledge in view of the fact that he had participated in the formulation of the contract.[13]

Another installment contract of the familiar type provided that in case the purchaser failed to pay an installment, the vendor would be relieved of the duty of executing a deed and the purchaser would then hold as a tenant at a stipulated rental. Upon default the vendor brought a special proceeding for the establishment of a landlord's lien for rent on the crops. The appellate court declared that the sole issue in this proceeding was whether rent was due and that the lower court had erred in deciding the issue in respect to the refunding of payments already made by the defaulting purchaser, the vendor having rescinded the contract. Since the purchaser had agreed to be bound at a stated rental in the event of a default, the court was of the opinion that the tenant, as he had become accord-

11. Robinson Co. v. Weathersby, 101 Miss. 724, 57 So. 983 (1912).
12. Sutton v. Graham, 80 Miss. 636, 31 So. 909 (1902).
13. Wilkins v. Fulcher, 9 Ga. App. 68, 70 S. E. 691 (1911).

ing to the contract, could not avoid payment of the rent at that figure. However, a disagreement among the members of the court developed with respect to the recovery of the payments. The opinion of the majority seems to deny recovery in the present controversy but appears to leave the way open for an independent action to recover the payments. The dissenting judge evidently thought that there should be no forfeiture and appeared to believe that an adherence to the principles announced in the majority opinion would leave the tenant without any means of redress. He also seemed to believe that the payments already made should be applied on the rent. However, he apparently misinterpreted the majority opinion, since the clear meaning of the language used therein leaves the way open for independent action to recover those payments.[14]

In North Carolina two interesting cases came before the court in the middle 'nineties. In one instance the person occupying the land under an installment contract defaulted and then made an agreement to pay rent. The original contract was not abandoned. It was held that the occupant's crops were subject to a landlord's lien, a tenancy having been established under the later agreement. However, it was said that the amounts paid for rent should be applied in discharge of the payments due on the contract to convey.[15] In the other case the question raised was whether a person who entered under a bond for title had abandoned his contract of purchase and made an agreement to become a tenant. He had made declarations that he had agreed to pay rent, but the notes he had given for the purchase price were still in the hands of the vendor. Furthermore, it also appeared that after making the declarations he had refused to surrender the land for the notes, as a condition to an agreement to rent the premises for another year. Under these circumstances it was ruled that the declarations were not sufficient evidence of an abandonment of the contract of sale and that the question of such an abandonment should not be submitted to a jury.[16]

An Arkansas tenancy developed out of a failure to redeem land which had been sold for taxes. In this instance a purchaser bought certain land at a tax sale. The statutory period for redemption was

14. Moore v. Moore, 126 S. C. 226, 119 S. E. 248 (1923).
15. Jones v. Jones, 117 N. C. 254, 23 S. E. 214 (1895).
16. Taylor v. Taylor, 112 N. C. 27, 16 S. E. 924 (1893).

about to expire, and the person entitled to redeem requested that an extension of time be granted him. He informed the purchaser that if he did not redeem by the date set, he would then be willing to pay rent on the premises for the current year. Accordingly he was permitted to occupy the land. It was held that he was bound by his agreement to pay rent for the entire year.[17]

A landowner by a written instrument transferred certain property for a term of ten years at a yearly "rental" of five bales of cotton. The agreement provided that if the "rent" and taxes were paid promptly, the cultivator could then purchase the land upon the payment of an additional fifty bales. It further stated that if any installment of the "rent" was not promptly paid, the cultivator's rights would then be forfeited and the landowner would have a right of re-entry. This arrangement was held to be an installment contract of sale. Upon the landowner's attempt to enforce a forfeiture for default in the payments, it was held that the cultivator might assert his equity and cause the land to be sold to pay the balance due on the purchase price. The court declared that installment contracts for the sale of land are similar to purchase-money mortgages. In neither relationship is the purchaser's equity destroyed by noncompliance with a stipulation for prompt payment, but upon default he is entitled to have the amount of the indebtedness ascertained and a judicial sale ordered, the surplus, if any, to be handed over to him.[18]

There seems to be no doubt that parties may make a contract creating a tenancy relationship and providing that at the end of the term and upon the performance of all stipulated conditions and covenants the lessor shall make an absolute deed to the property in the name of the lessee.[19] Such contracts are very much like leases with options to purchase, which will receive some further attention.

TENANCIES ARISING OUT OF COMMON OWNERSHIP

There is no rule of law that one coproprietor of land cannot lease from his co-owner. In fact it has been held that an agreement by which one coproprietor or tenant in common leases a portion of the common estate from another is perfectly lawful and creates the

17. Matthews v. Morris, 31 Ark. 222 (1876).
18. Hicks v. King, 150 N. C. 370, 64 S. E. 125 (1909).
19. Morris v. Bowman & Brown, 175 Ark. 1073, 1 S. W. (2d) 549 (1928); Frazier v. Nicks, 172 Ark. 1139, 292 S. W. 368 (1927).

relationship of landlord and tenant between them in respect to the undivided portion so leased.[20] However, the Florida court has declared that a tenancy relationship does not exist between one owner in common and his coproprietors where he occupies the common estate in his own right as co-owner and without a contract, express or implied, with the others.[21] Furthermore, the Louisiana Court has held that a joint proprietor of a plantation who cultivated half of the land on his own account, without trying to prevent his coproprietors from occupying and cultivating the other half, was not responsible to the latter for the rental of the common property. He had made an agreement with his co-owners, as part of a compromise involving other matters, to pay the sum of $600.00 as their share of the rents of the place during the year. The court decided that he had not paid this sum as rent, but as the "evident equivalent of revenues or rents from others to whom the place might have been possibly leased." Therefore there was no lease to serve as a basis for the tacit reconduction (renewal) for subsequent years which he was trying to show here.[22]

MORTGAGE TRANSACTIONS

Similar problems arise with respect to mortgage transactions, the mortgagor being in a like position to the vendee in the conditional contract of sale. Sometimes there may even be confusion in some controversy as to the exact status of the person who wishes to acquire the land. Thus a vendee may execute a mortgage back to the vendor and thereby become a mortgagor as well. In a case of this kind land was sold and the vendee executed a mortgage back to the vendor as security for the purchase price. The parties agreed that if the vendee did not pay the purchase-money note which would become due each year for a definite period, he must then pay the sum of $300.00 as rent, which on final settlement would be applied on the full purchase price. According to the court's analysis of this transaction, the vendee, upon his failure to make a payment when it was due, had the privilege of paying a stipulated rent, thus creating a tenancy relationship with all its rights and incidents. In the event of a failure to make his first payment, the contract was not to be canceled, but possession would be constructively delivered

20. Evans v. English, 61 Ala. 416 (1878).
21. Bird v. Earle & Perkins, 15 Fla. 447 (1875).
22. Balfour's Heirs v. Balfour, 33 La. Ann. 297 (1881).

to the vendor. The vendee, however, would remain as a tenant at the stipulated rental figure until the indebtedness was satisfied, or the mortgage foreclosed, and the right of the vendee to redeem was terminated. In case the vendee did redeem, his payments as rent must be accounted for in the manner in which similar payments are accounted for where a mortgagee takes possession of realty without a foreclosure proceeding.[23] Throughout the opinion the bargainee is spoken of as a vendee, and yet the court treats him very much like a mortgagor who has agreed to pay rent in the event of a default. In fact there is very little difference between the two with respect to the matter being considered here.

And now mortgage transactions proper must be discussed. This subject is best introduced by pointing to a controversial North Carolina case. Here the court in a split decision declared that, after default in the conditions of a registered real estate mortgage, the mortgagee can, by parol contract, become the landlord of the mortgagor and thereby avail himself of the incidents of the tenancy relationship, including the landlord's lien. It was said the subsequent lienholders are charged with knowledge of the mortgagee's right of entry. The fact that the mortgagee-landlord had rented the land to a person who happened to be the ex-mortgagor was said not to change the character of the possesion, which had become that of a tenant. The court declared that the entry of the mortgagee, being matter *in pais*, was incapable of registration, and that the agreement to rent, while it might have been recorded, was not required to be registered, as the contract was only for one year, with the parties having the privilege of extending it from year to year.[24] Mr. Justice Clark's dissent, in which one of his colleagues concurred, is very well reasoned. He argued that anyone who wished to extend credit to the mortgagor-tenant would have no means of knowing of the prior claim of the mortgagee-landlord on the crops. As he so ably points out in his opinion, to allow such a change in the relationship without making it a matter of record is fraught with danger to all supply merchants.

Of course where the mortgage has been forclosed and the mortgagee has acquired the land at a sale, any such agreement for rent is and clearly should be valid and effective, and the lessor should then have a lien prior to all subsequent liens or claims. However, the

23. Arant v. Adams, 16 Ala. App. 122, 75 So. 714 (1917).
24. Ford v. Green, 121 N. C. 70, 28 S. E. 132 (1897).

situation is somewhat altered where a claimant has obtained his lien or claim after the default in payment but prior to the foreclosure. Here the Alabama Court has decided that the mortgagor becomes a tenant at will or at sufferance, and that the former mortgagee, as landlord, will have a prior claim for rent. This is especially true where the estate has been converted into a contractual tenancy by a subsequent agreement.[25]

In an instance where lands were sold and conveyed and a mortgage taken to secure the payment of the purchase price, the parties entered into a subsequent agreement by which the mortgagors bound themselves, in the event of their failure to meet certain payments, to deliver three bales of cotton as rent. It was held that upon default a tenancy relationship was created between the parties, with its attendant rights and privileges. The mortgagee, having become a landlord entitled to a lien, might maintain an appropriate action against a purchaser of the crops who, with notice of the lien, had received and sold them.[26]

In Arkansas a contract was executed whereby a mortgagor's attorney, to whom the grantee of a purchaser at a foreclosure sale had conveyed the premises, gave the mortgagor the privilege of repurchasing the land within three years by paying the amount the attorney had advanced to pay the judgment under which the sale was ordered, the interest being payable from the rents. It was held that until redemption a tenancy was established at an annual rental figure equal to the amount of the annual interest charge on the purchase money. These circumstances were said to justify the attorney's attachment of the crop for the amount of the unpaid rent or interest.[27] Another case arose in Alabama where the mortgagor of land which had been sold under a mortgage leased it from the purchaser and then redeemed it, within the statutory period for redemption, but after the rent was due. The court declared that unless the mortgagee had entered, brought his action to recover possession, or had a receiver appointed on a bill to foreclose, this redemption was not a defense to the purchaser's action for rent. It also came to the conclusion that the fact that the mortgagor, after redeeming

25. First Nat. Bank of Dothan v. Federal Land Bank, 225 Ala. 387, 143 So. 567 (1932); Hughes & Tidwell Supply Co. v. Carr, 203 Ala. 469, 83 So. 472 (1919).

26. Thornton v. Strauss & Steinhardt, 79 Ala. 164 (1885).

27. Goode v. King, 189 Ark. 1093, 76 S. W. (2d) 300 (1934).

the property, had paid rent to another mortgagee with a prior claim during the period for which the purchaser had claimed rent did not constitute a valid defense, as such payment was purely voluntary. The senior mortgagee had made no effort to enter for condition broken and could not collect rent until he had at least taken some action in regard to the matter.[28]

The same kind of thing may happen where a purchaser buys land at a tax sale and the statutory period for redemption is about to expire. In an instance of this kind the person entitled to redeem requested that an extension of time be granted him. He informed the purchaser that if he did not redeem by the date originally set he would then be willing to pay rent on the premises for the current year. Accordingly, he was permitted to occupy the land. It was held that he was bound under the agreement to pay the purchaser rent for the entire year.[29]

Sometimes the existence of a tenancy will be disproved on principles of estoppel. Thus it has been said that a mortgagee is estopped by the record of his litigation with the mortgagor over the title and possession of certain land from claiming that a tenancy relationship existed during the period of litigation.[30]

LEASES WITH OPTIONS TO PURCHASE

At times a person wishing to buy land will want to test its fertility or its suitability for an intended use. The most practicable way in which this may be done is to have the landowner execute a lease with an option to purchase. Conditions may be attached to the privilege of exercising the option.[31] The contract commonly contains an agreement to pay rent until the option is exercised and specifies the price at which the conveyance will be made. It may stipulate that the rent payments are to be credited on the purchase price. Contracts of this general nature have been considered and approved by the courts in several of the Southeastern states.[32]

In the exercise of an option to purchase contained in a lease, time

28. Perkerson v. Snodgrass, 85 Ala. 137, 4 So. 752 (1888).
29. Matthews v. Morris, 31 Ark. 222 (1876).
30. Riley v. Hardy, 185 Miss. 765, 189 So. 514 (1939).
31. Frazier v. Nicks, 172 Ark. 1139, 292 S. W. 368 (1927).
32. Coley v. English, 209 Ala. 688, 96 So. 909 (1923); Mills v. Surrat, 185 Ark. 596, 48 S. W. (2d) 218 (1932); Foxworth v. Maddox, 103 Fla. 32, 137 So. 161 (1931); Spell v. Ward, 54 Ga. App. 273, 187 S. E. 720 (1936); Kinberger v. Drouet, 149 La. 986, 90 So. 367 (1922); Wise Supply Co. v. Davis, 194 N. C. 328, 139 S. E. 599 (1927).

is of the essence, whether the contract expressly so provides or not. The court cannot grant additional time nor can the lessee extend the prescribed period, merely by holding over and paying rent.[32-a]

It may be that a lease with an option to purchase will be held to exist even where a contract is worded in such a manner that the land goes to the transferee subject to the payment of installments of the purchase price, the transferee being required to pay a specified sum as rent in case the installment payments are not met as they become due. In two Georgia cases[33] where such a situation existed the landowner was allowed to claim a lien for rent and supplies advanced to make a crop. In both opinions it is said that the parties could not, by rescinding that portion of the contract concerning the sale, affect the intervening rights of third persons. But, in order to insist upon these rights, such persons must be without notice of the rescission and its effect upon the agreement. The language in both opinions is so confused that it is practically impossible to ascertain exactly what the relationship was at any given time. It is believed that all difficulty might have been avoided by holding that these contracts were sales agreements with provisions for the creation of tenancies upon default.

In another Georgia case the court went so far as to declare that a lease with an option to purchase was established even where the agreement provided that the instrument should not be construed as an option but as a contract for rent.[34] The court evidently believed that parties cannot change the nature of a relationship just by calling it something else.

When the tenant has breached the lease in several respects and has not availed himself of provisions in the lease to repair and compensate the breach until the time allowed therefor has expired, the tenant is not entitled to specific performance of an option to purchase, notwithstanding that he proposes to pay the landlord the full purchase price.[34-a]

An instrument may be worded in such a manner as to operate either as a sale or as a lease. Thus a contract may give the transferee, in the first instance, the opportunity to elect the desired relationship

32-a. Smith v. Carter, 213 Ark. 937, 214 S. W. (2d) 64 (1948).

33. Manley v. Underwood, 27 Ga. App. 822, 110 S. E. 49 (1921); Hodnett v. Mann, 10 Ga. App. 666, 73 S. E. 1082 (1912).

34. Spooner v. Dykes, 174 Ga. 767, 163 S. E. 889 (1932).

34-a. Smith v. Carter, 213 Ark. 937, 214 S. W. (2d) 64 (1948).

by a certain time, and on his failure to choose, the status of the parties is left to the election of the transferor.[35]

Other contracts provide that rent payments are to be credited on the purchase price in the event of the exercise of an option. It has been held that the idea of a tenancy status is not excluded by such an arrangement.[36]

It is suggested in one Alabama case that courts of equity will not be as liberal about enforcing these option contracts as they are with respect to ordinary contracts for the sale of land, the equities of the common vendee being much greater.[37]

There seems to be no doubt about the necessity that an option to purchase conform to the provisions of the Statute of Frauds, as an oral option has been held void and of no effect.[38]

A Georgia contract contained a promise to sell the land during the term of the lease. The tenant could purchase the property, if he so desired, at a stipulated price. He exercised his option before the expiration of the term, and the lessor received the full amount of the purchase money, with interest from the date of the sale. The court would not listen to the lessor's claim that he was entitled to receive rent for the term in addition to the purchase price.[39] However, quite a different result was reached where the tenant was already in possession and had agreed to pay rent under the lease and had renewed the promise at the time when a deed was given pursuant to an option to purchase granted during the one-year term. Upon the exercise of this option, the lessee was held liable for the full rent, even though the deed had been executed prior to the date when the rent fell due according to the terms of the lease.[40] In another instance the lessee was already on the premises under a contract when the option was granted. A controversy arose between an assignee of the rental contract and a merchant who had furnished supplies to the lessee. The option was conditioned upon the payment of rent in accordance with the provisions of the prior lease contract. It was shown that the lessee had not undertaken to exercise the option at any time prior to his purchase of supplies. Hence

35. Collins v. Whigham, 58 Ala. 438 (1877).
36. Foxworth v. Maddox, 103 Fla. 32, 137 So. 161 (1931); Burwell v. Cooper's Co-operative Warehouse Co., 172 N. C. 79, 89 S. E. 1064 (1916).
37. Coley v. English, 209 Ala. 688, 96 So. 909 (1923).
38. Minor v. Sutton, 73 Ga. App. 253, 36 S. E. (2d) 158 (1945).
39. Bentley v. Barrett, 26 Ga. App. 527, 106 S. E. 815 (1921).
40. Pate v. Gaitley, 183 N. C. 262, 111 S. E. 339 (1922).

it was ruled that a tenancy relationship still existed at that time and that the landlord's assignee would be enitled to a prior claim on the crop.[41]

A lessee with an option to purchase must fulfill all stipulations in the agreement which are construed as conditions precedent to the exercise of the option, such as the payment of rent and taxes, interest, and down payments or installments on the purchase price.[42] In one instance a lessee failed to make the last payment on the rent, giving as an excuse the fact that the lessor had failed to tender him a deed as required in the agreement. The court held that the failure to tender the deed was no valid excuse for the lessee's breach and refused to decide the case in his favor.[43]

Tendering the purchase price seems to be a necessary prerequisite to any attempt to take advantage of the option. The tender must be clear, prompt, and unequivocal. In one instance the lessee telegraphed that he was ready to accept the option and make payment. However, he made no tender and could not be found on the day on which the option expired. It was held that there had not been a sufficient compliance with the terms of the option.[44] In another case the contract was worded in such a manner as to give the lessee the refusal of the property if the lessor decided to sell to anyone. An offer was made by another party of a sum which was less than that called for by the option contract. The court declared that the lessee had a right to buy the property at the stated figure, but not for a smaller sum offered by another. The lessee made a tender of the smaller amount, but it was held that this was not sufficient compliance with the agreement and that he had no such equity as would prevent his eviction.[45]

However, a lessor may waive a tender of the purchase money. In one case the landowner had made it clear that she would not accept the purchase money even if offered, since she had conveyed the land to another. Under these circumstances it was held that the lessee was not required to make a tender.[46]

41. Wise Supply Co. v. Davis, 194 N. C. 328, 139 S. E. 599 (1927).
42. Coley v. English, 209 Ala. 688, 96 So. 909 (1923); Grummer v. Price, 101 Ark. 611, 143 S. W. 95 (1912); Carpenter v. Thornburn, 76 Ark. 578, 89 S. W. 1047 (1905); Spooner v. Shelfer, 152 Ga. 190, 108 S. E. 773 (1921); Crawford v. Cathey, 143 Ga. 403, 85 S. E. 127 (1915).
43. Carpenter v. Thornburn, 76 Ark. 578, 89 S. W. 1047 (1905).
44. Spell v. Ward, 54 Ga. App. 273, 187 S. E. 720 (1936).
45. Bennett v. Farkas, 126 Ga. 228, 54 S. E. 942 (1906).
46. Kinberger v. Drouet, 149 La. 986, 90 So. 367 (1922).

An option contract provided that the lessor would accept corn "on this land payment contract." It was held that this agreement would neither authorize nor permit the payment of corn as rent at a time prior to the date when the option was exercised.[47]

In one Louisiana case it was contended that a lessee with an option to purchase was estopped from setting up his rights to have the property deeded to him. Here the lessee had acceded to the sale of certain property, only partially covered by the option, to his sister-in-law. The instrument which had been drawn to effectuate this sale specified a certain method of payment, consideration, and rate of interest. The agreement under which the lessee claimed differed in all these respects. It appeared that the lessee had acted as his sister-in-law's agent in negotiating for the sale of the property to her, and there was even some evidence that he had agreed to join her in the purchase. Before the sale was actually put through, however, the lessee repudiated these co-operative acts and refused to sign away his rights. Since he had renounced all intention of joining her in the transaction before the deal was consummated, it was ruled that he was not estopped from asserting his rights under the prior contract.[48]

An Arkansas lessee with an option to purchase had consented to the sale of the whole farm to another party. The lessor made a sale of a portion of the property. It was held that a sale of this kind would not be permitted, since the lessee might object to the sale of only a part of the premises and yet have no aversion to the transfer of the entire tract. Hence the sale of a portion of the land constituted an eviction which would justify a refusal to pay rent.[49]

Sometimes a contract will give the tenant an option for an extension of the lease for a certain number of years. In one instance a landowner leased land to another for a term of one year and gave the lessee the privilege of continuing the tenancy for one period of five years and then for another five-year term. The contract provided a price for which the land would be sold at any time during the continuance of the tenancy. It was shown that the lessee had signified his intention of accepting the first five-year term, but there was no evidence with respect to the acceptance of the other options, either the one for the sale or the one for the second five-year period.

47. Mills v. Surrat, 185 Ark. 596, 48 S. W. (2d) 218 (1932).
48. Kinberger v. Drouet, 149 La. 986, 90 So. 367 (1922).
49. Nichol v. McDonald, 69 Ark. 341, 64 S. W. 263 (1901).

Hence it was held that both these further options had expired at the end of the first five-year term.[50] In another instance the term was for one year with an optional additional term of two years at the same rental figure. Upon the exercise of the option, the lessee, without the necessity of negotiating a new agreement, became entitled to an added two-year term.[51] In such cases the acceptance of the option must be prompt,[52] but it is not required to be in writing unless the contract so specifies.[53]

Again, a contract was said to have effected a lease at a stated sum per acre for a term of four years. After the first year the lessee was given the privilege of paying the "customary rental value" instead of the stated sum. Interpretating this contract, the court declared that the failure of the lessee to act at the end of the first year would automatically establish a tenancy at the stated rent.[54]

Sometimes a contract containing an option to purchase will be extended for an additional period by an indorsement upon the agreement itself. In one such case it was said that the entire agreement, including the option, was thereby extended. The purchaser's decision to exercise the option had not been taken until after the date of the agreement for an extension. Therefore the court held that the landowner was entitled to the yearly rent up to the time when the decision to buy the land was made. Under these circumstances, the transferee could not be responsible for the rent and taxes for the same period, and hence was not liable for the taxes accruing before the last extension of the leasing agreement. The court evidently looked upon him as a tenant up to that time and until the option to purchase was exercised.[55]

CONCLUSION

It may be said that contracts of the character considered here offer a signal opportunity for parties to a real estate transaction to shift out of one relationship into another which they may believe is better adapted to their needs. Contracts of this kind are well adapted to trying out persons with a view to testing their aptitude for the agricultural life, before committing them irrevocably to the life of a farmer. In other words, this type of agreement offers a practical way of applying the method of trial and error.

50. Atlantic Product Co. v. Dunn, 142 N. C. 471, 55 S. E. 299 (1906).
51. Neal v. Harris, 140 Ark. 619, 216 S. W. 6 (1919).
52. Atlantic Product Co. v. Dunn, *supra* Note 50.
53. Neal v. Harris, *supra* Note 51.
54. O'Kane v. McCuen, 146 Ark. 236, 225 S. W. 312 (1920).
55. Grummer v. Price, 101 Ark. 611, 143 S. W. 95 (1911).

V

Conditions and Covenants

STIPULATIONS in a lease contract may be considered as conditions or covenants according to their intended effect upon the relationship established by the agreement. The intention of the parties is to be gleaned from a consideration or perusal of the terms of the contract. A condition may be defined as a clause in an agreement which has for its object the rescinding, suspension, or modification of the principal obligation of the pact. In the case of a lease a condition differs from a covenant in that, upon its incidence, it brings to an end the estate or interest in the realty created by the lease contract. This result does not necessarily follow upon the breach of a mere covenant, which is only a promise to do or refrain from doing certain acts in respect to the land.

There have been very few references to conditions in farm lease cases from the Southeastern states, and the scope of this treatise is limited to a discussion of reported cases. Hence conditions will be touched upon only when they are referred to in some controversy which has come before the appellate courts.

The true nature of a covenant is a very important matter. It is dependent or independent according to the manner in which it is stated in the instrument creating the interest in the land. A covenant is dependent when it is operative only upon the performance of some act or promise by the other party. If this is not the case, the covenant is said to be independent, and a breach of its terms will not entail a forfeiture of all rights which the covenantor possesses under the lease contract. Hence in the latter situation he does not lose the benefit of the entire agreement and the other party is limited to an action for whatever damages he has sustained on account of the breach of that particular provision of the contract.

It has been said that where a person agrees, by covenant, to pay a certain sum of money for one year's rent, the covenant is dependent, and the enjoyment of the land must be a thing precedent to the obligation to pay the reserved rent.[1] In contrast to this decision is a

1. Thompson v. Gray, 2 Stew. & P. 60 (Ala., 1832). In this instance there

case where the landowner, upon the tenant's promise to pay rent, agreed to keep up the fences on the leased premises. Here the lower court had charged the jury that failure to keep up the fences would relieve the tenant from the obligation of paying the rent. This was held to be erroneous, the appellate court declaring that the covenants were independent. The tribunal was of the opinion that either party might recover damages for any injury resulting from the breach of covenant. It was held that the landlord's breach of his covenant to keep up the fences could not be pleaded as a defense to his action for the rent, it being necessary for the tenant to bring his own action to recover damages for the breach of the covenant relating to fences.[2]

The types of covenants and conditions in lease contracts are myriad. In fact it may be said that there is practically no limit to the variations which the parties incorporate into their agreements. Some of these contracts are very simple while others are extremely complicated. Some have only a few covenants and others may have hundreds. An exhaustive study of possible types will not be attempted here; it is believed that a treatment of the more usual types which have come before the courts in the Southeastern states will serve a more useful purpose.

COVENANTS CONCERNING FARM MANAGEMENT AND METHODS OF CULTIVATION

Among the most common of these covenants are those dealing with the management of the leased farm and with methods of cultivation and the division of crops and labor. Prominent among these is the type describing the crop which is to be raised on the land. Thus where a contract provided that the cultivator should receive one-half of the lint cotton, corn, and other produce, it was held that the lessee was not entitled to a half-share of the cotton seed, for the

---

was a general averment of performance, and the defendant pleaded that the plaintiff had not performed the agreement on his part. Issue was joined and the verdict was in favor of the plaintiff. The court held that the want of a special averment of performance on the part of the plaintiff would be cured under the statute of jeofails, which stated that no case is to be reversed, arrested, or otherwise set aside after verdict or judgment for any matter on the face of the pleadings which has not been previously objected to; provided, that the declaration contains averments amounting to a substantial cause of action, and that a material issue has been raised.

2. Smith v. Wiley, 60 Tenn. 418 (1872).

use of the term "lint cotton" would exclude any idea that the tenant would share in the seed.[3] A Mississippi lease provided that the tenants were to have the cotton raised, ginned, and baled, there being no gin on the lessor's plantation. It was declared that the lessor had impliedly consented to be responsible for ginning and baling out the cotton. This implied promise being for the common good of all parties interested in the crop, the charge for the same was ruled to be a lien on the crop superior to all other liens, whether of the lessor or other persons.[4]

An Arkansas tenant agreed to deliver to the landowner one-half of the crop or to pay its value in lieu of this rent in kind. Owing to the poorness of the crop, a part of it could not be gathered without much trouble and unusual expense. The court declared that only an act of God or the public enemy would justify a failure to account for the whole of the crop.[5] The dissenting judge argued that this should be true only when a tenant has agreed to pay as rent a fixed sum of money or a certain fraction of the produce. The amount of the rent would then depend upon the quantity of the crop raised, and that in turn would depend, not only upon the diligence and skill of the tenant and the fertility. of the soil, but also upon the many contingencies which may beset even the most prudent farmer. He argued that if the tenant had used due diligence in cultivating and gathering the crop, the landlord should then be entitled to no more than his contractual percentage of the portion of the crop which it was profitable for the tenant to harvest.

In one instance the contract left open the matter of selecting the seed, and the tenant chose a prolific variety which would sell at short staple prices. Instead of this variety the landlord furnished another kind of seed which was not prolific but would produce cotton which would sell at long staple prices. This substitution, without the tenant's consent, was prejudicial to the tenant's interest and very much to the advantage of the landlord, for, under the circumstances, the tenant would raise long staple cotton, with the disadvantage of a short yield, and would receive only short staple prices. On the other hand, the landlord would be able to sell at long staple prices cotton which he would receive at short staple prices, which were only about half as much. The tenant did not discover

3. Day v. Scott, 142 Ga. 50, 82 S. E. 442 (1914).
4. Duncan v. Jayne, 76 Miss. 133, 23 So. 392 (1898).
5. Johnson v. Bryant, 61 Ark. 312, 32 S. W. 1081 (1895).

that there had been a substitution until he was about ready to gather the crop. Under these circumstances the fact that he had actually gathered and delivered the crop did not constitute a ratification or waiver of the default on the part of the landlord. Where the fraud is discovered after the contract is executed either in whole or in part, the tenant's acts in continuing the performance of his obligations under the contract are not to be considered as a waiver of the landlord's fraudulent practices. Hence the landlord was made to account for the cotton at the prices actually realized in the market.[6]

Another lease provided that the tenant should not sublet the land or work it improperly but should keep the farm in good condition, cultivate it properly, and sow at least twenty acres of cowpeas. The instrument gave the lessor the right to re-enter in case of a violation of the contract. This evidently influenced the court to interpret these provisions as conditions subsequent rather than as ordinary covenants. Upon a breach the lease was to terminate and the burden of proving the violation was placed upon the lessor. The court declared that, by accepting one year's rent and permitting the lessee to remain in possession during that time, the lessor had waived his right to a forfeiture for alleged breaches occurring in that year.[7] The same kind of situation seems to have existed where there was a contract between a skilled farmer and an owner of land. The farmer agreed to oversee the work of two unskilled men, his son and son-in-law, and to supervise the planting, making, and gathering of the crops. It was evident that this was a personal service contract depending upon the skill of the farmer. The court held that contracts to perform personal service are considered to have been made upon the implied condition that the individual shall be alive and capable of performing the duties agreed upon, so that death, as in this instance, or serious disability will operate as a discharge.[8] Again, a tenant agreed to a forfeiture of crops if he should "voluntarily or involuntarily" leave the premises. The court refused to decree a forfeiture where it appeared that the landlord had forced the tenant to abandon the place because he had bought goods of persons other than the landlord.[9] It was evidently felt that the word "involuntarily" should not be given an interpretation which the parties obviously had not meant it to have.

6. Clark v. Lewis, 139 Ark. 308, 213 S. W. 746 (1919).
7. Clement v. Morris, 136 Ark. 624, 203 S. W. 1011 (1918).
8. Pope v. Dickerson, 205 Ala. 594, 89 So. 24 (1921).
9. Williams v. Cocke, 6 So. 774 (Miss., 1889).

An Alabama landowner agreed to give an overseer in return for his services "three-sixteenths of the cotton raised on the place, and to gin and haul his cotton, with his own, free of charge." The court decided that the overseer was entitled to the same proportion of the cotton seed. It declared him to be a co-owner of both the cotton and the seed until a proper division was made between the parties. A delivery of the seedless cotton, after ginning, would not operate as a full discharge of the obligations of the contract.[10] An Arkansas contract provided that the land was to be farmed in "corn and peanuts and all grain and crops." The tenant would receive two-thirds of the crops and the landlord one-third, and they were to furnish seed in the same proportion. It was held that the agreement covered only cultivated crops, and that a volunteer hay crop was not within the purview of the contract.[11]

Under a Louisiana lease, executed prior to the Bankhead Act of 1934[12] which fixed cotton allotments and provided for a tax on excess production, the rent was fixed at "1500 pounds of lint cotton without ginning or bagging charges." Since the amount of lint cotton free of these charges was to be paid in lieu of cash rent, the landlord was said to be entitled to that amount of lint cotton without the payment of any tax for excess production, the tenant being liable for such tax.[13]

A lease of Arkansas rice lands provided that the landlord should pay the expenses of operating a pumping plant and should put down a well. Furthermore, if he was not able to put down a well suitable for the purpose of irrigating the land, he should not then be liable to the tenant in damages but must pay the tenant the reasonable value of the "plowing and levee-fixing" up to the time when the tenant was given notice concerning the failure of the well project. In the landlord's action to enforce a lien for rent and supplies, it was held that the counterclaiming tenant could recover only the amount spent for plowing and for making new levees. The court stated that the term "plow" meant an agricultural implement drawn by horses or other power which makes a furrow and turns up the earth, and that the verb "to plow" meant to break or turn up of the surface of the land with a plow. Hence it was held that the tenant could not recover for money or labor expended in double-disking the land,

10. Allen v. Harper, 26 Ala. 686 (1855).
11. Porter v. Vail, 148 Ark. 642, 231 S. W. 3 (1921).
12. 48 Stat. 598 (1934).
13. Cardino v. Scroggins, 185 So. 109 (La. App., 1938).

cutting down old levees, or for dragging, drilling, harrowing, or rolling.[14]

Another Arkansas landlord breached a covenant to furnish water to irrigate his tenant's rice crop. The tenant failed to use due diligence in harvesting the crop actually produced. Here it was ruled that the tenant's damages would be calculated on the basis of his share of a sum representing the difference between what the land would have produced if proper irrigation had been furnished and what the tenant would have produced with proper husbandry, deducting from such difference the amount it would have cost to grow, harvest, and market the crop that would have been produced if the landlord had fulfilled his contract.[14-a]

The right to enforce such a covenant or stipulation in a lease contract may be waived. In one instance the method of cultivation to be employed was described in the lease, and the right to object because of improper husbandry was clearly authorized by the instrument. Here neither the lessor nor his duly appointed agent made any objection to the methods employed by the lessee until after the crop had been made, and the court ruled that it was then too late to do so. The lessor, by acts inconsistent with the lease, had caused the lessee to abandon the premises. He had then taken over the farm and had gathered and marketed the crop. Under these circumstances he was responsible to the lessee for the latter's portion of the produce.[15] Another instance of this sort arose in Arkansas where a covenant to live on the premises was regarded as waived because the tenant had lived for years, both before and after the lease contract was made, on adjoining land where he had a mercantile establishment, with no objection by the lessor.[16]

COVENANTS CONCERNING CLEARING AND IMPROVEMENT
OF PREMISES

One of the most common types of covenants concerning farm land is that which obligates a party to clear or improve the land. There have been many cases dealing with such stipulations. In one instance an Alabama lease required the tenant, during the term, to reduce an uncleared portion of the premises to cultivation. The in-

---

14. Leighton v. Lewis, 126 Ark. 83, 189 S. W. 672 (1916).
14-a. Gibson v. Lee Wilson & Co., 211 Ark. 300, 200 S. W. (2d) 497 (1947).
15. Young v. Gay, 41 La. Ann. 758, 6 So. 608 (1889).
16. Wales Riggs Plantations v. Banks, 101 Ark. 461, 142 S. W. 828 (1912).

strument gave the tenant the right to occupy the cultivated portions for a designated period. It was further stipulated that in the event of a sale during the term, the tenant should surrender the land on payment of "a reasonable valuation for the unexpired term." It is clear that a court of equity would have no right to issue an injunction to restrain the tenant from cutting timber on the land for the purposes authorized by the lease. The agreement permitted the tenant to use and occupy the portions which he cleared. This was said to be a covenant running with the land and therefore binding upon an assignee of the reversion, unless the situation was altered by the provision concerning the sale. The court declared that this clause merely reserved to the purchaser or assignee of the reversionary interest the privilege of determining the lease upon the performance of the condition concerning the payment of a reasonable valuation for the unexpired term. Until a payment or tender was made, the lessee would clearly have a right to the enjoyment of the premises and also a right to continue the clearing and cultivation according to the terms of the contract. No payment or tender having been made, there could be no interference with the activities of the tenant in furtherance of the agreement.[17]

A lease contract provided that the lessee should clear the land to the lessor's satisfaction by sawing up and burning all logs, brush, and other trash, and that he should put into cultivation not less than ten acres the first year. The court decided that under this instrument the lessee had to clear and cultivate ten full acres the first year, but that he had the whole term granted in the lease to burn and roll the timber and to perform the other required tasks.[18] Again, a lessee for a period of ten years agreed to clear and cultivate timber lands. At the time his case was brought before the court the work had not yet been done, but there was no evidence that the lessee intended to permit the term to pass without performing this portion of the agreement.[19] Another lease provided that the tenant might clear ten acres of woodland on a certain designated portion of the rented premises. The agreement specified the wood to be cut off this plot and gave the tenant the right to raise a crop thereon for the next year. The work was to begin on the side of the lot contiguous to other land which had been recently cleared. On the face of this

17. McDaniel v. Callan, 75 Ala. 327 (1883).
18. Stanley v. White, 132 Ark. 617, 201 S. W. 804 (1918).
19. Williams v. Shaver, 100 Ark. 565, 140 S. W. 740 (1911).

instrument it was held that the tenant's right to cut wood was limited to that on the named section of land, and that therefore the lower court had not erred in granting an injunction to prevent him from cutting it elsewhere on the premises.[20]

An owner of a tract of wild land leased it for eight years and agreed to deed a half interest in the property at the end of the term, provided the lessees performed their part of the contract. They agreed to put four hundred acres of the land into a state of good cultivation at the rate of fifty acres a year, to deaden the remainder of the tract, and to erect twelve tenant houses on the premises. Under this agreement the court said that the lessees would have the whole period of eight years to deaden the land and erect the houses. The court further held it was not a valid basis for rescission that at the end of a two-year period the lessees had put into cultivation only a small portion of one hundred acres, the amount of land which would have been under cultivation if the lessees had planned to do the job in equal stints. It was shown that the lessees had no intention of repudiating the contract or of abandoning the land. Neither could it be proved that the lessees would be unable to perform their obligations under the contract by the end of the eight-year period or that they could not respond in an action at law for damages. Hence it was held that the equitable remedy of rescission could not be maintained, the contract not having been broken in a matter vital to its existence or by its terms made of the essence of the agreement.[21]

A Tennessee lessor, having agreed to a three-year term in certain land in consideration of work done in clearing it, refused to perform the contract. The lessee was permitted to sue for labor done in carrying out the agreement and was allowed to recover a sum of money representing the enhancement of the value of the property. The lessor sought to avoid liability on the ground that the lessee had not planted the cleared land in corn as the former insisted he had agreed to do. The court declared that even if there was such a covenant, the lessor could not avoid liability under the contract. Under the provisions of the alleged agreement, the proceeds of the corn crop were to go exclusively to the lessee and there would therefore be no injury to the lessor. The lessee had merely declared his intention of planting the corn. In the process of clearing the land

20. Jones v. Gammon, 123 Ga. 47, 50 S. E. 982 (1905).
21. Mortimer v. Hanna, 82 Miss. 645, 35 So. 159 (1903).

the lessee had cut some timber, and he introduced evidence of a neighborhood custom which gave him the right to sell all severed timber from cleared land. The court also stated that where a contract is silent about a matter of this kind, a clearly established custom will prevail.[22]

Some covenants deal with buildings and other improvements on the land placed there by the lessor or the lessee. In one situation the contract provided that the lessor of a poultry plant should furnish cabins for the lessee's laborers. This covenant was held to have been fulfilled by making houses available at a place on the lessor's plantation within reasonable distance of the leased premises. It was proved that the plant was surrounded by the lessor's plantation, which had about seventy-five houses, some of them but a short distance from the plant, and that at all times there were houses available for the lessee's laborers within a reasonable distance.[23] In another instance a farmer employed a laborer and as part of the consideration agreed to furnish him a home at two dollars a month. The court declared that this was obviously a method of paying a portion of the laborer's wages, and that he could no more claim the right to occupy the house after a default in his own obligations than he would be entitled to any other wages.[24]

A common covenant to be found in agricultural leases is one which obligates the lessee or the lessor, usually the former, to build or keep up fences on the leased premises. In one instance a lease required the tenant to enclose the property with good wire fences. It was shown that on one of the boundaries there was a good line wire fence. The appellate court declared that the lower tribunal had acted properly in permitting the tenant to show that he had kept up the existing fence.[25] Another lease provided that the lessee should have the right to have all the timber cut from the tract, which he agreed to clear and fence. He was to have the use of the land for five years, but if, at the end of four years, he had not cleared and fenced the land as agreed, it was provided that he must surrender the premises. However, if he fulfilled his obligations, he would then have the right to remain for an additional year. After cutting all the timber from the tract, the lessee surrendered the premises to the

22. Duncan v. Blake, 77 Tenn. 534 (1882).
23. Shaw v. Knight, 16 La. App. 474, 134 So. 286 (1931).
24. McGee v. Gibson, 40 Ky. 105 (1840).
25. Hogg v. Frazier, 211 Ala. 218, 100 So. 95 (1924).

lessor without carrying out his obligations with respect to clearing and fencing. Under the theory advanced by the lessee, he would have been permitted to keep the land for four years, turn it back at the end of this time, and be rid of his obligations to clear and fence the tract. The court, however, refused to adopt this view and held that the lessee, when he abandoned the place at the end of the fourth year, remained liable for damages caused by the failure to clear and fence the land.[26] Under a lease the tenant was required to keep fences in repair, and an agreement was made for a definite type of galvanized barbed wire by a time certain. It was held that if the fences were not in the agreed condition by the time set forth in the lease, the tenant, or his surety, might be held liable to the extent of the sum of money necessary to put the fences in the required condition. The court further declared that the surety might put the fences in the proper condition and charge his principal, the tenant, a reasonable price therefor. He would not be permitted, however, to build a different kind of fence or repair particular portions of the existing fence one and two years after the termination of the lease, if the cost to the principal would amount to a greater sum than that which would have been required to repair the fences already on the premises in the first instance.[27]

In Arkansas a lessee agreed to construct a fence around the leased premises. He assigned the lease to a company with which he had formerly been connected. The lessor, with notice of the assignment and the severance of the business connection, accepted the rent from the assignee for several years, and in addition to this accepted the assignee's note as a *final* installment of rent due on the premises. It was held that although the acceptance of the rent, even with a knowledge of the true facts, would not be taken as a release of the lessee from his responsibility in respect to the fence and his secondary liability for the rent, the acceptance of the assignee's note as a final payment was a different matter and could be considered as an acceptance of the assignee as a tenant in place of the original lessee. This would operate as a release of the lessee from liability to pay the balance of the agreed rent but not from responsibility with respect to the fence. The lessee was not allowed to set off against this liability for the fence the expense of constructing various buildings on the premises prior to the assignment, since these buildings

26. Welborn v. Whayne, 163 Ky. 558, 174 S. W. 3 (1915).
27. Spann v. Spann, 105 Ark. 697, 150 S. W. 409 (1912).

had been sold to the assignee and were purchased by the lessor from one who bought them at a bankruptcy sale of the assignee's property.[28]

By the terms of a Tennessee lease the tenant had the privilege of paying the rent in money, or by the building of a good levee during the term. Much work had been done on the levee, but before completion it was washed away by high water. It was said that the tenant was not entitled to a credit for the work done, the loss falling upon him rather than upon the owner.[29] In another instance a lessor had agreed to clean out certain ditches, and it was shown that the failure to do this had caused the land to be flooded and had prevented the lessee from making a full crop. The court held that the lessee was entitled to recover, not merely the amount of money it would have cost to put the ditches into good condition, but also compensation for the decrease in the net yield of the land caused by the lessor's breach of contract.[30] Again, a lease required the landlord to do all necessary ditching, the tenant agreeing to obtain labor and materials and to superintend the work. The tenant promised to submit to the lessor an estimate of the cost of the work and to procure his assent to the project before beginning the job. The tenant failed to submit such an estimate, and it was held that he could not complain that the work had not been done. The fact that the landlord had voluntarily requested the county surveyor to run lines for levees and make an estimate of the cost of the ditching did not affect the outcome of the controversy, since this calculation had been rejected by the landlord as too costly.[31]

A Kentucky lessor agreed to build a tobacco barn, the contract being made in connection with a sublease entered into by the lessee with another. The lessor agreed to furnish the materials to build the barn and the lessee promised to hire the labor at a reasonable cost and superintend the work. The lessor failed to furnish the materials, and because of this the crops of both the lessee and the sublessee were heavily damaged. The sublessee sued for and recovered damages from the lessee who, after notifying the lessor of the suit and making a "reasonably efficient" defense, brought his own action against the lessor for the damages caused by the latter's breach of

28. Keith v. McGregor, 163 Ark. 203, 259 S. W. 725 (1924).
29. Clayton v. McKinney, 57 Tenn. 72 (1872).
30. Spencer v. Hamilton, 113 N. C. 49, 18 S. E. 167 (1893).
31. McKneely v. Hamm, 120 Ark. 631, 180 S. W. 478 (1915).

the original agreement. The lessee had also agreed to support the lessor's family, at that time consisting of the landlady, her husband, and her daughter. The lessor's son returned and became a member of the group without the lessee's consent. It was held that the lessor was liable for the injury to the crops of both the lessee and the sub-lessee caused by her breach of contract, she being responsible for whatever the lessee had lost in the sublessee's suit, and for the son's support as well.[32] In another instance the landlord had agreed to furnish "barn room" for the purpose of curing the tenant's tobacco. The roof of the barn was not completed when the time came for storing the crop, and the tobacco placed there was injured by rain and also by lack of proper drainage and ventilation. Evidence of these facts was held sufficient to sustain a verdict for damage to the tobacco. It was said that the proper measure of damages was the difference between the actual sales price and the market price of tobacco of similar quality which had been grown in the same neighborhood. Evidence that the price actually received was equal to the average price obtained on the market during the season was ruled inadmissible.[33]

Land had been sublet to a Georgia farmer who had agreed to pay a part of the rent in money or in kind and the other part by placing some improvements upon the premises. It was held that the land-owner might distrain for the rent against the subtenant and make an effort to collect a sum equal to the value of the improvements, they being considered just as much a part of the rent as the portion to be paid in money or in kind. In order to recover, however, the value of the improvements must be alleged in the affidavits accompanying the distress warrant.[34]

Provisions in lease contracts with respect to improving the premises may be worded as conditions, and where this is done a breach will entail a forfeiture,[35] unless it can be shown that there has been a waiver.[36]

COVENANT TO REPAIR

Another common covenant is one on the part of either lessor or lessee to keep the premises in repair or to make specific repairs to

32. Feland v. Berry, 130 Ky. 328, 113 S. W. 425 (1908).
33. McFall v. Carroll, 194 Ky. 678, 240 S. W. 367 (1922).
34. Fountain v. Whitehead, 119 Ga. 241, 46 S. E. 104 (1903).
35. Winn v. State, 55 Ark. 360, 18 S. E. 375 (1892).
36. Wales Biggs Plantations v. Banks, 101 Ark. 461, 142 S. W. 828 (1912).

farm buildings, fences, and the like. This covenant is often intertwined with one concerning improvements and has been held to run with the land, which means that it is binding upon all those in privity with the original parties to the lease.[37] Where a covenant required the landlord to furnish materials for making necessary repairs to the rented premises, it was held that the landlord was not thereby obligated to supply materials for the erection of new buildings.[38]

The owner of a South Carolina rice plantation leased it and agreed that $1,000.00 would be advanced in equal portions by himself and the lessee. Furthermore, the amount advanced by the latter would be credited on the rent until it was expended in repairs to the premises, if that amount was necessary to put the place into good condition. Should this sum prove insufficient to make the repairs thorough, the lessor would then have to advance additional funds to complete the job. The tenant agreed to return the plantation in good order at the end of the one-year term. In April an unusually high tide overflowed the river banks, flooding a portion of the premises, and it was necessary to mend certain flood-controlling levees in order that the plantation might be put into condition to produce a crop. It was shown that the repairs were necessary to the preservation of the whole plantation. Of course this required the expenditure of a large sum of money. The court held that under the agreement the landowner was responsible for this sum, since the contract, when considered as a whole, placed the burden of any large additional expense upon his shoulders.[39]

An Arkansas lease required the tenant of a fruit farm to make certain improvements and repairs and to gather the crop and deliver two-thirds of it to the landlord. Upon the failure of the tenant to perform his portion of the agreement, the landlord procured the appointment of a receiver. The tenant surrendered possession, and the crop was later gathered and sold, the landlord receiving much less than he would have if the tenant had carried out the terms of the agreement. The tenant sued for his share of the crop, but the court refused to permit a recovery.[40]

37. Shelby v. Hearne, 14 Tenn. 512 (1834).
38. Holton v. Blocker, 27 Ga. App. 104, 107 S. E. 550 (1921).
39. Mitchell v. Nelson, 13 S. C. 105 (1879).
40. Goldstein v. Biggs, 126 Ark. 627, 191 S. W. 219 (1917).

COVENANTS AGAINST DAMAGE CAUSED
BY NATURAL PHENOMENA

Sometimes the parties to a lease contract will insert a provision dealing with some natural phenomenon, like a freeze or a flood, which, according to past experience, is likely to occur during the term. A clause of this kind usually gives the lessee some exemption or reduction in obligation and is put in with the idea that he should not suffer too heavily where there has been a catastrophe which has wiped out the whole or even part of his investment.

An instance of this kind occurred where there was a lease of a Florida citrus grove for twenty years at an annual net rental, the lessees having an option to purchase. The instrument provided that in the event of a crop-destroying storm or freeze the lessees would be relieved from the payment of the rent until the new crop should equal the average production of any former four-year period. The court held that the word "destroy" as used in this lease would not be taken to mean a total loss, thus interpreting the clause as not requiring the property to be made useless for the purpose for which it was used or intended to be used.[41]

A common type of covenant in regions bordering on rivers or other streams or bodies of water is one by which the parties agree that if there should be an overflow of the leased land, even a partial one, the rent will be either excused entirely or reduced. Sometimes, in case of overflow, another form of payment, such as a share of whatever crop is raised on the reduced acreage or injured portion of the land, may be substituted for the cash rent required under the contract. In one case of this kind a lease provided that if the rented plantation should overflow after the fifteenth of May, the lessee would pay, instead of the yearly cash rental of $1500.00, one-fourth of the crop actually produced. During the term of the lease the plantation was inundated to the extent of one-third of its acreage. Although the provision of the lease related to the whole of the leased premises, the court held that, in accordance with the principles of fair construction, it would be possible to deduct from the rental figure a sum proportionate to the number of acres overflowed. Since one-third of the land actually overflowed, the lessor was

41. Umatilla Fruit Co. v. Campbell, 123 Fla. 484, 167 So. 370 (1936).

entitled to two-thirds of the rental figure plus one-fourth of the produce of the remaining third of the land.[42]

Another instance of a covenant concerning a change in terms because of an overflow is found in Arkansas. A lease contract provided that, in the event of a partial overflow, the lessee should notify the lessor on the first day of June of the current year if the former contemplated any claim for damage to the crop due to flood conditions. In the event of an overflow the lessor would receive as rent a stated portion of the crop instead of cash. He would also be permitted to use a building and certain machinery on the leased premises during that year. The court decided that it was not necessary to notify the lessor exactly on the first day of June, and that it was a sufficient compliance with the terms of the contract if the notice was sent by mail and was received by that date. Neither the fact that the lessee continued to use the machinery nor the fact that he had failed to cut and gather certain grass growing on the premises would be held to entail a forfeiture of his right to a reduction of the rent in the event of an overflow. The evidence being sufficient to show both overflow and notice, the lower court was held to have acted erroneously in rendering its judgment in favor of the lessor for the cash rent.[43] In a second hearing of this same case it was shown that the contract contained a provision stating that if no agreement could be reached concerning a reduction of the cash rent, the parties would then share the crop. In respect to this provision, the court said that neither party was required to attempt to bring about an agreement for reduction, and, if they did not do so, then the alternative proposition concerning the division of crops would become operative.[44]

COVENANTS CONCERNING NOTICE

The covenant concerning the giving of some form of notice is at times important in lease contracts. Thus in a Kentucky lease a clause stated that if the landlord sold the property during the term, the tenant would surrender possession at the end of the current year, provided he should have "notice of such sale before the first day of December." It was held that a mere notice of sale would

42. Furman v. Grounds, 125 La. 470, 51 So. 499 (1910).
43. Lacy Bros. v. Morton, 76 Ark. 603, 89 S. W. 842 (1905).
44. Morton v. Lacy Bros., 84 Ark. 396, 106 S. W. 200 (1907).

terminate the tenancy and justify the tenant in vacating the premises, although no actual sale was ever consummated.[45] Again, an Alabama lease provided that in case of a sale of the premises during the term, the lessee would surrender possession after a "reasonable notice" of the conveyance. The lessor was held to have given the required notice when he notified the tenant that he would require possession more than forty days before making the written demand necessary in an action of unlawful detainer.[46]

COVENANTS WITH RESPECT TO SIZE OF LEASED PREMISES

A familiar provision in farm leases is one which states the number of acres contained in the tract. While it is possible to word a provision of this kind in such a manner as to guarantee the acreage stated in the lease, such clauses are often taken as being merely descriptive of the premises and not as hidebound guarantees. A case in point is found in Arkansas, where a lease contract referred to the rented premises as "approximately 650 acres." Here it was held that the use of the word "approximately" made the recital of the acreage merely descriptive, and that it was never intended as a covenant of quantity.[47]

An Arkansas farmer rented a tract of land and executed a rent note which stated that he promised to pay the landlord one hundred and sixty dollars as the rental price of forty acres of land at four dollars an acre, "more or less." The court declared that the words "more or less" referred to the quantity of land, and that the instrument should be construed as a contract for renting by the acre and not as an agreement for a gross sum for the entire tract.[48]

Sometimes a tenant will be held to have waived his right to object to a shortage in acreage because he has had the opportunity to inspect the property and has failed to make his objection promptly. Thus in one instance a member of a tenant partnership was shown to have had several good opportunities to observe and inspect the leased premises during frequent trips made before the payment of the rent. The tenants were attempting to show that they had overpaid the rent because of a mistake in respect to acreage. The court applied the general rule of partnership law that all members of a

45. Lancaster v. Grant, 151 Ky. 465, 152 S. W. 251 (1913).
46. Gambill v. Cooper, 159 Ala. 637, 48 So. 691 (1909).
47. Cox v. Fisher, 146 Ark. 223, 225 S. W. 305 (1920).
48. Ayers v. Heustess, 94 Ark. 493, 127 S. W. 957 (1910).

firm are bound by the acts of any one partner. Anyone of average intelligence having sufficient information with respect to the claimed shortage would be deemed to know whatever could have been disclosed by an inquiry pursuant to such notice. In other words, the constructive knowledge of one partner was imputed to the others. The court concluded that tenants who voluntarily pay rent with knowledge of a shortage in acreage, or under circumstances whereby they are effected with such knowledge, cannot recover for any overpayment which they may have made.[49] Again a Georgia landlord made a representation, untrue but not fraudulent, with respect to the number of acres included in the leased premises. This statement was ruled to be no defense to the landlord's action on a note given as evidence of the debt for the rent, in spite of the fact that the tenant had had no opportunity to measure the tract. In other words, the statement did not amount to a warranty with respect to the true acreage of the tract.[50]

COVENANT OF QUIET ENJOYMENT

One of the most common provisions to be found in lease contracts is the covenant of quiet enjoyment. By this covenant the lessor contracts that the lessee shall not be disturbed in the enjoyment of the estate or interest granted under the lease. In fact it has been held by the Arkansas Court that a covenant of quiet enjoyment is implied in every mutual contract for the leasing of land.[51] In one instance a lease by the holder of a life estate contained a covenant of quiet enjoyment. The lessor died before the expiration of the term, and the lessee was thereupon evicted by the remainderman. The lessee was allowed to maintain an action against the lessor's administrator for breach of the covenant. The lessee had a privilege of renewal, but it was said that this would not affect the result where the eviction had occurred before the expiration of the original term and there had been no election to take the premises for the additional period.[52] In Alabama it was said that in suing on a covenant of quiet enjoyment the tenant must allege that the evictor is possessed of a title to the premises which is better than that of the lessor. It was further stated that where a lease has been made by a trustee in

---

49. Northcross v. Miller, 184 Ark. 463, 43 S. W. (2d) 734 (1931).
50. Bailey v. Tifton Buick Co., 44 Ga. App. 652, 162 S. E. 646 (1932).
51. Pickett v. Ferguson, 45 Ark. 177 (1885).
52. Duker's Adm'r v. Kaelin, 28 Ky. Law Rep. 900, 90 S. W. 959 (1906).

charge of the land of a beneficiary, the action must be brought against the trustee and not against the beneficiary. In this case the suit was for damages for being deprived of the land, and there was also a claim for special damages for expenses incurred while defending the eviction suit. A question arose as to whether in either or both types of action the lessee would be required to allege that he had notified the lessor that the eviction suit was pending, in order that the latter might make some effort to prepare a defense. The court declared that such an allegation was necessary in the action for special damages but not in the ordinary suit for breach of contract. In the action for special damages, moreover, it was said to be proper procedure to allege an express request that the lessor attend the trial and defend his title.[53]

It has been said that a tenant cannot withhold overdue rents or other sums of money due the landlord to cover expected damages from an apprehended eviction by someone with an alleged superior title to the leased property.[54]

There are expressions of opinion in one Alabama case that the covenant of quiet enjoyment is not a personal one and runs with the land.[55]

COVENANT OF RENEWAL

A usual type of covenant is that which makes it possible for the lessee to have an additional term if he so desires. Thus in one case an Arkansas tenant was given the right to renew the lease from year to year for one, two, three, or four years. This covenant was construed as giving the tenant an option to extend the term by merely holding over and paying the annual rental, and not to require a formal renewal each year.[56] In another case the lease was for eight years and provided that the tenant should have a right to renew for a term of ten years. The court declared that this instrument did not grant an eighteen-year term through an automatic extension but provided for a ten-year extension at the tenant's option, if he had not in the meantime forfeited his right. The use of the word "renew" was clearly indicative of a desire that the contract should expire at the end of eight years, with the tenant having the specific

53. Chestnut v. Tyson, 105 Ala. 149, 16 So. 723 (1894).
54. Pickett v. Ferguson, 45 Ark. 177 (1885).
55. McDaniel v. Callan, 75 Ala. 327 (1883).
56. Keith v. McGregor, 163 Ark. 203, 259 S. W. 725 (1924).

privilege to extend it for an additional ten-year term. However, the contract required the tenant to keep all the fences and improvements on the land in good repair and to deliver the property at the expiration of the term in as good condition as it was at the beginning. The tenant had failed to keep the property in repair during the eight-year term, and it was held that this constituted grounds for a refusal to renew the lease.[57]

In Kentucky a lease contract gave a seven-year term along with a renewal option for eight additional years. The instrument provided that certain buildings, to be erected on the premises by the lessee, should belong to the lessor at the end of the term. This provision was interpreted by the court as giving the lessor a right to these buildings at the end of the original seven-year term. If the lessee elected to renew the lease for the additional term, these improvements would become the property of the lessor at the end of that period. This contract did not provide in terms for a forfeiture of the leased premises for the lessee's failure to keep the buildings in good repair, and the court declared that no such covenant would be implied. It was held that, under the circumstances, the lessee's failure to keep the property in repair would not justify the lessor's refusal to renew the lease according to the terms of the contract. Even if there had been an effective covenant to keep up the property, it would no doubt be considered as independent. Hence the only action which could be maintained would be an action for damages which might result from a breach of this covenant. The instrument provided that if the parties could not agree on the rent for the additional term, the question should then be submitted to three disinterested parties, who would come to a conclusion in respect to a reasonable rent for the land. The evidence showed that the lessee had tried to get the lessor to abide by the agreement and had even tendered the amount of rent which had been agreed upon for each year of the original term. The court declared that the lessee was entitled to a renewal of the lease at a rental figure to be fixed as provided in the agreement.[58]

It appears to be settled that the covenant of renewal runs with the land and is binding upon all those in privity with the original parties.[59] In accordance with this principle it was ruled in Kentucky

57. Felder v. Hall Bros. Co., 151 Ark. 182, 235 S. W. 789 (1921).
58. Parsons v. Ball, 205 Ky. 793, 266 S. W. 649 (1924).
59. McDaniel v. Callan, 75 Ala. 327 (1883); Graham v. Rice, 203 Ky. 614, 262 S. W. 968 (1924).

that the death of the lessor did not destroy the lessee's right of renewal, which the latter could enforce against the lessor's personal representative.[60]

COVENANT TO PAY TAXES

In the absence of any mention of the payment of taxes on the leased premises the payment of such taxes is usually the responsibility of the lessor. Therefore, when the lessor wants to shift this burden, it is a common practice to insert in the lease contract a provision making the lessee liable for property taxes.

Under a covenant requiring the lessee to pay taxes it was held that there had been a breach when the time for the payment of the property taxes without penalty had passed with nothing having been done about the satisfaction of the claim.[61]

PROVISIONS FOR PAYMENT OF RENT

While it is entirely possible that a provision obligating the lessee to pay rent may be considered as a mere covenant,[62] a clause of this kind frequently is worded in such a manner that it must be considered a condition, any breach of which will authorize a forfeiture.[63]

MISCELLANEOUS PROVISIONS

The different types of covenants and conditions to be found in farm leases are of course manifold. In fact it would be impracticable to attempt an enumeration of all the various types. However, it might be useful to mention just a few of those which have been construed by the courts.

In one instance a lease contract gave the tenant the right to hold a certain meadow "so long as holding good or paying." It was said that this instrument called for the application of the maxim that a thing is certain which is capable of being made certain, and that it established a valid tenancy relationship. The contract stipulated that if all the land was not used as a meadow, the portion not so used would be cultivated. However, the court held that if the lessee failed to maintain the major portion of the land as a meadow, the lessor might then object and terminate the lease. During the

60. Graham v. Rice, 203 Ky. 614, 262 S. W. 968 (1924).
61. Ricou v. Hart, 47 La. Ann. 1370, 17 So. 878 (1895).
62. Morgan v. Chamberlain, 156 Ky. 369, 160 S. W. 1066 (1913).
63. Penney v. Burns, 226 Ala. 273, 146 So. 611 (1933); Sells v. Brewer, 125 Ark. 108, 187 S. W. 907 (1916).

term the lessor from time to time accepted the surrender of certain portions of the land which the lessee had ceased using as a meadow, thus progressively narrowing the estate. It was not shown that the reduced area had, in the words of the lease, ceased to hold good as a meadow. The testimony proved, on the contrary, that the land was still profitable as a meadow. Therefore, it was held that the lease was still in effect and that the lower court had erred in ruling that it was terminated.[64]

Under the cotton acreage reduction program of the early 'thirties, a contract with the Secretary of Agriculture required a Louisiana landowner to permit certain tenants to continue in occupancy, rent free, for a specified time, unless the tenants became a nuisance or a menace to the landowner's welfare. Rent was not paid by the tenants, and the landowner therefore attempted to eject them from the premises. The court refused to evict the tenants and declared that the failure to pay the rent had not made them a "nuisance" or a "menace" within the meaning of the agreement.[65]

A rather common type of covenant is the one by which the tenant agrees to deliver the possession of the premises to the landlord at the end of the term. In one case a covenant of this kind contained an agreement for liquidated damages in the event of a breach. The court declared that if the tenant abandoned the premises before the end of the term, he would not have performed the covenant and must pay damages, in this instance liquidated damages, for the breach. Such an abandonment might permit a stranger to make an entrance on the land and cause harm to the reversionary interest of the landlord.[66]

Another familiar type of covenant is the one by which a tenant agrees not to assign and/or sublet the leased premises. But a covenant not to assign does not seem to prevent a subletting of the lands.[67] Conversely, a covenant not to sublet is not broken by an assignment.[68]

There are numerous other covenants of varying importance. However, this discussion seems to have covered most of the common types, and there has been little comment upon the others by the courts.

64. Flinn v. Cullins, 143 Ark. 431, 220 S. W. 449 (1920).
65. Miller v. White, 163 So. 777 (La. App., 1935).
66. Bowling v. Ewing, 10 Ky. 616 (1821).
67. Hargrave v. King, 40 N. C. 430 (1848).
68. Rogers v. Hall, 227 N. C. 363, 42 S. E. (2d) 347 (1947).

VI

Particular Tenancies—Tenancy from Year To Year—Tenancy at Will— Tenancy at Sufferance

AT common law certain particular tenancies developed which had their beginnings in the old manorial system of feudal times. The rules established by the English courts concerning these tenancies were technical and not adapted to the more complex and tempestuous civilization of today. The colonists brought these rules with them when they settled in this country. As the state codes developed, much of this inherited law was bound to push its way into the statute books, and some of the technicalities still remain to plague the legal profession and others interested in the law of real property and landlord and tenant. In fact the early English statutes were often enacted verbatim by the lawmaking bodies of the colonies and states as they were settled.

A great deal of simplification is needed with respect to the laws governing tenancies from year to year, tenancies at will, and tenancies at sufferance. Statutes have been enacted in some jurisdictions with a view to a general modernization of the law concerning these tenancies. These laws seem to avoid at least some of the pitfalls and technicalities which had arisen under the common law and early statutes. Much still remains to be done, and yet a satisfactory start has been made toward a better system of law in respect to these tenancies.

TENANCY FROM YEAR TO YEAR

A tenancy from year to year may be created either by an express contract specifically establishing a tenancy of that type or by a lease for one or more years, the holding over of the tenant, and the payment of the stipulated annual rent after the first year without a new contract.[1] The establishment of such a tenancy by a mere hold-

1. Lamew v. Townsend, 147 Ark. 282, 227 S. W. 593 (1921).

ing over has been recognized in numerous instances.[2] Of course the implied consent of the landowner is necessary to the establishment of the tenancy.[3]

A Tennessee court has construed a written lease containing no stipulations as to length of term as running from year to year and as being terminable at the end of any year by either party.[4]

A Georgia tenant who had been in possession for several years, without saying anything to his landlord, left the rented premises in the hands of his son, who had formerly been his subtenant. The latter remained in possession for the rest of the current year and a portion of the succeeding year as well. It was held that the father had never abandoned the premises and was therefore responsible for the rent for both years. The tenant's failure to pay the rent for an entire year would not put the landlord upon implied notice that the tenant had abandoned the premises, since a tenant will often remain in possession for a year or more without paying the rent.[5]

Two Tennessee tenants were in joint possession of land which they had held continuingly from year to year. One of them agreed to give sole possession of a designated portion of the land to the other. The landowner, prior to the time when this contract would become effective, notified the promisee to vacate the premises. He then proceeded to lease the entire property to the other tenant, granting him permission to build thereon. The promisee sued his fellow tenant for a breach of contract. His recovery was limited by the lower court to damages for the year he had been in possession prior to the notice to vacate. From this decision he appealed, claiming that his recovery should not be so limited. The appellate court ruled against him and even expressed doubt as to whether he was entitled to any relief.[6]

A Mississippi tenant who had been in possession of a farm for some time was shown to have paid rent to the administrator after the death of the landlord. The question arose as to whether this payment should be considered a refusal to recognize the title of the

2. See Yancey v. Bruce, 109 Ark. 569, 160 S. W. 863 (1913); Beveridge v. Simmerville, 26 Ga. App. 373, 106 S. E. 212 (1921); Maynard v. Campbell, 115 S. C. 226, 105 S. E. 351 (1920); State ex rel. Sawyer v. Fort, 24 S. C. 510 (1885); Emerick v. Tavener, 9 Gratt. 220 (Va., 1852).

3. Yancey v. Bruce, 109 Ark. 569, 160 S. W. 863 (1913); Emerick v. Tavener, 9 Gratt. 220 (Va., 1852).

4. Stephens v. Stephens, 28 Tenn. App. 58, 185 S. W. (2d) 915 (1944).

5. Roberson v. Simons, 109 Ga. 360, 34 S. E. 604 (1899).

6. Boyd v. Mustin, 53 S. W. 225 (Tenn. Chan., 1899).

landlord or his heir. The court declared that such a payment would not have this effect and held that the tenant's continued possession of the premises would establish a tenancy from year to year.[7] Hence the payment to the administrator would not prevent the operation of the general rule in force in Mississippi [8] and elsewhere to the effect that a landowner's acceptance of rent for several years from a permissive occupant will establish a prima facie tenancy from year to year.

The Virginia Court declared that it is a mere presumption that a tenant holding over after the expiration of his term, with no objection from his landlord, becomes a tenant from year to year. This presumption may be rebutted by evidence which shows that his retention of the premises, though with the permission of the lessor, is not as tenant from year to year but in another capacity.[9] In the instant case the contract provided that the occupant should pay a sum in cash for the premises, and that if he failed to fulfill a certain condition in the instrument, then he should hold for the current year and the sum paid would be considered as rent. The occupant failed to fulfill the condition, and his holding over under these circumstances could not be considered as establishing a tenancy from year to year but only a tenancy for the current year.

A Louisiana statute [10] provides that if a person shall continue to occupy a predial estate (an estate for agricultural purposes) for one month after the expiration of his term without objection on the part of the lessor or someone claiming under him, the contract will be considered as renewed on the same terms for a year but no longer. However, this statute is not applicable where either party has announced his intention not to renew the lease contract on the same terms or for a full additional year. Here a rebuttable presumption is established. Where the lessee had definitely refused to renew the contract for another year and had only been permitted to hold over under an agreement to vacate on written notice to quit the premises, the presumption was declared to have been rebutted.[11]

Under the Kentucky statute [12] a tenant under contract for a term which is to expire on a day certain shall acquire no rights by holding

---

7. Richardson v. Neblett, 122 Miss. 723, 84 So. 695 (1920).
8. Hamilton v. Federal Land Bank, 175 Miss. 462, 167 So. 642 (1936).
9. Williamson v. Paxton, 18 Gratt. 475 (Va., 1868).
10. La. Civ. Code Ann. (Dart, 1932) Art. 2688.
11. Ashton Realty Co. v. Prowell, 165 La. 328, 115 So. 579 (1928).
12. Ky. Rev. Stat. (1946) §383.160.

over if proceedings to oust him are instituted within ninety days after the end of the term. However, if proceedings are not begun within that period, then the tenant cannot be ousted for a year from the day that the original tenancy expired. This statute has evidently altered the common law with respect to the effect of a tenant's continued occupation of land after his contract has expired.

A tenancy from year to year may be established where a farmer holds land under a lease contract which is invalid because of the Statute of Frauds. In one situation a Mississippi farmer contracted for the use of land under a five-year oral agreement which was invalid under the statute. He had given five annual rent notes to the landowner and had paid the periodic rent agreed upon for four years without objection. It was held that he had become a tenant from year to year and was therefore entitled to the statutory notice to quit.[13] This is evidently an application of the part-performance doctrine which seems to have been approved in an early Kentucky decision.[14] However, this doctrine cannot be employed in a situation where there has been no possession under the invalid oral contract.[15]

The common law required that a six-months notice be given before the end of the current period of tenure in order to terminate a tenancy from year to year. This rule was approved in early cases from Kentucky,[16] and North Carolina.[17] The above-mentioned Kentucky statute[18] has no doubt altered the law in this respect, at least to a certain degree, and the present North Carolina law requires a notice of a month or more before the expiration of the current year's term.[19] The statutory period for notice is three months in Florida[20] and Virginia[21] and two months in Mississippi.[22] Before the abolishment of the year-to-year tenancy by a recent statute in South Carolina,[23] that state required a reasonable notice,[24] and that

13. Scruggs v. McGehee, 110 Miss. 10, 69 So. 1003 (1915).
14. Morehead v. Watkyns, 44 Ky. 228 (1844).
15. White v. Levy, 93 Ala. 484, 9 So. 164 (1891).
16. Morehead v. Watkyns, 44 Ky. 228 (1844).
17. Irwin & Elmes v. Cox, 27 N. C. 521 (1845).
18. Supra note 12.
19. N. C. Gen. Stat. (1943) §42-14; Cherry v. Whitehurst, 216 N. C. 340, 4 S. E. (2d) 900 (1939).
20. Fla. Stat. Ann. (1941) §83.03.
21. Va. Code Ann. (Michie, 1936) §5516.
22. Miss. Code Ann. (1942) §946. See Hamilton v. Federal Bank, 175 Miss. 462, 167 So. 642 (1936); Scruggs v. McGehee, 110 Miss. 10, 69 So. 1003 (1915).
23. S. C. Stat. 1946, No. 873, §13.
24. Robison v. Barton, 113 S. C. 212, 102 S. E. 16 (1920).

it must look forward to the end of the calendar year.[25] An Arkansas judge made remarks which seem to indicate that a reasonable notice would be sufficient under the law of that state.[26] The reasonableness of the notice would clearly be an issue of fact for the jury.

Where a statute prescribes a certain period, the parties may agree upon another time for the giving of the notice.[27] If, after the commencement of a yearly term, an express lease is entered into between the parties for a definite time and it is agreed that the tenant shall quit the premises by that date, the form of the tenancy is superseded and notice is dispensed with.[28]

A Virginia landlord had notified his tenant from year to year that his rent for the next year would be a share of the crops rather than the fixed money rent he had been paying. The tenant had replied that he would do "what was right." Further notice was given the tenant to go ahead. It was held that the tenancy from year to year was not terminated by this exchange. The court was of the opinion that even if the notice and tenant's reply had been sufficient to end the relationship, the action of the landlord in afterward notifying his irresponsible tenant to stop drinking whiskey and go ahead with the job would constitute a waiver of the notice previously given.[29]

The Georgia Court has held that it is not necessary to give a tenant notice to vacate where the tenancy is for one year at a time.[30] However, it is probable that this contract was construed as establishing a continuous renewal agreement for one year at a time rather than a tenancy from year to year.

A study of the other periodic tenancies, such as from month to month and from week to week, is not appropriate here, since it is clear that no agricultural tenancy would be taken on these terms.

TENANCY AT WILL

A tenancy at will may be said to be a leasehold interest in land of uncertain duration which can be terminated at the wish of the landowner. Yet it has been said that a tenancy which is determinable at the will of one party is also determinable by the other.[31] A tenant

25. Maynard v. Campbell, 115 S. C. 226, 105 S. E. 351 (1920); Floyd v. Floyd, 4 Rich. 23 (S. C., 1850).
26. Lamew v. Townsend, 147 Ark. 282, 227 S. W. 593 (1921).
27. Cherry v. Whitehurst, 216 N. C. 340, 4 S. E. (2d) 900 (1939).
28. Williams v. Bennett, 26 N. C. 122 (1843).
29. Kellum v. Belote, 122 Va. 537, 95 S. E. 453 (1918).
30. Lee v. Beasley, 159 Ga. 527, 126 S. E. 290 (1925).
31. Mhoon v. Drizzle, 14 N. C. 414 (1831).

at will who holds over after a proper notice to quit the premises has been served upon him is no longer a tenant at will but becomes a tenant at sufferance.[32]

A tenancy at will may be established by an express provision of the lease contract. Thus an agreement by which the landowner permits a person to use the land with the understanding that the latter will move whenever requested to do so by the owner has been held to establish a tenancy at will.[33] The North Carolina court decided that such a tenancy existed where a landowner agreed to allow a prospective occupant to cultivate the soil during his life or for as long as he pleased.[34] One judge was of the opinion that this was a mere personal contract, and that no estate vested in the occupant.

The Louisiana court has held that a mere oral permission to occupy land during the lifetime of the owner without any rent or other charge would establish a tenancy at will terminable at the pleasure of the owner.[35] It may be that the court was influenced by a rule that parol evidence was only admissible to prove the simple fact of the permission to occupy the land and not to establish title or other such interest in the property itself, whether of ownership, use, or habitation, derived from or created by the owner's permission.

In a rather recent case from Mississippi one of several owners in common of an undivided tract of land, without authority from his co-owners, made a crop-sharing contract covering the entire premises with a person wishing to cultivate the land. The court refused to recognize the validity of this contract and ruled that the occupant was a tenant at will with respect to the undivided portions of the co-owners and would be responsible to them for the reasonable value of the use and occupation. The court reasoned that in this situation an occupant working under an invalid contract was a tenant at will.[36]

A Kentucky landowner employed a farm laborer for a term of one year at a stipulated sum per month. He agreed to keep the laborer's cow at a charge of one dollar a month and to furnish him a house at two dollars a month. After entering upon his duties the

32. Sappenfield v. Goodman, 215 N. C. 417, 2 S. E. (2d) 13 (1939).
33. Humphries v. Humphries, 25 N. C. 362 (1843); Harrison v. Middleton, 11 Gratt. 527 (Va., 1854).
34. Mhoon v. Drizzle, 14 N. C. 414 (1832).
35. Bailey v. Ward, 32 La. Ann. 839 (1880).
36. Vaughn v. McCool, 186 Miss. 549, 191 So. 286 (1939).

occupant refused to continue the work. The court definitely termed this a tenancy at will and declared that the tenant's interest was ended by his failure to perform the appointed tasks and that there was no need for any notice to quit the premises.[37] It would seem that the arrangement here might very well have been called a cropper relationship. In an instance where the occupant was clearly shown to have been a cropper, the Georgia court held that his subsequent failure to comply with the terms of the agreement did not make him a tenant at will, and as such, subject to be dispossessed under a summary warrant.[38]

As a general rule it may be said that a tenancy at will arises where a party is allowed to take possession of land under a contract of sale, written or oral, or under an unexecuted contract of lease.[39] The same is true where a mortgagor holds over after foreclosure with the consent of the mortgagee [40] or where possession has been obtained under a parol trust.[41] However, where it was shown that the occupant held the premises as a purchaser and not as a tenant, a possessory action based on the theory of a tenancy is not maintainable.[42]

In one North Carolina case [43] an occupant held under a deed of trust arrangement which contained a stipulation for the retention of the premises until they were sold under the terms of the trust. After the land had been sold the occupant remained in possession. The court declared that such an occupant is a tenant at will or at sufferance for some purposes but cannot be considered a tenant under a proper construction of the Landlord and Tenant Act [44] which authorizes dispossessory proceedings, since that statute is only intended to cover those cases where the occupant has entered under some express or implied contract of lease with the landowner or his assigns or where he is in privity with those who have so entered. This interpretation would seem to exclude from the operation of the statute vendors or mortgagors [45] retaining possession

37. McGee v. Gibson, 40 Ky. 105 (1840).

38. Robson v. Cofield, 113 Ga. 1153, 39 S. E. 472 (1901).

39. Dowd v. Gilchrist, 46 N. C. 353 (1854); Love v. Edmonston, 23 N. C. 152 (1840); Carson v. Baker, 15 N. C. 220 (1833); Jones v. Temple, 87 Va. 210, 12 S. E. 404 (1890).

40. Buchmann v. Callahan, 222 Ala. 240, 131 So. 799 (1931).

41. Wright v. Graves, 80 Ala. 416 (1885).

42. Thrift v. Schurr, 52 Ga. App. 314, 183 S. E. 195 (1935).

43. McCombs v. Wallace, 66 N. C. 481 (1872).

44. N. C. Gen. Stat. (1943) §42-26.

45. Culbreth v. Hall, 159 N. C. 588, 75 S. E. 1096 (1912); Greer v. Wilbar, 72 N. C. 592 (1875).

after a sale and also vendees [46] in possession under a contract for title which has not materialized.

An opposite construction seems to have been placed upon the Georgia Landlord and Tenant Act.[47] Here it has been said that where the interest of a landowner has been divested by a sale made pursuant to authority contained in a security deed, and he thereafter remains in possession, he becomes a tenant at sufferance of the purchaser and, as such, may be summarily dispossessed under the statute.[48]

This difference of opinion seems to prevail even where the security deed or other instrument contains a provision which states that the debtor will become a tenant upon a default and sale pursuant to the power provided for in the instrument. Thus the North Carolina court held that the action of summary ejectment authorized by the Landlord and Tenant Act could not be brought where the security deed stipulated that those in possession at the time of the sale would immediately become the tenants at will of the purchaser, the statute being applicable only in instances where a more conventional tenancy relationship existed.[49] On the other hand, a Georgia court has held that summary proceedings under the Landlord and Tenant Act may be brought where a security deed provides that the possession of the mortgagor or any person holding under him after a foreclosure sale shall be as "tenants holding over," for such a directive is clearly the intention of the parties.[50] The court also declared that the statutory rule [51] that a term of unspecified duration shall be presumed to be for the calendar year is not applicable to such a situation as is here presented.

It has been held that a tenancy at will is not created until the prospective occupant enters the premises, and that therefore the holder of a contract of tenancy who has never had possession is not allowed to maintain a possessory action.[52]

A South Carolina landowner leased certain premises to a tenant who afterwards assigned his interest to another with the owner's consent. After the assignee had gone into possession the landowner

46. Greer v. Wilbar, 72 N. C. 592 (1875).
47. Ga. Code (1933) §§61-301 et seq.
48. Atlantic Life Ins. Co. v. Ryals, 48 Ga. App. 793, 173 S. E. 875 (1934).
49. Prudential Ins. Co. v. Totten, 203 N. C. 431, 166 S. E. 316 (1932).
50. Price v. Bloodworth, 55 Ga. App. 268, 189 S. E. 925 (1937).
51. Ga. Code (1933) §61-104.
52. Pollock v. Kittrell, 4 N. C. 585 (1817).

agreed to execute a new lease to him personally. However, after the assignee had signed the instrument, the landowner refused to go through with the deal and would not sign. It was held that under these circumstances the assignee was not within the meaning of a statute [53] which authorized the ejectment of persons going into possession of land as tenants at will. This assignee did not in the first instance go on the land as tenant at will. It was also declared that the unexecuted agreement for a new term could not have the effect of making the assignee a tenant at will, since that instrument must be either entirely ignored or else regarded as having been carried into full force and effect according to the manifest intention of the parties at the time it was drawn up.[54]

A South Carolina statute provides that all persons, excepting domestic servants and farm laborers, using or occupying real estate without an agreement, either written or oral, shall be considered tenants at will.[55] It is also provided that the landowner may treat trespassers and others entering his property without right as tenants at will and collect a reasonable rent for the use and occupation of the premises.[56]

In Georgia, by express statutory provision,[57] a parol contract for the use of land for a term exceeding one year has the effect of establishing a tenancy at will.[58] In some instances the tenant can be shown to have paid a consideration, in money, labor, or improvements, for the privilege of cultivating the land. In one such case the tenant had made the improvements called for by a parol contract. The court declared that the character of the tenancy would not thereby be changed, but that the making of the improvements would operate as an estoppel upon the landlord to terminate the tenancy until the tenant had occupied the premises long enough for his outlay to offset the stipulated rent.[59] It also said the statute [60] providing that any rental contract of indefinite duration should be interpreted as a tenancy for a calendar year would have no applica-

53. S. C. Code Ann. (1932) §8812.
54. Morris v. Palmer, 44 S. C. 462, 22 S. E. 726 (1895).
55. S. C. Stat. 1946, No. 873, §3.
56. S. C. Stat. 1946, No. 873, §15.
57. Ga. Code (1933) §61-102.
58. See Beasley v. Lee, 155 Ga. 634, 117 S. E. 743 (1923); Abbott v. Padrosa, 136 Ga. 278, 71 S. E. 419 (1911); Sikes v. Carter, 30 Ga. App. 539, 118 S. E. 430 (1923); Beveridge v. Simmerville, 26 Ga. App. 373, 106 S. E. 212 (1921).
59. Sikes v. Carter, 30 Ga. App. 539, 118 S. E. 430 (1923).
60. Ga. Code (1933) §61-104.

tion when by necessary implication, as in this case, a minimum duration of the tenancy was fixed in excess of a year.

Suppose a tenant at will makes a sublease, assignment, or transfer of the premises to someone else. It is a general rule that the making of a lease to another by a tenant at will terminates the tenancy and converts the tenant into a trespasser. In Alabama, however, it has been held that it will have this effect only at the election of the landowner, and that no other person, including a tenant trying to avoid the payment of rent, has a right to regard the tenancy as terminated.[61]

It is clear that a tenant at will should be entitled to the growing crops planted before a notice to quit has been served and to the right of ingress and egress to work and harvest such crops.[62] But this does not give him the right to retain the premises or to live on the land after notice.

In respect to the notice which is necessary to terminate a tenancy at will, the laws in the several states differ widely. In North Carolina a tenant at will, if entitled to any notice at all, and in the absence of a statute setting up a different rule, is entitled to only a reasonable notice to quit.[63] In fact the court has said that a tenancy at will is terminable *instanter*.[64] According to the Mississippi statute [65] notice to quit is necessary where the term is of uncertain duration, but there is no definite requirement of time prescribed for quitting the premises where the tenancy is strictly at will. Hence it is likely that a reasonable time would be allowed. It is supposed that this would also be the effect of the Virginia statute.[66]

In the case of a predial or agricultural lease in Louisiana, a statute [67] provides that where no time or duration of the estate has been specified, the tenancy is presumed to be for one year, since that is the time usually needed to raise, gather, and market a crop. Therefore, it is probable that no lease of uncertain duration concerning agricultural lands would be considered as a strict ten-

61. Cook v. Cook, 28 Ala. 660 (1856).

62. Buchmann v. Callahan, 222 Ala. 240, 131 So. 799 (1931); Humphries v. Humphries, 25 N. C. 362 (1843).

63. Sappenfield v. Goodman, 215 N. C. 417, 2 S. E. (2d) 13 (1939).

64. Barbee v. Lamb, 225 N. C. 211, 34 S. E. (2d) 65 (1945); Love v. Edmonston, 23 N. C. 152 (1843).

65. Miss. Code Ann. (1942) §946.

66. Va. Code Ann. (Michie, 1936) §5516.

67. La. Civ. Code Ann. (Dart, 1932) Art. 2687.

ancy at will. Another statute [68] requiring ten days' notice in tenancies of uncertain duration would most likely not apply to agricultural leases.

A tenancy at will in Kentucky may be terminated by the landlord's written notice of one month.[69] South Carolina requires a written notice of twenty days.[70] According to a Georgia statute [71] the interest of a tenant at will does not expire until two months after the landlord's notice of his desire to end the relationship, while the tenant may terminate the status by one month's notice. It is not necessary that the notice be in writing.[72] Upon the issue being raised by the tenant, evidence showing a notice of two months is essential to the landlord's recovery of possession.[73]

A Florida statute [74] formerly provided that any lease not in writing or without the lessor's signature would be deemed to establish a tenancy at will; however, this was later altered, and such an occupancy now creates a tenancy at sufferance.[75] In this state all periodic tenancies, including those from year to year, which are created by a written contract are evidently to be deemed tenancies at will,[76] and three months' notice is required for the termination of such a tenancy.[77] Another statute[78] provides that the mere payment and/or acceptance of rent shall not be deemed to establish a renewed tenancy, but if the possession is continued with the written consent of the owner, a tenancy at will shall be established. This act seems to eliminate any possibility that a tenancy from year to year would arise from the payment and acceptance of rent in accordance with the general rule in effect in most of the Southeastern states.

How should the notice to terminate a tenancy at will be brought to the attention of the tenant? The Alabama Court has said that the notice must be given in such a way that the tenant may be made cognizant of the landlord's intent.[79]

68. La. Civ. Code Ann. (Dart, 1932) Art. 2686.
69. Ky. Rev. Stat. (1946) §383.140.
70. S. C. Stat. 1946, No. 873, §11.
71. Ga. Code (1933) §61-105.
72. Farlow v. Central Oil Co., 74 Ga. App. 349, 39 S. E. (2d) 561 (1946).
73. Harrell v. Souter, 27 Ga. App. 531, 109 S. E. 301 (1921).
74. Fla. Comp. Gen. Laws Ann. (Skillman, 1927) §5431.
75. Fla. Comp. Gen. Laws Ann. (Skillman, 1931 Supp.) §5431.
76. Fla. Comp. Gen. Laws Ann. (Skillman, 1931 Supp.) §5432.
77. Fla. Stat. Ann. (1941) §83.03.
78. Fla. Stat. Ann. (1941) §83.04.
79. Cook v. Cook, 28 Ala. 660 (1856).

There seems to be no doubt that a purchaser of the landlord's reversionary interest may, upon giving the required statutory notice, terminate the tenancy at will and proceed to oust the tenant.[80]

TENANCY AT SUFFERANCE

A tenancy at sufferance is not really a tenancy at all, the occupant being on the premises without any lawful claim. It exists where an occupant, who has been on the land rightfully, continues to hold over without any legitimate reason and with the mere sufferance of the owner. Thus where a tenant for an agreed term continues on after its expiration, a tenancy at sufferance is established.[81] In a situation where a tenant had held over in this manner, the court remarked that a tenant at sufferance is a wrongdoer in possession without the permission of the owner and because of his laches or neglect.[82] The Florida court has defined a tenant at sufferance as one who comes into lawful possession of land otherwise than by operation of law and who continues to occupy it after his right to do so is at an end.[83]

Where for a number of years a tenant had held under an oral lease, made subject to the right of the landlord to sell the property at any time, and the tenant continued on the land after being promptly notified of a sale, a tenancy at sufferance was created.[84] The same was true where a tenant at will in Georgia continued in possession for more than two months after the required statutory notice.[85] The rights of a tenant at will terminate at his death, and the Kentucky court has held that the wife of such a tenant thereafter remaining in possession was, if a tenant at all, merely a tenant at sufferance.[86]

A Georgia farmer occupied land under a cropping contract and remained in possession after the agreement had expired. Here the court declared that he held as a tenant at sufferance and could be proceeded against under the Landlord and Tenant Act, since he need not have entered originally as a tenant to be placed subse-

80. Tatum v. Padrosa, 24 Ga. App. 259, 100 S. E. 653 (1919).
81. Crawford v. Jones, 27 Ga. App. 448, 108 S. E. 807 (1921).
82. Willis v. Harrell, 118 Ga. 906, 45 S. E. 794 (1903).
83. Brady v. Scott, 128 Fla. 582, 175 So. 724 (1937); Coleman v. State, 119 Fla. 653, 161 So. 89 (1935). See also Baker v. Clifford-Mathew Inv. Co., 99 Fla. 1229, 128 So. 827 (1930).
84. Minor v. Sutton, 73 Ga. App. 253, 36 S. E. (2d) 158 (1945).
85. Crawford v. Jones, 27 Ga. App. 448, 108 S. E. 807 (1921).
86. Perry v. Veal, 142 Ky. 441, 134 S. W. 458 (1911).

quently in that category.[87] In this case the period of holding over before eviction proceedings were begun was only eight days, and the dissenting judge pointed out that to have the effect of changing the farmer's status to that of a tenant at sufferance, the subsequent occupancy should be of sufficient length to warrant an inference of consent to a different status. This seems a very reasonable attitude.

In Georgia a person entered upon certain premises as the tenant of another who held merely a beneficial interest in the land, his right to the property being subject to the claim of a third person holding a security deed with power of sale. The land was sold and the holder of the deed became the purchaser. The tenant remained in possession, and the court held that he was a tenant at sufferance and might be dispossessed.[88]

If the common law lessee of a life tenant is in possession at the time of the latter's death, and continues to hold the property, he thereby becomes a tenant at sufferance. Where, however, the lessee is not in possession when the life tenant dies, or does not hold over, a mere recognition on the part of the remainderman of the previously executed rental contract with the life tenant will not have the effect of making the occupant a tenant at sufferance, a necessary element of that tenancy being the continuance of possession.[89]

A tenancy at sufferance may arise out of other relationships. Thus where a real estate mortgagor remains in possession after forfeiture without the express assent or dissent of the new owner, he stays in possession without right and is a tenant at sufferance.[90] It has also been held that where all right, title, and interest of a landowner has been divested by a transfer made under the power of sale in a security deed, and he thereafter remains in possession, he becomes a tenant at sufferance and therefore subject to be dispossessed in a summary proceeding.[91]

Where a purchaser of land is given possession without payment of the price and remains in control after a default in the payment of the installments provided for by the contract, a tenancy at sufferance exists.[92] The same result follows where an occupant of land

87. Malone v. Floyd, 50 Ga. App. 701, 179 S. E. 176 (1935).
88. Williams v. Federal Land Bank, 44 Ga. App. 606, 162 S. E. 408 (1932).
89. Wright v. Graves, 80 Ala. 416 (1885).
90. Miller v. Faust, 250 Ala. 545, 35 So. (2d) 162 (1948); Buchmann v. Callahan, 222 Ala. 240, 131 So. 799 (1931).
91. Lowther v. Patton, 45 Ga. App. 543, 165 S. E. 487 (1932).
92. Bush v. Fuller, 173 Ala. 511, 55 So. 1000 (1911).

has entered under the terms of a purchasing contract providing that he is to vacate the premises on request after a default in the payment of purchase-money notes and then has held over after a failure to pay the first note.[93]

Sometimes a person whose land has been sold at an execution sale remains in control of the premises and his continued possession is merely tolerated by the purchaser, who at no time gives his consent to the extended occupancy. In a situation of this kind the court held that upon the consummation of the sale the former owner, who had led the purchaser to believe that he was going to quit the premises, became a tenant at sufferance. The mere fact that the purchaser had told the former owner that he would have to pay rent would not convert the holding into a tenancy at will.[94]

Again, a person made a purchasing contract with one who assumed to act as the agent of a landowner, the pact being subject to the latter's approval, and went into possession of the premises. The agreement was never ratified, however, and the occupant was held to be a tenant at sufferance.[95]

A Virginia tenant holding over after his term had come to an end gave a deed for the property to a third person. Here it was clear that a tenancy from year to year would result from the landlord's recognition of the occupant. If there had been no recognition, however, the uninterrupted possession would have made the occupant a tenant at sufferance, and the tenant's transferee would have had no more right to hold the property than had the tenant himself.[96]

Under a Georgia statute making a tenant holding over liable for double rent, it has been held that a tenant at sufferance does not become so liable until after a demand for possession.[97]

In Florida any lease is deemed to establish a tenancy at sufferance unless it is in writing and signed by the landowner.[98] In the event of the entrance of a tenant under a written lease and his continuance in possession after the term has expired, it would seem that the occupant will be considered a tenant at sufferance. However, if his pos-

---

93. Delph v. Bank of Harlan, 292 Ky. 387, 166 S. W. (2d) 852 (1942).
94. Hill v. Kitchens, 39 Ga. App. 789, 148 S. E. 754 (1929).
95. Smith v. Singleton, Hunt & Co., 71 Ga. 68 (1883).
96. Emerick v. Tavener, 9 Gratt 220 (Va., 1852).
97. Willis v. Harrell, 118 Ga. 906, 45 S. E. 794 (1903); Smith v. Singleton, Hunt & Co., 71 Ga. 68 (1883); Hill v. Kitchens, 39 Ga. App. 789, 148 S. E. 754 (1929).
98. Fla. Comp. Gen. Laws Ann. (Skillman, 1931 Supp.) §5431.

session is continued with the newly executed written consent of the landowner, then the occupant will become a tenant at will.[99]

Another Florida statute[100] in effect in the 'twenties made it a misdemeanor for a tenant whose term had expired to hold possession for more than fifteen days after the service of a written demand. The period is shortened to ten days by amending acts.[101] The validity of these laws was upheld in an opinion in which the court remarked that the ten-day statute would have no application to oral tenancy agreements, thus cutting down the usefulness of the act.[102]

A tenancy at sufferance continues until the landlord takes some affirmative action which will have the effect of transforming the holding into some other form of tenancy or until the interest is terminated.[103] Generally it may be said that no notice is required to end a tenancy at sufferance, the occupant having become a wrongdoer by holding over without any legitimate interest.[104] In contradiction of all reason, however, a Kentucky statute[105] provides for one month's notice in writing to terminate this tenancy. It would seem that an interest of this kind, being merely permissive and without right, should require no previous notice for a termination.

In Alabama it has been said that, although no notice is required to terminate a tenancy at sufferance, the service of a ten-day notice on such a tenant by necessary implication extends his lawful possession for that period, and that nothing short of a demand can make the possession unlawful until the stated time has elapsed. [106]. The court further declared that a landowner's mistaken idea that a person in possession was a tenant at will would not change a tenancy at sufferance into a tenancy at will. However, a notice by the landowner to the occupant, wherein it was recited that the tenancy was one at will, would justify an inference that the holding was in fact at will.

99. Fla. Comp. Gen. Laws Ann. (Skillman, 1931 Supp.) §5434.
100. Fla. Stat. Ann. (1941) §821.31. See Fla. Comp. Gen. Laws Ann. (Skillman, 1927) §7395.
101. See Fla. Laws 1933, c. 16066; Fla. Laws 1931, c. 15057.
102. Coleman v. State, 119 Fla. 653, 161 So. 89 (1935).
103. Willis v. Harrell, 118 Ga. 906, 45 S. E. 794 (1903); Crawford v. Jones, 27 Ga. App. 448, 108 S. E. 807 (1921).
104. Bush v. Fuller, 173 Ala. 511, 55 So. 1000 (1911); Miller v. Faust, 250 Ala. 545, 35 So. (2d) 162 (1948); Willis v. Harrell, 118 Ga. 906, 45 S. E. 794 (1903); Emerick v. Tavener, 9 Gratt. 220 (Va., 1852).
105. Ky. Rev. Stat. (1946) §383.140. See Delph v. Bank of Harlan, 292 Ky. 387, 166 S. W. (2d) 852 (1942).
106. Bush v. Fuller, 173 Ala. 511, 55 So. 1000 (1911).

CONCLUSION

As the written tenancy contract replaces the oral, the tenancy from year to year and the tenancy at will are disappearing from the law books to a great extent. They are carried over from the feudal law and the manorial system and are not adapted to this day of definite contracts. The need for certainty is one of the cornerstones of the movement for the modernization of the juridical system. Of course, the tenancy at sufferance will be with us as long as tenants hold over after their leases are terminated.

VII

Holding Over

MANY problems arise out of the "holding over" by a tenant after the expiration of a time certain marked out in the lease contract or, in the case of a tenancy of uncertain duration such as a tenancy at will, after the notice required by law. Needless to say, this holding over is rather common, and many suits grow out of such a continuation of possession.

HOLDING OVER IN GENERAL

The general rule seems to be that a tenant who holds over in this manner without any objection on the part of the landlord becomes a tenant for another year under the same covenants and restrictions and at the same rental provided for in the original lease contract.[1] Where the continued possession is with the tacit consent of the landlord, he cannot terminate the implied tenancy thus created by giving notice in the middle of the crop year. He must wait until the end of the current year to terminate the tenancy and take possession of the premises.[2] Under such circumstances the lessee thus continuing in possession becomes a tenant from year to year.[3] Furthermore, it does not seem to matter that the original term was for a period longer than one year.[4]

A person holding over under such circumstances is no less a tenant because the provisions of the contract have been impliedly renewed. Hence such an individual is prevented from disputing his landlord's title in accordance with the familiar rule of law to that effect.[5]

1. Abbeville State Bank v. Wiley Fertilizer Co., 224 Ala. 421, 140 So. 431 (1932); Ames v. Scheusler & Donnell, 14 Ala. 600 (1848); Linder v. Pope, 25 Ga. App. 332, 103 S. E. 265 (1920); Love v. Law, 57 Miss. 596 (1880); Usher v. Moss, 50 Miss. 208 (1874); Hobday v. Kane, 114 Va. 398, 76 S. E. 902 (1913). For an interesting discussion of the general problem presented here, see Voss v. King, 38 W. Va. 607, 18 S. E. 762 (1893).
2. Usher v. Moss, 50 Miss. 208 (1874).
3. Payne v. Woolfolk's Adm'x., 196 Ky. 550, 245 S. W. 151 (1922); Love v. Law, 57 Miss. 596 (1880); Seward v. Garner, 19 Tenn. App. 440, 89 S. W. (2d) 770 (1935).
4. Payne v. Woolfolk's Adm'x., 196 Ky. 550, 245 S. W. 151 (1922).
5. Linder v. Pope, 25 Ga. App. 332, 103 S. E. 265 (1920).

Moreover, it has been held that a landlord can recover rent where the cultivator has held over for a year under an agreement to sign a renewal lease.[6]

It has been held to be erroneous for a judge to charge a jury that it might *infer* that in holding over the tenant intended to occupy the premises for another year at the same rent. The appellate court objected to this charge on the ground that it gave the jury a discretion in arriving at a conclusion which would have been implied by law without any aid from that body. According to the principle announced in the charge, the jury might well have inferred that the tenant's intention to hold the land for another year at the same rental figure was a necessary element in making him responsible. The liability was in fact actually fixed by reason of his mere continuance of possession and entirely independent of his intention.[7]

The landlord may move promptly to oust the tenant holding over from the premises or he may treat the occupant as a tenant for the ensuing year.[8] A failure to act within a reasonable time has been taken as consent to the tenant's continued occupation for another year.[9] It may be said that the choice of the landlord in this matter may well be concluded by a short lapse of time or by acts of a minor nature indicating his wishes with respect to the continuation of the tenancy relationship.[10] Once the choice is indicated, however, the contract for the succeeding year is binding; and therefore a subsequent abandonment by the tenant, without the consent of the landlord, does not relieve the former from liability for the year's rent.[11]

The tenant has no such opportunity to elect what he will do, for his mere continuance of possession fixes his status for another year, provided the landlord wishes to insist that he be so considered.[12] Thus a crop mortgage given by a tenant holding over has been held to have priority over another mortgage given after the execution of a formal lease between the same two parties for another year.[13]

This view of the status of the tenant holding over has been approved in the Civil Law jurisdiction of Louisiana with the enact-

6. Southern Homestead Ass'n v. Perrin, 167 So. 135 (La. App., 1936).
7. Ames v. Scheusler & Donnell, 14 Ala. 600 (1848).
8. Ridgway v. Bryant, 8 Ga. App. 564, 70 S. E. 28 (1911).
9. Usher v. Moss, 50 Miss. 208 (1874).
10. Voss v. King, *supra* Note 1.
11. Ridgway v. Bryant, 8 Ga. App. 564, 70 S. E. 28 (1911).
12. Voss v. King, *supra* Note 1.
13. Abbeville State Bank v. Wiley Fertilizer Co., 224 Ala. 421, 140 So. 431 (1932).

ment of a statute[14] giving the parties practically the same rights to which they are entitled under the common law. Under this statute a holding over of a month or more with no objection by the lessor or some interested third person automatically continues the tenancy for the next year under the same covenants and conditions which had been incorporated into the original lease.

A slightly different approach is seen in the Virginia statute[15] which provides that a tenant holding over "shall not, by his mere failure to vacate the premises upon the expiration of the lease, be held as tenant for another term when such failure is not due to wilfulness, negligence or other avoidable cause." It was provided, however, that he shall be liable to the lessor in an action for use and occupation and responsible for all damages caused by his failure to surrender the premises at the stipulated time. Of course, this act would not be applicable in instances where the holding over is wilful.

According to a Kentucky statute,[16] a tenant holding over acquires no right to the tenancy for the following year until the expiration of ninety days from the termination of the original lease. He is then entitled to remain on the premises until the end of the current year, and so on from year to year, until he abandons the place, is turned out of possession at a proper time, or makes a new agreement with the landlord.[17]

A Florida statute[18] makes a lessee holding over a tenant at sufferance and provides that the mere payment or acceptance of rent shall not give him a right to a new term. If, however, the lessee continues to hold the premises with the consent of the lessor, then a tenancy at will is established. This statute is worded in such a manner that it seems to apply only where the original lease is in writing and the parties have failed to renew the contract in writing. Another statute[19] seems to make everyone holding under an oral lease a tenant at sufferance.

These statutes show the diverse efforts which have been made to find a satisfactory solution to the problem of the tenant holding

14. La. Civ. Code Ann. (Dart, 1932) Art. 2688.
15. Va. Code Ann. (Michie, 1936) §5517.
16. Ky. Rev. Stat. (1946) §383.160.
17. See Payne v. Woolfolk's Adm'x., 196 Ky. 550, 245 S. W. 151 (1922); Unger v. Bamberger, 85 Ky. 11, 2 S. W. 498 (1887).
18. Fla. Comp. Gen. Laws Ann. (Skillman, 1931 Supp.) §5434.
19. Fla. Comp. Gen. Laws Ann. (Skillman, 1931 Supp.) §5431.

over. It is very doubtful, however, that these novel schemes have improved very much on the common-law rules. A more manifest definiteness is the keynote of the Kentucky act, which seems to offer the soundest treatment of the problem.

Many diverse situations arise with respect to tenants holding over after their leases have expired. Some of these situations are important enough to merit consideration and analysis.

ATTEMPT AT NEW LEASE

In an Alabama case there was an intervening ineffectual negotiation for a sale of the leased premises to the tenant. It was held that such a negotiation would not interfere with the application of the rule that a tenant holding over is responsible, not for reasonable rent, but for the amount of rent reserved in the former lease.[20] This case is to be contrasted with one from Mississippi where the court found that there had been nothing amounting to negotiations for a new lease, despite the fact that the tenant had told the landlord's agent that, unless the rent were reduced, he would thereafter hold only from month to month. The landlord was trying to show that the occupant was liable under the general rule for the rent stipulated in the prior contract. The court seemed to believe that negotiations for a new lease would prevent the application of the general rule.[21] The only difference between the two cases is that in one instance the court is considering negotiations for a sale and in the other negotiations for the renewal of a lease, and it is extremely doubtful whether this would constitute a valid ground of distinction.

An Arkansas tenant, unable to agree upon terms for the succeeding year, except in respect to the amount of rent, remained in possession of the premises after the expiration of a prior term. The court held that holding over under these circumstances constituted an admission that the sum agreed upon was the proper amount to be charged.[22]

It has been declared that a clause in a lease reserving to the tenant the right to gather the crops after the expiration of the term would entitle him to a free means of ingress and egress to enable him to harvest the produce, but would not authorize him to hold over and exclude the landlord from rightful possession of the premises. In

20. Walker v. Gunnels, 188 Ala. 206, 66 So. 45 (1914).
21. Tonkel v. Riteman, 163 Miss. 216, 141 So. 344 (1932).
22. Dickenson v. Arkansas City Imp. Co., 77 Ark. 570, 92 S. W. 21 (1906).

this case the court held the tenant liable for all damages sustained by the landlord by reason of the former's continued possession.[23]

A tenant who had a lease which expired on a day certain held over after being notified to quit the premises. Pending an action of ejectment brought against him by the lessor, he left the place. The lessor sued him and recovered a reasonable sum for the use and occupation of the premises during the period that he had unlawfully remained in possession. Here the court refused to follow the tenant's theory that his possession after the contract had expired could be taken as evidence of a new tenancy from year to year. It was said, however, that the situation would have been entirely different if the money had been recovered or received as *rent*.[24]

JOINT HOLDING

Where an owner in common leases the land to his co-owner, a rather peculiar situation arises. It has been said that one owner in common in possession holds the premises for himself and his co-owner jointly. The relationship of landlord and tenant does not exist under these conditions unless a lease contract is entered into between them. Sometimes, however, such an agreement is made, but when the occupant holds over beyond the specified term, his possession again becomes the possession of both, and he is thereafter considered as co-owner and not as a tenant holding over.[25]

A lease may be made to two persons jointly, though only one of them actually occupies the land. In a situation of this kind the occupying tenant may hold over after the expiration of the term. Here the unlawful possession is deemed to be by both parties, and the nonoccupant can be held responsible unless he has given notice to the landowner that he has ceased to hold as tenant.[26]

DISCLAIMING TENANCY

Where there is a distinct disclaimer of any tenancy, the situation is vastly different. In one instance a tenant held over under a definite claim of ownership. Here the landowner was permitted to recover only the reasonable value of the use of the premises and was not allowed to recover rent at the rate stipulated in the expired agree-

23. Stoddard & Hewett v. Waters, 30 Ark. 156 (1875).
24. Stedman v. McIntosh, 27 N. C. 571 (1845).
25. Long v. Grant, 163 Ala. 507, 50 So. 914 (1909).
26. Fronty v. Wood, 2 Hill 367 (S. C., 1834).

ment.[27] In another case it was said that a tenant is not entitled to notice to quit where he, either by declarations or by acts, disavows the tenancy. Here the tenant, after the expiration of his term of one year, had continued in possession into a second year under no other contract than that which would be implied by law. He had refused either to pay rent or to give his note as he had previously done. These acts were held to constitute a clear disavowal of the tenancy. Hence he was not entitled to the notice which would be necessary to terminate a tenancy from year to year.[28]

CONTROVERSIES CONCERNING THIRD PARTIES

Sometimes a landlord will desire to change tenants and will make a contract with another while the former tenant is in possession under an unexpired lease. In this situation the Mississippi Court has held that the landlord who has not expressly contracted to give the second lessee possession has no right of action against the former lessee if he holds over, there being no implied covenant in that state guaranteeing that the premises will be open for occupancy at the beginning of the term.[29] This rule denying the existence of the implied covenant is known as the "American Rule," and under it the second lessee is the proper person to bring the suit. Under what is commonly called the "English Rule," which has been followed in Georgia[30] and North Carolina,[31] it is held that in the absence of express covenants dealing with the matter, there is an implied covenant in every lease, on the part of the landlord, that the premises will be open and ready for the tenant at the time fixed in the contract for the beginning of the term. Alabama also appears to have recognized the existence of such an implied covenant. In that state, however, it seems to extend only so far as to guarantee that the premises will be open to entry, and if the interference by a third person comes after the lessee is entitled to possession, whether he has actual possession or not, then the lessee and not the lessor is to be considered the wronged party. Where this is the case, the lessor is not to be held responsible for the actions of the third person.[32] Furthermore, in a later hearing of this same case, the court made remarks which do not

27. Thomas v. Thomas, 69 Miss. 564, 13 So. 666 (1891).
28. State *ex rel.* Biggers v. Steuart, 5 Strob. 29 (S. C., 1850).
29. McMillan v. Best, 171 Miss. 811, 158 So. 488 (1935).
30. Kokomo Rubber Co. v. Anderson, 33 Ga. App. 241, 125 S. E. 783 (1924).
31. Shelton v. Clinard, 187 N. C. 664, 122 S. E. 477 (1924).
32. King v. Reynolds, 67 Ala. 229, 42 Am. Rep. 107 (1880).

appear to be sound in principle. It seemed to declare that if there had been an express covenant, as distinguished from one which was implied, to put the lessee in possession, any trespass which occurred before he went into possession would be a wrong against the lessor, who might recover damages therefor.[33] This seems to be an unwarranted distinction, and it is doubted if it can be supported from the standpoint of reason. Why should there be a distinction of this kind with respect to express and implied covenants? Why should the legal consequences of one be different from the legal consequences of the other?

In Georgia a tenant was given permission to occupy certain premises until another tenant could be obtained for the next year. In this situation it is clear that the former tenant would be entitled to reasonable notice that another tenant had been obtained and was ready to move in. The court held that the consent of the landlord and the failure to give such notice would be a sufficient defense to any action by the landlord against his former tenant for holding over. If the real cause of action had been the breach of the terms of the landlord's consent, the violation should have been alleged in the pleading; but this was not done here. The testimony indicated that the new tenant suddenly appeared at the house carrying some of his belongings and expecting to take possesion immediately. Failing to be admitted, he claimed and exercised the right of canceling his lease contract with the landowner, thereby causing the latter to lose the benefit of a profitable transaction.[34]

DOUBLE RENT PENALTY

In seven of the Southeastern states, Alabama,[35] Arkansas,[36] Florida,[37] Georgia,[38] Kentucky,[39] Mississippi,[40] and South Carolina,[41] double rent or value may be recovered against the tenant who is holding over beyond his term. In Alabama, Arkansas, and South

---

33. Snodgrass, King's Adm'r. v. Reynolds, 79 Ala. 452, 58 Am. Rep. 601 (1885).
34. Sloat v. Rountree, 87 Ga. 470, 13 S. E. 637 (1891).
35. Ala. Code (1940) tit. 7, §977.
36. Ark. Dig. Stat. (Pope, 1937) §§8585-88.
37. Fla. Stat. Ann. (1941) §83.06.
38. Ga. Code (1933) §61-305.
39. Ky. Rev. Stat. (1946) §383.150.
40. Miss. Code Ann. (1942) §947.
41. S. C. Code Ann. (1932) §8800.

Carolina any such responsibility must be preceded by written notice to quit the premises. Mississippi demands notice, but the requirement that it be in writing is absent. In the other states there seems to be no specific requirement of this kind with respect to liability for double rent alone.

Alabama seems to hold that double rent cannot be recovered unless the term of the lease has expired by its own limitation. Therefore, the double sum is not to be assessed where the lease is terminated because of a provision of the instrument which called for a forfeiture under certain circumstances.[42] The Mississippi Court has decided that a landlord cannot maintain an action to dispossess a tenant after the land has been sold to another, and if the tenant holds over after the conveyance, the purchaser is the one to whom he is liable for double rent.[43]

Under the Arkansas statute double rent may be charged only where the holding over is done "wilfully." The court of that state has declared that when a tenant holds over under the bona fide belief that he has a right to do so, and there are reasonable grounds for his belief, even though he is mistaken, this is not a wilful holding over within the meaning of the statute.[44] The view taken here can at least be said to have something in its favor, and the opposing view that a tenant may act wilfully even though he is not influenced by a bad motive may not be worthy of consideration. Furthermore, this decision derives some support from a dictum in a Mississippi case to the effect that the word "wilfully" means not merely voluntarily, but with a malicious purpose as well. However, the word "wilfully" is not included in the Mississippi statute, and the court of that state decided that the double liability of a tenant holding over after proper notice to quit is absolute, without reference to his good or bad faith in so doing.[45] In contrast to this, however, the Florida court held in an early case that the holding over must be wilful and that the tenant was not responsible where he was in doubt in respect to the time when the rent should be paid.[46]

The Georgia courts have held that double rent may be recovered

42. Dillard v. Johnson, 201 Ala. 634, 79 So. 106 (1918).
43. Pinnix v. Jones, 127 Miss. 764, 90 So. 481 (1922).
44. Lesser-Goldman Cotton Co. v. Fletcher, 153 Ark. 17, 239 S. W. 742 (1922).
45. Weatherall v. Brown, 113 Miss. 887, 74 So. 765 (1917).
46. McLean v. Spratt, 20 Fla. 515 (1884).

even though the affidavit filed for the purpose of obtaining a possessory warrant makes no mention of rent.[47]

CONCLUSION

On the whole, the problems created by the tenant holding over have been capably handled by the courts. Some difficulties, however, have arisen, and the legislatures of some of the Southeastern states have attempted to codify and improve upon the common law. Except for a few clauses making periods of time and types of tenancies more definite, these attempts have not greatly influenced the over-all picture.

47. Pettis v. Brewster, 94 Ga. 527, 19 S. E. 755 (1894); Crider v. Hedden, 26 Ga. App. 737, 107 S. E. 345 (1921).

VIII

Possessory Actions

W HEN a tenant has forfeited his right to remain on leased premises or has held over beyond his term, how does the landowner obtain possession of the land? What is the procedure by which he may assert his right to the property? In all the Southeastern states a possessory action of some sort is authorized by statute. The justices of the peace or similar magistrates commonly have original jurisdiction of proceedings under these statutes, whether the action is called forcible detainer, as in Kentucky, unlawful detainer, summary ejectment, or some other appellation. The purpose of the action is to obtain possession of premises which the tenant has no longer any right to hold. In some states this action is tied in with the remedy provided for instances where there has been a forcible entry, but it is usually confined to cases where the entry has been permissive.

STATUTORY AUTHORIZATION OF REMEDIES

It is important to call attention to the proper statutory procedure in the various states. Unlawful or forcible detainer is the most common type of remedy in the states of this region and is authorized by the statutes of Alabama,[1] Arkansas,[2] Florida,[3] Kentucky,[4] Mississippi,[5] Tennessee,[6] and Virginia.[7] Of these Florida,[8] Mississippi,[9] and Virginia [10] have what seem to be alternative possessory remedies to be used where certain conditions exist. The other states, Georgia,[11]

1. Ala. Code (1940) tit. 7, §967 et seq.
2. Ark. Dig. Stat. (Pope, 1937) §6035 et seq.
3. Fla. Stat. Ann. (1941) §82.04.
4. Ky. Code of Prac. Ann. (Baldwin, 1938) §452 et seq.
5. Miss. Code Ann. (1942) §1033 et seq.
6. Tenn. Code Ann. (Williams, 1934) §9246 et seq.
7. Va. Code Ann. (Michie, 1936) §5445 et seq.
8. Fla. Stat. Ann. (1941) §§83.05, 83.20, 83.21-83.27, 83.28-83.38.
9. Miss. Code Ann. (1942) §948 et seq.
10. Va. Code Ann. (Michie, 1936) §5530.
11. Ga. Code (1933) §61-301 et seq.

Louisiana,[12] North Carolina,[13] and South Carolina,[14] provide possessory remedies which are very similar to unlawful detainer but are given some such name as summary ejectment. Several of the statutes setting up possessory remedies contain a clause stating that other remedies shall not be barred.[15] The majority of the acts make provision for a short period of notice as a prerequisite to a proceeding to oust a tenant for non-payment of rent.[16]

NON-PAYMENT OF RENT AS CAUSE FOR DISPOSSESSORY ACTION

Courts in several of the Southeastern states have held that non-payment of rent authorizes the institution of a possessory action of this type,[17] but some courts in earlier times refused to give this

12. La. Gen. Stat. Ann. (Dart, 1932) §§6597-6601.

13. N. C. Gen. Stat. (1943) §42-26 et seq.

14. S. C. Code Ann. (1932) §8811 et seq.

15. Ala. Code (1940) tit. 7, §978; Ark. Dig. Stat. (Pope, 1937) §5066; Ky. Code of Prac. Ann. (Baldwin, 1938) §468; La. Gen. Stat. Ann. (Dart, 1932) §6601 (for rent); Tenn. Code Ann. (Williams, 1934) §9277 (trespass); Va. Code Ann. (Michie, 1936) §5450.

16. Ark. Dig. Stat. (Pope, 1937) §6035 (3 days); Fla. Stat. Ann. (1941) §83.05, 83.20 (3 days); Ga. Code (1933) §61-306 (3 days, for any cause); Ky. Code of Prac. Ann. (Baldwin, 1938) §§454, 455 (3 days notice of hearing); La. Gen. Stat. Ann. (Dart, 1932) §6597 (5 days); Miss. Code Ann. (1942) §948 (3 days); S. C. Code Ann. (1932) §8813 (3 days). In Tennessee no notice to quit is required. Tenn. Code Ann. (Williams, 1934) §9254. The North Carolina and Virginia statutes are silent, and there seems to be no judicial interpretation. In Alabama it appears that two notices are required for maintenance of a dispossessory action, one the ten-day written demand provided for by Ala. Code (1940) tit. 7, §967, and the other a notice to terminate the tenancy, which must be served prior to the actual eviction at a time to be measured by the agreed interval between rent payments. Speer v. Smoot, 156 Ala. 456, 47 So. 256 (1908). But it is to be doubted that this would apply in a situation where there had already been a breach of the covenant for payment of rent, as the court has held that no notice to terminate a tenancy is required where the tenant is already in wrongful possession. Johnson v. Miller, 161 Ala. 632, 49 So. 858 (1909). Furthermore, it is held that notice to quit is not equivalent to the statutory ten-day demand. Brown v. Baker, 220 Ala. 45, 124 So. 87 (1929). Under the Arkansas statute it has been ruled that it is immaterial whether the lease makes the failure to pay the rent a ground of forfeiture. Martin v. Stratton, 157 Ark. 513, 248 S. W. 554 (1923). Also, a tenant holding over is not permitted to defeat an action of unlawful detainer, in so far as judgment for rent is prayed, because proper notice is not given. State v. Robinson, 143 Ark. 456, 220 S. W. 836 (1920). According to an early Kentucky case decided in 1817, it was not necessary at that time to give notice to quit the premises before applying for the issuance of a warrant. Harrison v. Marshall, 7 Ky. 524 (1817). In South Carolina the failure to give the statutory notice was said to be waived by the action of a tenant in answering a complaint and participating in the trial of the case on its merits. Majes v. Evans, 80 S. C. 362, 61 S. E. 216 (1908).

17. Lindsey v. Bloodworth, 97 Ark. 541, 134 S. W. 959 (1911); Parker v.

remedy where the lease contained no express forfeiture clause.[18] It is possible that this earlier view might even be followed today in the absence of a statute. The fact that the tenant has an option to purchase the premises upon specified terms in respect to time of payment does not prevent the landlord from maintaining a possessory action where the tenant has failed to pay the agreed rent.[19] Moreover, the bankruptcy of the tenant and his consequent absolution from the payment of rent will not prevent the landlord from regaining possession in an action of this type.[20] In this instance the rent was finally paid by the trustee in bankruptcy, but it was remarked that this subsequent payment would give an equity court no grounds for enjoining the execution of the possessory warrant.

A lease stated that the tenant was indebted to his landlord up to a certain amount for past due rent and that this sum, in addition to the regular rental, should be paid at the rate of five dollars a week. It made further provision that upon the failure of the tenant to pay this sum, the instrument would become null and void. A default having been made in respect to the weekly payments, the landlord was allowed to invoke the possessory remedy without serving any notice to quit the premises.[21]

According to the express provisions of the statutes of three states [22] arrears of rent are recoverable in a possessory action, and this is probably true in others as well. The acceptance or forced collection of rent in arrears at the time notice to quit is given does not deprive the landlord of the right to dispossess the tenant in accordance with the notice, the former being entitled to accept rent for the period between the notice to vacate and the issuance of the process. However, the landlord is not permitted to dispossess the tenant after instituting a proceeding to foreclose a landlord's lien with a view

---

Geary, 57 Ark. 301, 21 S. W. 472 (1893); State *ex rel.* Rich v. Ward, 135 Fla. 885, 185, So. 846 (1939); *Ex parte* Bienville Inv. Co., 102 Fla. 524, 136 So. 328 (1931); Ray v. Holden, 62 Ga. App. 554, 8 S. E. (2d) 703 (1940); Rakestraw v. Lubbock, 26 Ga. App. 330, 106 S. E. 190 (1921). The right is extended to the landlord's vendee. Veal v. Jenkins, 58 Ga. App. 4, 197 S. E. 328 (1938).

18. Buckner v. Warren, 41 Ark. 532 (1883); Meroney v. Wright, 81 N. C. 390 (1879).

19. Clifford v. Gresinger, 96 Ga. 789, 22 S. E. 399 (1895).

20. Carter v. Sutton, 147 Ga. 496, 94 S. E. 760 (1917).

21. Midimis v. Murrell, 189 N. C. 740, 128 S. E. 150 (1925).

22. Miss. Code Ann. (1942) §1043; N. C. Gen. Stat. (1943) §§42-30-32; Tenn. Code Ann. (Williams, 1934) §9261.

to obtaining rent not yet due, since it would be manifestly unjust to allow him to prosecute both remedies.[23]

NECESSITY FOR A DEMAND FOR POSSESSION

In stating a case under these statutes is it necessary to allege a demand for possession? Is such a demand a prerequisite to a successful proceeding to oust the tenant? These are important questions of pleading, and they have received the attention of both legislatures and courts.

In Alabama,[24] Arkansas,[25] Georgia,[26] and North Carolina,[27] statutes require a demand as a prerequisite to a possessory action, and the same seems to be true by judicial interpretation in Florida.[28]

The written demand required by the Alabama statute need not state any date of surrender, as the tenant is given ten days in which to leave the premises.[29] This ten-day demand is imperative, and no shorter period will suffice.[30] The written demand is required only where the remedy of unlawful detainer is being pursued and is not necessary in actions like ejectment, where the notice to quit may be oral.[31]

A Georgia landlord had made an unwarranted demand for possession of rented premises and had refused to accept rent when offered by the tenant. Here it was decided that the tenant could not be dispossessed for non-payment of rent unless the landlord had later indicated a willingness to accept it if tendered.[32]

In the absence of any issue respecting the making of such a demand, the courts have held that the demand will be presumed.[33]

23. Rich v. Rose, 124 Ky. 669, 99 S. W. 953 (1907).
24. Ala. Code (1940) tit. 7, §967 (10 days in writing.)
25. Ark. Dig. Stat. (Pope, 1937) §6035 (written); Lindsey v. Bloodworth, 97 Ark. 541, 134 S. W. 959 (1911); Parker v. Geary, 57 Ark. 301, 21 S. W. 472 (1893).
26. Ga. Code (1933) §61-301; Ricks v. Beacham, 131 Ga. 89, 62 S. E. 45 (1908); Ray v. Holden, 62 Ga. App. 554, 8 S. E. (2d) 703 (1940); Levens v. Arp, 23 Ga. App. 198, 97 S. E. 893 (1919).
27. N. C. Code Ann. (Michie, 1939) §2365; Gen. Stat. (1943) §42-26; Warren v. Breedlove, 219 N. C. 383, 14 S. E. (2d) 43 (1941).
28. State ex rel. Rich v. Ward, 135 Fla. 885, 185 So. 846 (1939); Ex parte Bienville Inv. Co., 102 Fla. 524, 136 So. 328 (1931).
29. See Smith v. Sharp, 210 Ala. 587, 98 So. 566 (1924).
30. McGuire v. Powell, 177 Ala. 137, 59 So. 60 (1912).
31. Harris v. Hill, 190 Ala. 589, 67 So. 284 (1914).
32. Fowler v. Logan, 41 Ga. App. 110, 151 S. E. 926 (1930).
33. Minor v. Sutton, 73 Ga. App. 253, 36 S. E. (2d) 158 (1945); Hennen v. Mitchell, 27 Ga. App. 293, 108 S. E. 131 (1921); Crider v. Hedden, 26 Ga. App. 737, 107 S. E. 345 (1921).

Where the point was raised and the demand denied by the tenant, however, it was erroneous for the trial judge to direct a verdict in favor of the landlord.[34]

BREACH OF A COVENANT

A question arises as to whether a possessory action is authorized where a covenant is broken. Although a tenant for years may be dispossessed by summary proceedings when he fails to pay the rent or holds over beyond his term, he cannot be ousted for the breach of such a provision as a covenant not to sublet the premises without the written consent of the landlord.[35] However, it is believed that all modern courts would agree with the reasoning in an early Arkansas case that where a tenant has indicated that he does not intend to perform the covenants, the landlord may then treat the lease as rescinded and bring an action to regain possession.[36]

It has been held that a possessory action of unlawful detainer could be maintained where an Arkansas tenant had abandoned and repudiated a lease by refusing to go on with a contract requiring him to plant as many strawberries as possible on a six-acre plot of a forty-acre farm. The failure to perform this portion of the contract was considered a total breach of his agreement and not a partial one for which he could not be ousted.[37]

In a situation involving a landlord's dispossessory warrant sued out for non-payment of rent, the Georgia court has held that the tenant may allege in his counter-affidavit that the landlord has violated the agreement in some particular manner and has thereby become liable for damages exceeding the amount of rent claimed. It is also stated that if this allegation is supported by the evidence, it is error for the trial court to direct a verdict for the double rent authorized where a tenant holds over without right.[38]

NECESSITY FOR TENANCY RELATIONSHIP

The actions authorized by the above statutes, whatever they may be called, are merely possessory in nature and cannot be brought where there exists a relationship other than that of landlord and tenant.[39] The relationship may be implied from the circumstances

34. Hindman v. Raper, 140 Ga. 775, 79 S. E. 945 (1913).
35. Rakestraw v. Lubbock, 26 Ga. App. 330, 106 S. E. 190 (1921).
36. Buckner v. Warren, 41 Ark. 532 (1883).
37. Leehy v. Fullerton, 150 Ark. 371, 234 S. W. 472 (1921).
38. Jefferson v. Glaze, 134 Ga. 842, 68 S. E. 580 (1910).
39. Holzman v. Gattis, 195 Ark. 773, 114 S. W. (2d) 3 (1938); White River

in which the parties find themselves, as in a case where a man permitted his daughter and her husband to occupy his land, and they stayed on after his death under his wife, who had a life estate in the property.[40] The sole issues in possessory actions of this sort are the determination of the right to possession between the alleged landlord and the alleged tenant, whether the tenancy exists, and whether the possessor is holding over,[41] and it is clear that the title to the land is not in issue.[42] Hence a tenant who is being proceeded against is estopped to deny the title of the person under whom he has entered in accordance with the familiar rule of tenancy law to that effect.[43] Moreover, the rule extends to persons claiming as successors of the tenant, such as his widow or heirs.[44] In a case from Arkansas, however, the court permitted an independent action of ejectment to try the title, as distinguished from a cross-action in an unlawful detainer proceeding.[45]

As a general rule, according to the usually adopted exception to this estoppel, a tenant may show that the title of the person under whom he has entered has expired and vested in another.[46] This

---

Land & Timber Co. v. Hawkins, 128 Ark. 277, 194 S. W. 9 (1917); Mason v. Delancy, 44 Ark. 444 (1884); Dortch v. Robinson, 31 Ark. 296 (1876); Hall's Ex'rs v. Robinson, 291 Ky. 631, 165 S. W. (2d) 163 (1942); Johnson v. Hauser, 82 N. C. 375 (1880); Lane v. Marshall, 8 Tenn. 255 (1827). According to Littleton v. Wynn, 31 Ga. 583 (1880), the same applies to an action for use and occupation. Where the rental contract covers only a portion of the tract occupied, unlawful detainer may be maintained only with respect to that part. Miller v. Turney, 13 Ark. 385 (1853).

40. Daily v. Rudy, 205 Ky. 658, 266 S. W. 347 (1924).

41. Hightower v. Phillips, 184 Ga. 532, 192 S. E. 26 (1937); Boatright v. Eason, 24 Ga. App. 364, 100 S. E. 764 (1919); Engle v. Tennis Coal Co., 125 Ky. 239, 101 S. W. 309 (1907); Mattox v. Helm, 15 Ky. 185, 15 Am. Dec. 64 (1824); Perry v. Perry, 190 N. C. 125, 129 S. E. 147 (1925).

42. Ala. Code (1940) tit. 7, §975, 8796; Ark. Dig. Stat. (Pope, 1937) §6054; Fla. Comp. Gen. Laws Ann. (Skillman, 1927) §5313; Tenn. Code Ann. (Williams, 1934) §9257. This is true without statute. Hamilton v. Darden, 58 Ga. App. 409, 198 S. E. 805 (1938); Moore v. Ramsey, 272 Ky. 582, 114 S. W. (2d) 1101 (1938); Hamel v. Lawrence, 8 Ky. 330 (1818).

43. Edwards v. Louisville & N. Ry. Co., 202 Ala. 463, 80 So. 847 (1919); Dunlap v. Moose, 98 Ark. 235; 135 S. W. 824 (1911); Washington v. Moore, 84 Ark. 220, 105 S. W. 253 (1907); Patrick v. Cobb, 122 Ga. 80, 49 S. E. 806 (1905); Calhoun v. Currie, 173 S. C. 429, 176 S. E. 324 (1934).

44. Cheney v. Haley, 142 So. 312 (La. App., 1932), overruling 138 So. 169 (La. App., 1931).

45. Denton v. Denton, 209 Ark. 301, 190 S. W. (2d) 291 (1945), with reference to Ark. Dig. Stat. (Pope, 1937) §6058.

46. Roberts v. Asher, 264 Ky. 73, 94 S. W. (2d) 289 (1936); Bowser v. Bowser, 29 Tenn. 49 (1849); Wood v. Turner, 27 Tenn. 685 (1848).

applies to a subtenant, where the original tenant's term has expired during the subtenancy.[47] Where the lease was executed after the owner's title had expired, however, the estoppel rule is in operation.[48]

A peculiar situation has developed in Alabama, where it seems that no inquiry into the title is permitted in an action of unlawful detainer, and that the usual exceptions to the estoppel are not even recognized.[49]

In this state a court of equity will not enjoin the execution of a judgment in an unlawful detainer action, even where the tenant has a defense which he was only prevented from using by the application of the rule that the title may not be questioned in a proceeding of this type.[50] However, where the action is not a possessory one but is for the purpose of recovering damages caused by the unlawful detention, all legal and equitable defenses may be invoked.[51]

It is a general rule that a defendant in a possessory action may show that the relationship of landlord and tenant does not exist in a given situation and that another relationship has been established.[52] Where the jury decides that there is no tenancy, all other issues in the case are only incidental and do not need to be discussed.[53] A Georgia court has even held that a possessory action cannot be maintained where the occupant proves that he is a cropper and not a tenant.[54] In fact, one court has declared that the affidavit in a possessory proceeding is not sufficient unless facts are averred from which a tenancy relationship may be inferred.[55]

47. Elms v. Randall, 32 Ky. 100 (1834).
48. Wood v. Turner, 27 Tenn. 685 (1848).
49. See Archer v. Sibley, 201 Ala. 495, 78 So. 849 (1918); Hill v. Harris, 179 Ala. 614, 60 So. 917 (1913); Shepherd v. Parker, 157 Ala. 493, 47 So. 1027 (1908); Patterson v. Folmar, 125 Ala. 130, 28 So. 450 (1900); Davis v. Pou, 108 Ala. 443, 19 So. 362 (1896); Nicrosi v. Phillippi, 91 Ala. 299, 8 So. 561 (1890); Vancleave v. Wilson, 73 Ala. 387 (1882); Norwood v. Kirby's Adm'r, 70 Ala. 397 (1881); Clark v. Stringfellow, 4 Ala. 353 (1842).
50. Davis v. Pou, 108 Ala. 443, 19 So. 362 (1896).
51. Ala. Code (1940) tit. 7, §975. See Archer v. Sibley, 201 Ala. 495, 78 So. 849 (1918).
52. State ex rel. Rich v. Ward, 135 Fla. 385, 185 So. 846 (1939); Foy v. McCrary, 157 Ga. 461, 121 S. E. 804 (1924); Holton v. Mercer, 65 Ga. App. 53, 15 S. E. (2d) 253 (1941); McLaurin v. McIntyre, 167 N. C. 350, 83 S. E. 627 (1914); Hauser v. Morrison, 146 N. C. 248, 59 S. E. 693 (1907).
53. Farmville Oil & Fertilizer Co. v. Bowen, 204 N. C. 375, 168 S. E. 211 (1933).
54. Collier v. Buice, 36 Ga. App. 198, 136 S. E. 287 (1927).
55. Bowles v. Dean, 84 Miss. 376, 36 So. 391 (1904).

A contract for the sale of real estate stipulated that, upon the failure of the purchaser to pay the price at maturity, the relationship of landlord and tenant would then arise between the parties. In this situation the occupant was liable for rent and could be dispossessed for failing to pay the rent as it came due.[56] A similar result was reached where a vendee had renounced his rights under a contract of sale and had entered into a new contract of lease, even though he did not surrender the possession and receive it again at the hands of the landowner.[57] Moreover, a possessory action was maintained where the parties to a conveyance had agreed that the vendor should remain in possession until a fixed date and he had refused to deliver the premises to the purchaser or his successor at that time.[58] However, where the contract provided that the purchaser should become a tenant upon default, it was ruled that the vendor could not maintain the action where he had waived his rights under this clause.[59]

A similar situation is seen in reference to mortgages. Thus a mortgagor may contract that in the event of a foreclosure he will become the tenant of the purchaser at the sale and that he will then be subject to possessory proceedings.[60] In one instance a Kentucky mortgagor was left in possession by permission of the mortgagee and had agreed to move. Here the mortgagee was permitted to maintain forcible detainer when the mortgagor failed to leave the premises.[61] In a somewhat similar case the Tennessee court rested its decision upon the theory of a constructive entry and possession.[62]

A Georgia landowner was alleged to have remained in possession after his title had been divested by a sale under a security deed, and the purchaser brought a dispossessory action against him. Here the court declared that if the plaintiff could show that this was the true situation, the defendant would then be a tenant at sufferance and therefore subject to be dispossessed. However, the alleged facts were not shown to be true, and therefore the action of the trial

56. Burns v. Warren, 194 Ark. 1155, 109 S. W. (2d) 432 (1937).
57. Riley v. Jordan, 75 N. C. 180 (1876).
58. Prichard v. Tabor, 104 Ga. 64, 30 S. E. 415 (1898); Sloan v. Sheffield, 31 Ga. App. 437, 120 S. E. 795 (1923).
59. Carlisle v. Prior, 48 S. C. 183, 26 S. E. 244 (1897).
60. Griffith v. Brackman, 97 Tenn. 387, 37 S. W. 273 (1896).
61. Pemberton v. Hardin, 258 Ky. 538, 80 S. W. (2d) 589 (1935).
62. Griffith v. Brackman, 97 Tenn. 387, 37 S. W. 273 (1896).

court in directing a verdict in the plaintiff's favor was reversed on appeal.[63]

In a fairly recent North Carolina case a mortgagee bank, after the mortgagor's default, foreclosed and had the land sold to one of its officers, who thereupon reconveyed the land to the bank. The corporation leased the land to a third person for the mortgagor's benefit and then subsequently leased it directly to the mortgagor himself. After procuring the lease the mortgagor entered into a consent judgment in the bank's summary ejectment proceeding and acknowledged that the bank was the owner of the land in fee. Here the court declared that the so-called mortgagor was estopped to assert a right to avoid the deeds as against the bank, a tenancy relationship existing rather than a mortgage arrangement. The mortgagor had claimed that the sale to the bank official and his reconveyance to the bank were void, but he was not permitted to show this because of the estoppel resulting from the tenancy.[64]

Contrasting with this is the holding by the North Carolina court in an early case that summary ejectment proceedings could not be maintained against a mortgagor who held over after a sale of the mortgaged premises.[65]

LIMITATIONS ON RIGHT TO BRING ACTION

Some of the statutes set up periods of time within which a possessory action may be brought.[66] It is interesting to note that a number of the statutes contain clauses stating that other remedies are not barred,[67] and that the Mississippi law has been construed in a similar manner with respect to trespass and ejectment.[68] It is also true that a judgment for the defendant in a possessory action is no bar to another action based on subsequent acts.[69]

63. Radcliffe v. Jones, 46 Ga. App. 33, 166 S. E. 450 (1932).

64. Shuford v. Greensboro Joint-Stock Bank, 207 N. C. 428, 177 S. E. 408 (1934).

65. McMillan v. Love, 72 N. C. 18 (1875).

66. Ala. Code (1940) tit. 7, §976 (3 years); Ark. Dig. Stat. (Pope, 1937) §6055 (3 years); Ky. Code of Prac. Ann. (Baldwin, 1938) §469 (2 years); Tenn. Code Ann. (Williams, 1934) §9250 (3 years); Va. Code Ann. (Michie, 1936) §5445 (3 years).

67. Ala. Code (1940) tit. 7, §978; Ark. Dig. Stat. (Pope, 1937) §6056; Ky. Code of Prac. Ann. (Baldwin, 1938) §468; La. Gen. Stat. Ann. (Dart, 1932) §6601; Tenn. Code Ann. (Williams, 1934) §9277 (trespass); Va. Code Ann. (Michie, 1936) §5450.

68. Richardson v. Callihan, 73 Miss. 4, 19 So. 95 (1895).

69. Peck v. Peck, 255 Ky. 835, 75 S. W. (2d) 522 (1934).

The proceeding authorized by these statutes is an action to recover real estate. It is not the proper remedy to recover personalty
and cannot be used for that purpose.[70]

What happens where the landlord is entitled to the possession of
only a portion of the property which is mentioned in the complaint? In an early Kentucky case a recovery *pro tanto* was allowed
in such a situation.[71]

JURISDICTION OF COURTS, INFERIOR AND SUPERIOR

The court of a justice of the peace or some other inferior tribunal
is commonly given original jurisdiction of possessory proceedings
under these statutes, whatever the name may be which the action
is called, unlawful detainer, forcible detainer, summary ejectment,
dispossessory proceedings, or something else. In Mississippi this is
true, even though the rental for the term exceeds the statutory jurisdictional limit, the jurisdiction being regarded as special.[72] In Alabama the justices' courts have original jurisdiction of unlawful
detainer actions and may render judgment for possession and
costs, subject to the limitation that damages or rent recoverable
shall not exceed the statutory jurisdictional amount of one hundred
dollars.[73] If the amount is greater than the jurisdictional amount,
the plaintiff must sue for it in a court of proper jurisdiction.[74] Concurrent original jurisdiction is given to justices of the peace under
the Tennessee statute.[75] In Louisiana they have concurrent jurisdiction with the district or parish courts when the monthly or yearly
rental figure does not exceed the sum of one hundred dollars.[76]
The situation presented here is comparable to the monetary jurisdictional limitations where a landlord is attempting to collect rent [77]
or enforce a lien for advances.[78]

Where the original proceeding before the justice has been improperly brought because title to the property is involved, an

70. DuBignon v. Tufts, 66 Ga. 59 (1880).
71. Ball v. Lively, 25 Ky. 181 (1829).
72. Simpson v. Boykin, 118 Miss. 701, 79 So. 852 (1918).
73. See Caldwell v. Hutchinson, 224 Ala. 136, 138 So. 833 (1931); Beck v.
Glenn, 69 Ala. 121 (1881).
74. Lykes v. Schwarz, 91 Ala. 461, 8 So. 71 (1890).
75. Tenn. Code Ann. (Williams, 1934) §9270.
76. La. Const., §48; La. Gen. Stat. Ann. (Dart, 1932) §6598. *Cf.* Campbell v.
Hart, 118 La. 871, 43 So. 533 (1907).
77. Dicus v. Bright, 23 Ark. 110 (1861).
78. Slaughter v. Manning, 11 Ga. App. 650, 75 S. E. 1059 (1912).

ordinary trial court cannot consider the case on appeal. It has no appellate jurisdiction since the justice's court had no right to try the issue in the first place.[79]

Another kind of limitation is to be noted in the Virginia statute. Here the justices' courts are given permissive jurisdiction where the tenancy or cropper contracts do not exceed a period of one year.[80] It is to be remarked that the statute expressly mentions croppers, and that therefore the possessory action would be available against a cropper in Virginia, a remedy which could not be pursued if such a case were tried in Georgia.[81]

In one instance a Georgia defendant in a possessory action filed an affidavit in which he claimed that he had legal title to the premises and a right to convey the same. However, he asked no affirmative relief, and the court said that the justice's court could not be deprived of its jurisdiction by such an allegation.[82] Neither was a justice's jurisdiction lost because of a South Carolina defendant's plea that there had been fraud in the procurement of the lease contract.[83]

The general theme here seems to be that possessory actions are usually to be originated in a justice's court or some other tribunal of similar judicial authority. The issues in these cases are ordinarily very simple and can be handled by men who are not technically trained in the intricacies of the law.

PARTIES WHO MAY BRING POSSESSORY ACTIONS

Questions often arise concerning the parties who bring the possessory action. The matter usually is discussed from the standpoint of the persons who, for one reason or another, are permitted to take the original landlord's place as the plaintiff in actions of this sort. The inquiry may lead into some rather interesting procedural problems.

According to the general rule, the successor to or purchaser from the landlord may bring a possessory proceeding to oust a tenant who is subject to removal.[84] A grantee holding title to an undivided

79. McLaurin v. McIntyre, 167 N. C. 350, 83 S. E. 627 (1914).
80. Va. Code Ann. (Michie, 1936) §5445.
81. Collier v. Buice, 36 Ga. App. 198, 136 S. E. 287 (1927).
82. Ray v. Holden, 62 Ga. App. 554, 8 S. E. (2d) 703 (1940).
83. Metropolitan Life Ins. Co. v. Stuckey, 194 S. C. 469, 10 S. E. (2d) 3 (1940).
84. Ish v. McRae, 48 Ark. 413, 3 S. W. 440 (1887); State ex rel. Rich v.

part of the leased premises may maintain the action,[85] and so may a widow with a dower right.[86] But a sale of leased land puts the purchaser in no better position than that occupied by the original landlord. Where the latter could not have maintained a possessory action against the tenant, it is clear that the purchaser should not be permitted to do so.[87]

In Florida a grantee who has never had possession is permitted to bring a possessory action.[88] In Mississippi the word "assigns" as used in the unlawful detainer statute [89] was interpreted to include within its meaning a grantee who had never been in possession and whose grantor, the original landlord, had months before served a notice to vacate on a tenant who had gone into possesion under a rental contract requiring him to leave on fifteen days' notice unless he paid all rent in arrears. Thus a grantee was permitted to bring the action without even having been in actual possession of the rented premises.[90] This is the usual and better rule, but it seems that at least one court at an early date declined to allow a possessory action on the basis of a constructive possession, although it refused to decide definitely that actual possession was essential.[91]

A peculiar rule was adopted in Alabama to the effect that an action of unlawful detainer must be brought by the original land-lord and not the transferee.[92] Under this rule the purchaser could not bring the action even though the tenant was estopped from denying the title.[93] The only apparent exception to this rule was in a situation where a lessor died and his heirs inherited the property. Here it was ruled that the heirs could maintain the possessory action

---

Ward, 135 Fla. 885, 185 So. 846 (1939); Marrow v. Sawyer, 82 Ga. 226, 8 S. E. 51 (1888); Veal v. Jenkins, 53 Ga. App. 4, 197 S. E. 328 (1938); Mason v. Bascom, 42 Ky. 269 (1842); Herndon v. Bascom, 38 Ky. 113 (1839); Dyer v. Wilson, 190 So. 851 (La. App., 1939); Williams v. Johnson, 175 Miss. 419, 167 So. 639 (1936); Cummings v. Kilpatrick, 23 Miss. 106 (1851); Marley v. Rodgers, 13 Tenn. 217 (1833).

85. Mason v. Bascom, 42 Ky. 269 (1842).

86. Moore v. Ramsey, 272 Ky. 582, 114 S. W. (2d) 1101 (1938).

87. Unger v. Bamberger, 85 Ky. 11, 2 S. W. 498 (1887).

88. Gray v. Callahan, 143 Fla. 673, 197 So. 396 (1940); State ex rel. Rich v. Ward, 135 Fla. 885, 185 So. 846 (1939).

89. Miss. Code Ann. (1942) §1033.

90. Williams v. Johnson, 175 Miss. 419, 167 So. 639 (1936).

91. Bradley v. Hume, 18 Ark. 284 (1857), interpreting McGuire v. Cook, 13 Ark. 448 (1853).

92. Hill v. Harris, 189 Ala. 614, 60 So. 917 (1913); Shepherd v. Parker, 157 Ala. 493, 47 So. 1027 (1908).

93. Devine v. Brown, 35 Ala. 596 (1860).

in place of their ancestor.[94] A statute now seems to give the transferee the right to bring an action of unlawful detainer against the tenant.[95] However, it has been said that the action is not maintainable unless the transferee proves actual prior possesion in himself or his grantor.[96]

Generally speaking, a present right to the possession of the premises seems to be essential, and a landlord who dwelt in Arkansas was not permitted to recover before the end of the term from a third person who had taken possession under an adverse claim of title with the permission of the tenant or those claiming under him.[97]

In an early case the Kentucky court decided that a person entering under one joint owner is considered to have entered under both. When this had been done, the two of them might bring a joint action of forcible detainer to oust him from the premises if such proceeding became necessary.[98] There seems to be no reason why this case should not be followed today.

It appears that a landowner's possessory action or right of entry is not barred because there is an outstanding executory contract to lease the land to another upon the expiration of the existing term.[99]

Questions sometimes arise concerning the legality of the acts of the landlord's agents or attorneys in instituting possessory actions against delinquent tenants. Although the Georgia statute [100] gives the landlord's agent or attorney at law or in fact authority to make oath to the facts on which a dispossessory warrant is to be based, it has been held that an attorney cannot lawfully execute the required affidavit in the landlord's name.[101] Even where the law would permit the affidavit to be so sworn, it would still be necessary to prove that the agent or attorney had the landlord's authorization. In Alabama, where a written demand is a prerequisite to a properly instituted action, it has been held that an attorney's authority to make such a demand must be clearly shown. The fact that the

94. Hill v. Harris, 189 Ala. 614, 60 So. 917 (1913); Kellum v. Balkum, 93 Ala. 317, 9 So. 463 (1891).
95. Ala. Code (1940), tit. 31, §10.
96. King v. Taylor, 40 So. (2d) 631 (Ala. 1949). See Thompkins v. Steagall, 247 Ala. 350, 24 So. (2d) 446 (1946).
97. King v. Duncan, 62 Ark. 588, 37 S. W. 228 (1896).
98. Haymes v. Adams, 10 Ky. 149 (1820).
99. Hall v. Harrell, 136 Ark. 329, 206 S. W. 435 (1918); Shelton v. Clinard, 187 N. C. 664, 122 S. E. 477 (1924).
100. Ga. Code (1933) §61-301.
101. Clark v. Smith, 142 Ga. 200, 82 S. E. 563 (1914).

attorney has brought the possessory proceeding is said not to be sufficient evidence of his authority to make the demand at the time it was actually made.[102] It might be argued from the language used that it was proper for the action to be brought by the attorney.

In Georgia it was said at an early date that the administrator of a deceased landlord might make the required affidavits to institute a possessory action against a tenant holding over.[103] In a recent case, however, the appellate court has made remarks which indicate that it would not approve the complimentary proposition that such an action would lie against the personal representative of a deceased tenant, saying that the proper party defendant was his successor in interest, his widow or heir.[104] Since the widow or heir of the tenant must defend a possessory action, the courts might find that under modern Georgia statutes the proper party to bring the action would be the widow or heir of a deceased landlord. The Alabama court has held that an administrator, though not actually in possession of the land, may maintain an action of unlawful detainer against a tenant who accepts a lease from him personally and then holds over.[105] Probably it would be best to allow the personal representative of the deceased to sue or be sued in possessory actions of this sort.

The possessory proceeding is a purely legal one, and in an early case the Kentucky Court has held that it was not maintainable by anyone with a mere equitable right like a bond for conveyance or title.[106] Whether modern courts would follow this decision seems to be a matter of the liberality of procedural rules. The Mississippi Court has held that an action of unlawful detainer cannot be maintained where the lease contract is not in proper form.[107] It is indicated in that opinion, however, that the landowner might maintain an action in equity to enforce his rights.

Prior to the time when a valid parol executory lease for an ensuing year is to take effect, the landlord is not entitled to disaffirm the contract on the ground that there has been no performance

102. Barnewell v. Stephens, 142 Ala. 609, 38 So. 662 (1905).
103. Moody v. Ronaldson, 38 Ga. 652 (1869).
104. Ray v. Holden, 62 Ga. App. 554, 8 S. E. (2d) 703 (1940).
105. Nicrosi v. Phillippi, 91 Ala. 299, 8 So. 561 (1890), also deciding that the administrator may bring an action based on use and occupation under the same circumstances. See also Norwood v. Kirby's Adm'rs., 70 Ala. 397 (1881).
106. Sullivan v. Enders, 33 Ky. 66 (1835).
107. Lobdell v. Mason, 71 Miss. 937, 15 So. 44 (1894).

and that neither party has acted to his prejudice because of it. In one instance arising in Georgia the landlord had instituted dispossessory proceedings against a person in possession as a tenant holding over and claimed rent which was admitted to be due. The judge instructed the jurors that even if they found that the tenant was entitled to retain possession, they could render a verdict in the landlord's favor for some amount of rent. The appellate court, however, declared this instruction to be erroneous in that the action was possessory in character and not one to recover rent. It would not be necessary to render a money verdict in this type of proceeding. Therefore, as the tenant was rightfully in possession under a valid lease, and the landlord was not entitled to disaffirm the contract, it was held that the possessory action would not lie.[108]

AGAINST WHOM MAY POSSESSORY ACTIONS BE BROUGHT?

A question may arise with respect to the persons who are subject to the proceedings authorized by these statutes. In other words, it may become important to ascertain exactly what types of persons can be dispossessed. Certain well defined principles are to be drawn from an analysis of the cases.

There seems to be no doubt that a tenant holding over beyond his term may be dispossessed.[109] In an early Kentucky case, however, the court declared that a mere continuance of possession could not be said to establish a refusal to restore possession to the landlord, nor could this be a fact from which the jury might infer a refusal. The court further remarked that there might be acts which would be the equivalent of a refusal, and that upon proof of these acts the tenant could be ousted in an action of forcible detainer.[110] The most reasonable interpretation of this language is that the landlord may not move to oust the tenant until at least some opportunity is given for the parties to indicate their intention. According to the present statute [111] the landlord has ninety days in which to oust the tenant before the latter acquires any right to hold the premises for the succeeding year. After this period has elapsed the possessory action cannot be maintained.

---

108. Roland v. Floyd, 53 Ga. App. 282, 185 S. E. 580 (1936).
109. Ray v. Holden, 62 Ga. App. 554, 8 S. E. (2d) 703 (1940); Hamel v. Lawrence, 8 Ky. 330 (1818).
110. Allison v. Thompson, 11 Ky. 31 (1822).
111. Ky. Rev. Stat. (1946) §383.160.

In Arkansas it seems that the possessory action is maintainable against a tenant in possession, though he may not have refused in so many words to quit the premises, if he holds over an unreasonable time after the demand required by statute. It appears, however, that he will be excused if the holding over is caused by circumstances beyond his control.[112]

A person entering under a lease contract which is void under the Statute of Frauds [113] or for some other reason [114] is considered a tenant and may be ousted in a possessory action.

The Louisiana [115] and Tennessee [116] statutes expressly authorize a possessory action against a subtenant, and the latter includes an assignee as well. Under the Alabama decisions it is clear that a subletting will not defeat an action of unlawful detainer.[117] In Arkansas an owner may oust a person who has entered under a tenant unrestricted in his right of subletting and has then held over after termination of the lease contract, notice to quit, and demand for possession.[118] In Georgia it would seem that a joint possessory proceeding is maintainable against both tenant and subtenant.[119] Therefore it can be said that a sublease will have little or no effect upon the possessory action of the landlord.

A Louisiana tenant's daughter and son-in-law moved into a rented farmhouse before the expiration of the lease and stayed on afterwards. Here the court declared that the entrance of the couple could not be used as the basis for a possessory action, but that they might be ousted for holding over after the term.[120]

In Kentucky it appears that forcible detainer is maintainable against a third person who, without the consent of the tenant, has taken possession of a portion of the rented premises.[121] This would seem to be a most radical extension with respect to the maintenance

112. Floyd v. Ricks, 11 Ark. 451 (1850).
113. Brubaker v. Poage, 17 Ky. 123 (1824); Harrison v. Marshall, 7 Ky. 524 (1817).
114. State v. Robinson, 143 Ark. 456, 220 S. W. 836 (1920).
115. La. Gen. Stat. Ann. (Dart, 1932) §6600.
116. Tenn. Code Ann. (Williams, 1934) §9281. See Bird v. Fannon, 40 Tenn. 12 (1859).
117. Edwards v. Louisville & N. Ry. Co., 202 Ala. 463, 80 So. 847 (1919); Giddens v. Bolling, 92 Ala. 586, 9 So. 274 (1891); Snoddy v. Watt, 9 Ala. 609 (1846).
118. Winkler v. Massengill, 66 Ark. 145, 49 S. W. 494 (1899).
119. Fletcher v. Fletcher, 123 Ga. 470, 51 S. E. 418 (1905).
120. Scott v. Kalip, 197 So. 205 (La. App., 1940).
121. Willis v. Whayne, 142 Ky. 194, 134 S. W. 150 (1911).

of a possessory action. A more suitable action would be ejectment or trespass.

In another modern Kentucky case involving a third person who had entered upon leased premises without any claim of title, the court declared that from the standpoint of the successful maintenance of the owner's possessory action it was immaterial whether the intruder had entered as a trespasser or as an assignee of the tenant.[122] This decision seems to reflect a change in attitude from those earlier cases wherein the court took the view that a person could not maintain forcible detainer proceedings unless the occupant entered under him.[123]

In Alabama, unless there has been an attornment, it has been decided that unlawful detainer proceedings are not maintainable where the defendants were in possession at the time the plaintiff's alleged possession began.[124] This seems to be in accord with the peculiar Alabama rule that the purchaser of a landlord's interest cannot bring the unlawful detainer action.[125] The Georgia court, on the other hand, has held that in a possessory action it is immaterial whether the occupant received the possession of the premises from the landlord or became a tenant after obtaining possession.[126]

The Georgia Court of Appeals, as has been seen,[127] has held that a possessory action will not lie against the personal representative of a deceased tenant, the proper party defendant being the widow or heir.[128] This is a matter of local significance only, and it is not known whether the same rule would be in effect in other jurisdictions. It might be supposed that the matter would be governed by local rules with respect to the administration of estates.

The fact that a non-resident tenant holding over has been guilty of repeated trespasses is no proper ground for the interference of

122. American Coal Land Co. v. Miller, 182 Ky. 51, 206 S. W. 18 (1918).

123. Kirk v. Taylor's Heirs, 47 Ky. 262 (1848); Morris v. Bowles, 31 Ky. 97 (1833); Norton v. Sanders, 30 Ky. 12 (1831); Brower v. Peed, 29 Ky. 494 (1831); Gray v. Gray, 13 Ky. 465 (1823); Nelson v. Cox, 9 Ky. 150 (1819). Under this doctrine a person who entered as a trespasser and that same day took a parol lease from the party in possession might be proceeded against by an action of forcible detainer after the lease expired. Fogle v. Chaney, 51 Ky. 138 (1851).

124. Barnewell v. Stephens, 142 Ala. 609, 38 So. 662 (1905).

125. Hill v. Harris, 179 Ala. 614, 60 So. 917 (1913); Shepherd v. Parker, 157 Ala. 493, 47 So. 1027 (1908). See also Note 92, *supra*.

126. Willis v. Harrell, 118 Ga. 906, 45 S. E. 794 (1903).

127. Note 104, *supra*.

128. Ray v. Holden, 62 Ga. App. 554, 8 S. E. (2d) 703 (1940).

a court of equity; the suitable action in such a situation is the possessory proceeding at law authorized by statute.[129] If the defendant had been a trespasser instead of a tenant, a court of equity would have had jurisdiction to prevent a multiplicity of suits. It has also been said that the poverty of the defending tenant and his inability to give bond furnish no grounds for equitable interference.[130]

Where the pleadings show clearly that a tenancy relationship exists between the parties, and that the occupant has entered under the plaintiff, no court of equity will enjoin an action to dispossess the occupant on the basis that the landlord has no valid claim to the property.[131] This is but another application of the usual estoppel rule.

CONCLUSION

On the whole, it may be said that the same general principles govern possessory actions, no matter what differences may appear in procedure and nomenclature. A simple possessory remedy of this type is an essential part of any well-ordered and thorough system of jurisprudence. While the tenant must receive adequate protection, the landlord should be able to dispossess a defaulting tenant without the necessity of involving himself in the technicalities and procedural quirks surrounding the older forms of action concerning real estate. The justice's court or its equivalent is probably the best place in which to try the simple eviction proceeding.

129. Montague v. Hood, 78 S. C. 222, 58 S. E. 767 (1907).
130. Napier v. Varner, 149 Ga. 586, 101 S. E. 580 (1919); Brown v. Watson, 115 Ga. 592, 41 S. E. 998 (1902).
131. Barnett v. Lewis, 194 Ga. 203, 20 S. E. (2d) 912 (1942).

IX

Wrongful Eviction of Tenant

IT may happen that a tenant will be evicted by his landlord for no legitimate reason. Inexcusable eviction often happens where the landlord supposes himself to have been wronged in some manner by the tenant. This is frequently due to a misconception respecting the rights of the parties under the lease contract. Hence a study of the decided cases concerning farm lessees who have been evicted from their homes in the middle of a term should prove helpful in determining the rights of such persons.

In an early Alabama case the court attempted to clarify the term "eviction" as it is employed in controversies of this type. Here it was declared that an eviction is not a mere trespass but something of a grave and permanent character, an act perpetrated with the definite intention of depriving the tenant of the possession of the leased premises. The tribunal was evidently of the opinion that the jury should decide whether the evidence established wrongful acts on the part of the landlord. In discussing the matter, however, the court laid down several guideposts for the jury to follow. Thus it stated that the tenant should have the uninterrupted occupancy and use of the whole of the premises. Furthermore, if he should be ousted from any material portion of the farm, such interference on the part of the landlord might very well be treated as a wrongful eviction. Should the tenant elect to stand on this basis, it is clear that he should be excused from the payment of rent and allowed to recover such damages as he has sustained.[1] A clearer description of the rights of the parties in eviction cases could scarcely be found.

The usual wrongful eviction case is decided upon the adequacy of the evidence. It is commonly a question of whether the allegations in the petition or the actual facts brought out in court will establish the wrongful eviction. All sorts of situations are encountered, and the evidential possibilities vary.

In one instance land was rented with a pasture attached. Relying

1. Rice v. Dudley, 65 Ala. 68 (1880).

upon the good faith of the landlord, the tenant plowed and fenced the land, sowed a crop of grain, repaired the house and barn, and made ready to carry out the terms of the contract. After cultivating the farm and using the pasture for five months, he was notified that the pasture had been rented to another party. He was warned not to put his stock in the pasture and threatened with violence against his own person as well as the animals if he disobeyed. The court considered this an eviction from a material portion of the leased premises and declared that it was a breach of contract which would discharge him from any further performance on his part. Under these circumstances he would be allowed to institute an action sounding in quasi contract to recover the value of such labor as he had performed in plowing, fencing, improving, and cultivating the premises. As an alternative, he might sue for a breach of the contract and recover the value of the lease.[2] It was alleged in another case that the landlord had used abusive language to the cultivator's children and had acted in such a manner as to make the whole family dissatisfied with living conditions on the farm. He had agreed to furnish certain stock for the cultivation of the premises but refused to permit the animals to be used by the children or others acting for the cultivator. Without stock or tools the latter was forced into an untenable position and was finally compelled by legal proceedings to vacate the premises. These facts were held sufficient to authorize a successful action against the landlord for eviction.[3]

During the term of a Virginia tenant it appeared that the landlord had entered a meadow on the premises and carried away the hay. This action was taken without the consent of the tenant, who, nevertheless, remained on the land for the rest of the term. It was held that the tenant might regard this as an eviction, and the fact that he had remained on the premises during the residue of the term was not taken as a waiver.[4]

When rent is not payable in advance, as it seldom is in agricultural tenancies, it is held that an unlawful eviction will not relieve the tenant from the payment of rent already due.[5]

If it can be shown that the tenant has harvested the entire crop

2. Roberson v. Allen, 7 Ga. App. 142, 66 S. E. 542 (1909).
3. Moore v. White, 26 Ga. App. 612, 107 S. E. 257 (1921).
4. Briggs v. Hall, 4 Leigh 484 (Va., 1833).
5. First Nat. Bank of Huntsville v. Carter, 231 Ala. 268, 164 So. 388 (1935).

for a certain year and was not evicted from any portion of the leased premises until the following winter, it is clear that there should be no abatement of the rent for that year.[6] But an abatement *pro tanto* has been decreed where the tenant was evicted or was not given possession of a rented tract because of an outstanding paramount title.[7] Where the lessor has deliberately ousted the tenant, however, no apportionment is allowed, for such an apportionment would permit the landowner to take advantage of his own wrongdoing.[8] The apportionment, when authorized, should be based on value and not on quantity.[9]

A lease authorized the lessor to take possession in case the lessee failed to pay the rent promptly. The court ruled that a demand for the rent was necessary in order that the lessee might be put on notice that the lessor would, in the event of the former's refusal or inability to pay, exercise his contractual right of re-entry.[10]

The general rule of damages in cases of eviction is commonly stated to be the difference between the fair rental value of the leased premises and the actual amount of rent agreed upon by the parties.[11] It has been said that "rental value" should not be measured by the probable profits which might accrue to the tenant if he were permitted to remain on the land and fulfill his obligations during the full term of the lease. It should be calculated on the basis of the amount of rent the land would bring or by evidence of other related circumstances from which the value of the term might be computed.[12] Where there was no evidence that the rental value exceeded the rent agreed to be paid, it was clear that there should be no recovery.[13]

---

6. Shaw v. Splane, 155 La. 686, 99 So. 530 (1924).

7. Shaw v. Splane, 155 La. 686, 99 So. 530 (1924); Cheairs v. Coats, 77 Miss. 846, 28 So. 728 (1900); Poston v. Jones, 37 N. C. 350 (1842). This view was taken by the dissenting judge in the early case of Briggs v. Hall, 4 Leigh 484 (Va., 1833), but a majority of the court held that the lessor would lose the benefit of the entire transaction and would be entitled to recover no part of the rent.

8. Cheairs v. Coats, 77 Miss. 846, 28 So. 728 (1900).

9. Cheairs v. Coats, *supra* Note 8.

10. First Nat. Bank of Huntsville v. Carter, 231 Ala. 268, 164 So. 388 (1935).

11. Heard v. Griffin, 188 Ark. 235, 66 S. W. (2d) 1060 (1933); Malone v. Wade, 148 Ark. 548, 230 S. W. 579 (1921); Reeves v. Romines, 132 Ark. 599, 201 S. W. 822 (1918); Watkins v. Haigwood, 41 Ga. App. 598, 153 S. E. 609 (1930); Palmer v. Ingram, 2 Ga. App. 200, 58 S. E. 362 (1907).

12. Reeves v. Romines, 132 Ark. 599, 201 S. W. 822 (1918).

13. McElvaney v. Smith, 76 Ark. 468, 88 S. W. 981 (1905).

A Georgia court has held that it was erroneous to base the measure of damages on the difference between the stipulated rental and the gross value of the products grown on the farm for the term, without making any deduction for costs of production.[14] According to the proposed measure of damages it might have been more profitable for the tenant if the landlord had broken his contract at the outset instead of fulfilling its terms.[15]

The evidence must conform to certain standards. If the court's instructions to the jury on the measure of damages are not as definite as the landlord may desire, a more descriptive version may be requested.[16] This would seem to suggest that too great particularization will not be required unless a request is made. The Kentucky court has held that the damages recovered are substantially correct if they are somewhere in the neighborhood of the loss sustained because of the eviction, a strict exactitude being unnecessary.[17]

Sometimes a tenant will set up damages resulting from an eviction as a counter measure. In one instance the tenant, in a plea of set-off, alleged that the landlord was indebted to him because of a breach of the lease contract. He alleged that the landlord, after the land was broken and prepared for plowing, had taken possession and refused to permit him to use the premises. The tenant stated that he had thereby been damaged to the extent of a sum certain representing the alleged value of profits which might have been made on the land. The court refused to uphold the plea because the damages asked were too speculative, declaring that a plea of set-off should be as certain in this respect as if it were an original action.[18]

A landlord will sometimes evict a tenant during the term and thereby prevent him from gathering the crops, reaping them himself despite the tenant's protests. Here the landlord is not entitled to be recompensed for the time and money spent in the process of harvesting.[19]

It seems to be clear that the expense of moving to another farm is a proper element of damage in eviction cases.[20] Furthermore,

14. Nicholson v. Williamson, 29 Ga. App. 692, 116 S. E. 321 (1923).
15. Palmer v. Ingram, 2 Ga. App. 200, 58 S. E. 362 (1907).
16. Smith v. Pearce, 174 Ark. 153, 294 S. W. 705 (1927).
17. Billiter v. Mounts, 147 Ky. 97, 143 S. W. 768 (1912).
18. Dawson v. Haygood, 24 Ala. App. 481, 136 So. 876 (1931).
19. Jefcoat v. Gunter, 73 Miss. 539, 19 So. 94 (1896).
20. Taylor v. Crowe, 190 Ark. 71, 77 S. W. (2d) 54 (1934); Heard v. Griffin, 188 Ark. 235, 66 S. W. (2d) 1060 (1933); Smith v. Pearce, 174 Ark.

where a tenant is unlawfully evicted in the dead of winter and is forced to provide a temporary abode for himself and his family until he can find a suitable farm to rent, he may recover for the expense of moving to a permanent home as well as the cost of moving to temporary quarters.[21]

The tenant may have done a great deal of work and made improvements on the premises with a view to cultivating the land. Under such circumstances an evicted tenant may recover the value of the improvements.[22]

It seems to be clear that mental pain and anguish can be considered as a proper element of damages in these eviction cases.[23]

Here we see the law protecting the tenant from hasty action on the part of the landlord. The remedy is not always adequate, but it is at least a deterrent to unwarranted action. In a proper case a court of equity will no doubt give the tenant relief by way of injunction. It is clear that the landlord cannot take the law into his own hands without risking the application of this remedy.

153, 294 S. W. 705 (1927); Franks v. Rogers, 156 Ark. 120, 245 S. W. 311 (1922); Malone v. Wade, 148 Ark. 548, 230 S. W. 579 (1921).

21. McElvaney v. Smith, 76 Ark. 468, 88 S. W. 981 (1905).

22. Heard v. Griffin, 188 Ark. 235, 66 S. W. (2d) 1060 (1933).

23. Walker v. Ingram, 37 So. (2d) 682 (Ala. App. 1948), aff'd 37 So. (2d) 685 (Ala. 1948).

X

The "Estoppel" to Deny the
Landlord's Title

IN every year many cases are decided by reference to that often-used axiom of tenancy law: A tenant is estopped to deny the title of his landlord. And yet it may be said that by terming it an estoppel judges have adopted a misnomer. Estoppel is defined as "a bar or impediment raised by the law, which precludes a man from alleging or denying a certain fact or state of facts, in consequence of his previous allegation or denial or conduct or admission, or in consequence of a final adjudication of the matter in a court of law." [1] While the term as thus defined might conceivably be construed in such a manner as to apply to the inability of the tenant under the law to deny his landlord's title, it is believed that it would be much better to say that, as a matter of law, the tenant is, generally speaking, not permitted to dispute the title of the person under whom he has accepted the possession of the leased premises. The term "estoppel," as used by courts today, has become associated in the professional mind with misleading conduct or failure to act in accordance with certain standards delineated by decency in human relationships. Hence the term as used in tenancy law does not fit the prevailing conception. In this treatise, however, the language of estoppel will be used, since this is the way that the judges, ancient and modern, have dealt with the problem in farm tenancy cases.

In all the Southeastern states it may be said that as a general proposition a tenant is estopped from questioning the title of his landlord.[2] The estoppel has been applied in an instance where former

1. Black's Law Dictionary (2d Ed.) p. 442 (1910).
2. Walden v. Bodley, 14 Pet. 156, 10 L. ed. 398 (1840); McWhorter v. Stein, 39 So. 617 (Ala., 1905); Cook v. Cook, 28 Ala. 660 (1856); Miller v. Bonsadon, 9 Ala. 317 (1846); Terry v. Ferguson, 8 Port. 500 (Ala., 1839); Bolin v. Drainage Dist., 206 Ark. 459, 176 S. W. (2d) 143 (1943); Casey v. Johnson, 193 Ark. 177, 98 S. W. (2d) 67 (1936); Jones v. Allen, 63 Fla. 204, 58 So. 784 (1912); Dixon v. Patterson, 135 Ga. 183, 69 S. E. 21 (1910); Hill v. Goolsby, 41 Ga. 289 (1870); Johnson v. Watkins, 26 Ga. App. 759, 107 S. E. 341 (1921); McGuire v. Lovelace, 128 S. W. 309 (Ky., 1910); Hardwick v. Karn, 33 Ky.

owners have continued in possession as tenants after a sale of the property under the power granted in a deed of trust. They had paid the rent stipulated in a written lease executed by the beneficiary under the deed, who had purchased the land at the foreclosure sale, and had remained on the property after his refusal to renew the lease.[3] The estoppel has been extended to include an additional tract of land where the landlord's testimony, unassailed by the tenant, purported to make the added bit subject to the tenancy contract.[4] Again, the rule is applied to a tenancy created by the executor of a deceased owner.[5]

The Tennessee court has declared that neither the tenant himself, nor a person to whom he has transferred his interest, whether with or without notice of the adverse claim of ownership, can dispute the title of the party under whom the tenant has entered.[6]

A tenant is not permitted, under the general rule, to set up an outstanding title in a third person.[7] This is true even where the title is really in the name of the landlord's deceased wife.[8] Nor can a tenant attorn to a title which is hostile to the landlord's claim.[9]

Law Rep. 776, 111 S. W. 293 (1908); Trabue v. Ramage, 80 Ky. 323 (1882); Farrow's Heirs v. Edmundson, 43 Ky. 605 (1844); Lively v. Ball, 41 Ky. 53 (1841); Connelley's Heirs v. Chiles, 9 Ky. 242 (1820); Swann v. Wilson, 8 Ky. 99 (1817); Stinson v. Marston, 185 La. 365, 169 So. 436 (1936); Harvin v. Blackman, 108 La. 426, 32 So. 452 (1902); Phelps v. Taylor, 23 La. Ann. 585 (1871); Tippet v. Jett, 10 La. 359 (1836); Richardson v. Scott, 6 La. 54 (1833); Lacaze v. Beeman, 178 So. 660 (La. App., 1938); State v. Mills, 2 La. App. 425 (1925); Simpson v. Ricketts, 185 Miss. 280, 186 So. 318 (1939); Bunn v. Holliday, 209 N. C. 351, 183 S. E. 278 (1936); Shell v. West, 130 N. C. 171, 41 S. E. 65 (1902); Conwell v. Mann, 100 N. C. 234, 6 S. E. 782 (1888); Springs v. Schenck, 99 N. C. 551, 6 S. E. 405 (1888); Davis v. Davis, 83 N. C. 71 (1880); Smart v. Smith, 13 N. C. 258 (1828); Maples v. Spencer, 97 S. C. 331, 81 S. E. 483 (1914); Lane's Lessee v. Osment, 17 Tenn. 86 (1836); Clarke v. McClure, 10 Gratt. 305 (Va., 1853). See Ala. Code (1940) tit. 31, §1.

    3. Joint Stock Land Bank v. Hardy, 211 N. C. 459, 190 S. E. 730 (1937).

    4. Benton v. Benton, 95 N. C. 559 (1886).

    5. Shell v. West, 130 N. C. 171, 41 S. E. 65 (1902).

    6. Lane's Lessee v. Osment, 17 Tenn. 86 (1836).

    7. Beck v. Johnson, 235 Ala. 323, 179 So. 225 (1938); Duncan v. Guy, 159 Ala. 524, 49 So. 229 (1909); Farris & McCurdy v. Houston, 74 Ala. 162 (1883); Bishop v. Lalouette's Heirs, 67 Ala. 197 (1880); Frazier v. Banks, 294 Ky. 61, 170 S. W. (2d) 900 (1943); Million v. Riley, 31 Ky. 359, 25 Am. Dec. 149 (1833); Conley's Heirs v. Chiles, 28 Ky. 302 (1831); Turly v. Rodgers, 8 Ky. 245 (1818); Thomas v. Jackson, 158 La. 1019, 105 So. 49 (1925); Pitman v. Hunt, 197 N. C. 574, 150 S. E. 13 (1929); Hobby v. Freeman, 183 N. C. 240, 111 S. E. 1 (1922); Davis v. Davis, 83 N. C. 71 (1880); Syme v. Saunders, 4 Strob. 196 (S. C., 1850).

    8. Hamer v. McCall, 121 N. C. 196, 28 S. E. 297 (1897).

    9. Duncan v. Guy, 159 Ala. 524, 49 So. 229 (1909); Simmons v. Robertson,

In one instance a Tennessee tenant sublet the rented premises to a person who later accepted a lease from the landowner, thus attorning to him. The tenant sued the subtenant for the agreed rent, and in this action it was held that estoppel prevented a denial of the tenant's right to the property, even though the property had been delivered to the landowner.[10] This is carrying the estoppel rule to absurd lengths.

As a general rule it may be said that the tenant is precluded from setting up title in himself without first relinquishing the possession to the landlord.[11] In a recent North Carolina case, however, it was said that this is true only where a hostile title is being set up. Moreover, where the landlord's title itself has been transferred to the tenant, the estoppel rule has no application. It was said that there is a merger of estates here.[12] This is a good rule and should be followed in other jurisdictions.

An outstanding title to land, purchased by a tenant in possession, is presumed to have been acquired to protect his possession of the property under the lease. The Alabama Court has said that the tenant's right to the property is subject to the landlord's right to reimburse the tenant for any sum of money expended. However, the court declared that the statutory limitation of two years on the landlord's right to redeem did not begin to run until the surrender of the land to the landlord.[13]

Sometimes a tenant may wish to set up a title to the rented

---

27 Ark. 50 (1871); Frazier v. Banks, 294 Ky. 61, 170 S. W. (2d) 900 (1943); Trabue v. Ramage, 80 Ky. 323 (1882); Pleak v. Chambers, 35 Ky. 60 (1837); Wells v. Hickman, 6 Rob. 1 (La., 1843); Federal Land Bank v. Spencer, 160 So. 175 (La. App., 1935); Belfour's and Henley's Heirs v. Davis, 20 N. C. 443 (1839).

10. Hammond v. Dean, 67 Tenn. 193 (1874).

11. Duncan v. Guy, 159 Ala. 524, 49 So. 229 (1909); Barlow v. Dahm, 97 Ala. 414, 12 So. 293 (1893); Farris & McCurdy v. Houston, 74 Ala. 162 (1883); Casey v. Johnson, 193 Ark. 177, 98 S. W. (2d) 67 (1936); Montgomery v. Massey, 145 Ark. 336, 224 S. W. 631 (1920); Pickett v. Ferguson, 45 Ark. 177 (1885); Jones v. Allen, 63 Fla. 204, 58 So. 784 (1912); Bullard v. Hudson, 125 Ga. 393, 54 S. E. 132 (1906); King v. Hill, 32 Ky. Law Rep. 1192, 108 S. W. 238 (1908); Kelsey v. Long, 7 Ky. Law Rep. 823, 13 Ky. Opin. 1121 (1886); Hodges v. Shields, 57 Ky. 828 (1857); Casey v. Gregory, 52 Ky. 505, 56 Am. Dec. 581 (1852); Drane v. Gregory's Heirs, 42 Ky. 619 (1843); Norton v. Sanders, 31 Ky. 14 (1833); Tippet v. Jett, 10 La. 359 (1836); Lacaze v. Beeman, 178 So. 660 (La. App., 1938); Pitman v. Hunt, 197 N. C. 574, 150 S. E. 13 (1929); Lawrence v. Eller, 169 N. C. 211, 85 S. E. 291 (1915).

12. Lofton v. Barber, 226 N. C. 481, 39 S. E. (2d) 263 (1946).

13. Kelly v. Kelly, 250 Ala. 664, 35 So. (2d) 686 (1948).

premises which he has acquired at a tax sale. There is a decided difference of opinion as to whether he may do so. In Alabama [14] and Kentucky [15] it is stated that a tenant cannot set up a title which he has obtained at a tax sale held during the tenancy. With this proposition the Mississippi Court agrees.[16] Where the tax sale precedes the tenancy, however, the court has come to a different conclusion. In an early case it was held that a tenant, who was not in possession when the land was sold for taxes but came into possession under a lease contract subsequent to the tax sale, was not precluded from buying in the title and setting it up against his landlord in the latter's action to recover possession of the premises.[17]

This right to buy at a tax sale has been affirmed in later cases.[18] However, it has been said that the tenant could only assert the title thus obtained after surrendering possession to his landlord pursuant to the rental agreement.[19] In accordance with these principles, the court decided that a tenant acquiring during his term the tax title from a purchaser at a tax sale held prior to the tenancy, and thereafter surrendering possession to the owner, could institute an unlawful entry and detainer action against the owner's subsequent tenants.[20] Further, it was said that such a tenant was liable to the landlord for the rent accruing each month that the tenant remained in possession, notwithstanding the fact that after the surrender the tenant could assert the purchased title against the landlord.[21]

In Arkansas it has been held that a tenant may not, while in possession of land under a lease, claim that his possession is adverse to the rights of the landlord.[22] In a later case, however, it was declared that a person entering as a tenant cannot be prevented from setting up an adverse claim based upon a possession which is subsequent to

14. Brunson v. Bailey, 245 Ala. 102, 16 So. (2d) 9 (1943); Bailey v. Campbell, 82 Ala. 342, 2 So. 646 (1887).

15. Morris v. Apperson, 11 Ky. Law. Rep. 838, 13 S. W. 441 (1890).

16. Johnson v. Carter, 193 Miss. 781, 11 So. (2d) 196 (1943); Walker v. Harrison, 75 Miss. 665, 23 So. 392 (1898).

17. Walker v. Harrison, 75 Miss. 665, 23 So. 392 (1898).

18. James v. Shaffer, 202 Miss. 565, 32 So. (2d) 749 (1947); McKay v. Shaffer, 202 Miss. 558, 32 So. (2d) 746 (1947); Johnson v. Carter, 193 Miss. 781, 11 So. (2d) 196 (1943).

19. James v. Shaffer, 202 Miss. 565, 32 So. (2d) 749 (1947); Simpson v. Ricketts, 185 Miss. 280, 186 So. 318 (1939); Johnson v. Langston, 175 Miss. 622, 176 So. 531 (1937).

20. McKay v. Shaffer, 202 Miss. 558, 32 So. (2d) 746 (1947).

21. James v. Shaffer, 202 Miss. 565, 32 So. (2d) 749 (1947).

22. Dickinson v. Arkansas City Improvement Co., 77 Ark. 570, 92 S. W. 21 (1906).

the alleged tenancy.[23] The court declared that to show such an adverse holding the tenant must have asserted an exclusive right in himself, evidenced by such acts of ownership as would afford the landlord actual notice of the claim. It was also said that an assignee of the tenant without notice of the relationship might succeed to the tenant's rights thereby obtained. Having referred to these decisions in a recent case,[24] the court went on to say that a tenant may become the purchaser of leased premises at a tax sale or may purchase such land from the state. In coming to this conclusion the court approved and followed two earlier cases in which it had declared that it is lawful for a tenant in possession to purchase the leased premises at a tax sale and set up his title against the landlord in a possessory action.[25]

In another instance a firm leased land to a tenant who occupied the land and paid rent under an express tenancy agreement. The tenant retained possession of the premises for ten years after receivers were appointed for the firm, without informing them of their valid claim to the property, which they had overlooked. He also failed to inform them of his purchase of the land at a sale made necessary by the foreclosure of a levee tax lien. Under these circumstances it was held that he occupied the premises under an "implied tenancy" after the appointment of the receivers, and that he was estopped to assert the title acquired at the tax sale as against a person to whom the receivers had transferred the property.[26] In this situation special circumstances would seem to be present. The tenant failed to inform the receivers, who did not even know of their ownership of the land, of his purchase at the tax sale. Therefore the tenant should not be allowed to set up the tax title as against them. In another recent case the evidence was to the effect that the tenant recognized the former owner as his landlord after acquiring the tax title, a circumstance which would clearly make it unjust to permit him to challenge the landlord's title in an action for rent or possession.[27]

In Florida the mere fact of tenancy does not necessarily prevent

23. Gee v. Hatley, 114 Ark. 376, 170 S. W. 72 (1914).

24. Sims v. Petree, 206 Ark. 1023, 178 S. W. (2d) 1016 (1944). See Billingsley v. Lipscomb, 211 Ark. 45, 200 S. W. (2d) 510 (1947).

25. Pickett v. Ferguson, 45 Ark. 177 (1885); Ferguson v. Etter, 21 Ark. 160 (1860).

26. Mann & Campbell v. Walker, 202 Ark. 211, 149 S. W. (2d) 935 (1941).

27. Ray v. Stroud, 204 Ark. 583, 163 S. W. (2d) 173 (1942).

the acquisition of an adverse tax title to land occupied under a contract of tenancy, and the occupancy may become adverse to the landlord without the surrender of possession. To be effective, however, the disclaimer and disavowal of the landlord's ownership must be brought home to him by notice which is clear, positive, and distinct.[28] This view of the law was reiterated in a recent case where a tenant, relying upon a tax deed, failed to prove that he had disclaimed the tenancy or challenged the landlord's title by positive act.[29]

A lessee of timber lands had continued to use the premises after purchasing tax certificates which entitled him to a claim on the property. He persisted in removing timber from the land in accordance with the terms of the lease but failed to pay the purchase price in the manner stipulated by the instrument. Here the court declared that the lessee was bound to credit the lessor with the amount due for the timber against the sum paid in respect to the taxes. It stated that a lessee cannot acquire any better right by purchasing tax certificates than he might obtain by paying the taxes. The only right he acquired was a lien for the amount expended in paying the taxes, even though he was not in default in the payments called for by the lease at the time he settled that claim.[30] Here there is no evidence of any disclaimer, and the tenant continued on the premises without any assertion of title in himself.

Further, it has been held in this state that a tenant who is under a contractual duty to pay the property taxes on leased premises can claim no title to the land which he buys at a tax sale at the suggestion or request of his landlord.[31] It is unjust to permit the tenant to obtain an advantage by paying a debt which he is already obligated to satisfy. This is in accordance with the general rule recognized by the courts and text writers.[32] Where there is no contractual duty to pay the taxes, the tenant can buy the land at a tax sale and set up the acquired title against the landlord.[33]

There are various ways in which the estoppel rule may be applied.

28. Armstrong v. Wilcox, 57 Fla. 30, 49 So. 41 (1909); Brown v. Atlanta B. & L. Ass'n, 46 Fla. 492, 35 So. 403 (1903).
29. Kilvert v. Clark, 152 Fla. 59, 10 So. (2d) 795 (1942).
30. Chicago Trust Co. v. Knabb, 142 Fla. 767, 196 So. 200 (1940).
31. Petty v. Mays, 19 Fla. 652 (1883).
32. Jackson v. King, 82 Ala. 432, 3 So. 232 (1887); Woods v. Woods, 226 S. W. (2d) 961 (Ark. 1950).
33. Woods v. Woods, 226 S. W. (2d) 961 (Ark. 1950); Hoch v. Ratcliff, 226 S. W. (2d) 39 (Ark. 1950); Bass v. John, 230 S. W. (2d) 946 (Ark. 1950).

Thus actual possession of land by a tenant does not give him a preference upon his application for a patent on the rented premises.[34] Moreover, another court held that a person in possession as a tenant cannot maintain a suit against his landlord to remove a cloud from an adverse title claimed by the tenant.[35] A bare peaceable possession under claim of title, though for a shorter period of time than would bar a real action by someone having an adverse claim, is sufficient to support an action of ejectment against either a trespasser or a tenant who is not in a position to dispute the claimant's title.[36] A tenant contended that it was lawful for him to deny his landlord's title if the evidence showed that the latter had not been actually seised of the premises at some previous time. However, the court denied the right of the tenant to set up an adverse title in a third person, even though the landlord had never been in actual possession of the land.[37] Furthermore, in a possessory action brought by an Arkansas landlord, the jurisdiction of a justice of the peace could not be defeated by a denial of the plaintiff's title to the land.[38] In North Carolina a farmer accepted a lease of land already in his possession. It was held that the estoppel rule would apply here just as though he had originally taken possession of the premises under the lease.[39]

The fact that the lease has expired and that the lessee may be classed as a tenant holding over does not prevent the operation of the estoppel.[40] This is especially true where the lessee holding over has become an express tenant by operation of law.[41]

A person in possession as a tenant cannot, either by consenting to possess for a third person, or by allowing others to take possession and cultivate the land, affect in any manner the rights of his land-

---

34. Kelsey v. Long, 7 Ky. Law Rep. 823, 13 Ky. Opin. 1121 (1886).

35. Gaines v. Russ, 60 Fla. 317, 53 So. 113 (1910).

36. Clarke v. Clarke's Adm'r, 51 Ala. 498 (1874).

37. Connelly's Heirs v. Chiles, 9 Ky. 242 (1820).

38. Nolen v. Royston, 36 Ark. 561 (1880).

39. Dixon v. Stewart, 113 N. C. 410, 18 S. E. 325 (1893).

40. Salter v. Fox, 190 Ala. 288, 67 So. 439 (1915); Bullard v. Hudson, 125 Ga. 393, 54 S. E. 132 (1906); Federal Land Bank v. Spencer, 160 So. 175 (La. App., 1935); Wilson v. Peacock, 111 Miss. 116, 71 So. 296 (1916); Holman v. Bonner, 63 Miss. 131 (1885); Hobby v. Freeman, 183 N. C. 240 111 S. E. 1 (1922); Taylor v. Kelly, 56 N. C. 240 (1857); Milhouse v. Patrick, 6 Rich. 350 (S. C., 1853); Watson v. Smith's Lessee, 18 Tenn. 476 (1837).

41. Smith v. Hardwick, 28 Ky. Law Rep. 615, 89 S. W. 731 (1905); Hammond v. Dean, 67 Tenn. 193 (1874).

lord.[42] The estoppel extends not only to the tenant, but to his privies in blood or estate.[43] The rule is applicable to an assignee,[44] licensee,[45] or subtenant.[46] A subtenant is not permitted to dispute the title of his landlord, the original tenant, by setting up the fact that the subtenancy has been created without the consent of the landowner.[47] Furthermore, it is no defense in an action for possession or rent that a sublessee, to protect his own interest in the premises, has been forced to purchase the land at a sale for the purpose of paying the landowner's debts. He is estopped from setting up an after-acquired title during his tenancy.[48] A claimant to the ownership of the land who has been admitted to defend a possessory action by a landlord against his tenant cannot set up any defense which is forbidden to the tenant, such as the title. He stands with, or in the place of, the tenant, and is entiled to the tenant's rights and subject to the tenant's disadvantages.[49] The estoppel has even been extended to the wife of a tenant in possession.[50] There is no estoppel, however, where the tenant is only a witness in a controversy between the alleged landlord and a third person but not a party to the suit.[51]

There are a good many well recognized exceptions to the estoppel rule. One group of these might be known as the "misconception"

42. Wells v. Hickman, 6 Rob. 1 (La., 1843).

43. McWhorter v. Stein, 39 So. 617 (Ala., 1905); Taylor v. Marble Savings Bank, 196 Ark. 1179, 119 S. W. (2d) 746 (1938); Blakeney v. Ferguson, 20 Ark. 547 (1859); Salter v. Salter, 80 Ga. App. 263, 55 S. E. (2d) 868 (1949); Lewis v. Adams, 61 Ga. 559 (1878); Frazier v. Banks, 294 Ky. 61, 170 S. W. (2d) 900 (1943); Russell v. McIntosh, 179 Ky. 677, 201 S. W. 33 (1918); Hardwick v. Karn, 33 Ky. Law Rep. 776, 111 S. W. 293 (1908); Green v. Wilson, 8 Ky. Law Rep. 601, 2 S. W. 564 (1887); Syme v. Sanders, 4 Strob. 196 (S. C., 1850); Lane's Lessee v. Osment, 17 Tenn. 86 (1836); Neff v. Ryman, 100 Va. 521, 42 S. E. 314 (1902).

44. Pate v. Turner, 94 N. C. 47 (1886); Lunsford v. Alexander, 20 N. C. 166 (1838).

45. Dills v. Hampton, 92 N. C. 566 (1885).

46. Coyle v. Leigh, 36 So. (2d) 68 (La. App. 1948). Bonds v. Smith, 106 N. C. 553, 11 S. E. 322 (1890); Lunsford v. Alexander, 20 N. C. 166 (1838); Thomson v. Peake, 7 Rich. 353 (S. C., 1854); Milhouse v. Patrick, 6 Rich. 350 (S. C., 1853).

47. Boyd v. Kinzy, 127 Ga. 358, 56 S. E. 420 (1907).

48. Montgomery v. Massey, 145 Ark. 336, 224 S. W. 631 (1920).

49. Belfour's and Henly's Heirs v. Davis, 20 N. C. 443 (1839).

50. Taylor v. Marble Savings Bank, 196 Ark. 1179, 119 S. W. (2d) 746 (1938); Tyler v. Niven, 194 Ark. 538, 108 S. W. (2d) 893 (1937).

51. South v. Deaton, 113 Ky. 312, 68 S. W. 137, 1105 (1902); Bartley v. McKinney, 28 Gratt. 750 (Va., 1877).

group. Thus it has been held that the estoppel is not operative where the contract of tenancy is tainted with fraud,[52] mistake,[53] or undue influence or imposition.[54] In Virginia the mistake must have been induced by fraudulent representations in order for the estoppel rule to be suspended.[55] Another exception allows the introduction of title papers in a situation where there is a boundary dispute.[56] Furthermore, the South Carolina court has held that a tenant, even prior to the termination of his tenancy, may acquire title by adverse possession to land which is outside the record title of his landlord.[57]

A tenant is precluded from questioning the title of his landlord's transferee[58] or from claiming a possession adverse to him.[59] The same holds true with respect to the remote vendees or transferees of both parties.[60] A tenant is not permitted to object that the title to the land has escheated to the state, at least as long as it continues in the possession of those who derive their claim from the administrator of a deceased landlord.[61] But he may attorn and take shelter under

52. Shaw v. Lacy, 199 Ala. 450, 74 So. 933 (1917); Farris and McCurdy v. Houston, 74 Ala. 162 (1883); Miller v. Bonsadon, 9 Ala. 317 (1846); Barnett v. Lewis, 194 Ga. 203, 20 S. E. (2d) 912 (1942) (dictum); Buckhorn Coal & Lumber Co. v. Woods, 228 Ky. 705, 15 S. W. (2d) 437 (1929) (dictum); Ball v. Lively, 34 Ky. 369 (1836), 38 Ky. 312 (1839), 41 Ky. 53 (1841); Givens v. Mullinax, 4 Rich. 590, 55 Am. Dec. 706 (S. C., 1851); Smith v. Zwicker, 136 Tenn. 77, 188 S. W. 595 (1916) (dictum); Allison v. Casey, 63 Tenn. 587 (1874); Locke v. Frasher's Adm'r, 79 Va. 409 (1884); Alderson v. Miller, 15 Gratt. 279 (Va., 1859).

53. Farris & McCurdy v. Houston, 74 Ala. 162 (1883); Pearce v. Nix, 34 Ala. 183 (1859); Lively v. Ball, 38 Ky. 312 (1839), 41 Ky. 53 (1841); Austin v. Crisp, 186 N. C. 616, 120 S. E. 199 (1923); Givens v. Mullinax, 4 Rich. 590, 55 Am. Dec. 706 (S. C., 1851); Smith v. Zwicker, 136 Tenn. 77, 188 S. W. 595 (1916); Hammons v. McClure, 85 Tenn. 65, 2 S. W. 37 (1886); Allison v. Casey, 63 Tenn. 587 (1874).

54. Farris & McCurdy v. Houston, 74 Ala. 162 (1883); Miller v. Bonsadon, 9 Ala. 317 (1846). See also Harvin v. Blackman, 108 La. 426, 32 So. 452 (1902).

55. Locke v. Frasher's Adm'r., 79 Va. 409 (1884); Alderson v. Miller, 15 Gratt. 279 (Va., 1859).

56. Richardson v. Scott, 6 La. 54 (1833); Smith v. Zwicker, 136 Tenn. 77, 188 S. W. 595 (1916).

57. Lucius v. DuBose, 114 S. C. 375, 103 S. E. 759 (1920).

58. Bishop v. Lalouette's Heirs, 67 Ala. 197 (1880); Casey v. Johnson, 193 Ark. 177, 98 S. W. (2d) 67 (1936); Lewis v. Harper, 149 Ark. 43, 231 S. W. 874 (1921); Thomson v. Peake, 7 Rich. 353 (S. C., 1854).

59. Brunson v. Morgan, 84 Ala. 598, 4 So. 589 (1888); Casey v. Johnson, 193 Ark. 177, 98 S. W. (2d) 67 (1936).

60. Russell v. McIntosh, 179 Ky. 677, 201 S. W. 33 (1918).

61. Bishop v. Lalouette's Heirs, 67 Ala. 197 (1880).

the title of his landlord's transferee or a person obtaining the land from the landlord by operation of law.[62]

The tenant cannot complain that the lease contract has been affected by usury [63] or champerty.[64] Sometimes, however, an equitable estoppel will prevent the operation of the rule, as in an Alabama case where a mortgagor was induced to accept a tenancy by the mortgagee's representations that the original mortgage relationship would be continued.[65] Here an estoppel prevents the operation of another estoppel, a confusion of terminology due to the fact that the rule which prevents a tenant from questioning his landlord's title is not a true estoppel. Furthermore, circumstances may be such that the landlord can be said to have waived the operation of the rule.[66] A waiver is not shown, however, where all he did was to fail to object to the evidence of title offered by the tenant.[67]

The estoppel to deny the landlord's title is made doubly effective where the instrument by which the tenancy was created recites the fact that the obligor is a tenant, this being an estoppel by deed.[68]

In a Tennessee case the defendant had been let into the possession of a tract of land by the plaintiff under an agreement to pay rent, in part by clearing ground, building houses, cribs, and fences, and making certain repairs. On being sued for his failure to perform this portion of the agreement, he sought to show that the title to the land was in a third person, who had forbidden the improvements to be made. It was held that this testimony was inadmissible, not because the defendant was estopped to deny his landlord's title, but for the reason that the landlord's title was not relevant to the merits of the action.[69]

The general rule seems to be that a tenant must surrender possession of leased premises before he can challenge his landlord's title. In other words, it has been said that the landlord can only be required to litigate the title with his tenant upon the vantage

62. Hodges v. Shields, 57 Ky. 828 (1857); Melchor v. Casey, 173 Miss. 67, 161 So. 692 (1935) Galloway v. Inglis, 138 Miss. 350, 103 So. 147 (1925); Rhyne v. Guevara, 67 Miss. 139, 6 So. 736 (1889).

63. King v. Murray, 28 N. C. 62 (1845).

64. McIntire v. Patton, 28 Tenn. 447 (1848).

65. Bank of New Brockton v. Dunnavant, 204 Ala. 636, 87 So. 105 (1920).

66. Wood v. Chambers, 3 Rich. 150 (S. C., 1846).

67. Milhouse v. Patrick, 6 Rich. 350 (S. C., 1853).

68. Hall v. Haun's Heirs, 35 Ky. 55 (1837).

69. Long v. Douglass, 59 Tenn. 147 (1873).

ground of possession.[70] Such has been the holding in Alabama,[71] Arkansas,[72] Georgia,[73] Kentucky,[74] Louisiana,[75] Mississippi,[76] South Carolina,[77] and probably Tennessee.[78] It is probable that the same

70. Howard v. Jones, 123 Ala. 488, 26 So. 129 (1899).

71. Childress v. Smith, 227 Ala. 435, 150 So. 334 (1933); Layton v. Hamilton, 214 Ala. 329, 107 So. 830 (1926); Anders v. Sandlin, 191 Ala. 158, 67 So. 684 (1914); Sayers v. Tallahassee Falls Mfg. Co., 167 Ala. 553, 52 So. 892 (1910); Howard v. Jones, 123 Ala. 488, 26 So. 129 (1899); Barlow v. Dahm, 97 Ala. 414, 12 So. 293 (1893); Robinson v. Holt, 90 Ala. 115, 7 So. 441 (1890); Crim v. Nelms, 78 Ala. 604 (1885); Littleton v. Clayton, 77 Ala. 571 (1884); Bishop v. Lalouette's Heirs, 67 Ala. 197 (1880).

72. Denton v. Denton, 209 Ark. 216, 190 S. W. (2d) 291 (1945); Ray v. Stroud, 204 Ark. 583, 163 S. W. (2d) 173 (1942); Taylor v. Marble Savings Bank, 196 Ark. 1179, 119 S. W. (2d) 746 (1938); Tyler v. Niven, 194 Ark. 538, 108 S. W. (2d) 893 (1937); Lewis v. Harper, 149 Ark. 43, 231 S. W. 874 (1921); Gibson v. Allen-West Commission Co., 138 Ark. 172, 211 S. W. 142 (1919); Waggener v. McLaughlin, 33 Ark. 195 (1878); Hughes v. Watt, 28 Ark. 153 (1873).

73. Ga. Code (1933) §61-107; Barnett v. Lewis, 194 Ga. 203, 20 S. E. (2d) 912 (1942); Smith v. Aldridge, 192 Ga. 376, 15 S. E. (2d) 430 (1941); Bullard v. Hudson, 125 Ga. 393, 54 S. E. 132 (1906); Newton v. Roe, 33 Ga. 163 (1862); Cowart v. Maddox, 22 Ga. App. 197, 95 S. E. 719 (1918).

74. Finlayson v. Cuyuga Coal & Coke Co., 173 Ky. 763, 191 S. W. 486 (1917); Mullins v. Hall, 112 S. W. 920 (Ky., 1908); King v. Hill, 32 Ky. Law Rep. 1192, 108 S. W. 238 (1908); Saunders v. Moore, 77 Ky. 97 (1878); Hodges v. Shields, 57 Ky. 828 (1857); Norton v. Sanders, 31 Ky. 14 (1833). The word "renounce" is used in two cases. Miller v. South, 12 Ky. Law Rep. 351, 14 S. W. 361 (1890); Patterson v. Hansel, 67 Ky. 654 (1868). The main proposition is probably not affected by what is said about the adverse possession of a tenant in the following cases: Frazier v. Banks, 294 Ky. 61, 170 S. W. (2d) 900 (1943); South's Heirs v. Marcum, 22 Ky. Law Rep. 641, 58 S. W. 527 (1900); Farrow's Heirs v. Edmundson, 43 Ky. 605 (1844); Sebastian v. Ford's Heirs, 36 Ky. 436 (1838).

75. Harvin v. Blackman, 112 La. 24, 36 So. 213 (1904).

76. Simpson v. Ricketts, 185 Miss. 280, 186 So. 318 (1939); Johnson v. Langston, 179 Miss. 622, 176 So. 531 (1937); Holman v. Bonner, 63 Miss. 131 (1885). True as general proposition, although probably limited somewhat by what is said in other decisions. See Galloway v. Inglis, 138 Miss. 350, 103 So. 147 (1925); Greenwood v. Moore, 79 Miss. 201, 30 So. 609 (1901).

77. Pinckney v. Knowles, 112 S. C. 7, 99 S. E. 354 (1919); Milhouse v. Patrick, 6 Rich. 350 (S. C., 1853); Wilson v. Weathersby, 1 Nott & McCord 373 (S. C., 1818). In Thomas v. Willison, 3 Pet. 43, 7 Law Ed. 586 (1830), the Federal Supreme Court seems to have failed to carry the proposition decided here to its logical conclusion, preferring to engraft an opposing doctrine of its own in a factual situation which seemed to call for only a slight extension of the principles announced by the South Carolina Court in Wilson v. Weathersby, *supra*. See also Walden v. Bodley, 14 Pet. 156, 10 Law Ed. 398 (1840). In respect to the tenant's claim of adverse possession against his landlord, see Trustees of Wadsworthville School v. Jennings, 40 S. C. 168, 18 S. E. 257 (1893).

78. Phillips' Lessee v. Robertson, 6 Tenn. 101 (1818). There are remarks

general rule would prevail in Florida,[79] although in that state it has been definitely declared that a tenant may, without surrendering possession, disclaim the tenancy and hold adversely, provided the disclaimer is definite and is brought to the attention of the landlord.[80] In North Carolina all the early cases appear to be in accordance with the general rule requiring a surrender.[81] In a recent case, however, it is said that a surrender is necessary only where a hostile title is being set up. It is not obligatory where the title under which the tenant entered has been transferred to a third person or to the tenant himself.[82] In Virginia a tenant, in order to make his possession adverse, is not forced to surrender possession of the land. He may make a clear, positive, and continued disclaimer of the tenancy and a disavowal of the landlord's title, notice of which must be brought home to the landlord.[83]

The surrender, to be effective, must be to the landlord and no one else. Hence a tenant's conveyance of leased realty, purchased by him from a mortgagee who had bought it at a foreclosure sale, and a surrender to the persons to whom he had conveyed, could not be effective as a proper surrender to the landlord.[84]

In general it may be said that possession as a tenant is not adverse.[85] For the tenant's possession to be deemed adverse, the fact that he is holding adversely must generally be brought to the landlord's atten-

---

in later cases which would indicate that a tenant might make his possession adverse by a disclaimer of the tenancy brought to the notice of the landlord. See Watson v. Smith's Lessee, 18 Tenn. 476 (1837); Duke v. Harper, 14 Tenn. 279, 27 Am. Dec. 462 (1834).

79. See State v. Hutchins, 118 Fla. 220, 158 So. 716 (1935); Jones v. Allen, 63 Fla. 204, 58 So. 784 (1912).

80. Little v. Kendrick, 152 Fla. 720, 12 So. (2d) 899 (1943); Armstrong v. Wilcox, 57 Fla. 30, 49 So. 41 (1909); Brown v. Atlanta Bldg. & Loan Ass'n, 46 Fla. 492, 35 So. 403 (1903).

81. Pitman v. Hunt, 197 N. C. 574, 150 S. E. 13 (1929); Hobby v. Freeman, 183 N. C. 240, 111 S. E. 1 (1922); Lawrence v. Eller, 169 N. C. 211, 85 S. E. 291 (1915); Bonds v. Smith, 106 N. C. 553, 11 S. E. 322 (1890); Pate v. Turner, 94 N. C. 47 (1886); James v. Russell, 92 N. C. 194 (1885); Abbott v. Cromartie, 72 N. C. 292 (1875); Taylor v. Kelly, 56 N. C. 240 (1857).

82. Lofton v. Barber, 226 N. C. 481, 39 S. E. (2d) 263 (1946).

83. Neff v. Ryman, 100 Va. 521, 42 S. E. 314 (1902).

84. Kelly v. Kelly, 250 Ala. 664, 35 So. (2d) 686 (1948).

85. LeMoyne v. Neal, 158 Ky. 316, 164 S. W. 964 (1914); Lucas v. New Hebron Bank, 181 Miss. 762, 180 So. 611 (1938); Eubanks v. McLeod, 105 Miss. 826, 63 So. 226 (1913); Pitman v. Hunt, 197 N. C. 574, 150 S. E. 13 (1929), citing N. C. Code Ann. (Michie, 1927) §433, setting up a particular rule in respect to this matter of adverse possession by one who has entered as a tenant.

tion in some manner.[86] The Arkansas court, however, has declared
that such notice is unnecessary and that the adverseness of the claim
can be established by outward acts of an unequivocal nature.[87] In a
South Carolina case it was declared that a possession under a recorded deed is sufficient notice of an adverse holding, the record
acting as constructive notice. An examination of the dissenting
opinion and rehearing, however, makes it clear that this cannot be
taken as anything more authoritative than a dictum.[88] In Kentucky
it is said that while a tenant may acquire title by adverse possession
against his landlord, such an antagonistic claim must be manifested
by some open, notorious, and public act of disclaimer, such as holding over in opposition to the title of the landlord and against his
will or some forcible act of expulsion.[89]

The surrender of the premises by the tenant to the landlord must
not be collusive.[90] The same principle applies where a third person
attempts to set up a title after collusive planning with the tenant.[91]

After surrender, of course, the tenancy is terminated and the
estoppel no longer applies.[92] The same is true where the tenancy is
terminated for other reasons.[93] Thus a former tenant may assert a
title which he acquired during the term.[94] The surrender must be an
accomplished fact before the start of the action, and it is not
enough that the tenant removed from the premises before the trial
of the case.[95]

86. Pender v. Cheaves, 104 Ala. 307, 16 So. 145 (1894); Winn v. Strickland,
34 Fla. 610, 16 So. 606 (1894); Williams v. Cash, 27 Ga. 507 (1859); Trustees of
Wadsworthville School v. Jennings, 40 S. C. 168, 18 S. E. 257 (1893); Watson
v. Smith's Lessee, 18 Tenn. 476 (1837); Duke v. Harper, 14 Tenn. 279, 27 Am.
Dec. 462 (1834); Neff v. Ryman, 100 Va. 521, 42 S. E. 314 (1902); Reusens v.
Lawson, 91 Va. 226, 21 S. E. 347 (1895).

87. Blakeney v. Ferguson, 20 Ark. 547 (1859).

88. Trustees of Wadsworthville School v. Jennings, 40 S. C. 168, 18 S. E.
257, 891 (1893).

89. Frazier v. Banks, 294 Ky. 61, 170 S. W. (2d) 900 (1943).

90. Littleton v. Clayton, 77 Ala. 571 (1884); Eversole v. Barker, 203 Ky.
572, 262 S. W. 946 (1924); Pate v. Turner, 94 N. C. 47 (1886).

91. Pleak v. Chambers, 35 Ky. 60 (1837); Bonds v. Smith, 106 N. C. 553,
11 S. E. 322 (1890). See also Springs v. Schenck, 99 N. C. 551, 6 S. E. 405 (1888).

92. Childress v. Smith, 227 Ala. 435, 150 So. 334 (1933); Kelso v. Robinson,
172 Miss. 828, 161 So. 135 (1935); Henning v. Warner, 109 N. C. 406, 14 S. E.
317 (1891); Smart v. Smith, 13 N. C. 258 (1828); Wild's Lessee v. Serpell, 10
Gratt. 405 (Va., 1853).

93. Gore v. Stevens, 31 Ky. 201, 25 Am. Dec. 141 (1833); Burbank v. Harris,
30 La. Ann. 487 (1878); Vanzant v. Morgan, 181 So. 660 (La. App., 1938);
Wild's Lessee v. Serpell, 10 Gratt. 405 (Va., 1853).

94. Williams v. Garrison, 29 Ga. 503 (1859).

95. Dixon v. Patterson, 135 Ga. 183, 69 S. E. 21 (1910).

The estoppel has been held not to apply where the landlord's title has been conveyed, voluntarily or involuntarily, or has come to an end by operation of law.[96] In North Carolina a tenant, against whose landlord a judgment in ejectment has been recovered, may, after such judgment and before eviction under it, purchase the title of the true owner and hold the premises as his own under his newly acquired title.[97] A Kentucky case declared that a tenant against whom a possessory action had been brought could introduce in evidence a court's decree in a previous suit between the same parties deciding that the title was in the tenant, thus depriving the landlord of any right he might have had to recover the premises.[98] If the title of the landlord has been divested at the time of the initiation of the possessory proceedings, the fact that he has reacquired the property prior to the trial cannot prevent the tenant from introducing proof that the landlord had parted with the ownership, thus entitling him to avoid the estoppel.[99] The estoppel does not apply where the tenant has been evicted under a paramount title asserted by some other person,[100] and this eviction may be constructive.[101] A tenant may terminate the lease and extinguish the title of his lessor by purchasing the rented premises at a voluntary or forced sale.[102] He may also protect himself against the termination of the lessor's interest because of the latter's failure to pay taxes by paying them himself, thereby becoming entitled to a lien on the property.[103] In an Alabama case it is said that the estoppel rule applies only to the title at the inception of the tenancy, and not to a situation in which the ownership has been transferred to another during the term.[104]

96. Childress v. Smith, 227 Ala. 435, 150 So. 334 (1933); Duncan v. Guy, 159 Ala. 524, 49 So. 229 (1909); Sadler v. Jefferson, 143 Ala. 669, 39 So. 380 (1905); Farris & McCurdy v. Houston, 74 Ala. 162 (1883); English v. Key, 39 Ala. 113 (1863); Terry v. Ferguson, 8 Port. 500 (Ala., 1839); Winn v. Strickland, 34 Fla. 610, 16 So. 606 (1894); Raines v. Hindman, 136 Ga. 450, 71 S. E. 738 (1911); Hodges v. Shields, 57 Ky. 828 (1857); Casey v. Gregory, 52 Ky. 408, 56 Am. Dec. 581 (1852); Gregory's Heirs v. Crab's Heirs, 41 Ky. 234 (1842); Melcher v. Casey, 173 Miss. 67, 161 So. 692 (1935); Rhyne v. Guevara, 67 Miss. 139, 6 So. 736 (1889); Wolf v. Johnson, 30 Miss. 513 (1855); Lassiter v. Stell, 214 N. C. 391, 199 S. E. 409 (1938); Lancashire v. Mason, 75 N. C. 455 (1876).

97. Clapp v. Coble, 21 N. C. 177 (1835).

98. Swann v. Wilson, 8 Ky. 99 (1817).

99. Backey v. Grew, 38 Ga. App. 154, 142 S. E. 913 (1928).

100. Farris & McCurdy v. Houston, 74 Ala. 162 (1883); English v. Key, 39 Ala. 113 (1862); Pate v. Turner, 94 N. C. 47 (1884).

101. Galloway v. Inglis, 138 Miss. 350, 103 So. 147 (1925).

102. Pickett v. Ferguson, 45 Ark. 177 (1885).

103. Waggener v. McLaughlin, 33 Ark. 195 (1878).

104. Sadler v. Jefferson, 143 Ala. 669, 39 So. 380 (1905).

Applying the estoppel rule, a tenant is precluded from attorning to an adverse claimant under a hostile title,[105] and this is true even where the tenant is holding over after the lease has expired.[106] The same principle applies where a subtenant takes a lease from the original lessor during the term stated in the original lease, the subtenant not being permitted to set up the second lease in an action for rent brought against him by the original tenant.[107] Where the landlord consents, the tenant may attorn to another;[108] but where this consent is lacking, an attornment is not effective,[109] even where the person attorned to was the landlord's vendor asserting a right to the premises.[110] When the landlord's estate has been terminated by eviction, purchase, or operation of law, however, the tenant may attorn to the succeeding owner.[111] In Kentucky it has been said that if a sale of land be made while it is in the possession of a tenant, he, and everyone coming into possession under him, thereby becomes the tenant of the vendee and cannot thereafter attorn to a stranger to the title under which he entered.[112] There is an automatic attornment here, brought about by operation of law. An interesting situation is presented in a recent Arkansas case in which it was declared that a person who is in possession of land under claim of ownership

105. Duncan v. Guy, 159 Ala. 524, 49 So. 229 (1909); DeJarnette v. McDaniel, 93 Ala. 215, 9 So. 570 (1891); Elliot v. Dyche, 78 Ala. 150 (1884); Simmons v. Robertson, 27 Ark. 50 (1871); Williams v. McMichael, 64 Ga. 445 (1879); Backey v. Grew, 38 Ga. App. 154, 142 S. E. 913 (1928); Frazier v. Banks, 294 Ky. 61, 170 S. W. (2d) 900 (1943); Trabue v. Ramage, 80 Ky. 323 (1882); Pleak v. Chambers, 35 Ky. 60 (1837); Wells v. Hickman, 6 Rob. 1 (La., 1843); Belfour's Heirs v. Davis, 20 N. C. 443 (1839); Camden Orphan Society v. Lockhart, 2 McMul. 84 (S. C., 1841).

106. Federal Land Bank v. Spencer, 160 So. 175 (La. App., 1935).

107. Hammond v. Dean, 67 Tenn. 193 (1874).

108. Hill v. Williams, 41 S. C. 134, 19 S. E. 290 (1894); Moore v. Johnston, 2 Speers 288 (S. C., 1844).

109. Ratcliff v. Belfont-Iron Works Co., 87 Ky. 559, 10 S. W. 365 (1888); Payne v. Vandever, 56 Ky. 14 (1856).

110. Broxton v. Ennis, 96 Ga. 792, 22 S. E. 945 (1895).

111. Hines v. Lavant, 158 Ga. 336, 123 S. E. 611 (1924); Evans' Adm'r v. Lytle, 102 Ky. 146, 42 S. W. 1110 (1897); Lunsford v. Turner, 28 Ky. 104, 20 Am. Dec. 248 (1830); Foster v. Morris, 10 Ky. 609, 13 Am. Dec. 205 (1821); Bank of Coushatta v. Williams, 10 La. App. 571, 121 So. 646 (1929); Gilliam v. Moore, 44 N. C. 95 (1852); Bowser v. Bowser, 27 Tenn. 23 (1847). The apparent contrariety of Pugh v. Davis, 103 Ala. 316, 18 So. 8 (1895), to this principle can probably be explained by the fact that the Alabama Court does not permit tenants to question titles in actions of unlawful detainer. Ala. Code. Ann. (1940) Tit. 7, §975; Dent v. Stovall, 200 Ala. 193, 75 So. 94 (1917).

112. Breeding's Heirs v. Taylor's Heirs, 52 Ky. 477 (1852).

may attorn to and become the tenant of another claiming to be the owner, thereby bringing into play the estoppel rule.[113]

In Georgia a purchaser of land at a sale under a security deed gave an attorning tenant a warranty to defend the title and possession. The court said that this warranty could be invoked against a claim for rent by the original landlord. The tenant petitioned for an injunction against the claim for rent, alleging an offer to pay the rent money into court and the insolvency of both the original landlord and the purchaser. This petition was held to state proper grounds for equitable intervention.[114]

The application of the estoppel rule is not affected by the fact that the lessee had been in possession at the time of the lease.[115] Neither is it affected by the fact that either or both parties know that the title is in another.[116] Of course the tenant may avoid the estoppel by showing that the tenancy relationship does not exist between the parties.[117] There are indications in at least two opinions that the same could be said where the existence of the tenancy is in dispute.[118] Furthermore, it has been declared in Arkansas that there can be no estoppel where the landlord himself asks or indicates a desire that the title be litigated.[119]

The general rule that a tenant is estopped to deny the title of his landlord is applicable in courts of equity as well as in courts of law.[120] In North Carolina the court allows certain equitable rights to be pleaded in proceedings under the Landlord and Tenant Act. A defendant in such an action is not estopped to show that he holds

113. Bolin v. Drainage District, 206 Ark. 459, 176 S. W. (2d) 143 (1943).

114. South Georgia Trust Co. v. Barlow, 172 Ga. 166, 157 S. E. 326 (1931).

115. Barnett v. Lewis, 194 Ga. 203, 20 S. E. (2d) 912 (1942); Woods v. Garrard, 292 Ky. 233, 138 S. W. (2d) 325 (1940); Bowles v. Gillespie, 212 Ky. 463, 279 S. W. 669 (1926); Saunders v. Moore, 77 Ky. 97 (1878); Patterson v. Hansel, 67 Ky. 654 (1868); Ball v. Lively, 34 Ky. 369 (1836); Boling v. Ewing, 33 Ky. 132 (1835); Locke v. Frasher's Adm'r, 79 Va. 409 (1884).

116. Clark v. Long, 25 Ga. App. 807, 105 S. E. 654 (1921).

117. Stephens v. Stark, 232 Ala. 485, 168 So. 873 (1936); Crim v. Nelms, 78 Ala. 604 (1885); State v. Hutchins, 118 Fla. 220, 158 So. 716 (1935); Garrick v. Tidwell, 151 Ga. 294, 106 S. E. 551 (1921); Wilborn v. Whitfield's Exec'rs, 44 Ga. 51 (1870); Leverette v. Jeffries, 8 Ga. App. 798, 70 S. E. 177 (1911); Stewart v. Keener, 131 N. C. 486, 42 S. E. 933 (1902); Brown v. Grayson, 160 Tenn. 374, 24 S. W. (2d) 894 (1930).

118. Pheland v. Candee, 105 Ala. 235, 16 So. 696 (1894); Conelly v. Rosen, 144 Ark. 442, 222 S. W. 716 (1920).

119. Swift v. Ivory, 147 Ark. 141, 227 S. W. 600 (1921).

120. Bank of New Brockton v. Dunnavant, 204 Ala. 636, 89 So. 105 (1920); Conley's Heirs v. Chiles, 28 Ky. 302 (1831).

under instruments or contracts which make it inequitable for the landlord to take advantage of the estoppel. Therefore, to avoid the necessity of initiating an entirely new proceeding in equity, the defendant is permitted to set up the facts constituting his equitable defense.[121]

However, it is not every equitable right which may be set up in this manner.[122] The court is very unspecific about the kinds of equities the defendant will be allowed to plead, but the cases seem to permit him to plead such defenses when they come about as the result of rights to the property growing out of the contract under which he is supposed to have entered as a tenant. Thus the defendant may show that the true relationship is that of vendor and purchaser,[123] or mortgagor and mortgagee.[124] In one instance the court permitted such a showing to be made where the defendant's claim was based on a contractual right to remove fixtures placed upon the premises during the tenancy.[125] Again, the court evidently considered a claim under a prior deed an equitable defense and permitted the defense to be interposed in a possessory action.[126] The allowance of these equitable defenses does not interfere with the application of the ordinary rules of estoppel where such equities do not exist.[127] Some of these cases involve the jurisdiction of the justices' courts under the Landlord and Tenant Act and not estoppel, but similar treatment is accorded to both.

Some of the other Southeastern states have permitted defenses of this kind to be pleaded in actions under the several Landlord and Tenant Acts. The Kentucky Court has declared that a tenant may prove that he himself has become the owner of the land, either by a voluntary alienation on the part of the landlord or by a coercive sale under execution.[128] In Georgia the alleged tenant may show that the

121. Allen v. Griffin, 98 N. C. 120, 3 S. E. 837 (1887); Turner v. Lowe, 66 N. C. 413 (1872). See also Prudential Ins. Co. v. Totten, 203 N. C. 431, 166 S. E. 316 (1932).

122. Hahn v. Guilford & Lathan, 87 N. C. 172 (1882).

123. Hughes v. Mason, 84 N. C. 472 (1881).

124. Hauser v. Morrison, 146 N. C. 248, 59 S. E. 693 (1907); Forsythe v. Bullock, 74 N. C. 135 (1876).

125. Springs v. Atlantic Refining Co., 205 N. C. 444, 171 S. E. 635 (1933).

126. Allen v. Griffen, 98 N. C. 120, 3 S. E. 837 (1887).

127. Buckhorne Land & Timber Co. v. Yarbrough, 179 N. C. 335, 102 S. E. 630 (1920); Lawrence v. Eller, 169 N. C. 211, 85 S. E. 291 (1915); Davis v. Davis, 83 N. C. 71 (1880).

128. Casey v. Gregory, 52 Ky. 505, 56 Am. Dec. 581 (1852).

contract was one of purchase with provisions added to change the relationship into a tenancy upon a default in the payment of the purchase price.[129] Under a Florida decision the occupant may set up the fact that he is the holder of an option to purchase the land under a contract independent of the lease.[130] The Tennessee court allows the alleged tenant to prove that he is in possession under a parol contract of purchase,[131] and in Georgia he may show a parol gift[132] or a prescriptive right in the land.[133] The Alabama Court has said that the estoppel rule does not apply when the agreement to be a tenant and to pay rent was incident to the same transaction in which equitable rights of the tenant were created.[134]

CONCLUSION

Hence it appears that the courts are getting more and more liberal with respect to the application of the estoppel rule, thus preventing much delay and inconvenience to litigants. The tendency of modern law is to break away from ironclad semiprocedural rules of this kind and to make the practice more flexible. A further liberalization of the estoppel rule is to be expected in future tenancy controversies.

129. Leverette v. Jeffries, 8 Ga. App. 798, 70 S. E. 177 (1911).
130. State v. Hutchins, 118 Fla. 220, 158 So. 716 (1935).
131. Brown v. Grayson, 160 Tenn. 374, 24 S. W. (2d) 894 (1930).
132. Garrick v. Tidwell, 151 Ga. 294, 106 S. E. 551 (1921).
133. Smith v. Wynn, 111 Ga. 884, 36 S. E. 970 (1900), on demurer to defensive cross-action.
134. Holman v. Hall, 248 Ala. 541, 28 So. (2d) 629 (1946).

XI

Emblements—Right to Crops—Manure—
Timber—Estovers—Fixtures

A TENANT enters upon leased premises and lives there for a time which is certain or uncertain depending upon the nature or type of the tenancy contract. While working on the land it is usually his home, and he brings to the place not only his worldly possessions but his urge to create, his desire for survival in this world of formidable competition, and his ambition to better his position, economic and social, among his fellow men. With these purposes in view he brings his abilities to bear upon the task of making a living for himself and those dependent upon his intelligence and industry. To accomplish this he seeks to harvest from the farm the best crop the land is capable of producing. While he often fails for one reason or another to reach that goal, it is very rare for him not to have had at least the desire to do the best job possible under the circumstances. A one-horse farmer may start his crop with a desire for success which is just as great as that of the lessee of a thousand-acre plantation.

The lawmakers should recognize that he brings to the arrangement with the landowner something which should have an importance at least equal to the latter's property rights. Doctrines like that of emblements were developed to guarantee to the tenant the product of his efforts. The particular purpose of the doctrine of emblements is the protection of the tenant in situations where the landlord, for reasons connected with the historical development of the law of real property, had been given a distinct advantage over the tenant. As time went by it became more and more necessary and expedient to find some lawful means of protecting the tenant population from the machinations of profit-seeking and sometimes dishonest landlords. The task has not been completed, but a start has been made toward this goal. The landowners have been on the whole antagonistic toward any changes which would curtail their rights. Therefore it has been difficult to obtain needed reforms.

RIGHTS TO EMBLEMENTS IN GENERAL

A right to "emblements" is the right to the vegetable products or crops grown on the land, not spontaneously, but by the industry and labor of man.[1] In other words, the term has practically the same significance as the term *"fructus industriales."* In a more limited sense it may be used to denote the right of the occupier of land to the "way-going" crop, that is, the crop which is in the ground when the tenancy comes to an end.

The general rule is that a tenant with a lease for a time certain is not entitled to emblements, since he knows at what time the term will end and would be absolutely without right in planting a crop which he knew would not mature in time to harvest by the end of the term.[2] In an early case the North Carolina court held that a tenant from year to year was not entitled to emblements, because at that time the landlord was required to give six months' notice in order to terminate this tenancy effectively, and therefore the tenant would be given sufficient notice of the end of his interest in the land to prevent the application of the reason of the rule giving the right to emblements.[3] However, in some states, including North Carolina, the period of notice to terminate a tenancy from year to year has been shortened,[4] and under these circumstances the tenant would not know that the tenancy was coming to an end in time to keep him from planting a crop which would mature after the tenancy had been terminated by the landlord. Therefore, where such is the case, the tenant should be allowed to claim the right to emblements.

Under this reasoning a tenant at will whose estate had been terminated by the landlord would clearly be entitled to emblements,[5] and the same applies to any other tenancy where the interest of the lessee has been put an end to without his fault or desire.[6] However, where the tenancy is terminated by the act of the lessee or because of some failure on his part to live up to the terms of the contract,

1. McClain v. Gilbert, 30 Ala. App. 261, 4 So. (2d) 203 (1941).
2. Huckaby v. Walker, 141 Ark. 477, 217 S. W. 481 (1920); Sanders v. Ellington, 77 N. C. 255 (1877); Mason v. Moyers, 2 Rob. 606 (Va., 1844). See also Florala Sawmill Co. v. Parrish, 155 Ala. 462, 46 So. 461 (1908).
3. Sanders v. Ellington, 77 N. C. 255 (1877).
4. See Ch. 6, Notes 18-25.
5. Buchmann v. Callahan, 222 Ala. 240, 131 So. 799 (1931); Humphries v. Humphries, 25 N. C. 362 (1843).
6. Price v. Pickett, 21 Ala. 741 (1852); Dollar v. Roddenbury, 97 Ga. 148, 25 S. E. 410 (1895).

then his claim for emblements should not be allowed.[7] After the tenancy at will has been terminated, a tenant having a valid claim to emblements is entitled to the privilege of ingress to and egress from the land for purposes of cultivating and harvesting the crops.[8]

With respect to a tenancy terminating at a certain time, it is clear that the tenant should not be allowed to claim emblements where there is an immature crop when the term ends.[9] Where the crop is mature, however, there seems to be a difference of opinion. In this situation the courts of Alabama [10] and Mississippi [11] have held that the tenant should be given a reasonable time after the term ends to remove the crop. According to the Alabama decision, weather conditions and opportunity for removal will be taken into consideration in the computation of this reasonable time. However, this doctrine with respect to mature crops has been repudiated by the courts in Arkansas [12] and North Carolina,[13] the latter in a case where the tenant was prevented from harvesting the crop by a heavy snow. The Arkansas court intimated that the situation might be changed by sufficient proof of local custom, but this proposition seems to have been repudiated in a case from Virginia.[14] In fact there seems to be a general rule of law that a custom cannot be used to contradict an absolute right conferred by state law. In one Georgia case [15] a tenant introduced a local custom to the effect that tenants were permitted to gather mature crops after the expiration of the term. His opponent argued that the right to the crops was specifically denied by a particular statute,[16] which, if applicable, would certainly seem to deny this right. The court ruled, however, that this statute was applicable only to the peculiar Georgia estate for years [17] and not to the relationship of landlord and tenant. Since there was no specific rule of law contradicting the tenant's right to the crops, the court held that proof of the custom was admissible.

7. Lingerfelt v. Gibson, 161 Tenn. 477, 32 S. W. (2d) 1047 (1930).
8. Buchmann v. Callahan, 222 Ala. 240, 131 So. 799 (1931); Humphries v. Humphries, 25 N. C. 362 (1843).
9. Harris v. Carson, 7 Leigh 632 (Va., 1836).
10. McClain v. Gilbert, 30 Ala. App. 261, 4 So. (2d) 203 (1941).
11. Opperman v. Littlejohn, 98 Miss. 636, 54 So. 77 (1911).
12. Huckaby v. Walker, 141 Ark. 477, 217 S. W. 481 (1920).
13. Sanders v. Ellington, 77 N. C. 255 (1877).
14. Harris v. Carson, 7 Leigh 632 (Va., 1836).
15. Carter v. Booth, 25 Ga. App. 796, 104 S. E. 910 (1920).
16. Ga. Code (1933) §85-804.
17. See Ch. 3, Note 143.

Unless they are specifically excepted in the lease contract, a tenant is entitled to the unmatured vegetable products or crops growing on the land at the time when the agreement goes into effect.[18] The same seems to be true of the fruit of the trees on the rented premises ripening during the term.[19]

In an early Alabama case [20] it is said that at common law a distinction is drawn between the right to emblements and the cost of preparing the ground for the planting of the seed. Hence if the tenancy was terminated before the actual planting of all the land, the tenant could claim the right to emblements only with respect to those crops which were seeded before the happening of the uncertain event which terminated the estate.

An interesting situation is presented where a tenant abandons the leased premises to the landlord before the expiration of his term, leaving a growing crop on the land. In this situation no right nor interest remains in the tenant. The abandonment amounts to a surrender upon the landlord's re-entry, and the right of property in the crop passes to the landlord as an incident to the restoration of possession and the termination of the tenancy.[21]

A Tennessee tenant, occupying premises under a lease for an indefinite period, sowed a crop of oats in the autumn, harvested it in the spring, and then plowed in the stubble to get a new crop for the next year. A short time after the plowing his tenancy was terminated without reservation or objection on his part. In the spring of the following year he claimed the right to harvest the crop which had grown as a result of plowing in the stubble. The court denied him this right, declaring that plowing in the stubble was not equivalent to growing a new crop, though it had produced a similar result.[22]

In a Mississippi case [23] it has been said that the doctrine of emblements has no application as between a person claiming title to land which was actually owned by the United States government and an occupant who had taken possession under a contract of lease, because neither party had any right to the land or the crops under a contract which was illegal.

18. Friskkorn v. Ogden, 16 Ala. App. 358, 77 So. 970 (1918).
19. Quiggle v. Vining, 125 Ga. 98, 54 S. E. 74 (1906).
20. Price v. Pickett, 21 Ala. 741 (1852).
21. Shahan v. Herzberg, Simpson & Co., 73 Ala. 59 (1882).
22. Hendrixson v. Cardwell, 68 Tenn. 389, 40 Am. Rep. 396 (1876).
23. Ellis v. Sutton, 126 Miss. 102, 88 So. 519 (1921).

RIGHT OF LIFE TENANT'S LESSEE TO EMBLEMENTS

According to the common law, the estate of a life tenant terminated at his death, subject to the lessee's right to emblements, which included all crops planted or seeded before the termination of the life estate, but not those sowed after the particular estate came to an end.[24] Even though the tenant had plowed and fertilized the land, upon being ousted he was not entitled to emblements and lost the labor and materials which had gone into these preparatory stages of the farming enterprise.[25] Under this state of the law he could be thrown out of his rented home and nothing could be done about it. There was no provision for the apportionment of the landlord's share of the project, whether it was a share of the crop or money rent, between the estate of the life tenant and the remainderman. Hence a movement developed in many quarters for legislation which would remedy these difficulties and inequalities.

Eight of the Southeastern states have enacted statutes [26] in which some attempt has been made to apportion the rent between the life tenant's estate and the remainderman. In another state, Georgia, the statute [27] seems merely to guarantee to the tenant the right to remain in possession of the land until the end of the year in which the life estate terminates, along with the right to emblements, there being no specific mention of the apportionment of the rent. In its interpretation of the law, however, the Georgia Court of Appeals seems to have adopted the principle of apportionment. In the leading case [28] a life tenant died without collecting the rent or doing any act to which the law would give the effect of a collection. The court declared that the lessee, who was entitled under the statute to hold the premises until the end of the year, was accountable to the remainderman for such a proportion of the rent as the interval between the life tenant's death and the end of the year bore to the entire year. It was further said that if the life tenant had taken a

24. See Price v. Pickett, 21 Ala. 741 (1852); Hays v. Wrenn, 167 N. C. 229, 83 S. E. 356 (1914); King v. Foscue, 91 N. C. 116 (1884); Thompson v. Thompson, 6 Munf. 514 (Va., 1820).

25. Price v. Pickett, 21 Ala. 741 (1852).

26. Ala. Code (1940) tit. 31, §14; Ark. Dig. Stat. (Pope, 1937) §8579; Ky. Rev. Stat. (Cullen, 1946) §§383.190, 395.350, 395.360; Miss. Code Ann. (1942) §901; N. C. Gen. Stat. (1943) §42-7; S. C. Code Ann. (1932) §§8797-99; Tenn. Code Ann. (Williams, 1934) §§8406-07; Va. Code Ann. (Michie, 1942) §§5543.

27. Ga. Code (1933) §§85-606, 85-607.

28. Butt v. Story, 5 Ga. App. 540, 63 S. E. 658 (1909).

negotiable promissory note for the year's rent and transferred it for value to a third person, this would be equivalent to payment. The lessee could then claim the benefit of a satisfaction of the indebtedness as against the remainderman. On the other hand, it was said that the taking of a non-negotiable note, though it had been assigned, would not necessarily be equivalent to a satisfaction of the debt, for the assignee would hold it subject to the existing equities between the two original parties. The note in the instant case was found to be non-negotiable, and the court corrected its own erroneous impression in an earlier hearing that the note was a negotiable one. In this former hearing [29] the court declared that the life tenant had been the agent of the remainderman with respect to the lease and that therefore the latter was bound by the contract. The lessee would have a correlative duty to comply with the terms of the agreement. If he performed his obligations in a satisfactory manner and paid the rent, which the court later found he had not done, he could not then be held accountable to the remainderman, though the life tenant died before the crop was sown. The remainderman could no doubt obtain satisfaction from the estate of the life tenant.

A life tenant in another Georgia case [30] rented land for a year to a lessee who was also the remainderman, taking a negotiable promissory note for the rent. He transferred the note to a third person for value and afterwards died during the term without collecting any of the rent. The note had been transferred to secure the payment of indebtedness which the life tenant owed the transferee. In this situation the transferee could recover the amount of the debt, accounting to the remainderman for the excess. Furthermore, the lessee was said to have the right to show these facts, with the result that recovery should be limited to the actual amount of the indebtedness.

A somewhat similar case [31] arose in Alabama when a life tenant leased her interest to the remainderman for certain annual installments, payable during her lifetime. Upon the death of the life tenant, the remainderman was held liable for a just proportion of the annual rent for the year in which the life tenant died.

As late as 1900 a Tennessee court [32] recognized the distinction

29. Story v. Butt, 2 Ga. App. 119, 58 S. E. 388 (1907).
30. Michell v. Rutherford, 9 Ga. App. 722, 72 S. E. 302 (1911).
31. Saint v. Britnell, 206 Ala. 533, 91 So. 310 (1921).
32. Collins v. Crownover, 57 S. W. 357 (Tenn. Chan. App., 1900).

between lands actually planted before the termination of the life estate and those which were only prepared for planting and cultivation. The fact that an interest may be retained by the lessee after the death of the life tenant because of the doctrine of emblements will give the lessee no right to retain other portions of the premises which are included in the lease but are not planted before the life tenant's death. In such instances the apportionment statute does not authorize a lease to extend beyond the life estate, and a right to recover rents due upon the termination of the life interest is the only right possessed by the life tenant's personal representative. In another case[33] it was held that the remainderman was entitled either to disaffirm the lease contract or to ratify it and share the rent *pro tanto*. In this instance the remainderman sought to recover possession of the land and also damages or compensation for use and occupation. Since there was no ratification of the lease, the lessees were entitled to emblements, consisting of the yearly crop of grain which had required an outlay of labor and industry, without payment of any compensation for the use of the land in harvesting the crops. In a much earlier case[34] a husband had a life estate in his wife's lands during coverture and had rented them to another for a year. Upon the husband's death the court ruled that the widow at once became entitled to the rents; and, if the husband's personal representative had collected the rents which accrued after his death, the representative would then be liable to the widow therefor.

The Kentucky court has remarked that the lessee's right of possession under a contract with a life tenant would terminate upon the latter's death.[35] However, the statutes provide that if the life tenant dies after March 1, the lessee may remain on the premises until the end of the year. He is also given the right to claim emblements. Furthermore, the principle of apportionment is clearly recognized. In one situation a life tenant permitted his lessee to sow a field of wheat, each party agreeing to furnish one-half of the fertilizer. According to the contract, the crop would be equally divided between them after it was threshed. The life tenant died during the year's term. After deducting the value of the seed supplied by the life tenant before his death, the court apportioned the remainder of the one-half share of the crop payable as rent between the personal representative

33. Turner v. Turner, 132 Tenn. 592, 179 S. W. 132 (1915).
34. Arnold v. Hodges' Adm'r, 29 Tenn. 38 (1849).
35. Avey v. Hogancamp, 172 Ky. 675, 189 S. W. 917 (1916).

and the remainderman.[36] The amount to which the representative is entitled is in proportion to the time the life tenant lived after the term began.[37]

In North Carolina the statute [38] continues the lease to the end of the current year in order to enable the lessee to gather his crop, and the remainderman is entitled to a part of the rent proportionate to the part of the year elapsing after the life tenant's death.[39] In one instance a life tenant rented the land, and the lessee sublet it at a much higher rate. Upon the life tenant's death during the year's term, the court ruled that the remainderman could take only a proportionate part of the rent reserved in the lease contract and was not entitled to a proportionate part of the rent actually paid by the subtenant.[40] It is evident that the lease is continued to the end of the year in lieu of emblements.[41]

A South Carolina statute [42] provides that upon the death of a person holding a life interest in land after March 1 in any given year, the crops grown on land occupied by the deceased will be assets in the hands of his administrators. The date was evidently picked because the growing season begins at about that time. Under this statute it was held in an early case [43] that the lessee's possession of land leased from a life tenant could not be disturbed if the latter died after March 1, the lessee being required to secure to the remainderman that proportion of the rent accruing after the death of the life tenant. The South Carolina apportionment statute [44] authorizes a distribution to the interested parties, the personal representative of the life tenant and the remainderman. It provides further that the lessee, who cannot be dispossessed until the end of the crop year, shall secure the payment of the rent when it comes due. Under this portion of the act it has been held that the remainderman is entitled to compel the lessee to secure the payment of the rent for the unexpired portion of the year.[45]

36. Redmon v. Bedford, 80 Ky. 13 (1882).
37. Haynes v. Harris, 14 Ky. Law Rep. 303 (1893).
38. N. C. Gen. Stat. (1943) §42-7.
39. King v. Foscue, 91 N. C. 116 (1884).
40. Hays v. Wrenn, 167 N. C. 229, 83 S. W. 356 (1914).
41. Hays v. Wrenn, 167 N. C. 229, 83 S. E. 356 (1914); King v. Foscue, 91 N. C. 116 (1884).
42. S. C. Code Ann. (Michie, 1942) §8996.
43. Freeman v. Tompkins, 1 Strob. Eq. 53 (S. C., 1846).
44. S. C. Code Ann. (Michie, 1932) §§8797-99.
45. May v. Thomas, 94 S. C. 158, 78 S. E. 85 (1913).

In a case decided under both statutes a husband, in the right of his wife, rented out her lands for a year, reserving six acres which he had decided to cultivate himself. The wife died on March 9, thus terminating her life interest in the lands. Applying these statutes, it was held that the rent owing by the lessee immediately became the property of the remainderman and the personal representative of the life tenant. The remainderman would have to look for remuneration to the lessee, and not to the husband, who had no control of the crops or responsibility for the rent. The ninth of March would be the dividing line for the apportionment. In respect to the six acres which were not leased but cultivated by the husband in the right of the wife, the crops raised thereon would then be assets in the hands of the life tenant's executors or administrators, they, in preference to the remainderman, being entitled to both lands and crops for the rest of the year. The court declared that a planting by March 1 was not essential to the exercise of this right by the personal representatives.[46] It was also held that the statute [47] providing for double rent where a party in possession refuses to surrender to the landlord at the termination of the tenancy would not apply to the situation presented here.

Somewhat similar problems arise under the Kentucky statutes.[48] An apportionment is decreed, and if the life tenant dies after March 1, the lessee is permitted to remain on the land until the end of the year. It is stated that the emblements of a person dying after this date shall be assets in the hands of his personal representative; but, if the death occurs before March 1, the emblements growing on the lands shall pass to the remainderman. Applying this to the situation where a life tenant leases the property and then dies, it probably means nothing more than a simple apportionment of the landlord's share of the crop according to the provisions of the law. To establish his claim, however, the personal representative must show, not only that his deceased principal had died after March 1, but also that the crops had been severed before the last day of the following December. In one case the assignee of a third person's life estate under an instrument executed in September, 1903, made a contract to lease the land to a tenant for a term of one year beginning the following March. A month later, in October, the life tenant

46. Newton v. Odom, 67 S. C. 1, 45 S. E. 105 (1903).
47. S. C. Code Ann. (Michie, 1942) §8800.
48. Ky. Rev. Stat. (Cullen, 1946) §§383.190, 395.340, 395.350, 395.360.

died. Previous to that event, although his term had not begun, the prospective tenant took possession of the land and planted a crop of wheat. Ignoring the fact that he had entered before the lease had gone into effect, the court decided that, although the life tenant had died after March 1 of the year the crop was planted, the tenant could claim no right to emblements under the statute because the wheat would not mature and hence could not be severed by the last day of December.[49] It seems impossible to explain why the court ignored the fact that the tenant had no right on the land until the following March. It may be that the court was merely taking this opportunity to interpret the statute, since the decision was going against the tenant anyway.

In an Alabama case, possession of previously leased property was taken by a grantee of the life tenant, who had taken a rent note from the lessee prior to the transfer and assigned it to a third person, to whom the lessee had actually paid the rent. Upon the death of the life tenant during the year for which the note was given, the remainderman sued the grantee of the life interest for the rent of the land. It was held that the remainderman was not entitled to recover.[50] The issue as to whether he could recover from the lessee was not presented by the record. The Alabama statute gives the personal representative the right to recover whatever rent is due at the time of the life tenant's death; but, where the life estate terminates before the rent is due, an apportionment is in order. This apportionment statute does not have the effect of creating a tenancy relationship between the remainderman and the life tenant's lessee.[51] The statutes of Arkansas [52] and Mississippi [53] closely resemble the Alabama law.

The Virginia statute [54] allows the lessee to remain on the land and apportions the rent between the representative of the life tenant and the remainderman. If the rent is payable in kind, however, it must be paid to the personal representative; and he, in turn, is required to pay a reasonable money rent to the remainderman for the period between the death of the life tenant and the end of the cur-

49. Devers v. May, 124 Ky. 387, 99 S. W. 255 (1907).
50. Terrell v. Reeves, 103 Ala. 264, 16 So. 54 (1894).
51. Jones v. Scott, 249 Ala. 336, 31 So. (2d) 361 (1947).
52. Ark. Dig. Stat. (Pope, 1937) §8579, construed in Smithwick v. Oliver, 94 Ark. 451, 127 S. W. 706 (1910).
53. Miss. Code Ann. (1942) §§901-902.
54. Va. Code Ann. (Michie, 1936) §5543.

rent year. This sum is a preferred charge on the rent in kind received from the lessee by the personal representative. The provision concerning the payment of a reasonable rent to the remainderman merely confirms the holding of the Virginia court in an early case, decided under the common law, that such a sum could be recovered by the remainderman.[55]

Generally, it may be said that the problems arising under these statutes have been effectively dealt with by the courts. The injustices of the common law have been eradicated to a great extent, and the rights of the parties marked out and clarified. Perhaps the term "emblements," when used in these laws, should be given a more positive definition. Nothing so important as the principle of apportionment should be left to judicial interpretation, as was done by the Georgia legislators. All future legislative efforts along this line should be drafted with these defects in mind.

DISPOSITION OF TENANT'S CROPS WHERE
OWNERSHIP OF LAND IS TRANSFERRED

What is the desirable result where a tenant has raised a crop or is in the process of raising one on rented land transferred to a new owner during the term of the lease? Some very interesting problems have arisen where such transfers of leased property have been made. The conveyances may be either voluntary or involuntary, and the crop may be either mature or immature at the time of the transfer.

Sometimes a tenant is in possession of leased land which is sold at an execution sale pursuant to a judgment against the landlord, or under a power of sale contained in a security deed. Where the tenant's crop has matured before the sale, the courts of Louisiana,[56] Mississippi,[57] and North Carolina [58] have decided the issue in respect to the produce in favor of the tenant and against the transferee at the sale. By statute in Mississippi [59] a defaulting vendee under a contract of purchase, or a mortgagor after foreclosure under a power of sale in a security deed, is given the right to crops planted by him and grown or growing on the land at the commencement of the forfeiture or foreclosure suit. He is also given the right to enter after eviction in order that he may complete cultivation, gather, and re-

55. Thompson v. Thompson, 6 Munf. 514 (Va., 1820).
56. Porche v. Bodin, 28 La. Ann. 761 (1876).
57. Wood v. Pace, 164 Miss. 187, 143 So. 471 (1932).
58. Dail v. Freeman, 92 N. C. 351 (1885).
59. Miss. Code Ann. (1942) §§1045, 1056.

move the crops, but it is provided that he must pay a reasonable compensation for the use of the land. Moreover, the Mississippi Court has declared that prior to the foreclosure sale the mortgagee has no interest in the land, except the lien of the security deed.[60]

With respect to a growing and immature crop, the Georgia court has held that the tenant's claim is superior to the right of a purchaser of the landlord's interest at an execution sale.[61] The same result was reached in a somewhat similar case in which the landlord's property had been sold under the power contained in a security deed of earlier date than the Georgia statute[62] which declares that growing crops are personalty. It is evident that the crops were considered as real property, and yet this was not allowed to influence the decision of the court, which was in favor of the tenant.[63] The argument in favor of this position is that the purchaser should not acquire any greater interest than the landlord or mortgagor had at the time of the sale. To give the purchaser the growing crops under these circumstances would amount to an unjust enrichment at the expense of a person who was innocent of any wrong.

The opposing view is that an unmatured crop is real property, that it is transferred with the land at the sale under the security deed, and that the doctrine of emblements does not apply in such cases. The Tennessee[64] and Virginia[65] courts have taken this view of the matter, and a similar result has been reached at a rehearing before an appellate court in Louisiana. Here the court had decided in favor of the tenant at the original hearing on the basis of reasoning which is very similar to that employed by the Georgia courts.[66] The argument used at the rehearing was based on constructive notice of prior encumbrances on everything attached to the mortgaged realty, such notice being supplied by the records.

In taking its stand against the tenant the Tennessee court[67] used the dubious argument that the tenant stood in the shoes of the mortgagor-landlord and was bound by the latter's act in permitting default. Such a view imputes the failure or negligence of another to the tenant, who certainly has no means of controlling his action or

60. Wood v. Pace, 164 Miss. 187, 143 So. 471 (1932).
61. Dollar v. Roddenbury, 97 Ga. 148, 25 S. E. 410 (1895).
62. Ga. Acts 1922, p. 114, now Ga. Code (1933) §85-1901.
63. Chason v. O'Neal, 158 Ga. 725, 124 S. E. 519 (1924).
64. Lingerfelt v. Gibson, 161 Tenn. 477, 32 S. W. (2d) 1047 (1930).
65. Armour Fertilizer Works v. Taylor, 129 Va. 1, 105 S. E. 574 (1921).
66. Deville v. Couvillion, 5 La. App. 519 (1926).
67. Lingerfelt v. Gibson, *supra* Note 64.

nonaction in this situation. As a practical matter this decision would force every tenant into a situation where it would not be safe for him to lease farm land on which there is a recorded mortgage and would throw upon him the burden of having the record examined, a task requiring the technical skill of an attorney. Tenants in the South are not sufficiently educated to understand the problems presented, and few of them would be able to bear the burden of the expense.

The holder of an agricultural lien on the tenant's crop is in the same position as the tenant with respect to the matters just discussed and can claim only what the tenant can.[68]

Even under the Georgia rule, the purchaser at the foreclosure or execution sale is entitled to a landlord's lien on the tenant's crop. In the situation where there has been an agreement without consideration between the original landlord and tenant to the effect that no rent shall be paid, this pact does not bind the purchaser, and he is entitled to a reasonable sum as compensation for the use of the land.[69] In this case the arrangement was made by the insolvent original landowner with the idea of defrauding creditors.

A recent case from Kentucky presents an interesting sidelight with respect to this matter of the right to crops on land which is changing hands. In this instance a landowner had sown a certain portion of his acreage in grain and straw in the fall of the year. The next February he leased to a tenant all such land as would be "available for producing crops." Later the landowner harvested the grain and straw at his own expense and paid the tenant for the sacking and hauling. Here the court held that the tenant could claim no interest in these crops, which were evidently not meant to be included within the scope of the tenancy agreement.[70]

PROPERTY CLASSIFICATION OF GROWING CROPS

At common law a growing crop, before its severance from the land, was considered as a part of the realty. This is true in spite of remarks to the contrary in two Tennessee cases.[71] In Arkansas it has been declared that crops may be levied upon in execution, and the

68. Dail v. Freeman, 92 N. C. 351 (1885); Armour Fertilizer Works v. Taylor, 129 Va. 1, 105 S. E. 574 (1921).
69. Chason v. O'Neal, 158 Ga. 725, 124 S. E. 519 (1924).
70. McHargue v. Conrad, 312 Ky. 434, 227 S. W. (2d) 977 (1950).
71. Langford v. Hudson, 146 Tenn. 309, 241 S. W. 393 (1922); Edwards v. Thompson, 85 Tenn. 720, 4 S. W. 913 (1887).

inference is that this may be done whether they be mature or immature.[72] Under Georgia laws, however, while matured crops may be levied upon, it is not proper to allow a levy to be made upon crops which have not reached maturity.[73] In fact a court in this state has held [74] that immature crops cannot be levied upon, even though a statute [75] provided that all crops, mature or immature, were to be considered as personal property. Before the enactment of this statute in 1922 [76] it had been held that a deed to land passed title to the crops, mature or immature, to the transferee.[77] In Tennessee the distinction between mature and immature crops in respect to execution seems to have been recognized at a rather early date.[78] Under the statute in effect today [79] a levy may be made on the growing crop, but not until the fifteenth of November following maturity, and then only subject to the landlord's lien. However, if the owner of the crop absconds or conceals himself, the levy may be made at any time.

In Louisiana standing or growing crops and fruit on trees are, before severance, to be considered as part of the realty or immovable property; but, when severed, they become movables.[80] In South Carolina unsevered crops are regarded as a part of the realty, with certain statutory exceptions. It has been held here that an action of claim and delivery, which is designed to recover personalty, will not lie for the purpose of obtaining possession of ungathered produce.[81]

It is a commonly accepted principle that real property cannot be the subject of larceny. The Alabama Court has approved this view of the law but has declared that, after severance of a growing crop,

72. Munson v. Wade, 174 Ark. 880, 298 S. W. 25 (1927).
73. Hester v. Shrouder, 64 Ga. App. 572, 13 S. E. (2d) 875 (1941); Barnesville Bank v. Ingram, 34 Ga. App. 269, 129 S. E. 112 (1925).
74. Barnesville Bank v. Ingram, *supra* Note 73.
75. Ga. Code (1933) §85-1901.
76. Ga. Acts 1922, p. 114.
77. Here the purchaser of the land was the tenant himself, but the language of the court would seem to include any purchaser within the scope of the decision. The dissenting judge seemed to consider the portion of the crop due the landlord as a *chose in action* and hence as personalty which would not pass with the land. Newton County v. Boyd, 148 Ga. 761, 98 S. E. 347 (1919).
78. Edwards v. Thompson, 85 Tenn. 720, 4 S. E. 913 (1887).
79. Tenn. Code Ann. (Williams, 1934) §8894.
80. La. Civ. Code Ann. (Dart, 1932) Art. 465. See Porche v. Bodin, 28 La. Ann. 761 (1879); Colligan v. Benoit, 13 La. App. 612, 128 So. 688 (1930).
81. Norwood v. Carter, 176 S. C. 472, 180 S. E. 453 (1935).

larceny may be committed by an act which is independent of the original severance.[82] In an effort to improve the law in this respect, several of the Southeastern states have made the taking of growing crops with felonious intent a specific statutory crime, sometimes termed larcency and sometimes something else.[83]

Hence a general movement is seen away from the common law notion that growing crops were to be considered as real property. It is believed that this movement will continue and that the day will come when the products of a farmer's arduous toil are no longer so considered for all purposes.

MANURE

The general rule is that manure from the droppings of animals becomes an accretion to the realty and cannot be removed by the tenant at the termination of the lease. In fact the courts of four Southeastern states, Georgia,[84] Kentucky,[85] Mississippi,[86] and South Carolina,[87] have so held. North Carolina seems to be the only state in this section of the country which holds that the tenant is entitled to the manure, and in so deciding it has taken the position that a trespass was not committed where, in the process of removal, it became necessary to rake up a small amount of dirt with the manure. In the case [88] in which this position was taken the court declared that the lessee would lose his right to the manure if he left the farm without removing it. An agreement had been made that the lessee might carry away everything that he brought on the premises. In this situation it might be possible to argue that since the lessee had brought the animals on the property, he would be entitled to the excretions from their bodies. This is a rather weak argument, how-

82. Adams v. State, 159 Ala. 115, 48 So. 795 (1909).

83. Mississippi and North Carolina term it larceny. Miss. Code Ann. (1942) §2246; N. C. Gen. Stat. (1943) §14-78. In South Carolina it is called a misdemeanor. S. C. Code Ann. (Michie, 1942) §1172. Florida penalizes the taking of crops from the land and does not mention the crime's classification. Fla. Stat. Ann. (1941) §821-12. This statute, however, has been held not to shield the culprit from prosecution for larceny where circumstances would warrant such action. McKenna v. State, 119 Fla. 576, 161 So. 561 (1934).

84. Brigham v. Overstreet, 128 Ga. 447, 57 S. E. 484 (1907); Hammond v. Driver, 30 Ga. App. 216, 117 S. E. 264 (1923).

85. Stuart v. Clements, 186 Ky. 9, 216 S. W. 136 (1919).

86. Williams v. Gardner, 157 Miss. 252, 128 So. 111 (1930).

87. Roberts v. Jones, 71 S. C. 404, 51 S. E. 240 (1905).

88. Smithwick v. Ellison, 24 N. C. 326 (1842).

ever, and it does not appear that this agreement influenced the court in its decision.

The general rule that the landlord is entitled to the manure does not seem to be applicable where there is a local custom to the contrary. An existing local custom of this sort has been held to have been incorporated into lease contracts by implication.[89]

The tenant's right to remove manure is an exceptional right, and hence it can hardly be said that the landlord's vendee would be charged with notice that the right existed, there being nothing to bring the matter to his attention. In a state where the general rule with respect to manure prevails, the right to remove it, however derived, cannot be said to be binding on someone who does not know of its existence. Therefore, a Georgia court has held that a vendee in this position cannot be bound and is entitled to maintain an action against the tenant for the removal of the manure.[90] In Mississippi it was shown that certain manure had accumulated from the droppings from stock owned by a lessee and fed from foodstuffs produced by him on other lands. This manure had been kept separate from other manure dropped by the lessor's stock which had been loaned to the lessee to make the crop. The court held that these circumstances made no difference, and that the general rule that the lessor is entitled to the manure would prevail.[91]

RIGHTS TO TIMBER AND ESTOVERS

With respect to the timber on leased land, it seems to be generally recognized in the Southeastern states that trees and underbrush may be removed by a lessee who wishes to clear the land for purposes of cultivation.[92] The farm lessee is also entitled to estovers, the right to cut timber for purposes of general farm maintenance, including certain specific uses such as firewood and the repairing of fences and buildings.[93]

A tenant may sell the timber which he has cut in the process of clearing and cultivating rented lands and may apply the proceeds

89. Stuart v. Clements, 186 Ky. 9, 216 S. W. 136 (1919).
90. Hammond v. Driver, 30 Ga. App. 216, 117 S. E. 264 (1923).
91. Williams v. Gardner, 157 Miss. 252, 128 So. 111 (1930).
92. Higgins v. State, 58 Ga. App. 480, 199 S. E. 158 (1938); Moss Point Lumber Co. v. Board of Supervisors, 89 Miss. 448, 42 So. 290 (1906); Ward v. Sheppard, 3 N. C. 283 (1803).
93. Field v. Jones Mercantile Co., 182 Ga. 142, 184 S. E. 882 (1936); Higgins v. State, 58 Ga. App. 480, 199 S. E. 158 (1938); Loudon v. Warfield, 28 Ky. 196 (1830).

to his own use, provided that the cutting can be shown to have been good husbandry.[94] However, he must leave enough timber on the land to supply the needs of the holder of the reversionary interest or future tenants.[95] The tenant must not cut timber merely for purposes of sale for profit.[96] This cutting of timber for commercial purposes has been held to constitute waste,[97] and a tenant who has threatened to take such action may be enjoined from doing so.[98]

An Alabama statute[99] places a certain penalty upon the cutting of designated species of trees and a lesser penalty upon the severance of trees of other types. This statute has been interpreted to penalize the cutting of trees by a tenant on leased land.[100] A tenant is liable under the statute unless authority for the destruction of the trees is contained in the lease contract or is to be implied therefrom.[101] Even where he is given the right to cut the timber in the process of cultivation, he cannot cut and sell timber from other portions of the property which he is not clearing; and anyone claiming under him is subject to the same disability.[102] The landlord not being in possession, an action of trespass is not maintainable against the tenant; and the proper remedy, none being specifically provided by the statute itself, is an action of debt or an action for the conversion of the logs after severance.[103]

The general rule is that after severance the timber becomes personal property, and that anyone who converts the logs to his own use with felonious intent is guilty of larceny.[104]

94. See Higgins v. State, 58 Ga. App. 480, 199 S. E. 158 (1938); Board of Supervisors v. Gans, 80 Miss. 76, 31 So. 539 (1901).

95. Moss Point Lumber Co. v. Board of Supervisors, 89 Miss. 448, 42 So. 290 (1906); Board of Supervisors v. Gans, 80 Miss. 76, 31 So. 539 (1901).

96. Higgins v. State, 58 Ga. App. 480, 199 S. E. 158 (1938); Loudon v. Warfield, 28 Ky. 196 (1830); Board of Supervisors v. Gans, 80 Miss. 76, 31 So. 539 (1901); Ward v. Sheppard, 3 N. C. 283 (1803).

97. Moss Point Lumber Co. v. Board of Supervisors, 89 Miss. 448, 42 So. 290 (1906); Ward v. Sheppard, 3 N. C. 283 (1803).

98. Loudon v. Warfield, 28 Ky. 196 (1830).

99. Ala. Code (1940) tit. 47, §272.

100. Garrett v. Berry, 205 Ala. 309, 87 So. 340 (1921); Ladd v. Shattock, 90 Ala. 134, 7 So. 764 (1890).

101. Garrett v. Berry, 205 Ala. 309, 87 So. 340 (1921).

102. Ladd v. Shattock, 90 Ala. 134, 7 So. 764 (1890).

103. Rodgers v. Brooks, 99 Ala. 31, 11 So. 753 (1892), 101 Ala. 111, 13 So. 386 (1893).

104. Higgins v. State, 58 Ga. App. 480, 199 S. E. 158 (1939).

FARM FIXTURES

The usual rules of law concerning fixtures are applicable in farm tenancy cases. Of the few instances where questions with respect to farm fixtures have arisen in the Southeastern states, it may be said that the intention of the tenant in affixing the buildings or appliances on the land is controlling. In one instance a landowner had installed a sugar cane mill, a sugar boiler, an old boiler to be used as a watering place for stock, a storehouse with shelves fastened and nailed to the wall, a large meat box, and several heavy tables and counters. Afterwards he lost the land and became a tenant of the premises. These appliances having been placed upon the land while he was the owner, the right of property in them was held to have been transferred along with the land, and no removal was permitted.[105] Where the appliances are brought upon the land by the tenant with the idea of increasing the production of the farm and with the definite intention of removal at the termination of the lease, they are to be considered as well within the category of "trade fixtures," and hence removable at that time. This has been held to be true with respect to farm buildings in Mississippi [106] and poultry houses and fences in North Carolina.[107] However, where Arkansas tenants, without consulting the landlord, moved a house onto farm land to be used to facilitate sawmill work, and then failed to remove the building after the sawmill had served its purpose, the court held that the landlord was justified in acting upon the assumption that the tenants did not expect to claim the house as their own.[108]

CONCLUSION

The material presented has shown that many controversies develop over things which are grown or placed upon or attached to leased land in the course of the tenant's farming operations. On the whole it may be said that the rules of law herein stated represent a practicable and, in most instances, a fair treatment of the legal problems involved.

105. Brigham v. Overstreet, 128 Ga. 447, 57 S. E. 484 (1907).
106. Waldauer v. Parks, 141 Miss. 617, 106 So. 881 (1926).
107. Causey v. Orton, 171 N. C. 375, 88 S. E. 513 (1916).
108. Pearce v. Williamson & Caldwell, 216 Ark. 413, 208 S. W. (2d) 8 (1947).

XII

Improvements and Repairs

THE law concerning improvements and repairs made by tenants on leased land, growing as it did out of the feudal system, is to a certain extent archaic. It cannot be said to have been framed with the idea of protecting the interest of the tenant with as much exactness as it does the interest of the landlord. One of the chief reasons for this is that for a long while the landed aristocracy of both England and America was greatly influential in the governments of the respective countries. Only in the last century has the right to vote been freed from all property qualifications. The landed gentry were not well disposed toward legislation which would limit their rights in respect to their relations with the tenants who were one of their most important sources of labor and income. Progress is rather difficult for the proponents of reform legislation when they are met with the opposition of the owners of large estates, who are a powerful and influential group in any Southern legislature. These landlords are not disposed to favor legislation curtailing their rights and privileges. Some of the more conservative members of this group are very likely to take the view that any interference with the legal *status quo* is an attempt to hurt their financial interests.

These people are not cognizant of the true purpose of reform legislation and fail to realize that a tenant who can claim compensation for improvements will work much harder to improve the land and appurtenances than one who knows that he will be deprived of the fruits of his labor when the lease expires. This is particularly true of short-term leases. It is but human that a tenant who is going to be ousted or has no assurance that he will be permitted to remain on the land for another year should wish to get all he can from the premises with the least possible outlay in money and labor. This natural conduct of tenants with short-term leases, oral or written, is a chief cause for the deterioration of farm land so deplored by many agriculturalists. A change in the law which could guarantee compensation for labor and materials used by the tenant in making improvements on the land would go a long way toward encouraging better farm management. The tenant would then have an incentive to do all he could to increase the fertility of the land, since he would stand less chance of losing the fruits of his forethought and toil. His interest in the farm project would be increased, and he would be more co-operative in carrying out the schemes of the landlord to add fertility or other advantages to the premises. It is to be hoped that far-sighted landlords will realize that the old system is making their land less fertile, and that their most valuable asset, the land itself, is being wasted and allowed to wash away.

IMPROVEMENTS

At common law, in the absence of special agreement, the tenant is not permitted to remove improvements from the leased premises at the end of the term and cannot claim compensation therefor. The application of this doctrine to farm lands has been affirmed in Alabama,[1] Arkansas,[2] Kentucky,[3] and North Carolina.[4] It is probable that the other Southeastern states with common law antecedents would hold the same way. Anyone claiming under the tenant, such as a creditor, is also denied any right to the improvements.[5]

An Alabama tenant made an attempt to use the theory that the law implies an obligation to pay a reasonable price for valuable services rendered by one person and knowingly accepted by another. The court held, however, that this rule is inapplicable to cases involving a tenant's improvements on leased land.[6]

In an early case the South Carolina Court seems to have adopted the general common law rule with respect to improvements.[7] Later, however, the court appears to have applied a bit of fireside equity. The son-in-law of a landowner leased land from him and made valuable improvements on the premises with the expectation that the daughter would inherit the property from her father, who had raised no objections when the additions were made. After a domestic quarrel the couple separated, and much ill-will developed between

1. Lawler v. Stanford, 26 Ala. App. 416, 161 So. 265 (1935).
2. Gocio v. Day, 51 Ark. 46, 9 S. W. 433 (1888).
3. Tuck v. Sharer, 234 Ky. 296, 28 S. W. (2d) 22 (1930); Guthrie v. Guthrie, 25 Ky. Law Rep. 1701, 78 S. W. 474 (1904); Gudgell v. Duvall, 27 Ky. 229 (1830).
4. Pitt v. Speight, 222 N. C. 585, 24 S. E. (2d) 350 (1943); Dunn v. Bagby, 88 N. C. 91 (1883); Pomeroy v. Lambeth, 36 N. C. 65 (1840).
5. Pitt v. Speight, 222 N. C. 585, 24 S. E. (2d) 350 (1943).
6. Lawler v. Stanford, 26 Ala. App. 416, 161 So. 265 (1935).
7. Smith v. Brown, 5 Rich, Eq. 291 (S. C., 1853).

the father and the son-in-law, who claimed that he was entitled to be recompensed for the improvements. The court decided in favor of the son-in-law and declared that he was entitled to compensation for such improvements as had increased the rental value of the land.[8] It is evident that the majority of the court felt that injustice would be done if no compensation were awarded. The dissenting judge took the strictly legal view and advocated a denial of the son-in-law's claim.

A somewhat similar case arose in Kentucky, when a landowner made a parol gift of a homesite to his daughter and son-in-law. Valuable improvements were placed upon the land with the idea of making the place a permanent home and with no thought of making it pay through cultivation. After the couple had been in possession for eleven years, the donor, because of family difficulties, demanded a return of the property, there having been no effective conveyance. The court, treating the son-in-law as a sort of quasi lessee, ruled that the father was entitled to a reasonable rent from the time that possession was demanded. The son-in-law set up a claim for improvements as a set-off against the claim for rent. Here the court decided that he was entitled only to a sum representing the enhanced value of the property by reason of the improvements and not to their actual cost.[9]

In a case from Arkansas the court used language which would seem to indicate a refusal to countenance compensation for a tenant's improvements on a minor's homestead where there was no evidence that the additions had increased the rental value of the premises, but intimating that an award would have been made had the value been enhanced thereby.[10] There are cases decided both before and after this controversy which reiterate these principles with respect to the occupiers of a minor's homestead, but it is significant that in all these instances[11] the occupier of the homestead was not a tenant but was on the land in some other capacity. Therefore it is extremely doubtful if the dictum in the principal case would be permitted to override the common law doctrine concerning improvements which has, as is noted above, been approved by

8. Coggins v. McKinney, 112 S. C. 270, 99 S. E. 844 (1919).
9. Bourne v. Odam, 17 Ky. Law Rep. 696, 32 S. W. 398 (1895).
10. Reynolds v. Reynolds, 55 Ark. 369, 18 S. W. 377 (1892).
11. Warren v. Henson, 171 Ark. 162, 283 S. W. 19 (1926); Gatlin v. Lafon, 95 Ark. 256, 129 S. W. 284 (1910); Sparkman v. Roberts, 61 Ark. 26, 31 S. W. 742 (1895); McLoy v. Arnett, 47 Ark. 445, 2 S. W. 71 (1886).

the Arkansas court. The court was probably not thinking of a tenancy when the remark was made, and a thorough reading of the opinion seems to indicate that such was the case.

Under the Louisiana law the lessee, unless it is otherwise stipulated in the rental contract, is entitled to remove improvements, provided he leaves the premises in the same condition in which he received them. If the improvements or additions are made with lime and cement in such a manner as to be affixed to the land, the lessor may retain them upon the payment of a fair price.[12]

Where, however, the improvements made by the tenant are, by the terms of the lease, to be included as a part of the rent, the landlord is entitled to them.[13] It has also been held that additions made by the tenant cannot be removed when there are arrears of rent to be paid, such improvements being liable to be taken therefor.[14]

It is seen that the Civil Law, from which the Louisiana system of jurisprudence stems, is much more favorable to the tenant in this particular matter than is the English common law, which is the basis of the juridical systems of the other Southeastern states.

Georgia has adopted a statute [15] making the landlord "liable" for all substantial improvements which the tenant has placed upon the leased premises with the former's consent. It is supposed that this would be interpreted as a guarantee of compensation. Georgia seems to be the only Southeastern state which has handled the problem in this particular manner.

In an early North Carolina case it was said that a tenant who was under no misapprehension as to the nature of his interest in the leased premises was not entitled to claim an equity in additions and improvements he had made on the land.[16] Some years later the same court refused to give any relief to a tenant who, without any objection on the part of the landlord, had made improvements under the mistaken belief that he had an interest in the property for the lessor's life.[17] The court declared that this was not a case for the application of the doctrine that, where title is in dispute, compensa-

12. La. Civ. Code Ann. (Dart, 1932) Art. 2726. See Penn v. Citizens' Bank of Louisiana, 32 La. Ann. 195 (1880); Fernandez v. Soulie, 28 La. Ann. 31 (1876); D'Armand v. Pullin, 16 La. Ann. 243 (1861); Kean v. Chaney, 3 La. App. 512 (1925).

13. Kean v. Chaney, 3 La. App. 512 (1925).

14. Davidson v. Fletcher, 130 La. 668, 58 So. 504 (1912).

15. Ga. Code (1933) §61-111.

16. Pomeroy v. Lambeth, 36 N. C. 65 (1840).

17. Dunn v. Bagby, 88 N. C. 91 (1883).

tion will be made for improvements. In another instance, however, this court said that one who was induced to enter upon and improve land by a parol promise that it would be settled upon him, as an advancement or gratuity, would not be evicted until compensation had been given him for any improvements he had made.[18] This doctrine has been extended to include instances where improvements have been made by a tenant in possession according to the terms of a parol lease which is unenforceable under the Statute of Frauds.[19]

Lease contracts often contain provisions concerning improvements. They are usually placed in the agreements with the idea of protecting the tenant or landlord in some manner. A common type of covenant is the one which protects the tenant from losing the benefit of improvements which he may have placed upon the land. In one situation it was agreed that improvements made by the lessee should be retained by him if they were "promptly removed." Upon cancellation of the lease because of a sale of the lessor's property in bankruptcy, it was held that the lessee should be given a reasonable time, four months, within which to remove such improvements as he had made.[20] However, where a reasonable interpretation of a lease contract gave the tenant the right to claim a credit for improvements made in contemplation of a purchase, the Alabama court declined to give compensation for thirty loads of manure placed on the land in the ordinary course of cultivation, declaring that this was not an "improvement" within the fair interpretation of that term as used in the agreement.[21]

In Kentucky a lease contract for a five-year term gave the tenant the right to remove any improvements he might make. Upon the expiration of this term the tenant remained in possession under a new lease, but there was no evidence or allegation that the new agreement contained any reference to the covenant concerning improvements. The court held that the tenant lost or waived any right he might have had in the improvements by not reserving the right to remove them in the second lease. Furthermore, the rent under the new lease was cut in half, and it was said that this indicated that it had been reduced to compensate the tenant for the failure to

18. Hedgepeth v. Rose, 95 N. C. 41 (1886).
19. Poole v. Johnson, 31 Ky. Law Rep. 168, 101 S. W. 955 (1907); Fredell v. Ormand Mining Co., 176 N. C. 475, 97 S. E. 386 (1918).
20. Celeste Sugar Co. v. Dunbar-Dukate Co., 160 La. 694, 107 So. 493 (1926).
21. Walker v. Gunnels, 188 Ala. 206, 66 So. 45 (1914).

include the provision concerning the improvements.[22] While this argument may have little to support it, there may have been other circumstances which indicated that such was the true intention of the parties.

The general agent of an Alabama landlord made an agreement with a tenant that a credit would be allowed on the rent for work done by the lessee in constructing several houses on the leased premises. Here it was held that the landlord, after accepting the benefits of the agreement and thereby ratifying it, could not avoid being bound by its terms.[23]

An Arkansas lease required the landlord to make certain improvements and obliged the tenant to attend personally to the work. Under this agreement it was ruled that the tenant was the landlord's agent and was authorized to purchase materials to do the repair job at the landlord's expense. There was an understanding that the value of the materials should be deducted from the amount due the landlord as rent. The court held that this understanding would have no effect upon the agency of the tenant or the liability of the landlord.[24]

In Mississippi a lease provided that the lessee should not have the right, at the expiration of the contract, to remove three specifically identified houses which he would construct on the premises. The lessee built these and other houses on the land during the term. The fact that the lease mentioned the three houses specifically was taken as an indication of an intention to exclude any other houses the lessee might build from the provisions of the covenant. However, as the rent had not been paid and the lessee was insolvent, the court held that equity would not permit him to remove the remaining houses, and these became personalty and liable to seizure for rent.[25]

Questions arise with respect to the measure of damages applicable where the lessor breaks his covenant to make improvements on rented premises. Such a situation arose in Arkansas, and it was said that the lessee was entitled to the difference between the rental value of the land with the proposed improvements and the rental value without them. The court evidently regarded this as a better measure of damages than a calculation on the basis of what the lessee had suf-

22. Unz v. Price's Devisees, 22 Ky. Law Rep. 791, 58 S. W. 705 (1900).
23. Sweetser v. Shorter, 123 Ala. 518, 26 So. 298 (1899).
24. Davis v. Osceola Lumber Co., 168 Ark. 584, 270 S. W. 960 (1925).
25. Galbreath v. Thayer, 147 Miss. 556, 113 So. 180 (1927).

fered as a result of the failure on the part of the lessor to make the agreed improvements.[26] In Tennessee a lessor agreed to build two new cross-fences, to furnish timber for rails to keep the old fences in repair, and to pay the lessee for the labor required to perform the task. Upon a breach of this covenant and the destruction of the lessee's crops because of the lessor's failure to perform the agreement to build the cross-fences, the court held that the proper measure of damages was the difference between the value of the land without the cross-fences and its rental value as stipulated in the lease contract. It was declared that any measure of damages which was based on the cost of the cross-fences would be too harsh.[27]

There may also be specific covenants in a lease which favor the landlord. In an early Louisiana case the lessee agreed to allow all machinery and fixtures put on the premises by him to remain on the land at the expiration of the lease. The court declared that the lessee would have no right to move the improvements but did not by such an agreement waive his right to claim compensation therefor under the general law of Louisiana, provided he left the premises in the same condition in which he had received them at the beginning of the term.[28] In a later case it was agreed that another Louisiana lessee could make all the improvements he chose at his own expense, the improvements to revert to the lessor at the expiration of the term. There was also an agreement that the lessor would pay nothing therefor. The lessee abandoned the property because the lessor dedicated a strip of land through the premises for another purpose, and because of this breach a claim was set up for the entire value of the improvements. The court refused to uphold the lessee's claim and restricted its award to a sum representing the value of the improvements for the unexpired term. Without the agreement that there should be no payment for the improvements, the case would have been governed by the decision in the earlier controversy, since the Louisiana law makes the lessor responsible in a situation where there has been no such agreement. But in this instance the right to compensation was given up by contract and expressly waived according to the testimony of the lessee himself.[29]

A rather unusual situation came before the Louisiana court when

26. Brunson v. Teague, 123 Ark. 594, 186 S. W. 78 (1916).
27. Parker v. Meadows, 86 Tenn. 181, 6 S. W. 49 (1887).
28. Ross v. Zuntz, 36 La. Ann. 888 (1884).
29. McWilliams v. Harper, 159 So. 454 (La. App., 1935).

one of two joint owners deserted the land and the other proprietor took possession and cultivated a portion of the premises which did not exceed half the total area. There was no mention of any lease or agreement to pay rent. It was ruled that the joint owner in possession was under no obligation whatever to the absent co-owner. It was also held, however, that the co-owner could not be compelled to pay for any improvements or repairs which the occupant made to aid him in raising a crop.[30]

Since a lessor's covenant to make improvements or repairs is usually considered as independent, a breach of its terms can only be used as the basis for a counterclaim and cannot be relied upon as a total bar to an action for the rent.[31] Furthermore, it has been said that under the Civil Law of Louisiana a lessee may set up a claim for improvements to offset claims made by the lessor under the lease contract.[32]

It is imperative that legislation be enacted in the several states which would give the tenant the right, under specified circumstances, to remove certain types of improvements from the leased premises at the expiration of the term. For more permanent improvements a system of compensation could be arranged. Such legislation should be framed to include all the more usual situations which may arise; hence a rather elaborate statute would be required in order to insure an equitable settlement in all cases. The enactment of such legislation should be urged upon the legislators of all the Southeastern states.

REPAIRS

According to the common law rule, the lessor, in the absence of a special agreement concerning the matter, is under no obligation to keep the rented premises in repair. This view has been specifically adopted with respect to leases of land in Alabama,[33] Arkansas,[34]

30. Becnel v. Becnel, 23 La. Ann. 150 (1871).

31. Frazier v. Riley, 215 Ala. 517, 111 So. 10 (1926); Culver v. Hill, 68 Ala. 66 (1880); Lee v. Ellis, 169 Ark. 556, 275 S. W. 889 (1925); Varner v. Rice, 39 Ark. 344 (1882).

32. Fernandez v. Soulie, 28 La. Ann. 31 (1876); D'Armand v. Pullin, 16 La. Ann. 243 (1861).

33. Bethea-Starr Packing & Shipping Co. v. Douglass, 12 Ala. App. 561, 68 So. 515 (1915). See also Brown v. Dwight Mfg. Co., 200 Ala. 376, 76 So. 292, L.R.A. 1917F 997 (1917).

34. Rundell v. Rogers, 144 Ark. 293, 222 S. W. 19 (1920); Jones v. Felker, 72 Ark. 405, 80 S. W. 1088 (1904).

Kentucky,[35] North Carolina,[36] and South Carolina.[37] The Arkansas court has declared that a local custom to the contrary cannot be shown.[38] In fact an Alabama tenant has the burden of showing a specific covenant to repair on the part of the landlord,[39] and this would probably be true in other states as well. Generally speaking, the duty to make ordinary repairs of a minor nature rests upon the shoulders of the tenant,[40] but the South Carolina court has declared that, in the absence of statute or covenant, no duty to repair is imposed on either party.[41]

In Louisiana it seems that the lessor is responsible for the repairs which become necessary because of decay or the happening of unforseen events.[42] The lessee may, with notice to the lessor, make the repairs himself and deduct the cost from the rent.[43] The lessor must be put in default by a request that the repairs be made. It has been held that this requirement must be satisfied in order that liability may be imposed upon the lessor for such repairs made by the lessee.[44] The lessor is also required to pay for the cleaning of wells and toilets.[45] The repairs to the interior of the house are mostly to be borne by the lessee.[46] In fact he is required to deliver the premises at the termination of the lease in the same condition in which he received them from the lessor, except for ordinary wear and tear and damages caused by unavoidable accidents.[47] An overflow of the land by a stream has been held to be an "unavoidable accident" within the meaning of this provision, [48] though it is not one within the act authorizing an abatement of rent under such circumstances.[49]

In Georgia the general duty to repair has been shifted to the land-

---

35. Montgomery v. Blocher, 194 Ky. 280, 239 S. W. 46 (1922).
36. Duffy v. Hartsfield, 180 N. C. 151, 104 S. E. 189 (1920).
37. Williams v. Salmond, 79 S. C. 459, 61 S. E. 79 (1908).
38. Rundell v. Rogers, 144 Ark. 293, 222 S. W. 19 (1920).
39. Bethea-Starr Packing & Shipping Co. v. Douglass, 12 Ala. App. 561, 68 So. 515 (1915).
40. Nixon v. Gammon, 191 Ky. 175, 229 S. W. 75 (1921).
41. Williams v. Salmond, 79 S. C. 459, 61 S. E. 79 (1908).
42. La. Civ. Code Ann. (Dart, 1932) §§2693, 2717.
43. La. Civ. Code Ann. (Dart, 1932) Art. 2694.
44. Hennen v. Hayden & Kelly, 5 La. Ann. 713 (1850).
45. La. Civ. Code Ann. (Dart, 1932) Art. 2718.
46. La. Civ. Code Ann. (Dart, 1932) Art. 2716.
47. La. Civ. Code Ann. (Dart, 1932) Art. 2719.
48. Payne v. James, 45 La. Ann. 381, 12 So. 492 (1893).
49. Hollingsworth v. Atkins, 46 La. Ann. 515, 15 So. 77 (1894).

lord by statute.[50] Where the peculiar Georgia estate for years[51] exists, however, the common law rule still applies, and the duty to repair is on the lessee.[52] This duty to "repair" has been held not to require the replacement of a building which is totally destroyed by fire.[53] In other words the landlord is not responsible if the building burns down completely but is liable if it is only partially destroyed. The landlord might allow some old shack or cabin to burn to the ground rather than make an effort to save it, even if the loss to the tenant was very great. Of course there would be no such motive where the house was a good one. Where the tenant had agreed to be responsible for repairs except for fire or unprecedented events, the shoe would be on the other foot. It is clear that no general liability to repair on the part of the landlord could result from the mere exception of damage by fire or unprecedented events from the tenant's covenant to repair.[54]

Where the general duty to repair has been placed on the landlord, as it has in Georgia, questions arise with respect to his liability for injuries caused by unrepaired defects in the leased premises. With respect to patent defects which are obvious to both landlord and tenant at the time of renting there is no liability to repair or responsibility for injuries caused thereby.[55] In fact the landlord does not even have to repair a patent defect known to the tenant when renting, even after notice has been given by the tenant.[56] Should anything happen to a crop because of a patent defect in some structure like a fence, the loss is a common one and should be borne by both landlord and tenant.[57]

With respect to latent defects the landlord is not liable unless it can be shown that he actually knew or should have known of such defects.[58] The tenant must bring the defect to the attention of the

50. Ga. Code (1933) §61-111.
51. See Ch. 3, Note 143.
52. Mayer v. Morehead, 106 Ga. 434, 32 S. E. 349 (1899).
53. Mayer v. Morehead, 106 Ga. 434, 32 S. E. 349 (1899).
54. Mayer v. Morehead, 106 Ga. 434, 32 S. E. 349 (1899).
55. Aiken v. Perry, 119 Ga. 263, 46 S. E. 93 (1903); Driver v. Maxwell, 56 Ga. 11 (1876); Chastain v. Reserve Loan Life Ins. Co., 43 Ga. App. 91, 158 S. E. 448 (1931); Godard v. Peavy, 32 Ga. App. 121, 122 S. E. 634 (1924); McGee v. Hardacre, 27 Ga. App. 106, 107 S. E. 563 (1921).
56. Chastain v. Reserve Loan Life Ins. Co., 43 Ga. App. 91, 158 S. E. 448 (1931).
57. Driver v. Maxwell, 56 Ga. 11 (1876).
58. Godard v. Peavy, 32 Ga. App. 121, 122 S. E. 634 (1924); Cohen Bros. v.

landlord, who is given a reasonable time in which to make the repairs.[59] The knowledge of a particular defect charges the landlord with notice of all other defects which might have come to light if he had made a prompt inspection and makes him liable for injuries which are caused thereby.[60] But his responsibility does not extend to injuries caused by latent defects not connected or associated with the defect pointed out by the tenant.[61] Moreover, where the latent defect is in the construction of the building or structure in question, there is no liability unless the landlord actually erected the structure or had notice of the defect.[62] If the tenant has been in possession of the premises under a former landlord, he has the burden of showing that the injury occurred after he had entered into a contract with the second landlord.[63]

Of course the tenant who has been injured because of a latent defect is not permitted to recover where he could have avoided injury by the use of ordinary care.[64] In one instance it was said that the rule of comparative negligence is applicable here, and that the tenant is under a duty to lessen the damages by the exercise of ordinary care and diligence.[65]

A Louisiana statute[66] makes the lessor liable for injuries resulting from defects in the premises which prevent them from being used, even if it should appear that he knew nothing of the defects at the time the lease was made. The act also makes him liable for any defect which has arisen since that time, provided the lessee is not responsible therefor in any way.

Covenants to repair houses or other structures on the leased premises are often included in rental contracts. These covenants may be general or specific and may obligate either the lessor or the lessee to make the repairs. The variety of these provisions is very great, and

---

Krumbein, 28 Ga. App. 788, 113 S. E. 58 (1922); McGee v. Hardacre, 27 Ga. App. 106, 107 S. E. 563 (1921).

59. Veal v. Hanlon, 123 Ga. 642, 51 S. E. 579 (1905); Cohen Bros. v. Krumbein, 28 Ga. App. 788, 113 S. E. 58 (1922); McGee v. Hardacre, 27 Ga. App. 106, 107 S. E. 563 (1921).

60. McGee v. Hardacre, 27 Ga. App. 106, 107 S. E. 563 (1921).

61. Godard v. Peavy, 32 Ga. App. 121, 122 S. E. 634 (1924).

62. Godard v. Peavy, 32 Ga. App. 121, 122 S. E. 634 (1924).

63. Aiken v. Perry, 119 Ga. 263, 46 S. E. 93 (1903).

64. Henley v. Brockman, 124 Ga. 1059, 53 S. E. 672 (1906); Veal v. Hanlon, 123 Ga. 642, 51 S. E. 579 (1905); Finley v. Williams, 45 Ga. App. 863, 166 S. E. 265 (1932).

65. Cohen Bros. v. Krumbein, 25 Ga. App. 788, 113 S. E. 58 (1922).

66. La. Civ. Code Ann. (Dart, 1932) Art. 2695.

it is important that the covenants coming before the courts be studied with a view to interpretive analysis.

Sometimes a lease will bind the tenant to make repairs which will put the premises in the same condition at the termination of the contract as they were in when it was executed. Thus a Louisiana lessee agreed to keep the property in good repair and to surrender it at the expiration of the lease in the same good order in which he had received it. Under this covenant it was held that before the expiration of the lease the lessee could not be held responsible for not making the repairs which were needed, he being entitled to delay the work until that time.[67] The Arkansas Court has said that the lessee is entitled to delay the agreed repairs until such time as they are usually made according to the customs of the community and the dictates of good husbandry.[68]

In another instance a Louisiana lessee covenanted to deliver the property at the end of the term in good repair. Here it was held that the lower court had not erred in refusing to allow the lessee to prove the state of disrepair on the premises when he went into possession. It was clear that he was under a duty to deliver the property in a state of good repair, and that the condition of the premises at the time of the lessee's entrance made no difference. It was declared, however, that the lower court had erred in refusing to permit the lessee to establish that the lessor had expressed himself as being satisfied with the condition of the premises at the time the settlement for the rent was made. The appellate court also ruled that it had been proper to reject testimony offered to prove that the fences on the farm were in just as good condition as those of the neighbors; that they were sufficient to keep the stock in as well as out; and that their state of dilapidation was the result of natural decay. These items were inadmissible since the prime issue of the controversy was whether the premises were in good condition at a specified time, namely, at the expiration of the lease. The point was also made that the trial judge had erred in sustaining an objection to the introduction of the lessee's evidence to the effect that the boards which had been used by him in repairing one side of the house were as good as new, it making no difference whether the lumber was new or old. The important thing, of course, was whether the lessee had repaired the premises in accordance with the agreement.[69]

67. Payne v. James, 42 La. Ann. 230, 7 So. 457 (1890).
68. Whipple v. Driver, 140 Ark. 393, 215 S. W. 669 (1919).
69. Grayson v. Buie, 26 La. Ann. 637 (1874).

Under an Arkansas lease the tenants undertook to build, repair, and keep in good condition houses of sufficient number to accommodate the laborers necessary to cultivate the premises, and to erect, repair, and maintain fences which could protect the crops to be grown thereon. Here the court held that the tenants were liable for a failure to deliver the houses and fences in good condition at the expiration of the lease.[70]

In an early Kentucky case the tenant agreed to restore the premises to the landlord at the end of the term "in good tenantable repair in every respect." An action was brought by the landlord for breach of this covenant. The appellate court ruled that it had been error for the lower court to refuse to allow the landlord to prove that at the expiration of the lease the premises were not in good repair and to confine him to proof of damage done or waste permitted by the tenant during the term and left unrepaired. It was evident that the natural meaning of this covenant was that it bound the tenant to put the premises in tenantable condition, irrespective of their condition when he had gone into possession under the lease.[71] A few years later an unsuccessful attempt was made to persuade the court that a similar decision should be rendered where the tenant covenanted to keep the farm in good repair and leave it in the same good order at the end of the term, the basis for the decision being that the word "keep" indicated an intention to maintain the *status quo*.[72]

Often the contract will contain a simple specific covenant to repair certain structures on the leased premises. In an early Alabama case the lessor was declared to have broken such a covenant. Here the court stated that the lessee was under no compulsion to make the repairs himself, and that he would be allowed to recover all such damages as were the natural and proximate result of the breach.[73] In one situation the Arkansas court seems to have taken a similar view and decided that the lessor must be given a reasonable time to make the repairs after notice.[74] Only recently, however, it refused to approve the acts of tenants who had moved away from the leased premises because of the breach of the landlord's covenant to repair farm buildings. The tenants could have made the repairs themselves

70. Franklin v. Triplett, 79 Ark. 82, 94 S. W. 929 (1906).
71. Brashear v. Chandler, 22 Ky. 150 (1827).
72. West v. Hart, 30 Ky. 258 (1832).
73. Vandergrift v. Abbott, 75 Ala. 487 (1883).
74. Bowling v. Carroll, 122 Ark. 23, 182 S. W. 514 (1916).

and charged them to the landlord.[75] Sometimes it is impractical for the tenants to make these repairs, and where this is the case, they may recover such damages as they may have suffered by reason of the breach of the covenant.[76]

In some instances the lessee will agree to make the repairs and the lessor will promise either to pay for them or to allow the lease to run until the lessee's claim against him is offset by the rent which will become due according to the agreement. In one case of this type it was held that the lessor could not maintain a possessory action for the recovery of the land without showing that he had paid or tendered the amount by which the cost of the repairs exceeded the rent due and unpaid.[77] A covenant of this sort will of course have the same effect as a lessor's covenant to make the repairs generally. This accompanying covenant to pay the cost of the repairs is not usually present, however, and where it is absent, a lessee's covenant to make the repairs will be interpreted as requiring him to pay the cost of the job.[78]

An Arkansas tenant agreed to keep the fences on the premises in repair, and the landlord consented to furnish the materials to do the repair work. The covenants were held to be dependent, and it was said that the tenant could not be required to live up to his part of the bargain if the landlord failed to perform his agreement.[79] Furthermore, it has been held that where land was rented upon condition that the tenant should make certain repairs, and he failed to perform the condition, the landlord might consider the contract rescinded and recover from the tenant in an action for use and occupation.[80]

Several cases have arisen with respect to the application of the parol evidence rule in situations where the lease contract is in writing and an oral agreement to make repairs is introduced in evidence. Where the written lease can be said to express an agreement which seems to be entire, it is probable that no parol promise to make repairs, whether it be by landlord or tenant, will be admissible in evidence. However, where the written instrument does not purport to express the entire agreement, the parol promise will then be admis-

75. Childress v. Tyson, 200 Ark. 1129, 143 S. W. (2d) 45 (1940).
76. Idem.
77. Jones v. Overton, 7 Ky. 334 (1816).
78. Von Berg v. Goodman, 85 Ark. 605, 109 S. W. 1006 (1908).
79. Barnes v. Lindsey, 100 Ark. 629, 140 S. W. (1911).
80. Tate v. McClure, 25 Ark. 168 (1867).

sible in accordance with a well-defined exception to the rule.[81] Furthermore, where it can be shown that the parol promise to make the repairs is an additional consideration in inducing the lease contract, the fact that this promise is not included in the written agreement is not fatal to its admissibility in evidence. The promise, therefore, will be considered a separate and distinct consideration in addition to that expressed in the written instrument, namely, the rent on one side and the use of the leased premises on the other.[82] An even stronger case is made where the agreement to make repairs has been omitted from the written lease because of the mistaken belief of both parties that the landlord was responsible for repairs in the absence of any agreement to that effect.[83]

A rather important point of law was raised in an early Kentucky case. A tenant occupied farm land under a five-year lease, and one of the fences on the premises was destroyed by a freshet. The landlord, who was evidently under the impression that the tenant had a right to terminate the lease because of this occurrence, promised to repair the fence if the tenant would remain on the land. Acting upon this promise, the tenant planted a crop which was destroyed because of the failure of the landlord to repair the fence. The court held that, as the tenant was bound to continue on the premises even after the destruction of the fence, there had been no detriment to him in agreeing to remain on the place and hence no consideration to support the landlord's promise, thereby rendering it null and void.[84] The only way in which such a promise might be supported is by an application of the doctrine of promissory estoppel. It might be argued that there was a detriment to the tenant in his reliance on the promise, since it was his privilege to abandon the premises and subject himself to an action for breach of contract. However, it is rather doubtful whether such a doctrine would be applicable in the instant case, where the supposed consideration for the promise was an act which the promisee was already obligated to perform. Yet the courts of today are much more liberal than were the tribunals at the time this case was decided in accordance with the strict rules of contract law. At least some support for a broadening of the doctrine of

81. Vandergrift v. Abbott, 75 Ala. 487 (1883).
82. Williams v. Salmond, 79 S. C. 459, 61 S. E. 79 (1908).
83. Montgomery v. Blocker, 194 Ky. 280, 239 S. W. 46 (1922).
84. Proctor v. Keith, 51 Ky. 252 (1851).

promissory estoppel can be found by those who would like to give it freer rein.[85]

Sometimes buildings, fences, or other fixtures on rented land are destroyed by fire, and by the terms of the lease the tenant is under a general contractual duty to repair. According to the common law the tenant would not be excused from his obligation in a situation of this kind. In fact the Arkansas court has ruled that he remains responsible and is not relieved of his agreement to repair.[86] This is of course very hard on the tenant, and in some jurisdictions an effort has been made to remedy the situation. In six of the Southeastern states statutes[87] have been enacted which would seem to excuse a tenant who is under a statutory, common law, or contractual duty of this kind from all obligation to make repairs in case of fire or other unavoidable accident. Under the North Carolina act[88] the damage by fire must amount to more than one-half of the value of the building hurt by the flames to excuse the tenant from his contractual duty to repair the structure. Generally speaking, of course, the tenant is not relieved of responsibility where the fire or other accident came about through his own fault or negligence.

With the principles of the common law requiring the tenant to shoulder much of the burden of keeping the premises in a state of good repair, he would be wise to include a specific covenant relating to this matter in every lease he signs. Under an oral lease it would be necessary to have a definite understanding with the landlord concerning the responsibilities of both parties.

CONCLUSION

There is no doubt that the common law rules concerning improvements and repairs are antiquated and unfair to the tenant. The occupant of rented premises is discouraged from making needed improvements which would promote the interests of both the landlord and himself. The tenant should be given at least some return of a permanent nature from any unexhausted improvements which he has placed upon the land during the term. However, the Georgia

85. See Restatement on Law of Contracts §90.
86. Whipple v. Driver, 140 Ark. 393, 215 S. W. 669 (1919).
87. Ky. Rev. Stat. (1946) §383.170; La. Civ. Code Ann. (Dart, 1932) Arts. 2716, 2723; Miss. Code Ann. (1942) §898; N. C. Gen. Stat. (1943) §§42-9, 10; Tenn. Code Ann. (Williams, 1934) §7620; Va. Code Ann. (Michie, 1936) §5180.
88. N. C. Gen. Stat. (1943) §42-9.

statute is not elaborate enough to adjust all the equities among the parties. The advantage of a more detailed system for the adjustment of varied interests is readily apparent when one compares the Louisiana law with that of states of common law antecedents. The amount of detail that should be placed in a statute is a problem which taxes the ingenuity of reforming legislators.

XIII

Torts and Crimes Incident to the Farm Tenancy Relationship

THE establishment of the landlord-tenant relationship creates numerous rights and correlative duties among the parties to the lease contract, their agents or employees, and other persons who, for divers reasons, are brought into contact with either party. The courts have given much attention to the interrelation of these rights and duties. Many cases have arisen concerning willful and negligent acts leading to injuries. Various forms of action sounding in tort have been analysed and their appropriateness discussed. Some criminal statutes dealing with tenants are also given attention.

There are many types of cases in which matters of this sort are important. Some of the more common ones involve problems with respect to trespass and related matters, nuisance, waste, and enticement. There are also other categories, such as the cases marking out and discussing the rights of the cropper in the event of unauthorized incursions upon land in his rightful possession, and those in which an injured party seeks to hold the landlord responsible for the wrongful acts of his cropper or tenant.

TRESPASS

There are many problems that may arise out of trespasses to land which is being cultivated by a person who has contracted with the landowner for the use of the premises. Some of these problems are procedural in nature, while others are decided by the application of the principles of substantive law. In most instances the trespass is committed or alleged to have been committed by a third person who is a stranger to the lease contract.

When this is the case, the most important thing seems to be a determination of the proper scope of recovery for the lessor and the lessee. Can both bring actions for injuries to their respective interests in the land? The answer to this question appears to be in the affirmative.[1] The usual rule is that the landlord cannot recover unless there has been some injury to the freehold interest in the land.[2] For an injury to the possession alone the right of action is in the tenant, and the landlord may not maintain an action of trespass based upon an infringement of a right of this sort.[3]

In a recent case from Arkansas an opulent farmer employed an airplane pilot to spray his rice crop with chemical dust. Knowing that this dust was harmful to broad-leaf plants, the farmer instructed the pilot not to release the dust if there was any wind. During dusting operations a rather strong breeze arose, but the pilot, disregarding instructions, continued to release the dust until the farmer succeeded in stopping the process. Meanwhile the dust drifted and caused considerable damage to a cotton crop on another party's farm a mile or more distant. The owner of this land had employed another to make a cotton crop under an agreement to divide the proceeds after the payment of all expenses. Here it was decided that if the jury came to the conclusion that the rice farmer was negligent in respect to the spraying operations, the owner of the land on which the cotton had been grown was the proper party to recover the whole amount of damages to the crop.[4] It would seem that the court was of the opinion that the party who planted the cotton was an employee of the landowner.

In North Carolina it has been held that it is permissible but not necessary to join the landlord and the tenant in the same action as parties plaintiff.[5] In the usual situation, however, the rights of action of landlord and tenant are separate and distinct, one for the injury to the freehold and the other for the damage to the lessee's interest.[6]

Where the injury is to the possessory interest, the real party in

1. Gibbons v. Dillingham, 10 Ark. 9 (1843); Beasley v. Central of Georgia Ry. Co., 17 Ga. App. 615, 87 S. E. 907 (1916); Central of Georgia Ry. Co. v. Kelley, 7 Ga. App. 464, 67 S. E. 118 (1910); Dills v. Hampton, 92 N. C. 566 (1885).

2. Seaboard Air Line Ry. Co. v. Brown, 158 Ala. 630, 48 So. 48 (1908); Smith v. Fortiscue, 48 N. C. 65 (1855).

3. Walden v. Conn, 84 Ky. 312, 1 S. W. 537 (1886).

4. Burns v. Vaughn, 224 S. W. (2d) 365 (Ark. 1949).

5. See Tripp v. Little, 186 N. C. 215, 119 S. E. 225 (1923); Dale v. Southern Ry. Co., 132 N. C. 705, 44 S. E. 399 (1903).

6. Beasley v. Central of Georgia Ry. Co., 17 Ga. App. 615, 87 S. E. 907 (1916); Central of Georgia Ry. Co. v. Kelley, 7 Ga. App. 464, 67 S. E. 118 (1910); Dills v. Hampton, 92 N. C. 566 (1885).

interest is the tenant, and any action for injuries to crops[7] or household goods[8] must be brought by him. This rule would not be changed in a case arising under the North Carolina statute[9] which vests the landlord with the right to the possession of the crops until the rent and advances are paid.[10] Even where the occupant is a tenant at will or at sufferance, the Kentucky court has declared that the right of action is in him and not in the landlord.[11] But recovery was allowed a landowner where a former tenant had remained only temporarily on certain premises in Alabama until he could find a new home.[12]

These doctrines are sound, for, during the life of a lease, the lessee holds an outstanding leasehold estate, which for all practical purposes is equivalent to a temporary ownership, while the lessor holds only a reversionary interest, which will ripen into a perfect title only when the lease expires.[13]

An Arkansas landlord was not permitted to recover where the only injury complained of was that the right of way to a spring was obstructed by a fence erected by the defendant railway company, since the tenant alone was injured thereby.[14] It has also been held that a North Carolina landlord could not recover where the sole injury alleged was the treading down of grass.[15] The same result was reached where grass was damaged because of an Alabama railway's failure to maintain a stock gap, the court saying that no injury had been done to the land itself.[16]

In contrast to these cases is the North Carolina decision that broom straw growing wild on leased premises shall be treated as *fructus naturalis* and not as *fructus industrialis*, and that any action for an injury thereto must be brought by the landlord and not by

7. Dale v. Southern Ry. Co., 132 N. C. 705, 44 S. E. 399 (1903); Bridgers v. Dill, 97 N. C. 222, 1 S. E. 767 (1887).

8. Pruitt v. Williams, 21 Tenn. App. 171, 106 S. W. (2d) 892 (1937).

9. N. C. Gen. Stat. (1943) §42-15.

10. Bridgers v. Dill, 97 N. C. 222, 1 S. E. 767 (1887).

11. Louisville & N. R. R. Co. v. Moore, 31 Ky. Law Rep. 141, 101 S. W. 934 (1907).

12. Garrett v. Sewell, 108 Ala. 521, 18 So. 737 (1895).

13. Rogers v. Martin, 87 Fla. 204, 99 So. 551 (1924).

14. Kansas City F. S. & M. Ry. Co. v. King, 63 Ark. 251, 38 S. W. 13 (1896).

15. Smith v. Fortiscue, 48 N. C. 65 (1855).

16. Seaboard Air Line Ry. Co. v. Brown, 158 Ala. 630, 48 So. 48 (1908).

the tenant.[17] It might be argued from this that broom straw and grass are not in the same category.

In one instance a railway company had permitted dry grass, leaves, and other combustible materials to remain near its track in North Carolina. These were ignited by sparks emitted from a locomotive which had no spark arrester. The resultant fire extended to land occupied by a tenant, causing damage to the premises. Here it was declared that the landlord, through his tenant, was prima facie the owner of the land, and that he was entitled to recover damages for the injury to his proprietary and possessory rights.[18] Since this case involved an injury to the reversionary interest, there can be no doubt that it was correctly decided. However, some of the language employed, when tested by the above principles, would seem to be inaccurate.

Generally it may be said that the landlord will not be permitted to recover for injuries to crops,[19] that right being reserved for the tenant.[20] In one instance, however, the Alabama court used language which would seem to allow the landlord a recovery to the extent of his share of the crop. A decision in his favor was reversed only because the judge's charge to the jury would have authorized a consideration of the injury to the entire crop in estimating the damages.[21] If the wrongful act was the direct and proximate cause of a devastating injury to the crop, the tenant is entitled to recover for the complete failure to harvest any produce and is not limited in his recovery to such a sum as would make repairs, put the damaged property in order, and cover the injury done to the crop before he learned of the trespass.[22]

A Georgia court has refused to permit a tenant to recover for damage to standing timber or for the burning of trash and litter which had been allowed to injure the land, since it could not be said that such injuries constituted damage to the tenant's usufructuary interest or right to use the property.[23]

17. Chauncy v. Atlantic Coast Line R. R. Co., 195 N. C. 415, 142 S. E. 327 (1928).
18. Aycock v. Raleigh & Augusta Air-Line R. R. Co., 89 N. C. 321 (1883).
19. St. Louis, A. & T. Ry. Co. v. Trigg, 63 Ark. 536, 40 S. W. 579 (1897); Gibbons v. Dillingham, 10 Ark. 9 (1849); Louisville & N. Ry. Co. v. Nanny, 137 Ga. 607, 73 S. E. 1052 (1912).
20. Chauncy v. Atlantic C. L. R. R., 195 N. C. 415, 142 S. E. 327 (1928).
21. Atlanta & B. Airline Ry. Co. v. Brown, 158 Ala. 607, 48 So. 73 (1908).
22. Bridgers v. Dill, 97 N. C. 222, 1 S. E. 767 (1887).
23. Beasley v. Central of Georgia Ry. Co., 17 Ga. App. 615, 87 S. E. 907 (1916).

An Alabama tenant was allowed to recover even where he had consented that a third person might come upon the leased premises and remove a fence, as the consent was of no effect because it constituted a breach of the duty of fealty which he owed to his landlord.[24] In a North Carolina case where the act complained of constituted waste and would have been actionable if perpetrated by the tenant, a recovery by the landlord was not prevented by the fact that the tenant had given the third party defendant a license to do the tortious act.[25]

A cropper in possession under a South Carolina tenant was permitted to recover damages from a trespasser who had improperly and unlawfully come onto the premises assigned to the cropper and gathered and hauled away certain specified portions of the crops.[26] A dissenting judge was of the opinion that the cropper did not have a sufficient interest in the land to support an action of trespass.

The right of the lessee to recover against a tort-feasor is not to be denied because the actual tortious act was done by an independent contractor in the employ of the tort-feasor.[27] Neither the lessee nor the lessor is to be denied a recovery where the trespasser, in removing a partition fence, stood on his own land and did not come over the line onto the leased premises.[28]

A tenant has a right of exclusive possession of the leased premises, and the landlord is liable for any act of his own which constitutes a trespass.[29] Under the old system of pleading an action of trespass *quare clausum fregit* would have been the proper remedy here, but under the modern codes of civil procedure the remedy is a civil action sounding in tort.[30]

It seems that a cropper, though having a somewhat nebulous interest in the land, may maintain an action sounding in tort against the landlord where there have been breaches by the latter of obligations or duties created by the cropping contract between the parties. In a Georgia case a recovery was allowed where a landowner, without cause and after the cropper had performed a major

24. Brown v. French, 159 Ala. 645, 49 So. 255 (1909).
25. Dills v. Hampton, 92 N. C. 566 (1885).
26. Childers v. Verner, 12 S. C. 1 (1878).
27. Clark v. St. Louis, S. F. & N. O. Ry. Co., 79 Ark. 629, 94 S. W. 930 (1906); Fair Lumber Co. v. Weems, 196 Miss. 201, 16 So. (2d) 770 (1944).
28. Garrett v. Sewell, 108 Ala. 521, 18 So. 737 (1895).
29. Barneycastle v. Walker, 92 N. C. 198 (1885); Hatchell v. Kimbrough, 49 N. C. 163 (1856). See also State v. Piper, 89 N. C. 551 (1883).
30. Barneycastle v. Walker, 92 N. C. 198 (1885).

portion of the agreement, had refused to allow him to complete the cultivation and harvesting of the crops and had compelled him to leave the premises.[31]

In an action initiated by the landlord for rent, the practice today is to allow the tenant to counterclaim for injuries sustained by him as a result of the landlord's wrongful acts. Thus counterclaims have been allowed against landlords who had unlawfully permitted their cattle to enter and commit depredations upon the leased premises.[32] In one instance of this kind the landlord testified that the tenant had consented to the entrance of the livestock upon the land. Here it was held that it was error for the judge to charge that the tenant was entitled to set off the damages occasioned thereby, since such a charge might be interpreted by the jury as taking the issue out of its hands. The testimony had been given before the court, and it was for the jury to determine its truth or falsity.[33] In another case the damage had been done by the tenant's own cattle which had been permitted to enter the tenant's fields due to the landlord's negligence in failing to repair a fence as he had agreed to do. Under these circumstances it was held that it was erroneous for the judge to charge the jury that the tenant could not recover on his counterclaim for the damage done by his own cattle.[34]

It may be said in general that the mere ownership of land confers no right to the possession and disposal of the crops raised upon it by a tenant. The right given to the landlord in respect to his claim for rent must be asserted and perfected under the provisions of the law designed to protect his rights.[35]

In a controversy from the State of Georgia a landowner broke open a locked outhouse and took certain cotton raised on the leased premises and some effects which the tenant had sold to him but had never delivered. The owner had found out where the property was stored and had gone upon the premises and placed another lock on the outhouse, thus depriving the tenant of the use of this portion of the premises. Still having made no demand for the delivery of the purchased goods, he then broke into the outhouse and carried the

31. Payne v. Watters, 9 Ga. App. 265, 70 S. E. 1114 (1911).
32. Johnson v. Aldridge, 93 Ala. 77, 9 So. 513 (1891); Smith v. Glover, 135 Ark. 531, 205 S. W. 891 (1918). But see contra Hulme v. Brown, 50 Tenn. 679 (1871).
33. Johnson v. Aldridge, 93 Ala. 77, 9 So. 513 (1891).
34. Rowe v. Baber, 93 Ala. 422, 8 So. 865 (1891).
35. Robinson v. Kruse, 29 Ark. 575 (1874).

property away. It was held that this conduct amounted to a trespass for which the landowner was liable for punitive as well as compensatory damages.[36]

In North Carolina a tenant from year to year had waived his right to a notice to quit and had gone out of possession. Afterwards he decided to return and get some planks which he had placed loosely upon the sills of a cabin he had been engaged in putting up before his abandonment of the premises. The planks were shown never to have been nailed down. In spite of this fact, however, it was held that a person who had no idea of returning to the farm as a tenant could not lawfully enter the premises and take these planks, since his conduct had invested the owner with a rightful possession which he could defend against all intruders, including his former tenant.[37] A different situation exists where the tenant has only temporarily abandoned the leased premises. Here the Mississippi court seemed to be of the opinion that the tenant should be allowed to recover. It held, however, that the judge's instruction to the jury to fix the tenant's damages at the amount which it might believe he had been injured was not sufficiently clear, since it failed to limit the recovery to those damages which had proximately flowed from the eviction by the landlord. Moreover, as the landlord had been given the impression that the tenant had no intention of returning, it was held that no punitive damages could be recovered.[38]

As a general rule, a mere trespass on leased premises will not be enjoined where there is an adequate remedy at law. In one instance an Arkansas lessee sought an injunction to restrain a supposedly solvent lessor from turning horses and cattle onto fields which were being cultivated by the lessee. There being no allegation of insolvency and no evidence that the lessee would suffer any irreparable damage, it was held that he had an adequate remedy at law and that equity could not interfere.[39] In another instance a Georgia landowner was desirous of getting rid of a cropper. In order to facilitate his purpose of forcing the cropper to break his contract and compelling him to abandon a practically matured crop, the landlord sought to intimidate the cropper by threatening mob violence. He made it known that he would continue the display of force with

36. Shores v. Brooks, 81 Ga. 468, 8 S. E. 429 (1888).
37. Torrans v. Stricklin, 52 N. C. 50 (1859).
38. Gardner v. Heflin, 188 Miss. 790, 196 So. 256 (1940).
39. Caplinger v. Hickerson, 175 Ark. 1105, 1 S. W. (2d) 548 (1928).

the avowed purpose of dislodging the cropper from the premises. Evidence of these facts evidently persuaded the court that there was no adequate remedy at law, and therefore the landlord, though solvent, was enjoined from continuing the objectionable conduct.[40]

MEASURE OF DAMAGES WITH RESPECT TO TRESPASS ON LAND
LEASED TO TENANT

Where there has been a trespass on rented premises which is actionable by the lessee, the usual measure of damages is the difference in the value of the term before and after the trespass.[41] Sometimes the acts of a trespasser may cause either a direct injury to a tenant's livestock or give him trouble of a serious nature by contributing to the animals' escape. In one such situation a trespasser was held liable for the loss of the cattle, the expense of corralling and renting a temporary enclosure in which to put the recaptured animals, the loss of subrentals on the pasture, the expense incurred and time lost by the lessee in trying to prevent other cattle from escaping through the break in the fence, and punitive damages for the malicious act.[42] In another instance where the acts of the trespasser caused a lessee's cattle to escape, the measure of damages was said to be the difference between their fair market value at the time they were returned and their value at the time when the trespasser's acts had caused their dispersal. Here it was said that the jury might consider evidence concerning the nervous condition of the cattle, for it is a well known-fact that cattle in such a condition do not fatten well.[43]

In Georgia it has been held that where for any reason, such as the tenancy being at will, the term has no market value, the damages must be calculated by the jury in the light of all the relevant facts and circumstances.[44] In an Arkansas case involving a tenancy at will, however, the court remarked that the proper way to compute damages was to arrive at the usable value of the property at the time of the trespass and its value after the tortious act complained of, and to calculate the difference with emphasis upon how much damage had been done down to the time of the trial.[45]

A North Carolina landlord was held responsible for the loss of

40. Bussell v. Bishop, 152 Ga. 428, 110 S. E. 174 (1921).
41. Daniel v. Perkins Logging Co., 9 Ga. App. 842, 72 S. E. 438 (1911).
42. Fair Lumber Co. v. Weems, 196 Miss. 201, 16 So. (2d) 770 (1944).
43. Petroleum Exploration v. White, 237 Ky. 10, 34 S. W. (2d) 738 (1931).
44. Daniel v. Perkins Logging Co. 9 Ga. App. 842, 72 S. E. 438 (1911).
45. St. Louis, I. M. & S. Ry. Co. v. Hall, 71 Ark. 302, 74 S. W. 293 (1903).

his tenant's eye caused by exposure and cold experienced when the
landlord removed the roof to the house where the tenant resided.[46]
An Arkansas tenant was unlawfully evicted and proved that his
household goods had been exposed to bad weather conditions because no other house could be found into which the family could
move. Here it was held that evidence tending to show what the
tenant had paid for the articles of furniture, the length of time he
had used them, and their present value and condition, was relevant
and admissible on the issue of damages.[47]

QUESTION OF LANDLORD'S RESPONSIBILITY

FOR TORTS OF TENANT OR CROPPER

Generally it may be said that a landlord who has rented land and
has neither possession nor control of the leased premises is not responsible for the torts of his tenant. Thus an Arkansas landlord
was held not to be liable for an injury to adjoining land caused by
the closing of a cut in a levee on premises leased to a tenant, who had
closed the cut without the landowner's license or consent.[48] Where
the farmer is a cropper, however, the possibilities of an agency are
increased, since the landlord has more control of his employee's
actions. To establish the agency the act must be shown to lie within
the scope of some employment authorized by the landlord. In a recent South Carolina case[49] it is said that a cropper is a "laborer" or a
"servant" but is not generally considered the agent of his landlord,
who is not liable for his torts unless at the time of the alleged tort
the cropper was performing some act or mission at the request or
command of the landlord. In this instance the plaintiff had been injured in a collision with the cropper, who had been hauling wood at
the time of the accident. He introduced evidence of a declaration
made by the cropper at the time of the accident to the effect that the
landlord had sent him to haul hay on the day the collision occurred.
Declarations of an agent are usually inadmissible to establish agency
except where they are used as corroborative testimony. Therefore,
the court held that the declaration alone would not support a verdict
for the plaintiff against the landlord where the cropper had later
testified otherwise and the other evidence in the case seemed to sup-

46. Hatchell v. Kimbrough, 49 N. C. 163 (1856).
47. Stanley v. Smith, 135 Ark. 502, 205 S. W. 889 (1918).
48. Baker v. Allen, 66 Ark. 271, 50 S. W. 511 (1899).
49. Powers v. Wheless, 193 S. C. 364, 9 S. E. (2d) 129 (1940).

port the view that no agency existed. In another instance the decision in favor of the landlord does not appear to have been so clearly justified. Here a Georgia cropper was preparing the land for cultivation. Certain trash and rubbish needed to be burned, and the cropper set out fires at many points on the premises. The fires got out of hand and caused injury to the property of the third-party plaintiff. The cropping contract provided that the cultivator and his family should work the crop "under the direction and control" of the landlord.[50] It might well be argued, however, that the cropper had implied authority to do whatever was necessary for the proper management and cultivation of the farm, and that therefore he was within the scope of his employment when he started the fires. Why wouldn't the burning of rubbish be within the scope of the implied authority given to him by the landlord?

CONSPIRACY AND MALICIOUS MISCHIEF

Sometimes a landlord or third person will do something which has a tendency to break up the tenancy relationship. It may be that under the circumstances of a particular case such conduct will be considered unlawful.

In one instance of this sort an Arkansas lessee claimed that the lessor had entered into a conspiracy with a third person with a view to ousting him from the land. The lease provided that the term should come to an end upon a sale of the premises, and the lessor had in fact executed a deed to the third person. The lessee further claimed that this was not a bona fide transaction, and that a conspiracy to oust him was indicated. It was held that the lessee would have the burden of showing that this claim was true, which burden of proof the court decided he had not sustained. However, the court remarked that if the allegations of the petition had been shown to be true, a recovery would have been allowed and an injunction against a threatened incursion of the lessee dissolved.[51]

In Louisiana it was shown that a third person had officiously and mischievously attempted to make trouble between a landlord and his tenant by throwing suspicion upon the authenticity of the landlord's title and creating doubts in the minds of tenant and subtenants as to whether, in view of pending litigation, they would realize anything for their labor and past and prospective improvements. This con-

50. Cook v. Brown, 23 Ga. App. 284, 98 S. E. 92 (1919).
51. Du Fresne v. Paul, 144 Ark. 87, 221 S. W. 485 (1920).

duct caused a general demoralization of the workers on the leased plantation and a consequent failure of the landowner to receive the amount of produce expected by him as a result of his bargain with the tenant. On the basis of these facts the landlord was allowed to recover against the third person.[52]

INJURIES CAUSED BY THE DIVERSION OF WATER AND THE OBSTRUCTION OF ITS NATURAL FLOW

The right of action for damage solely to the possession of leased land which has been injured by a diversion of surface water from its natural channel seems to be in the tenant and not in the landowner, and the tenant must do everything within reason to minimize the damages.[53] However, it has been decided that ordinary care did not require a Mississippi lessee to dig a large ditch to protect his crop from backwater caused by a roadbed which had obstructed the natural flow of water, the tenant having no right or duty to construct a new ditch of this sort. Furthermore, the decision was not altered by the fact that the tenant had agreed to keep all the ditches on the premises and their banks clear and unobstructed.[54]

NUISANCES ON FARMS

Sometimes in tenancy cases a plot of land will be used in such a manner as to constitute a nuisance. In an instance of this kind a cow was killed by a fall into an open well upon premises which had been leased to a tenant with the understanding that the well would be made safe. It was claimed that this promise to make the well safe had made an agent out of the tenant, who had put up an inadequate fence around the watering place The court evidently came to the conclusion that the tenant was the agent of the landowner. It was said that to authorize a recovery here the third-party plaintiff must show that the failure to put up an adequate fence constituted conduct amounting to a nuisance or negligence, and that the alleged nuisance had come about as the result of the particular negligent act complained of in the pleadings. Such questions were not for the court but for the jury, and if they were decided in favor of the plaintiff, the landowner would then be held responsible. In passing

52. Martin v. Sterkx, 146 La. 489, 83 So. 776 (1920).
53. Louisville & N. Ry. Co. v. Moore, 31 Ky. Law Rep. 141, 101 S. W. 934 (1907).
54. Yazoo & M. V. Ry. Co. v. Sultan, 106 Miss. 373, 63 So. 672 (1913).

the court remarked that a landlord might be held liable for a nuisance which had existed prior to the lease but not for one created and maintained by the tenant after he had gone into possession.[55]

An owner of real estate claimed that certain fruit tress on premises leased to another were injured by the constant diffusion over the orchard of noxious fumes from a third person's fertilizer factory. The trees were stunted in their growth, a definite retardation was noted in the maturity of the fruit, and the quantity and value of the yield was materially diminished. These fumes were held to constitute a nuisance. The injury being to the reversionary interest in the land as well as to the tenant's interest, it was decided that the landowner could maintain an action to abate the nuisance.[56]

An Alabama landowner had stored dynamite caps in an outhouse which served as a toolshed. These dynamite caps were taken away by a tenant's children, who were afterwards injured through their explosion. It was shown that the children frequented the path beside the toolhouse and even went into the shed on occasion. The court held the landowner liable, declaring that he owed a duty to exercise a degree of care commensurate with the dangerous quality of the stored articles. His inaction in allowing the children to play in and about the toolshed amounted to an implied invitation. In such a situation he would be required to exercise extraordinary precautions. This he did not do and hence was held responsible for the injury to the children.[57] This decision can probably be justified under the attractive nuisance doctrine.

WASTE

There are instances where a tenant commits some form of depredation on the leased premises. Acts of this type are sometimes punishable under statutes interdicting wasteful acts on leased land by tenants. Several of the Southeastern states have such laws.[58] The Kentucky and North Carolina statutes provide for treble damages, and the Virginia law for double damages increased to treble where the injury to the property occurs during the pendency of any action

55. Bailey v. Dunaway, 8 Ga. App. 713, 70 S. E. 141 (1911).
56. Bigbee Fertilizer Co. v. Scott, 3 Ala. App. 333, 56 So. 834 (1911).
57. Bryan v. Stewart, 194 Ala. 353, 70 So. 123 (1915).
58. Ky. Rev. Stat. (1946) §381.350; La. Civ. Code Ann. (Dart, 1932) Art. 2722; N. C. Gen. Stat. (1943) §§1-533-538; Va. Code Ann. (Michie, 1936) §§5506, 5509-11.

to recover or to charge the land. A Tennessee statute[59] interdicts the use of timber on leased premises in excess of the amount actually needed for repair and firewood purposes. This act also includes the destruction or removal of any buildings or fences on the land. Another Tennessee statute[60] recognizes that waste is actionable by stating that nothing mentioned therein shall take away the right to an action for damages or for an injunction where irreparable waste is being committed on the property. Alabama[61] and Mississipi[62] statutes recognize the landlord's right to object to waste by providing that the landlord's assignee is invested with such a right. A South Carolina statute[63] recognizes the existence of the remedy by referring to assessment of damages in waste actions. In fact wrongful waste on the part of the lessee is mentioned in the peculiar Georgia statute[64] recognizing an estate for years as distinguished from the usual relationship of landlord and tenant.

Some interesting cases concerning waste on farm lands have come before the courts in the Southeastern states. In one instance a Virginia landlord attempted to enjoin his tenant from committing alleged waste on the leased premises. The tenant had incited the ire of his landlord by plowing up and cultivating in corn a certain river bottom which had been set in blue grass. There was nothing said in the lease about the noncultivation of any portion of the premises. However, the lease did provide that the land should be farmed in such a manner as not to injure it in any way which could reasonably be prevented. It was shown that this particular plot sowed in blue grass had no peculiar characteristics setting it apart from other portions of the farm and that it had actually been the custom of the country that all fields should be plowed up alternately and planted in corn. There were plenty of grass lands on the place which could be used for pasturage and sod purposes. Here the court declared that under such circumstances it could not be presumed, without something being said in the lease, that the parties had intended that any restrictions should be engrafted with respect to the cultivation of

59. Tenn. Code Ann. (Williams, 1934) §7745.
60. Tenn. Code Ann. (Williams, 1934) §9320.
61. Ala. Code Ann. (1940) Tit. 31, §10.
62. Miss. Code Ann. (1942) §904.
63. S. C. Code Ann. (1942) §8866.
64. See Ga. Code (1933) §85-803, making reference to §85-604. See Ch. 3, Note 143.

any one or more of the fields on the leased premises.[65] It might well
be argued that the doctrine of this case would not go so far as to
protect a lessee who threatened to destroy turf that had been planted
for some specific purpose connected with the chosen use of the land.
In this same case the lessee had erected a stable on the premises without consulting the lessor. It was claimed that this would constitute
waste, in that a stable might easily be considered a liability and not
an asset because of the peculiar nature of the property. However,
it had been agreed that the stable would be removed at the expiration of the lessee's term. Under these circumstances the court
ordered an injunction against the alleged waste dissolved.

An Arkansas tenant contracted with a third person to erect a
sawmill on a rented farm. An understanding was reached whereby
the third person agreed to cut the timber for his mill on a certain
part of the land. It was shown that he had not only cut the timber
on the agreed area and sold it without making the improvements he
had consented to provide, but had also cut about three acres of
timber outside of the specified area. In addition to this the tenant
himself, without obtaining the landlord's consent, had also cut
timber to which he had no right. The rental contract had expressly
provided against waste, and it was held that these facts clearly
showed that there had been depredations on the land.[66]

IMPROPER USE OF LEGAL PROCESS

Sometimes a landlord will start a legal proceeding to oust a
tenant without having any legitimate right to do so. There seems
to be no doubt that a tenant may maintain an action for malicious
use of legal process where a possessory action has been unsuccessfully brought against him, maliciously and without probable cause.
In one such instance a tenant had been put to great expense for
attorney's fees and a bond to arrest the proceedings. Furthermore, it
was claimed that by so bringing an action against him the landlord
had broken the covenant of quiet enjoyment contained in the lease
contract. A recovery was allowed on the count for malicious use
of legal process, but since the dispossessory proceeding had been
unsuccessful, it could not be said as a matter of law there had
been any interference with the tenant's enjoyment of the premises,
either actually or constructively.[67]

65. Hubble v. Cole, 85 Va. 87, 7 S. E. 242 (1888).
66. Yarbrough v. Hurt, 131 Ark. 593, 199 S. W. 911 (1917).
67. Morris v. Battey, 33 Ga. App. 422, 126 S. E. 854 (1925).

If a person claiming to be a landlord enters upon an alleged tenant by means of a valid legal process, irregularly sued out, issued, and executed, the latter cannot lawfully maintain an action of trespass or its equivalent, claiming that he is the owner and not a tenant, and his proper remedy is an action for suing out the process maliciously and without probable cause.[68] However, where the landlord takes possession of land, as against his tenant, by virtue of a void writ, he stands in the same position as if he had acted without a writ and cannot be held responsible in an action for malicious use of legal process.[69]

ASSAULT AND OTHER VIOLENT CONDUCT IN PROTECTING RIGHTS

How far can a landowner go in protecting himself against defaulting tenants? Can he resort to self-help or is it necessary to call for the aid of law-enforcement officers? There have been a few cases in which questions of this kind have arisen.

In a recent case from Tennessee, for example, it was shown that a so-called tenant, who was probably merely a cropper, had continued to live on his landlord's plantation after being lawfully discharged. The landlord ordered him out of one of the plantation houses at the point of a pistol, and a member of the landlord's family shot through the window, thus frightening the farmer's wife, who suffered a miscarriage. It was held that the landlord had no right to take the law into his own hands in this manner, for an ordinary possessory action should have been employed to oust the defaulting farmer. Therefore the landlord and the member of his family involved in the shooting were held liable for an assault, and damages were assessed against them.[70] In contrast to this is the North Carolina case where a landlord attempted to protect himself from financial loss by threatening to beat with a stick certain persons who were unlawfully attempting to remove his tenant's crop. In this instance it was shown that the landlord had used only an amount of personal force sufficient to prevent the crop from being removed. The North Carolina statute [71] vests possession of the crop in the landowner until the rent and advances are paid. Though the

68. Melson v. Dickson, 63 Ga. 682 (1879).
69. Vinson v. Flynn, 64 Ark. 453, 43 S. W. 146, 46 S. W. 186 (1897).
70. Schumpert v. Moore, 24 Tenn. App. 695, 149 S. W. (2d) 471 (1940).
71. N. C. Gen. Stat. (1943) §42-15.

landlord was indicted for an assault, the court held that he was not guilty.[72]

LAWS MAKING TRESPASS IN VARIOUS FORMS A CRIME

There are a few statutes enacted by Southeastern states which make it a criminal offense for anyone to commit a trespass on land under certain specified conditions. These statutes have been applied in a few cases where farm tenants were involved.

For instance, an Alabama statute [73] makes it a crime for anyone to go on the premises of another after being warned not to do so. In a case arising under this act evidence was introduced which tended to show that the discharged cultivator of the land of another had left his gear and plow upon the premises after a warning had been given him to stay off the place. The fact that the gear and plow were on the place after a warning was said to indicate that the cultivator himself had been there also.[74]

A similar Georgia statute [75] makes it a criminal offense for anyone to "wilfully enter, go upon, or pass over any field, orchard, garden, or other enclosed or cultivated land of another, after being personally forbidden so to do by the owner or person entitled to the possession for the time being, or authorized agent thereof." In a case arising under this statute a landowner had forbidden the husband of his female tenant to come on the land or across it, a thing which it is clear he had no right to do, since a tenant could most assuredly have whoever he or she wanted on the leased premises, together with the right to a means of ingress and egress. In this instance, however, the husband walked across one of the landlord's cultivated fields. Here the court held that, while the tenant had a right to have anyone visit her by the ordinary thoroughfares or roadways, the husband had no right to make his way across the cultivated land. Hence the husband's conviction was upheld by the appellate court.[76]

INJURY TO TENANT CAUSED BY DEFECTIVE APPLIANCE
SUPPLIED BY LANDLORD

Sometimes a tenant is injured while operating some tool or appliance which has been supplied to him by the landlord. In one

72. State v. Austin, 123 N. C. 749, 31 S. E. 731 (1898).
73. Ala. Code (1940) tit. 14, §426.
74. Arrington v. State, 168 Ala. 143, 52 So. 928 (1910).
75. Ga. Code (1933) §26-3002.
76. Horsely v. State, 16 Ga. App. 136, 84 S. E. 600 (1915).

case of this kind the injury occurred when a hammer mill fell apart or exploded in the process of operation by tenants. The court declared that there could be no recovery if the injury was caused by a latent or hidden defect in the appliance of which the landlord had no notion.[77]

LAWS AGAINST ENTICING TENANTS

In the Southeastern states, with the single exception of Virginia, statutes have been enacted against the practice of enticing tenants, croppers, and other laborers away from their landlords or employers. These laws vary to a certain extent as to details, but are all aimed at the practice of tenant-stealing, which in periods of labor shortage is rather common in agricultural communities.[78] Some of these laws create both civil and criminal liability.

These statutes are not framed to punish persons who hire tenants or croppers who have already given up their previous employment,[79] and this is true even where the tenant has never entered upon his duties under his agreement with the first landlord.[80]

In order to justify a conviction or verdict under these statutes the tenant, cropper, or laborer must be at the time of the persuasion under a contractual obligation to work for the landowner.[81] If, before a person has approached the tenant or cropper, the latter has decided of his own free will to break the contract, then the hirer

77. Larkin v. Baker, 308 Ky. 304, 214 S. W. (2d) 379 (1948).

78. Ala. Code (1940) tit. 26, §§332-333; Ark. Dig. Stat. (Pope, 1937) §8600; Fla. Stat. Ann. (1941) §448.02; Ga. Code (1933) §66-9904-05; Ky. Rev. Stat. (1946) §433.310; La. Gen. Stat. Ann. (Dart, 1932) §§4384-85; Miss. Code Ann. (1942) §2129; N. C. Gen. Stat. (1943) §§14-348, 14-359; S. C. Code Ann. (1932) §1314; Tenn. Code Ann. (Williams, 1934) §§8559-60. One of the North Carolina acts outlaws the hiring of a tenant who has unlawfully left his employer, while the other is a local act applying to certain named counties and punishing anyone harboring a delinquent tenant. However, the North Carolina act punishing the enticement of servants has been held not to apply to tenants. State v. Etheridge, 169 N. C. 263, 84 S. E. 264 (1915), interpreting N. C. Gen. Stat. (1943) §14-347. Neither the Kentucky nor Tennessee statutes apply specifically to tenants or croppers, but the Tennessee act has been applied in a case involving a cropping contract on shares. McCutchin v. Taylor, 79 Tenn. 259 (1883). The same was held with respect to a Mississippi cropping contract where the statute mentioned only laborers and renters. Armstrong v. Bishop, 151 Miss. 353, 117 So. 512 (1928).

79. Simonson v. Butler, 171 Ark. 1189, 289 S. W. 1014 (1926); Johns v. Patterson, 138 Ark. 420, 211 S. W. 387 (1919); Hill v. Duckworth, 155 Miss. 484, 124 So. 641 (1929); Waldrup v. State, 154 Miss. 646; 122 So. 771 (1929).

80. Evans v. State, 121 Miss. 252, 83 So. 167 (1919).

81. Orr v. Hardin, 4 Ga. App. 382, 61 S. E. 518 (1908); Griffin v. State, 160 Ark. 166, 254 S. W. 469 (1923).

cannot be held responsible for employing him.[82] The hirer's knowledge of his former employment would make no difference,[83] and neither would the fact that the cropper was still sleeping on his former employer's farm.[84]

If the contract is still in effect, however, proof of knowledge of its pre-existence has been ruled to be an essential element to a conviction under the Mississippi statute.[85]

Where a landlord was under no legal obligation to furnish meat or clothing to his tenant, his failure to provide these articles could not be used as a justification by an enticer who, knowing of the tenancy, had employed the tenant on his own place.[86]

In one case it was shown that a landlord had accepted a payment on his cropper's past-due account from a person who had persuaded the cropper to leave his employment. It was held that this acceptance would not constitute acquiescence in the acts of the enticer and could not be used as a defense in a criminal action under the statute.[87]

A female Negro cropper, prior to harvesting her crop, started negotiations with another person for employment on the latter's place. She sent a message to her prospective employer saying that she had obtained her landlord's consent to leave and that she wished him to settle her account with the landlord before the move was made. The prospective employer testified that a general statement of the account in writing had been sent to him and that he had considered it. However, the court refused to recognize this as a valid defense to an enticement suit, ruling that the cropper had not left her original employment in such a manner as to excuse a definite act of hiring.[88]

An employer who had contracted with another person's tenant without knowing of the previous employment, upon being informed that the tenant was under contract, attempted to make him return to his former landlord. The latter told the prospective employer that if the tenant would find a substitute, he would be released from all liability as an enticer. He was told by the tenant that a proper sub-

82. Coolidge v. Howe, 180 Ark. 952, 23 S. W. (2d) 609 (1930); Johns v. Patterson, 145 Ark. 46, 223 S. W. 382 (1920).

83. Coolidge v. Howe, 180 Ark. 952, 23 S. W. (2d) 609 (1930).

84. Johns v. Patterson, 145 Ark. 46, 223 S. W. 382 (1920).

85. Haney v. State, 38 So. 284 (Miss., 1905).

86. Petty v. Leggett, 38 So. 549 (Miss., 1905).

87. Griffen v. State, 160 Ark. 166, 254 S. W. 469 (1923).

88. Armstrong v. Bishop, 151 Miss. 353, 117 So. 512 (1928).

stitute had been found, and, acting in reliance on this assertion, kept the tenant in his employ. Under these circumstances it was held that he was not responsible as an enticer.[89] Again, an alleged enticer was held not to be responsible where a renter had abandoned his landlord because of the latter's refusal to allow certain laborers, whom the renter had employed to help with the crop, to remain on the place.[90]

One controversy arose in Georgia where an alleged enticer rented land to the wife of another's tenant. The statute was held not to apply here, since the tenant and his wife could not be identified as one and the same person.[91]

A landlord may be guilty of interfering with the laborers of his tenant. Thus a South Carolina landowner was held responsible where he moved about twenty Negroes out of his tenant's fields and put them to work on his own unrented land, thereby depriving the tenant of the means of harvesting the crops.[92]

The Mississippi act provides that the enticer shall be liable for the value of advances made by the landlord to the tenant or laborer. This right, however, was held not to include advances made in a previous year which remained unpaid.[93]

A question of damages may be brought up in controversies arising under these laws. In one instance of enticement a plaintiff sought to recover the value of the rent lost and the damage to the land owing to a growth of weeds which had resulted from his inability to secure other tenants or labor of any kind. The evidence of damage to the property was said to be admissible, and the plaintiff was allowed to recover.[94]

The Alabama statute is worded in such a manner as to make the enticer liable only where the original lease contract is in writing.[95] The only other statute subject to this interpretation is one [96] of the Georgia Acts, but its companion Act,[97] which also punishes enticement, is specifically applicable to parol contracts as well as to writ-

89. Snead v. Gilman, 44 So. 830 (Miss., 1907).
90. Mahoney v. McNeil, 77 Miss. 406, 27 So. 528 (1900).
91. Stewart v. Hill, 134 Ga. 596, 68 S. E. 328 (1910).
92. Winthrop v. Allen, 116 S. C. 388, 108 S. E. 153 (1921).
93. Wheeler v. Pannell, 96 Miss. 382, 51 So. 598 (1910).
94. Wagner v. Ellis, 85 Miss. 422, 37 So. 959 (1905).
95. See Murrell v. State, 44 Ala. 367 (1870).
96. Ga. Code (1933) §66-9904.
97. Ga. Code (1933) §66-9905.

ten contracts. All the other statutes either refer specifically to parol contracts or are silent about the matter. In Mississippi, however, the required release from the obligation of the prior contract must be in writing.[98]

It has been held that a statute making it an offense to entice farm laborers is a legitimate exercise of the police power.[99] It is not violative of due process of law,[100] equal protection of the laws,[101] or the thirteenth amendment or federal peonage laws.[102] Since such a statute is directed only at the breach of a civil duty and does not interfere with the undeniable right of the laborer to break his contract and subject himself only to civil liability therefor, it seems that no constitutional objection can be raised.[103] Any interpretation of such a statute which went beyond this would make the act invalid, since it would create involuntary servitude.[104] In a South Carolina case a judge's instruction to the jury was subject to the interpretation that the enticer could be held responsible even though the solicited tenant or employee had broken his contract of his own volition and the attempt to hire him had not been made until after the breach. The court held that such an interpretation would countenance involuntary servitude. The tenant would be compelled by economic necessity to continue his employment, since anyone with whom he sought work would be faced with an enticement suit if a job should be given him.[105]

Another somewhat similar situation is presented by a Georgia Act prohibiting any person from employing or renting lands to any tenant, cropper, or laborer who is under contract to another. This was held to be an unreasonable restriction upon the individual's right to contract with respect to his own labor. The statute was also said to be invalid in that it peremptorily forbade the renting of land to the tenant or cropper of another without regard to the relationship existing between the cultivator and his landlord and the effect of the statute upon it. The court also employed the fol-

98. Miss. Code Ann. (1942) §2129.
99. State v. Hurdle, 113 Miss. 736, 74 So. 681 (1917).
100. State v. Nix, 165 Ala. 126, 51 So. 754 (1910).
101. Hoole v. Dorroh, 75 Miss. 257, 22 So. 829 (1897).
102. Johns v. Patterson, 138 Ark. 420, 211 S. W. 387 (1919).
103. Thompson v. Box, 147 Miss. 1, 112 So. 597 (1927); Hoole v. Dorroh, 75 Miss. 257, 22 So. 829 (1897).
104. Thompson v. Box, 147 Miss. 1, 112 So. 597 (1927).
105. Shaw v. Fisher, 113 S. C. 287, 102 S. E. 325 (1920).

lowing additional argument: The tenant may have rented from his landlord a farm of insufficient size to engage the full attention of himself and the other members of his family. If he has done so and the statute could be supported as a valid piece of legislation, no other landlord could rent the cultivator any more land without making himself liable to the penalties provided by the Act. This would certainly be an unreasonable restriction on the right to contract.[106]

CONCLUSION

On the whole, it may be said that the law in relation to trespass and the other subjects treated herein is in a satisfactory condition. Hence there is little of a constructive nature which needs to be done in respect to this matter. It is to be noted that familiar principles of law are applicable, and that the cases have usually been fairly decided.

106. Fortune v. Braswell, 139 Ga. 609, 77 S. E. 818 (1913).

XIV

Agricultural Liens—Their Origin, Scope, and Limitations

IN the pre-Civil-War South there was little need for legislation establishing liens on the tenant's property, including the crops raised on the leased premises. As a general rule the production of agricultural commodities was carried on by the large plantation owners with slave labor. It was neither necessary nor profitable for the owners of large estates to hire tenants or croppers to perform the labor essential to a prosperous economy.

During the chaotic political and economic conditions which followed the war, the southern planters were compelled to find a new system of farming which would permit them to make a profitable use of their one remaining important asset, the land. The Negroes were trained in the rudiments of farming but were unable to employ their capabilities without land and supervision. Therefore it was expedient for these two groups, the landowners and the freedmen, to make arrangements by which each group could utilize skills possessed in abundance by the other.

Furthermore the Southern planters were influenced by the desire to find a method of preserving at least some vestige of their former way of life, with its long leisure hours and freedom from arduous labor. These ex-slaveholders, accustomed to absolute authority, naturally wished to devise a scheme by which as much of that authority as possible might be preserved. The tenancy or cropper contract was deemed the best method to accomplish this purpose, and at the same time to provide a remedy of some sort for the broken economy of the war-torn South.

The contracts necessarily varied as to terms. Sometimes the agreement provided for a cash rental, while in other instances a "standing rent," a certain number of units of the commodity to be raised, was required. Under the prevailing type of contract, however, the rent consisted of a fractional portion of the crops grown on the leased premises.

ORIGIN OF THE AGRICULTURAL LIENS

It is indicated in several opinions [1] that in the early days of the region the lien on crops for rent and/or advances did not exist as a common-law right. The remedy of distress, however, was available in some of the states, but in others, notably Alabama [2] and North Carolina,[3] this remedy had been abolished by statute or had never been put into effect.

In these early times crop mortgages were used to some extent to secure the landlord's or merchant's interest. A growing crop, however immature its state, was the subject of a mortgage at common law.[4] A mortgage on an unplanted crop was void at law,[5] although a court of equity would recognize such a mortgage and enforce it whenever the crop came into existence and matured.[6] One court even held that by taking a mortgage the landlord acquired the title to the crop, thereby applying the title theory of a real estate mortgage to immature produce.[7]

The landowners were anxious to find some method by which they would be assured of collecting the rent. It was generally believed, and not without reason, that the freedmen were not sufficiently conversant with business practices to be financially responsible, and that they would break their contracts and dispose of the crops to another party, leaving the landlord with an uncollectible debt. Seeking to prevent such acts on the part of tenants and to guarantee the landowner security for the indebtedness, a common form of legislation was provided affording the landlord a lien for rent and advances on the crops grown on the leased premises. Thus the common-law remedy of distress, in the states where it was available, was supplemented and the rights of the landlord made more secure.

1. Etheredge v. Hester, 32 Ala. App. 321, 25 So. (2d) 523 (1946); Frazier v. Thomas, 6 Ala. 169 (1844); Weed v. Standley, 12 Fla. 166 (1867); Johnson v. Emanuel, 50 Ga. 590 (1874); Arbuckle v. Nelms, 50 Miss. 556 (1874); Deaver v. Rice, 20 N. C. 567 (1839).
2. Frazier v. Thomas, 6 Ala. 169 (1844).
3. Dalgleish v. Grandy, 1 N. C. 161 (1800).
4. Booker v. Jones' Adm'x, 55 Ala. 266 (1876).
5. Roberts v. Jacks, 31 Ark. 597 (1876).
6. Booker v. Jones' Adm'x, 55 Ala. 266 (1876); Roberts v. Jacks, 31 Ark. 597 (1876); Hamlett v. Tallman and Graves, 30 Ark. 505 (1875).
7. Booker v. Jones' Adm'x, 55 Ala. 266 (1876).

STATUTORY LIENS FOR RENT AND ADVANCES

In every Southeastern state the landlord was given a statutory lien on crops raised on the leased premises for rent and advances made to aid in their production.[8] Any debt created with the furtherance of the crop in mind was usually considered as an advance covered by the statutes. This included the whole process of growing the crop, from the preparation of the land for cultivation to the marketing of the produce.

In some jurisdictions even this was deemed insufficient. There was still the supply merchant to be protected; so the legislatures of some of the states passed laws which gave anyone making agricultural advances a lien on the crops. At present four Southeastern states, Florida,[9] Louisiana,[10] North Carolina,[11] and Virginia,[12] give a crop lien to merchants and others who advance supplies to farmers. In two other states a somewhat limited merchant's supply lien is given. Under the present South Carolina act the lien is limited to a preference which attaches to the supplies or articles themselves and is in effect only so long as they are not consumed in the use intended by the farmer.[13] A Tennessee statute gives the merchant a supply lien only where advances are made in aid of a tobacco crop,[14] and it would seem that this limitation excludes all possibility of a lien where the advances were made in aid of any other crop.

Thus the planters and merchants of the South, who were dominant in the political set-up of the post-Reconstruction period, pro-

---

8. Ala. Code (1940) tit. 31, §15 *et seq;* Ark. Dig. Stat. (Pope, 1937) §§8845-46; Fla. Stat. Ann. (1941) §§83.08, 83.10; Ga. Code (1933) §§61-202-03; Ky. Rev. Stat. (1946) §§383.070, 383.110; La. Civ. Code Ann. (Dart, 1932) Arts. 3218-21, La. Gen. Stat. Ann. (Dart, 1932) §5058; Miss. Code Ann. (1942) §§857-858; N. C. Gen. Stat. (1943) §42-15; S. C. Code Ann. (1932) §8771; Tenn. Code Ann. (Williams, 1934) §§8017-19; Va. Code Ann. (Michie, 1936) §6454.

9. Fla. Stat. Ann. (1941) §85.22.

10. La. Civ. Code Ann. (Dart, 1932) Art. 3217.

11. N. C. Gen. Stat. (1943) §§44-52-64.

12. Va. Code Ann. (Michie, 1936) §§6452-53, 6455.

13. S. C. Code Ann. (1932) §8779. Formerly there was a statute which was not so limited. S. C. Code (1902) §3059. However, this was repealed in 1909. 26 S. C. Stat. 1909, No. 112, p. 178. At this time the legislature provided that all statutes inconsistent with this statute should be void and of no effect. But it is to be noted that the codifiers of later Codes have not as yet removed all the redundant provisions from the other portions of the lien statute, one of which mentions this lien with respect to priorities. S. C. Code Ann. (1932) §8779.

14. Tenn. Code Ann. (Williams, 1934) §§6670-75.

tected their own interst and decreased the risk of loss from unfore-
seen events and dishonest, lazy, or unfortunate tenants. That there
was some justification for their attitude is seen in the fact that,
at the beginning of any period of agricultural depression, many uncollectible debts pile up on the books of the Southern landlords and
merchants. In fact, even in ordinary times, there are always some
bad debts. Yet these liens are undoubtedly hard on the tenant in
that they limit his control of the product of his labor and often
keep him from disposing of the crop to his best advantage. Nevertheless, some sort of security is needed to protect the landlord and
merchant.

The solution of this most difficult problem challenges the inventiveness of state legislators who are interested in tenancy reform.
Is it possible to find a formula which will protect the interests of
all parties? In finding an affirmative answer to this question lies
much of the hope that the South will be able to improve the status
of its farm tenants.

QUESTIONS INVOLVING TITLE TO CROPS

Many cases arise where some issue respecting the title to the
crops grown on the rented premises becomes the bone of contention.
Does the lien of the landlord invest him with the legal title to the
crop? When does the title to the crop pass? Such questions must be
answered in order that a clear picture can be obtained of the status
of the parties to a tenancy contract.

Generally speaking, it may be said that the legal title to the crops
is in the tenant, subject to the landlord's lien for rent and/or advances, and that the lien is to be enforced by the method pointed
out in the statute of the particular state where the proceeding is
initiated.[15] The lien does not invest the landlord with a *jus in re* or a
jus ad rem, and he possesses only a prior right of payment—the
right to have so much money carved out of the proceeds when the
crop is sold.[16] Therefore the holder of a landlord's lien can maintain no action against a wrongdoer which is grounded upon the
right of property or possession.[17] Thus it is held that no landlord,
before the division of the crop, can maintain actions such as trover

15. Watson v. State, 20 Ala. App. 284, 102 So. 598 (1924); Upham v. Dodd,
24 Ark. 545 (1866); Worrill v. Barnes, 57 Ga. 404 (1876).
16. Armstrong v. Blackwood, 227 Ala. 545, 151 So. 602 (1933).
17. Norton v. Orendorff, 191 Ala. 508, 67 So. 683 (1914).

or conversion,[18] trespass,[19] detinue,[20] replevin,[21] a statutory claim suit,[22] or, waiving the tort, an action for money had and received.[23] Of course the landlord's assignee is affected with the same disabilities as his assignor in actions of this kind.[24] On the other hand the tenant, who is invested with the title, may maintain a possessory action of this nature.[25]

Sometimes a lease contract will stipulate that the title to the crop shall vest and remain in the landlord until he shall have been fully paid. The Georgia court has held that a contract of this kind extending over a period of years is not invalid with respect to the crops grown during the last year, as a transfer of property not in existence, the transaction simply amounting to a reservation by the landlord of the fruits of his own land.[26]

A similar situation is seen under the North Carolina statute.[27] In this state it is provided that, unless otherwise specified in the lease contract, possession of all crops raised on premises rented for agricultural purposes shall be deemed to be vested in the lessor or his assigns until he or they shall have been paid the rent and advances and all stipulations of the lease shall have been performed. There seems to have been some confusion with respect to the identity of the titleholder under this statute. While the better view appears to be that the landowner is merely a trustee in constructive possession

18. Baker v. Cotney, 142 Ala. 566, 38 So. 131 (1905); Martin v. Scott, 14 Ala. App. 230, 69 So. 309 (1915); Manilla Supply Co. v. Tiger Bros., 126 Ark. 105, 189 S. W. 675 (1916); Anderson & Co. v. Bowles, 44 Ark. 108 (1884); Worrill v. Barnes, 57 Ga. 404 (1876); Schoenlau-Steiner Trunk Top & Veneer Co. v. Hilderbrand, 152 Tenn. 166, 274 S. W. 544 (1925).

19. Baker v. Cotney, 142 Ala. 566, 38 So. 131 (1905).

20. First Nat. Bank of Stevenson v. Crawford, 227 Ala. 188, 149 So. 228 (1933); aff'g. 25 Ala. App. 463, 149 So. 230 (1933); Killian v. Hall Auto Co., 25 Ala. App. 518, 149 So. 716 (1933). But see Gafford v. Stearns, 51 Ala. 434 (1874).

21. Knox v. Hellums, 38 Ark. 413 (1882). Cf. Titsworth v. Frauenthal, 52 Ark. 254, 12 S. W. 498 (1889); Scarborough v. Lucas, 119 Miss. 128, 80 So. 521 (1919).

22. Jackson v. Bain, 74 Ala. 328 (1883); Treadway v. Treadway's Ex'rs, 56 Ala. 390 (1876).

23. Anderson & Co. v. Bowles, 44 Ark. 108 (1884); Worrill v. Barnes, 57 Ga. 404 (1876).

24. First Nat. Bank of Stevenson v. Crawford, 227 Ala. 188, 149 So. 228 (1933), aff'g. 25 Ala. App. 463, 149 So. 230 (1933).

25. Williams v. Sykes, 170 Miss. 88, 154 So. 727 (1934).

26. DeVaughn v. Howell, 82 Ga. 336, 9 S. E. 173 (1889).

27. N. C. Gen. Stat. (1943) §42-15.

and that he has no title to the crop prior to a settlement,[28] there is some authority for the proposition that the title as well as the right to possession is vested in the landlord.[29] The view first stated would be more in accord with the usual holding in respect to the tenancy relationship and does not differ greatly from the view taken prior to the enactment of the statute.[30]

In one instance arising under this statute a lessor had agreed to take a stated sum of money or a portion of the crop as rent, and it was shown that he had actually received a part of the rent in money. It was held that the lessor was entitled to hold the crop until the rent was paid in full.[31] Whether the crop is in the hands of the tenant or a third party, the landlord may maintain an action for his part of the crop, the fact that he is suing for only a portion making no difference.[32] Furthermore, where no time was fixed for a division of the produce, it was ruled that the landowner did not have to wait until the entire crop had been gathered and fully harvested before bringing the possessory action authorized by the statute.[33]

In Tennessee, unless the lease provides otherwise, the title to the part of the crop reserved to the landlord as rent is deemed vested in him, and this is true whether the crop be divided or undivided.[34] Louisiana statutes provide that the right of the lessor is of a higher nature than a mere privilege, the Louisiana term for a lien, and that his share of the crop is at any and all times vested in him, thus enabling him to take possesion of the property and retain it until payment is made.[35] In authorizing a recovery for crop injury by a third person, a Kentucky statute provides that the right to that portion of the crop to which the landlord is entitled by agreement shall vest in him, though the crop may have been planted or

28. Tobacco Growers Ass'n v. Bissett, 187 N. C. 180, 121 S. E. 446 (1924); State v. Copeland, 86 N. C. 692 (1882).

29. Adams v. Growers' Warehouse, 230 N. C. 704, 55 S. E. (2d) 331 (1949); Batts v. Sullivan, 182 N. C. 129, 108 S. E. 511 (1921); McGhee v. Breedlove, 122 N. C. 277, 30 S. E. 311 (1898); Smith v. Tindall, 107 N. C. 88, 12 S. E. 121 (1890).

30. Ross v. Swaringer, 31 N. C. 481 (1849).

31. McGhee v. Breedlove, 122 N. C. 277, 30 S. E. 311 (1898).

32. Boone v. Darden, 109 N. C. 74, 13 S. E. 728 (1891).

33. Rich v. Hobson, 112 N. C. 79, 16 S. E. 931 (1893); Smith v. Tindall, 107 N. C. 88, 12 S. E. 121 (1890).

34. Tenn. Code Ann. (Williams, 1934) §8027.

35. La. Gen. Stat. Ann. (Dart, 1932) §5065; La. Civ. Code Ann. (Dart, 1932) Art. 3218.

raised by a person other than the original tenant.[36] The effect of the
Louisiana and Kentucky provisions upon the question of title
generally can only be surmised.

There have been quite a few cases concerning the transfer of
title to crops from one party to another. Often issues of this kind
arise in situations where a tenant is indicted for larceny. In one
instance it was decided that a landlord, although possessed of a
prior lien on his tenant's crop, could not acquire title simply by
taking possession. After he had done so, the tenant appropriated
the crop to his own use. It was held that this was not larceny, and
that the prosecution must proceed under the statute making it a
crime for a tenant to remove lien-encumbered property.[37] A North
Carolina tenant was hauling seed cotton to his lessor's gin. He
threw a sack of it off the wagon by the side of the road, returned
to the spot at night, and carried it away to his own home. The act
of throwing the sack off the wagon was not considered an abandonment of his own possession. Hence the subsequent nocturnal seizure
was no trespass upon the possession of the lessor and therefore not
larceny. It was said that if the cotton had been delivered to the
lessor at the gin, giving him actual possession, and the tenant had
then taken it away, the latter would have been guilty of the crime
of larceny.[38]

The issue of transfer of title may arise in other situations as well.
Thus it is ruled that where there is a contract of sale for parcels
of cotton and an agreement that they shall be counted, weighed,
measured and/or separated from a larger bulk before dominion
over them is turned over to another, the sale is not complete and
the title does not pass until the counting, weighing, measuring,
and/or separation takes place.[39] In this instance, however, the court
declared that it might be possible to have a complete sale without
these formalities, and even without an agreement with respect to the
price, when such was the understanding of the parties and the
transaction was consummated by delivery. In another instance there
was an attempted transfer of a quantity of cotton, part of a crop
that had not been ginned. Neither had it been delivered, separated
from the bulk, or otherwise identified. It was ruled that this mere-

36. Ky. Rev. Stat. (1946) §383.120.
37. Teel v. State, 7 Ga. App. 600, 67 S. E. 699 (1910).
38. State v. Copeland, 86 N. C. 692 (1882).
39. Aderholt v. Embry, 78 Ala. 185 (1884).

ly amounted to an agreement to sell, and that the intended transferee acquired no title to the cotton.[40]

An Arkansas landlord was held to have no property right in his
tenant's corn crop, though there was some evidence that it had been
set apart as intended for him, where there was nothing in the testimony to indicate that the rent was payable in corn, or that he had
accepted it in payment, or even knew that it had been so set apart.[41]
However, where an Alabama tenant set aside certain bales of cotton
sufficient to cover the rent, notified the landlord that he had done
so, and was instructed to sell them and apply the proceeds to the
latter's account, it was held that there had been such a constructive
delivery as would transfer the title.[42]

PROBLEMS RELATING TO EXTENT OF LIEN IN GENERAL

Many problems arise concerning the scope of agrictultural liens,
particularly the landlord's lien for rent and/or advances. New
questions are continually making their appearance, and a rather
variegated and complex pattern of cases has come before the courts.

First it may be said that a landlord's lien on the crops exists
whether the rent is reserved in money or is to be paid in a fractional
part of the produce.[43] Furthermore, a tenant's agreement to pay the
property taxes on the leased premises may be construed as a contract
to pay them as a part of the rent, so as to give the landlord a lien
therefor.[44] The lien has been held to cover the sum received for the
use of a dwelling house located in a nearby town about a mile and
a half from the leased farm, the important issue being whether the
dwelling was reasonably essential for the proper fulfillment of the
tenant's contract to carry on farming operations.[45] In another instance a landlord rented farm land and a nearby store building for a
percentage of the crops and forty dollars. The appellate court stated

40. Upham v. Dodd, 24 Ark. 545 (1866).
41. Bell & Miller v. Matheny, 36 Ark. 572 (1880).
42. Belser v. Youngblood, 103 Ala. 545, 15 So. 863 (1894).
43. Schoenlaw-Steiner T. T. & V. Co. v. Hilderbrand, 152 Tenn. 166, 274
S. W. 544 (1925). Under an early Mississippi statute, Miss. Laws 1873, p. 79, a
landlord who reserved rent payable in money, and not in kind, did not have
a lien unless the contract so provided. Phillips v. Douglass, 53 Miss. 175 (1876).
Under the more modern Mississippi statute, however, this distinction is no
longer recognized, and the landlord has a lien no matter how the rent is
paid. See Seavy & Sons v. Godbold, 99 Miss. 113, 54 So. 838 (1911).
44. Gedge v. Shoenberger, 83 Ky. 91 (1885); Roberts v. Sims, 64 Miss. 597,
2 So. 72 (1887).
45. Dale v. Webb, 166 Miss. 309, 146 So. 875 (1933).

that the trial judge had laid too much stress upon the contention of the landlord that the transaction was an entire one. The land and store could be leased by the same instrument, and yet the contract might still be severable. If, upon another trial, the contract was found to be severable, the forty-dollar item would be held to cover the store rent and hence not secured by a lien on the crops.[46] In another case it was held that even though the lease apportions the rent between the farm and the dwelling house on an adjoining farm, the rent for both is a lien on the crops.[47]

A proceeding to enforce an Arkansas landlord's lien for rent may be maintained, although it is stipulated in the leasing agreement that the sum claimed is for the hire of certain personal property as well as for rent. Here it is unnecessary to state the amount due on each item, especially if it is alleged that the hire of the personalty is worth nothing.[48]

At an early date the Mississippi court decided that the statute of that state then in effect gave the landlord a lien on all the agricultural products of the leased premises, paramount to all other liens, claims, or demands of any kind, to secure the payment of the rent and any indebtedness for supplies furnished the tenant, and declared that the right of the landlord to enforce this lien was not prejudiced or in any way diminished by the termination of the lease and the removal of the tenant. It was said that in either event the lien continued in effect until it was extinguished by the elapsing of the period prescribed by law for its enforcement, just as if there had been no removal of the tenant, or of the produce. The court also remarked that there was a different rule of law with respect to goods and chattels which were not agricultural products grown on the leased premises. It was said that the landlord had no lien on such property, but only a right of seizure by attachment or distress.[49]

The Virginia court has held that crops raised in the ordinary course of husbandry upon land previously set apart as a homestead are exempt from levy to the same extent as the land itself.[50] A few courts, however, have held that the tenant's personal property exemption does not prevail over the landlord's lien for rent and/or

46. Reynolds v. Tayler, 144 N. C. 165, 56 S. E. 871 (1907).
47. Scroggins v. Foster, 76 Miss. 318, 24 So. 194 (1898).
48. Dickenson v. Harris, 48 Ark. 355, 3 S. W. 58 (1887).
49. Fitzgerald v. Fowlkes, 60 Miss. 270 (1882), *approving* Henry v. Davis, 60 Miss. 212 (1882).
50. Neblett v. Shackelton, 111 Va. 707, 69 S. E. 946 (1911).

supplies, and that therefore the crops cannot be held against a claim of this nature.[51] The reason for this is that claims of this kind are in the nature of purchase money and are therefore not affected by the exemption.[52] However, where an attempt was made to extend this doctrine to a claim under a farm laborer's lien, the Georgia courts refused to do so, notwithstanding the fact that the amount due the laborer was for work done in raising the products which were alleged to be exempt.[53] This would seem to be an unjust discrimination in favor of the landlords and merchants. Surely a farm hand's labor is as valuable to the growing of the crop as the land upon which it is grown or the supplies which go into its production.

The Federal Bankruptcy Act[54] renders void liens obtained by legal proceedings within four months of the filing of the petition in bankruptcy. A question arose in respect to the enforceability of the landlord's lien where the tenant is a bankrupt. It was held that under the Georgia law a landlord's lien does not ripen until foreclosure and hence cannot be said to have been obtained through legal proceedings barring it within the meaning of the Federal statute.[55] According to this view of the law, therefore, the lien is not cut off by the petition in bankruptcy.

Sometimes a tenant will give his landlord a rent note which includes an agreement to pay an attorney's fee in the event that the instrument should have to be placed in the hands of an attorney for collection. In such an instance the Mississippi court was of the opinion that such an indebtedness was not covered by the lien and that the tenant's crop was not impressed with a preferred claim.[56] Moreover, the Louisiana court has held that a lessor can claim no privilege in an instance where he desires to be reimbursed for dam-

51. Moseman v. Comer, 160 Ga. 106, 127 S. E. 406 (1925); Tift v. Newsom, 44 Ga. 600 (1872); Smith & Hollis v. Youngblood, 23 Ga. App. 640, 99 S. E. 143 (1919); Harrell v. Fagan, 43 Ga. 339 (1871); Taliaferro v. Pry, 41 Ga. 622 (1871); Davis v. Meyers, 41 Ga. 95 (1870); Hamer v. McCall, 121 N. C. 196, 28 S. E. 297 (1897); Durham v. Speeke, 82 N. C. 87 (1880); Hill v. George, 38 Tenn. 394 (1858).

52. Tift v. Newsom, 44 Ga. 600 (1872); Smith & Hollis v. Youngblood, 23 Ga. App. 640, 99 S. E. 143 (1919).

53. Watson v. Williams, 110 Ga. 321, 35 S. E. 344 (1900).

54. Bankruptcy Act (1898) §67f.

55. Henderson v. Mayer, 225 U. S. 631, 32 Sup. Ct. 699 (1912); Moseman v. Comer, 160 Ga. 106, 127 S. E. 406 (1925); Turner v. Sitton, 160 Ga. 215, 127 S. E. 847 (1925).

56. Williams Bros. v. Bank of Blue Mountain, 132 Miss. 178, 95 So. 843 (1923); O'Keefe v. McLemore, 125 Miss. 394, 87 So. 655 (1921).

ages inflicted upon certain mules the hire of which was included in the contract for the lease of a plantation.[57] Again, in an early Alabama case, the court declared that the note or obligation then required to be executed for agricultural advances was vitiated as a foundation for a statutory crop lien by the inclusion therein, knowingly and intentionally, of a debt which was contracted for a separate and distinct purpose, and which constituted a substantial portion of the consideration for the instrument.[58] The dissenting judge believed that there should be only a *pro tanto* vitiation, and this is probably a more practical view.

Where a tenant voluntarily places his crop in the possession of the landlord for the avowed purpose of securing the lien, the Kentucky court has declared that it would be folly to require the latter to go through the useless and expensive process of instituting an action to enforce the claim.[59] In a recent case, however, it was held that an agreement to turn over the year's potato crop to be applied on the landlord's unpaid rent would not constitute a valid claim in the absence of evidence that there had been a delivery. Here it was shown that the tenant had turned over to the landlord certain receipts given to him by a produce exchange to which he had delivered the crop for sale in the market, and not for storage. It was said that this transaction constituted at most a pledge of the crop, which was constructively delivered by the transfer of the receipts, and that any claim the landlord might have did not amount to a lien. The court refused to consider the receipts as warehouse receipts and declared that the produce exchange, with a right to deduct a debt due it from the sale of the crop, was liable for the costs of the action because it had made no tender of the balance of the money in its hands.[60]

In Louisiana it was held that a lessor, who had terminated the lease contract by buying the lessee's right of occupancy at a sale under execution, had not retroactively surrendered his claim to the lessee's movable property which had been seized and sold by the sheriff in partial satisfaction of a judgment for rent.[61] In this state

57. Griffith v. Keller, 147 La. 540, 85 So. 233 (1920).

58. Comer v. Daniel, 69 Ala. 434 (1881).

59. Barlow v. Fuller, 157 Ky. 582, 163 S. W. 742 (1914); Marquess v. Ladd, 30 Ky. Law Rep. 1142, 100 S. W. 305 (1907).

60. Martin v. St. Matthew's Produce Exchange, 265 Ky. 26, 95 S. W. (2d) 1119 (1936).

61. Ranson v. Voiron, 176 La. 718, 146 So. 681 (1933).

it has been remarked that the lessor has a twofold right—a right of pledge, with its attendant authority to hold the chattel and the resultant preference, plus a right of privilege, distinct from the pledge.[62]

Under Louisiana statutes [63] giving the lessor a right of pledge on the lessee's movables, the tools and instruments by which the lessee makes his living are exempted from the pledge. In 1935 the Louisiana intermediate appellate court ruled that farming tools and implements which the lessee of a strawberry farm used in tilling the soil could not be deemed to be within the exemption, the statute being construed as applicable to lessees engaged in some trade or occupation of an industrial or professional nature.[64] When the question reached the state Supreme Court a year later, however, the majority of a divided court took the view that the tools and implements of a farmer are just as much within the reason and spirit of the exemption as the implements of some artisan or professional man.[65]

The landlord's lien under the North Carolina statute has been held to extend to and include the costs of such legal proceedings as are necessary to enforce the claim for rent.[66]

Under the laws of Kentucky only the personal property of the lessee or his assignee or subtenant is liable to distress, and in view of the statutes concerning the rights of married women [67] a landlord cannot claim a lien for rent against property belonging to the tenant's wife which had been brought upon the premises before it was mortgaged to a claimant bank.[68] This is of course the modern view in common-law states, but in Louisiana the lessor's privilege seems to be enforceable against property belonging to third persons which has been placed in the hands of the lessor or the lessee, unless it can be proved that the lessor knew that the articles did not belong to the lessee.[69]

---

62. O'Kelley v. Ferguson, 49 La. Ann. 1230, 22 So. 783 (1897).
63. La. Civ. Code (Dart, 1932) Art. 2705; La. Code Prac. (Dart, 1942) Art. 644.
64. Vento v. Amici, 159 So. 751 (La. App., 1935).
65. Young v. Geter, 185 La. 709, 170 So. 240 (1936). Three judges dissented.
66. Slaughter v. Winfrey, 85 N. C. 159 (1881).
67. Ky. Rev. Stat. (1946) §404.010.
68. First Nat. Bank of Hopkinsville v. Trimble, 229 Ky. 280, 17 S. W. (2d) 223 (1929).
69. La. Civ. Code Ann. (Dart, 1932) Art. 3260.

IMPACT OF FEDERAL LEGISLATION

During the economic depression of the 'thirties many federal laws were enacted which had as their object the relief of the agricultural classes in the communities. The Agricultural Adjustment Administration was set up in 1933, and various bureaus were established. In order to help the farmers in their battle against economic collapse crop control legislation and other devices were put into effect. Among these were some which collided with state laws concerning landlords' liens. There have been a few cases in which the landlord's interest in the crops of his tenant or cropper has been affected or alleged to be affected by this federal legislation.

In one instance an Arkansas landlord claimed a lien on the proceeds of certain cotton in the hands of the tenant's mortgagee and not credited to the tenant's account. It was alleged and proved that the mortgagee, knowing that the land on which the cotton was grown belonged to the landlord, had assisted the tenant in wrongfully appropriating it by acting as his agent in placing it in a government loan. Notwithstanding the fact that the landlord had authorized the tenant to sell the cotton, it was held that the landlord was entitled to a lien on the proceeds in the mortgagee's possession.[70] In another Arkansas case a landlord and his tenant entered into a contract to divide the rent received from land leased to the Federal Government with respect to any amount over eight dollars per acre. The court held that crops raised by persons under contract to the tenant were not subject to the landlord's lien with respect to that portion of the rent owed to the landlord for the land leased to the government, and that such was the case irrespective of the true status of the cultivators, whether they were considered as subtenants or sharecroppers.[71]

Under the Agricultural Adjustment Administration set-up a tenant was allowed the privilege of subleasing the rented premises to the Secretary of Agriculture. In one instance two hundred and seventy acres of Mississippi farm land so leased had been taken out of cotton production and a government check for the rent delivered to the tenant and paid in full. Here it was held that after the government's interest in the transaction had terminated, the tenant would not have a claim to this money, representing the rent

70. Lee Gin Co. v. Archillion, 198 Ark. 564, 129 S. W. (2d) 952 (1939).
71. Dulaney v. Balls, 193 Ark. 701, 102 S. W. (2d) 88 (1937).

of the sublessee, to the exclusion of the landlord whose land had been involved. The landlord, having an interest in the crop, and in the contract of sublease as well, for the satisfaction of the amount of rent due him from the original lessee, could not be neglected. The court also ruled that the tenant's shares of a production credit association's stock, purchased by the tenant with money realized from the sale of agricultural products grown on the leased premises, should be subjected to the claim of the landlord for rent. However, it was declared that certain surplus cotton tax exemption certificates, received by the tenant as trustee under a declaration executed by him pursuant to the provisions of the Cotton Control Act [72] and the regulations of the Secretary of Agriculture, were exempt and therefore free from being levied upon to satisfy the landlord's lien for rent.[73]

An Arkansas farm tenant made an agreement with the Secretary of Agriculture to plow up and destroy cotton growing on leased land, the Secretary promising to allow him certain cotton options. The landlord filed a claim against a check and the options in the possession of the Secretary's local agents. He alleged that the tenant had agreed to pay as rent a certain amount of cotton at date of delivery, that no part of the cotton or its proceeds had been paid, and that the tenant, in pursuance of the agreement with the Secretary of Agriculture, had destroyed the crop on which the landlord had a lien. The landlord claimed the right to garnishee the check in the hands of the local agents to satisfy his lien for rent. It was held that a court of equity had jurisdiction in this instance to enforce the lien and to allow the landlord to bring garnishment proceedings, since a landlord's lien cannot be impaired in such cases by the acts of third persons, even though they happen to be government agents. The court further declared that "it may be said that the impounding and compulsory assignment of this check to the one rightfully entitled thereto under the laws of this state is no interference with the public interest, for the reason that, when this check is issued and delivered to the local agent of the Secretary of Agriculture for delivery to the payee or the one entitled to the proceeds thereof under the laws of this state, the government agencies' interests therein are at an end."[74] Much the same reasoning

72. 48 Stat. 598
73. Life Ins. Co. of Virginia v. Page, 178 Miss. 287, 172 So. 873 (1937).
74. Graves Bros. v. Lasley, 190 Ark. 251, 78 S. W. (2d) 810 (1935).

appears to have been employed in the Mississippi decision mentioned above.

A Kentucky lease provided for a cash rent, thus leaving the products of the farm to the lessee. A clause stated that if the lessee grew more than one acre of tobacco, which was base acreage under federal regulations, the lessor should not be penalized for any excessive amount of tobacco grown on the land. The lessee grew more than one acre of tobacco on the premises, and the lessor claimed that he was entitled to share in the excess. The court declared that the above clause would not be construed as mandatorily limiting the amount of tobacco the lessee might grow. Hence there was no violation of the lease contract, and the lessor was not permitted to share in the proceeds of the crop from the excess acreage. The only effect of the clause was to absolve the lessor from any penalty which might be inflicted as a result of the violation of the governmental regulations.[75]

In one rather novel controversy the attorney of an Arkansas tenant attempted to avoid the landlord's lien by using the Frazier-Lemke Act. He sought an order of the Federal Conciliation Commissioner, who had authority under the act to postpone certain indebtedness, permitting the tenant to sell a crop which had been attached by the landlord in an effort to enforce his lien for rent and advances. The court declared that the Frazier-Lemke Act had been enacted to protect home owners during the national emergency caused by the depression by authorizing the federal courts to postpone the foreclosure of real estate mortgages on homes. The act had not been passed to aid tenants in schemes which were aimed at cheating their landlords and preventing them from collecting rent and supply bills justly due. The court held both the tenant and his attorney liable for conversion in taking possession of the crop for their own purposes.[76]

More cases of this type would undoubtedly have arisen if World War II and the events leading up to that greatest of all conflagrations had not initiated economic prosperity and its aftermath of scarcities in many major commodities, including agricultural products. However, an economic depression will bring forth other efforts to help the farm population, and cases similar to the ones here discussed will perhaps be more frequent.

75. McLin v. Johnson, 302 Ky. 705, 196 S. W. (2d) 381 (1946).
76. Clemmons v. Byars, 197 Ark. 300, 122 S. W. (2d) 652 (1938).

EXTENSION OF LIEN TO CROP OF SUBTENANT

To what extent is the lien of the landlord on the products of the farm affected by a sublease of the property? The courts' answers to this and other related questions form a basis for some of the most interesting problems of farm tenancy law. While there is a similarity about the way in which all of the Southeastern states have dealt with this matter, there are many local differences which prevent generalizations being made to any great extent. The results reached in two or more jurisdictions may be very much alike, and yet the manner of arriving at these conclusions is often very dissimilar. Sometimes strange quirks appear. For this reason a state-by-state survey of the decisions in the various jurisdictions is necessary.

ALABAMA

In Alabama, for instance, a statute [77] makes the crop of the subtenant subject to the landlord's lien, and this is true though there is no privity of contract between them.[78] Here the lien extends to all crops grown on the leased premises, whether produced by tenant or subtenant.[79] This statute further provides that the crop of the tenant in chief must be exhausted before the landlord can lawfully proceed against the crop of the subtenant. Another statute [80] provides that if there is any danger that the tenant in chief's crop may be dissipated, the subtenant may notify the landlord of the facts, and if the landlord does not then act expeditiously, the subtenant is relieved of liability. This statutory right to compel the landlord to proceed against the crop of the tenant in chief until it is exhausted has been applied in several instances by the courts.[81] If the landlord does not exercise his claim against the tenant in chief within a reasonable time after receiving the above-mentioned notice, he loses his right of action for the deficiency against the crop of the subtenant.[82] The landlord has the burden of proving that the crop of

77. Ala. Code Ann. (Michie, 1928) §8810, as interpreted in Drinkard v. State, 12 Ala. App. 184, 68 So. 553 (1915).

78. Moneyham v. Herring, 204 Ala. 332, 85 So. 390 (1920); Robinson v. Lehman, Durr & Co., 72 Ala. 401 (1882).

79. Chandler v. Burk, 211 Ala. 93, 99 So. 727 (1924); Foster v. Goodwin, 82 Ala. 384, 2 So. 895 (1887); Givens v. Easley, 17 Ala. 385 (1850).

80. Ala. Code (1940) tit. 31, §27.

81. Chandler v. Burk, 211 Ala. 93, 99 So. 727 (1924); Lehman Bros. v. Howze & Creagh, 73 Ala. 302 (1882).

82. Derrick v. Pollard, 117 Ala. 654, 23 So. 659 (1898).

the tenant in chief is not sufficient to satisfy the lien.[83] The right of demanding that the crop of the tenant in chief be exhausted before the subtenant's liability accrues is personal and does not arise in favor of a creditor of the subtenant.[84] There is also a statutory provision [85] that a subtenant who is forced to discharge the landlord's lien because of the tenant in chief's default is subrogated to the rights of the landlord against the tenant.

In an early case a sheriff, after levying on enough of the crop of the tenant in chief to satisfy the landlord, suffered the tenant and his family to retain and dispose of it. It was ruled that the officer was not thereby rendered liable to a subtenant for a subsequent seizure and sale of the crop raised by the latter on a portion of the premises which had been sublet to him by the original lessee.[86] A modern court would probably hold the levying officer responsible here. It would seem that the officer had been guilty of actionable negligence in allowing the produce to be dissipated.

Again, certain rent notes, given by subtenants to the tenant in chief, were indorsed for value to a third person before maturity. Here it was held that the landlord, who had filed a bill in equity to enforce a crop lien, must aver and prove that money used in paying the notes had come from the sale of crops grown on the rented premises, along with notice to the indorsee that such was the case. He failed to sustain this burden. It was held that the innocent purchaser of the notes was entitled to protection.[87]

Another controversy involved the application of the parol evidence rule to situations of this kind. It was said that the rule forbidding the introduction of parol testimony to vary or contradict instruments in writing applies only to parties to the contract and their privies. Strangers to a written agreement, who have neither assented to the truth of the statements contained therein nor agreed that they should be a memorial of facts admitted to exist, are not bound by the contract and may, whenever it is introduced to affect their rights, contradict it by parol. Therefore, the court declared that a subtenant, not being a party or privy to a written obligation for the payment of a "standing rent" to the landlord agreed to by

83. Plunkett v. Dendy, 197 Ala. 262, 72 So. 525 (1916).

84. Baker v. Cotney, 187 Ala. 137, 65 So. 799 (1914); Baker v. Allen, 161 Ala. 288, 44 So. 847 (1909); Robinson v. Lehman, Durr & Co., 72 Ala. 401 (1882).

85. Ala. Code (1940) tit. 31, §26.

86. Givens v. Easley, 17 Ala. 385 (1850).

87. Webb & Aigner v. Darrow, 227 Ala. 441, 150 So. 357 (1933).

the tenant in chief, might, on the trial of his motion to vacate the levy of the landlord's attachment on the subtenant's crop, show by parol what the true consideration for the agreement had been.[88]

ARKANSAS

Under Arkansas law the subtenant is liable for the rent of only that portion of the land which he actually occupies or cultivates.[89] The tenant, before collecting rent from the subtenant, must obtain from the landlord a written directive stating the amount of rent which he is authorized to collect from the said subtenant.[90] Other statutes [91] authorize the amount paid out upon this written directive to be deducted from the *pro rata* amount of rent for which the land cultivated by the subtenant would otherwise be liable. Under these laws a tenant in chief who collects unlawfully from the subtenant is held criminally responsible.

A chattel mortgage on all crops, given by a tenant in chief for supplies furnished him by the landlord, was held to constitute no lien on the subtenant's crop, the tenant in chief not having a claim on this crop beyond one for a *pro rata* amount of rent.[92]

Another controversy arose where a tenant turned over to the landlord a bill of sale on cotton raised by subtenants, in satisfaction of a rent claim when it became due. Here it was held that the landlord was responsible to the subtenants and their mortgagees for the amount which he had received in excess of the rent due him, notwithstanding the fact that at the time of the transfer the cotton was not worth the amount of the rent, and that it had been necessary for him to hold it for some time before being able to sell it for a sum in excess of the claim for rent.[93]

The Arkansas law may be summed up by saying that, regardless of the terms of the agreement between the tenant and subtenant, the landlord has a lien on all the crops grown on the leased premises, subject, of course, to the above-mentioned proportional limitation.[94]

88. Lehman Bros. v. Howze & Creagh, 73 Ala. 302 (1882).

89. Ark. Dig. Stat. (Pope, 1937) §8848; Watkins v. Wells, 172 Ark. 696, 290 S. W. 593 (1927); Morgan v. Russell, 151 Ark. 405, 236 S. W. 602 (1922); Storthz v. Smith, 109 Ark. 552, 161 S. W. 183 (1913); Jacobson v. Atkins, 103 Ark. 91, 146 S. W. 133 (1912).

90. Ark. Dig. Stat. (Pope, 1937) §8850.

91. Ark. Dig. Stat. (Pope, 1937) §§8851-52.

92. Watkins v. Wells, 172 Ark. 696, 290 S. W. 593 (1927).

93. West v. Cook Mercantile Co., 157 Ark. 600, 249 S. W. 561 (1923).

94. Watkins v. Wells, 172 Ark. 696, 290 S. W. 593 (1927).

GEORGIA

In Georgia the subtenant's crop, when it matures, is subject to the lien of the landlord for the rent owed to him by the original tenant. The lien may be collected on a distress warrant directed against the tenant.[95] The courts have adopted very much the same proportional basis [96] as is used in determining the liability of the subtenant under the Arkansas statutes.

The landlord may adopt the subtenant as his own and enforce his lien for the rent primarily due him from the tenant in chief.[97] Where this has been done, the subtenant becomes the substitute for the original tenant, at least to such an extent that the lien of the landowner for supplies furnished the original tenant to make the crop cannot be defeated by the contract of subletting. Under such circumstances the landlord is entitled to a lien, not only for the rent, but for the supplies advanced to make the crop as well.[98]

Where the tenant in chief defaults, the subtenant, in order to protect himself against double liability, may discharge his own rent obligation by applying on the debt due to the landlord from the original tenant so much of his crop or its proceeds as it takes to pay his rent. After being so discharged, he cannot be compelled to pay the rent, or any part of it, a second time.[99]

In this jurisdiction it is said that a tenant has no power to consent to an application by the landlord of the subject matter of the lien for rent in such a way that it would leave that claim in force to the prejudice of a subtenant; nor can the landlord apply the proceeds of the tenant's crop to an indebtedness of the tenant to the disadvantage of the subtenant.[100]

Sometimes, in satisfaction of the rent agreed upon, a subtenant will give his negotiable promissory note to the tenant in chief, who later transfers it to a third person. Here it is held that the landlord may proceed by distress warrant to subject the subtenant's crop to

95. Leonard v. Fields, 143 Ga. 479, 85 S. E. 315 (1915); Thompson v. Commercial Guano Co., 93 Ga. 282, 20 S.E. 309 (1893); Horton v. Union Store, 19 Ga. App. 184, 91 S. E. 214 (1917).

96. Leonard v. Fields, 143 Ga. 479, 85 S. E. 315 (1915).

97. McConnell v. East Point Land Co., 100 Ga. 129, 28 S. E. 80 (1897); Long v. Clark, 16 Ga. App. 355, 85 S. E. 358 (1915); Nash v. Orr, 9 Ga. App. 33, 70 S. E. 194 (1911).

98. Nash v. Orr, 9 Ga. App. 33, 70 S. E. 194 (1911).

99. Thompson v. Commercial Guano Co., 93 Ga. 282, 20 S. E. 309 (1893).

100. Leonard v. Fields, 143 Ga. 479, 85 S. E. 315 (1915).

his lien, although doing so might result in the latter's double liability.[101] If the note were non-negotiable, no such double liability would exist.[102]

KENTUCKY

A Kentucky statute [103] provides that rent may be recovered from a subtenant, but the latter is responsible only for the amount accrued after his interest begins. It is probable that an agricultural landlord's lien would be limited accordingly.

LOUISIANA

A Louisiana statute extends the right of pledge to the effects of a subtenant in so far as he is indebted to the principal tenant, although payment in anticipation does not release him from the landlord's claim.[104] Nothing is said in this act which would indicate that the same could not be said with respect to the privilege. But it has been held that a lessor of farm land can recover nothing from a subtenant who has delivered to the tenant in chief the share of the crop called for by the sublease.[105]

MISSISSIPPI

Crops grown on leased premises in Mississippi are subject to the landlord's lien for rent, whether they are raised by the tenant or by a subtenant to whom the tenant had rented the land.[106] The subtenant is in the position of a surety [107] and may compel the landlord to resort first to the crop of the original tenant in order to satisfy his lien.[108] It is clear that the ordinary rules of suretyship law apply.

101. Barlow v. Jones, 117 Ga. 412, 43 S. E. 690 (1903).

102. Thompson v. Commercial Guano Co., 93 Ga. 282, 20 S. E. 309 (1893).

103. Ky. Rev. Stat. (1946) §383.010.

104. La. Civ. Code Ann. (Dart, 1932) Art. 2706.

105. Pellachino v. Cryer, 160 So. 167 (La. App., 1935).

106. Hooks v. Burns, 173 Miss. 413, 160 So. 910 (1935); 168 Miss. 723, 152 So. 469 (1934); Dale v. Webb, 166 Miss. 309, 146 So. 875 (1933); Powell v. Tomlinson, 129 Miss. 354, 92 So. 226 (1922); Applewhite v. Nelms, 71 Miss. 482, 14 So. 443 (1894). See also case involving vendee. Maynard v. Cocke, 15 So. 788 (Miss., 1894).

107. Dale v. Webb, 166 Miss. 309, 146 So. 875 (1933); Applewhite v. Nelms, 71 Miss. 482, 14 So. 443 (1894).

108. Hooks v. Burns, 168 Miss. 723, 152 So. 469 (1934); Dale v. Webb, 166 Miss. 309, 146 So. 875 (1933); Newman, Inc. v. Delta Grocery & Cotton Co., 138 Miss. 683, 103 So. 373, 104 So. 157 (1925); Applewhite v. Nelms, 71 Miss. 482, 14 So. 443 (1894).

Thus where the landlord and the tenant in chief made a new agreement whereby the former took additional security and extended the date of payment, the subtenant was released and his crops were freed from the claim of the landlord.[109]

In an early case[110] the court used language which indicated that a subtenant was responsible only for the rent of the portion of the premises which he had subleased, and in a more recent opinion[111] the same view appears to have won approval. It is doubtful, nevertheless, if the court, when faced with the direct issue, would not hold that the subtenant's crop could be taken if needed to complete the sum which would satisfy the landlord's lien, for, as noted in the previous paragraphs, the crops grown on the premises, by whomsoever raised, can be seized to satisfy the landlord's claim.

In one instance a tenant subleased a part of the land rented to him, agreeing to pay the rent for that portion, but not promising in writing to be responsible for advances made to the subtenant. The landlord charged the goods advanced to a separate account in the name of the subtenant. The tenant was named as surety, although his written consent had not been obtained. This evidence was said to prove only an oral promise to pay the debts of another, which was void under the Statute of Frauds, and hence the tenant could not be held responsible for the advances.[112]

NORTH CAROLINA

Under North Carolina decisions the landlord's right to the crop to secure payment of the rent is not impaired by a tenant's act of subletting.[113] The lien of the landlord is paramount, and hence the subtenant's crop may be subjected to a double claim. The landlord has been held to have a prior claim where the subtenant, with the tenant's consent, carried the crop from the land and took it to a gin,[114] or where the subtenant gave a mortgage on his entire interest in the crop.[115]

The North Carolina statute[116] giving the landlord's lien states that

109. Powell v. Tomlinson, 129 Miss. 354, 92 So. 226 (1922).
110. Harris v. Frank & Reinach, 52 Miss. 155 (1876).
111. Hooks v. Burns, 173 Miss. 413, 160 So. 910 (1935).
112. Poindexter v. Cunningham Bros., 41 So. 3 (Miss., 1906).
113. Never Fail Land Co. v. Cole, 197 N. C. 452, 149 S. E. 585 (1929); Montague v. Mial, 89 N. C. 137 (1883).
114. Montague v. Mial, 89 N. C. 137 (1883).
115. Never Fail Land Co. v. Cole, 197 N. C. 452, 149 S. E. 585 (1929).
116. N. C. Gen. Stat. (1943) §42-15.

the claim is effective until he "shall be paid for all advancements made, and expenses incurred, in making and saving said crops." Under this provision a claim by a landowner for supplies advanced by him to a sublessee, without the knowledge, assent, or privity of the original tenant, is not entitled to a priority over a third person's advances procured by the tenant for the sublessee's use.[117] In fact expressions in the opinion seem to indicate that the landlord would not even be entitled to a *pro rata* share.

SOUTH CAROLINA

Only one case has arisen in South Carolina in which it was necessary to discuss the rights of the agricultural subtenant. In this instance the landlord was sued for converting the subtenant's crop. The judge presiding over the lower court instructed the jury that if the landlord allowed the tenant to subrent to the plaintiff and notified him that if he paid the tenant in chief he would then be relieved of liability to the landlord, the lien on the subtenant's crop would be released. This instruction was said to state the law correctly and was ruled to be responsive to the issue.[118]

TENNESSEE

There has been very little comment upon this matter in the Tennessee cases. At an early date it was decided that the possessor of an interest in land, himself holding under a lease for years, was entitled to a lien on the crop of the sublessee of his tenant, although the sublessee had already paid the rent due under his contract with the tenant, his immediate lessor.[119] Furthermore, in a much later case,[120] the intermediate appellate court held that a purchaser of a subtenant's crop, subject to a landlord's lien, was liable to the assignees of a rent note to the extent of the value of the crop, in spite of the fact that the subtenant had deposited one-third of the proceeds of the sale to the credit of the original tenant, who had known that the note was outstanding. Thus we see the Tennessee courts going about as far as any other jurisdiction in protecting the interests of the landlord.

117. Moore v. Faison, 97 N. C. 322, 2 S. E. 169 (1887).
118. Hatchell v. Chandler, 62 S. C. 380, 40 S. E. 777 (1902).
119. Rutlege v. Walton, 12 Tenn. 458 (1833).
120. Lee v. Spence, 5 Tenn. App. 363 (1927).

VIRGINIA

A Virginia statute[121] provides that a distress warrant for rent may be levied upon any goods of the lessee, his assignee, or subtenant which are found on the premises, or which may have been removed therefrom not more than thirty days previously. This would seem to include other property as well as crops. With respect to property used for agricultural purposes, moreover, the tenant's goods are not to be removed from the premises unless the rent obligations for twelve months or a shorter period are paid; but a subtenant or one claiming under him may obtain a release of his goods from the lien by paying the rent which is in arrears.[122]

Hence it is seen that the Southern legislatures and courts have usually favored the interests of the landowner in cases where there is a clash between two non-defaulting parties, the landlord and the subtenant. The chief theme of the law here is that all crops raised on the leased farm, by whomsoever raised, are subject to the lien of the landlord.

APPLICATION OF LIEN TO CONTRACTS OF GUARANTY AND SURETYSHIP

Sometimes a question arises as to whether a landlord who has promised to be responsible for advances made to his tenant or cropper is entitled to a lien on the tenant's crop for the amount of these advances. The answer to this query is usually governed by the nature of the liability. It seems to be a matter of great moment whether this liability is primary or secondary.

Except in Mississippi, where it has been declared that there is no lien in favor of the landlord whether the contract is one of guaranty or suretyship,[123] a landlord who guarantees the payment of or is primarily responsible for advances to his tenant made by third parties is permitted a lien on the crops.[124] The Mississippi court, in refusing the lien, declared that it did "not decide that the

---

121. Va. Code Ann. (Michie, 1936) §5523.
122. Va. Code Ann. (Michie, 1936) §§5524-25.
123. Ellis v. Jones, 70 Miss. 60, 11 So. 566 (1892).
124. Walker v. Rose, 153 Ark. 599, 241 S. W. 19 (1922); Hatcher v. Ballard, 149 Ark. 669, 233 S. W. 1078 (1921); Foster v. Bradney, 143 Ark. 319, 220 S. W. 811 (1920); Rodgers v. Black, 99 Ga. 139, 25 S. E. 23 (1896); Stubbs Co. v. Waddell, 4 Ga. App. 264, 61 S. E. 145 (1908); Henderson v. Hughes, 4 Ga. App. 52, 60 S. E. 813 (1908); Powell v. Perry, 127 N. C. 22, 37 S. E. 71 (1900).

lien exists only when the landlord deals directly with the tenant."
In fact, if he made the advances through a third person, no reason is
seen why there should be no lien. "But, in any event, the circumstances must be such as to create a debt due from the tenant to
the landlord. It is not sufficient that the tenant and the landlord
be indebted to some third person." [125]

Where the landlord is only secondarily liable for the advances,
as in the case of a surety, there seems to be a more definite difference of opinion. The better view is probably that there is no lien
in such a case, as is held in Arkansas [126] and Georgia; [127] but a contrary view seems to have been taken in Alabama [128] and North Carolina. [129] The Alabama decision seems to have been influenced by
the peculiar language of the statute in effect in that state, and the
North Carolina court evidently overlooked the dissimilarity between a guarantor and a surety, since the difference is not mentioned, and the decision is said to be controlled by a case involving
a guaranty contract. [130]

Even in Alabama, however, when the circumstances show that
the advances have been made by the supplyman with the understanding, either express or implied, that he shall look to the tenant
for payment, there can be no lien, since there is no liability on the
part of the landlord, even though the supplies were furnished at his
instance and request. [131] In other words, to establish the liability
upon which the lien rests, the promise to be responsible must be of
a definite character. [132]

Under the rule that the surety has no lien, there may be attending circumstances which warrant interference by a court of equity.
Thus where the landlord had paid the note as surety, and the purchase of certain rice bags had inured to the benefit of the obligee
as well as to that of the landlord and the tenant, the Arkansas court
held that the landlord had been primarily liable and gave appro-

125. Ellis v. Jones, 70 Miss. 60, 11 So. 566 (1892).
126. Morrilton Cotton Oil Co. v. Frauenthal & Schwarz, 162 Ark. 597, 258
S. W. 628 (1924); Kaufman & Willson v. Underwood, 83 Ark. 118, 102 S. W.
718 (1907).
127. Brimberry v. Mansfield, 86 Ga. 792, 13 S. E. 132 (1891); Swann v. Morris, 83 Ga. 143, 9 S. E. 767 (1889); Scott v. Pound, 61 Ga. 579 (1878).
128. Kelly v. Woodley, 228 Ala. 401, 153 So. 745 (1934).
129. Ransom v. Eastern Cotton Oil Co., 203 N. C. 193, 165 S. E. 350 (1932).
130. Powell v. Perry, 127 N. C. 22, 37 S. E. 71 (1900).
131. Bell & Co. v. Hurst & McWhorter, 75 Ala. 44 (1883).
132. Griffith & Warren v. Biggers, 206 Ala. 565, 90 So. 798 (1921).

priate relief.[133] It might be possible to argue that when the land-lord paid the note, he was subrogated to the rights of the obligee against the tenant, and if the obligee had a lien, the landlord could pursue the usual remedies.

For the liability to be primary it must appear that the supplies were furnished on the landlord's credit, it making no difference whether the goods actually passed through his hands, or whether a note creating a joint and several liability on the part of both land-lord and tenant was given for the purchase price of the supplies.[134] If the landlord signs as surety and the circumstances are such as to indicate that, in spite of this, the liability is primary, there is a lien.[135] In any case, the question of the primary or secondary liabil-ity of the landlord is one for the jury.[136]

An Alabama landlord was held to have no lien for the price of mules sold to his tenant by a third person, where the evidence showed that he was not legally bound for the payment of the debt but had merely promised to see that the third person was paid in case the tenant made anything over and above the landlord's claim.[137] In this instance the landlord had testified that he was not liable at all and that he had said he would not satisfy the claim unless the tenant made more than enough to pay his own debt, and then only out of the tenant's share of the crop.

It has been held that when a landlord, without the knowledge, request, or consent of the tenant, assumes a liability to a third person for advances made by the latter to the tenant, and pays or becomes liable to pay the indebtedness, he is not entitled to a lien on the tenant's crop.[138] Thus the landlord, arbitrarily and of his own will and without the concurrence of the tenant, cannot acquire a lien for such an indebtedness.

In one instance a Georgia landlord had brought fertilizer and turned it over to the tenant, with directions that it be held to await the former's orders. It was shown that the tenant possessed the bill

---

133. Bank of Gillett v. Botts, 157 Ark. 478, 248 S. W. 573 (1923).

134. Phillips v. Freeman, 30 Ga. App. 450, 118 S. E. 404 (1923).

135. Rodgers v. Black, 99 Ga. 139, 25 S. E. 23 (1896).

136. Scott v. Pound, 61 Ga. 579 (1878); Phillips v. Freeman, 30 Ga. App. 450, 118 S. E. 404 (1923); Stubbs Co. v. Waddell, 4 Ga. App. 264, 61 S. E. 145 (1908).

137. Willis v. Wilson Mercantile Co., 16 Ala. App. 263, 77 So. 245 (1917).

138. Clanton v. Eaton, 92 Ala. 612, 8 So. 823 (1891); Rodgers v. Black, 99 Ga. 139, 25 S. E. 23 (1896); Henderson v. Hughes, 4 Ga. App. 52, 60 S. E. 813 (1908).

of lading. In spite of this testimony, however, the court held that the title to the fertilizer had not passed. Delivery was essential to the perfection of the sale, and there had been no actual or constructive delivery to the tenant. Therefore this was not the case for a lien.[139]

Again, a firm of merchants had furnished rice seed to an Arkansas farmer upon a bank's agreement that the firm would be paid. The bank failed without meeting the debt, which had become due because of the farmer's default. Here the firm was said to be entitled to the benefit of a crop lien and also a chattel mortgage taken by the bank. It was allowed to recover the same proportion of the fund derived from the sale of the rice that the debt for the seed bore to the cost of production.[140] The court applied the general proposition that a creditor has a right to claim the benefit of a security given by his debtor to a surety for the latter's indemnity, to be used, if necessary, for the payment of the indebtedness. The security is in the nature of trust property. The right of the creditor, however, arises from the natural justice of allowing him the privilege of having the property applied to the discharge of the debt.

Another important point to discuss concerning primary and secondary liability is the application of that section of the Statute of Frauds which requires that a contract to pay the debt of another must be in writing. Thus, where the liability is primary, the undertaking is said to be original and therefore not void under the statute.[141] However, where the liability is secondary, the undertaking is unenforceable unless it is in writing.[142]

NATURE AND SCOPE OF SUPPLY LIEN IN GENERAL

In respect to the supply lien of the landlord or merchant there are many generalizations which may be made. Much has been said concerning the lien and its nature and incidents. There is a surprising uniformity about the decisions of the several courts, and very few exceptions mar the orderly pattern. Of course there are a few differences in the statutes of the various states, but they are comparatively trivial and unimportant.

139. Mutual Fertilizer Co. v. Moultrie Banking Co., 36 Ga. App. 322, 136 S. E. 803 (1927).
140. Morris v. Bowman & Brown, 175 Ark. 1073, 1 S. W. (2d) 549 (1928).
141. Gardner v. Jarrett, 121 S. C. 328, 113 S. E. 493 (1922).
142. Neal v. Brandon, 70 Ark. 79, 66 S. E. 200 (1902). But see Neal v. Bellamy, 73 N. C. 384 (1875), where such an undertaking was considered an order and not a promise to pay the debt of another.

For instance the general clauses which describe the scope of the lien differ only in language, their meaning being much the same. The variance is therefore more fancied than real. However, it may prove useful to analyse these provisions in detail.

The statutes of Arkansas,[143] Georgia,[144] and Tennessee [145] give a lien for all advances which are necessary to the raising of the crop. In a Georgia case [146] it was said that the proper interpretation of this general provision involved the answers to the following questions: Were the articles furnished by the landlord used in making the crop? Was the use of the articles supplied essentially necessary to the growing of the crop?

The Alabama provision confers the lien where the advance contributes to the "sustenance or well being of the tenant or his family, or for preparing the ground for cultivation, or for cultivating, gathering, saving, handling, or preparing the crop for market."[147] There is a similar law in effect in Florida.[148] In Kentucky the statute gives the lien for advances "to the tenant to enable him to raise the crop, or to subsist whilst carrying out his contract of tenancy."[149] The North Carolina act provides a lien "for all advancements made and expenses incurred in making and saving said crops."[150]

These general provisions have received a certain amount of interpretative analysis. For instance, the Alabama court has held that it is essential to the existence of the lien that the articles furnished be in the statutory class.[151] However, it is unnecessary for the pleader to particularize to any great extent respecting the items of an account.[152] In an early case[153] it was decided that the lien did not exist where the obligation was partially founded on consideration other than those articles specifically contemplated under the state statute. In later decisions, however, it was said that such a claim

143. Ark. Dig. Stat. (Pope, 1937) §8846.
144. Ga. Code (1933) §61-202.
145. Tenn. Code Ann. (Williams, 1934) §§8018-19.
146. Boyce v. Day, 3 Ga. App. 275, 59 S. E. 930 (1907).
147. Ala. Code (1940) tit. 31, §15.
148. Fla. Stat. Ann. (1941) 83.10.
149. Ky. Rev. Stat. (1946) §383.110.
150. N. C. Gen. Stat. (1943) §42-15.
151. Cockburn v. Watkins, 76 Ala. 486 (1884); Bell & Co. v. Hurst & McWhorter, 75 Ala. 44 (1883).
152. Ragsdale v. Kinney, 119 Ala. 454, 24 So. 443 (1898); Cockburn v. Watkins, 76 Ala. 486 (1884).
153. Bell & Co. v. Hurst & McWhorter, 75 Ala. 44 (1883).

was not vitiated because one unimportant item was not of the character for which the lien was given.[154] The requirements of the attachment affidavit are discussed in another decision. Here the court refused to sustain the affidavit since it failed to set forth the nature and kinds of articles advanced and did not state that the advances were made for the sustenance and well being of the family, or to enable the tenant to make a crop.[155]

In North Carolina the term "advancements" has been said to embrace anything of value supplied by the landlord in good faith, for the purpose of making or saving a crop.[156] The Arkansas court has declared that the supplies must be reasonably necessary to enable the tenant to make or gather the crop. The tribunal evidently believed that the advances, though apparently unreasonable, were essential to the success of the venture.[157]

It is unnecessary to prove that supplies, furnished for the purpose of making a crop, are actually used for that purpose. It is sufficient to show that the landlord really furnished the supplies and intended them to be so used.[158] It is immaterial whether the tenant could or could not have made a crop without supplies other than those furnished.[159] In one instance certain supplies were furnished to a Georgia tenant by an organization from which he could buy and the landlord could not. This organization was in the nature of a co-operative association of buyers. Three or four months later the landlord furnished money to pay for the fertilizer, already purchased from the association and partially used, which had been bought as a part of the supplies. Since the money had been furnished later and was not essential to the successful growing of the crop, and since the fertilizer had definitely been supplied on the tenant's credit, the court ruled that the landlord had no lien on the crop for this indebtedness.[160] From the point of view of time, the court makes an unwarranted distinction here. What difference does the time of the advance make? The money had been used to pay a debt which was

154. Ligon v. Roberts, 192 Ala. 31, 68 So. 319 (1915); Giddens v. Bolling, 93 Ala. 92, 9 So. 427 (1891).
155. Ballard v. Stephens, 92 Ala. 616, 8 So. 416 (1890).
156. Windsor Bargain House v. Watson, 148 N. C. 295, 62 S. E. 305 (1908).
157. Smith v. Johnson, 153 Ark. 262, 239 S. W. 1056 (1922).
158. Buxton v. Hickman, 18 Ga. App. 260, 89 S. E. 380 (1916); Nash v. Orr, 9 Ga. App. 33, 70 S. E. 194 (1911).
159. Ferniman v. Nowlin, 91 Ark. 20, 120 S. W. 378 (1909).
160. Landers v. Touchstone, 27 Ga. App. 310, 108 S. E. 125 (1921).

incurred in the process of growing the crop, and this should be the controlling consideration. However, it may be that the court was influenced to a greater extent than indicated by the fact that the credit was definitely made to the tenant and not to the landlord. Perhaps a crop mortgagee who had no notice should be protected in a case of this kind. An earlier case in a similar vein must be considered at this point. Here it was said that a landlord could not take a lien for supplies already furnished by a third person on the tenant's credit. A special contract for a lien had been executed by the tenant and landlord in writing, and then assigned by the landlord after the supplies had all been furnished. The court held that this claim had no validity against the other creditors of the tenant. It made no difference that the special contract for the lien had been agreed upon, the writing prepared for execution, and the assignment of it promised before the supplies were furnished, inasmuch as, under then-existing legislation, an assignable lien could be created only by a special contract in writing, actually executed by the necessary parties.[161]

Advances to a tenant, made before he puts in his crops, and while he is waiting for the cultivating season to begin, have been held to be the proper subject of a landlord's lien.[162]

In one instance a Georgia tenant, holding a rental agreement, was in possession of certain mules under a contract of purchase with a third person. To keep the mules as a necessary adjunct of the venture, the landlord agreed to advance a certain portion of the purchase price of the animals, although as yet the tenant had not taken over. Upholding the lien in favor of the landlord, the court remarked that it was not essential to the existence of the lien that the tenant should enter into actual possession of the leased premises before the advance was made.[163]

Another important point is illustrated by a case from Kentucky. Here a merchant advanced supplies to a tenant cultivating land on shares, who then turned his crop over to the landlord in payment of certain debts. The merchant was not permitted to apply the crop or its proceeds to the amount owed for supplies to the prejudice of the landlord, even though the tenant had told him that the crop could be taken for the amount due, and it was shown that the land-

161. Elliott v. Parker, 94 Ga. 620, 20 S. E. 106 (1894).
162. Ragsdale v. Kinney, 119 Ala. 454, 24 So. 443 (1898).
163. Lowe & Pittard v. Warbington, 144 Ga. 181, 86 S. E. 537 (1915).

lord knew that the statement had been made. A debtor's promise that his creditor's account shall be paid out of a certain fund is not sufficient to give a lien. There appears to have been no ground for an estoppel here, since mere knowledge of the statement is not enough.[164] Needless to say, Kentucky gives no supply lien to merchants. Furthermore, if the landlord and tenant undertake by collusion and fraud to create a lien under color of advancements to the tenant, to the prejudice of other creditors, the transaction will not be sustained.[165]

In a rather early case it was said that a Mississippi landlord, knowing that a merchant had agreed to furnish necessary supplies to his tenant and that the merchant had taken a deed of trust on the crop, had no right to furnish the supplies himself and take possession of the crop without notifying the merchant that, if he failed to furnish the necessary goods, the landlord would do so.[166]

A sum of money supplied to enable a tenant to obtain the release of certain produce from the claim of a former landlord has been held to be an advance of a sort which might create a lien.[167] But the lien has been denied where a landlord had advanced a small sum of money for an undisclosed purpose.[168] Hence we see that it is essential to show the purpose for which the supplies were furnished. Where the advance was made after the crop had matured, the lien could not be established.[169]

MERCHANTS' LIENS

With respect to the merchant's lien[170] which is in effect in some states, certain principles were enunciated in an early North Carolina case.[171] Here the court enumerated the essential features of a valid lien of this kind. According to the analysis it must appear that the advances consisted of money or supplies; that they were made after an agreement was perfected; that they were made to an individual who was engaged, or was about to engage, in the cultivation of the soil; and that they were made to be expended with

164. Quigley v. Franklin, 143 Ky. 92, 136 S. W. 129 (1911).
165. Ledbetter v. Quick, 90 N. C. 276 (1884).
166. Paxton v. Meyer, 58 Miss. 445 (1880).
167. Landrum & Co. v. Wright, 11 Ala. App. 406, 66 So. 892 (1914).
168. Ligon v. Roberts, 192 Ala. 31, 68 So. 319 (1915).
169. Whitfield v. DePriest, 6 Tenn. App. 200 (1927).
170. See *supra*, notes 9-14.
171. Clark v. Farrar, 74 N. C. 686 (1876).

respect to the crop of the particular year. It was decided that the real purpose of the transaction under consideration was to secure an antecedent indebtedness, which had been carried over from the previous year, and that therefore the agreement could not take effect as a merchant's agricultural lien. Since the instrument was founded on a consideration not expressed but concealed and disguised, it could not be supported as a chattel mortgage. The contract professed to create an agricultural lien in form and substance, and it must have that effect or none at all.

The lien of the furnisher of supplies is limited to the share of the crop belonging to the party who has contracted for the goods. When the supplies have been furnished and delivered to the landlord and the tenant has received no benefit therefrom, the tenant is entitled to hold his share of the crop free from the lien of the supplyman.[172]

One of the most progressive and forward-looking provisions in the field of farm tenancy law is contained in the North Carolina act conferring the merchant's lien.[173] Under the statute merchants or other persons advancing money or supplies are prevented from making interest or commission charges of more than ten per cent on the actual sum advanced or the retail cash prices of the articles sold. The landlord is also required to conform to this rule of law.[174] It is provided that the ten-per-cent commission shall not be deducted from the advance, but shall be added to the indebtedness created. Anyone who violates the statute forfeits his lien. However, it has been said that the lien is void only with respect to the particular items for which the overcharge was made.[175]

The only important case which has arisen under this statute is one in which a bank made just such a ten-per-cent discount as is prohibited by the statute, the deduction being $150.00 from an advance of $1500.00. The loan was evidenced by the tenant's $1500.00 note payable to the bank, with the landlord signing as surety. This instrument was secured by another note for a like amount with the tenant as the maker and the landlord as the payee. At maturity, the landlord paid the bank but could collect only a small sum from the tenant on the other note. The tenant had deliv-

172. Rouse v. Wooten, 104 N. C. 229, 10 S. E. 190 (1889).
173. N. C. Gen. Stat. (1943) §§44-52-64.
174. N. C. Gen. Stat. (1943) §42-15.
175. Slade, Rhodes, & Co. v. James, 194 N. C. 240, 139 S. E. 240 (1927).

ered the crop to a junior lienholder. It was held that the landlord, although merely a surety who had been forced to pay an indebtedness created at his own request, was entitled to enforce the lien at the expense of the junior lienholder, even though the arrangement was an illegal one.[176] There are indications in the opinion that the result might have been different if there had been collusion between the bank and the landlord, who seems to have been blameless here.

The only other controversy of this sort appears to be in an Alabama case where excessive interest charges paid on advances were held not to be usurious when no agreement to pay such charges had been made. In spite of the fact that such a transaction did not constitute usury, these excessive charges were said to be admissible in evidence to reduce the amount due on the account.[177]

That merchants of the South are guilty of making excessive charges on advances to ignorant tenant farmers has been emphasized in song and story. However, the merchant's lien often serves a useful purpose in keeping a dishonest tenant from escaping his just debts. The North Carolina provision, with all its imperfections, is a step in the right direction. At least a merchant or landlord cannot go "hog wild" and charge any price he wishes.

ADMISSIBILITY OF ACCOUNT BOOKS IN EVIDENCE

Account books in which landlords and merchants keep entries of advances made to tenants or croppers are admissible in evidence under a familiar exception to the hearsay rule. Yet it has been held erroneous to admit an account book without some preliminary proof of its correctness.[178]

In one instance it was shown that the plantation journal and cash book were kept in the regular course of business. The journal entries of the advances made to the tenants were transferred daily from blotters, upon which the original entries had been recorded contemporaneously with the several transactions by persons having intimate knowledge thereof. In an action for the advances the court approved the admission of the journal entries, when properly authenticated, though not accompanied by the blotters. Any error in admitting the journal entries without the blotters was ruled harmless, since the latter were afterwards admitted without objection

176. Ransom v. Eastern Cotton Oil Co., 203 N. C. 193, 165 S. E. 350 (1932).
177. Donaldson v. Wilkerson, 170 Ala. 507, 54 So. 234 (1910).
178. Powell v. State, 84 Ala. 444, 4 So. 719 (1888).

by the opposing party. The properly authenticated blotters were of course admissible, in spite of the fact that the entries had been afterwards transferred to the journal.[179]

A Tennessee statute[180] requires the account to be sworn to and itemized by the holder of the lien. In fact it has been ruled that a claim not so sworn to cannot become the basis of a valid lien.[181]

SPECIFIC ARTICLES SUBJECT TO LIEN

What specific articles or services are to be classed as necessary to a tenant farmer in carrying on his occupation or in giving him and his family the needed sustenance while he is engaged in raising a crop? Relevance to the farming operations seems to be the chief test used in determining the answer to this question. Needless to say, there have been many cases where specific articles or services have been held to be either within or without the general provisions respecting advances.

Cash advanced to further the farming operations or to sustain the family of the tenant is certainly within the judicial definition of the term "supplies" or "advances" which has been employed in the statutes.[182] The lien is for the amount of money advanced and not for the value of the property purchased with the money.[183] There is a lien for sums advanced to do the necessary picking, ginning, baling, and wrapping of cotton,[184] but not for money supplied for a pleasure trip to visit relatives.[185] Money furnished to pay interest on a debt connected with the farming operations may also be considered an "advance."[186]

The landlord has a lien for livestock such as mules or horses advanced to the tenant.[187] A lien is also given a landlord for pasturing

179. Donaldson v. Wilkerson, 170 Ala. 507, 54 S. E. 234 (1910).

180. Tenn. Code Ann. (Williams, 1934) §8022.

181. Rochelle v. Mullins, 12 Tenn. App. 363 (1930); Whitfield v. DePriest, 6 Tenn. App. 200 (1927).

182. Walls v. Skelton, 215 Ala. 357, 110 So. 813 (1926); Lunsford v. Skelton, 169 Ark. 547, 275 S. W. 901 (1925); Somerville v. Delta Grocery & Cotton Co., 159 Miss. 252, 130 So. 95 (1929).

183. Walls v. Skelton, 215 Ala. 357, 110 So. 813 (1926).

184. Earl Bros. v. Malone, 80 Ark. 218, 96 S. W. 1062 (1906); Strauss v. Baley, 58 Miss. 131 (1880).

185. Etheridge v. Bird Bros., 176 Ark. 649, 4 S. W (2d) 9 (1928).

186. Hinton v. Barton, 32 Ala. App. 563, 28 So. (2d) 213 (1946).

187. Trimble v. Durham, 70 Miss. 295, 12 So. 207 (1892); Strauss v. Baley, 58 Miss. 131 (1880); Ledbetter v. Quick, 90 N. C. 276 (1884); Wofford v. Hooper, 149 Tenn. 250, 259 S. W. 549 (1924). See Haralson v. Boyle, 22 La.

the animals.[188] To sustain the lien, it is unimportant whether the livestock has been sold or hired to the tenant.[189] In one instance a corporate landlord advanced money to its tenant to buy a cow. Several exchanges were made, the tenant finally receiving, after a series of barterings, a mule. The court ruled that the mule was subject to the landlord's lien, regardless of how many exchanges there had been.[190]

A sewing machine,[191] wagons,[192] farm implements,[193] and a set of blacksmith's tools[194] have been held to be necessary articles within the statutes. However, the lien has been refused in the case of buggies not used in the farm enterprise.[195]

An Alabama court has declared that a supply lien will attach where the landlord has furnished seed, feed, and fertilizer, and provided facilities for moving the tenant to the farm, harrowing the land and hauling cotton to a gin.[196]

Several courts have held that a lien exists in favor of a landlord who has agreed to furnish board for his tenant.[197] Professional medical services have also been held to be within the statute, the court being of the opinion that the good health of the tenant and his family is necessary to proper husbandry and good manage-

---

Ann. 210 (1870), where mules and other movable property in Louisiana, used by the lessee in working the land, had been provisionally seized for the rent and then released on bond before judgment. Here the privilege was not lost, for the same property might be seized a second time and sold to satisfy the claim. It has been held in Louisiana that mules, horses, and other work animals, together with farm implements, stand as a pledge to the lessor for the payment of the rent, even though they belong to the lessee. Johnson v. Tacneau, 23 La. Ann. 453 (1871).

188. Hinton v. Barton, 32 Ala. App. 563, 28 So. (2d) 213 (1946); Earl Bros v. Malone, 80 Ark. 218, 96 S. W. 1062 (1906).

189. Drinkard v. State, 12 Ala. App. 184, 68 So. 553 (1915); Boyce v. Day, 3 Ga. App. 275, 59 S. E. 930 (1907).

190. Butler-Kyser Oil & Fertilizer Co. v. Howle, 4 Ala. App. 312, 58 So. 115 (1912).

191. Earl Bros. v. Malone, 80 Ark. 218, 96 S.W. 1062 (1906).

192. Ledbetter v. Quick, 90 N. C. 276 (1884).

193. Wofford v. Hooper, 149 Tenn. 250, 259 S. W. 549 (1924). See Johnson v. Tacneau, *supra* Note 187.

194. Holladay v. Rutledge, 145 Ala. 656, 39 So. 613 (1905).

195. Brown v. State, 2 Ga. App. 657, 58 S. E. 1070 (1907); Field v. Newburn, 91 Miss. 861, 45 So. 573 (1908), interpreting La. Stat.

196. Hinton v. Barton, 32 Ala. App. 563, 28 So. (2d) 213 (1946).

197. Jones v. Eubanks, 86 Ga. 616, 12 S. E. 1065 (1891); Brown v. Brown, 109 N. C. 124, 13 S. E. 797 (1891); Wofford v. Hooper, 149 Tenn. 250, 259 S. W. 549 (1924).

ment.[198] However, where the doctor's services cannot be shown to have been for the tenant, his family, or his laborers, there is no lien.[199] In one instance it was decided that no lien existed where the landlord had bought up a debt for medical services rendered by a physician hired by the tenant.[200]

The Louisiana court has declared that articles like tobacco, pipes, playing cards, whisky, and perfumery are in no sense supplies necessary to the raising of a crop and therefore cannot be the basis for any privilege.[201] At an early date the Alabama tribunal took this same view with respect to tobacco and whisky,[202] but under a more modern statute the lien was upheld in a case involving tobacco and snuff.[203]

It is evident that the courts usually follow a policy of not deciding the status of any specific article until a case involving such an article comes before the court. In this way they are better able to avoid the pitfalls into which they would be likely to fall if any serious attempts to generalize were made.

LIMITATIONS ON LIEN

In considering the scope of the lien, it is proper to discuss the ways in which it may be limited. The restrictions fall into well-defined categories. Thus a lien may be limited by contract[204] or by operation of law. In the latter classification are time and property limitations. The types of contract limitations are of course myriad. It is enough to point out that cases arising under such agreements are governed by the usual rules of contract law.

TIME LIMITATIONS

Questions are continually arising concerning time in relation to agricultural liens. It seems to be the general rule that the lien extends only to the crops of the particular year for which the rent and advances were charged.[205] In fact it has been said that in order for

198. Moak v. Moak, 150 Miss. 289, 116 So. 286 (1928).
199. Ligon v. Roberts, 192 Ala. 31, 68 So. 319 (1915).
200. Brown v. State, 2 Ga. App. 657, 58 S. E. 1070 (1907).
201. Stafford v. Pearson, 26 La. Ann. 658 (1875).
202. Marcus v. Robinson, 76 Ala. 550 (1884).
203. Donaldson v. Wilkerson, 170 Ala. 507, 54 So. 234 (1910).
204. For example, N. C. Gen. Stat. (1943) §42-15 provides for a lien if the lease contract does not state otherwise.
205. Mills v. Pryor, 65 Ark. 214, 45 S. W. 350 (1898); Ware v. Blalock, 72 Ga. 804 (1884); Lee v. Payne, 61 Ga. App. 16, 5 S. E. (2d) 592 (1939); Wim-

supplies to constitute a valid lien, they must have been advanced for the purpose of raising the crop upon which the lien is alleged to attach.[206] In respect to the lien for rent, it has been said that a landlord who wishes to enforce his claim must establish that the crops were grown on the leased premises during the term.[207] That it is necessary to plead that the crops were raised at a certain time is to be seen in a South Carolina case[208] where an affidavit failed to state when the crops were grown or that the rented land was in the county where the action was brought. The court held, however, that as the affidavit of defense stated these facts, the defects of the original affidavit were cured.

Under the general rule, advances made during a preceeding year are not commonly held to be a lien upon the crops of the current year,[209] but where the advances are made late in one year to be used in raising a crop for the next year, the lien has been held to attach.[210] Moreover, a winter wheat crop which was planted one year and harvested the next has been held subject to a lien for advances furnished by the landlord prior to the sowing of the wheat.[211]

The general rule is not in force in Alabama, where the lien is carried over and attaches to the crops of the succeeding year[212] and continues over from year to year, for any balance due, as long as the tenancy continues.[213] The claim of the landlord is a specific lien on specific property and is limited to the price or value of the articles advanced for the current year. It cannot be extended to include any increase in the price or value of the articles in a suc-

berly v. Ocmulgee Guano Co., 21 Ga. App. 270, 94 S. E. 288 (1917); O'Kelley v. Ferguson, 49 La. Ann. 1230, 22 So. 783 (1897); Sprouse v. Davis, 141 Miss. 564, 106 So. 824 (1926); Eastern Cotton Oil Co. v. Powell, 201 N. C. 351, 160 S. E. 292 (1931); Ballard v. Johnson, 114 N. C. 141, 19 S. E. 98 (1894); Clark v. Farrar, 74 N. C. 686 (1876); Bramlett v. Hurley, 160 Tenn. 653, 28 S.W. (2d) 633 (1930).

206. Woodlief v. Harris & Parham, 95 N. C. 211 (1886).

207. Federal Land Bank v. Strickland, 227 Ala. 116, 148 So. 799 (1933).

208. Tinman v. McMeekin, 42 S. C. 311, 20 S. E. 36 (1894).

209. Camp v. Matthews, 143 Ga. 393, 85 S. E. 196 (1915); Lee v. Payne, 61 Ga. App. 16, 5 S. E. (2d) 592 (1939); Heaton v. Graham Co., 21 Ga. App. 613, 94 S. E. 829 (1918); Mullins v. Dowling, 20 Ga. App. 138, 92 S. E. 763 (1917).

210. Lowe & Pittard v. Warbington, 144 Ga. 181, 86 S. E. 537 (1915); Johnson v. McDaniel, 138 Ga. 203, 75 S. E. 101 (1912); Byrd v. State, 32 Ga. App. 334, 123 S. E. 33 (1924); Sprouse v. Davis, 141 Miss. 564, 106 So. 824 (1926).

211. Brooks v. Garrett, 195 N. C. 452, 142 S. E. 486 (1928).

212. Ala. Code (1940) tit. 31, §17; Reese v. Rugeley, 82 Ala. 267, 2 So. 441 (1887); Thompson v. Powell, 77 Ala. 391 (1884).

213. Cockburn v. Watkins, 76 Ala. 486 (1884).

ceeding year.[214] Furthermore, a landlord is not permitted to carry over an indebtedness against an ex-tenant who has assumed an entirely different relationship on the land for the succeeding year.[215]

As a usual thing, it may be said that an agreement to give a lien for advances does not cover pre-existing indebtedness.[216] However, it may be that the parties have agreed that prior advances shall be included under the lien for the current year, and agreements of this kind appear to have been approved by the North Carolina court.[217] In a case[218] arising just after the turn of the century, the Georgia Supreme Court decided that a balance of indebtedness for a prior year could not be included as a valid item in a foreclosure proceeding based on a lien for supplies, even where the parties made an agreement at the beginning of the second year that such balance should be included, along with future indebtedness, as an advance for the current year. It was said to be immaterial that the landlord might have foreclosed the lien for this indebtedness at the proper time. At a later date, however, the intermediate appellate court rendered several decisions in which agreements of this kind seem to have been approved.[219] In one of these instances the decision of the court seems to have been based on the theory of constructive delivery and re-delivery.[220] It was said that if there had not been enough property on hand to repay the landlord at the time of the agreement an entirely different situation would have been presented, since there could be no constructive delivery of a shortage. The State Supreme Court did not rule upon any of these cases, and therefore it is not known whether it would reverse itself in respect to this matter.

Of course, where money is advanced after a crop has matured, there is no lien upon the harvested produce.[221] Furthermore, it has been said that a party who has furnished money to pay for gather-

214. Burgess v. Hyatt, 209 Ala. 472, 96 So. 222 (1923).
215. Baker v. Patterson, 171 Ala. 88, 55 So. 135 (1911).
216. Lowdermilk v. Bostick, 98 N. C. 299, 3 S. E. 844 (1887).
217. Windsor Bargain House v. Watson, 148 N. C. 295, 62 S. E. 305 (1908); Thigpen v. Maget, 107 N. C. 39, 12 S. E. 272 (1890).
218. Parks v. Simpson, 124 Ga. 523, 52 S. E. 616 (1905).
219. Barnett v. Culberson, 62 Ga. App. 582, 8 S. E. (2d) 900 (1940); Thornton v. Hinson, 30 Ga. App. 200, 117 S. E. 273 (1923); Fletcher Guano Co. v. Vorus, 10 Ga. App. 380, 73 S. E. 348 (1912).
220. Fletcher Guano Co. v. Vorus, supra, Note 219.
221. Whitfield v. DePriest, 6 Tenn. App. 200 (1927).

ing a tenant's cotton crop has no lien upon other cotton grown at another time.[222]

As a general rule and in the absence of an agreement to the contrary, it may be said that the landlord's right to collect his portion of the crop, as well as his right to demand payment for any supplies he may have furnished, accrues upon the maturity of the crop and is not postponed until the end of the year.[223] It appears that the lien accrues as soon as there is any crop upon which it may attach, and that the landlord does not have to wait until the rent falls due.[224] The North Carolina court has said that where a lease of a farm on shares is indefinite in that no time is fixed for a division of the crops, the lessor is entitled to so much of the produce as is necessary to settle the debt for rent and advances and is not required to wait until a full harvest. In other words, the lessor might, if he so desired, take his share in installments as the crops matured, without waiting for the maturity of all the crops at the end of the year.[225] The question arises whether this is fair to the tenant in an instance where the crop is destroyed by some accident or other outside agency after the lessor has harvested his share. In another case where no time for the division was fixed, it was said that the fact that the crop was only partially gathered at the commencement of the lessor's possessory action was no bar to the maintenance of the suit.[226]

Sometimes a landlord will agree to advance money or property to a tenant without any specific provision in respect to the time of repayment. In one case of this kind there was nothing in the agreement to show that repayment was to be postponed until the crops were harvested and sold, and the tenant had promised to make a settlement for cash advances, generally or on demand. It was held that the debt became due simultaneously with the promise and could be enforced, it having become apparent that the tenant was about to leave the premises without making any arrangement to make payment, though the rent was not then due.[227]

In one instance a Mississippi landlord, at the time of leasing the premises, had allowed the tenant to keep some corn then on the

222. Goodwin v. Mitchell, 38 So. 657 (Miss., 1905).
223. Wimbush v. Curry, 8 Ga. App. 223, 68 S. E. 951 (1910); McAlister v. Tucker, 103 S. C. 204, 87 S. E. 1000 (1916).
224. Sevier v. Shaw, Barbour & Co., 25 Ark. 417 (1869).
225. Smith v. Tindall, 107 N. C. 88, 12 S. E. 121 (1890).
226. Rich v. Hobson, 112 N. C. 79, 16 S. E. 931 (1893).
227. Thomson v. Tilton, 22 Ky. Law Rep. 1004, 59 S. W. 485 (1900).

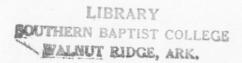

place, which was to be paid for, or replaced, in one year's time. The time for payment was afterwards extended another year. Here the court held that, to constitute an advance within the meaning of the statute, the landlord must furnish, or cause to be furnished, something which was not the tenant's property before the lease. It was said that mere forbearance to demand something due the landlord in one year did not give him a lien for the same debt on the argricultural products raised on the land in a future year, as against one who had a deed of trust, regardless of his rights against the tenant. The corn due from the tenant was not delivered but continued to be the tenant's property, and the transaction between the two amounted to no more than a forbearance on the part of the landlord to demand what was due him.[228]

The Tennessee statute cannot be fairly construed as giving a lien on the current crop for the entire sale value of stock, the animals having a more or less permanent or recurring use. Furnishings of this character are not productive of the current crop in any such proportion of their value as to come within the contemplation of the statute in full measure.[229]

In one early Alabama case a farmer went into possession of land under a contract of sale. In the autumn the parties became dissatisfied with the arrangement and decided to change the relationship to that of landlord and tenant. The occupant had planted a crop which was sold before the rescission of the contract of sale and the establishment of the tenancy, but which was not removed from the premises until afterwards. In the first hearing of this case it was held that the landowner could not enforce a claim to the crop, the lien and remedy by attachment being dependent upon the existence of the tenancy relationship.[230] In a later hearing, however, the court seemed to qualify this proposition by saying the lien applied to crops growing on the land at the time the tenancy was established, although they might have been planted at a time previous to the creation of the relationship.[231]

A discussion of this subject would be incomplete without at least some mention of the application of the statute of limitations to liens

228. Lumbley v. Gilruth, 65 Miss. 23, 3 So. 77 (1887).
229. Bramlett v. Hurley, 160 Tenn. 653, 28 S. W. (2d) 633 (1930).
230. Hadden's Exec'rs v. Powell, 17 Ala. 314 (1850).
231. Powell v. Hadden's Exec'rs, 21 Ala. 745 (1852).

of this type. In this category are the state statutes which prescribe a certain period of time after removal of the crop within which the landlord's lien may be enforced. In Kentucky[232] and Louisiana[233] the period of time after removal is fifteen days, while in Mississippi[234] and Virginia[235] the period is thirty days.

In some jurisdictions there are statutes which limit the duration of certain agricultural liens. In Kentucky, for example, the landlord is not permitted to recover for any rent which has been due more than eleven months[236] nor for any advances which have been due more than one hundred and twenty days.[237] In Tennessee the liens for rent and advances expire on the first day of July of the year following the one in which the tenancy was entered into,[238] a former limitation of six months[239] having been abrogated. In Arkansas the rent lien continues for six months from the time the rent becomes due,[240] and an action to enforce it is barred after this period of time has expired.[241] This was held not to be true, however, where the landlord had instituted proceedings within six months and was prevented from getting the property because the tenants had unlawfully converted it during the pendency of the suit.[242]

In one instance an Arkansas landlord brought suit against a bank which had taken possession of the tenant's crop to satisfy an indebtedness of the tenant to the bank. It was shown that the bank had promised to pay the rent when certain collections were made. Since there was no consideration for this promise, and no basis for an estoppel, the court held that the running of the six-month statute of

232. Ky. Rev. Stat. (1946) §383.070.
233. La. Civ. Code Ann. (Dart, 1932) Art. 2709; La. Code Prac. Ann. (Dart, 1932) Art. 288.
234. Miss. Code Ann. (1942) §921.
235. Va. Code Ann. (Michie, 1936) §6416.
236. Ky. Rev. Stat. (1946) §383.070.
237. Ky. Rev. Stat. (1946) §383.110; Marquess v. Ladd, 30 Ky. Law Rep. 1142, 100 S. W. 305 (1907).
238. Tenn. Code Ann. (Williams, 1934) §8021.
239. See Biggs v. Piper, 86 Tenn. 589, 8 S. W. 851 (1888); Davis v. Wilson, 86 Tenn. 519, 8 S. W. 151 (1888); Hardeman v. Shumate, 19 Tenn. 398 (1838).
240. Ark. Dig. Stat. (Pope, 1937) §8845.
241. Taylor v. Crawford, 187 Ark. 316, 59 S. W. (2d) 484 (1933); King and Clopton v. Blount, 37 Ark. 115 (1881); Valentine v. Hamlett, 35 Ark. 538 (1880).
242. Clemmons v. Byars, 197 Ark. 300, 122 S. W. (2d) 652 (1938).

limitations was not suspended by the promise. The landlord was not allowed to enforce his lien after the prescribed period of time had elapsed.[243]

LIMITATION OF LIEN TO PROPERTY INCLUDED UNDER CONTRACT

As a general rule it may be said that the agricultural liens on a tenant's crop are limited in such a manner that the lienor can claim an encumbrance only upon produce raised on land specified or included in the lease or agreement which is the basis of the lien. In other words, it must be clear that the produce from a certain tract was intended to be the subject of the lienor's claim. An interesting North Carolina case illustrates the fact that the location of the land referred to in the agreement must be capable of ascertainment. Here the written agreement provided that the lien would attach to crops grown on lands particularly specified, and also to any crops raised by the cultivators on other lands in the county. A crop not grown on the specified land was sold and afterwards claimed under the lien. The court refused to allow the lien to be enforced. It was said that the lien was operative only in respect to the crop raised on the specified farm, the general clause being much too uncertain to have any effect.[244]

Sometimes a landlord undertakes to insure that he will receive the full value of the leased premises, whether the tenant cultivates all the land or not, by stipulating in the contract that money rental is to be paid by the tenant for any land included in the lease but not cultivated. Such a situation was presented in a case which arose in Arkansas. Here the court held the contract to be an entire one, in that the crop lien on the land cultivated would apply to all the leased premises, whether cultivated or not. Moreover, the court concluded that the provision for money rental was not defeated by such a construction, since the landlord, by inserting this provision in the contract, was protecting himself against the contingency that the crop lien would be insufficient to pay him the rental due on the entire tract of land leased to the tenant.[245] It has also been held that the lien attached to all the tenant's crops, though he had

243. Bottrell v. Farmers' Bank & Trust Co., 172 Ark. 1165, 291 S. W. 832 (1927).
244. Gwathmey v. Etheridge, 99 N. C. 571, 6 S. E. 411 (1888).
245. Stephenson v. Lewis, 152 Ark. 361, 238 S. W. 61 (1922).

agreed to set apart a specific portion of them for the payment of the rent.[246]

In one instance an Alabama landlord made separate rental contracts with respect to the leasing of distinct parcels of land to the same tenant. The court held that the landlord had a lien on the crops grown on each parcel for the rent of that particular parcel, and for that parcel only.[247] Here, of course, there were two distinct transactions, and it was clear that the parties intended the situation to be so understood.

In Mississippi the lien seems to cover all crops grown under the lease contract, though all the land cultivated may not have been included in the original demise. In one instance where such a decision was reached, portions of the property originally leased were flooded, and the landlord had procured other land which was turned over to the tenant under the original agreement. This land had been obtained from a third person by a separate leasing arrangement and then sublet to the tenant. Perhaps the special circumstances of this case influenced the court in its decision that the lien covered the entire crop.[248]

A landlord seeking to assert a lien on a certain crop or the proceeds from its sale must prove that the crop on which he is seeking execution was produced upon the leased property. In one instance a Georgia landlord introduced evidence to show that he had rented to certain persons, that these persons, or one of them, had consigned a cotton crop to named factors, and that cotton was one of the crops grown on the leased premises. This evidence was held insufficient to relieve the landlord of the burden of proving that the cotton sought to be levied upon was grown on the leased premises. The defendants, third persons in possession of the cotton or its proceeds, were not required in this situation to prove that the cotton was not grown on the land covered by the lease.[249] Where the affidavit, warrant, or levy fails to show that the crops were raised on the leased premises, the landlord cannot maintain his action.[250] In fact it appears that it is absolutely essential to the maintenance of

---

246. State v. Reeder, 36 S. C. 497, 15 S. E. 544 (1892).
247. Nelson v. Webb, 54 Ala. 436 (1875).
248. McGee, Dean & Co. v. Crawford, 131 So. 341 (Miss., 1930).
249. Saulsbury, Respess & Co. v. McKellar, 55 Ga. 323 (1875).
250. Smith & Hollis v. Youngblood, 23 Ga. App. 640, 99 S. E. 143 (1919); Tinman v. McMeekin, 42 S. C. 311, 20 S. E. 36 (1894).

the proceeding to enforce the lien that the landlord sustain the burden of proof that the crop was grown on the leased premises.[251]

The Louisiana court has held that the lessor of a plantation has no privilege on sugar and molasses manufactured on the place from cane belonging to third persons, grown on another plantation. The third persons here had merely used the sugar mill on the leased plantation to manufacture their cane into a more refined and disposable product. The sugar and molasses became mixed and confused with similar products belonging to the lessee, but it was decided that the extraneous owners, having had no opportunity to effect a separation, were entitled to be reimbursed out of the proceeds of the products, the money having been paid into court.[252] In another instance it was held that the lessor of a cotton press had no lien, pledge, or privilege for the payment of the rent upon cotton sent to the plant by third persons and transiently stored with the lessee, to be re-pressed.[253] Thus it is seen that property which is only incidentally upon the leased premises is not subject to the lien or privilege.

It is clear that there should be some such limitations upon the scope of the lien as those noted here. The decisions of the courts have reflected a desire of the judges to keep the lien within reasonable bounds and not to allow it to apply to property which is definitely beyond the intended scope of the security device.

CONCLUSION

In conclusion it may be remarked that courts and legislatures in the Southeastern states have done an excellent job in protecting the landlord against the machinations of unscrupulous tenants. By giving him the lien they have given him a very potent weapon, but care should be taken to see that he does not use this weapon as a club to beat the tenant into a state of bondage little better than slavery. Of course the landlord has to have protection, but so does the tenant. It is for our legislators to devise some scheme by which the interests of all parties may be protected. In a later chapter an attempt will be made to point out some ways and means of attaining this goal.

251. Shehee v. Johnson, 2 La. App. 91 (1925).
252. Lesseps v. Ritcher, 18 La. Ann. 653 (1866).
253. Rea v. Burt, 8 La. 509 (1835).

XV

Priorities in Respect to Liens on Agricultural
Products

QUESTIONS are continually arising concerning priorities with respect to liens on agricultural products. Some of the problems are simple, while others involve complicated theories like the two-fund doctrine of marshalling securities. In some instances the rights of crop mortgagees or judgment creditors are discussed. A tangle of conflicting claims is often presented, and it is the duty of the courts to unravel the knots. In a few states apparent conflicts in the decisions have arisen, and it is rather difficult to ascertain the true picture. However, certain general and local rules can be definitely stated, and one may obtain a degree of familiarity with the principles of law governing the priority of crop liens.

Except in Alabama, where the ginner's lien has been held to be paramount,[1] and in Louisiana, where a preference is given to the farm laborer's privilege[2] and perhaps to that of the overseer as well,[3] the landlord's lien for rent is superior to other private liens or encumbrances on the crops grown on the leased premises.[4] In fact the lien for rent and/or advances is superior to an ordinary chattel mortgage[5] or a farm laborer's lien[6] on the tenant's crops.

1. Etheredge v. Hester, 32 Ala. App. 321, 25 So. (2d) 523 (1946).
2. Reed v. Andrepont, 142 So. 184 (La. App., 1932); Saloy v. Dragon, 37 La. Ann. 71 (1885).
3. La. Civ. Code Ann. (Dart, 1932) Art. 3259; Laporte v. Libby, 114 La. 570, 38 So. 457 (1905); Duplantier v. Wilkins, 19 La. Ann. 112 (1867). But see La. Gen. Stat. Ann. (Dart, 1932) §5064, discussed in Flower & King v. Skipwith, 45 La. Ann. 895, 13 So. 152 (1893), where the overseer's privilege is made inferior to that of the lessor.
4. First Nat. Bank of Gadsden v. Burnett, 213 Ala. 89, 104 So. 17 (1925); Toler v. Seabrook, 39 Ga. 14 (1869); Storm v. Green, 51 Miss. 103 (1875).
5. J. C. Wilson & Son v. Curry, 149 Ala. 368, 42 So. 753 (1907); Keith v. Ham, 89 Ala. 590, 7 So. 234 (1890); Dunlap v. Steele & Vandergrift, 80 Ala. 424 (1885); Hamilton v. Maas & Brother, 77 Ala. 283 (1884); Burkart & Co. v. Bell, 24 Ala. App. 516, 137 So. 322 (1931); Ferniman v. Nowlin, 91 Ark. 20, 120 S. W. 378 (1909); Kaufman & Wilson v. Underwood, 83 Ark. 118, 102 S. W. 718 (1907); Watson v. Johnson, 33 Ark. 737 (1878); Lambeth v. Ponder, 33 Ark. 707 (1878); Tomlinson v. Greenfield, 31 Ark. 557 (1876) Gedge v.

The landlord's lien for rent and/or advances is also superior to the claims of the subtenant's mortgage or execution creditors.[7] A rather peculiar situation presented itself in an interesting case from Arkansas. Here a landlord had liens for rent and for supplies furnished to a tenant who had subrented a portion of the land to another. An attempt was made to apply the crop of the tenant in chief to the lien for supplies rather than to the lien for rent. The plan was to use the subtenant's crop to satisfy the lien for rent to the extent of his proportionate liability therefor under the Arkansas law. The court ruled in favor of this scheme, and a mortgagee of the subtenant's crop was held to have an inferior claim. The liens for rent and supplies were declared to be of equal dignity, and the action of the landlord was approved, since the claim for rent did not have to be satisfied first.[8]

In Mississippi a statute which conferred a supply lien has been construed to give the landlord a prior lien, even though when he furnished the supplies he had notice of the deed of trust under which his merchant opponent claimed.[9]

In an Alabama case there were conflicting claims on cattle grazed on leased premises. The court said that although intervening mortgagees are not permitted to prevail against a landlord's lien for rent existing under a prior contract, the lien of a mortgage created before the execution of a new lease is superior to the landlord's lien under the renewal, since the landlord had either knowledge or constructive notice of the mortgage at the time of entering into the new lease.[10]

A Mississippi landowner made a contract for the sale of land, giving a bond for title. The agreement included an alternative proposition stating that the other party would pay rent if he failed to pay the purchase money. It was held that a merchant, who had taken a deed of trust on the crop to be grown on the premises as security for certain advances made by him, without notice of the alternative proposition, had relied on the bond for title at his peril. His claim,

---

Shoenberger, 83 Ky. 91 (1885); Wilczinski v. Lick, 68 Miss. 596, 10 So. 73 (1891); Storm v. Green, 51 Miss. 103 (1875); Arbuckle v. Nelms, 50 Miss. 556 (1874); Perry v. Perry, 127 N. C. 23, 37 S. E. 71 (1900).

6. Hudson v. Wright, 1 Ala. App. 433, 56 So. 258 (1911), 3 Ala. App. 290, 57 So. 90 (1911); Alston v. Wilson, 64 Ga. 482 (1880).

7. Lunsford v. Skelton, 169 Ark. 547, 275 S. W. 901 (1925).

8. Morgan v. Russell, 151 Ark. 405, 236 S. W. 602 (1922). See *infra* p. 296.

9. Strauss v. Baley, 58 Miss. 131 (1880).

10. Payne v. Boutwell, 231 Ala. 311, 164 So. 755 (1935).

therefore, was subordinate to the landlord's lien, which had arisen when the alternative proposition became operative. The bond for title was said not to be such evidence of ownership as would estop the landlord, since it was incumbent upon a person dealing with the tenant to inquire into the character of the right by which he held the property. The court declared that information, to bind the landlord, must have been derived from him, and not from the tenant.[11]

The courts have held that a landlord's lien for rent is superior to the lien of another person for supplies furnished to the tenant.[12] Moreover, the landlord's lien for advances has been held in Alabama to be superior to the lien of any merchant or other person who makes advances to the tenant.[13] Such an interpretation is evidently meant to be placed upon the statutes in at least two of the other Southeastern states, North Carolina[14] and Virginia.[15] However, in South Carolina it would seem that the limited supply lien is superior to all other liens.[16]

A tenant sold cotton before it had been set apart for the landlord, without his permission or instructions. It was held that the purchaser was liable to a person holding a mortgage on the crop, though the tenant had paid the proceeds of the sale to the landlord.[17] Again, a lessee of a cotton plantation deposited the rent contracts of his subtenants, payable in cotton, with a merchant who had notice of the landlord's lien. The lessee placed the cotton, as received, in the warehouse of a factor, who, having notice of the merchant's lien but not of the landlord's, paid a check of the tenant's in favor of the merchant and charged it to the tenant's account, before the cotton was sold. In this situation the landlord was allowed to maintain an action sounding in quasi contract against the merchant for the money received on the check.[18]

11. Bacon v. Howell, 60 Miss. 362 (1882).

12. Brown v. Hamil, 76 Ala. 506 (1884); Carroll v. Bancker, 43 La. Ann. 1078, 1194, 10 So. 187 (1891); Goodwin v. Mitchell, 38 So. 657 (Miss., 1905); Rhodes v. Smith-Douglass Fertilizer Co., 220 N. C. 21, 16 S. E. (2d) 408 (1941); Wise Supply Co. v. Davis, 194 N. C. 328, 139 S. E. 599 (1927); Ballard v. Johnson, 114 N. C. 141, 19 S. E. 98 (1894).

13. Brown v. Hamil, 76 Ala. 506 (1884); Lake v. Gaines, 75 Ala. 435 (1883); Coleman v. Siler, 74 Ala. 435 (1883); Wells v. Thompson, 50 Ala. 83 (1873).

14. N. C. Code Gen. Stat. (1943) §§42-15, 44-52. See Rhodes v. Smith-Douglass Fertilizer Co., 220 N. C. 21, 16 S. E. (2d) 408 (1941).

15. Va. Code (Michie, 1936) §6454.

16. S. C. Code Ann. (1932) §8779.

17. Belser v. Youngblood, 103 Ala. 545, 15 So. 863 (1894).

18. Burnett v. Warren, 82 Ala. 557, 2 So. 457 (1886).

Another interesting case arose when a tenant delivered a portion of his crop to a surety on a note for rent, to be used in paying the rent. The surety forwarded the produce to commission merchants for that purpose. The merchants, in violation of instructions, applied the produce in payment of their advances made to the tenant. It was said that the surety might, after paying the rent, recover the value of the portion of the crop placed in his hands. Since the rent was the paramount charge, the surety had a property in and a right to hold the crop, applying it to the payment of the rent. Hence he was permitted to recover its value, the lien for rent being superior to the merchants' claim for advances made to the tenant.[19]

As a usual thing, the landlord's lien is superior to the claim of an execution or seizing creditor,[20] and this is true to a certain extent even in Georgia,[21] where a rather strange situation has developed.

According to the Georgia rule a foreclosed landlord's supply lien is the equivalent of the common-law distress warrant for rent.[22] It may also be said that crops produced upon rented premises are by operation of law encumbered with a landlord's supply lien, although the lien has not been foreclosed as provided for by the statute.[23] The lien exists from the time the supplies are furnished but does not ripen until foreclosure.[24] In the leading case[25] dealing with the necessity for a foreclosure to preserve the lien for rent, it is said that the landlord's lien is superior in dignity to the lien of a common-law judgment. However, the landlord must assert the priority of his lien by a foreclosure proceeding in order to claim the crop levied upon by the judgment creditor. Furthermore the lien must be foreclosed prior to the sale of the property under the judgment. Otherwise the lien cannot be enforced. The same has been reaffirmed in two later cases concerning the asserted priority of supply liens over judgments.[26] Where the foreclosed lien was placed in the hands of

19. Shields v. Atkinson, 67 Ala. 244 (1880).
20. Sevier v. Shaw, Barbour & Co., 25 Ark. 417 (1869); Arick v. Walsh & Boisseau, 23 La. Ann. 605 (1871); Harmon v. Juge, 6 La. Ann. 768 (1851); Rabb v. Wagner, 5 La. Ann. 111 (1850); Robinson v. Staples, 5 La. Ann. 712 (1850); Okolona Sav. Inst. v. Trice, 60 Miss. 262 (1882).
21. See Colclough v. Mathis, 79 Ga. 394, 4 S. E. 762 (1887).
22. Turner v. Sitton, 160 Ga. 215, 127 S. E. 847 (1925).
23. Streetman v. Turner, 32 Ga. App. 733, 124 S. E. 549 (1924).
24. Turner v. Sitton, 160 Ga. 215, 127 S. E. 847 (1925).
25. Duncan v. Clark, 96 Ga. 263, 22 S. E. 927 (1895).
26. Lathem & Sons v. Stringer, 145 Ga. 224, 88 S. E. 941 (1916), rev'g. 17 Ga. App. 585, 87 S. E. 840 (1916); Hawkins v. Smith, 24 Ga. App. 464, 101 S. E. 311 (1919).

the levying officer before the sale under the execution of the judgment creditor, it was ruled that the lien of the landlord was preserved.[27] Furthermore, in an early case it was held that a distress warrant, issued in December, based on a landlord's special lien, took precedence over an attachment against the tenant, levied in September, and put in judgment in the previous October. Until maturity, the crop could not be legally levied upon by way of execution or attachment. The crop having been levied upon in September, before it matured, the landlord was held to be entitled to hold the crop.[28]

What is the result when a Georgia landlord gets possession of the crop by some method other than foreclosure and before the levy under the execution? Where the rent is payable in money, there seems to be no doubt that a voluntary delivery of the crop for the purpose of satisfying the lien will not take the place of a foreclosure and does not preserve the priority of the landlord.[29] The title passes to the landlord, however, where the rent is payable in kind and there has been an actual delivery of the landlord's share of the crop by the tenant. This transferred portion of the crop is not subject to a later claim of a general judgment creditor of the tenant. The court remarked that if the landlord's lien had been foreclosed, the claim under it would have been superior to the judgment in claiming a superior right to a fund arising from a sale of the crop. It further stated that there was no reason why a voluntary delivery should not have the same effect as a foreclosure in transferring title.[30] In other words, why should a landlord be required to go through the expensive procedure of foreclosure when his tenant had fulfilled the agreement by delivering in kind the share of the crop called for by the express terms of the contract itself? But even where the method of paying the rent is in kind, the necessity for a timely foreclosure is not dispensed with. Even where there was an oral agreement that the entire crop, without delivery, should be and remain the property of the landlord until a debt for supplies was entirely paid off,[31] or where the landlord had purchased the crop from the tenant at a private sale,[32] there must be a foreclosure. While there is a rather

27. Cochran v. Waits, Johnson & Co., 127 Ga. 93, 56 S. E. 241 (1906); Hill-Atkinson Co. v. Hasty, 17 Ga. App. 569, 87 S. E. 839 (1916).
28. Hopkins v. Pedrick, 75 Ga. 706 (1885).
29. Duncan v. Clark, 96 Ga. 263, 22 S. E. 927 (1895); Carr v. Morris, 17 Ga. App. 45, 86 S. E. 94 (1915).
30. Durdin v. Hill, 75 Ga. 228 (1885).
31. Almand v. Scott, 80 Ga. 95, 4 S. E. 892 (1888).
32. Lightner v. Brannen, 99 Ga. 606, 27 S. E. 703 (1896).

thin line of distinction here, there is some difference in the situations presented. In one case the initiative for fulfilling the contract came from the tenant, while in the others the landlord desired to protect himself more fully and took action with that purpose in view.

In another somewhat similar situation there was a controversy between a landlord and a holder of a bill of sale executed by the tenant. The parties agreed that the landlord might retain and dispose of the crop and that he should pay his opponent its value, if he was found to be indebted to him in a settlement of the matter before the court, the landlord's liability to depend upon whether his lien was superior to the bill of sale. The appellate court held that the effect of the agreement was to take the case out of the rule of law requiring a foreclosure, and that the lower court had erred in giving a priority to the holder of the bill of sale.[33] Of course where the relationship of landlord and cropper exists, the rule could have no application, since the title to the crop would have been in the landlord from its inception.[34]

In Louisiana, except for the above-mentioned conflict with respect to the overseer's privilege, a well-ordered system of priorities has been set down in the statutes. This order makes a laborer's privilege superior to the privilege of the lessor, followed by pledges of the crop, and then by the privileges of supply merchants.[35] Under this system the privilege of the lessor has been held to be superior to the right of pledge of a factor who had made advances to the tenant.[36] The lessor's privilege covers not only the crops but also the other movables of the lessee. It has been held that the lessor's privilege on various work animals, carts, and plantation supplies is superior to the claim of a third person who purchased the movables after the lease had been executed.[37] The statute establishing the order of priorities cannot be given a retroactive operation. Therefore the pledge of a tenant's crop authorized by a former act is not given preference over the antecedent privilege of a merchant who has furnished the tenant with supplies. The statute refers only to privileges that arise subsequent to the pledge. In the case under discussion the land had been held under a conditional agreement of sale, afterwards sup-

33. Cofer v. Barnett, 99 Ga. 307, 25 S. E. 651 (1896).
34. Almand v. Scott, 80 Ga. 95, 4 S. E. 892 (1888).
35. See La. Gen. Stat. (Dart, 1932) §5064; Flower v. Skipwith, 45 La. Ann. 895, 13 So. 152 (1893).
36. Carroll v. Bancker, 43 La. Ann. 1078, 1194, 10 So. 187 (1891).
37. Davis v. Thomas, 23 La. Ann. 340 (1871).

planted by a lease not executed until after the supplies had been furnished. This situation could not be affected by the subsequent
change in arrangements. The lessor's privilege, having arisen after
the date of the lease, had taken effect only as the situation then
stood, his claim being subject to the antecedent privilege. When
the supply privilege was created, the agreement was one of sale, and
it could not be changed afterwards to give the vendor-lessor a
prior claim.[38]

The merchant supplying farming utensils receives a priority over
the lessor's privilege under a Louisiana statute.[39] It was decided that
a steam thresher, necessary for the harvesting of a plantation rice
crop, was within the meaning of this statute.[40] The act was said to
create an exception to the right of the lessor to movables conferred
under another statute.[41] A steam engine, used in connection with a
pump for purposes of irrigation, with a thresher for threshing, and
possibly with plows and harness for cultivating a crop of rice, has
been held to be a farming utensil within this statute.[42] The engine
was not shown to have been used for other purposes. The decision
would have been the same whether the engine was acquired as a
part of the pump or at another time and from another source. The
court declared that the character of the apparatus was to be determined, for the purpose of the point under consideration, by its use
and not by the source from which it was obtained or the time of its
acquisition.

In another case from Louisiana the lease provided that any building erected on the premises by the lessee should belong to the lessor.
The parties agreed that the lessor could have a barn erected by the
lessee on the premises in payment of rent past due. It was said that
this agreement constituted a completed delivery and sale of the
building, though the lease had not expired and the premises were still
in the lessee's possession. A third person had furnished lumber to
build the barn and claimed that he had a privilege on the structure.
The court decided in favor of the lessor but declared that the decision would have been otherwise had there been no agreement or
delivery.[43] Another reason for the decision in favor of the landlord

38. Flower v. Skipwith, 45 La. Ann. 895, 13 So. 152 (1893).
39. La. Civ. Code (Dart, 1932) Art. 3259.
40. Laporte v. Libby, 114 La. 570, 38 So. 457 (1905).
41. La. Civ. Code (Dart, 1932) Art. 3263.
42. Lahn v. Carr, 120 La. 797, 45 So. 707 (1908).
43. Carroll Lumber Co. v. Davis, 133 La. 416, 63 So. 93 (1913).

was that the materialman's claim had not been recorded within seven days, as required by statute for such privileges.[44]

The North Carolina lien statute gives the lessor a right to hold the crops until he "shall be paid for all advancements made, and expenses incurred, in making and saving said crops." In considering this statute, the state court has ruled that advances made by a landlord to a sublessee, without the knowledge, assent, or privity of the lessee, are not entitled to priority over other advances procured by the lessee from another party for the use of the sublessee.[45] The opinion seems to indicate that the landlord is not even entitled to a pro rata apportionment in a case of this kind.

PRIORITY OF DEBTS—MARSHALING OF SECURITIES

In an Alabama case[46] the court enunciated certain principles respecting priorities which are important here: Thus it is said that where a debtor who owes several debts to one creditor makes a payment without directing how the money shall be applied, the creditor may apply it to any debt he chooses. But where the debtor owes several distinct debts to the same person, one of which is secured by mortgage and the others not, a payment made from the proceeds of a sale of the mortgaged property cannot, without the consent of both parties, be applied to any debt except the mortgage debt, until the satisfaction of that claim. Another general principle announced is that where no particular application of partial payments is directed or made by either party, such payments will be applied first to the oldest items of the indebtedness.

In the principal case an owner rented his farm land for five years at an agreed annual rental payable at a certain date in each year. The lessee was given an option to purchase the property during the lease at a stipulated price, on the condition that he pay each yearly rental promptly as it fell due. The lessor made advances to the tenant at various times and secured them either by mortgage or by lien on the crops, these security devices also covering the rent. Each year the tenant, on or before the date the rent became due, paid the landlord a sum exceeding the amount of the rent but less than the entire amount due for rent and advances combined, without directing the particular debt to which the payment should be applied. The land-

44. La. Civ. Code (Dart, 1932) Art. 3274.
45. Moore v. Faison, 97 N. C. 322, 2 S. E. 169 (1887).
46. Brown v. Larry, 153 Ala. 452, 44 So. 841 (1907).

lord applied the funds first to the satisfaction of the debt for advances and gave receipts showing that the sum had been so applied, the tenant having made no objection at the time. The lessor then declared the rent in default and claimed that the tenant had thereby lost his option to purchase. The court agreed with this theory of the case and held that there was a forfeiture under the terms of the contract, even though the landlord at a later date received the payment of the amount due as rent. The court also refused to adopt the theory of waiver set up by the tenant and insisted that time was of the essence in respect to the option. Although this decision might be approved as in strict conformity with the principles of contract law, it is a hard case in view of the fact that the tenant was evidently under a misapprehension as to the effect of his first payments on the transaction as a whole. It seems unjust to make him forfeit the option because of his failure to see that the receipts noted that the advances and not the rents were paid, especially in view of the later payment and acceptance. The necessity for a direction on the part of the tenant to assure application to the desired indebtedness was also stated in an earlier Alabama case.[47]

The Arkansas court has also upheld the application of a tenant's property to a contemporaneous debt for advances in a case involving an eviction for nonpayment of rent due to the failure of the landlord to apply the funds in his hands to the rent rather than to the advances.[48] The Georgia court, however, has declared that where it appears that other property has been levied upon and sold under a landlord's supply lien, and no credit has been entered upon the execution papers, it is incumbent upon the landlord to account for the proceeds before he can subject other property, upon which there is an adverse claim, to the full amount of a second execution. Here the landlord testified that he had applied a portion of the proceeds of the sale to the satisfaction of unsecured debts which were owed to him by the tenant. It was said that he had no right to apply the proceeds in this manner and that the levying officer should have credited them on the indebtedness secured by the lien. Therefore the claimant was allowed to prove that this had not been done in this case.[49]

In Arkansas the court has said that a creditor having a lien on

47. Aderholt v. Embry, 78 Ala. 185 (1884).
48. Malone v. Wade, 148 Ark. 548, 230 S. W. 579 (1921).
49. Smith v. Smith, 105 Ga. 717, 31 S. E. 754 (1898).

certain property for a debt cannot, even by agreement, apply any portion of the property to a debt which is not a lien upon it, to the prejudice of the holder of a junior lien on the same property. He must apply it only to the lien debt, leaving the residue, after its payment, for the satisfaction of the junior claim. This is what is known as the doctrine of marshaling securities or the two-fund doctrine. Where a creditor has no lien on the property at the time of its application, he cannot object to its appropriation to another unsecured indebtedness. In the principal case it was decided that while a landlord must refrain from active injury to the holder of a junior lien on the tenant's crop, he is under no legal obligation to collect his debt for him, or to husband the crop in order that both debts may be paid. The court stated that if a portion of the crop was dissipated by the tenant, the landlord would have a right to take the residue to satisfy his rent claim.[50]

In South Carolina a tenant who was required by contract to deliver certain cotton at a warehouse sold to the defendant cotton on which the landlord had a lien. The purchaser claimed that the landlord's rights could be defeated, proffering the erroneous argument that he should have first sought satisfaction in all possible ways before trying to subject the cotton which had been sold. The court said that the two-fund doctrine was applicable only in cases where there are at least two parties and two funds, and that such was not the case in this instance.[51] In another case the two-fund doctrine was also said to have no application where the proceeds of the tenant's crop were insufficient to pay the entire claim of the landlord, whose security also included a claim on a mule covered by a recorded mortgage in favor of the landlord. The animal was also covered by an unrecorded mortgage in favor of a third person. As the second mortgage had been executed after a settlement between the landlord and tenant, the doctrine was not deemed to be involved here.[52]

A Georgia landlord sought a distress warrant to be levied on a portion of the tenant's crop which had been seized by another claimant to whom the tenant was indebted. The other portion of the crop was subject to the equity of the beneficiaries of a homestead exemption right in the tenant. However, the claimant argued that, under

50. Hammond v. Harper, 39 Ark. 248 (1882).
51. Markert v. North Augusta Warehouse Co., 107 S. C. 135, 92 S. E. 201 (1917).
52. Sellers & Moore v. Campbell, 103 S. C. 207, 87 S. E. 999 (1916).

the doctrine of marshaling, the landlord must try to satisfy his debt out of the portion of the crop claimed by the beneficiaries before he could seize the part in the claimant's possession. This was not a proper case for the application of the two-fund doctrine, the court declaring that the general rule in such cases cannot be applied to the detriment of third persons with equities equal to or greater than the equity of the person seeking to invoke the doctrine. It was stated that the beneficiaries of the homestead possessed such equities.[53]

In another instance the landlord proposed to his tenant that he perform fixed acts of labor and be paid in advances of goods instead of money, the contract being entirely aside from the main tenancy agreement. The Alabama court ruled that there was no lien for such advances.[54] This court declared that crops raised by a tenant, and delivered by him to his landlord, must be applied to the debt covered by a landlord's lien on the crops. The only debt for which a lien could be claimed was for rent, though the landlord had other demands against the tenant.

In a Louisiana case negotiable warehouse receipts for cotton were sold, the lessor and lessee consenting, with the understanding that the proceeds should be applied to the payment of the lessor's privilege. A furnisher of supplies sued to enforce his inferior privilege on the crop. The evidence disclosed that the furnisher of supplies had sustained no injury and did not have any equitable cause of complaint, since, had the lessor pressed his suit to enforce the superior privilege, then his claim would have been the first to be paid out of the proceeds of the sale. The record indicated that had such a course been followed, there would have been nothing left to be applied on the furnisher's claim after payment of the superior privilege and costs. Under this evidence the court held that the purchaser of the warehouse receipts took the property free from the junior privilege of the supply furnisher.[55] However, it was also said that the mere fact that the cotton was deposited in a public warehouse and the receipts transferred to another would not prevent the supply merchant's privilege from following the cotton into the hands of the other person.

A tenant made a payment to the landlord which, if it had been applied to the rent as requested by the tenant, would have satisfied

---

53. Mulherin v. Porter, 1 Ga. App. 153, 58 S. E. 60 (1907).
54. Powell v. State, 84 Ala. 444, 4 So. 719 (1888).
55. Dunn Mercantile Co. v. Hudson, 17 La. App. 529, 136 So. 626 (1931).

the claim for rent. Instead of so applying it, however, the landlord attempted to credit it on the tenant's note to a third person on which the landlord was a surety. This note had been assigned to the landlord after the tenant's crop was harvested. The court declared that such an application of the payment was unjustified and held that the landlord had no lien on the tenant's crop to secure the amount of the debt represented by the note.[56]

A surety on a rent note received from the tenant a portion of the cotton crop to be used in the payment of claims for rent and advances. He was held to have a right to demand that the cotton be applied to the payment of the rent. If, contrary to the surety's instructions, a commission merchant to whom the cotton had been forwarded applied the proceeds to the payment of advances, the surety, after paying the rent, might recover from the commission merchant the value of the cotton, since the rent was the paramount charge.[57]

RECORDATION

It has been held that a landlord's claim on the tenant's crops for rent does not have to be recorded in order to be effective as a valid lien or privilege.[58] One reason for this is that the landlord's lien arises by operation of law.[59]

The supply lien statutes of North Carolina[60] and Virginia[61] provide for the recordation of the liens, and it is clear that recording is necessary in order to protect lienors against the claims of third persons.[62] An agricultural lien duly registered takes precedence over a mortgage of prior date and registration which is not in the proper form to constitute a valid supply lien itself.[63] The North Carolina court has held that registration of an agricultural lien is not essential to its validity as between the original parties to the contract.[64]

---

56. Carberry v. Howell, 114 Miss. 549, 75 So. 383 (1917).

57. Shields v. Atkinson, 67 Ala. 244 (1880).

58. White v. First Nat. Bank of Opp, 236 Ala. 589, 183 So. 875 (1938); Flower v. Skipwith, 45 La. Ann. 895, 13 So. 152 (1893); Arick v. Walsh & Boisseau, 23 La. Ann. 605 (1871).

59. I. M. Scott & Co. v. Ward, 21 Ga. App. 535, 94 S. E. 863 (1918).

60. N. C. Gen. Stat. (1943) §44-52.

61. Va. Code Ann. (Michie, 1936) §6452.

62. Gay v. Nash, 78 N. C. 100 (1878).

63. Eastern Cotton Oil Co. v. Powell, 201 N. C. 351, 160 S. E. 292 (1931).

64. Gay v. Nash, 78 N. C. 100 (1878); Reese & Co. v. Cole, 93 N. C. 87 (1885).

A South Carolina judge said it was not necessary as between the original parties to "index" the lien of the landlord for the rent of agricultural lands. As between the landlord and tenant, the contract was binding with or without recordation. The court seemed to doubt the necessity of recording the landlord's lien, even though there had been a claim by a third person. It further declared that the language of the lien statute indicated that the contract was enforceable, whether it was written or oral. It is impossible for a parol lien to be recorded, and hence the tribunal argued that the lien was effective without registration.[65]

At present a Louisiana statute[66] provides for the recordation of liens, privileges, and pledges, and it has been intimated that a proper registration will give protection against the claims of third persons.[67] It has also been said that pledges are to be considered in the order of their recordation.[68] However, it has been held that the privilege of the furnisher of supplies to a tenant need not be recorded to retain its priority over a subsequent chattel mortgage.[69] In making this decision the court took an opposite view from that which it had taken some years earlier with respect to a lessor's privilege for supplies.[70] In this instance the court seemed to differentiate between a privilege of this kind and a pledge on livestock and farming implements to secure the rent, holding that the pledge was effective without recordation. Furthermore, it had been held that the lessor's pledge need not be recorded to give it a preference over the privilege of a furnisher of supplies.[71] At least one of the cases declaring that registration is unnecessary was decided after the enactment of the recording act.

Thus a rather confused picture is presented with respect to the necessity for recording privileges and pledges in Louisiana. The state legislature should be urged to clarify the matter at the earliest possible moment.

65. Davis v. Days, 42 S. C. 69, 19 S. E. 975 (1894).
66. La. Gen. Stat. Ann. (Dart, 1932) §5063.
67. See Traylor v. Murphy, 2 La. App. 593 (1925).
68. Flower & King v. Skipwith, 45 La. Ann. 895, 13 So. 152 (1893).
69. Purity Mills Feed Co. v. Moore, 152 La. 393, 93 So. 196 (1922).
70. Dictum in Johnson v. Tacneau, 23 La. Ann. 453 (1871).
71. Burnett v. Cleneay, 24 La. Ann. 143 (1872). The lessor would prevail whether the property belonged jointly to lessees acting as partners in the planting business, or to one of them. Hynson v. Cordukes, 21 La. Ann. 553 (1869).

CONCLUSION

The whole body of the law concerning the priority of agricultural liens has been very much complicated by local rules. In fact there are only a few general rules which could be fitted into the scheme of priorities in all the states of the Southeastern group. A number of peculiarities seem to interfere with the clarity and decisiveness which should be demanded of legal opinions on this subject. It might be necessary for each legislature to work out the system of priorities best suited to local needs. A suggestion meriting some consideration is an act on the order of a uniform priorities law with exceptions to meet the needs of the particular locality.

XVI

Waiver of Lien and Estoppel

OFTEN there is a waiver of the landlord's lien for rent or supplies or both. Thus a landlord may either expressly waive or be considered to have impliedly waived his statutory right to have the crops grown upon the leased premises applied primarily to his own indebtedness. Circumstances may also arise which raise an equitable estoppel against the landlord, and in such a case he is not allowed to assert his lien. A waiver may be conditional or it may be limited in some manner by the terms expressed at the time it was put into effect. What constitutes a waiver or an estoppel is a matter to be determined in each individual case. The situations are numerous and varied, and some are complicated. The decisions will be reviewed with the idea of determining the kind of evidence which will make the courts decide in favor of or against the waiver or estoppel claimed by the proponents. Frequently a merchant advances supplies to the tenant or cropper relying upon the promise of the landlord to surrender or limit his prior claim to crops grown on the premises.

In introducing this subject it seems important to ascertain just what will constitute a waiver. With regard to this matter it is necessary to inquire into the type of evidence from which a waiver is deduced. Some comment has been made about this evidential phase in the opinions of the judges of the Southeastern region. Thus it has been declared that a landlord does not waive his lien by merely telling one of the tenant's other creditors that the crops are to be delivered to him as security, but subject to the landlord's lien.[1]

It has been held to be proper for a judge to instruct a jury that if the landlord allows his tenant to sublet the leased premises and then notifies the subtenant that a payment to the original tenant will relieve him of any liability to the landlord, the latter's lien upon the subtenant's crop will be released thereby.[2]

1. Foster v. Bradney, 143 Ark. 319, 220 S. W. 811 (1920).
2. Hatchell v. Chandler, 62 S. C. 380, 40 S. E. 777 (1902).

On the other hand, it may be said that the lien is not waived by the landlord's acceptance, in part payment of the rent, of a portion of the money paid by a purchaser of the tenant's crop. Although the landlord knew, at the time of acceptance, that it was a part of that sum, the lien would not be waived unless it could be shown that the landlord had consented to the sale or that he had been a party to the transaction between the tenant and the purchaser.[3] Furthermore, it has been held that mere knowledge on the part of the landlord that the tenant was being furnished supplies by a third person would not of itself constitute a waiver.[4] Again, there was no waiver where the testimony showed that one holding a landlord's lien on certain cotton had in effect permitted a substitution of one tenant for another, upon the latter tenant's promise to pay the rent and an amount due for supplies.[5] A similar result was reached where a landlord was shown to have had knowledge that certain mortgagees of cotton grown on rented premises had arranged with the growers to have it shipped out of the state.[6]

The Arkansas court has stated that the landlord's lien is not lost on account of the form of execution by which he seeks to enforce it, by the refusal of the county court to recognize it, by the failure to enforce it in the manner prescribed by law, or by an assignment of the tenant's property for the payment of his debts. Neither is it lost because the goods were in official custody at the time the attachment was sued out to enforce the lien, or because the property was converted into money at the order of a receiver appointed by the court itself.[7]

Sometimes a landlord may agree that if a merchant will make advances to his tenant, he will forego his right to do likewise. In one instance of this kind an Alabama landlord subsequently made advances to his tenant. The court held that he was not entitled to a crop lien which was superior to the claim of the merchant who had advanced supplies to the tenant on the faith of the agreement.[8]

3. Volmer v. Wharton, 34 Ark. 691 (1879).
4. Lee Gin Co. v. Archillion, 198 Ark. 564, 129 S. W. (2d) 952 (1939); Fletcher v. Dunn, 188 Ark. 734, 67 S. W. (2d) 579 (1934).
5. First Nat. Bank v. Duvall, 156 Ark. 377, 246 S. W. 471 (1923).
6. Sledge & Norfleet Co. v. Hughes, 156 Ark. 481, 247 S. W. 1077 (1923).
7. Blackwood v. Farmers' Bank & Trust Co., 200 Ark. 738, 141 S. W. (2d) 1 (1940).
8. Coleman v. Siler, 74 Ala. 435 (1883).

CONSENT TO SALE OR REMOVAL OF
CROP AS WAIVER

The general rule seems to be that a sale and removal of the crops with the consent of the landlord will be taken as a waiver of his lien.[9] The Georgia court has ruled in favor of a waiver where the testimony showed that the landlord was present and had consented to the sale of the crop by the tenant, permitting the warehouseman to make out a check in the name of the tenant, but later persuading him to stop payment on the check after a dispute arose over the division of the proceeds.[10] Therefore it seems that a landlord may not recall his consent after it has been acted upon.

To make the title of the purchaser of the produce at a permissive sale valid as against crop mortgages, however, the transaction must not only be made with the landlord's consent, but also on his account and for the purpose of satisfying his claim.[11]

Consent to the removal of crops from rented premises cannot always be said to constitute a waiver, inasmuch as a great deal depends upon the purposes of the removal and the intent with which the consent was given.[12] Consent to a sale is not a waiver where it is understood that the proceeds are to be used to settle the landlord's claim.[13] A lessor has been held not to have relinquished his lien, as against junior lienholders, by permitting his tenants to take corn and seed raised on the rented premises to another farm where they were to be stored in preparation for the planting of a second crop.[14] Furthermore, it has been said that consent of the landlord that the crops shall be cribbed on lands rented to the tenant and under his control does not authorize the latter to turn them over to a subten-

9. Foxworth v. Brown, 120 Ala. 59, 24 So. 1 (1898); May v. McGaughey, 60 Ark. 357, 30 S. W. 417 (1895); Webb v. Arnold, 52 Ark. 358, 12 S. W. 707 (1890); Lee v. Melton, 173 N. C. 704, 91 S. E. 697 (1917).

10. Hall v. Cain, 37 Ga. App. 170, 139 S. E. 130 (1927).

11. Gay & Bruce v. Smith, 211 Ala. 358, 100 So. 633 (1924).

12. Tuttle v. Walker, 69 Ala. 172 (1881).

13. Johnson v. Pruitt, 239 Ala. 44, 194 So. 409 (1939), rev'g 29 Ala. App. 174, 194 So. 406 (1939); Rose City Mercantile Co. v. Miller, 171 Ark. 872, 286 S. W. 1010 (1926). But in Alabama where the proceeds were not so used it was held that the landlord must sue in contract upon the promise to settle the claim and could not recover in a tort action for the appropriation. McCarthy v. Roswald, 105 Ala. 511, 17 So. 120 (1895).

14. Earl Bros. & Co. v. Smith, 169 Ark. 525, 275 S. W. 765 (1925).

ant to remove and store beyond the reach of either party to the original rental agreement.[15]

In a recent Kentucky case[16] a landlord, possessed of a lien upon his tenant's tobacco crop, took a chattel mortgage on the same crop as additional security. He agreed that the tenant might sell the tobacco, which was also covered by the attachment of a creditor, and stipulated that the proceeds should remain in the hands of a warehouseman until the rights of the respective claimants were definitely ascertained. The court declared that ordinarily, when property subject to a lien is sold with the consent of the lienor, the lien is waived and hence does not fasten itself upon the proceeds of the sale to the prejudice of the attaching creditor. In this instance, however, the terms of the agreement made it clear that there had been no abandonment of the lien.

With respect to consent to the sale and removal of goods subject to a lien as a waiver, a rather puzzling situation has developed in Louisiana. This matter is complicated by the influence of the Civil Law and the two-fold right of pledge and privilege which the lessor possesses under that system of jurisprudence. It is further complicated by contradictory statements in the opinions of the courts.

In a case which arose near the end of the past century, the State Supreme Court declared that while the consent of the lessor to the removal of a crop and the consequent loss of possession will forfeit the right of pledge, the same will not necessarily entail the loss of the privilege as well. It is argued that the two rights are conferred by separate statutes and are distinct. The pledge gives rights, including the right of detention, beyond those of a mere privilege. It is nonetheless in some respects a more precarious right than the privilege, which does not depend upon possession. The court held that the lessor, having permitted the property to escape from his grasp, had thereby lost the right of pledge. He could, however, still fall back upon his privilege, unless it had been extinguished for some other reason.[17]

In a much earlier case the same court, the Supreme Court of Louisiana, had come to a contrary conclusion respecting the loss of the privilege in an instance where the lessor had merely stood by and

---

15. Chandler v. Burk, 211 Ala. 93, 99 So. 727 (1924).
16. Jackson v. Coons, 285 Ky. 154, 147 S. W. (2d) 45 (1941).
17. O'Kelley v. Ferguson, 49 La. Ann. 1230, 22 So. 783 (1897).

allowed the property to be taken away without making any objection, thereby giving his tacit consent.[18]

Recently the question was raised again in a case which came before the intermediate appellate court of the State. In that instance the lessee's crops were removed with the express consent of the lessor. The court, ignoring the latest opinion of the higher tribunal, and basing its opinion upon the earlier case and the interpretation given certain statutes[19] giving fifteen days after removal for the assertion of the lienholder's rights, held that the loss of possession and removal with the consent of the lessor had the effect of cutting off the right of privilege as well as that of pledge. It was said that these two statutory rights or remedies are in reality merely two expressions of the same right, and that the loss of one necessarily entails the loss of the other. The court further declared that a lessor could not waive his right of pledge and retain his privilege or lien on the crops.[20] In other words, the Court of Appeals deliberately disregarded the latest opinion of the Supreme Court and adopted the view taken by that court in an earlier case where the consent was tacit and not express as it was in the instant case. Considering the two kinds of consent as the same, there can be no doubt that the earlier opinion of the Supreme Court is authority for the proposition stated here. But this certainly is strange procedure.

To this view one commentator has definitely acceded, basing his opinion upon an analysis of the French law and the Louisiana stat-

18. Desban v. Pickett, 16 La. Ann. 350 (1861).

19. La. Civ. Code (Dart, 1932) Art. 2709; La. Code Prac. (Dart, 1932) Art. 288, interpreted by Carroll v. Bancker, 43 La. Ann. 1078, 10 So. 187 (1891); Conrad v. Patzelt, 29 La. Ann. 465 (1877); General Motors Acceptance Corp. v. Hand, 16 La. App. 488, 133 So. 466 (1931); Madonia v. Meyer, 9 La. App. 71, 119 So. 96 (1928).

20. Boylston v. Jones, 153 So. 53 (La. App., 1934). In accord is the later case of Reed v. Walthers, 193 So. 253 (La. App., 1940). The property in the *Desban* case, *supra* Note 18, was furniture, and in the *Boylston* case the court ruled that the same doctrine would apply to crops. In the latter case it is said that the phrase "without his consent," employed in La. Code Prac. Ann. (Dart, 1932) Art. 288, does not limit the situations in which the statute may apply to instances where no consent is given, but that it would also apply where consent is shown. The court argued that the meaning would be the same without the alleged superfluous phrase. This is one interpretation that might be made, but it ignores the fact that the legislature, which is not in the habit of employing ineffectual language, had actually used this particular phraseology here. A matter such as this one is not settled until the court of last resort expresses its opinion, and therefore it cannot be said that the point is definitely decided.

utes and decisions.[21] He was evidently of the opinion that the decisions of the State Supreme Court were in hopeless conflict and that therefore the judges of the appellate court were justified in taking the view which they were convinced would give the best results. While this is probably the better opinion from the standpoint of the principles of law involved, it can hardly be said that the state law is settled, especially in view of the fact that Louisiana's highest tribunal, in its latest discussion of the matter, expressed itself in such definite language as being of a different opinion.

In summing up the matter of consent there seems to be no doubt that the sale and removal of farm produce from leased premises, when it is done with the permission of the landlord, should be considered as a waiver of any right he may have to the crops, including the landlord's lien. The courts have commonly adopted this principle as a guidepost to fair dealing.

COURSE OF DEALING AS WAIVER

The courts of two states, Alabama[22] and Mississippi,[23] have held that when by a course of dealing over a number of years a landlord has permitted his tenant to dispose of the crops grown on the leased premises, the landowner is considered to have waived his lien and therefore cannot be allowed to enforce it to the prejudice of a purchaser from his tenant. This is particularly important in Mississippi, where a bona fide purchaser of the tenant's crop is not protected.[24] In order to take advantage of this defense the purchaser must allege and prove the facts constituting this course of dealing, and it is not necessary for a landlord seeking to enforce his lien to negate such a course of dealing in the complaint.[25]

Where a landlord has allowed his tenant to store the crop in a warehouse and permitted him to take negotiable warehouse receipts therefor, thereby clothing him with apparent ownership, he is considered to have waived his lien. A purchaser of these receipts from

21. Note (1935) 9 Tulane Law Rev. 442.
22. Pelzer v. Mutual Warehouse Co., 217 Ala. 630, 117 So. 165 (1928); Patterson v. Vest, 216 Ala. 298, 113 So. 59 (1927).
23. Federal Land Bank v. Southern Credit Corp., 188 Miss. 192, 192 So. 827 (1940); Crutcher v. Commercial Bank, 146 Miss. 404, 111 So. 569 (1927); Judd v. Delta Grocery & Cotton Co., 133 Miss. 866, 98 So. 243 (1923); Phillips v. Thomas, 128 Miss. 729, 91 So. 420 (1922).
24. Warren v. Jones, 70 Miss. 202, 14 So. 25 (1892).
25. Pitts v. Baskin, 140 Miss. 443, 106 So. 10 (1925).

the tenant can hold the property free from the landlord's claim.[26] However, where the circumstances show that the tenant has stored the crops and taken the warehouse receipts without the express or implied consent of the landlord, the lien is not waived, and the landlord may enforce it by either taking the property or recovering damages for the conversion of the receipts.[27]

In a recent North Carolina case the landlord delivered his Agricultural Adjustment Administration card to the tenant for the purpose of enabling the tenant to sell his tobacco through a warehouse without incurring a penalty. It was held that by so doing the landlord had lost his prior claim on the crop and had no recourse against the warehousemen.[28]

CONDITIONAL WAIVER

It seems to be true that where a mortgagee has been authorized by the waiver of a landlord's lien to take and dispose of crops, he cannot be considered to have committed a wrong by reason of any act in reference to the crops which was warranted by the contract and was done while it was in force. To bring himself within this rule, however, the mortgagee must show that he himself has performed all such acts as have been made a condition of the landlord's responsibility.[29] For instance, a landlord may have consented to a sale of produce by his tenant's mortgagee on condition that the latter should account to the extent of the landlord's advances. Here it is ruled that the lien is not waived in such a manner as to defeat the landlord's right to an accounting.[30]

LIMITED WAIVER

A waiver may also be limited, that is, it may be worded in such a manner as to apply only up to a certain amount. In fact this form of waiver is rather common. It is usually made for the purpose of obtaining a limited amount of goods from a merchant who would

26. Phillips v. Box, 204 Miss. 231, 37 So. (2d) 266 (1948). Crutcher v. Commercial Bank, 146 Miss. 404, 111 So. 569 (1927); McGee v. Carver, 141 Miss. 463, 106 So. 760 (1926).

27. Tennessee Joint Stock Land Co. v. Bank of Greenwood, 179 Miss. 534, 172 So. 323 (1937); Schmitt v. Federal Compress & Warehouse Co., 169 Miss. 589, 153 So. 815 (1934); Campbell v. Farmers' Bank, 127 Miss. 668, 90 So. 436 (1922).

28. Adams v. Growers' Warehouse, 230 N. C. 704, 55 S. E. (2d) 331 (1949).

29. Stoekler v. Wooten, 80 Ala. 610, 2 So. 703 (1887).

30. Pinckard & Lay v. Roland, 211 Ala. 157, 99 So. 910 (1924).

not otherwise extend credit to the tenant. A landlord may be willing to execute a limited waiver, whereas he could not be persuaded to make one that was unlimited.

Apparently where a landlord waives his lien up to a limited cash amount or a certain number of units of the commodity to be produced, his lien upon the remainder of the crops is not extinguished and continues to be effective.[31] In a Mississippi case a merchant supplied the tenant up to the stated amount and also took a deed of trust covering the crops and other property as well. A subtenant gave the tenant a rent note which was later transferred to the landlord and collected out of the proceeds of the subtenant's crop. The merchant sued the landlord and was permitted to recover to the extent of the amount stated in the waiver.[32]

Such a waiver may sometimes be included in the lease contract for the purpose of facilitating the credit machinery. In one instance an Arkansas lease gave just such a waiver of the landlord's claim for rent in favor of anyone who would furnish money up to a stated amount. The court construed this as a present waiver and not as an agreement to waive on future demand. The landlord contended that the waiver stated in the contract was purely for the tenant's benefit and that hence a third person could not take advantage of it. However, the court ruled that a person who had furnished money for the production and harvesting of the crops could enforce the contract and take advantage of the waiver according to its terms.[33]

THE TAKING OF ADDITIONAL SECURITY AS A WAIVER

Frequently a landlord, not satisfied with the security which is provided by his lien for rent and/or advances, will require the tenant to give additional security, which commonly takes the form of a note or mortgage or both. In considering situations in which such security is given, the courts inevitably encounter questions similar to the following one. Under what circumstances will the taking of such additional security constitute a waiver of the landlord's lien

31. Varner v. Ross, 121 Ala. 603, 25 So. 725 (1899); Blackwood v. Farmers' Bank & Trust Co., 200 Ark. 738, 141 S. W. (2d) 1 (1940); Jacobson v. Atkins, 103 Ark. 91, 146 S. W. 133 (1912); Bigham v. Cross, 69 Ark. 581, 65 S. W. 101 (1901); Lemay v. Johnson, 35 Ark. 225 (1879); Hamilton v. Blanton, 107 S. C. 142, 92 S. E. 275 (1917).

32. H. & C. Newman, Inc. v. Delta Grocery & Cotton Co., 138 Miss. 683, 103 So. 373, 104 So. 157 (1925).

33. Lee Wilson & Co. v. Fleming, 203 Ark. 417, 156 S. W. (2d) 893 (1941).

on the crop? There is a lack of unanimity in the decisions of the Southeastern states in respect to this important matter.

The view that the lien is waived seems to have been recognized by decisions from Alabama,[34] Arkansas,[35] and Tennessee.[36] According to the opinions in the first two states, however, it would appear that the lien is not waived unless an election has clearly been made and there is a definite intention to consider the other security as a substitute. The Kentucky court has ruled that there will be no waiver implied from the taking of personal security which is not inconsistent with the statutory lien.[37]

There has been quite a bit of discussion in Mississippi concerning this matter. In a rather early case a landlord's agent, not content with the security of the supply lien, took a deed of trust on the tenant's prospective crop in his own name. Thus the agent had carved out and required another apparently inconsistent security which, on its face, secured an indebtedness to a person whose agency for the landlord was not disclosed by the instrument. The premises had been subrented to subtenants who had raised a crop thereon. The court declared that the landlord must confine himself to the security afforded by the deed of trust. He was not permitted to recover the value of the crop, since the principal tenant could not thus encumber the subtenants' produce, even though it had been grown on the leased premises. In other words, the court appeared to believe that the parties had dealt with the subject matter in such a manner as to make it inequitable for the landlord to repudiate the security selected by his agent and fall back on the lien.[38] This argument seems to be based upon something very much akin to estoppel.

In a much later case a Mississippi landlord sold certain personalty to his tenant for use on the leased premises and had a purchase-money lien thereon. Not being satisfied with respect to the security, he took a deed of trust on the personalty. Here it was decided that by this action the landlord had waived neither the lien on the crop for advances nor his purchase-money lien for the balance of the purchase price of the articles furnished.[39] The court appears to have

34. Johnson v. Thompson, 185 Ala. 666, 64 So. 554 (1914).
35. Cole v. Turner, 108 Ark. 537, 158 S. W. 493 (1913).
36. Bramlett v. Hurley, 160 Tenn. 653, 28 S. W. (2d) 633 (1930); Pettigrew v. Hodges, 5 Tenn. App. 599 (1927).
37. Smith v. Wells' Adm'x., 67 Ky. 92 (1868).
38. Gaines v. Keeton, 68 Miss. 473, 10 So. 71 (1891).
39. Thompson v. Hill, 147 Miss. 489, 112 So. 697 (1927).

followed a similar case where the earlier controversy concerning the subtenants was differentiated as a situation in which the security taken was inconsistent with the lien.[40] The rule as enunciated in these two cases is said by the court to be the established law in Mississippi but contrary to the weight of authority. In view of what other Southeastern courts have said concerning this rule of law it is doubtful that the decision is contrary to current opinion.

Furthermore, it appears that a Mississippi landlord does not waive the lien by taking both a rent note and a note for the price of certain mules advanced by him, where the instruments recite that he will retain a lien on both the crop and the mules until the indebtedness is paid.[41]

This discussion may be summed up by saying that the hint of conflict of opinion here is more fancied than real. A thorough analysis shows that the courts do not differ so very much.

WAIVER AS AFFECTING RIGHT OF DISTRESS

In a South Carolina case there was a provision in a lease fixing the amount of the landlord's claim on the crop, a clause which was treated by the court as a waiver of everything above the set amount. A question arose as to the effect of such a waiver upon the landlord's right to the remedy of distress. It was ruled that such a provision in a lease applied only to the rights and remedies given the landlord under the Agricultural Lien Law, and that therefore he was not deprived of his right, independent of statute, to distrain the tenant's property for rent due. Evidently, the court was of the opinion that this important right of the landlord would not be considered as waived without some definite language which was clearly expressive of such an intent, and that no such language had been used here.[42]

ORAL OR WRITTEN WAIVER

Ordinarily an oral waiver is sufficient to release a landlord's lien on the tenant's crops. In fact such a result had been reached in Arkansas[43] before the legislature of that State decided to change the law. In 1936 a statute was enacted which provides that any

40. See Smith & Vaile Co. v. Butts, 72 Miss. 269, 16 So. 242 (1894).
41. Trimble v. Durham, 70 Miss. 295, 12 So. 207 (1892).
42. Parrot v. Malpass, 49 S. C. 4, 26 S. E. 884 (1897).
43. Meyer v. McKenzie, 189 Ark. 76, 70 S. W. (2d) 505 (1934); Wilson v. Citizens' Bank of Osceola, 170 Ark. 1194, 282 S. W. 689 (1926).

waiver of a landlord's lien is invalid against a subsequent mortgagee, purchaser, or assignee, unless the person procuring such waiver makes sure that the existence of the waiver is recited in the instrument under which he claims.[44] Even before this date a written waiver was required where the landlord wished to waive his lien in favor of an employee of his tenant,[45] or where he wanted to surrender his right to keep the tenant from collecting rent from a subtenant before a final settlement with the owner had been reached.[46]

A Tennessee statute[47] requires payment for the tenant's crop to be made to the landlord and tenant jointly in instances where the landlord has given his written consent to the sale. Any check or other written instrument used to make the payment shall be made payable to both. In addition it is necessary that the genuine signature of the landlord or his authorized agent be placed upon the back of the instrument before it is paid. Moreover, there is a provision in the Tennessee statute which might possibly be construed as requiring all waivers of landlords' liens to be in writing, but it is not believed that the courts will so construe it.

CONSIDERATION FOR WAIVER

There is no necessity for a consideration in the case of a waiver which has been acted upon.[48] However, it is different with an executory contract to waive. Here the landlord may revoke the waiver at any time before it has been acted upon, provided there was no consideration for the agreement to give up the lien.[49] Where there is consideration a different situation exists. This may be illustrated by a case where a Georgia landlord agreed to waive his lien in favor of a laborer who had contracted with the tenant to work on the crops. The proponent of the waiver argued that the promise to waive was supported by a valuable consideration, namely, the benefit accruing to the landlord from the procurement of the laborer to cultivate the land. The court was of the opinion that the laborer's efforts would improve the prospect of a good

44. Ark. Dig. Stat. (Pope, 1937) §8857.
45. Ark. Dig. Stat. (Pope, 1937) §8847.
46. Ark. Dig. Stat. (Pope, 1937) §8850.
47. Tenn. Code Ann. (Williams, 1934) §8028. See First Citizens' Nat. Bank v. Cottonseed Products Co., 11 Tenn. App. 269 (1930).
48. Cohn v. Smith, 64 Miss. 816, 2 So. 244 (1887); Sugg v. Farrar, 107 N. C. 123, 12 S. E. 236 (1890).
49. Cohn v. Smith, 64 Miss. 816, 2 So. 244 (1887); Sugg v. Farrar, 107 N. C. 123, 12 S. E. 236 (1890).

yield and give the tenant a better opportunity to pay the rent, even after a full satisfaction of the laborer's claim.[50] This decision is fully in accord with well-established principles of the law of contracts.

WAIVER OBTAINED BY FRAUD

Sometimes a tenant will obtain a waiver of the landlord's lien by misrepresentation or fraud. In one such case an Arkansas credit association had been induced to loan money to a tenant by a waiver of such a lien which had been obtained from the landlord by fraudulent conduct on the part of the tenant. It was shown that the association was ignorant of the fraud at the time when it had accepted the waiver and extended its credit to the tenant. The landlord claimed that he was entitled to rescind the waiver because of this fraud and that he could recover from the association for the alleged conversion of the crop. The court refused a recovery for the reason that the association neither knew nor had any reason to suspect that the waiver had been obtained by fraudulent means. It said that the association had a right to rely upon a waiver which it had no reason to believe was tinged with the chicanery of the tenant.[51]

INTERPRETATION OF WAIVER OR AGREEMENT TO WAIVE

Sometimes an instrument which contains a waiver of a landlord's lien or an agreement to waive it is couched in such vague language that misunderstandings arise with respect to the exact definition of the words used. When these disputes come before the courts, it is necessary for the judges to interpret the agreements and arrive at some conclusion concerning the meaning of the language employed. At times the terminology of the agricultural and warehouse trade is used, and the courts, therefore, may find it necessary to interpret the meaning of a technical or trade term in the agreement. More frequently, however, it is just a matter of determining the extent of the waiver and the meaning of ordinary language.

Where there was a simple waiver of a landlord's lien, in favor of one who had furnished supplies to tenants for the current year, the court held it did not operate as a relinquishment of an ante-

50. Nelson v. Fuqua, 46 Ga. App. 754, 169 S. E. 206 (1933).
51. White River Production Credit Ass'n v. Fears, 213 Ark. 75, 209 S. W. (2d) 294 (1948).

cedent claim against the tenants, unless it was clear that such was the interpretation placed upon the contract by the parties themselves.[52] In fact, it seems that the presumption is always against the waiver.[53]

A South Carolina merchant induced a landlord to indorse a lease in the following language: "I hereby waive my landlord's lien for rent to the extent of $75.00, reserving the right to give or take the first bale weighing 400 pounds, and bale about afterwards." The court decided that this was no general waiver but only a relinquishment of the lien on alternate bales as indicated in the latter portion of the agreement.[54] Again, an Alabama landlord agreed to waive his lien for rent on one bale of his tenant's cotton for a specified year. This was interpreted as a waiver on only one bale of the crop, leaving the remainder subject to the lien for the amount stated in the rent contract. The effect was merely to give the tenant the privilege of disposing of one bale of the cotton crop free from the lien. With respect to the remainder of the crop, the lien was still in force and superior to the chattel mortgage of the person to whom the waiver had been given.[55]

An Arkansas landlord waived his lien on his tenants' crops to a stated amount in favor of a bank which was financing the tenants. The cotton crop had been delivered to a compress company and released to the tenants and a surety on their bond, with a directive to pay the landlord if he were adjudged to have a lien. Although the bank, before its withdrawal from the case, was capable of providing the necessary proof of the tenants' debt, it had not only failed to do so, but had also advanced additional sums to the tenants. As it is not the policy of banks ordinarily to grant new loans to irresponsible debtors, the court assumed, in the absence of proof to the contrary, that the debt had been satisfied and that the bank had no further interest in the matter. It was further held that the waiver was in favor of the bank alone, and that no one else, including the tenants and their surety, could set it up as a defense in the landlord's action to enforce the lien. In other words, the waiver did not extinguish

52. Napier v. Foster, 80 Ala. 339 (1885); Silbernagel & Co. v. Taliaferro, 186 Ark. 470, 53 S. W. (2d) 999 (1932).
53. Blackwood v. Farmers' Bank & Trust Co., 200 Ark. 738, 141 S. W. (2d) 1 (1940).
54. Boag v. Woodward, 33 S. C. 247, 11 S. E. 726 (1890).
55. Varner v. Ross, 121 Ala. 603, 25 So. 725 (1899).

the lien but rendered it dormant in favor of the person or institution to whom it had been given.[56]

In a Louisiana case a lessee obtained a waiver of the lessor's privilege or lien for the purpose of obtaining credit at a bank. The inducement for the waiver was a promise to ship the cotton crop to a factor designated by the lessor. Subsequently, the lessee borrowed money from a third person and made an agreement to ship the cotton to him. The note executed in this transaction was discounted at the bank. The court declared that there was no obligation on the bank, upon discounting the note, to see that the lessee lived up to his agreement to ship the cotton to the selected factor or to see that the rent was paid. As between the lessor and the bank, the only obligation created was the former's promise to forego his privilege in favor of the latter.[57]

A Mississippi tenant gave a mortgage on his crop to secure certain notes given to a merchant furnishing supplies. A landlord's waiver was included in the instrument, relinquishing the rent lien and any other lien until the notes were paid. The court held that this waiver was not a general one, and that it merely postponed the payment of the tenant's indebtedness to the landlord until the debt secured by the mortgage was paid. Therefore neither the mortgagee nor anyone else could derive from the waiver any right to purchase the crop.[58]

Another landlord agreed to waive his lien in favor of a merchant if he would "sell all supplies necessary for the furnishing of his tenants" in the raising of the crops. There were three separate cash advances to the tenants. Two of these items, one advanced to pay a subtenant's fine and the other to purchase horses and mules afterwards sold at a profit, the proceeds being applied on the indebtedness to the merchant, were held not to be within the terms of the waiver. The third item was for supplies necessary to proper cultivation and was held to be within the language employed, although it was contended that a cash advance should not come within the purview of the term "sell" as used in the waiver.[59]

56. Burke v. International Life Ins. Co., 179 Ark. 651, 17 S. W. (2d) 314 (1929).

57. Raccourci Co. v. Louisiana State Bank, 128 La. 1074, 55 So. 679 (1911).

58. Pitts v. Baskin, 140 Miss. 443, 106 So. 10 (1925).

59. Somerville v. Delta Grocery & Cotton Co., 159 Miss. 252, 130 So. 95 (1929).

WHAT CONSTITUTES AN ESTOPPEL

Sometimes a landlord is guilty of conduct which makes it inequitable for him to enforce his prior lien for rent and/or advances. This is what is known as an estoppel *in pais*, or an equitable estoppel. It frequently occurs where the landlord has said or done something which has misled another person to the latter's detriment. This estoppel presents itself not only when the words or conduct of the landlord are intended to be acted upon, but also when it is reasonable for him to anticipate a change in the other person's position as a result of reliance on the landlord's misrepresentation.[60] There are quite a few instances of estoppels of this nature which have arisen in the courts of the Southeastern states.

A simple example of this type of estoppel is seen where an Alabama landowner represented to a merchant that a certain tenant had been permitted to cultivate a plot free from rent and that he had no claim upon the crop, thereby persuading the merchant to make advances. The court held that the landowner could set up no claim for either rent or supplies furnished by himself.[61]

In one instance a Mississippi landlord waived his lien on his tenant's cotton and thereby subordinated it to a claim for supplies furnished by a merchant, who received a deed of trust as security. The landlord then took possession of a part of this cotton and mingled it with his own. Under these circumstances it was held that the landlord was estopped to deny that a particular bale of cotton seized under legal process by the trustee at the instance of the merchant was in fact produced upon the leased premises.[62] Again, a landlord induced a third person to extend credit by waiving all liens on crops raised by or for his tenant. He thereby led him into believing that by taking a deed of trust he would acquire a paramount claim on all crops grown on the leased premises. Here the court held that the landlord was estopped from contending that the third person did not acquire a valid claim to crops raised by a subtenant, since the landlord had failed to disclose the tenant's prior

60. 21 C. J., p. 1120. In Colvin v. Payne, 218 Ala. 341, 118 So. 578 (1928), this statement is quoted, but the latter portion of the definition is not included, thereby creating the erroneous impression that there can be no estoppel without a definite intent to deceive.

61. Chancellor v. Law & Edmonds, 148 Ala. 511, 41 So. 514 (1906).

62. Alexander v. Ziegler, 84 Miss. 560, 36 So. 536 (1904).

assignment to the landlord of the subtenant's rent note and its subsequent payment. Hence the third person was permitted to recover the amount of the note as money had and received in an action sounding in quasi contract, a promise to pay being implied.[63]

Where a landlord holding a lien for both rent and advances receives the rent out of the proceeds of his tenant's cotton crop and at the time of the sale gives no notice of his additional claim for advances, he is thereafter estopped from making the claim that the tenant had no authority to dispose of the crop and give a title free from any supply lien he might have.[64]

Something in the nature of an estoppel may arise even in criminal proceedings. A tenant was indicted under a Tennessee statute[65] which imposed a fine upon anyone who sold property subject to the lien of a landlord with the intention of depriving him of the security upon which the lien existed. It was stated in the opinion that the landlord had either expressly agreed that the tenant might sell the crop and use the proceeds, or had led him to believe that, in view of the fact that personal security had been taken, the lien was no longer a matter of any particular concern, thereby persuading him that there had been a waiver. Under these circumstances a conviction of the tenant for appropriating the crop in alleged violation of the statute was reversed for want of criminal intent.[66]

In other cases it has been held that the evidence was not of the right sort or quality to establish an estoppel. For instance, a Mississippi tenant wrote his landlady a note asking that he be relieved of paying the rent when it fell due. The landlady wrote an answer stating that if he would pay a portion of the rent, the remainder would be allowed to go over to the next year. Without the landlady's permission the tenant showed this letter to a merchant with whom he had been dealing, and the latter made further advances to him. It was evidently the opinion of the court that this communication written by the landlady did not contain such statements as she would suppose anyone could make the basis of a claim of estoppel. It was declared that the statement of the merchant that he was induced by this letter to change his position to his detriment

63. H. & C. Newman, Inc. v. Delta Grocery & Cotton Co., 144 Miss. 877, 110 So. 686 (1927).

64. Seavey & Sons v. Godbold, 99 Miss. 113, 54 So. 838 (1911).

65. Tenn. Code Ann. (Williams, 1934) §8025.

66. State v. Hoskins, 106 Tenn. 430, 61 S. W. 781 (1901).

looked very much like a pretext and an afterthought in an effort to defeat the landlord's just claim.[67]

A woman from South Carolina held a preferred lien for rent on crops made by her husband on lands which she had leased to him. It was held that she was not estopped from asserting her lien, as against a third person's claim for supplies which had been furnished the husband, because of payments made by him out of the crops on either the third person's claim or other indebtedness.[68] In other words, the marital relationship cannot be used in this situation as the basis for an estoppel.

The mere fact that the landlord knows that a mercantile firm, which has furnished supplies to the tenant and taken chattel mortgages as security, is receiving cotton from the tenant does not estop him from asserting a lien upon the proceeds of the cotton in the hands of the firm. He is entitled to assume that there would be no attempt to convert the proceeds to his prejudice.[69]

Mere silence would hardly be taken as the basis for an estoppel except in very unusual cases. An illustration can be seen in a recent Arkansas case where a landlord stood silently by and did nothing while his tenant told a merchant that the latter would have a first lien on the crop. The merchant claimed that this silence had been a tacit approval of the transaction and that he had thereby been induced to extend credit to the tenant who had then agreed to give him a first mortgage lien on the produce. Here the court refused to hold that there was any basis for an estoppel.[70]

PROMISSORY ESTOPPEL

An Alabama court has said that a statement made by a landlord to a mortgagee of the tenant's crop that he would not advance any supplies to the tenant did not estop the landlord from making a claim based on supplies he afterwards advanced. Reliance upon the promise of another with respect to his future conduct is not to be given the effect of an estoppel, however liable the promissor may be for a breach of contract.[71] While this proposition concerning a promise

67. Houston v. Witherspoon, 68 Miss. 188, 190, 8 So. 515 (1891).
68. Carter v. DuPre, 18 S. C. 179 (1882).
69. Lee Gin Co. v. Archillion, 198 Ark. 564, 129 S. W. (2d) 952 (1939); Fletcher v. Dunn, 188 Ark. 734, 67 S. W. (2d) 579 (1934).
70. Woods v. Pankey, 214 Ark. 236, 215 S. W. (2d) 292 (1948).
71. McAdams & Co. v. Smith, 8 Ala. App. 515, 62 So. 1000 (1913). Cf. Coleman v. Siler, *supra* Note 8, for a similar situation in respect to waiver.

of future conduct is true as a general rule, the courts have now developed the doctrine of promissory estoppel to take care of just such a situation. Under this doctrine an estoppel will be permitted if the promise or representation was made to induce action or was calculated to induce action and has in fact done so.[72]

Another Alabama case furnishes an interesting comparison. In this instance the landlord stated to a third person that if the latter would furnish his tenant with supplies, he would claim no prior lien on the crop. Thereupon the third person advanced the supplies, taking a parol mortgage which was invalid by statute. Afterwards the landlord took a mortgage in writing as additional security. It was held that the landlord was not estopped from asserting his mortgage lien on the crop because of the above statement. Again the court indicated that the third person's only remedy lay in an action for breach of contract. If we assume that the promise not to claim a lien included the mortgage lien as well as the landlord's statutory lien, the case agrees with the situation just discussed and hence is subject to the same criticism.[73]

In a case stronger from a different angle, certain factors who held a mortgage on a farmer's property asked a landowner to rent the farmer a tract of land and promised that their mortgage would be secondary to the landowner's lien for rent. The factors also agreed to furnish the farmer with supplies to run the place. Upon the faith of these assurances the landowner let the farmer have the land. Here it was held that the factors were estopped from claiming any of the funds realized from the sale to the exclusion of the landowner's lien.[74]

IS A CHANGE IN TERMS OF LEASE A BASIS FOR AN ESTOPPEL?

Sometimes a landowner and a tenant who is continuing on the land for another year will change the terms of the lease contract in such a way that the landowner will get a better slice of the crop than the contract of the previous year had given him. It is clear that the mere fact that the landlord and tenant have changed the terms of the rental agreement should not in itself create an estoppel

72. 31 C. J. S., Estoppel, §80, p. 290. See Thom v. Thom, 208 Minn. 461, 294 N. W. 461 (1940).

73. Weaver v. Bell, 87 Ala. 385, 6 So. 298 (1889).

74. Crime & Daniel v. Davis, 68 Ga. 138 (1881).

in favor of a merchant who has not been informed of the new terms. An illustration of this sort of thing occurred in an Arkansas case where the land had been rented in previous years for one-fourth of the cotton crop, and the rental terms were changed to six hundred dollars in cash for the next year. Neither the landlord nor the tenant did anything to induce the merchant furnishing supplies to believe that there had been no change of terms for the coming year. In fact, nothing was said about the matter. The court held that there was no basis for an estoppel here.[75] The same result was reached where a Georgia landlord had informed a merchant that his tenant would owe him one thousand pounds of lint cotton as rent and subsequently leased the tenant additional lands, making the total rent fourteen hundred pounds for the year. It was held that the landlord was not estopped by this statement from claiming a prior lien for the entire sum, and that there was no duty to inform the merchant of the change in the agreement.[76]

A different situation presents itself, however, where there is evidence of collusion on the part of the landlord and tenant to keep the merchant ignorant of the change in terms. The court held that such collusive silence is fraudulent and declared that the landlord was "estopped" from asserting a lien for the increased rental.[77] The true ground of this decision is really fraud, and the use of the term "estoppel" seems out of place, since ordinarily there can be no reliance upon silence. That there must be such reliance is shown in an Alabama case where the landlord informed a prospective mortgagee of his tenant's crop that the terms of the rental agreement gave him one-fourth of the cotton and one-third of the corn. The court was asked to instruct the jury that the landlord's statement would estop him from claiming additional amounts in accordance with a change in the terms of the lease contract. It was held that this instruction was properly refused, there being no mention of any reliance on the part of the mortgagee upon the landlord's statement. The court made it clear that it considered reliance to be an essential element of an equitable estoppel.[78]

75. Payne v. Seymour, 181 Ark. 1083, 29 S. W. (2d) 287 (1930).
76. Madison Supply & Hardware Co. v. Richardson, 8 Ga. App. 344, 64 S. E. 45 (1910).
77. Reeves v. B. T. Williams & Co., 160 Ga. 15, 127 S. E. 293 (1925).
78. McAdams & Co. v. Smith, 8 Ala. App. 515, 62 So. 1000 (1912).

The law in respect to estoppel has developed over an extended period of years but as yet cannot be said to have reached a point where no improvement is possible. Cases are continually arising which require the extension of the doctrine to new situations. Illustrations have shown how the adoption of the doctrine of promissory estoppel prevented injustices with respect to the enforcement of the landlord's lien, and there may be other phases of tenancy law where the doctrine could be applied advantageously.

CONCLUSION

On the whole it may be said that the law with respect to waiver and estoppel in cases pertaining to the landlord's lien is in a fairly satisfactory condition. Of course, there are a few situations which need clarification. The courts of the Southeastern states must study the past opinions of the judges with a view to broadening the law and putting aside outworn theories.

XVII

Transfer of Interest—Effect upon Lien

IN the modern world of business, property interests are continually shifting from one person to another. With respect to the matter of crop liens, questions are constantly arising concerning changing ownership and assignment. What affect does an assignment of a lien or rent note have upon the relationship of parties involved in a particular controversy? What results are engendered by the transfer, conveyance, or mortgage of the reversionary interest of the landlord? Answers to questions of this kind may be complicated by the application of laws in an entirely new field of jurisprudence. For instance, the assignment of a rent note will often bring the law of negotiable instruments into controversy. Hence many of the cases presented in this discussion are complicated by the introduction of several parties and by involved fact situations.

ASSIGNMENT

A presentation of the subject of assignment of liens and rent notes must be given a geographical and chronological emphasis, since the law has changed many times in most of the Southeastern states, and the development has not been uniform.

With the exception of Kentucky and Louisiana, these states now have statutes authorizing an assignee to enforce the landlord's lien for rent.[1] An assignee of the landlord's lien for advances is also expressly authorized to enforce the lien by these same statutes in Alabama, Mississippi, North Carolina, and South Carolina.

In most of these states no particular form of assignment, such as an assignment in writing, appears to be necessary. This is illustrated by the Alabama cases, in which it is said that the assignment of the landlord's claim may be by parol, by delivery of the note or obligation to the assignee, or by appropriate words or other instrument

1. Ala. Code (1940) tit. 31, §24; Ark. Dig. Stat. (Pope, 1937); §§8858-59; Fla. Stat. Ann. (1941) §83.08; Ga. Code (1933) §§61-206-07; Miss. Code Ann. (1942) §910; N. C. Gen. Stat. (1943) §42-15; S. C. Code Ann. (1932) §8771; Tenn. Code Ann. (Williams, 1934) §8017; Va. Code Ann. (Michie, 1936) §5520.

granting to the assignee the rents due to the landlord for a given period of time.[2] Such an assignment need not be recorded,[3] but it must be couched in such language as to indicate a present intention to transfer the lien.[4] In Georgia, however, the assignment must be in writing,[5] and this is true whether the rent contract between the landlord and tenant is in writing or not.[6] In one case a landlord's lien for supplies was created by a special contract in writing, executed by the tenant before any supplies were furnished. A third person afterwards extended credit to the tenant and furnished him with supplies as the result of a parol agreement with the landlord for an assignment of the existing landlord's lien. It was held that the assignment was effective, in spite of the fact that a written assignment was not actually executed until after the greater portion of the supplies had been furnished by the assignee.[7] It has also been held that it makes no difference if the lien is transferred on the day it was made and before any supplies had been furnished by the landlord, the object of the assignment being to enable the latter to comply with his part of the contract.[8]

ALABAMA

In an early Alabama case the court of that State denied the writ of attachment to the assignee of a rent note, holding that this remedy was one which only the original landlord could pursue.[9] This case again came before the appellate court two years later, and this time the court ruled that the lien for rent existed as a right independent of the remedy by attachment given to the landlord to enforce it. Therefore the assignee could maintain either an action at law for money had and received or a suit in equity against one who purchased the crop from the tenant with notice of the lien.[10] In this same year of 1877 the legislature amended the statute to give the

2. Strickland Co. v. Lesesne & Ladd, 160 Ala. 213, 49 So. 233 (1909); Bennett v. McKee, 144 Ala. 601, 38 So. 129 (1905); Wells v. Cody, 112 Ala. 278, 20 So. 381 (1896).

3. Bennett v. McKee, 144 Ala. 601, 38 So. 129 (1905).

4. Strickland Co. v. Lesesne & Ladd, 160 Ala. 213, 49 So. 233 (1909).

5. Ga. Code (1933) §61-206; Scott & Co. v. Ward, 21 Ga. App. 535, 94 S. E. 863 (1918); Benson v. Gottheimer, 75 Ga. 642 (1885).

6. Scott & Co. v. Ward, 21 Ga. App. 535, 94 S. E. 863 (1918).

7. Baldwin v. McCarthern, 94 Ga. 622, 21 S. E. 578 (1894).

8. Benson v. Gottheimer, 75 Ga. 642 (1885).

9. Foster v. Westmoreland & Trousdale, 52 Ala. 223 (1875).

10. Westmoreland & Trousdale v. Foster, 60 Ala. 448 (1877).

assignee the benefit of attachment in such cases.[11] The assignee's right to maintain an action against anyone destroying the lien was reaffirmed in a later case.[12] Under the statute the assignment is effective,[13] and the landlord may make a valid mortgage of the interest he has under his rent lien, the assignee having the same remedies that the landlord had prior to the transfer.[14]

However, it has been repeatedly held that a landlord who would be entitled to a lien for future advances which he might make to his tenant cannot make a valid transfer or assignment to another of his right to make such advances and have a lien therefor.[15] In one case it was shown that the landlord had signed an instrument by which he attempted to transfer to a third person the right to a lien given him by operation of law. He promised that he would claim nothing except the rent until the third person was paid in full by the tenant. The court declared that, to effect a subrogation of the third person to rights under the landlord's lien, it was essential that the tenant should at the time of the attempted transfer have knowledge of the landlord's request to the third person to make the advances and the consequent arrangement made by them, or that the tenant should ratify the transaction after being notified that such a situation existed.[16] In support of its position the court cited an earlier case in which a landlord, without the consent or knowledge of his tenant, assumed responsibility to a third person for advances made by him to the tenant and was shown to have actually paid the debt.[17]

The facts of these two cases are so dissimilar that it is difficult to see how one could be cited in support of the other. The reasoning which, in the earlier case, stressed the lack of notice to the tenant is not germane to the issues involved in the later controversy. How is it possible that the actions of the tenant could influence the decision in this case? The court seems to indicate that had the tenant

11. Ala. Acts 1876-77, No. 60.

12. Hawkins v. Damson & Abraham, 182 Ala. 83, 62 So. 15 (1913).

13. Leslie v. Hinson, 83 Ala. 266, 3 So. 443 (1888).

14. Ballard v. Mayfield, 107 Ala. 396, 18 So. 29 (1895). Whatever is said to the contrary in Leslie v. Hinson, 83 Ala. 266, 3 So. 443 (1888), is here specifically overruled.

15. Whaley v. Bright, 189 Ala. 134, 66 So. 644 (1914); Gerson v. Norman, 111 Ala. 433, 20 So. 453 (1896); Henderson v. State, 109 Ala. 40, 19 So. 733 (1896); Leslie v. Hinson, 83 Ala. 266, 3 So. 443 (1888).

16. Gerson v. Norman, 111 Ala. 433, 20 So. 453 (1896).

17. Clanton v. Eaton, 92 Ala. 612, 8 So. 823 (1891).

had knowledge of the arrangement when it was made, or had he ratified it after becoming cognizant of it, the third person would have been subrogated to the rights of the landlord. There is a *non sequitur* here which is very bad reasoning indeed. The later case is rightly decided, however, in view of the fact that neither the knowledge nor the ratification of the tenant was proved, and the court emphatically denied that the lien existed in favor of the alleged transferee.

Sometimes a rent note is given with the provision that it is payable not in money but in a specified portion of the commodity to be grown by the tenant on the leased premises. In such a case the note is nonnegotiable and is open to defenses which exist between the maker and the payee prior to transfer. In one instance a land-lady at first took no rent note but afterwards sent her son to procure one from the tenant. Without being authorized to do so, the son fraudulently took a note payable to himself and assigned it to another. Ordinarily the law is that a tenant is estopped to deny the title of one whom he has acknowledged as landlord and, conse-quently, from setting up a lack of consideration for a note executed and given to the supposed landlord as evidence of the debt for rent. However, if the tenant had not received the possession of the premises from the supposed landlord and was induced to acknowl-edge him as such through fraud, misrepresentation, or mistake, he may deny the supposed landlord's title and set up a want of con-sideration for a rent note. Hence the tenant in this instance could not be held liable on the note.[18] Had the note been negotiable, the tenant would not have been allowed to set up defenses of this kind.

ARKANSAS

In an early Arkansas case it is said that a lien is neither property nor a debt, but only a right to have satisfaction of a particular indebtedness out of a specific bit of property, and that it is not the subject of sale or assignment.[19] The transfer of a rent note, either with or without indorsement, was held not to transfer the landlord's lien on the crop for the payment of the rent;[20] hence the transferee had no right of attachment in such a case.[21] Therefore the assign-

18. Davis v. Douglass, 12 Ala. App. 581, 68 So. 528 (1915).
19. Roberts v. Jacks, 31 Ark. 597 (1876).
20. Block v. Smith, 61 Ark. 266, 32 S. W. 1070 (1895); Nolen v. Royston, 36 Ark. 561 (1880).
21. Nolen v. Royston, 36 Ark. 561 (1880).

ment of such a rent note as collateral security for an indebtedness of the landlord gave the assignee no lien upon the property.[22] But where the tenant delivered the crop in order to pay the note to one holding it as collateral, the title and possession of the latter was upheld against the claim of the holder of a chattel mortgage on the crop given by the tenant to a third person.[23] Furthermore, a retransfer of the note after the debt for which it was pledged had been settled revivified the lien in the hands of the landlord.[24]

A mortgagor of certain chattels assigned rent notes to the mortgagee to secure the mortgage indebtedness. It was held that the mortgagee was under no obligation to attempt to collect the notes, nor was he liable for any loss suffered by the mortgagor which came about as a result of the failure to collect the notes.[25] In another case a landlord assigned a rent note to a bona fide purchaser for value prior to a transfer of the reversion. This was said to operate as a severance of the rent from the reversion. Hence the rent did not pass to the transferee of the reversionary interest in the property, who had obtained the interest by way of a mortgage. Before the expiration of the lease the mortgage was foreclosed by the mortgagee and a receiver appointed. It was held that the holder of the rent notes was entitled to the proportion of the rent which had become due at the time the receiver qualified.[26]

This was the state of the law of Arkansas until 1935, when the legislature enacted a statute making the landlord's lien for rent assignable and giving the transferee, endorsee, mortgagee, pledgee, or holder of the note or contract the right to enforce the lien.[27]

GEORGIA

In an early case from Georgia the assignee of a note given for rent attempted to sue out a distress warrant against a tenant who was preparing to remove the crop from the leased premises. It was held that only the landlord might distrain for the rent, and that therefore the holder would not be permitted to do so.[28] A few years

22. Cravens v. Barr, 123 Ark. 528, 185 S. W. 1084 (1916); Roberts v. Jacks, 31 Ark. 597 (1876).

23. Meyer v. Bloom, 37 Ark. 43 (1881).

24. Dickinson v. Harris, 52 Ark. 58, 11 S. W. 965 (1889); Varner v. Rice, 39 Ark. 344 (1882).

25. Cravens v. Barr, 123 Ark. 528, 185 S. W. 1084 (1916).

26. Deming Inv. Co. v. Bank of Judsonia, 170 Ark. 65, 278 S. W. 634 (1926).

27. Ark. Laws 1935, No. 12, which is now Ark. Dig. Stat. (Pope, 1027) §§8858-59.

28. Scott v. Berry, 46 Ga. 394 (1872).

later, however, it was said that where the proprietor of a farm gave to an assignee the right to lease the premises and collect the rent therefrom, the latter might distrain for the rent.[29]

Where a landlord assigned a lien on his tenant's crop to enable the tenant to carry on operations on the leased farm for the benefit of both, and the assignee, in reliance on the assignment, furnished supplies to the tenant, it was held that the landlord was estopped from attacking the validity of the lien in the hands of the assignee.[30]

During this same period it was held that, there being no assignment of the lien per se in writing, a mere assignment of a rent note in writing did not transfer the lien to the assignee.[31] The court said that the statute in force at this time seemed to contemplate the retention of the lien by the original landlord, unless he specifically assigned the lien itself in writing. To assign the debt or the evidence of the debt was said not necessarily to entail an assignment of the lien also. The court declared that this was especially true where the assignor became liable as the endorser of the note, since he might wish to retain the lien for his own protection. In an earlier case, moreover, a landlord transferred a rent note by an indorsement which stated that he should retain the right to collect the rent and pay it to the transferee, the note being left in the landlord's possession. Since the indorsement of the note was qualified and not absolute, it was decided that a distress warrant would lie in the landlord's favor against the defaulting tenant.[32]

A few years after the court's decision that a lien was not to be transferred to the assignee, the legislature, in 1883, enacted a statute giving a lien for rent to the transferee of a rent contract.[33] Under this act it was held that after the transfer of a rent note there was a special lien for rent in effect in favor of the transferee which would be enforceable when the crop matured, provided the transfer was made in writing before such maturity.[34] The court declared that it made no difference that the transfer of the negotiable note was as collateral security for a debt owed to the transferee, since a transfer

29. Keaton v. Tift, 56 Ga. 446 (1876).
30. Zachry v. Stewart, 67 Ga. 218 (1881).
31. Lathrop & Co. v. Clewis, 63 Ga. 282 (1879).
32. Bolton v. Duncan, 61 Ga. 103 (1878).
33. Ga. Acts 1882-83, p. 109.
34. Andrew v. Stewart Bros., 81 Ga. 53, 7 S. E. 169 (1888). Therefore the statement in Rawls v. Moye, 98 Ga. 564, 25 So. 582 (1896), to the effect that all the transferee got was the obligation for the rent, citing Lathrop & Co. v. Clewis, *supra* Note 31, is at least misleading if not entirely erroneous.

for that purpose passes the legal title. This statute applied in specific terms only to the assignment of a rent contract, but by the decision in this case it was interpreted to apply also to an assignment of a rent note by indorsement.[35]

A landlord assigned his lien at the tenant's request to enable the latter to obtain supplies. The assignee, in reliance on the lien, furnished the tenant with supplies and charged them to his account. It was held that the assignee could enforce the lien against the tenant's crop.[36] Another landlord made an assignment "without recourse" of his lien for supplies advanced to aid in the making of the crop. The transferee failed to foreclose the lien, a right which he undeniably had, evidently preferring to rely upon the landlord's oral promise to pay the debt of his cropper, to whom the advances had been made. The crop was sold and the proceeds were in the hands of the landlord. It was held that the transferee could not force the application to his debt of any portion of the proceeds due to the cropper as wages, nor could he recover in a tort action against the landlord for his refusal to turn over the cropper's share, when the latter had not authorized any such application of the portion due him as wages according to his contract with the landlord.[37] It might be possible to argue that the oral promise could estop the landlord from claiming his own share of the crop, even though the oral promise was void according to the Statute of Frauds.

In 1896 a controversy arose where a tenant executed and delivered to his landlord a contract embracing a promise to pay a specified amount of cotton as rent. This agreement created a lien in the landlord's favor to secure payment for whatever advances he might make to aid the tenant in producing a crop on the rented premises during the ensuing year. On the day the contract was executed, an entry was written thereon, which the landlord signed, reciting that, "for value received, the within rent note is hereby transferred" to a named person. The landlord was indebted to the transferee upon a promissory note which he had given as evidence of a debt created by his purchase of the rented land. The assignment of the rent con-

35. Accordingly, a statement in the later case of Beall v. Patterson, 146 Ga. 233, 91 S. E. 71 (1916), to the effect that prior to the act of 1899 the transfer of a rent note payable to the order of the landlord, by simple indorsement, was ineffectual to assign the landlord's lien, and citing Lathrop & Co. v. Clewis, *supra* Note 31, was probably made without due regard to the 1883 act and Andrew v. Stewart, *supra* Note 34.

36. Mercer v. Cross, 79 Ga. 432, 5 S. E. 245 (1888).

37. Lyon v. Griffin, 16 Ga. App. 725, 86 S. E. 86 (1915).

tract was made as collateral security for the payment of this note. In the contract for the sale of the land it was stipulated that, if the note was not paid when due, the land would remain the property of the vendor, and that the vendee's tenant would then become his tenant. The purchase money, however, was paid before the maturity of the indebtedness. Upon this state of facts, it was held that the assignment of the contract did not operate to pass to the assignee the special lien in the landlord's favor for advances, nor did it authorize the assignee to furnish the tenant with supplies and then collect the price of them by foreclosing the alleged lien. The court declared that an express assignment was indispensably necessary to transfer the landlord's lien for supplies.[38]

This was no doubt an accurate statement of the law at that time, since the statute of 1883 applied specifically only to contracts for rent and did not mention the indebtedness and lien for advances. However, the court used some unfortunate language which seemed to indicate that the lien was nonassignable even in a case where it secured a claim for rent. The 1883 act was not mentioned, and the case which had denied the assignability of the lien just prior to the enactment of the statute was cited in support of the decision. That this was the general interpretation placed upon the language of the court in respect to advances is shown by what is said about the decision in a case decided a few years later. In this instance the court used the following language: "That case dealt with a paper which was a rent note, and also a written lien for supplies. The transfer was only of the rent note, and it was held this did not authorize the transferee to foreclose for advancements."[39] In the later case, however, there was an agreement between the original landlord and the transferee of the note that the former should retain the right to foreclose the lien for his own protection. The landlord exercised this right, and both the tenant and the transferee assented. The reservation of the lien was held to be a legitimate transaction and was said to be the crux of the matter here, since, had there been no reservation, the lien would have passed to the transferee by authority of the act of 1883.

Quite a confused picture is presented here, and the legislature evidently had this in mind when it enacted the statute of 1899, an act which was somewhat broader in scope than its predecessor. This

38. Rawls v. Moye, 98 Ga. 564, 25 S. E. 582 (1896).
39. Strickland Bros. v. Stiles, 107 Ga. 308, 33 S. E. 85 (1899).

statute[40] provides that when an instrument which is secured by mortgage or lien, or out of which there springs a lien by operation of law, is transferred by assignment, the lien can be foreclosed by the transferee in his own name. Under this act no reason is seen why the transferee of a note given for advances could not maintain an action in his own name to enforce the lien which secures the debt assigned to him. But the statute would scarcely be interpreted to give the assignee the right to furnish supplies to the tenant and then claim a lien for the price of these advancements, since that is an entirely different matter, and the right has been denied in decisions from other states, notably Alabama.[41]

After the passage of this act, the right of the assignee to enforce the lien by distress warrant was approved by the courts.[42] It has also been decided that an innocent purchaser of the note who takes it as collateral security for a debt stands on the same footing as any other innocent purchaser and may enforce the lien.[43] The court declared, in accordance with the previous decisions, that a purchaser of a negotiable rent note, although with notice of an equity as between the maker and the original payee, was protected if he purchased the note from one who did not have notice of the equity.

As decided in Alabama[44] a rent note payable in a specified portion of the crops was held to be non-negotiable. In a case involving such a note it is stated that the Act of 1883 did not enable the assignee to enforce the special lien for rent where the assignor himself could not have enforced it due to a superior claim.[45]

In some instances the consideration for the rent note fails because of the tenant's eviction by a transferee of the landlord's interest in the land at a voluntary or forced sale or because of the tenant's eviction by someone having a better title to the property. Even where the assignment of the note or rent contract occurs before maturity of the debt, the assignee has been held not to have a right to enforce the lien.[46] In another controversy the owner of a tract of land rented

40. Ga. Laws 1899, p. 90, which is now Ga. Code (1933) §§67-1706-07, 67-2302. The 1883 act is now Ga. Code (1933) §§61-206-07.

41. Note 15, *supra*.

42. Beall v. Patterson, 146 Ga. 233, 91 S. E. 71 (1916); International Agricultural Corp. v. Powell, 31 Ga. App. 348, 120 S. E. 668 (1923).

43. Veal v. Jenkins, 58 Ga. App. 4, 197 S. E. 328 (1938).

44. Davis v. Douglass, *supra* Note 18.

45. Thompson v. Commercial Guano Co., 93 Ga. 282, 20 S. E. 309 (1893).

46. Garner v. Douglasville Banking Co., 136 Ga. 310, 71 S. E. 478 (1911); Camp v. West, 113 Ga. 304, 38 S. E. 822 (1901).

to a tenant, who sublet a portion of the premises for a specific price and took a negotiable note for the indebtedness. The original tenant transferred the note to a third person. It was held that the landlord could elect to treat the subtenant as his own tenant and proceed against him directly by distress warrant.[47] The court went even further, however, and said that the holder of the note could enforce his claim against the subtenant. This could not have been done, according to the opinion, if the note had been nonnegotiable.[48]

Where a landlord, after the rent was due, took a note for rent payable at a future date, he was not prevented from obtaining final judgment in a distress warrant proceeding, where the note was surrendered to the maker or was sufficiently accounted for by proof that the maker would incur no further risk of being held liable thereon.[49] This would seem to be an equitable decision, since it prevented the tenant from being held doubly liable.

However, there is another case along these same lines where the language of the court is not so favorable to the tenant. In this situation a landlord was given two negotiable notes for the rent and transferred one of the notes to a third person, retaining the other. It was said that in the absence of an agreement to the contrary, the right to enforce the lien was split, and the interests of the landlord and his transferee thereby made several. As a result of this separation, the interest of the transferee was not subject to the landlord's control. The tenant sold and disposed of a portion of the crops raised during the year and paid the entire proceeds to the landlord, the transferee giving no assent to the sale. Of course the landlord could not produce the transferred note. The court declared that such an application would not estop the transferee from asserting the sale and removal as a ground for distraining for the amount of rent represented by the note in his possession, since it was transferred before maturity. It was further stated that the tenant, having given the negotiable notes, was required to beware lest, in dealing with the landlord, he should violate the rights of the transferee.[50] Moreover, irrespective of this rule, it appeared that in this instance the tenant had actual knowledge that one of the notes had been transferred.

47. Barlow v. Jones, 117 Ga. 412, 43 S. E. 690 (1903).
48. Thompson v. Commercial Guano Co., 93 Ga. 282, 20 S. E. 309 (1893).
49. Brooks v. Jackins, 38 Ga. App. 57, 142 S. E. 574 (1928).
50. International Agricultural Corp. v. Powell, 31 Ga. App. 348, 120 S. E. 668 (1923).

About this matter it is submitted that the court should adopt a rule that would avoid the double liability, if this is possible without violating the general theory of the law concerning the landlord's lien. Of course it can be said that the cases are not wholly analogous, since in one of them the tenant had actual notice of the transfer.

A tenant, before the maturity of his crop, was interrogated by a third person about to purchase a negotiable note not yet due, but purporting on its face to be given for rent. He admitted the execution of the note, and that it was in fact given for rent. If the person making the inquiry acted upon this information in purchasing the note, the tenant would be estopped to deny either the execution of the note or its consideration. In this instance the purchaser had started a distress warrant proceeding against the tenant to enforce the special lien on the crops. The court declared however, that there would be no estoppel unless it was made to appear, either directly or from the attending circumstances, that at the time of answering the inquiry the person interrogated either knew or had good reason to believe that a purchase of the note was being contemplated, and that the inquiry was not being made out of mere curiosity, or in the interest of the payee or anyone else already having or claiming an interest in the subject matter. It was also declared that the question in respect to the purpose of the inquiry was an issue for the jury. Furthermore, the court stated that in charging the jury the judge had failed to give any consideration to the state of mind of the tenant at the time he had the conversation with the transferee. Because of this omission, the case was reversed and sent back for a new trial.[51]

Again, it was shown that the owner of a tract of land, on January 24, 1911, entered into a contract by which he leased the land to certain tenants for a period of three years, commencing on January 1, 1912. As provided in the contract, notes for the annual rent were given by the tenants. On May 12, 1911, subsequent to the execution of the rent contract but prior to the beginning of the term, the owner executed a warranty deed containing a power of sale, conveying the land to a creditor for the purpose of securing a debt. On July 12, 1912, and before the maturity of the crops raised on the rented land in that year, the grantee in the security deed, by virtue of the power of sale, conveyed the land to a purchaser, who thereby acquired the right and title of the original owner. Before the execu-

51. Freeny v. Hall, 93 Ga. 706, 21 S. E. 163 (1894).

tion of the deed containing the power of sale, the original owner, the payee in the rent notes, had transferred the notes to a bank. In October, 1912, the tenants, surmising that the purchaser of the land at the sale would insist upon collecting the rent for that year, and believing that the bank would also claim the right to collect on the rent notes, filed a petition for injunction and interpleader, offering to pay the rent into court to await judicial decision in the matter. The lower court decided in favor of the bank, but the State Supreme Court reversed this and rendered a decision for the purchaser. The court declared that the purchaser, who had become the owner of the rented land before the maturity of the crops, was entitled to recover the rent. While under the provisions of the statute relating to the transfer of liens, the bank was in as good a position as the transferor in respect to the enforcement of the landlord's lien, it was, nevertheless, in no better position as a result of the transfer. Since the original landlord had parted with the title to the land before the maturity of the crop, he was clearly in no position to enforce the lien, and consequently the transferee bank could not do so. The court decided, therefore, that the right to enforce the lien for rent had arisen in favor of the purchaser of the land and no one else.[52] Hence it seems that the transferee of the rent notes was not entitled to any remedy that the landlord did not acquire prior to the sale of the land, the lien not attaching because the crops had not matured prior to the sale.

In later cases the Court of Appeals affirmed the proposition that the purchaser of the land under a power of sale in a security deed executed by the landlord succeeded to the latter's rights, including the lien on the crops, to the exclusion of the rights of a transferee of the rent note.[53] It has also been said that the claim of the purchaser of the land before the maturity of the crops cannot be extinguished by the act of the tenant in paying the specified amount of rent to the transferee of a rent note made out to the original landlord.[54] It has been stated[55] that, notwithstanding the statute of 1922[56] declaring all growing crops to be personalty, the purchaser of lands at a sale under a mortgage of older date than the act, the sale having been

52. Ball v. Citizens' Bank of Rome, 143 Ga. 55, 84 S. E. 122 (1915).
53. Schnedl v. Langford, 40 Ga. App. 190, 149 S. E. 102 (1929); Brooks v. Causey, 36 Ga. App. 233, 136 S. E. 282 (1926).
54. Brooks v. Causey, 36 Ga. App. 233, 136 S. E. 282 (1926).
55. Brooks v. Causey, 36 Ga. App. 233, 136 S. E. 282 (1926); Chason v. O'Neal, 158 Ga. 725, 124 S. E. 519 (1924).
56. Ga. Acts 1922, p. 114.

consummated after the passage of the act, could acquire a good title to the crops grown on the land after the passage of the act, if they were raised and owned by the former owner of the lands. However, if the former owner had in fact, prior to the sale, rented the lands in good faith to tenants, who then raised the crops, the purchaser at the sale would not obtain title to the fruits of the property but would acquire only the rights of the former owner in respect to the crops, notably the landlord's lien.

KENTUCKY

In Kentucky there is no statute expressly authorizing an assignee to enforce the lien transferred to him by the landlord. Regarding the rights of the assignee, however, it has been held that an assignee of a note given for rent, who is not also the assignee of the reversion, cannot avail himself of the remedies of distress and attachment under the statutes permitting these remedies to be used by landlords.[57] Whether the assignee of a rent note would be permitted to maintain an action of the type allowed to landlords in a later decision,[58] as differentiated from the remedies of distress and attachment, was left to future consideration.

In an earlier case the landlord's assignee sued the tenant on a rent note. The defendant entered a plea that the note had been given for the rent and that the lease contract had been rescinded, without any averment that under the terms of the contract of rescission the note was to be surrendered. It was further alleged that the defendant had performed his part of the latter agreement. This plea was held not to be an effective discharge of the defendant's obligation on the note, since the rescission of the rent contract did not in itself release him from liability thereon.[59]

LOUISIANA

In a leading Louisiana case the lessee gave his notes in advance for the rent of property on which there was a registered mortgage, the registration giving him constructive notice of the claim on the property. Proceedings were instituted afterwards to foreclose the mortgage. The lessee feared that the notes would fall into the hands of a bona fide holder, thus subjecting him to double liability. He

57. Hutsell v. Deposit Bank of Paris, 102 Ky. 410, 43 S. W. 469 (1897).

58. Brown v. Noel, 21 Ky. Law Rep. 648, 52 S. W. 849 (1899).
59. Childers v. Smith, 49 Ky. 235 (1850).

therefore instituted a suit in equity for the purpose of arresting the negotiation of the notes in the hands of the lessor and demanding security to protect himself against excessive loss. According to the Louisiana law, it seems that the lease is dissolved at the time of the mortgage sale and not at the moment when the suit to foreclose is begun. Therefore it was decided that the lessee owed the rent to the lessor up to the time of the sheriff's seizure of the premises, or, if not so seized, until the moment of the sale of the property under judicial process. The court declared it would be manifestly unjust and inequitable to permit the lessor to prosecute his suit for the amount due as rent for the property sold under mortgage, and also to retain the notes, without giving some security to indemnify the lessee against the liability which would result from a transfer of the notes to an innocent holder, who, according to the law in respect to negotiable instruments, could enforce payment in spite of the fact that the consideration had partially failed. The court further said that if, before the seizure or sale, the lessee had refused to pay the rent, the landlord would have the right to enforce the lessor's privilege. It was declared that a case like the one under discussion would be remanded to await the result of the suit to foreclose the mortgage or, in lieu of that, the expiration of the lease, with both parties being required to give bond.[60] In this case the Louisiana court rendered a decision which might well be followed in other states. The practice of waiting until the rights of the parties are crystallized is very helpful where the notes are still in the landlord's hands and have not already been transferred.

The danger of giving rent notes is illustrated by the following cases: In the first it was held that the purchaser of a plantation which had been leased before the sale was entitled to rent notes given to the lessor as evidence of the rent obligation for a year subsequent to the sale. The court also declared that a purchaser is not entitled to recover the rent for that portion of a year which is prior to the transfer of the reversionary interest.[61] With this case for a background, another case came before the intermediate appellate court a few years later. In this instance a judgment creditor of a lessor of certain land seized the property under a writ of execution. The property was held under an unrecorded lease by a lessee who had executed negotiable rent notes and delivered them to the lessor.

60. Thompson v. Flathers, 45 La. Ann. 120, 12 So. 245 (1893).
61. Lesseigne v. Cedar Grove Realty Co., 150 La. 641, 91 So. 136 (1921).

Here the court held that, notwithstanding the prior execution and delivery of the notes, the judgment creditor might require the lessee to pay all the rent accruing after the sale under the writ of execution.[62]

MISSISSIPPI

At an early date a Mississippi landlord assigned the rent and lease contract to a third person as collateral security for a debt. It was held that this assignment carried with it the lien on the tenant's crop given by the act of 1873,[63] thus protecting the assignee against the claim of the holder of a subsequent deed of trust given by the landlord.[64] But the court was not yet willing to permit the assignee to have all the rights of the landlord. Some years later it refused to allow the assignee of a rent note to sue out a writ of attachment, declaring that this remedy was limited by the attachment statute to those persons who occupied a relationship to the land.[65] A year later, however, in spite of the fact that the law did not authorize an attachment, the court ruled that the lien passed to the assignee of a rent note and could be enforced by an action to subject the crops to the payment of the indebtedness.[66] In this instance certain merchants had made advances to a tenant on the security of a deposit with them of the tenant's rent note which the landlord had indorsed in blank and surrendered to the tenant to use as he saw fit. Soon pressure was brought upon the legislature to give the assignee a right to a writ of attachment in such a situation, and in 1890 this amendment to the attachment law was enacted.[67]

The Mississippi Court has adopted the same view taken by the Alabama tribunals in respect to the matter of assignment of the right to make advances and the denial of a lien therefor. A plaintiff's intestate, the transferee of a tenant's rent note, consented before his death to furnish the tenant with supplies in return for an agreement that he would recognize the intestate as his landlord. It was said that such an agreement did not create the relationship of landlord and

---

62. Bank of Coushatta v. Williams, 10 La. App. 571, 121 So. 646 (1929).
63. Miss. Acts 1873, p. 79.
64. Taylor v. Nelson, 54 Miss. 524 (1877).
65. Gross v. Bartley, 66 Miss. 116, 5 So. 225 (1888).
66. Newman v. Bank of Greenville, 66 Miss. 323, 5 So. 753 (1889).
67. Miss. Laws 1890, c. 51. See Miss. Code Ann. (1942) §910; Hollingsworth v. Hill, 69 Miss. 73, 10 So. 450 (1891); Coker v. Britt, 78 Miss. 583, 29 So. 833 (1901).

tenant between the parties. The plaintiff's intestate was not the land-lord and could only become such by purchasing the land leased by the tenant. Since no tenancy relationship existed, the court refused to allow the plaintiff to have an attachment.[68]

Two other Mississippi cases merit discussion in connection with assignment. In one of these cases a person holding certain rent notes given by a tenant concealed his ownership of the notes from a mer-chant and represented to him that, by securing a waiver of the landlord's lien, he would obtain a prior claim for any advances he might make to the tenant. It was held that the holder of the notes, having led the merchant, a mortgagee, to believe that this was the true state of affairs, was estopped from setting up his claim under the lien acquired by the assignment of the notes to him.[69] In the other case the landlord conveyed certain leased premises to his wife and then made advances to his erstwhile tenant. He retained the rent note, but the court declared that the conveyance would carry the ownership of the note with it as an incident of the reversion. The court denied that he had a lien on the tenant's crops for advances made by him to the tenant after the conveyance to his wife. It was also declared that his wife's reconveyance to him, by an unrecorded deed, did not in this case revitalize his rights, since such a reconvey-ance was void with respect to the intervening claims of third par-sons, who were entitled to rely upon the apparent circumstances.[70]

NORTH CAROLINA

In North Carolina there have been two fairly recent cases in which the rights of assignees have been considered. In the first of these cases the assignee of a rental contract was held to be entitled to a superior lien on the tenant's crops, the landlord's lien being made expressly superior to the supplyman's lien under the statute author-izing and establishing the latter encumbrance.[71]

The other case shows that there is much to be done in the im-provement of our lien laws in the Southeast. In this instance a land-owner leased a farm to a tenant for a stipulated cash rental. Later the landlord, desiring supplies to run all his farms, gave an agricultural supply lien to a farmers' supply house, the instrument indicating that

68. Coker v. Britt, 78 Miss. 583, 29 So. 833 (1901).
69. Dreyfus v. W. A. Gage & Co., 84 Miss. 219, 36 So. 248 (1904).
70. Watkins v. Duvall, 69 Miss. 364, 13 So. 727 (1891).
71. Wise Supply Co. v. Davis, 194 N. C. 328, 139 S. E. 599 (1927), inter-preting N. C. Code Ann. (Michie, 1939) §§2355, 2480.

the lien covered the crops raised on all the lands of the landlord, including those leased to this particular tenant. The testimony showed that these supplies were never received by the tenant nor used on the land which he had rented. A short while after the execution of the supply lien the tenant gave the landlord a negotiable rent note which the latter assigned to another person. Both the assignee of the note and the supply house claimed to be entitled to the amount of the rent, which the tenant had voluntarily paid to the assignee. The court ruled in favor of the supply house and decided that it was entitled to the proceeds of the crops to the amount of the rent.[72] This left the tenant in a predicament, since he had been deprived of the landlord's share of the crops, and there was still the agricultural lien outstanding which must be taken care of in some way. Hence, through no fault of his own, he was subjected to a double liability from which there seemed to be no escape under the law as it now is in North Carolina.

One commentator[73] has indicated that there are three possible situations which might develop with respect to the assignment of the lien and the rent note to separate persons: (1) The note for the rent is received and assigned before the assignment of the landlord's lien; (2) The note is received before the assignment of the lien but not assigned until afterwards; (3) The note is both received and assigned subsequent to the assignment of the lien. In the first case the lien would follow the note,[74] but in the other two an entirely different situation is seen. Under the law as it is today it seems that the tenant would be subject to a double liability in both instances. As the above-mentioned commentator pointed out, the landlord, by merely juggling the order of the assignments, can place an undesirable risk on the tenant's doorstep. The fact that the tenant may have a remedy against the landlord after expensive and time-consuming litigation is no adequate solution, for the situation in which he is placed calls for immediate redress.

In the second situation mentioned above, the risk of double liability might be obviated by a "ruling that when the landlord accepted the rent note the lien became attached to the note itself as additional security for its payment."[75] The holder of the note would

72. Rhodes v. Smith-Douglass Fertilizer Co., 220 N. C. 21, 16 S. E. (2d) 408 (1941), commented upon in Note (1942) 20 N. C. Law Rev. 216.

73. Note (1942) 20 N. C. Law Rev. 216, 220.

74. Wise Supply Co. v. Davis, 194 N. C. 328, 139 S. E. 599 (1927); Avery v. McNeill, 77 N. C. 50 (1877); Lee v. Spence, 5 Tenn. App. 363 (1927).

75. Op. cit., *supra* Note 73, at 221.

then automatically become the holder of the lien, and a subsequent assignee of the lien would consequently take nothing.

However, this would not solve the problem where the lien is assigned, not only before the assignment but also before the acceptance of the note by the landlord, which is the case in the third situation mentioned above and also in the North Carolina case under discussion. The commentator suggests that the only solution with respect to this situation is through statutory revision, for obviously the rights of a prior assignee of the lien "should not be impaired by any subsequent action of the landlord or tenant." The law of negotiable instruments would also demand that an obligation like this rent note should be free from various defenses when it is transferred to a holder in due course.

The commentator suggests that a solution might lie in "a statutory proviso that the landlord's lien may not be assigned without the service of written notice on the tenant," thus placing the tenant on his guard against any subsequent execution or assignment of a rent note. If the decision stands, as seems to be the case, for the proposition that the landlord can execute a valid agricultural lien on the whole of the tenant's crop without delivering the supplies obtained in the deal to the tenant, it is certainly taking unfair advantage of the tenant. In fact it was ruled in an early case involving an agricultural lien that the supplies must be extended to the "persons engaged, or about to engage in the cultivation of the soil."[76] If this were not true, the landlord could "encumber the crops without even the actual knowledge of the tenant,"[77] and "it should not be necessary for the tenant continually to resort to the courthouse to see if a lien has been recorded on his crop."[78] The instant case seems to put too much of a burden on the tenant. It seems unjust to force him into a situation where he has so little to say about a matter which is very much his affair.

More protection for the tenant's interests is demanded by a wise and enlightened public policy. In all the Southeastern states where the laws are somewhat similar to the North Carolina statutes as interpreted in this case, the legislative bodies should amend the statutes and the courts so interpret the laws that decisions of this kind, in accordance with some jurists' strict interpretation of these statutes

76. Clark v. Farrar, 74 N. C. 686 (1876).
77. Op. cit., *supra* Note 73, at 222.
78. Op. cit., *supra* Note 73, at 222.

but really based on reactionary economic views, could not be rendered. The law should be a shield for those who are unable to protect themselves adequately and not a weapon in the hands of those in a better bargaining position.

SOUTH CAROLINA

In South Carolina a statutory amendment[79] gives the assignee the right to enforce the landlord's lien. This statute appears to have been enacted as a result of a decision which seemed to permit the assignee to enforce the rent claim in an action on the contract but denied him a lien for the rent.[80] Again, it is said that a mere assignment of unpaid rent does not carry with it the right to distrain.[81] This seems to be true notwithstanding the above amendment to the statute. In this respect the South Carolina court, despite the statutory amendment, apparently has taken the same view of the matter that the Kentucky court did in the absence of such a statute.

TENNESSEE

In Tennessee it has been decided that an assignee of a rent note given by a tenant to his landlord, the assignor, is entitled to the rights of the landlord with respect to the landlord's lien on the tenant's crops.[82]

CONCLUSIONS

The law as it has developed in each state having been presented, the task is to ascertain what inequities are present and what may be done to improve the law with respect to the situations which have arisen. It is clear that the tenant is not adequately protected in respect to the assignment of rent notes which he has given to the landlord prior to the date when the rent falls due. As suggested in the discussion of the North Carolina law, a requirement that the tenant be notified of any contemplated transfer of the lien would go a long way toward solving one of the knottiest problems. The tenant would then know the person to whom the rent should be paid. An-

79. S. C. Stat. 1906, No. 58.
80. State v. Elmore, 68 S. C. 140, 46 S. E. 939 (1904). This case is apparently a criminal indictment based on a civil statute. At least the opinion states that the indictment is based upon the above statute as it appeared in the 1902 Revision. S. C. Code (1902) §3057.
81. Staton v. Guillebeaux, 123 S. C. 363, 116 S. E. 443 (1923).
82. Biggs v. Piper, 86 Tenn. 589, 8 S. W. 851 (1888); Lee v. Spence, 5 Tenn. App. 363 (1927).

other improvement would result from a more definite codification of the law concerning assignment and its incidents. This would tend to make the rights of the parties more certain and be a springboard from which the law of assignments could be improved by methods of trial and error. As it stands today, the law is too uncertain even in the states where there are many decisions on the point.

TRANSFER OF REVERSIONARY INTEREST BY LANDLORD

Oftentimes an owner of leased land will wish to convey or mortgage it while it is leased to another. Sometimes the property is mortgaged even before the premises are rented and then subsequently sold under a foreclosure proceeding. One can readily see that transfers of this kind create many problems concerning the rights of the lessee with respect to land and crops. Situations developing out of such conveyance and mortgage transactions are among the most interesting in farm tenancy law.

CONVEYANCES

Ordinarily, when there is a sale, the rent follows the reversion.[83] It has been held that the grantee obtaining the land at such a sale is entitled to enforce a landlord's lien on the tenant's crop.[84] In Arkansas a landlord who had furnished his tenant with supplies sold the land to another who, as part of the consideration, paid the tenant's account. The sale was consummated before the crop was planted. Under these circumstances it was held that the purchaser was entitled to a landlord's lien, as against crop mortgagees, the transaction between the purchaser and the landlord not amounting to an assignment, which at that time did not transfer the lien in Arkansas.[85] In another instance a South Carolina landlord rented

83. Ingram v. Roberts, Euther & Co., 224 Ala. 314, 140 So. 369 (1932); Westmoreland & Trousdale v. Foster, 60 Ala. 448 (1877); Tubb v. Fort, 58 Ala. 277 (1877); Rose City Mercantile Co. v. Miller, 171 Ark. 872, 286 S. W. 1010 (1926); Bloodworth v. Stevens, 51 Miss. 475 (1875).

84. Simmons v. Fielder & Sessions, 46 Ala. 304 (1871); Rose City Mercantile Co. v. Miller, 171 Ark. 872, 286 S. W. 1010 (1926). In the *Simmons* case, however, it is said that the rent claim could not be thus enforced against a subtenant in a proceeding based on the rent contract made by the tenant in chief with the landlord prior to the sale. If the undertenant is sued, he must be proceeded against in an action based upon his contract with the tenant in chief, and it must be shown that this contract had been transferred to the purchaser.

85. Oberste Bros. v. Crabtree, 175 Ark. 107, 299 S. W. 6 (1927). See *supra* Notes 19 *et seq.*

two mules along with the land for a gross sum, with no separate rental fixed for each. Here the court held that the purchaser of the reversionary interest in the land could not enforce a claim for the rent in a distress warrant proceeding.[86] It was said that the purchaser might maintain an action against the tenant for use and occupation of the land but would not be permitted to have the remedy of distress in a case of this kind.

In Alabama there can be no apportionment of the rent between the original landlord and the purchaser. It is therefore unnecessary, in order to perfect the purchaser's right to the entire rent which afterwards falls due and to discharge the tenant from all liability therefor to the original landlord, that the tenant shall agree to become the tenant of the purchaser or that he shall be evicted by him.[87] Also where a purchasing grantee rents the entire tract to the grantor, the grantee's right to recover the rent is limited to the sum payable by the grantor, the right to collect rent from the grantor's tenants being in the nature of security.[88]

Sometimes a case arises, however, where a rent note given by the tenant to the landlord is negotiated to another person before the sale of the land to the purchaser. This has been said to constitute a severance of the rent from the reversion, and the purchaser cannot claim that the tenant is responsible to him therefor, the holder of the note being entitled to that debt.[89] This is true even where the purchaser of the reversion is the lessee himself.[90]

MORTGAGES

The following Alabama rules have been stated with respect to the rights of a mortgagee of rented premises: Where a mortgage giving the mortgagee a defeasible estate in land is made subject to a lease, it operates as a transfer of the reversionary interest to the mortgagee. As transferee of the reversion the mortgagee is entitled, after default or forfeiture, to receive the rent, income, and profits from the time when, by proper entry on the land, by legal notice, or by proceeding, the intent so to claim them is specifically manifest. How-

---

86. Stewart v. Gregg, 42 S. C. 392, 20 S. E. 193 (1894).
87. English v. Key, 39 Ala. 113 (1863).
88. Ingram v. Roberts, Euther & Co., 224 Ala. 314, 140 So. 369 (1932).
89. Alabama Gold Life Insurance Co. v. Oliver, 82 Ala. 417, 2 So. 445 (1887); Bank of Moundville v. Walsh, 216 Ala. 116, 112 So. 438 (1927); Cheatham v. Beck, 96 Ark. 250, 131 S. W. 699 (1910).
90. Alabama Gold Life Insurance Co. v. Oliver, 78 Ala. 158 (1884).

ever, where the lease is made subject to the mortgage, a tenant is not liable to a mortgagee out of possession for the rent accruing under the lease, there being no privity of estate between the mortgagee and the tenant; and this is true although the mortgage operates as a grant of the legal title to the property.[91] In a later hearing of this same case it was said that one entitled to the reversion when the rent falls due is also entitled to the rent unless it has been previously severed. Moreover, the purchaser at a foreclosure sale was held to have a right to the proceeds of the tenant's rent notes which became due and were paid to the assignee of the mortgagor after the foreclosure sale, the assignee being charged with notice of the mortgage and of the fact that it might be foreclosed before the maturity of the indebtedness for rent.[92]

However, for the mortgagee to have a valid claim, the foreclosure sale must not have been an illegal one. In one instance the mortgagee had induced a third person to purchase the equity in the mortgaged premises by falsely assuring him that the time for the payment of the indebtedness had been extended. It was said that the mortgagee, having purchased the property at a foreclosure sale made unlawful by this deceptive conduct, was estopped from gaining any advantage thereby. The court declared that the mortgagee was liable to the purchaser of the mortgagor's equity for damages to the premises resulting from the acts of himself, his agent, or the immediate tenant placed by him on the land. It was said that the mortgagee, whose tenants had possession of the premises in his name, was entitled to credit for reasonable expenditure in making repairs, as distinguished from improvements, and for the payment of taxes, and had the right to deduct these items from charges for waste and the loss of rents and profits. This damage was measured in the case of the rents and profits by the losses which had resulted from willful default or gross negligence.[93]

The real estate mortgagee has no basis for a recovery where the mortgagor's tenant has paid the rent in advance at the time of the execution of the lease, there being no valid claim for rent here. Therefore the mortgagee could have no lien in an instance of this sort where the prospective tenant had no notice of the mortgagee's claim.[94]

91. Bank of Moundville v. Walsh, 216 Ala. 116, 112 So. 438 (1927).
92. Walsh v. Bank of Moundville, 222 Ala. 164, 132 So. 52 (1930).
93. Smith v. Stringer, 220 Ala. 353, 125 So. 226 (1929).
94. Cassady v. Williams, 234 Ala. 299, 174 So. 485 (1937).

Sometimes the mortgagee of the reversionary interest will merely notify the tenant that he claims the rent. An Alabama court has held that, without an attornment of the tenant to the mortgagee, such a notice is not sufficient to create the relationship of landlord and tenant between these parties,[95] and the mortgagee is therefore not entitled to a landlord's lien.[96] In other words, the mortgagee is not entitled to the rent until he has some understanding with the tenant that the rent is due to him and not to the mortgagor, the tenant's original landlord.

A clause in a real estate mortgage given by the owner of leased land made provision for the transfer of "the rents that may accrue to us in said years." The court declared that this constituted a valid assignment of the rent. This assignment was said not to be inoperative because it related to the rent for a succeeding year. The mortgagee was held to have a lien on cotton grown on the rented land, and his claim was said to prevail over the claim of a bank which had taken an assignment of the tenant's subsequently-issued rent note. The fact that the assignee bank had possession and control of the cotton crop did not entitle it to assert that its claim of a lien had ripened into legal title unless a superior claim could be shown.[97]

In Arkansas, although a mortgage on land does not include the crops grown by a tenant, the mortgagee may impound rents and profits from the time the foreclosure suit is begun on showing that the value of the land is not sufficient to cover the mortgage indebtedness.[98] Also the mortgagor has a right, without the mortgagee's consent, to lease the land subject to the lien of the mortgage, and the mortgagee can foreclose on default of payment of the debt secured. A covenant of quiet enjoyment was necessarily implied in this contract for leasing lands covered by a mortgage. The court also declared that the purchaser at a sale foreclosing a mortgage on the leased premises became entitled to subsequently accruing rents and had a right to require that the payments be made to him. The transferee of rent notes given to the mortgagor by the tenant took them in payment of an existing indebtedness with knowledge of circumstances showing that the consideration for the notes had failed. The mortgage on the leased land had been foreclosed before the rent

95. Mack v. Beeland Co., 21 Ala. App. 97, 105 So. 722 (1925).
96. Drakford v. Turk, 75 Ala. 339 (1883).
97. Herren v. Burns, 217 Ala. 692, 117 So. 417 (1928).
98. O'Connell v. St. Louis Joint-Stock Land Bank, 170 Ark. 778, 281 S. W. 385 (1926).

notes, given by the lessee for rent to become due in the future, had reached maturity. The notes were subject to cancellation in the hands of the transferee.[99]

Again where there was no mention of the rents and profits in the mortgage, they belonged to the mortgagor or a third person claiming under him, subject, of course, to the rights of the mortgagee. The mortgagor might lease, sell, or deal with the land as the owner so long as he was permitted to remain in possession; but every person taking under him took the property subject to all the rights of the mortgagee. Hence the bona fide holder of rent notes transferred to him by the mortgagor, the original landlord of the maker, was entitled to the proportion of the rent which was due when a receiver took possession of the premises under foreclosure proceedings.[100] This theory of dividing the rent proportionately between the mortgagee or his receiver and the holder of the rent contract or notes has been approved in two later cases.[101] Somewhat the same result was reached in a Louisiana case involving a purchase of land leased to a tenant.[102]

A Kentucky real estate mortgage provided that in case of default the mortgagee could have a receiver appointed during the pendency of foreclosure proceedings. The instrument gave the mortgagee a lien on the rents and profits. On bringing foreclosure proceedings, the mortgagee was held to have a right to a lien on the tenant's crops both under the terms of the mortgage and under a statute[103] which gave relief to a mortgagee in such a situation where there is a threatened loss.[104]

In North Carolina, a state in which it is well settled that the real estate mortgagee has title to the land, the state of the law is somewhat confused with respect to his rights to crops raised by a mortgagor in possession or a tenant of such mortgagor. In 1888 it was said that the mortgagee was entitled to possession of the land, and in the absence of an agreement to the contrary, was entitled to the crops produced thereon, until the debt was discharged. Furthermore, his

99. Wallin v. Donnahoe, 175 Ark. 791, 300 S. W. 428 (1927).

100. Deming Inv. Co. v. Bank of Judsonia, 170 Ark. 65, 278 S. W. 634 (1926).

101. Cantley v. Turner, 191 Ark. 607, 87 S. W. (2d) 42 (1935); Purvis v. Elder, 175 Ark. 780, 1 S. W. (2d) 36 (1927).

102. Matthews v. Alsworth, 45 La. Ann. 465, 12 So. 518 (1893).

103. Ky. Civ. Code Prac. (1938) §299.

104. Brasfield & Son v. Northwestern Mut. Life Ins. Co., 233 Ky. 94, 25 S. W. (2d) 72 (1930).

rights were not abridged by an unnecessary and superfluous clause in the mortgage contract which expressly conveyed the crops to him and provided that they should not be removed in any year until the installment of the indebtedness due for that year had been paid.[105] In a case decided in the same year, it was held that a mortgagor in possession after condition broken could not, as against the mortgagee, create a valid agricultural lien which would be superior to the latter's claim. Moreover, where the mortgagor subsequently accepted a lease of the premises from the mortgagee, the landlord's statutory lien on the crops, in this case unsevered, took precedence.[106] Almost immediately the legislature enacted a statute[107] authorizing a mortgagor or trustor in possession to give a valid agricultural lien on the crops, but the act states nothing about priorities being affected.

In the same year that the statute was passed the Killebrew case[108] came before the court. This controversy involved a vendee in possession under a contract of sale, but the court treated it in exactly the same way as if it were a case concerning a mortgagor-mortgagee relationship, contending that it amounted to the same thing. The majority opinion ruled that the mortgagee, or rather the vendor, had no landlord's lien on the crops grown on the land until they were sequestered. Therefore he could not maintain a possessory action for the crops against the vendee (mortgagor) or a third person claiming under or in relation to him; and, even after sequestration, the vendor's (mortgagee's) lien was subject to agricultural liens for advances executed by the vendee (mortgagor) or third person. The court cited an earlier case[109] to the effect that a mortgagor in possession or his assignee has the right to appropriate the profits arising from the land to his own use, or to lease to another and take the accruing rent, and that this right remains effective until it is divested by some positive interference by the mortgagee. Hence it was argued that "it is only when the mortgagee enters that he is entitled to the possession of the growing crops." The court also declared that "equity makes the mortgage, as between the mortgagor and mortgagee, a charge upon the rents and profits," and that the crops

105. Coor v. Smith, 101 N. C. 261, 7 S. E. 669 (1888).
106. Brewer v. Chappell, 101 N. C. 251, 7 S. E. 670 (1888).
107. N. C. Pub. Laws 1889, c. 476, afterwards N. C. Consol. Stat. (1919) §2481.
108. Killebrew v. Hines, 104 N. C. 182, 10 S. E. 159 (1889).
109. Dunn & Co. v. Tillery, 79 N. C. 497 (1878).

"cannot be said to be incumbered so as to give a preference to the mortagee or vendor claiming a lien upon the land *as against another creditor*, who may obtain an express lien upon the crops under the statute, or by chattel mortgage or execution." Therefore it was argued that, prior to some definite act by the vendor (mortgagee) to assert his rights, he had no lien upon the crops and could not recover them in the possessory action of replevin, either against the vendee (mortgagor) or third persons acquiring rights prior to the act. The court evidently believed that to allow the mortgagee to claim the crops without some such action on his part would make it difficult for farmers with mortgages on their land, of whom there are always many, to obtain credit facilities, and that this would have a bad effect on agriculture in general. The majority opinion evidently considered the two earlier cases as being at least somewhat in conflict with the ruling in the case being decided here, for it was distinctly stated that, insofar as they were inconsistent therewith, they were overruled. It was also stated that the above-mentioned statute of 1889, protecting agricultural lienors in such a situation, was merely "declaratory of a correct exposition of existing laws."

There was a clause in the contract providing that the vendor (mortgagee) was to "hold everything made on the land." It was held that this provision could not be given the effect of conferring a lien on subsequently made crops, and should it constitute a valid mortgage on them, it was subordinate to subsequently executed agricultural liens, even though the lienholders had actual notice. The contract also provided that it would be void on the failure of the vendee to make payments for two successive years and that, after such a default, the vendee would then pay rent. The court held that the vendors could claim no landlord's lien on the crops, which had been removed by the vendee in possession, before the expiration of the two-year period specified by the contract of sale.

One judge, however, delivered a concurring opinion[110] in which he declared that the decisions in the two earlier cases are not inconsistent with the present case, thus disagreeing with the majority of the court, which had definitely intimated that there was a conflict. Following the title theory, he reached the conclusion that the mortgagee is entitled to the products of the premises. He seemed to distinguish the present case from the earlier decisions on the ground that

110. Killebrew v. Hines, 104 N. C. 182, 194, 10 S. E. 251 (1889).

in the present case the crops were severed before action was taken by the vendor (mortgagee). He stated that "where the vendor allows the vendee to remain in possession of the land, and make a crop and *sever* the same, the former cannot recover the *severed* crop from the latter or third persons, and this rests upon the ground of the presumed assent of the vendor to allow the vendee to make and take the crop." Whether this distinction based on severance is a valid one is problematical. The question has probably been rendered academic with respect to the particular point involved by the statute of 1889 which, according to the concurring judge, gave mortgagors in possession the right to give agricultural liens and made such claims superior to the rights of the mortgagee. He declared, however, that the statute "does not give them the right to so mortgage their crops for other purposes." Certainly the opinion of this concurring judge is at least reasonable in some respects if the title theory of the mortgage is followed to its logical conclusion.

Some years later a real estate mortgagee, after the default of the mortgagor, made an oral agreement whereby he became the landlord and the mortgagor the tenant. The mortgagor, in possession after condition broken, had given a chattel mortgage on the crops to be raised on the land before the oral agreement had been made. The court decided that while the mortgagee might make a valid parol agreement with the mortgagor and thereby acquire a landlord's lien for supplies furnished to the newly-made tenant, this right was subject to the prior lien of the chattel mortgagee, whose claim had been duly executed and registered as required by the agricultural lien law.[111] Evidently the court was of the opinion that the Killebrew case was a controlling authority and failed to mention the act of 1889, which would probably have furnished a better basis for the decision, considering all that has been said above.

In a case which had arisen years before, the court had said that after default in the conditions of a registered real estate mortgage, the mortgagee could, by parol contract, become the landlord of the mortgagor, and might thereafter avail himself of the landlord's lien, subsequent lienholders being charged with notice of the mortgagee's right of entry. This case, however, is distinguishable from the above decision by reason of the fact that the mortgagor had surrendered possession to the mortgagee four years or more before the adverse

111. Warrington v. Hardison, 185 N. C. 76, 116 S. E. 166 (1923).

claimant, the holder of a chattel mortgage, had acquired his lien on the crops.[112]

In another case a purchaser bought the land at a foreclosure sale and entered upon the property before the crop in question was planted. He rented the land to the mortgagor, who was still in possession at that time. Before the sale considerable advances had been made to the mortgagor by a third person. The crux of the matter here seemed to be that the purchaser took possession of the land before the crop was planted, and the court, in deciding the case in his favor, made this the criterion in distinguishing the Killebrew case. The lien of the third person had not attached to the crop at the time when the purchaser bought the land at the foreclosure sale and took over the property by renting it to the mortgagor. The third person attempted to set up a claim under certain apportionment statutes. One of these statutes[113] provides that when rents are payable to successive owners, and the right of any owner is terminable by death or other uncertain event, the next payment shall be apportioned among the said owners. The other statute in point[114] provides that when a farm lease is terminable by the happening of an uncertain event cutting short the estate of the lessor, the lessee shall continue occupying the land until the end of the year and shall pay to the succeeding owner a proportionate share of the rent. The court declared that a foreclosure was not such an uncertain event as to entitle one to claim an apportionment of a crop which was planted after the sale, and on which he had made advances with knowledge of the foreclosure decree.[115]

Again, the North Carolina court held that a purchaser at a foreclosure sale under a real estate mortgage was entitled to recover possession of the land from a lessee of the mortgagor claiming to hold under a lease made after the maturity of the mortgage indebtedness, the mortgage not having been foreclosed immediately. The court declared that where the mortgagee had not entered after the maturity of the debt, or where the crops were severed before entry, he would then have no right to claim them as his own. It further said that, generally speaking, if a mortgage foreclosure sale is completed and title is vested in the purchaser while a crop is still growing and

---

112. Ford v. Green, 121 N. C. 70, 28 S. E. 132 (1897).
113. N. C. Gen. Stat. (1943) §42-6.
114. N. C. Gen. Stat. (1943) §42-7.
115. Spruill v. Arrington, 109 N. C. 192, 13 S. E. 779 (1891).

unsevered, and there has been no waiver of the right to the crop, the title and right to it passes to the purchaser along with the land. This is true as against the mortgagor, his execution creditors, and the lessee holding under a contract executed at a time subsequent to the mortgage. The court remarked there was no statute in North Carolina giving the lessee of a mortgagor after default any right to the crop for the year in which it was planted. It suggested that it might be wise to have such legislation, but declared that this is a matter for the legislature and not for the courts. Moreover, it was said that whenever a person takes a mortgage or deed of trust on a farm, he does so with notice of the State Agricultural Lien Law providing for a lien for advances within one year from the date of the agreement, if the statute is complied with, and stating that the mortgage or deed of trust, whether the indebtedness secured thereby be due or not, is subject to the provisions of the law.[116] The aforesaid apportionment statute[117] was invoked by the tenant claiming under the mortgagor. The statute was held not to defeat the right of the purchaser at the foreclosure sale to recover the possession of the property from the mortgagor's tenant, who claimed to have a superior right under a lease made after the maturity of the mortgage indebtedness.[118] Here at least the court seems to approve the reasoning concerning severance in the concurring opinion of the Killebrew case and also indicates that it would refuse to enlarge upon the rights of agricultural lienors as approved by the court in that decision.

Two years later the Agricultural Lien Law was amended in such a manner as to give the tenants, lessees, or croppers of a mortgagor in possession the right to execute a valid and superior agricultural lien on the crops raised upon the rented premises.[119]

Thus it appears that there has been a tendency on the part of North Carolina legislators to try to protect agricultural lienors, who derive their rights through the mortgagor or his tenants, at the expense of the mortgagee, whose rights the court has seemed to give preference.

This North Carolina controversy, with its clashing interests, may be considered as typical of what to expect in other jurisdictions when similar questions arise. It is to be hoped that the courts will be

116. N. C. Code Ann. (Michie, 1927) §§2480-81.
117. N. C. Gen. Stat. (1943) §42-7. See Note 114, *supra*.
118. Collins v. Bass, 198 N. C. 99, 150 S. E. 706 (1929).
119. N. C. Pub. Laws 1931, c. 173 (N. C. Code Ann. (Michie, 1939) §2481).

able to work out these problems and any other similar ones which call for just decisions. In doing so, the conflicting interests of the ultimate landowner, the cultivator, and any intermediate creditors should be given the best possible protection under existing theories of law. Should these theories prove unequal to the task of achieving the desired end of justice for all, then new theories might be tried with a view toward a more equitable solution for everyone concerned.

EFFECT OF MULTIPLE TRANSFERS

OF INTERESTS IN LAND

Sometimes a case arises where there have been several transfers of the interests of the landlord or tenant in the land. Only a very few instances of this sort have come before the courts of the Southeastern states.

A Mississippi tenant was in possession of land under a lease for one year. A purchaser of the property, in September of that year, made an oral lease to the tenant for the next year. In December the land was again sold, and the intermediate owner at the same time rented the premises from his transferee. The possession of the land by the tenant was said to put the ultimate purchaser on notice, not only with respect to the lease for the first year, but concerning the oral lease for the following year as well. Under these circumstances it was declared that the tenant occupied the premises during the second year under his oral contract of lease with the intermediate owner, and not as a sublessee, his rights under the oral lease being prior to the lease made in December by the ultimate purchaser.[120]

A tenant in Virginia, himself an assignee, assigned his interest to another, who reaped and enjoyed a crop sown before the last assignment, which was supported by an adequate consideration. The ultimate assignee was evicted because of a defect in the title of the original lessor, who had made a special covenant or agreement to be responsible if any flaw appeared. The intermediate assignee was said to be under no obligation to restore the purchase money which had been paid to him for the transfer of his interest. The court declared that this was especially true here, where the possibility of an eviction had been in the minds of both parties at the time of the assignment, and where no proper effort had been made to show that the original

120. Frye v. Rose, 120 Miss. 778, 83 So. 179 (1919).

lessor was insolvent. It was indicated that a recovery might have been had against the original lessor.[121]

CONCLUSION

This matter of assignability is very complicated and offers many problems to farmers and their attorneys. Some effort should be made to level some of the pitfalls into which both landlords and tenants may step in wandering through the maze of assigned liens, rent notes, and reversionary interests. The law needs more codification here.

121. McClenahan v. Gwynn, 3 Munf. 556 (Va., 1811).

XVIII

Removal and Conversion of Lien-Encumbered Crops

OFTEN a crop upon which there is a lien will be removed or appropriated by landlord, tenant, or third person. Many problems arise out of arbitrary assumption of control over the products which the tenant has raised upon the rented premises. The situations are many and varied and are continually coming before the courts in the principal areas which produce cotton and tobacco.

In general it may be said that a disposal or removal of crops or other property subject to a lien for rent or advances, without the consent of the lienholder, is unlawful and subjects the parties responsible therefor to civil and, in some jurisdictions, criminal liability for such action. Of course this principle of law applies only when the lien has not been satisfied by payment or in some other manner. Usually the holder of a landlord's lien is permitted to step in even before the maturity of the indebtedness where there are circumstances which would seem to indicate that he might be injured by the removal of the property from the leased premises. Thus it has been said that the landlord may attach the crop of the tenant when the latter has removed it, or any portion of it, from the premises without the landlord's consent, or when he is about to remove it from the place without paying the rent.[1] Of course all removals of crops are not illegal, and there are many instances in which the appropriation may be explained. In one case a crop was subject to two liens, in favor of the landlord and a mortgagee respectively. An arrangement was made by the landlord and tenant to sell to a third person certain cotton subject to both liens, and the proceeds were applied to settle the landlord's claim. The court held that this was a lawful sale for the purpose of clearing away an indebtedness superior to the mortgagee's claim and passed a good title to the purchaser. The mortgagee was not permitted to object because the proceeds were used to pay the prior claim.[2]

1. Masterton v. Bentley, 60 Ala. 520 (1877).
2. Gay & Bruce v. Smith, 211 Ala. 358, 100 So. 633 (1924).

REMOVAL BY TENANT OR THIRD PERSON

Of frequent occurrence is the removal or conversion by a tenant or third person of a crop upon which there is a landlord's lien. Various questions arise concerning the rights of these persons and also those of crop mortgagees. It is to be noted that the situations are many and the problems interesting.

As a general rule it may be said that removal of agricultural products or other property subject to a landlord's lien does not interfere with the landlord's right to enforce his claim.[3] In Kentucky[4] and Louisiana[5] the lien can be enforced only if the lessor takes action within fifteen days of the time when the property is removed from the leased premises, while in Mississippi[6] and Virginia[7] the period is thirty days. However, the Louisiana Court has remarked that the time limit will not be enforced if the tenant and the person to whom the property has been delivered have conspired to defraud the lessor.[8]

According to the statutes of Alabama,[9] Arkansas,[10] Georgia,[11] and Mississippi,[12] the landlord is expressly permitted to enforce his lien on the crop either when the tenant has removed it, or any portion of it, without the consent of the landlord, or when the tenant is about to remove it from the leased premises without satisfying the landlord's claim, even though the debt for which the lien is claimed is not due. It is also probable that the North Carolina,[13] South Caro-

3. Craven v. Phillips, 214 Ala. 430, 108 So. 243 (1926); Boggs v. Price, 64 Ala. 514 (1879); Stone v. Yount, 174 Ark. 825, 296 S. W. 717 (1927); Tennessee Joint Stock Land Bank v. Bank of Greenwood, 179 Miss. 534, 172 So. 323 (1937); Scarborough v. Lucas, 119 Miss. 128, 80 So. 521 (1919); Jordan v. Bryan, 103 N. C. 59, 9 S. E. 135 (1889); Hamilton v. Stubbs Co., 105 S. C. 157, 89 S. E. 554 (1916).

4. Ky. Rev. Stat. (1946) §383.070; Stone v. Bohm Bros. & Co., 79 Ky. 141 (1880).

5. La. Civ. Code Ann. (Dart, 1932) Art. 2709; La. Code Prac. Ann. (Dart, 1932) Art. 288; Odier v. Schexnaydre, 164 La. 989, 115 So. 57 (1927); Carroll v. Bancker, 43 La. Ann. 1078, 10 So. 187 (1891); Worrell v. Vickers, 30 La. Ann. 202 (1878); Haralson v. Boyle, 22 La. Ann. 210 (1870).

6. Miss. Code Ann. (1942) §921.

7. Va. Code Ann. (Michie, 1936) §6416.

8. Dictum in Carroll v. Bancker, 43 La. Ann. 1078, 10 So. 187 (1891).

9. Ala. Code (1940) tit. 31, §20.

10. Ark. Dig. Stat. (Pope, 1937) §8853.

11. Ga. Code (1933) §61-401.

12. Miss. Code Ann. (1942) §§897, 908, 921.

13. N. C. Gen. Stat. (1943) §42-15.

lina,[14] and Virginia[15] statutes are subject to a like interpretation. If either of the above situations exists, the landlord may step in and enforce the lien.[16] The decisions of the courts in Kentucky[17] and Louisiana[18] are in accord with the principles of law contained in these statutes. Furthermore, it has been said that the landlord may interfere where legal process, not in favor of the landlord, or controlled by him, or levied at his instance or procurement, is being enforced against the property subject to the lien.[19]

According to a Kentucky decision, the landlord is not bound to wait until there is barely enough property on the premises to satisfy his claim; he must have reasonable grounds for apprehension but cannot be compelled to delay action until his belief ripens into an absolute conviction.[20] The Louisiana court has said that he has a right to determine for himself whether he is sufficiently protected by the property which remains upon the premises, and the tenant has no right to determine this for him.[21] To sustain a writ of sequestration in this State it is unnecessary to prove the fear of loss, since the fact that the tenant has the power to part with, conceal, or dispose of the property is all that is required.[22] Where there is danger that the landlord or his assignee will be injured if the tenant or a purchaser from him is allowed to remove the crop subject to the lien, a court of equity will enjoin the removal, particularly when

14. S. C. Code Ann. (1932) §8817.

15. Va. Code Ann. (Michie, 1936) §6416.

16. Masterton v. Bentley, 60 Ala. 520 (1877); Valentine v. Washington, 33 Ark. 795 (1878); Vaughn v. Strickland, 108 Ga. 659, 34 S. E. 192 (1899); Daniel v. Harris, 84 Ga. 479, 10 S. E. 1013 (1890); James v. Benjamin, 72 Ga. 185 (1883); Payne v. Holt, 61 Ga. 355 (1878); Rosenstein v. Forester, 57 Ga. 94 (1876); Peterman v. Dunaway, 32 Ga. App. 171, 122 S. E. 727 (1924); Dyer v. Cannon, 27 Ga. App. 793, 110 S. E. 415 (1921); Payne v. Braswell, 25 Ga. App. 380, 103 S. E. 688 (1920); Kimball v. Rogers, 22 Ga. App. 763, 97 S. E. 205 (1918); Little v. Lary, 12 Ga. App. 754, 78 S. E. 470 (1913); Leonard v. Brockman, 46 S. C. 128, 24 S. E. 96 (1896).

17. Browning v. Crawford, 145 Ky. 279, 140 S. W. 530 (1911); Thomson v. Tilton, 22 Ky. Law Rep. 1004, 59 S. W. 485 (1900); Porter v. Sparks, 19 Ky. Law Rep. 1211, 43 S. W. 220 (1897); McLean v. McLean, 73 Ky. 167 (1873).

18. Millot v. Conrad, 112 La. 928, 36 So. 807 (1904); Thomas v. Dundas, 31 La. Ann. 184 (1879); Wilcoxen v. Bowles, 1 La. Ann. 230 (1846); LeBlanc v. Guy, 14 La. App. 162, 128 So. 715 (1930).

19. Payne v. Braswell, 25 Ga. App. 380, 103 S. E. 688 (1920).

20. McLean v. McLean, 73 Ky. 167 (1873).

21. Millot v. Conrad, 112 La. 928, 36 So. 807 (1904).

22. LeBlanc v. Guy, 14 La. App. 162, 128 So. 715 (1930). See Gueydan v. T. E. Ranch Co., 156 La. 397, 100 So. 541 (1924).

there is, in addition to the lien, a mortgage on the crop in favor of the landlord himself.[23]

The Georgia courts have held that the purpose and intent of the removal are unimportant and immaterial.[24] In a case where this rule was generally recognized, it was held that it did not apply because the contract stipulated that the cotton crop must be delivered at a certain warehouse beyond the boundaries of the leased premises.[25] A similar result was reached in a comparatively recent Kentucky case where the contract had authorized the tenant to sell the tobacco crop and a creditor of the tenant had attached it. The court pointed out that the creditor stood in the shoes of the tenant and was possessed of all rights which the latter had at the time of the attachment.[26] The contract provided that the tenant should sell the crop and pay the rent, and it was said that the landlord had no equity in the proceeds of the property which had been deposited in a bank.

It has been stated that even where the crop has been carried only so far as other lands belonging to the same landlord, the removal cannot be justified.[27] In a case involving a criminal indictment, however, it was said that where the defendant had merely gathered the crop and put it in a crib on the land on which it was grown, and it remained in the control of the lessee, the act was not unlawful, no intention appearing of depriving the lessor of his share of the crop.[28] In another case a tenant had mortgaged his share of a tobacco crop for more than it ultimately brought in the market and had moved it to his barn on other premises for stripping. The court held such acts were sufficient grounds for a reasonable belief on the part of the landlord that he would lose his claim for rent and therefore an adequate basis for the issuance of an attachment.[29]

In North Carolina it has been held that a removal of the tenant's share of a crop after a division has been made cannot be objected to by the landlord.[30] This rule is not applicable to a situation where the

23. Valentine v. Washington, 33 Ark. 795 (1875).

24. Daniel v. Harris, 84 Ga. 479, 10 S. E. 1013 (1890); Little v. Lary, 12 Ga. App. 754, 78 S. E. 470 (1913).

25. Wheeler v. Mote, 37 Ga. App. 547, 140 S. E. 904 (1927).

26. Day's Exec'x v. Traders' Nat. Bank, 232 Ky. 662, 24 S. E. (2d) 576 (1930).

27. Masterton v. Bentley, 60 Ala. 520 (1877).

28. Varner v. Spencer, 72 N. C. 381 (1875).

29. McLemore v. Treadway, 191 Ky. 306, 230 S. W. 56 (1921).

30. Jordan v. Bryan, 103 N. C. 59, 9 S. E. 135 (1889).

division was not an absolute but a provisional one for the purpose of giving the tenant and his family an opportunity to strip that portion of the tobacco crop set aside to him.[31]

It has been said that commingling the crops from the rented premises with others and selling or consuming them so as to destroy or endanger the landlord's security is an illegal disposal of them.[32]

The fact that sufficient cotton remains in the field to satisfy the landlord's claim does not justify the tenant in selling some of the cotton raised on the leased premises before delivering the prescribed share to the landlord.[33] Indeed it has been said that a tenant's removal of any portion of the crop, even for honest purposes, without the consent of the landlord, would justify attachment proceedings. This is true even though enough of the crop remains upon the premises to satisfy the lien for rent, and it is shown that the tenant does not intend to remove the crop in bulk.[34]

In North Carolina it was held that the landlord may bring claim and delivery proceedings, the proper remedy in that State, not only where the crops are removed from the leased premises, but also where the tenant, or any other person, takes the crops into his absolute possession and denies the rights of the landlord thereto. It was said that a different interpretation would violate the spirit of the statute and lead the tenant to defy the landlord and consume the crops on the premises, or sell them to another, who could do likewise.[35] On the other hand, there is a Louisiana case in which it was shown that the tenant had taken a part of the corn crop and ground it into meal to use for the purpose of feeding his family, who had no other means of sustenance. The landlord had stopped advancing supplies because he claimed the tenant was not working as actively as he should and had abandoned some of the cotton. He felt that the tenant was not working the balance sufficiently, and that he had also unnecessarily delayed the picking. In the absence of proof that the tenant would not have made the seized corn good in a final settlement with the landlord, it was stated that this appropriation was no lawful ground for a writ of sequestration, a common remedy in Louisiana for the enforcement of privileges. However, it was held that the evidence concerning abandonment of the crop was suffi-

31. Jarrell v. Daniel, 114 N. C. 212, 19 S. E. 146 (1894).
32. Chandler v. Burk, 211 Ala. 93, 99 So. 727 (1924).
33. LeBlanc v. Guy, 14 La. App. 162, 128 So. 715 (1930).
34. Randolph v. McCain, 34 Ark. 696 (1879).
35. Livingston v. Farish, 89 N. C. 140 (1883).

cient reason for the issuance of the writ.[36] In a Georgia case, there was evidence that a tenant had gathered a small portion of the wheat crop and had had it ground. Part of the wheat he used as flour for his family, and the other part, consisting of a twenty-four pound sack, he exchanged for twenty-four pounds of commercial flour to be used by the family. This seizure was not considered substantial enough to authorize the issuance of a distress warrant.[37]

In Alabama it has been said that a purchaser of the crop cannot be held personally liable unless it appears that he has disposed of the property or its proceeds in such a manner that it will be impossible for the landlord to enforce his lien.[38] Hence it seems probable that no intermeddling with the property is or can be injurious to the landlord's rights which stops short of the destruction or impairment of his lien. Moreover, it may be said that in order to authorize a recovery the landlord must be shown to have suffered some loss.[39]

In a case in which the plaintiff is not asking for punitive or vindictive damages, the motive with which the defendant has acted in converting the property is unimportant.[40] Where punitive damages are demanded, however, the absence of a bad motive may bar the recovery thereof.[41]

In Arkansas certain crops upon which there was a landlord's lien for rent had been turned over to crop mortgagees on their promise to pay the amount due. It was held that the mortgagees could not relieve themselves of liability by delivering the crops to a receiver in a foreclosure proceeding. The court declared that their act constituted a conversion for which the mortgagees were responsible.[42]

It cannot be affirmed as a general rule that the mere consent of a landlord to the removal of a crop from the rented premises is a waiver of the lien. In this situation a great deal depends upon the aims of the removal and the purposes for which the consent was given.[43] For instance, the landlord's consent that the crops shall be cribbed on the lands rented to the tenant and under his control does

36. Dixon v. Alford, 143 So. 679 (La. App., 1932).
37. Dyer v. Cannon, 24 Ga. App. 304, 100 S. E. 723 (1919).
38. Griffis v. Wilson, 18 Ala. App. 449, 92 So. 907 (1922).
39. McWhorter v. Jordan, 237 Ala. 327, 186 So. 698 (1939).
40. Lavender v. Wall, 60 Ala. 214 (1877); Hussey v. Peebles, 53 Ala. 432 (1875).
41. Hussey v. Peebles, 53 Ala. 432 (1875).
42. Silbernagel v. Taliaferro, 173 Ark. 141, 289 S. W. 764 (1927).
43. Tuttle v. Walker, 69 Ala. 172 (1881).

not authorize the tenant to turn them over to a subtenant to remove and store beyond the control of both landlord and tenant in chief.[44]

There is a rule of evidence that what a person says contemporaneously with the doing of a particular act generally may be proved as constituting a part of the *res gestae*, where it is explanatory of or tends to characterize the act. Hence it was held that when an attachment had been sued out against a tenant's crop on the ground that he was about to remove it without paying the rent, and he afterwards sued on the bond for damages for illegal attachment, it was permissible for him to prove, as a part of the *res gestate*, that, by the terms of the contemplated sale, the purchaser was to pay the rent before removing the crop.[45]

In cases involving affidavits in support of attachments under the Alabama law concerning the removal of a tenant's crops from rented premises, it has been held that such affidavits must allege that the removal was without the consent of the landlord;[46] must state the year for which the rent is due and that the lands have been rented from the plaintiff;[47] must allege that the crop was removed from the leased premises;[48] and must aver a demand for the sum due as rent and/or advances alleged to be due and unpaid.[49] The last allegation would hardly be required in Georgia, since a demand for payment there is not a prerequisite of a recovery in removal cases.[50]

It has been decided in Mississippi that a person merely receiving, on an account against the tenant, money realized from the sale of agricultural products on which there is a lien for rent, cannot be held liable for such rent. Here he did not purchase the cotton, but his collector merely received the proceeds of the sale in money after the consummation of the transaction.[51] Furthermore, the holder of a deed of trust on crops, who took no part in the sale of certain cotton by a tenant but was simply holding negotiable warehouse receipts as security for the indebtedness until the sale of the cotton could be completed, was held not to have converted the cot-

44. Chandler v. Burk, 211 Ala. 93, 99 So. 727 (1924).
45. Masterson v. Phinizy, 56 Ala. 336 (1876).
46. Robinson v. Holt, 85 Ala. 596, 5 So. 350 (1889); Busbin v. Ware, 69 Ala. 279 (1881); Shield v. Dothard, 59 Ala. 595 (1877); DeBardeleben v. Crosby, 53 Ala. 363 (1875).
47. DeBardeleben v. Crosby, 53 Ala. 363 (1875).
48. Knowles v. Steed, 79 Ala. 427 (1885).
49. Robinson v. Holt, 85 Ala. 596, 5 So. 350 (1889).
50. Vaughn v. Strickland, 108 Ga. 659, 34 S. E. 192 (1899).
51. Jones v. Stevens & Busick, 12 So. 446 (Miss., 1892).

ton as against an assignee of a rent note of which he had no notice.[52] However, it has been held in this State that a person purchasing cotton from a lessee, with notice of the tenancy, is liable to the landlord, whether the purchaser has or has not joined with the tenant in removing the property from the premises.[53]

Tennessee statutes authorize a landlord to recover from a purchaser of a crop upon which he has a lien the value of the products delivered to or taken possession of by the purchaser before the first of July following the year in which the crop is raised, and also from a factor, commission merchant, broker, or other person who, with or without notice, sells the crop and applies the proceeds to the tenant's indebtedness to himself, the liability being the same in both cases.[54] In one instance it was said that a factor acting as an agent only, who had not resorted to the indicated subterfuge to become himself the beneficiary of the sale of a lien-encumbered crop, did not become liable under the statute.[55] Again, it was said that in the absence of fraud, only the first purchaser from the tenant could be held liable, although under another section of the lien statute the landlord might levy upon the crop in the hands of anyone.[56] A landlord had a choice of bringing an action against the defendant for selling a cotton crop or for purchasing it. The court held that he could not be required to elect which remedy he would pursue, and that both might be prosecuted to judgment, though satisfaction could be had on one only.[57]

In Louisiana a tenant had sent rice raised on leased premises to certain merchants with a direction to sell and apply the proceeds on advances made to the tenant. The merchants had notice of the

---

52. Crutcher v. Commercial Bank, 146 Miss. 404, 111 So. 569 (1927).

53. Cohn v. Smith, 64 Miss. 816, 2 So. 244 (1887). In an earlier case under Miss. Laws 1872, c. 107, and Miss. Laws 1873, c. 75, it was decided that the landlord did not have a right of action against the purchaser of a crop on which there was a lien, although the crop might be followed and seized, just as property which is subject to a judgment lien may be followed and seized. Westmoreland v. Wooten, 51 Miss. 825 (1876). A question was raised with respect to the liability of a person who fraudulently colluded with a tenant and aided him in defeating the lien of a landlord by a sale and removal of a crop subject to the lien, but the court did not decide the point.

54. Tenn. Code Ann. (Williams, 1934) §§8023-24. See Hunter v. Harrison, 154 Tenn. 590, 288 S. W. 355 (1926).

55. Hunter v. Harrison, 154 Tenn. 590, 288 S. W. 355 (1926).

56. Decker v. Rice, 137 Tenn. 478, 194 S. W. 87 (1917).

57. Schoenlau-Steiner Trunk Top & Vaneer Co. v. Hildebrand, 152 Tenn. 166, 274 S. W. 544 (1925).

landlord's privilege for rent. It was intimated by the court that they would have been personally liable therefor if the landlord had exercised his rights within the fifteen-day period prescribed by law.[58]

A Georgia case involved land that had been leased for a rental of six thousand pounds of lint cotton. The evidence for the tenant would have authorized a finding that there had been a new agreement, a novation, that the tenant should pay as rent one-fourth of the crops produced. The landlord testified that he did not so agree but had told the tenant, when they had the conversation about the change in the terms, that he "would consider it." There was also evidence that the tenant had not properly cultivated the crops and that the new agreement was conditioned upon proper husbandry. Conceding but not deciding that a valid agreement to alter the terms of payment was established, it could not be shown that the condition to its vitalization had been met. Therefore, under any view of the evidence, the novation was never effected. This being the case, a removal of the crop without payment of the amount called for by the original contract was unlawful and made it subject to distress proceedings immediately.[59]

The holder of a chattel mortgage has a claim inferior to that of the landlord and hence is not permitted to remove the crop until the latter's superior claim is satisfied. It has been held that a mere allegation that a chattel mortgagee has taken possession of a tenant's corn crop upon which the plaintiff landlord had a lien for rent and has removed the crop from the leased premises and disposed of it, thereby preventing the plaintiff from enforcing his lien, is a sufficient statement of a cause of action.[60]

In Georgia it was shown that a tenant had asked permission to remove the crops from the leased premises and that the landlord had refused to allow it. The intention of the tenant in removing the crops did not appear. The judge instructed the jury that if the tenant was moving the crops, the landlord might sue out a distress warrant. It was held that the instruction need not be qualified by adding that, if the removal was made with the landlord's consent, or if such action was necessary to enable the tenant to pay the rent, then the distress warrant could not be supported.[61] In another

58. Odier v. Schexnaydre, 164 La. 989, 115 So. 57 (1927). See Chapter 14, Note 233.
59. Peterman v. Dunaway, 32 Ga. App. 171, 122 S. E. 727 (1924).
60. Donohoo v. Zellner, 17 Ala. App. 209, 84 So. 556 (1919).
61. Jones v. Eubanks, 86 Ga. 616, 12 S. E. 1065 (1891).

instance there was evidence of an actual removal of one bale of a tenant's cotton crop and of failure to pay the rent. It was said that this might be looked upon as a circumstance indicating that more of the cotton would follow, although the rest of the crop had been taken no further than a gin which was located on the premises.[62]

Under a South Carolina statute[63] an affidavit is required in support of a warrant of seizure used in enforcing liens. The court has stated that the requirements are satisfied by an affidavit which alleges that the land has been rented, that a note has been given for a specified amount of rent, that the note is justly due the plaintiff, and that the defendant has refused payment, even though there be no specific averment that a cause of action exists. It was further averred that the defendant had sold a portion of his crop and had refused to pay the rent with the intention of defeating the plaintiff's lien. This was said to be equivalent to a statement that the defendant intended to defraud his creditor. The court also ruled that an allegation that the plaintiff owned the land was not assailable upon evidence showing that the plaintiff had owned the property and had died.[64]

A comparison of two other South Carolina cases illustrates some of the difficulties of the pleader in instances where removal is involved. In an early case the affidavit stated that the landlord had reason to believe, and did believe, that the debtor had disposed of, or was about to dispose of, his crops, the effect of which would be to defeat the landlord's lien. A statute provided that the affidavit must allege facts of a character which, if true, would *prima facie* warrant the belief. The court declared that the affiant must state the facts upon which the belief was founded, and that these facts must be of such character as would support the belief. There was no positive allegation of either an intent on the part of the defendant to dispose of his crops to defeat the lien, or of an "act of disposition" for that purpose. The court held the affidavit to be insufficient.[65] In a later case, however, a somewhat similar affidavit was held to state a cause of action. The affiant alleged that the tenant was gathering the crop and putting it out of sight, forbidding the entrance of the landlord upon the premises, and telling him that he was going

62. Payne v. Holt, 61 Ga. 355 (1878).
63. S. C. Code Ann. (1932) §8777.
64. Monday v. Elmore, 27 S. C. 126, 3 S. E. 65 (1887).
65. Baum v. Bell, 28 S. C. 201, 5 S. E. 485 (1888).

to leave. The defendant claimed this affidavit was defective in that it did not state the sources of the information upon which the belief was founded or the facts upon which the fear of loss was based. The court decided that it was unnecessary to elaborate further and that a cause of action was stated.[66] In this later controversy the court evidently believed that the affidavit stated enough facts to give the defendant sufficient advance notice of the nature of the action which he would be required to meet. The court in the earlier case, however, did not so believe, and there is a great deal to be said in favor of this difference in the handling of the two cases.

RIGHTS OF A BONA FIDE PURCHASER

What is the result when a crop which is subject to a landlord's lien is sold to a purchaser who is ignorant of the fact that there is such a lien? The answer is neither simple nor clear-cut. In fact there is a decided difference of opinion in respect to this matter, and the problem is beclouded with much discussion of a definitive nature concerning the buyer and his classification as a bona fide purchaser.

As a matter of law, a person in that category is protected in some of the Southeastern states but not in others. He is shielded by the law of Alabama,[67] Arkansas,[68] Georgia,[69] Kentucky,[70] and at least to a certain extent in South Carolina,[71] although it has been indicated

66. Faust v. Bonnett, 110 S. C. 435, 96 S. E. 489 (1918).

67. Bellingrath v. Samuel, 219 Ala. 263, 122 So. 27 (1929); Craven v. Phillips, 214 Ala. 430, 108 So. 243 (1926); Scaife & Co. v. Stovall, 67 Ala. 237 (1880); Governor v. Davis, 20 Ala. 366 (1852); Worthington v. Long, 9 Ala. App. 617, 64 So. 174 (1913).

68. Medendorp v. Washington, 191 Ark. 1077, 89 S. W. (2d) 730 (1935); Van Etten v. Lesser-Goldman Cotton Co., 158 Ark. 432, 250 S. W. 338 (1923); Hunter v. Mathews, 67 Ark. 362, 55 S. W. 144 (1900); Bledsoe v. Mitchell, 52 Ark. 158, 12 S. W. 390 (1889); Puckett v. Reed, 31 Ark. 131 (1876).

69. Lancaster v. Whiteside, 108 Ga. 801, 33 S. E. 995 (1899); Worrill v. Barnes, 57 Ga. 404 (1876); Elder v. First Nat. Bank of Jefferson, 29 Ga. App. 455, 115 S. E. 922 (1923); Collins v. Harrison, 24 Ga. App. 404, 100 S. E. 794 (1919). See also Atchison v. Taliaferro County, 65 Ga. App. 177, 15 S. E. (2d) 534 (1941); McCommons-Thompson-Boswell Co. v. White, 33 Ga. App. 20, 125 S. E. 76 (1924).

70. Stone v. Bohm Bros. & Co., 79 Ky. 141 (1880). Cf. the early case of Craddock v. Riddlesbarger, 32 Ky. 205 (1834), where it was said that a purchaser, with or without notice of the landlord's lien, of the tenant's property which is subject to the lien, under a *fieri facias* sale of the property, gets it free from the lien. The court evidently believed that the landlord's remedy was against the levying officer who, if he was shown to have had notice of the lien, was said to be liable for the arrears of rent, whereas if he had no notice he was not responsible at all.

71. See Graham v. Seignious, 53 S. C. 132, 31 S. E. 51 (1898); Brewster v.

in the latter State that notice given soon after the purchase and before a second transfer of the crop would be sufficient to preserve the lien.[72] On the other hand, Mississippi[73] and North Carolina[74] have held that notice is immaterial, and that the lienholder can claim the property in the hands of the purchaser whether or not he had actual or constructive knowledge of the encumbrance. The Mississippi court has also declared that notice or lack of notice no more affects the liability of a foreign purchaser than it affects the home-state buyer.[75] The question of the position of the bona fide purchaser of a tenant's crop does not seem to have arisen in Florida or Virginia.

Under a Tennessee statute of 1825[76] the purchaser of a tenant's crop could not be held personally liable by the landlord, whether the former had notice of the lien[77] or not.[78] In interpreting an act of 1857[79] the court held that a landlord might attach a tenant's crop when in the possession of third persons and that the lien related back to the date of the contract and was superior to any right acquired by a purchaser of the crop, although the latter was without notice of the lien. If, however, the landlord elected to proceed against the purchaser for the value of the property, and not for the property itself, he could not recover if the purchaser had no notice of the lien.[80] In another instance a factor sold cotton for a tenant and

McNab, 36 S. C. 274, 15 S. E. 233 (1892); Drake v. Whaley, 35 S. C. 187, 14 S. E. 397 (1892). The repeal of S. C. Code (1932) §8819, which protected bona fide purchasers from distress, by S. C. Acts 1946, No. 873, §50, would probably not affect the general law with respect to this matter.

72. Markert v. North Augusta Warehouse Co., 107 S. C. 135, 92 S. E. 201 (1917); Park v. Laurens Cotton Mills, 70 S. C. 274, 49 S. E. 871 (1904).

73. Tennessee Joint Stock Land Bank v. Bank of Greenwood, 179 Miss. 534, 172 So. 325 (1937); Warren v. Jones, 70 Miss. 202, 14 So. 25 (1892); Jones v. Stevens & Busick, 12 So. 446 (Miss., 1892); Dunn v. Kelly, 57 Miss. 825 (1880). In Wooten v. Guinn, 56 Miss. 422 (1879), Justice Simrall was of the opinion that a bona fide purchase cut off the lien, but Justice Chalmers disagreed with him, and the latter's view was adopted in the later cases.

74. Belcher v. Grimsley, 88 N. C. 88 (1883). See also Burwell v. Cooper's Cooperative Warehouse Co., 172 N. C. 79, 89 S. E. 1064 (1916), in which a recovery was allowed without any mention of notice.

75. Millsaps v. Tate, 75 Miss. 150, 21 So. 663 (1897).

76. Tenn. Acts 1825, c. 21.

77. Bryan v. Buckholder, 27 Tenn. 561 (1847). The court remarked that the statute would allow an unprincipled tenant to defeat the lien but concluded that this was one of the many instances where no remedy was provided.

78. Lawrence v. Jenkins, 15 Tenn. 494 (1835); Ballantine & Kercher v. Greer, 14 Tenn. 267 (1834); Davis v. Parks & Campbell, 14 Tenn. 252 (1834).

79. Tenn. Acts 1857-58, c. 52, §3.

80. Phillips v. Maxwell, 60 Tenn. 25 (1872).

appropriated the proceeds to a debt due him from the tenant, with the latter's consent and with knowledge of the tenancy. It was held that the factor was not responsible to the landlord, since he was not considered a purchaser within the meaning of the act.[81] In 1879 the legislature amended the statute by deleting the clause making notice a prerequisite for a successful action against the purchaser.[82] This was the state of the law for some time.[83] At present, following a statutory change,[84] the action can be maintained only if the crop is delivered to or taken possession of by the purchaser before the first day of July of the following year and if the lienholder brings his suit within one year after the transfer.

Another statute was enacted which provides that any factor, commission merchant, broker, or other person selling the crop of a tenant or sharecropper, with or without notice of the landlord's lien, and before the statute of limitations has run, who applies the proceeds to the payment of the tenant's indebtedness to himself, shall be liable as a purchaser to the holder of the lien for rent or supplies.[85] Thus the law as announced in the above case concerning the liability of the factor was changed in order that the landlord's interest in the crop might be more fully protected. It has also been held that the action against the purchaser may be maintained before the rent is due and prior to any successful action against the tenant.[86] The final result of all these decisions and legislative enactments seems to be that the landlord is given the right to recover from the purchaser and that the lack of notice makes no difference. Therefore it may be said that the law of Tennessee is very much like that of Mississippi in this respect.

In Louisiana the holder of a lessor's privilege or an agricultural supplyman's privilege for advances may follow the tenant's crop into the hands of an immediate purchaser,[87] but is not permitted to hold the latter personally liable for the rent or advances secured by his privilege.[88] However, the privilege is lost altogether when the

81. Armstrong v. Walker, 77 Tenn. 156 (1882).
82. Tenn. Acts 1879, c. 72.
83. Davis v. Wilson, 86 Tenn. 519, 8 S. W. 151 (1888).
84. Tenn. Code Ann. (Williams, 1934) §8023.
85. Tenn. Code Ann. (Williams, 1934) §8024.
86. Richardson & Nelson v. Blakemore, 79 Tenn. 290 (1883).
87. Loeb v. Collier, 131 La. 377, 59 So. 816 (1912).
88. Duke v. Crawford, Jenkins & Booth, 150 La. 1023, 91 So. 440 (1922); Union Seed & Fertilizer Co. v. Supple's Sons Planting Co., 139 La. 692, 71 So. 949 (1916). In the *Duke* case it is stated that the purchaser acted in good faith at all times.

purchaser sells the crops and they enter the channels of trade as merchandise.[89] The original purchaser is chargeable with presumptive knowledge of the privilege resting upon the crops. Moreover, it is said in one case that allegations of actual knowledge of the privilege are unnecessary and mere surplusage, for proof of such allegations would not affect the decision in any manner whatsoever.[90]

Even in the states holding that a sale of the tenant's crop to a bona fide purchaser cuts off the lien, notice or knowledge of the landlord's claim prevents a purchaser from being placed under the protection of the rule.[91] In other words, to make a third person liable for the loss of a landlord's lien through the removal of crops subject thereto, it must be shown that he had notice, actual or constructive, of the existence of the claim.[92] The Alabama Court has held that the burden of proving notice of the lien is upon the plaintiff landlord,[93] especially where it has been shown that value has been paid by the buyer and he is claiming to be a bona fide purchaser.[94] The complaint must allege notice on the part of the defendants themselves, it being insufficient to state that the tenant has delivered the crop to the defendants who have sold it to persons without notice of the encumbrance.[95] If notice is not alleged, the complaint is demurrable and cannot be made the basis of a successful action.[96]

89. Loeb v. Collier, 131 La. 377, 59 So. 816 (1912).
90. Weill v. Kent, 107 La. 322, 31 So. 761 (1902).
91. City Nat. Bank v. Nelson, 218 Ala. 90, 117 So. 681 (1928); 214 Ala. 297, 107 So. 849 (1926); Bank of Ramer v. Derden, 211 Ala. 666, 101 So. 594 (1924); Baker v. Cotney, 142 Ala. 566, 38 So. 131 (1905); Bush v. Willis, 130 Ala. 395, 30 So. 443 (1901); Foxworth v. Brown, 120 Ala. 59, 24 So. 1 (1898); Robinson v. Lehman, Durr & Co., 72 Ala. 401 (1882); Hussey v. Peebles, 53 Ala. 432 (1875); Dulany v. Dickerson, 12 Ala. 601 (1847); Mt. Vernon-Woodberry Mills v. Union Springs Guano Co., 26 Ala. App. 136, 155 So. 710 (1934); Bank of Marion v. Beck, 199 Ark. 668, 136 S. W. (2d) 188 (1940); Lee Gin Co. v. Archillion, 198 Ark. 564, 129 S. W. (2d) 952 (1939); Taylor v. Crawford, 187 Ark. 316, 59 S. W. (2d) 484 (1933); Silbernagel v. Taliaferro, 173 Ark. 141, 289 S. W. 764 (1927); Gould-Galbraith Supply Co. v. Triplett, 167 Ark. 125, 266 S. W. 937 (1924); Sledge & Norfleet Co. v. Hughes, 156 Ark. 481, 247 S. W. 1077 (1923); Solomon v. Keesee, 156 Ark. 387, 246 S. W. 469 (1923); Judge v. Curtis, 72 Ark. 132, 78 S. W. 746 (1904); Hunter v. Matthews, 67 Ark. 362, 55 S. W. 144 (1900); Merchants' & Planters' Bank v. Meyer, 56 Ark. 499, 20 S. W. 406 (1892); Saulsbury, Respess & Co. v. McKellar, 59 Ga. 301 (1877); Streetman v. Turner, 32 Ga. App. 733, 124 S. E. 549 (1924); Drake v. Whaley, 35 S. C. 187, 14 S. E. 397 (1892).
92. Street v. Treadwell, 203 Ala. 68, 82 So. 28 (1919).
93. Webb & Aigner v. Darrow, 227 Ala. 441, 150 So. 357 (1933).
94. Patton v. Darden, 227 Ala. 129, 148 So. 806 (1933).
95. Gurley v. Henderson Nat. Bank, 21 Ala. App. 569, 110 So. 63 (1926).
96. Gurley v. Henderson Nat. Bank, *supra* Note 95.

To hold a purchaser of the tenant's crop responsible to the land-lord in a state which protects the bona fide purchaser, actual notice is not essential,[97] for it is sufficient if facts are shown which, if true, will put the purchaser on notice that the lien exists.[98] The circumstances are deemed sufficient if they tend to put the purchaser or other person on inquiry in respect to the existence of the lien.[99] In Alabama the question at issue seems to be whether the purchaser had knowledge of such facts as would put an ordinary prudent man on inquiry and which, if followed up, would have disclosed the lien.[100] The known facts should direct the purchaser to the possible existence of the lien.[101] The South Carolina court appears to require knowledge of such facts as would, if pursued with due diligence, lead to the discovery of the lien.[102] Mere knowledge that the crops to be purchased were grown on rented land has been ruled admissible in a few instances.[103]

In one case an Alabama tenant leased land on shares, and the landlord executed a deed to the tenant, expressly reserving crops. The deed was recorded. It was held that this deed did not have the effect of destroying the landlord's lien, but, under a state statute,[104] operates as notice of the lien to all persons dealing with the tenant.[105] In contrast to this, however, a clause in a mortgage describing crops as including cotton grown "on farm, or any other places cultivated by me, or in which I have an interest," was held not in itself to show

97. City Nat. Bank v. Nelson, 214 Ala. 297, 107 So. 849 (1926); Lomax v. LeGrand Co., 60 Ala. 537 (1877).

98. City Nat. Bank v. Nelson, 218 Ala. 90, 117 So. 681 (1928); 214 Ala. 297, 107 So. 849 (1926); Polytinsky v. Johnston, 211 Ala. 99, 99 So. 839 (1924); Merchants' & Planters' Bank v. Meyer, 56 Ark. 499, 20 S. W. 406 (1892); Collins v. Harrison, 24 Ga. App. 404, 100 S. E. 794 (1919).

99. Polytinsky v. Johnston, 211 Ala. 99, 99 So. 839 (1924); Lomax v. Le-Grand, 60 Ala. 537 (1877); Gould-Galbraith Supply Co. v. Triplett, 167 Ark. 125, 266 S. W. 937 (1924); Judge v. Curtis, 72 Ark. 132, 78 S. W. 746 (1904); Pape v. Steward, 69 Ark. 306, 63 S. W. 47 (1901); Hunter v. Matthews, 67 Ark. 362, 55 S. W. 144 (1900); Collins v. Harrison, 24 Ga. App. 404, 100 S. E. 794 (1919); Graham v. Seignious, 53 S. C. 132, 31 S. E. 51 (1898).

100. City Nat. Bank v. Nelson, 218 Ala. 90, 117 So. 681 (1928).

101. Etheredge v. Hester, 32 Ala. App. 321, 25 So. (2d) 523 (1946).

102. Graham v. Seignious, 53 S. C. 132, 31 S. E. 51 (1898).

103. City Nat. Bank v. Nelson, 214 Ala. 297, 107 So. 849 (1926); Sloan v. Hudson, 119 Ala. 27, 24 So. 458 (1898); Kelly v. Eyster, 102 Ala. 325, 14 So. 657 (1894).

104. Ala. Code (1942) tit. 47, §102.

105. Hooper v. Farmers' Union Warehouse Co., 21 Ala. App. 91, 105 So. 725 (1924).

notice that a certain cotton crop had been raised on rented land.[106]

A farmer represented to the defendant, a crop mortgagee, that he was on land which he had purchased conditionally and was paying rent and satisfying claims for advances made by the plaintiff, the original landowner. He further stated that his crops would be worth little to the defendant unless he could obtain money to pay for the land. The court held that this was sufficient to make it the duty of the defendant, before disposing of the crops in his possession, to inquire as to the existence of a landlord's lien.[107]

The fact that the crops were bought in open market seems to have influenced the Arkansas court in favor of the person claiming to be a bona fide purchaser,[108] especially where the tenant owned other land and had for several years sold freely cotton raised on both pieces of ground.[109] But in another case the court seems to have ignored the fact that the crops were purchased in the open market.[110]

Evidence of the knowledge or dealings of the parties in previous years has been ruled admissible on the issue of notice in both Alabama[111] and Arkansas,[112] although in one Alabama appellate court decision it was held that evidence showing that on previous occasions the defendant had been compelled to pay the landlord for cotton bought from his tenants was immaterial and therefore inadmissible.[113] In South Carolina, although such evidence is admissible where there is a lease contract which is continuous through a number of years, it is inadmissible where a new lease for the very same land has been entered into by the landlord and tenant.[114]

Testimony of agents of individuals or corporations, and of officers of corporations, concerning their knowledge of the tenancy or of facts which, if examined thoroughly, would lead to such knowledge is also held to be admissible on the issue of notice.[115]

106. Bellinggrath v. Samuel, 219 Ala. 263, 122 So. 27 (1929).

107. Manasses v. Dent, 89 Ala. 565, 8 So. 108 (1890).

108. Medendorp v. Washington, 191 Ark. 1077, 89 S. W. (2d) 730 (1936).

109. Van Etten v. Lesser-Goldman Cotton Co., 158 Ark. 432, 250 S. W. 338 (1923).

110. Walker v. Rose, 153 Ark. 599, 241 S. W. 19 (1922).

111. Foxworth v. Brown, 120 Ala. 59, 24 So. (1898); Kelly v. Eyster, 102 Ala. 325, 14 So. 657 (1894); Mt. Vernon-Woodberry Mills v. Union Springs Guano Co., 26 Ala. App. 136, 155 So. 710 (1934).

112. Lesser-Goldman Cotton Co. v. Miller, 169 Ark. 1099, 277 S. W. 865 (1925); Judge v. Curtis, 72 Ark. 132, 78 S. W. 746 (1904).

113. Worthington v. Long, 9 Ala. App. 617, 64 So. 174 (1913).

114. Graham v. Seignious, 53 S. C. 132, 31 S. E. 51 (1898).

115. City Nat. Bank v. Nelson, 218 Ala. 90, 117 So. 681 (1928); 214 Ala.

In one situation an Arkansas bank received money on deposit without notice of any lien thereon. The court held that the institution was bound to pay checks drawn upon the account by the depositor and hence in so doing did not become liable to the person holding the lien.[116] It also declared, however, that it did not mean to state that a bank, having such notice or knowledge, would or would not, under all circumstances, be bound to pay a customer's check to the extent of the deposit, since that question was not presented in the case before it. There seems to be no reason why a bank should be allowed to avoid liability here any more than other persons who are charged with notice of the lien.

An early Alabama opinion stated that the landlord's lien for advances had been placed by statute on an equality with his lien for rent.[117] Either the lien for advances or the lien for rent is sufficient to support an action against one who has converted the crop to his own use, and hence the lienholder cannot be forced to prove that both exist.[118] In two other early cases the Alabama court held that notice of the tenancy relationship operated as constructive notice of the lien for rent, but not of the lien for advances.[119] However, this proposition has been reversed in later decisions, and at present knowledge of the tenancy operates as notice of both types of liens.[120]

In an unusual case a friend helped a sick tenant by carrying cotton to the compress, receiving tickets and samples, offering it for sale, and then paying the proceeds to him. It was shown that he was acting entirely in good faith and had no knowledge of the landlord's claim. The court held that, since the tenant's friend had committed no wrongful act, he could not be held personally liable for damages sustained by the landlord.[121]

Sometimes the tenant's crop is placed in storage and warehouse

---

297, 107 So. 849 (1926); Gurley v. Henderson Nat. Bank, 21 Ala. App. 569, 110 So. 63 (1926); First Nat. Bank v. Duvall, 156 Ark. 377, 246 S. W. 471 (1923); Walker v. Rose, 153 Ark. 599, 241 S. W. 19 (1922).

116. Merchants' & Planters' Bank v. Meyer, 56 Ark. 499, 20 S. W. 406 (1892).

117. Thompson v. Powell, 77 Ala. 391 (1884), interpreting Ala. Laws 1878-79, p. 72 and the then existent Code. Ala. Code (1876) §3469.

118. Mt. Vernon-Woodberry Mills v. Union Springs Guano Co., 26 Ala. App. 136, 155 So. 710 (1934).

119. Coleman v. Siler, 74 Ala. 435 (1883); Wilson v. Stewart, 69 Ala. 302 (1881).

120. Walls v. Skelton, 215 Ala. 357, 110 So. 813 (1926); Atkinson v. James, 96 Ala. 214, 10 So. 846 (1892).

121. Norton v. Orendorff, 191 Ala. 508, 67 So. 683 (1914).

receipts or other kinds of receipts are taken and negotiated to different persons. In Alabama[122] and Georgia[123] it is indicated that the purchaser of a warehouse receipt is in practically the same position as the ordinary purchaser of the tenant's crop in respect to the law concerning the knowledge or lack of knowledge of the lien. In an early case the Arkansas court took the same view.[124] In this State, however, the practical results of the decision evidently did not satisfy the landlords, for a statute was enacted which provided that the purchaser of the receipt of any warehouseman, ginner, factor, or other bailee of farm products should not be deemed a bona fide purchaser and that such a transfer should not cut off the lien of the landlord or laborer.[125] Recently the court took the view that this novelty was in conflict with the Uniform Warehouse Receipts Act which had been adopted in Arkansas a few years later. This statute protected a bona fide purchaser of a negotiable warehouse receipt, the purpose of the act being to create throughout the nation a uniform system of law governing business transactions of this type. The provisions of the Uniform Act[126] were said to repeal the above act giving priority to the landlord's lien and to protect the innocent purchaser of a ginner's, factor's, or warehouseman's receipt which is negotiable. Under the Uniform Act a purchaser must be honest rather than free from negligence in order to be classed as a bona fide purchaser. Therefore it was said that a purchaser who had made no investigation of title other than to inquire whether anyone else had any interest in the property would be entitled to prevail over the landlord's lien.[127]

In contrast to this ruling with respect to the effect of the Uniform Act is the holding by a Mississippi court that the claim of the landlord is preferred over the rights of the bona fide holder of a negotiable warehouse receipt.[128]

122. City Nat. Bank v. Nelson, 218 Ala. 90, 117 So. 681 (1928).
123. Elder v. First Nat. Bank, 29 Ga. App. 455, 115 S. E. 922 (1923).
124. Puckett v. Reed, 31 Ark. 131 (1876).
125. Ark. Dig. Stat. (Pope, 1937) §8849. See Lynch v. Mackey, 151 Ark. 145, 235 S. W. 781 (1921); Jackson v. Atkins, 103 Ark. 91, 146 S. W. 133 (1912); Noe v. Layton, 69 Ark. 551, 64 S. W. 880 (1901); Hunter v. Matthews, 67 Ark. 362, 55 S. W. 144 (1900). But cf. Commodity Credit Corp. v. Usrey, 199 Ark. 406, 133 S. W. (2d) 887 (1939), where the facts seem to indicate that the statute should have been applied but it was not done.
126. Ark. Dig. Stat. (Pope, 1937) §§14413 et seq.
127. Grauman v. Jackson, 225 S. W. (2d) 678 (Ark. 1950).
128. Phillips v. Box, 204 Miss. 231, 37 So. (2d) 266 (1948).

In Louisiana it was held that the privilege of a person who furnished money or supplies for the making of a crop was superior to the rights of the holder of a warehouse receipt issued when the crop was placed in storage.[129]

In Alabama it seems that a crop mortgagee, with or without actual or constructive notice of the landlord's lien, cannot claim to be considered in the same category as a bona fide purchaser for value,[130] although there is an opinion in which the mortgagee's lack of notice seems to have been given undue emphasis.[131] It has been decided in Georgia that where a warehouse receipt has been transferred to secure a loan made simultaneously with a pledge of the property represented by the receipt, the pledgee stands in the same position as a bona fide purchaser of the property and is therefore protected.[132] In this same State, however, it was held at an earlier date that innocent junior lienholders would not be protected against the claim of the landlord for rent.[133]

An early Alabama opinion stated that an execution was levied on a crop of cotton after it had been removed from the leased premises and stored in a warehouse by the tenant. This levy was permitted to prevail over an attachment subsequently enforced on the cotton at the suit of the landlord, the execution creditor having no notice of the lien, and it not being intended that creditors without notice should be cut off.[134] From what has been said before in respect to the status of the bona fide mortgagee in this State, it is extremely doubtful if this decision would be followed at the present time. In fact this is practically assured, and the landlord's lien would no doubt prevail.

SHIPMENTS ACROSS STATE LINES

What is the result when a crop subject to a landlord's lien is carried into another state? Is it possible for the landlord to follow the produce under these circumstances? What are the rights of the

---

129. Purity Feed Mills Co. v. Moore, 152 La. 393, 93 So. 196 (1922).

130. Metropolitan Ins. Co. v. Reconstruction Finance Corp., 230 Ala. 580, 162 So. 379 (1935); Bellingrath v. Samuel, 219 Ala. 263, 122 So. 27 (1929); McLellan v. Roberson, 171 Ala. 120, 55 So. 99 (1911); Waite v. Corbin, 109 Ala. 154, 19 So. 505 (1896). A fortiori, where the mortgage had been given for an antecedent debt. Gafford v. Stearns, 51 Ala. 434 (1874).

131. Colvin v. Payne, 218 Ala. 341, 118 So. 578 (1928).

132. Elder v. First Nat. Bank, 29 Ga. App. 455, 115 S. E. 922 (1923).

133. Smith v. Fouche, 55 Ga. 120 (1875).

134. Governor v. Davis, 20 Ala. 366 (1852).

out-of-state buyer or factor? These queries pose interesting and complicated problems.

First let it be said that state statutes establishing the landlord's lien have no extraterritorial effect.[135] The Mississippi court has held this to be true whether the crop has been shipped out of the State to a foreign mortgagee,[136] a purchaser,[137] or a factor or commission merchant,[138] and it cannot be said that any of these are personally liable to the landlord. A different conclusion is called for, however, where the conversion takes place before the goods leave the borders of a state, and in these circumstances the right of the landlord can be enforced in the courts of another state, although the laws of that state will govern with respect to the remedy to be employed.[139]

In one instance a Mississippi tenant delivered a crop of tomatoes to certain merchants with whom he had an open account, with the understanding that they were to ship the crop out of the State and credit the proceeds to the account, a direction which the merchants carried out. The Mississippi Court held that these acts constituted a conversion within the State and rendered the merchants liable to the extent of the landlord's lien.[140] The Arkansas court concluded that a conversion had taken place in that State when by prearrangement a cotton crop was delivered to a common carrier and shipped to a mortgagee domiciled in another state, to be applied to the shipper's account, and in addition it was shown that the mortgagee had an interest in the property.[141] In this situation there seems to

135. J. T. Fargason Co. v. Furst, 287 Fed. 306 (C. C. A. 8th, 1923); Millsaps v. Tate, 75 Miss. 150, 21 So. 663 (1897). In a North Carolina case a Virginia tenant farmer carried produce into North Carolina, and it was there attached by a merchant who had made advances. The landlord claimed the crop because of a lien for rent and advances under the laws of Virginia. His claim for rent was allowed, but it was said that he had not sufficiently proved his claim for supplies. The North Carolina court ignored the conflict of laws aspects of the controversy. Adams v. Caudle, 188 N. C. 185, 124 S. E. 127 (1924). It would seem that the Virginia statute should have no extraterritorial effect here.

136. Millsaps v. Tate, 75 Miss. 150, 21 So. 663 (1897).

137. Ball, Brown & Co. v. Sledge, 82 Miss. 749, 35 So. 447 (1903).

138. Chism v. Thomson, 73 Miss. 410, 19 So. 210 (1896); Hernandez v. Aaron, 16 So. 910 (Miss., 1895). But see Cocke v. Maynard, 16 So. 908 (Miss., 1895), where evidence that defendants had told the tenant to draw on them in favor of the plaintiff landlord was said to be admissible.

139. Security Bank & Trust Co. v. Bond, 132 Ark. 592, 201 S. W. 820 (1918).

140. Peets & Norman Co. v. Baker, 95 Miss. 576, 48 So. 898 (1909).

141. Sledge & Norfleet Co. v. Hughes, 156 Ark. 481, 247 S. W. 1077 (1923).

have been a definite scheme to escape the payment of the landlord's prior claim, notice on the part of the mortgagee being clearly shown. It was said that mere knowledge of the shipment would not constitute a waiver by the landlord. In another instance the out-of-state factor to whom the crop was shipped by the tenant held a mortgage thereon and had knowledge of the landlord's lien. Under these circumstances it was said that a delivery to a carrier for transportation to his business address would make the mortgagee guilty of conversion at the place of shipment.[142] However, where these circumstances do not exist and the factor is innocent of any conniving or overt act in the state of shipment, a delivery to a carrier will not make him guilty of a conversion.[143]

In an early case in the Federal Supreme Court, an Arkansas lessee had shipped his cotton crop to a broker in Louisiana without satisfying the landlord's lien. The landlord sued to recover the crop. The court held that the law of Louisiana, which gave the consignee a right of pledge for advances where goods were delivered to him in this manner by a carrier, should govern the controversy and compel a decision in favor of the broker.[144]

REMOVAL OR CONVERSION BY LANDLORD

The landlord, as well as the tenant or third person, may be responsible for a conversion or removal of the produce of the tenant grown on the leased premises. In fact cases of this sort are continually arising and form a counterpart to instances where the tenant has been guilty of tortious conduct.

North Carolina has recognized the existence of such conduct on the part of landlords by the enactment of a statute [145] authorizing an action of claim and delivery, the same remedy given to landlords under similar circumstances, in cases where a landlord has converted the tenant's crops to his own use without a proper consideration for the latter's rights. In the other Southeastern states the courts have been left to deal with problems of this sort as they arise.

Several cases have arisen under the North Carolina statute. In one instance a tenant died after the crop matured but before it was gathered. His share of the produce had been alloted to his wife as the year's support to which she was entitled under the law of this

142. J. T. Fargason Co. v. Furst, 287 Fed. 306 (C. C. A. 8th, 1923).
143. Driver v. J. T. Fargason Co., 288 Fed. 671 (C. C. A. 8th, 1923).
144. Walworth v. Harris, 129 U. S. 355, 9 Sup. Ct. 340 (1889).
145. N. C. Gen. Stat. (1943) §42-16.

State.[146] Here the widow was permitted to recover from the landlord, who had appropriated the crop to his own use.[147] In another situation a landlord who had received the value of his tenant's interest in a crop upon which the plaintiff supplyman had an agricultural lien and had failed to account therefor was held liable for the amount due.[148] Moreover, where a landlord gave a supply lien on crops to be raised on his land, the person who had raised them under a share contract was said to be entitled to his share free from any claim of the supplyman.[149] Again, an action was brought against an offending landlord for the value of a portion of the crop which, it was alleged, he had wrongfully converted. Here a motion to dismiss the action was held to have been properly denied, since under the allegations of the complaint the landlord would be compelled to account for the value of the crop in excess of the sum secured by the lien.[150]

Generally it may be said that in the other Southeastern states the principles of law concerning conversion by the landlord are in accordance with the interpretation given this North Carolina statute. In Alabama, for example, landlords have been held responsible for converting the entire crop.[151] A similar result was reached in South Carolina.[152]

In one instance a Mississippi landlord, without the tenant's consent, commingled the latter's cotton with his own and sold it to a cotton association. There was no evidence that the rent had not been paid, and the only valid claim the landowner had was for such supplies as had been advanced to the tenant in aid of the crop. Hence it was held that the cotton association was responsible to the tenant's assignee for all the cotton in excess of this valid claim.[153] Even where the tenant has given his consent to the removal of the crop by the landlord, such an appropriation is unlawful if it prejudices other creditors of the tenant, such as crop mortgagees or pledgees.[154]

146. N. C. Gen. Stat. (1943) §30-15.
147. Parker v. Brown, 136 N. C. 280, 48 S. E. 657 (1904).
148. Glover v. Dail, 199 N. C. 659, 155 S. E. 575 (1930).
149. Rouse v. Wooten, 104 N. C. 229, 10 S. E. 190 (1889).
150. Crinkley v. Egerton, 113 N. C. 142, 18 S. E. 341 (1893).
151. Marlowe v. Rogers, 102 Ala. 510, 14 So. 790 (1894); Townsend v. Bussey, 30 Ala. App. 259, 4 So. (2d) 199 (1941).
152. Hatchell v. Chandler, 62 S. C. 380, 40 S. E. 777 (1902).
153. Mississippi Cooperative Cotton Ass'n v. Walker, 186 Miss. 870, 192 So. 303 (1939).
154. Cofer v. Benson, 92 Ga. 793, 19 S. E. 56 (1894); Landreneaux v. Dergin, 19 La. App. 542, 134 So. 283 (1931).

Furthermore, it has been said that where a tenant has assigned his interest in the crop to another before maturity without obtaining the landlord's consent, it is not considered an appropriation which will prevent the assignee from maintaining a tort action for conversion against the landlord.[155]

In Georgia it has been held that a tenant may maintain an action against his landlord for a stated sum of money alleged to be the value of the crops, and that the landlord may set off the plaintiff's indebtedness to him for the current year and a preceding one, both action and set-off being considered as arising *ex contractu* and not *ex delicto*.[156] Therefore it is seen that an action sounding in contract may be brought in situations of this kind as well as the more common tort action.

One court has authorized punitive damages in instances where the landlord has converted the crop to his own use and in so doing has acted in a wanton, reckless, or malicious manner.[157]

Generally speaking, it is held that even though the landlord might have attached or otherwise lawfully seized the tenant's crop by virtue of his lien, his appropriation of the produce without instituting legal proceedings was unlawful and made him liable for a conversion.[158] However, a different situation is presented where the landlord has come into possession without trespass, with the tenant's consent, for the purpose of securing the rent, or where the crop has been deposited with a like motive in the hands of other persons. Here the rent must be fully tendered before the crop can be repossessed by the tenant or his creditors.[159] If the tender is not forthcoming, the landlord's refusal to turn over the crop is justified and cannot be considered as a waiver of the lien.[160] In no event is the landlord liable for more than the tenant's share of the crop.[161]

Sometimes a landlord will obtain possession of his tenant's crop on

155. Enley v. Nowlin, 60 Tenn. 163 (1873).

156. Carswell v. Smith, 145 Ga. 588, 89 S. E. 698 (1916).

157. Hatchell v. Chandler, 62 S. C. 380, 40 S. E. 777 (1902).

158. Donaldson Mercantile Co. v. First Nat. Bank of Brantley, 213 Ala. 213, 104 So. 394 (1925); Marlowe v. Rogers, 102 Ala. 510, 14 So. 790 (1894); Townsend v. Bussey, 30 Ala. App. 259, 4 So. (2d) 199 (1941); Hudson v. Burton, 158 Ark. 619, 250 S. W. 898 (1923); Buck v. Lee, 36 Ark. 525 (1880); Hall v. McGaughey, 114 Ga. 405, 40 S. E. 246 (1901). But see Nickleson v. Lofton, 16 Ala. App. 672, 81 So. 192 (1919).

159. Buck v. Lee, 36 Ark. 525 (1880). See also Donaldson Mercantile Co. v. First Nat. Bank of Brantley; Nickleson v. Lofton, *supra* Note 158.

160. Nickleson v. Lofton, *supra* Note 158.

161. Skelton v. Baker, 189 Ala. 512, 66 So. 695 (1914).

which a third person has a mortgage. In a situation of this kind the Arkansas Court held that the landlord must, after discharging his own prior lien, account to the mortgagee for the surplus.[162] Also it has been said that the mortgagee cannot obtain possession from the landlord without first paying the amount due for rent.[163]

In Georgia a landlord was shown to have received enough of his tenant's crop to satisfy the claim for rent. Instead of paying that debt, however, he insisted upon applying this portion of the produce to the payment of an unsecured open account. It was held that the landlord, even with the tenant's consent, would not be permitted to do this where the rights of a crop mortgagee would be prejudiced thereby.[164] In a somewhat similar North Carolina case a landlord took possession of certain cotton raised by his tenant. The court held that this cotton must be applied to the satisfaction of the rent note before it could be used to discharge an unsecured account between the parties.[165]

Testimony that a Mississippi landlord had appropriated the crop of his tenant, after agreeing to waive his lien and consenting that the crop be applied to the payment of a third person's account, was held not to support an action against the landlord on the account. However, the court made it clear that this evidence would support a more appropriate proceeding, such as an action on the case or a suit for money had and received.[166]

All sorts of situations of this general nature may arise. A Georgia tenant had agreed to pay rent in cotton raised on the land. After the crop had been harvested the tenant died, and by agreement with the landlord his widow proceeded to carry out the contract. The cotton was placed in the ginhouse of the landlord, who had it ginned, packed, and carried to town for her. There, by inadvertence, the cotton was left at the warehouse of one of the landlord's creditors, who sought to apply it to an independent indebtedness. It was said that a landlord's creditor could not, without the consent of the parties, take a tenant's cotton and pay the landlord's debt. Therefore, it was held that the widow was entitled to recover from the warehouseman.[167] An Alabama landlord gained possession of certain

162. Peeples v. Hayley, Beine & Co., 89 Ark. 252, 116 S. W. 197 (1909).
163. Roth & Co. v. Williams, 45 Ark. 447 (1885).
164. Cofer v. Benson, 92 Ga. 793, 19 S. E. 56 (1894).
165. Avera v. McNeill, 77 N. C. 50 (1877).
166. Chism v. Alcorn, 71 Miss. 506, 15 So. 73 (1894).
167. Flournoy, Hatcher & Co. v. Wardlaw, 67 Ga. 378 (1880).

warehouse receipts representing a crop on which he had a lien and refused to deliver them to the tenant on demand. It was held that this act of appropriation amounted to a conversion and rendered the landlord responsible for the resultant loss.[168]

In a case where an Arkansas landowner had taken possession of a rice crop, the plaintiff cultivator had offered to settle his claim out of the proceeds as expressly provided for in the contract. After the plaintiff had initiated an action the landowner offered to let him take and sell the crop, and it was thereupon sold at a sum less than it would have brought on the date of the unlawful seizure. It was held that this offer and acceptance would not excuse the conversion and would be considered only in mitigation of damages. The court also refused to dismiss the action because the plaintiff had failed to repay money advanced to grow the crop.[169]

It may be seen that any landlord who wrongfully appropriates the fruits of his tenant's labor can be haled into court and made responsible for his unlawful conduct. In respect to this matter the courts, lacking statutory direction, have developed rules of their own to cover the situations as they have arisen.

CRIMINAL PROSECUTIONS

Most of the Southeastern states have statutes making the tenant's unlawful removal of crops from rented premises a misdemeanor.[170] The intention to defraud the landlord or lienholder has been held to be an essential element of the offense under the statutes of Alabama,[171] Arkansas,[172] Georgia,[173] and Mississippi,[174] while in North Carolina it is stated in one case that the intent is implied

168. Compton v. Sims, 209 Ala. 287, 96 So. 185 (1923).

169. Papan v. Thomason, 156 Ark. 231, 246 S. W. 15 (1922).

170. Ala. Code (1940) tit. 14, §363; Ark. Dig. Stat. (Pope, 1937) §§3212-15; Fla. Stat. Ann. (1941) §812.03; Ga. Code (1933); §§61-9902-03; La. Gen. Stat. Ann. (Dart, 1932) §5061; Miss. Code Ann. (1942) §§2250-52; N. C. Gen. Stat. (1943) §42-22; S. C. Code Ann. (1932) §§1276-77; Tenn. Code Ann. (Williams, 1934) §8025; Va. Code Ann. (Michie, 1936) §4455a. It would seem that Kentucky has no such statute.

171. Money v. State, 89 Ala. 110, 7 So. 841 (1890); Dillehay v. State, 18 Ala. App. 271, 90 So. 332 (1921); Drinkard v. State, 12 Ala. App. 184, 68 So. 553 (1915).

172. Royal v. State, 159 Ark. 601, 252 S. W. 601 (1923).

173. White v. State, 24 Ga. App. 74, 100 S. E. 39 (1919); Smith v. State, 17 Ga. App. 554, 87 S. E. 829 (1916); Kellam v. State, 2 Ga. App. 479, 58 S. E. 695 (1907).

174. Dolph v. State, 111 Miss. 668, 71 So. 911 (1916); Edwards v. State, 8 So. 464 (Miss., 1891).

from the removal[175] and in another that it is immaterial.[176] At least a knowledge of the tenancy agreement seems to be essential in order to obtain a conviction under the North Carolina act.[177] The South Carolina court has held that the motive of the removal is immaterial, the disposal of the property with knowledge of the lien implying fraud, and that it is no defense that in the act of appropriation the defendant has followed the advice of counsel.[178] The necessity for an allegation of fraudulent intent, wherever essential, is not met by an averment that the act was committed to "defeat payment."[179]

The intent must exist with respect to the exact property alleged to have been removed. In one instance it was said that evidence was admissible to show that the tenant understood that the lien applied only to the cotton and corn and not the potatoes. The court declared that as a usual thing the tenant on a cotton and corn farm is entitled to the horticultural products, and hence it would be reasonable to assume that the contract had been so understood. The jury, with such evidence before it, might well have believed that there had been no intent to defeat or impair the lien.[180]

In a state where it is necessary to show fraud, the prosecution has the burden of proving it and the fact that the property is subject to the lien.[181] If the intent to defraud is present, the tenant defendant is guilty notwithstanding the fact that he had agreed to deliver the cotton crop to a certain gin, a portion of the contract which he had effectually performed.[182] Under the Alabama act it is necessary for the prosecution to show that the defendant acted with knowledge of the lien and that the removal was with the intention of hindering, delaying, or defrauding the lienholder.[183] Removal with knowledge of the existence of the lien would raise the presumption of the intent to defraud.[184]

In a Georgia case of considerable sociological interest a tenant delivered two bales of cotton to his landlord, who had a lien on the crops for rent and advances, but these two bales satisfied the rent

175. State v. Williams, 106 N. C. 646, 10 S. E. 901 (1890).
176. State v. Crook, 132 N. C. 1053, 44 S. E. 32 (1903).
177. State v. Sears, 71 N. C. 295 (1874).
178. State v. Reeder, 36 S. C. 497, 15 S. E. 544 (1892).
179. Edwards v. State, 8 So. 464 (Miss., 1891).
180. Dolph v. State, 111 Miss. 668, 71 So. 911 (1916).
181. Drinkard v. State, 12 Ala. App. 184, 68 So. 553 (1915).
182. Money v. State, 89 Ala. 110, 7 So. 841 (1890).
183. Drinkard v. State, 12 Ala. App. 184, 68 So. 553 (1915).
184. Kent v. State, 41 So. (2d) 194 (Ala. App. 1949).

claim only. As far as appears, this was the only cotton raised on the place. There was a debt for fertilizer and also a pre-existing indebtedness, entered into before the contract under consideration was executed. The tenant offered the landlord some corn and fodder, which he refused to accept because he considered it worthless. The tenant then turned over his mule, buggy, and harness, the proceeds of the sale of these articles being applied to the debt. In addition the tenant had sold the seed from one cotton bale for $5.16, the evidence showing that he had been compelled to do this in order that his family might have bare living expenses, since the landlord had not furnished him with food. The landlord prosecuted the tenant for disposing of the cotton seed. The lower court convicted the tenant, but the appellate tribunal declared that a criminal intent was lacking, and as this was an essential element of the offense, there had been no crime committed.[185] In this case, though the court did not have as good a foundation for its opinion under general principles of law as it might have had, it was willing to stretch a point and render a just decision.

Where the proceeds of property sold by an Alabama defendant were paid over to the holder of a mortgage on the property, executed by the defendant and his landlord, the court declared that, since the landlord had joined in the mortgage, the evidence would not sustain a conviction.[186] In another instance there were a landlord's lien and two mortgages on a cotton crop. The tenant necessarily sold the crop according to the directions of the prior lien-holders with the purpose of satisfying their claims, offering the residue to the second mortgagee, who had notice of the prior claims. It was held that there was no basis for a conviction. The appellate court declared that to permit a conviction to stand in this instance would, in effect, be an affirmation of guilt for the tenant's failure to make a crop of sufficient value to satisfy all the secured debts and not for a fraudulent disposition of the crop after it had been produced.[187]

In one instance evidence was introduced that the defendant had rented land from an owner, that a crop-sharing agreement had been made, and that he had made a cotton crop and disposed of it without paying the rent. It was held that this testimony made out an indict-

185. Kellam v. State, 2 Ga. App. 479, 58 S. E. 695 (1907).
186. Smith v. State, 139 Ala. 115, 36 So. 727 (1904).
187. Conner v. State, 97 Ala. 83, 12 So. 413 (1893).

able offense under the statute penalizing a fraudulent conversion.[188] However, a failure to prove that the crop had been raised on premises rented from the landlord is fatal, and in such a case an affirmative charge for the defendant must be given.[189]

The establishment of the value of the crop converted is said to be necessary to a successful prosecution under the statutes of both Alabama[190] and Arkansas.[191] The act of removal is punishable as larceny in Alabama, and the value is important in determining whether it is grand or petit. However, it is only necessary to show that the property has some value, and exactitude is not essential.[192]

In South Carolina it has been held that the removal must be one for which the defendant himself is responsible. A sale of a cotton crop by a constable under a crop warrant proceeding instigated by the landowner is not such an act as will subject the latter to a prosecution under the statute.[193]

An averment that a lease agreement has been made is pregnant with the suggestion that a lien exists. An indictment which did not specifically charge that the landlord had a lien on the crop has been held to be sufficient under the North Carolina statute, lessors being given a lien in all such cases by implication.[194]

Under Arkansas laws an indictment for removing mortgaged property was said not to be fatally defective because the proof offered by the prosecution tended to show that the property was subject to a landlord's lien. The gravamen of the offense was the removal of the lien-encumbered goods, the type of lien being unimportant.[195]

Criminal statutes are usually strictly construed, and hence the courts are particular, though not overly so, that every important element of the offense charged be carefully alleged and proved. Very little variance is permitted in cases arising under the type of statute considered here, the important issue being what it is necessary to allege and prove and just how much variance will be allowed. Sometimes a charge to the jury will also lack an essential element of the offense charged.

188. Pate v. State, 29 Ala. App. 78, 191 So. 640 (1939).
189. McWhorter v. State, 16 Ala. App. 168, 76 So. 325 (1917).
190. Dillehay v. State, 18 Ala. App. 271, 90 So. 332 (1921).
191. Royal v. State, 159 Ark. 601, 252 S. W. 601 (1923).
192. Drinkard v. State, 12 Ala. App. 184, 68 So. 553 (1915).
193. State v. Johnson, 51 S. C. 268, 28 S. E. 905 (1898).
194. State v. Smith, 106 N. C. 653, 11 S. E. 166 (1890).
195. Murry v. State, 150 Ark. 461, 234 S. W. 485 (1921).

Usually the pleader is required to make the indictment follow very closely the ingredients of the offense as outlined in the particular statute under consideration. Thus it was ruled that the words of the North Carolina act "before satisfying all liens held *by the lessor or his assigns* on said crop" should be strictly followed, and that an allegation charging a defendant with removal of the produce "without satisfying *all* liens on said crop" was defective.[196] It has also been held in this State that an indictment should state the relationship of the landowner or his assigns to the cultivator or his assigns, the liens on the crops, and the fact that the defendant as lessee, his assigns, or a third person, as the case may be, has removed the crops or a part of them from the premises "without the consent of the lessor or his assigns," without giving him or his agent five days' notice of the intended removal, and before satisfying all liens held by the "lessor or his assigns" on the crops.[197] From this it may be reasoned that an essential element of the indictment is the negation of the five-day notice of the contemplated removal,[198] and the burden of proving its absence rests upon the prosecution.[199] However, an averment that the crop had been taken away without "any notice" has been held equivalent to an allegation that the removal had been made without "five days notice."[200]

It was ruled in one instance that a judge's instruction to the jury stating that the defendant would be guilty if he had removed hay from the leased premises was, if error, harmless, where the jury found him guilty of removing both cotton and hay.[201]

In Georgia the offense aimed at by the statute must be well described in the indictment and its various elements supported by proof. Some of the most important of these elements which must be alleged and proved are the existence of the tenancy relationship, the absence of the landlord's consent to the removal, the fraudulent intent, and the subsequent loss or damage to the landlord.[202] Furthermore, under a somewhat similar statute[203] concerning the illegal sale

196. State v. Merrit, 89 N. C. 506 (1883).

197. State v. Rose, 90 N. C. 712 (1884).

198. State v. Williams, 106 N. C. 646, 10 S. E. 901 (1890).

199. State v. Harris, 161 N. C. 267, 76 S. E. 683 (1912); State v. Crowder, 97 N. C. 432, 1 S. E. 690 (1887).

200. State v. Powell, 94 N. C. 920 (1886).

201. State v. Crook, 132 N. C. 1053, 44 S. E. 32 (1903).

202. See Morrison v. State, 111 Ga. 642, 36 S. E. 902 (1900); White v. State, 24 Ga. App. 74, 100 S. E. 39 (1919); Thompson v. State, 12 Ga. App. 201, 76 S. E. 1072 (1913).

203. Ga. Code (1933) §61-9904.

of produce by a cropper, it was ruled that a judge's failure to charge that the sale must have been completed without the landlord's consent necessitated the granting of a new trial, especially as the evidence with respect to consent was in sharp conflict.[204] Two essential allegations which must be made in an indictment under this statute are the year in which the crop was grown and the portion of the crop disposed of by the cropper.[205]

In a case arising under the tenancy statute, the bill of indictment stated that the defendant had rented the land from the landowner. Actually, at the trial it was shown that another person, his wife, had leased the premises and given her obligation for the payment of the rent. The court held that this constituted a fatal variance, and that it was not sufficient merely to show that the accused had cultivated the crop.[206] In a later case arising under the statute concerning croppers, however, it was said that it was unnecessary to show that the person under whom the defendant claimed had a fee simple title to the premises, since the evidence was positive that the defendant had contracted with the alleged landlord and had occupied the premises as his cropper. Here it was decided that the prosecution would have to go no further than this for the purpose of establishing the relationship.[207] A similar view of the matter was taken in a case arising in North Carolina. In this instance the indictment alleged an agreement on the part of the defendant to raise a crop on the land of one Godfrey. The proof, however, was to the effect that the title to the property was in another, who had rented it to Godfrey, who in turn had subrented it to the defendant. The court held that there was no fatal variance, since, with respect to the defendant, Godfrey was the landlord, and, in accordance with the State law, vested with the right of possession of the crop. Therefore, until the rent was paid, it could not be removed without the notice required by the statute.[208] The latter view is more in accord with the liberal rules of modern procedure.

The Georgia courts have held that an averment of a fraudulent sale is not supported by proof of either a fraudulent loan[209] or a fraudulent pledge.[210] It was also held that an indictment charging

204. Moon v. State, 42 Ga. App. 467, 156 S. E. 640 (1931).
205. Walker v. State, 29 Ga. App. 54, 113 S. E. 37 (1922).
206. Hackney v. State, 101 Ga. 512, 28 S. E. 1007 (1897).
207. Freeman v. State, 30 Ga. App. 133, 116 S. E. 920 (1923).
208. State v. Foushee, 117 N. C. 766, 23 S. E. 247 (1895).
209. Bugg v. State, 17 Ga. App. 211, 86 S. E. 405 (1915).
210. Gilbert v. State, 16 Ga. App. 249, 85 S. E. 86 (1915).

the defendant with the unlawful sale of cotton weighing 582 pounds might be supported by proof that the defendant had sold 588 pounds of cotton, the variance being negligible.[211] However, where the indictment alleged that the removal had been accomplished "without having paid the rent due the landlord and for supplies to make said crop," it was said to be necessary to show that the landlord had actually furnished the supplies.[212]

The penalties of the Georgia laws are directed against any sale by a tenant of property subject to a landlord's lien for rent and/or advances, and they apply as well when the sale is effected by indirection as when the actual delivery of the encumbered property is contemporaneous with the illegal contract of sale. In applying these principles it was said not to be erroneous for a trial judge to instruct the jury that the transfer by an accused tenant of rent notes, taken by him from subtenants and payable to himself in cotton which was subject to the landlord's lien, would be equivalent to the sale of cotton actually grown by the accused on the leased premises, provided the transfer of the notes was without the consent of the landlord and that the latter sustained a loss.[213]

Under the cropper statute, it was held that a conviction was not authorized where the landlord made no objection to the sale, ratified it afterward, and, before any prosecution was instituted, accepted the proceeds of the sale from the cultivator. Here, while the landlord did not expressly authorize the sale in the first instance, he did subsequently consent to it and accepted his half of the proceeds. The court declared that it would be shocking to common justice to allow a landlord to prosecute his cropper after ratifying the sale and taking his half of the money. Here the law implies consent in the first instance.[214] However, a court upheld the conviction of a tenant who had sold his crop at a price which was less than the sum offered by the landlord and had given a check for the rent, leaving certain advances unpaid. It was said that the landlord's acceptance of the check could not be considered as a satisfaction of the whole claim, for, at the time he took the check, he had demanded that the tenant come to see him and settle for the advances, which the latter promised to do but never did.[215]

211. Sims v. State, 43 Ga. App. 438, 158 S. E. 913 (1931).
212. Byrd v. State, 32 Ga. App. 334, 123 S. E. 33 (1924).
213. Bell v. State, 14 Ga. App. 425, 81 S. E. 253 (1914).
214. McGarr v. State, 13 Ga. App. 80, 78 S. E. 776 (1913).
215. Davis v. State, 53 Ga. App. 325, 185 S. E. 400 (1936).

One of several cotenants disposed of a portion of the crop without the landlord's consent and before a settlement had been made for his rent and advances. The cotenant so disposing of the crop was guilty under the Georgia statute, whether the other cotenants participated in the sale or not.[216] In Alabama a tenant and his cropper had given a mortgage on the crop raised by the latter for certain supplies furnished by a merchant. This mortgage was signed by both tenant and cropper but not by the former's brother, who was a cotenant. Later the brothers executed another mortgage to a bank, and, when the crop was gathered and sold, the proceeds were paid to the bank in discharge of its claim. The facts were held to support an inference that the tenant, having joined in the second mortgage with the knowledge that he had signed the prior instrument, had intended to defraud the first mortgagee, whether the payment to the bank was made by himself or by the cotenant with his co-operation and aid. Therefore a conviction was upheld.[217]

An Alabama tenant was indicted for the wrongful removal of lien-encumbered property. The landlady testified that her son, acting as her agent, had notified the tenant not to remove it. Evidence was introduced that the landlady had surrendered the rent note and had told the tenant that she would leave it to his honor to pay the balance due. The lower court refused to charge that, under this view of the circumstances, there could be no conviction unless the jury could be made to believe that *she* had notified the defendant not to remove the property before he actually did so. The appellate court declared that this charge was calculated to impress the jury with the erroneous belief that the notice would not be effective unless it was given by the landlady herself in person. Therefore a reversal was ordered.[218]

Under the North Carolina removal statute it has been held that a tenant may be found guilty where he removes cotton from the leased premises before the rent is paid and without the landlord's knowledge or consent, though it be with the intent of storing and preserving the crop, for which purpose no adequate means existed on the leased premises.[219] In another instance the tenant had merely gathered the crop and put it in a crib on the premises on which it was grown. Though the crib was under the tenant's control, an

216. Smith v. State, 17 Ga. App. 554, 87 S. E. 829 (1916).
217. Courtney v. State, 10 Ala. App. 141, 65 So. 433 (1914).
218. Wilson v. State, 39 So. 776 (Ala., 1905).
219. State v. Williams, 106 N. C. 646, 10 S. E. 901 (1890).

indictable offense was not shown, no intention of converting the crop appearing.[220] With respect to another count in the same indictment, however, the situation was different. Here it was alleged that after putting the crop in the crib he had taken a portion of it and fed it to his stock. This was held to be an unlawful removal within the meaning of the statute. In another case concerning an indictment under the Alabama act, the undisputed testimony disclosed that the defendant had merely hauled cotton for hire without knowledge of any controversy concerning it. This evidence was held insufficient to sustain a conviction for selling the cotton with an intent to defeat the landlord's lien.[221]

Problems may arise where the tenant removes the crops from one county to another. A Georgia cropper carried a portion of the crop raised by him from one county to another, the second county being the one in which he then resided, and it was held that this action was not a violation of the statute.[222] However, the court declared that the crossing of a state line would probably make a difference, since that would involve jurisdictional difficulties. In another instance a cropper, at night, and without the consent of the landlord, removed a portion of a crop from the county in which it was grown and thereafter sold or otherwise disposed of it in another county. The court held that the proper tribunals of the county from which the crop was removed would have jurisdiction of the offense. It was said that in such a case the actual sale or removal of the property might authorize the court to infer that the intent to dispose of the crop in this manner was originally in existence and operative in the mind of the defendant when he first removed the crop. Any overt act in pursuance of this design and thereafter successfully accomplished would merely complete the offense.[223]

Under the North Carolina act it was formerly held that a tenant indicted for the removal of crops could prove that the landlord had been guilty of breaches of contract causing the tenant extensive damages and wiping out any indebtedness to the landlord at the time the crop was converted. A landlord had promised to repair the buildings on the premises, which he had not done, and his tenant had offered to testify that the landlord had agreed to let him

220. Varner v. Spencer, 72 N. C. 381 (1875).
221. Griffin v. State, 26 Ala. App. 473, 162 So. 547 (1935).
222. Scott v. State, 6 Ga. App. 332, 64 S. E. 1005 (1909).
223. Curry v. State, 17 Ga. App. 272, 86 S. E. 533 (1915).

have more land and that damages had resulted from the latter's failure to carry out the promises.[224] Three years later, however, the court overruled this case and declared that it is no defense to an indictment under the statute to show that the defendant tenant has been damaged by the failure of the landlord to carry out the terms of the contract.[225] This later decision is more in accord with the general principles of law governing this type of case, for breaches of contract by the other party to the agreement are not usually considered a valid defense to an indictment under a criminal statute.

A North Carolina statute[226] provides for a criminal action against the landlord as a complement to the criminal action against the tenant. The landlord is made criminally liable for a misappropriation of the tenant's share of the crop. Under this act it has been held that the unlawful seizure of a growing crop by a landlord is an indictable offense.[227] Moreover, a Georgia statute[228] provides that any landlord who refuses to make a delivery of the cropper's share of the produce, after a demand and the payment of advances, shall be guilty of a misdemeanor. The fact that other states do not have such laws is a reflection on the sense of fairness of their legislators.

CONCLUSION

On the whole, it may be said that the subject of removal and conversion of crops has been adequately dealt with in the courts and legislative halls of the Southeastern states. As pointed out, however, there are some inadequacies, such as the failure of the legislators to provide a pattern of dealing with respect to conversion by the landlord and the lack of laws providing for his criminal prosecution in a case of intentional removal. Legal reformers should give their attention to these inadequacies and attempt to persuade the lawmakers that fair and equal treatment is essential to good government.

224. State v. Neal, 129 N. C. 692, 40 S. E. 205 (1901).
225. State v. Bell, 136 N. C. 674, 49 S. E. 163 (1904).
226. N. C. Gen. Stat. (1943) §42-22.
227. State v. Townsend, 170 N. C. 696, 86 S. E. 718 (1915).
228. Ga. Code (1933) §61-9904.

XIX

Remedies Provided for Enforcement of Landlords'
Liens—Distress—Attachment—Foreclosure—
Warrants of Seizure—Claim and Delivery—
Provisional Seizure—Sequestration.

NOW that the liens growing out of the tenancy relationship
have been examined and the rights of landlords, tenants, and third
persons described and analyzed, it is important that there be a discussion of the various methods and procedures by which the several
Southeastern states have provided for the enforcement of these
rights. By far the most common of these remedies are attachment,
distress, and foreclosure, although a study would be incomplete without at least some discussion of possessory warrants, claim and delivery, and the Louisiana Civil Law remedies of provisional seizure
and sequestration. In some jurisdictions all of the reported cases
may have been commenced under one form of procedure, while in
others two or more may have been employed. In Louisiana the Civil
Law remedies seem to have been exclusively used, and this might be
expected, in view of the continental origin of the law of that State.

Since distress is the most ancient of these remedies, it is but natural
that its use should be surrounded with an unusual amount of
technicality, the quantity being determined by the extent to which
the procedure has been liberalized by statute in the particular
jurisdiction. However, it may be said that the other remedies are
also replete with procedural quirks of a troublesome nature. Needless to say, the procedure is complicated and differs in many ways.
It is never exactly the same in any two states, and yet there is a
certain uniformity about the various remedies and forms, a sameness
that makes one believe that these differences are unimportant and
that the procedural variations are more apparent than real.

It is hoped that a detailed discussion of the various procedures
employed in the courts of the Southeastern states today will bring
about a popular demand for simplification and brevity.

DISTRESS

The analysis begins with a discussion of the common-law right of distress and the manner in which it has been modified to meet the needs of an evolving jurisprudence and the conditions under which it has been applied to the growing agricultural community. In the first place, it may be said that in four of the Southeastern states with a common-law background distress is not in use as a means of enforcing a landlord's lien for rent. In Alabama the right of distress for rent was abolished by statute in 1812.[1] The North Carolina court has declared that a landlord cannot distrain for rent, as this process has never been adopted.[2] In Arkansas and Tennessee no reference has been found to a distress for rent, the common remedy being a writ of attachment. Hence it is supposed that distress is not an authorized remedy in these states.

Before the enactment of laws giving the landlord a special lien on the tenant's crop, and in the absence of any contractual provision to that effect in the lease, the landlord had no preferential claim on the crop until the levy of a distress warrant was made thereon.[3] But an express provision conferring the right of distress was unnecessary, and the warrant could be enforced without such authorization.[4]

A distress warrant will not issue unless the relationship of landlord and tenant exists between the parties.[5] However, the termination of the relationship will not bar the remedy of distress with respect to rent which has already accrued.[6] Where, for a valuable consideration, the proprietor of the farm confers the right to let the premises and collect the rent on an assignee, and the assignee has acted in accordance with the authority thus given him, a distress warrant may be issued in the latter's name.[7]

1. Folmar & Sons v. Copeland, 57 Ala. 588 (1877); Frazier v. Thomas, 6 Ala. 169 (1844).
2. Dalgleish v. Grandy, 1 N. C. 161 (1800). See Reynolds v. Taylor, 144 N. C. 165, 56 S. E. 871 (1907); Howland v. Forlaw, 108 N. C. 567, 13 S. E. 173 (1891); Deaver v. Rice, 20 N. C. 567 (1839). With respect to distress and its gradual disappearance from American law, see Note (1886) 15 Am. Dec. 584.
3. Johnson v. Emanuel, 50 Ga. 590 (1874).
4. Williams v. Howard, 3 Munf. 277 (Va., 1812).
5. Culpepper v. Cunningham, 142 Ga. 164, 82 S. E. 549 (1914); Hearn v. Huff, 6 Ga. App. 56, 64 S. E. 298 (1909).
6. Owens v. Wilson, 58 Fla. 335, 50 So. 674 (1909); Tyner v. Slappey, 74 Ga. 364 (1884).
7. Keaton v. Tift, 56 Ga. 446 (1876).

Unless payable in advance, a rare thing in farm tenancy cases, rent is not usually recoverable before the crop matures. In order for the landlord to effect a recovery before maturity, it is ordinarily necessary for him to allege that the tenant has removed or is about to remove the property from the leased premises.[8] In fact, according to a Mississippi decision,[9] the proceeding will not be effective if it is based merely upon the landlord's belief that the tenant is preparing to remove the property; there must be evidence of facts upon which such a belief could be reasonably based. In the rare case in which the rent is payable in advance, the distress warrant may issue on the day when the rent is due.[10]

In an early case from South Carolina it was held that a lessee, who had parted with his full term, would not be permitted to collect the rent by distress warrant proceedings against the transferee, there being a lack of privity of contract as well as a desire on the part of the court to prevent a multiplicity of suits.[11] However, it is believed that this action would be permitted under more modern procedural rules. In fact the Georgia court has held that a tenant who subleases land to a third person is the subtenant's landlord and that he may enforce his claim in a distress warrant proceeding.[12]

The right to enforce a landlord's claim for rent is not affected by the fact that the tenant has given his note for the indebtedness[13] nor by an option to purchase the leased premises in the hands of the tenant.[14]

The fact that the rent is to be paid in "specifics" or in a fixed portion of the crops cannot be urged against the issuance of a distress warrant, this being a sufficiently plain description of the subject matter to enable the court to make an accurate calculation in judging the adequacy of the landlord's affidavit.[15] This is particularly true of a commercial crop like cotton, where the value of various grades is given daily and far-reaching publicity throughout

8. Beall v. Hill, 42 Ga. 172 (1871).
9. Bricoe v. McElween, 43 Miss. 556 (1871).
10. Williams v. Howard, 3 Munf. 277 (Va., 1812).
11. Ragsdale v. Estis, 8 Rich. 429 (S. C., 1832).
12. Harrison v. Guill, 46 Ga. 427 (1872).
13. Hilley v. Perrin, 3 Ga. App. 143, 59 S. E. 342 (1907).
14. Spooner v. Dykes, 174 Ga. 767, 163 S. E. 889 (1932); Crawford v. Cathey, 143 Ga. 403, 85 S. E. 127 (1915).
15. Tucker v. Cox, 65 Ga. 700 (1880); Rosenstein v. Forester, 57 Ga. 94 (1876); Toler v. Seabrook, 39 Ga. 14 (1869); Faircloth v. State, 69 Ga. App. 441, 26 S. E. (2d) 118 (1943).

the nation.[16] In one instance there was no mention of the specific share the tenant had contracted to pay as rent. This omission is not necessarily fatal to a distress warrant sued out for the purpose of collecting the rent, since in some localities there is a custom that all land shall be rented for particular portions of various crops, such as one-third of the corn and one-fourth of the cotton.[17] Hence the term "third and fourth renter."

It has been said that when the rent is already due, it is unnecessary to state in the affidavit the particular premises on which the crops were grown. However, where the rent is not due and there is an attempt to remove the crops from the premises, then there is a reason to designate the land in a more definite manner.[18]

Usually it is necessary for the proof to follow the pleading to a very marked degree. However, the courts are not too strict about this. Thus there was no fatal variance where the affidavit upon which a distress warrant was based was to the effect that the defendant owed a sum certain as rent, but the proof showed that he had contracted to pay as rent a certain number of bales of cotton, which were valued at that sum.[19]

It is settled law that the landlord may not distrain his tenant's goods when the rent is not due unless he can show that a removal is contemplated.[20] A mere belief that the removal is imminent is not sufficient, and facts on which a reasonable conclusion may be based must be alleged and proved. Without such evidence a distress is wrongful.[21]

The Kentucky court has decided that no personal property other than that belonging to the tenant or subtenant is subject to a distress warrant. Hence a landlord was not permitted to claim the property of his tenant's wife, which had been mortgaged before it had been brought on the premises, the goods being hers under the Married Woman's Separate Property Act.[22] Since the act of 1811 property belonging to other persons has not been subject to distraint even if found on the leased premises.[23] This appears to be the modern

16. Brooks v. Cunningham, 49 Miss. 108 (1873).
17. Scruggs v. Gibson, 40 Ga. 511 (1869).
18. Scruggs v. Gibson, 40 Ga. 511 (1869).
19. Renew v. Redding, 56 Ga. 311 (1876).
20. Little v. Lary, 12 Ga. App. 754, 78 S. E. 470 (1913).
21. Briscoe v. McElween, 43 Miss. 556 (1871).
22. Bank of Hopkinsville v. Trimble, 229 Ky. 280, 17 S. W. (2d) 223 (1929).
23. Mitchell v. Franklin, 26 Ky. 477 (1830).

rule in South Carolina[24] and undoubtedly is in force in the other states as well.

According to the English common law, livestock which had slept on the leased premises, *levant et couchant*, were subject to distraint, even though they were not the property of the tenant. In an early case the South Carolina court refused to apply this doctrine, saying that it did not conform to the agricultural usages of this country. The court decided, however, that cattle which had been put upon the premises with the consent of the owner were liable to distraint, and that it did not matter that the landlord was informed that they did not belong to the tenant.[25] But even this limited view would no doubt be out of date at present, for such an interpretation of the right of distress is inconsistent with modern jurisprudence.

When the common-law rule permitting the property of third persons to be distrained for rent if the goods were physically present on the premises was abrogated by statute in Mississippi, the act provided that the only way in which the true owner could claim his property was by an action of replevin prosecuted before the sale of the goods under the distress warrant.[26] In a case arising under this act certain mules and other property belonging to a third person were taken in a distress warrant proceeding prosecuted by a Mississippi landlord against his tenant. The third person was a resident of Tennessee and started an action of trover in that State for the conversion of the property, naming as a defendant the surety on a bond given by the landlord at the request of the sheriff, who had been unwilling to proceed with the sale unless some security was given, as he knew there was an unsatisfied claim. The Tennessee court held that the Mississippi statute was operative only upon the remedy authorized by the laws of the latter State and that the right of redress was not extinguished. Therefore the third person was permitted to recover in an action of trover for the conversion.[27] That trover is a proper remedy in a situation of this sort is affirmed in a Kentucky decision.[28]

All property of the tenant or subtenant located on the leased premises is distrainable to satisfy the landlord's general lien for rent, as distinguished from the special lien on the crops. At least

24. Fidelity T. & M. Co. v. Davis, 158 S. C. 400, 155 S. E. 622 (1930).
25. Reeves v. McKenzie, 1 Bailey 497 (S. C., 1830).
26. See Punchard v. Rundell, 2 Miss. 508 (1837).
27. Hunt v. Walker, 59 Tenn. 551 (1873).
28. Hall v. Amos, 21 Ky. 89 (1827).

this appears to be the law in Florida,[29] Georgia,[30] and Virginia.[31] South Carolina is in the same category, except that the statute makes no specific mention of the property of the subtenant.[32] In Mississippi it seems that the distress is directed to be levied upon the agricultural products, and, if they prove insufficient to satisfy the debt, then on the other property of the tenant.[33]

As a general rule the property must have been on the leased premises in order to be legally subject to distraint.[34] However, under modern statutes the landlord can follow the crops when they have been removed without his consent. Nevertheless, this would be true to the fullest extent only in those jurisdictions where a bona fide purchase fails to cut off the landlord's lien. Where the opposite view is followed, as in Georgia[35] and Kentucky,[36] the right of distress is cut off by a bona fide purchase.

A novel South Carolina statutory provision[37] authorizes the landlord to pay off a purchase-money debt on chattels which have not been completely paid for by the tenant and to subject the chattels to the claim for rent in distress proceedings.

If the tenant's property is already in the hands of the sheriff, the landlord's distress warrant cannot be levied upon it. At least this was true where a South Carolina landlord had seized the property for the rent and the tenant had instituted claim and delivery proceedings. The officers took custody after the seizure and would return the property to the tenant only after he had paid the whole amount of the rent.[38] The distress warrant may be placed in the hands of the officers and may be considered along with other claims against the tenant in the process of marshaling his assets.[39] In one instance a tenant's personal property had been seized under execu-

29. Fla. Stat. Ann. (1941) §83.08.

30. Ga. Code (1933) §61-203.

31. Va. Code Ann. (Michie, 1936) §5523.

32. S. C. Acts 1946, No. 873 §§31-32. This act, §33, exempts personal clothing, food within the dwelling, bedsteads and bedding, and cooking utensils.

33. Miss. Code Ann. (1942) §913.

34. Price v. Hughes, 69 Ga. 739 (1882); Taliaferro v. Pry, 41 Ga. 622 (1871); Bradley v. Piggot, 1 Miss. 348 (1829).

35. Atchison v. Taliaferro County, 65 Ga. App. 177, 15 S. E. (2d) 534 (1941).

36. Mitchell v. Franklin, 26 Ky. 477 (1830).

37. S. C. Acts 1946, No. 873, §49.

38. Williams v. Wolfe, 130 S. C. 227, 126 S. E. 41 (1925).

39. Mulherin v. Porter, 1 Ga. App. 153, 58 S. E. 60 (1907).

tions in the hands of a constable. Later the landlord had notified the constable that the rent for the current year had not been paid and claimed the proceeds of a sale of the property. Testimony was introduced to the effect that the landlord had lost his right to enforce the lien on the crops because he had been lulled into a false sense of security by assurances that the lien would be first discharged. The court declared that he was remitted to his right of distress and entitled to a judgment for the proceeds, amounting to a sum smaller than the claim for rent.[40]

An agreement by a Mississippi tenant to pay his landlord a past indebtedness, as rent, in addition to the regular rent agreed upon, could not be construed as converting the past-due debt into rent, and therefore a distress warrant would not lie for the additional sum.[41]

Where the rent is to be paid for in services to the landlord and no definite value has been put upon such services in the pleading, a distress warrant will not lie. For such a claim to form the basis for a distress warrant the value of the stipulated services must be stated with a certain degree of accuracy.[42] Often these services consist of repairs to the buildings on the leased premises and the farming equipment. It is probable that no modern court would deny relief to the landlord in instances where the value of these repairs was capable of reasonably definite calculation and ascertainment. But a distress warrant will not be enforceable unless it can be shown that the repairs or other services were a portion of the rental price agreed upon.[43] The same is true with respect to livestock, machinery, and tools supplied by the landlord, for to constitute "rent" such property must have been hired and not purchased.[44]

Suppose a distraining landlord has failed to comply with certain covenants of the leasing agreement, and at the trial the tenant wishes to set off damages which have occurred because of this dereliction. In an early case the Georgia court held that a set-off of this kind would not be permitted.[45] In later cases, however, a set-off was allowed where the claim was sufficiently connected with the lease

---

40. Sullivan v. Ellison, 20 S. C. 481 (1883).
41. Paxton v. Kennedy, 70 Miss. 865, 12 So. 546 (1893).
42. Briscoe v. McElween, 43 Miss. 556 (1871).
43. Wilkins v. Taliaferro, 52 Ga. 208 (1873).
44. Sapp v. Elkins, 125 Ga. 459, 54 S. E. 98 (1906); Cranston v. Rogers, 83 Ga. 750, 10 S. E. 364 (1889); Toler v. Seabrook, 39 Ga. 14 (1869).
45. McMahan v. Tyson, 23 Ga. 43 (1857).

contract,[46] but not where the item was entirely independent of and separate from the agreement.[47] Thus the usual rules of law with respect to set-off and counterclaim seem to be applicable here.

In an early case from South Carolina a landlord sued out a distress warrant and then died before a levy was made. The court declared that a distress warrant was merely a power of attorney which expired along with the landlord, and that therefore the landlord's personal representative had no authority to distrain for rent which had accrued before his death.[48] With respect to rent accruing before the death of the landlord, it was said that an English statute[49] empowering executors and administrators to distrain had never been adopted in South Carolina. In a case decided in 1923[50] this doctrine was reaffirmed in a situation where the warrant was issued after the death of the landlord. Here the court made it plain that in the absence of express authority conferred by will, the devisee and not the personal representative was the proper person to distrain for rent which had accrued either before or after the devisor's death. The devisee and the executrix in this particular instance were one and the same person, and it was unsuccessfully argued that the right of distress could be considered as having been transferred by herself as executrix to herself as the beneficiary under the will. It was said, however, that this would put her in no better position, since the mere assignment of unpaid rent could not be said to carry with it the right to a distress warrant. A much better rule is that contained in the Kentucky[51] and Mississippi[52] statutes, where the personal representative of a deceased landlord is given full rights with respect to matters of this nature.

According to the law in Georgia, the lien of a distress warrant, upon property other than the crops raised on the leased premises, attaches only from the date of the levy and therefore differs from the lien of a common-law judgment, which binds the tenant's property from the time it is rendered.[53] Therefore it may be said that it

46. Johnston v. Patterson, 86 Ga. 725, 13 S. E. 17 (1891); 91 Ga. 531, 18 S. E. 350 (1893).
47. Little v. Lary, 12 Ga. App. 754, 78 S. E. 470 (1913).
48. Bagwell v. Jamison, Cheves 249 (S. C., 1840).
49. 32 Henry VIII, c. 37.
50. Staton v. Guillebeaux, 123 S. C. 363, 116 S. E. 443 (1923).
51. Ky. Rev. Stat. (1946) §383.010.
52. Miss. Code Ann. (1942) §§902-903.
53. Wimberly v. Ocmulgee Guano Co., 21 Ga. App. 270, 94 S. E. 288 (1917).

is incumbent upon a Georgia landlord to see that his distress warrant is promptly levied upon the tenant's general property, or he may lose his claim to another who has acted with greater dispatch in obtaining and enforcing his judgment. Under an early Florida statute[54] a lessor had no lien for rent until a distress warrant was issued according to stipulations contained in the act.[55] The present Florida statute[56] provides that the landlord's lien on agricultural products raised on the leased premises is superior to all other liens, though they may be of earlier date. The act states that the lien on other property of the tenant or subtenant which is kept upon the premises is superior to any lien acquired subsequent to the time when the property was brought on the land. Hence it can be said without doubt that the above decision is not the law of Florida today.

Other early Florida statutes[57] authorized a special proceeding in which a distress warrant was employed to enforce the landlord's claims for both rent and advances. In a case arising under these acts it was said that the landlord's liens for rent and advances might be enforced by a single distress warrant, the claim for rent being a lien on both the crops and the other property of the tenant kept on the premises, while the claim for advances must be satisfied out of the crops alone.[58] It would seem that this may still be the law under a reasonable interpretation of the present Florida statute.[59] Such an interpretation has been placed upon the Alabama act authorizing the use of the writ of attachment in enforcing liens,[60] a remedy which will be discussed at greater length elsewhere.

In Georgia it was held that a distress warrant for the rent might be levied on any of the tenant's property, and that the filing of a counter-affidavit by the tenant was an admission that the property levied upon belonged to him and was thus subject to the warrant.[61] In another case, on the trial of the issue the plaintiff testified to a positive agreement with respect to the amount of the rental. The court held that the trial judge had acted correctly in refusing to

54. Fla. Laws 1865-66, c. 1498.
55. Patterson v. Taylor, 15 Fla. 336 (1875).
56. Fla. Stat. Ann. (1941) §83.08.
57. Fla. Laws 1879, c. 3131; Fla. Laws 1881, c. 3247.
58. Blanchard v. Raines' Exec'rs, 20 Fla. 467 (1884).
59. Fla. Stat. Ann. (1941) §§82.15-82.16.
60. Ala. Code Ann. (Michie, 1928) §8804; Ragsdale v. Kinney, 119 Ala. 454, 24 So. 443 (1898); Ballard v. Stephens, 92 Ala. 616, 8 So. 416 (1890).
61. Price v. Thompson, 4 Ga. App. 46, 60 S. E. 800 (1908).

admit the plaintiff's testimony concerning the reasonable rental value of the premises, since the agreement made such evidence unnecessary.[62]

It was formerly held that in seeking to enforce a special lien for rent on the tenant's crop a Georgia landlord must allege a prior demand and a refusal to pay the indebtedness. The court stated, however, that such an averment was unnecessary where the landlord was attempting to enforce a general lien for rent on the tenant's property as a whole or on some particlular chattel.[63] Soon after this decision was rendered, the statute was altered in such a manner that it was no longer necessary to allege a demand and refusal, even where the lien was a special one.[64]

According to the Florida statute,[65] the distress warrant is used to enforce the lien for advances as well as the lien for rent, and the same appears to be true of the statutes authorizing the alternative remedies of distress and attachment for rent and/or advances in Kentucky,[66] Mississippi,[67] and Virginia,[68] and the statutes denominating attachment as the proper remedy for claims of both kinds in Alabama,[69] Arkansas,[70] and Tennessee.[71] The procedure in Georgia and South Carolina is much alike on this point, both states authorizing distress as the proper remedy where rent is involved,[72] while a claim for advances is enforced by foreclosure proceedings.[73] Neither Louisiana nor North Carolina use attachment or distress as a method of enforcing the landlord's lien, both states employing other forms of action.

It is clear that a landlord should not be allowed to distrain for

62. Bohannon v. Poage, 24 Ga. App. 108, 100 S. E. 27 (1919).
63. McDougal v. Sanders, 75 Ga. 140 (1885).
64. Ga. Acts 1887, p. 34; Almand v. Scott, 83 Ga. 402, 11 S. E. 653 (1889).
65. Fla. Stat. Ann. (1941) §§83.11-83.13.
66. Ky. Rev. Stat. (1946) §§383.010, 383.040, 383.030, 383.110.
67. Miss. Code Ann. (1942) §910 et seq.
68. Va. Code Ann. (Michie, 1936) §§5526, 6454. According to §6454 distress is the proper remedy where the claim for rent is due, and attachment where it is not due.
69. Ala. Code (1940) tit. 31, §20 et seq.
70. Ark. Dig. Stat. (Pope, 1937) §8853 et seq.
71. Tenn. Code Ann. (Williams, 1934) §8022.
72. Ga. Code (1933) §61-205; S. C. Code Ann. (1932).
73. Ga. Code (1933) §§61-202, 67-2401; S. C. Code Ann. (1932) §§8771, 8775. In South Carolina, Sec. 8775 authorizes the use of a warrant to enforce the lien, and, in interpreting these statutes, the court has said that this is the warrant to foreclose the supply lien mentioned in Sec. 8771. Faust v. Bennett, 110 S. C. 435, 96 S. E. 489 (1918).

damages caused by his tenant's breach of contract, for such a claim could not conceivably be called rent. Thus a distress warrant could not be issued lawfully where the landlord was claiming damages caused by the tenant's failure to plant or cultivate the farm which he had leased.[74]

A purchaser of the interest of a landlord in the rented premises succeeds to the rights of his vendor and therefore has the right to distrain his tenant's property to satisfy a claim for rent.[75] This substantiates the rule that no one except a landlord or a person to whom his interest has been assigned is entitled to this remedy.[76]

What is the result when a landlord sues out a distress warrant for a sum greater than the amount due as rent? The Kentucky court has held that the distress is not unlawful and that the excessive claim will not bar the recovery of the sum which is actually due.[77]

The grounds upon which the distress warrant is based must be clearly stated to authorize a recovery. In a case from Georgia a tenant had agreed in writing to "pay rent money out of the first cotton gathered." He made a cotton crop on the rented premises. Under the contract the rent did not become due until the tenant had gathered, or had had a reasonable opportunity to gather, cotton of sufficient value to satisfy the claim for rent, or until it was ascertained that the entire crop, when harvested, was not sufficient to accomplish that purpose. Under these circumstances it was incumbent upon the landlord to introduce evidence that the rent was due and that his claim had matured before the distress warrant was issued. At the trial he introduced testimony tending to prove that the defendant had removed the crops and other personalty from the leased premises. The distress warrant had not been sued out on any such theory, and the court ruled that the verdict in the plaintiff's favor was contrary to the law and the evidence, and ordered a new trial.[78]

May a distress warrant be considered a complaint against the tenant for not complying with the contract in respect to the payment of rent? In Georgia a warrant alone, without counter-affidavit or bond, forms no issue for adjudication, even where the landlord fails to

---

74. Ayers v. Claridy, 149 Ga. 498, 101 S. E. 292 (1919).
75. Burton v. Bearden, 25 Ga. App. 380, 103 S. E. 737 (1920).
76. McCulloch v. Good, Small & Co., 63 Ga. 519 (1879).
77. Whitney v. Carle, 47 Ky. 171 (1848).
78. Holt v. Licette, 111 Ga. 810, 35 S. E. 703 (1900).

object to their absence.[79] After the answer to the distress warrant, the counter-affidavit, has been duly filed, the landlord must prove his claim, for the warrant alone is not considered prima facie evidence.[80] The filing of the counter-affidavit converts the proceeding into an action for rent.[81]

UNLAWFUL DISTRESS

What is the result when an unlawful or exorbitant distress is levied upon the property of the tenant? What redress has the tenant under such circumstances? In some of the Southeastern states there are statutes authorizing the recovery of damages where the seizure is wrongful.[82] Kentucky and Mississippi allow the tenant to recover double damages, and in the former State the damages are trebled where the property is seized while it is in the hands of a person having "legal custody" thereof. In a case arising in Mississippi a landlord made the proper affidavit for a distress warrant, but both the court and the parties treated the proceeding as though it were a writ of attachment. Thereafter the tenant attempted to recover such double damages as would have been authorized had there been an unlawful distress. The court refused to permit an altered view of the proceeding, and no recovery was allowed.[83]

The law normally provides a method by which a tenant whose property has been levied upon under a distress warrant can regain possession of it while waiting for the trial of an issue raised by the pleadings. Usually he may do this by giving a forthcoming or replevy bond, and this security takes the place of the released chattel as the sole resort of the landlord in case the indebtedness is not paid.[84] The failure of a tenant to have his bond meet statutory requirements authorizes the levying officer to retake the property and sell it again, although the distress warrant has been returned and is not in his hands at the moment of recapture.[85] With respect to the chattel which has been so released from the lien of the distress war-

79. Brown v. Brown, 99 Ga. 168, 25 S. E. 95 (1896).
80. Reid v. Brinson, 37 Ga. 63 (1867).
81. Ayers v. Claridy, 149 Ga. 498, 101 S. E. 292 (1919).
82. Ky. Rev. Stat. (1946) §383.020; Miss. Code Ann. (1942) §925; S. C. Code Ann. (1932) §8824; Va. Code Ann. (Michie, 1936) §5783.
83. Hawkins v. James, 69 Miss. 361, 11 So. 654 (1892).
84. Andrews v. Sims, 27 Ga. App. 338, 108 S. E. 258 (1921); Thompson v. Hill, 152 Miss. 390, 119 So. 320 (1928).
85. Grubb v. McCoy, 59 Ky. 486 (1859).

rant, it has been held that the person to whom it is pledged obtains a good title.[86]

It is unnecessary that there be statutory authorization for an action of unlawful distress. Thus in the absence of a statute the Georgia courts gave relief in cases of this kind. In one instance a landlord unlawfully sued out a distress warrant and had it levied upon the crops of his tenant. The issue having been raised by the pleadings, a judgment was rendered in the tenant's favor. Pending these proceedings the levying officer had incurred expenses in gathering, protecting, and marketing the crops. He had hired the tenant to aid him in gathering a portion of the produce. The appellate tribunal ruled that the lower court had erred in taking a portion of the proceeds derived from the sale of the crops to pay any of the expenses so incurred by the officers. It did not matter that the levying officer had hired the tenant to aid him in gathering the crops, paying him for his services as he would any other laborer. The landlord had illegally seized the crops and had thus prevented the tenant from marketing the produce. A judgment was authorized in favor of the tenant for the whole of the costs and expenses created by the unlawful proceedings. If the proceeds derived from the sale of the landlord's share of the crops were insufficient to meet these liabilities, then a personal judgment should be rendered for the balance.[87]

It is always necessary that the landlord be connected with the illegal seizure. In one instance a Georgia tenant alleged that "officers" had wrongfully closed the doors of a tobacco barn, thus causing a great deal of damage to the tenant's crop which had been placed therein. It was ruled that this allegation did not make it plain that the landlord was being held responsible. A further allegation that the property levied upon was in the sole possession of the landlord was said to be a mere conclusion of the pleader in the absence of any showing that the landlord had acquired possession after the levy.[88]

In actions for wrongful distress, the true measure of damages is the value of the property at the time of the seizure, with interest until the date of the trial. But if there exists proof of fraud, malice,

86. Andrews v. Sims, 27 Ga. App. 338, 108 S. E. 258 (1921).
87. Reynolds v. Howard, 113 Ga. 349, 38 S. E. 849 (1901).
88. Pitts v. First Nat. Bank of Valdosta, 44 Ga. App. 828, 163 S. E. 305 (1932).

oppression, or wilful wrong, either in respect to the taking or detention, the measure of damages is left for the jury.[89]

ATTACHMENT

Another remedy in common use with respect to the enforcement
of the landlord's lien is attachment. In Kentucky, Mississippi, and
Virginia, as has been shown,[90] attachment is employed as an alternative remedy to distress. Sometimes, as in Alabama and Arkansas,
attachment seems to be practically the exclusive remedy.

In respect to this remedy courts have held that certain jurisdictional facts, such as the tenancy relationship, the existence of an
unpaid indebtedness, the lien-establishing nature of the claim, the
existence of one of the causes for which the writ will issue, the
demand for payment, where it is required by local law, and other
necessary averments, are essential to a recovery by the landlord.[91]
All such jurisdictional facts must be stated in the attachment affidavit. Following this rule, one court has held that a statement in the
affidavit that the tenant has "removed a part of the crop grown on
the rented premises" will not justify the issuance of a writ of attachment to enforce a lien established under a statute authorizing an
attachment where the removal has been without the consent of the
landlord and before the rent has been paid. It is necessary to include
an allegation of the latter two elements of the offense in the affidavit.[92] The court will consider only the defects pointed out in the
plea or answer.[93] However, it is not every minor defect that will
invalidate an attachment.[94] It is unnecessary that the plaintiff in his
pleading deny a motive of harrassing or vexing the tenant.[95]

It has been decided that in an instance where the landlord is
claiming both rent and advances the attachment affidavit may state
the amount due in lump sum.[96] A plaintiff's right to an attachment

89. Briscoe v. McElween, 43 Miss. 556 (1871).
90. *Supra* Notes 66, 67, 68.
91. Ragsdale v. Kinney, 119 Ala. 454, 24 So. 443 (1898); Ballard v. Stephens,
92 Ala. 616, 8 So. 416 (1890); Knowles v. Steed, 79 Ala. 427 (1885); Gunter v.
DuBose, 77 Ala. 326 (1884); Bell v. Allen, 76 Ala. 450 (1884); Fitzsimmons v.
Howard, 69 Ala. 590 (1881); Hawkins v. Gill, 6 Ala. 620 (1844); Bishop v.
McQuerry, 76 Ky. 417 (1877); McRae v. Browning, 119 Miss. 427, 81 So. 123
(1919); Dougherty v. Kellum, 71 Tenn. 643 (1879).
92. Baxley v. Segrist, 85 Ala. 183, 4 So. 865 (1888).
93. Bell v. Allen, 76 Ala. 450 (1884).
94. Ellis v. Martin, 60 Ala. 394 (1877).
95. Hawkins v. Gill, 6 Ala. 620 (1844).
96. Ragsdale v. Kinney, 119 Ala. 454, 24 So. 443 (1898).

is not impaired because he has included in his affidavit a claim for which he has no lien.[97] Furthermore, where an affidavit is sufficient in respect to rent, but insufficient in respect to advances, averments with respect to the latter shall be treated as surplusage, and the attachment for the rent sustained.[98]

Where an attachment is sued out for a cause of action which is not authorized by statute, the validity of the attachment cannot be questioned by either a plea in abatement or a motion to quash. The proper method of reaching such an irregularity is an application for a rule to make the plaintiff show cause against the dissolution of the writ and its levy, such an application being required to precede a plea to the merits of the controversy.[99]

Most courts today allow a plaintiff to amend his complaint provided the cause of action is not radically changed thereby. This liberalized procedure made its appearance in some states at an earlier date than in others. Thus the Arkansas court allowed amendments to an attachment for rent as early as 1878.[100] Two years earlier the Alabama court had refused to permit amendments with respect to certain jurisdictional facts, the allegation of the tenancy relationship and the matters concerning the nature of the indebtedness.[101] Under more modern procedure in this State, however, it was said to be error to refuse to permit an amendment to a writ of attachment issued for the purpose of being levied against the general estate of a tenant. The correct procedure was an attachment against the crop alone.[102] Moreover, the Arkansas court has held that pleadings and the affidavit in an attachment proceeding to enforce a landlord's lien may be amended at any time before the trial in order to include the name of the tenant.[103]

In Alabama an attachment whose mandate runs merely against the crops of a tenant in chief authorizes the levy of the writ, not only upon the tenant's crops, but also upon crops grown by a subtenant.[104] This would no doubt be true in other jurisdictions as well.

In Kentucky it is said that a landlord suing out a specific attach-

97. Kurtz v. Dunn, 36 Ark. 648 (1880).
98. Ballard v. Stephens, 92 Ala. 616, 8 So. 416 (1890).
99. Drakford v. Turk, 75 Ala. 339 (1883).
100. Rogers v. Cooper, 33 Ark. 406 (1878).
101. Staggers v. Washington, 56 Ala. 225 (1876).
102. Wright v. DuBose, 17 Ala. App. 207, 84 So. 432 (1919).
103. Sellers v. Bowie, 183 Ark. 726, 38 S. W. (2d) 560 (1931).
104. Agee v. Mayer Bros., 71 Ala. 88 (1881).

ment for rent under the lien laws is not to be held to the same strictness of proof as persons who are proceeding under the general attachment law to secure ordinary debts. In one instance where the court adhered to this view a tenant promised to give a mortgage on a crop of tobacco raised on the leased premises as soon as it could be housed. For a week after the housing had been completed the landlord made diligent efforts to ascertain the whereabouts of the tenant, that the mortgage might be executed as agreed. Failing to find him, the landlord applied for a writ of attachment. The tenant was shown to have left the State temporarily, and the tobacco was stored in an open barn with a bad roof, which was likely to be blown down in a storm. Here it was held that the landlord had good reason to believe that he might lose his rent unless an attachment issued.[105] In another case where the proceeding was under the general law of attachment the tenant had absconded from the county, leaving no word concerning the date of his return. It was shown that he had planned to dispose of his property with fraudulent intent to hinder and delay the landlord in the collection of the lawful indebtedness. The court declared that a mere showing that the defendant had departed from the State was insufficient to justify an attachment on the grounds provided by statute. It must further appear that the property was concealed or removed from the State with the intention of defrauding creditors. The lower court had properly discharged the attachment because there had been a total lack of proof to sustain the grounds set up in the application for the writ.[106]

The specific attachment authorized by such laws as those of Kentucky and Arkansas provides a remedy which is wholly distinct from the general attachment provided by the general law of the jurisdiction. In Kentucky the remedies are said to be cumulative,[107] and it is probable that the tenant could have either remedy, since the court remarked that to deny general attachment to a particular class of creditors would be discriminatory. An Arkansas landlord filed the affidavit for specific attachment, but by mistake filed the general attachment bond. The clerk issued a general writ of attachment, which was levied upon the tenant's general property. Here the court held that the writ should be quashed, since the plaintiff had failed

105. Ward v. Grigsby, 21 Ky. Law Rep. 1406, 55 S. W. 436 (1900).
106. Bush v. Niblack, 241 Ky. 113, 43 S. W. (2d) 505 (1931).
107. Browning v. Crawford, 145 Ky. 279, 140 S. W. 530 (1911).

to do all the things required for the enforcement of either remedy.[108] In a later case, however, it was said that a mistake of this kind could not be raised after the tenant had executed a bond to discharge the attachment, no levy having been made on the tenant's general property.[109] Furthermore, if a removal of the crop is threatened, a landlord may have a specific attachment against the crop before the rent is due; but if he proceeds by general attachment before that time, then no recovery will be allowed.[110]

Two early Alabama cases illustrate the effect which the death of the tenant had upon the landlord's right to pursue the remedy of attachment. In one instance it was said that if the tenant died after the levy of the attachment, and his estate was declared insolvent, the lien of the attachment could not be considered dissolved or destroyed.[111] In the other case the court declared that the death of the tenant had made it impossible for the landlord to pursue the remedy by attachment, and that therefore no remedy at law existed. Hence the court ruled that a court of equity might intervene and enforce the claim.[112] It may be that under modern statutes the landlord would have a legal remedy here. If so, it is clear that a court of equity would have no jurisdiction in such a case. The point would depend upon the general law of the particular state with respect to the administration of estates.

An attachment, like distress in a state where that remedy is a proper one, may be issued in any instance where the known facts give a basis for a true calculation of the sum due to the landlord as rent or for any other claim for which he has this type of lien.[113] In Kentucky, as has been shown, attachment and distress are alternative remedies in enforcing landlords' liens. An old and defunct Kentucky statute[114] provided that distress could only be had where the rent was reserved in *money*. Another statute[115] provided that an attachment would issue where the tenant removed his effects so that "no distress for the said rent can be made." This was interpreted to mean that an attachment would issue only where circumstances were

108. Edwards v. Cooper, 28 Ark. 466 (1873).
109. Sellers v. Bowie, 183 Ark. 726, 38 S. W. (2d) 560 (1931).
110. Tignor v. Bradley, 32 Ark. 781 (1878).
111. McDonald's Adm'r v. Morrison, 50 Ala. 30 (1873).
112. Abraham v. Hall, 59 Ala. 386 (1877).
113. Cole v. Tipton, 196 Ark. 1177, 114 S. W. (2d) 464 (1938).
114. Stat. Law, 1356.
115. Stat. Law, 1353.

such that a distress warrant proceeding might have been maintained. Therefore, where the rent had been reserved in *corn*, the remedy by attachment was considered unavailable.[116]

A Tennessee landowner rented a farm for one-third of the crop. Owing to poor cultivation the tenant raised only three bales of cotton. The landlord attempted to attach more than the one-third of the cotton due him according to the contract. He claimed the extra amount on the theory that the tenant had violated the implied covenant of good husbandry which is a part of every such lease. It was held that damages for the breach of such a covenant could not be recovered by attachment for rent, the landlord being entitled to only one-third of the crop, be it much or little.[117]

An Arkansas share tenant abandoned rented premises in debt to his landlord and left a partially-raised crop. After the landlord had taken over the crop and finished it, he attached the tenant's property, claiming that the tenant owed him an additional sum. The court declared that, while it was proper to measure the amount of the indebtedness by the outcome of the crop as handled by the landlord, it was error to make the validity of the attachment dependent thereon, since that should depend upon the market value of the crop at the time when the tenant vacated the premises. It might have been that the market value of the crop at that time was not the equivalent of the debt and that the landlord, by good husbandry, had increased its value to such an extent that the proceeds would pay the indebtedness, in which event the attachment should be sustained. On the other hand, the crop might have been at the time of the abandonment of a market value sufficient to have paid the landlord's claim in full. If, on account of neglect or poor husbandry, he would not receive enough money from a sale of the crop to pay the debt, then the attachment ought not to be sustained. There was another issue in this case with respect to the payment of the indebtedness, and the lower court confounded the two issues and made the fate of the attachment hang upon the outcome of the landlord's efforts with the abandoned crop. It was proper to determine the issue of indebtedness in this manner, but the issue with respect to the attachment should not have been so determined.[118]

116. Poer v. Peebles, 40 Ky. 1 (1840).
117. Patterson v. Hawkins, 71 Tenn. 483 (1879).
118. Southern Orchard Planting Co. v. Turner, 87 Ark. 382, 112 S. W. 956 (1908).

Where the crop removed by a third person is still available, it would seem that specific attachment would be the proper remedy.[119] However, where the property has been disposed of and cannot be reached, other remedies, such as an action on the case or a bill in equity, must be employed.[120] In Mississippi a landlord brought attachment proceedings for rent against a tenant's goods and chattels, situated off the leased premises, within thirty days of their removal, as provided by statute.[121] It was held to be unnecessary that the removal from the premises be stated in the attachment affidavit.[122]

With respect to the nature of the writ, it has been said that the lien on the crop of the tenant is created by statute and not by the issuance or levy of the attachment, which is only the remedy provided by law for the enforcement of the lien.[123]

It is evident that writs of attachment have been authorized because of the peculiar relationship of the parties and because of the difficulties of landlords in the collection of their rent. In summing up, it may be said that a judge's instruction to the jury which denounced as harsh this right to the writ of attachment to enforce the lien, a remedy specifically passed upon by the legislature, is inappropriate and harmful to the cause of the landowner.[124]

UNLAWFUL ATTACHMENT

What is the result where the attachment is wrongfully or prematurely sued out? On the whole the procedure here is very much like that which is employed where there has been a wrongful distress. In common practice the landlord is required to file an attachment bond before he is permitted to take possession of the property. This bond is necessary in order to insure the tenant against loss. Where the tenant wishes to keep the property in his possession pending the outcome of the proceeding he is generally permitted to give a replevy or forthcoming bond, and may hold the

119. Atkinson v. James, 96 Ala. 214, 10 So. 846 (1892); Dulany v. Dickinson, 12 Ala. 601 (1847); Reavis v. Barnes, 36 Ark. 575 (1880).

120. City Nat. Bank v. Nelson, 218 Ala. 90, 117 So. 681 (1928); Thompson v. Powell, 77 Ala. 391 (1884); Reavis v. Barnes, 36 Ark. 575 (1880). Cf. Erhman v. Oates, 101 Ala. 604, 14 So. 561 (1893); Hussey v. Peebles, 53 Ala. 432 (1875); Blum v. Jones, 51 Ala. 149 (1874) for peculiarities of Alabama procedure.

121. See Chap. 14, Note 234.

122. Henry v. Davis, 60 Miss. 212 (1882).

123. Ellis v. Martin, 60 Ala. 394 (1877).

124. Randolph v. McCain, 34 Ark. 696 (1879).

property until the court has come to a decision upon the issues raised before it.

In one instance where a tenant sued on an attachment bond, it was decided that he must aver and prove the falsity of the facts stated in the attachment affidavit as the basis for the landlord's claim. The burden of proof would be upon the tenant, though the averment was negative in form and involved proof of a negative.[125]

Sometimes a third person will put in a claim for the property demanded by the landlord. Here the claimant has the burden of proving ownership. Such evidence shifts the burden to the landlord to prove that the goods, when the claimant acquired his interest in them, were and continued to be subject to the landlord's lien for rent.[126]

An attachment need not be both wrongful and vexatious or malicious to give rise to an action on the bond. But it has been held that if the tenant actually alleges that the attachment is both wrongful and malicious, then he must prove both allegations.[127] This seems to be a rather illogical conclusion, since proof of a nonessential allegation is required. If the tenant was seeking punitive damages, then the issue would become important, but no mention is made of any such attempt.

In Kentucky[128] and Mississippi,[129] just as in the case of a distress warrant, the tenant may recover double the value of the property illegally seized in attachment proceedings. In Mississippi, however, a recovery can be had only where the property seized has been sold under the attachment.[130]

In an early case from Arkansas[131] the recovery of attorney's fees in an action for unlawful attachment was denied, but in later controversies in Alabama[132] and Mississippi[133] such a claim for legal services was allowed. The latter view is clearly the better one.

By statute in Alabama the twenty-fifth day of December was set as the day, in the absence of contrary agreement, on which rent and

125. Harrison v. Emens, 235 Ala. 319, 179 So. 219 (1938).
126. Dunn v. Hart, 120 Miss. 132, 81 So. 795 (1919).
127. Harrison v. Emens, 235 Ala. 319, 179 So. 219 (1938).
128. Ky. Rev. Stat. (1946) §383.020.
129. Miss. Code Ann. (1942) §925.
130. Thornton v. Gardner, 99 So. 131 (Miss., 1924).
131. Patton v. Garrett, 37 Ark. 605 (1881).
132. Penny v. Burns, 230 Ala. 124, 159 So. 835 (1935).
133. Wigginton v. Moore, 147 Miss. 169, 113 So. 326 (1927).

advances became due.[134] In one case arising under this statute an attachment was levied upon the tenant's property nearly two months before that date. The court held that this attachment was premature. It declared also that an affidavit is fatally defective which does not show by positive averment, or by reasonable intendment, that a refusal to pay occurred after the landlord's claim for rent and/or advances became due.[135] The date on which such claims become due has been changed and has now been set at November 1.[136]

A rather peculiar situation was presented in a case from Alabama. Here a tenant sued in equity and alleged that he was entitled to a farm under a lease for five years, implying that he had agreed to cultivate the land during the term. The action was brought to restrain the landlord from further prosecution of an attachment proceeding, which the tenant claimed had interfered with his possession and cultivation of the land. Objection was made that the tenant had not stated facts sufficient to warrant interference by a court of equity. The court disagreed and declared that a cause of action had been stated.[137]

FORECLOSURE OF LIEN

The same general principles respecting allegations and form may be seen in a study of foreclosure and the other miscellaneous remedies given by the statutes, presently effective or ineffective, of the several Southeastern states. The foreclosure procedure is used to a great extent in Georgia to enforce the landlord's claims for advances. Foreclosure may be defined as a method by which property upon which there is a mortgage or other lien may be sold and the proceeds applied to the indebtedness for which the property is security.

In an action to foreclose a Georgia landlord's lien for supplies, misjoinder of parties defendant was found where one of the persons against whom the proceeding was brought was not a tenant but had merely joined in the execution of the instrument manifesting an indebtedness which had been incurred by both the tenant and himself.[138] Thus an averment of the landlord-tenant relationship is a

134. Ala. Code (1876) §3468.
135. Dozier v. Robinson, 82 Ala. 408, 3 So. 45 (1887).
136. Ala. Code (1940) tit. 31, §16.
137. Watkins v. Smith, 211 Ala. 151, 99 So. 907 (1924).
138. Saterfield v. Moore, 110 Ga. 514, 35 S. E. 638 (1900).

necessary allegation in this type of action, just as it is in distress and attachment.

The necessary allegations in such an action were outlined in an early decision. Here it was said that the foreclosure affidavit stated all the necessary facts. The affidavit set out fully the tenancy relationship and the facts surrounding the advancing of supplies for a given year and averred the amount claimed, the demand on the cultivator, and his refusal to pay after the debt became due. The court stated that it was not necessary to set out or describe the property on which the lien was claimed, since execution must be issued against the property subject to the lien, and the law specified that the crops for the current year could be subjected.[139] Where any of these allegations are not correctly stated, the affidavit filed with the foreclosure proceedings may be amended.[140]

In a rather unusual case a creditor obtained an ordinary judgment against a tenant and caused the process issued thereon to be levied upon certain cotton which was subject to the landlord's lien for rent. The landlord then foreclosed his lien and caused it to be levied on the same cotton. The tenant replevied the crop, giving a forthcoming bond with the landlord as surety. On the appointed day the cotton was not produced, and an action was brought by an officer on behalf of the judgment creditor. Judgment was secured against the tenant as principal and the landlord as surety. The landlord paid the amount due on this judgment to the sheriff and made a claim to the fund on the strength of the foreclosed lien for rent. The court held that the judgment creditor was entitled to the fund, since that was the way the controversy would end in any case. If the money should be awarded to the landlord, then that would leave the creditor's judgment against him as surety unpaid, and the creditor could immediately proceed to raise the sum due thereon out of his property.[141] Here the judgment creditor is preferred because of the peculiar Georgia rule.[141-a]

WARRANTS OF SEIZURE

Another form of action for the enforcement of liens is the writ or warrant of seizure, a procedure which is much like attachment.

139. Ware v. Blaylock, 72 Ga. 804 (1884).
140. Johnson v. Lock, 36 Ga. App. 620, 137 S. E. 910 (1927); Sharp v. Morgan, 9 Ga. App. 487, 71 S. E. 766 (1911).
141. Linder v. Sanders, 77 Ga. 57 (1886).
141-a. See Chap. 15, Notes 25 and 26.

Such a proceeding was authorized by the Mississippi Agricultural Lien Law of 1876.[142] In a case arising under this statute it was decided that a writ which commanded the seizure of agricultural products, but neither named a defendant nor contained a personal summons, was not void, and that an officer who had seized property under it might hold it.[143] In South Carolina an act of 1885 [144] authorized a warrant of seizure to enforce a landlord's lien. This act provided that the affidavit to be filed in this proceeding should conform as nearly as possible to the practice regulating the issuance of warrants of attachment. In a case arising under this statute, it was said that a landlord who was seeking to enforce a lien for rent must prove by affidavit, to the satisfaction of the clerk of court, that the tenant was about to dispose of the crops or was proposing to defeat the lien in some other manner. The court declared that an affidavit simply stating that the tenant was "about to sell and dispose of said crop, subject to said lien, and to defeat the same," without the averment of any fact which would tend to show that the act alleged was about to be done, was insufficient, since the affidavit must have necessarily rested upon belief alone.[145]

A South Carolina officer took possession of a tenant's property under a warrant of seizure to enforce a lien for rent. The person from whom the property was taken was rightfully in possession, and the property was not subject to the lien. A statute authorized such a person whose property had been thus unlawfully seized, on entering into a required bond, to institute claim and delivery proceedings to recover immediate possession of the property so seized. It was held that the third person in possession of the property when seized might have the remedy of claim and delivery, and he was permitted to recover.[146]

CLAIM AND DELIVERY

In North Carolina the action of claim and delivery is the proper remedy for the enforcement of the landlord's lien and for the enforcement of the tenant's rights in an action for the conversion of the crops by the landlord.[147] A statute authorizes a proceeding

142. Miss. Acts 1876, p. 113.
143. Dogan v. Bloodworth, 56 Miss. 419 (1879).
144. 19 S. C. Stat. 429.
145. Sharp v. Palmer, 31 S. C. 444, 10 S. E. 98 (1889).
146. Southern Ry. Co. v. Sarratt, 58 S. C. 98, 36 S. E. 504 (1900).
147. N. C. Gen. Stat. (1943) §§42-15, 42-16; Powell v. Perry, 127 N. C. 22, 37 S. E. 71 (1900); Field v. Wheeler, 120 N. C. 264, 26 S. E. 812 (1897).

to settle disputes between the parties.[148] Under the provisions of this statute it has been held that a suit in equity may be brought by the landlord for the recovery of the crop and the appointment of a receiver, and this in spite of the fact that the plaintiff has a legal remedy in the action of claim and delivery.[149] According to the North Carolina law, the right to the possession of the crop is vested in the landlord,[150] and hence the following difficulty which arose in South Carolina may never come before the courts of her sister state to the North.

The usual holding is that a landlord must have title or right to possession in order to maintain a possessory action like detinue or replevin, the earlier counterpart of claim and delivery, or even trover, and that a crop lien is not a sufficient interest upon which to base such actions.[151] In 1917, however, a difficulty arose in South Carolina concerning the availability of the remedy of claim and delivery in actions by landlords to enforce crop liens. While the requested relief was denied in the controversy under consideration because it was shown that the indebtedness had been satisfied, the majority of the court made it plain that they considered claim and delivery a proper remedy.[152] However, the court used some confusing language with respect to the form of action. It is plain from the context that the court confused claim and delivery with distress, and the opinion cannot be read without a suspicion that the case was being presented as a distress warrant proceeding. In fact, in one place it was actually said that the plaintiff had chosen to proceed by distress rather than to follow the procedure provided by statute. Of course this was untrue, as it is clearly stated elsewhere that the action was one of claim and delivery, but it is indicative of the confusion in the minds of the judges. The one dissenting judge, the Chief Justice, took the usual view that the landlord must have more than a mere lien to maintain a possessory action like claim and delivery and that he should have followed the statutory procedure which would have given him adequate relief. This would be true even though distress was unavailable for some reason. In the principal case the property had gotten into the hands of a third person.

148. N. C. Gen. Stat. (1943) §43-17.
149. Talbot v. Tyson, 147 N. C. 273, 60 S. E. 1125 (1908).
150. Rouse v. Wooten, 104 N. C. 229, 10 S. E. 190 (1889).
151. See Chap. 14, Notes 18-21.
152. Hamilton v. Blanton, 107 S. C. 142, 92 S. E. 275 (1917). *Cf.* Hamilton v. Stubbs Co., 105 S. C. 157, 89 S. E. 554 (1916).

This point was evidently deemed important in the decision of two other cases[153] in which plaintiffs in claim and delivery were allowed to recover in situations very similar to that in the 1917 decision. Here it is possible that the court wished to draw a distinction between those instances where the crop or other property was still in the hands of the tenant and those where it had been transferred to another person. However, this ignores the main theory of the dissenting judge that a mere landlord's lien is not a sufficient interest upon which to base a possessory action like claim and delivery. When the best legal theory is applied to this problem, it is doubted that the view of the majority, although clearly the law of South Carolina, could be supported.

PROVISIONAL SEIZURE AND SEQUESTRATION

In Louisiana the common remedy which is used to enforce a right of pledge or privilege on the crop or other property of a lessee is provisional seizure.[154] This remedy seems to be the Civil Law equivalent of proceedings like distress and attachment, which are in effect in jurisdictions where the common law is the basis of the jurisprudence. Provisional seizure is justified where the lessee has removed the property from the rented premises,[155] or where the lessor has reason to believe that it will be removed.[156] However, it has been intimated that the lessor must have some basis for his belief and cannot act arbitrarily.[157] In discussing this point the Supreme Court of the State remarked that the law "wisely provides the landlord with drastic remedies for a lessee's failure to pay the rent, and it is as much in the interest of one as of the other. Tenants are more numerous than proprietors. He who has no house of his own to shelter his family, or no land of his own to cultivate, has need to use that of others, and can more easily obtain it and on easier terms if the law assures the landlord the payment of his rent by affording him exceptional facilities for enforcing its payment." A more succinct statement of the paternalistic attitude of Southern conservatives toward the tenant farmer could not be found. This attitude is still prevalent

153. Bookhart v. Langford, 128 S. C. 350, 122 S. E. 866 (1924); Sumter County Duroc Stock Farm v. Dubose, 127 S. C. 551, 121 S. E. 673 (1924).
154. La. Code of Prac. (Dart, 1932) Art. 287.
155. LeBlanc v. Guy, 14 La. App. 162, 128 So. 715 (1930).
156. Nesbitt v. Givens, 2 La. App. 298 (1925); Wilcoxen v. Bowles, 1 La. Ann. 230 (1846).
157. Dillon v. Porier, 34 La. Ann. 1100 (1882).

in the South today and is one of the chief stumbling blocks to progress of a real and permanent nature.

In Louisiana the failure to pay rent alone authorizes the dissolution or termination of the lease contract but does not authorize the
issuance of a writ of provisional seizure. As a prerequisite for the issuance of the writ it must be shown in addition that the lessor believed that the lessee intended to remove the property. Therefore
the writ could not lawfully be issued in an instance where the lessee
had virtually placed the property in the hands of the lessor in such
a manner as to guarantee that the proceeds derived from its sale
would be used in satisfying the claim for rent.[158] Moreover, a writ
has been held to have been properly dissolved where a lessee had offered either to deliver stored ginhouse cotton to the lessor, this cotton being sufficient to satisfy the claim for rent, or to give a draft for
its value.[159] Thus it is seen that an offer to satisfy a claim for rent has
the same effect as making the property available to the lessor. Recently, however, a court held that the refusal to pay rent coupled
with the sale of a cotton crop to a third person justified the conclusion that the lessee was not going to pay the rent, and that under
these circumstances a writ of provisional seizure had been rightfully
issued.[160]

The writ of sequestration, a remedy which is very much like attachment in a common-law state, may be used either alone or along
with provisional seizure whenever a lessee is attempting to remove
or has sold or taken away property covered by a lessor's privilege.[161]
The writ is not enforceable with respect to immovable property, including crops standing in the fields before severance from the
land.[162] It seems, however, that standing crops are subject to provisional seizure.[163]

Legal process of this sort may not be used to prevent a tenant
from doing anything which could be considered as an aid to the
chief purpose of the tenancy contract, namely, the raising of the

158. Nesbitt v. Givens, 2 La. App. 298 (1925).
159. Browne v. Clarke, 35 La. Ann. 290 (1883).
160. Hunter v. Rudisill, 155 So. 29 (La. App., 1934).
161. La. Code Prac. Ann. (Dart, 1932) Art. 275, §8; La. Acts 1912, No. 190;
Dixon v. Watson, 143 So. 683 (La. App., 1932); Dixon v. Alford, 143 So. 679
(La. App., 1932); LeBlanc v. Guy, 14 La. App. 162, 128 So. 715 (1930).
162. La. Code Prac. Ann. (Dart, 1942) Art. 275; La. Civ. Code Ann. (Dart,
1932) Art. 465; Dixon v. Watson, 143 So. 683 (La. App., 1932); Dixon v.
Alford, 143 So. 679 (La. App., 1932).
163. Colligan v. Benoit, 13 La. App. 612, 128 So. 688 (1930).

crops. For instance, the lessor cannot lawfully interfere in this manner with the picking of the cotton or the gathering of the corn.[164] Where, in spite of the illegality of the process, the property is nevertheless provisionally seized, the lessee may recover the value of the property thus unlawfully taken.[165]

In Louisiana, as in states in which the common law is the basis of the jurisprudence, provision is duly made for the lessee to regain possession of the seized property by giving a forthcoming bond with proper sureties.[166] The bondsmen are liable only for articles which are not returned to the officers after a recovery by the lessor, and for these only if they have an actual value.[167] Where only a portion of the goods is turned back to the sheriff, the lessor is entitled to a judgment on the bond for the difference between the amount of the bond and the appraised value of the property returned.[168] This bond is a substitute for, and stands in the place of, the released property, and any subsequent lessor who has acquired a lien or privilege on the property possesses a claim superior to that of the prior lessor.[169] If no such claim exists, the privilege is not lost, and the property may be seized a second time and sold to satisfy the privilege recognized by the judgment in his favor, provided the lessee has not parted with the possession of the property more than fifteen days prior to the last seizure.[170]

USE OF CIVIL ACTION IN ENFORCING LIENS

It is not thought wise to conclude the subject of remedies without at least an allusion to what was said in a Kentucky case decided in 1899. Here the court stated that the authorization of the Kentucky statute[171] for the enforcement of the landlord's lien by distress or attachment is merely cumulative, and that the right of the landlord to enforce the lien by civil action is not taken away.[172]

164. Dixon v. Watson, 143 So. 683 (La. App., 1932).
165. Cox v. Meyers, 4 La. Ann. 144 (1849).
166. La. Code Prac. Ann. (Dart, 1932) Art. 287.
167. Valley v. Causey, 1 La. App. 179 (1924).
168. Honeycutt v. Whitten, 152 La. 1045, 95 So. 216 (1923).
169. Conrad v. Patzelt, 29 La. Ann. 465 (1877).
170. Haralson v. Boyle, 22 La. Ann. 210 (1870).
171. Ky. Rev. Stat. (1946) §383.110.
172. Brown v. Noel, 21 Ky. Law Rep. 648, 52 S. W. 849 (1899).

CONCLUSION

So many different remedies are being used to enforce the landlord's lien that sometimes a great confusion appears, even in the minds of the judges. It might very well be urged that all these different forms be scrapped and that a uniform procedure be adopted in cases of this type. Such a change would certainly be a boon to all concerned and would avoid a great amount of bewilderment with respect to the rights of both landlord and tenant. Thus far, the state legislatures have neglected to make a study with a view to unifying all these types of actions under one head. When this has been done, an educational program should be started to get the results of this research before the people in such a way as to persuade them that it would be to their interest to demand a simplification of the procedure in this respect.

XX

The Rights of the Cropper—Laborers' Liens

WHAT are the rights of the farmer under a cropping agreement as distinguished from those he is entitled to under a lease or
tenancy contract? Under the two arrangements the title to the crops
is in different persons, and this makes a fundamental difference in
the treatment accorded to the respective relationships. A better
understanding of the cropper's status will be obtained by referring
to the cases dealing with the cropping contract as it evolved out of
the confusion created by the aftermath of the Civil War. During
this period the laws enacted were usually inspired by the desire of
the landowners to protect their interests in the lands and crops.
Among the rights given to property owners was the landlord's lien
on crops grown by a tenant. But certain fair-minded legislators
realized that the landlord was not the only person who needed protection. Hence many of the states adopted statutes giving the
laborer, which of course included the cropper, a lien upon the crop
he had worked to produce. A detailed analysis of the law dealing
with the cropper relationship is now in order.

TITLE AND RIGHT TO POSSESSION

Where a tenancy relationship exists and there has been no settlement of the rights of the parties, it is usually held that the title to the
crops and the exclusive right to possession is in the tenant.[1] On the
other hand, where a cropper relationship obtains, the title and right
to possession are in the landlord until a settlement is duly arrived at
by the parties.[2] The cropper will not be vested with the title until

1. Heaton v. Slaten, 25 Ala. App. 81, 141 So. 267 (1932); Bryant v. Pugh,
86 Ga. 525, 12 S. E. 927 (1891); Flynt v. Barrett, 73 Ga. App. 396, 36 S. E. (2d)
868 (1946); De Laigle v. Shuptrine, 28 Ga. App. 380, 110 S. E. 920 (1922).
2. Farrow v. Wooley & Jordan, 138 Ala. 267, 36 So. 384 (1903); Hardeman
v. Arthurs, 144 Ark. 289, 222 S. W. 20 (1920); Hendricks v. Smith, 12 S. W.
781 (Ark., 1889); Fields v. Argo, 103 Ga. 387, 30 S. E. 29 (1898); Folds v.
Harris, 34 Ga. App. 445, 129 S. E. 664 (1925); Cowart v. Dees, 7 Ga. App. 601,
67 S. E. 705 (1910); Holmes v. Payne, 4 La. App. 345 (1926); McNeeley v.
Hart, 32 N. C. 63 (1849); Smith v. Williamston Mills, 136 S. C. 9, 134 S. E. 145
(1926); Lipscomb v. Johnson, 123 S. C. 44, 115 S. E. 753 (1923); Dacus v.

the produce has been actually divided.[3] He is entitled to hold possession of the crop for the satisfaction of his claim against the landlord and for no other purpose.[4] It is unlawful for the cropper, without the landlord's consent, to sell or otherwise dispose of the crop and apply the proceeds to his own use prior to the setting aside of the landlord's agreed portion.[5]

THE LABORER'S LIEN

Since the landlord is given a lien on the crops in a tenancy relationship, consistency would seem to demand that the cropper should be given a laborer's lien on the crop which his labor has been a main factor in producing. To deny such a lien would be a clear indication that the lawmakers were more sympathetic to the landed interests than they were to propertyless farm laborers. Therefore a laborer's or cropper's lien is authorized by statute in most of the Southeastern states.[6] In a case arising before the fusion of the tenancy and cropper relationships in Alabama,[7] a court in that State re-

Williamston Mills, 118 S. C. 245, 110 S. E. 393 (1922); Parrish v. Commonwealth, 81 Va. 1 (1894).

3. Sivley v. Moore, 20 Ala. App. 269, 101 So. 513 (1924); Hammock v. Creekmoore, 48 Ark. 264, 3 S. W. 180 (1887); Welch v. Lindsey, 27 Ga. App. 164, 107 S. E. 891 (1921); Holmes v. Payne, 4 La. App. 345 (1926); Hardwick v. Page, 124 S. C. 111, 117 S. E. 204 (1923); Loveless v. Gilliam, 70 S. C. 391, 50 S. E. 9 (1905); Zimmerman v. Dean, 54 S. C. 90, 31 S. E. 884 (1899).

4. Crow v. Beck, 208 Ala. 444, 94 So. 580 (1922).

5. Williams v. Mitchem, 151 Ga. 227, 106 S. E. 284 (1921); Godwin v. Allman, 25 Ga. App. 74, 102 S. E. 645 (1920).

6. Ala. Code (1940) tit. 33, §18. (See also Ala. Code (1907) §4743; Ark. Dig. Stat. (Pope, 1937) §§8834-44; Fla. Stat. Ann. (1941) §85.04; Ga. Code (1933) §§67-1801-03; La. Civ. Code Ann. (Dart, 1932) Art. 3217; Miss. Code Ann. (1942) §336; S. C. Code Ann. (1932) §§8772-73; Tenn. Code Ann. (Williams, 1934) §§8014-16. Kentucky and Virginia appear to have no statutes specifically giving the cropper a lien upon the produce of the farm. In North Carolina it may be said that there was formerly such an act, references to it being found in N. C. Gen. Stat. (1943) §§44-41, 44-52. See also Whitaker v. Smith, 81 N. C. 340 (1879), where the court denied an overseer a lien of this kind and stated that it did so because the task was not a manual one. It appears that a manual laborer would have been entitled to a lien. In this State, where N. C. Gen. Stat. (1943) §42-15 has fused into one the tenancy and cropper relationships, the cultivator has been given a remedy by claim and delivery. Id. §42-16. In practice this takes the place of the laborer's lien in crop-sharing cases. However, this remedy is not available to ordinary farm laborers who work for wages and not for a share of the crop, and therefore the need for a laborer's lien on crops is not wholly obviated. It might be that the Mechanic's Lien Statute, N. C. Gen. Stat. (1943) §43-50, which gives a lien for labor performed on any property, real or personal, would be construed to fill the gap.

7. See Chap. 2, Note 2.

marked that the cropper or laborer had a lien for the value of his share of the crop, which had the same effect and might be enforced in the same manner as the landlord's lien for rent and/or supplies.[8]

Before a cropper's crop lien can be enforced, it must be shown that he has completed his agreed task,[9] unless he has a legitimate excuse like interference by the minions of the law.[10] Sometimes the completion of the work is prevented or waived by the acts of the landlord and/or a third person. Thus in one instance a landlord, with the aid of a contesting creditor, interfered with his cropper, whose lien was said to be effective even though the agreed task had not been fully performed in accordance with the terms of the contract. The court declared that by his interference the landlord had impliedly waived his right to demand a satisfactory performance. Therefore it was unnecessary for the cropper to show a full compliance with the contract before starting proceedings for the enforcement of his lien.[11]

It has been determined that a cropper is entitled to a lien for work done by his minor children.[12] He may also claim a lien for money spent for the employment of extra labor used at critical periods during the growing season.[13] In one case the testimony was silent about the age of a daughter claimed to be a minor, but the child was present in court as a witness in full view of the judge and jury. From observation the jury might have determined that she was a minor. In so far as the verdict for the cropper was predicated upon the services of a minor child, it could not be said to be without evidence to support it.[14]

PRIORITY OF LIENS

In most of the Southeastern states the lien of the landlord is superior to the claim of the cropper or laborer, whether or not the latter has a tenure status immediately under the landowner.[15] The

8. Hudson v. Wright, 1 Ala. App. 433, 56 So. 258 (1911).

9. Rand v. Walton, 130 Ark. 431, 197 S. W. 852 (1917); Gardner v. Smith, 39 Ga. App. 224, 146 S. E. 648 (1929); Alabama R. R. Co. v. Bass, 29 Ga. App. 475, 115 S. E. 923 (1923); Harney v. Lewis, 19 Ga. App. 655, 91 S. E. 1052 (1917).

10. Lewis v. Owens, 124 Ga. 228, 52 S. E. 333 (1905).

11. Ballard v. Daniel, 18 Ga. App. 449, 89 S. E. 603 (1916).

12. McElmurray v. Turner, 86 Ga. 215, 12 S. E. 359 (1890); Howard v. Franklin, 32 Ga. App. 737, 124 S. E. 554 (1924).

13. McElmurray v. Turner, 86 Ga. 215, 12 S. E. 359 (1890).

14. Howard v. Franklin, 32 Ga. App. 737, 124 S. E. 554 (1924).

15. Hudson v. Wright, 1 Ala. App. 433, 56 So. 258 (1911); DuRant v.

only state which gives superiority to the claim of the laborer is Louisiana.[16] A laborer's lien is superior to a crop mortgage given by the landlord which is prior in point of time. [16-a]

Sometimes conflicting claims arise in cases involving liens of landowners and laborers or croppers who are employed by tenants to work the crops. The paramount position of the landlord's lien in such cases has received recognition in decisions from Alabama[17] and Arkansas.[18] In fact the Alabama court declared that in an action by the landlord to enforce his claim it was not even necessary to make the laborer a party. Furthermore, in an instance where the crops had been turned over to the landlord in payment of advances which he had made to the tenant, the Arkansas court remarked that there was nothing remaining on which the laborer's lien could attach.[19]

A Georgia laborer employed by a tenant to work the crops attempted to assert a lien on cotton raised in a certain field. By agreement the produce of this field had been promised to him as compensation for work done in helping the tenant raise crops on other portions of the rented premises. It was shown that the landowner had known nothing of this agreement and had in no way assented to the arrangement. The tenant delivered the crops raised on this particular plot to the landowner, who in good faith accepted them in satisfaction of a lien for supplies furnished the tenant. It was held that the laborer could not, in an action at law, recover from the landowner the value of the crops. Nowhere in the opinion is there any statement that the laborer would have been more successful had he sued in equity. The court declared that even if the landlord's lien had been inferior to the laborer's lien, a supposition clearly contrary to accepted principles, the laborer would certainly not be permitted to assert his claim by bringing an ordinary suit at law against the landlord, who had acted in good faith in making the settlement with the tenant.[20]

Bank of Barnwell, 129 S. C. 283, 124 S. E. 12 (1924); Birt v. Greene & Co., 127 S. C. 70, 120 S. E. 747 (1924).

16. La. Gen. Stat. Ann. (Dart, 1932) §5064; Saloy v. Dragon, 37 La. Ann. 71 (1885); Reed v. Andrepont, 142 So. 184 (La. App., 1932). Even in that State the law was formerly in accord with the general rule, the change coming with the statute of 1867. See Bres & O'Brien v. Cowan, 22 La. Ann. 438 (1870); Moore v. Gray, 22 La. Ann. 289 (1870).

16-a. Carraway v. Phipps, 191 Ark. 326, 86 S. W. (2d) 12 (1935).

17. Hudson v. Wright, 1 Ala. App. 433, 56 So. 258 (1911).

18. Campbell v. Anderson, 189 Ark. 671, 74 S. W. (2d) 782 (1934).

19. Burgie v. Davis, 34 Ark. 179 (1879).

20. Rousey v. Mattox, 111 Ga. 883, 36 S. E. 925 (1900).

A South Carolina farm was leased and the rent reserved in cotton. The tenant made an agreement with a cropper to let him have the use of a portion of the land. To enable the tenant to obtain fertilizer, the landlord joined him in executing a mortgage on the entire crop grown on the land to a third person not involved in the controversy under discussion. The cropper gave a mortgage on his share of the crop, four bales, to the defendant. The tenant's portion of the cropper's produce, twenty-three bales, was turned over to the landlord and used to pay off the joint mortgage. The landlord then sought to collect the rent by seizing the four bales, the share of the cropper, which were in the possession of the defendant. It was the opinion of the court that the landlord's lien for rent covered the share of the cropper and that, in ordinary cases, the landlord would have a right to follow these four bales of cotton into the hands of the defendant and recover them. It was admitted that the cropper had a laborer's lien on the crop. The court held that by signing the mortgage along with his tenant the landlord had waived his prior lien for rent to the amount necessary to pay the mortgage indebtedness. Since more than enough cotton had been delivered to satisfy the claim for rent and the laborer's lien gave him an interest superior to the claim of the joint mortgagee, the court declared that the four bales could not be taken from the cropper.[21]

No recordation of the agricultural laborer's lien is usually required.[22] Under the Arkansas statute, however, a contract for labor must be recorded, and it is provided that no third person shall be prejudiced by the existence of the lien unless it is so filed. A question arose about the efficacy of the lien where the agreement was a parol one. The court declared that contracts not requiring writing under the Statute of Frauds, of which the agreement under consideration was one, need not be recorded, and that the liens growing out of these contracts were in the same category with respect to filing. Therefore the court ruled that under such an agreement the lien of a laborer was superior to the lien of a chattel mortgage on the crop, even though the mortgage had been recorded before the making of the cropping contract out of which the laborer's lien arose.[23]

21. Hamilton v. Blanton, 107 S. C. 142, 92 S. E. 275 (1917).
22. See Powell v. Smith, 74 Miss. 142, 20 So. 872 (1896).
23. Watson v. Day, 62 Ark. 435, 35 S. W. 1108 (1896).

RIGHTS OF THIRD PARTY PURCHASER

The Arkansas court has held that one who purchases a land-owner's crop upon which there is a laborer's lien, with notice that the lien exists, cannot defend his claim when an action is brought by the holder of the lien.[24] A similar decision was reached where the produce had been delivered to a South Carolina crop mortgagee with notice.[25] In the Arkansas case it was intimated that an innocent purchaser without notice would be protected, since such a sale would cut off the equitable right of the laborer. The same view would probably be taken in all jurisdictions where the landlord's lien is cut off by a bona fide purchase.[26] Since such is not the case in Mississippi, however, a decision[27] in that State that a laborer's lien might be enforced against a purchaser of the crop in open market, whether he had notice or not, would not be indicative of what would be held in a jurisdiction which protects bona fide purchasers in the case of the landlord's lien.

It is different, however, where the purchase is made from the cropper. Here it has been held that the landlord may rely upon his legal title to the crop and maintain an action for conversion, even when the purchase is without notice of the landlord's claim.[28] In this situation the law is different from that obtaining in tenancy cases, where the bona fide purchaser is protected.[29] The reason for the difference in treatment is that in a cropper relationship the land-lord has the legal title to the crops, while in a tenancy he has only a lien which is of an equitable nature. The rights of the parties are determined in accordance with the familiar rule that a bona fide purchase will cut off an equitable right but not one which is strictly legal in character.

WAIVER AND ESTOPPEL

A laborer may waive his lien or be guilty of conduct which amounts to an estoppel. In a rather interesting Mississippi case the lessee of a large farm was authorized by laborers working under him

24. Jonesboro Trust Co. v. Beaty, 133 Ark. 599, 199 S. W. 73 (1917).
25. DuRant v. Bank of Barnwell, 129 S. C. 283, 124 S. E. 12 (1924).
26. See Chap. 18, Notes 67-71.
27. Powell v. Smith, 74 Miss. 142, 20 So. 872 (1896).
28. Valentine v. Edwards, 112 Ark. 354, 166 S. W. 531 (1914); Franklin v. Tanner, 34 Ga. App. 254, 129 S. E. 114 (1925); Kirkland v. Wallace, 29 Ga. App. 238, 114 S. E. 649 (1922).
29. See Chap. 18, Notes 67-71.

to sell the crops free from any liens which they might have thereon. The lessee was directed to turn the purchasers' checks over to the lessor, who had agreed to return to the lessee all sums due the laborers under their contracts. Under these circumstances it was held that the laborers' liens, though waived as to purchasers of the crops, had not been waived with respect to the proceeds of the sale in the hands of either the lessee or the landowner. Such funds were said to be impressed with a trust in the hands of the landowner, and he was not permitted to apply the money on notes which the lessee had given him.[30] In another instance a laborer had taken a note for wages due at a certain time. Here it was held that his acceptance of the note could not be considered a waiver of the laborer's lien on the crop which his labor had aided in producing.[31]

A laborer's lien may be unenforceable because of conduct which amounts to an estoppel. A tenant's son had remained silent during a conversation which his father had concerning the priority of a merchant's claim for supplies. As a result of this conduct the son was said to have abandoned his laborer's lien on the crop by tacitly agreeing to his father's statement that the merchant's claim would be paid immediately after the landlord's demands were satisfied.[32]

An Arkansas statute[33] provides that in situations involving contracts of a sharecropping nature no mortgage or conveyance of any portion of the crops, made by the person cultivating the land, shall have any validity unless executed with the consent of the landlord, and that such assent must be indorsed on the mortgage or conveyance. In an early case[34] it was declared that the purpose of this act was not to impose an absolute restriction upon the farm laborer's power of alienation, the object being merely to protect the landlord. If the landlord gives a valid authorization to sell the crop, the purchaser obtains a good title, although the laborer afterwards converts the proceeds of the sale to his own use.[35] When the respective rights of the parties have been ascertained and adjusted and a settlement reached with the setting aside of the laborer's or cropper's share, he may mortgage or dispose of it as he will, without reference to the

30. Jackson v. Jefferson, 171 Miss. 774, 158 So. 486 (1935).
31. Powell v. Smith, 74 Miss. 142, 20 So. 872 (1896).
32. Reed v. Andrepont, 142 So. 184 (La. App., 1932).
33. Ark. Dig. Stat. (Pope, 1937) §8844.
34. Parkes v. Webb, 48 Ark. 293, 3 S. W. 521 (1887).
35. Valentine v. Edwards, 112 Ark. 354, 166 S. W. 531 (1914).

landlord's desires. A mortgage made under these circumstances, without the landlord's consent, would prevail over the rights of a subsequent purchaser.[36]

This statute requiring a *written* indorsement or waiver by the landlord is applicable only to situations where a cropper or laborer is involved. An oral waiver is sufficient in the case of a tenancy.[37]

NO APPLICATION OF STATUTE OF FRAUDS

The South Carolina court has held that the contract between the landlord and the cropper need not be in writing.[38] It is very probable that the courts of other states would follow this decision, since there is clearly no clause in the Statute of Frauds which could be construed to outlaw parol contracts of this kind.

CONSTRUCTION OF GARNISHMENT STATUTE

A Georgia statute[39] exempted from the process of garnishment the daily, weekly, or monthly wages of day laborers. In applying this statute a court held that the net amount due a cropper after a full settlement with his landlord was a wage paid to a laborer within the meaning of the statute and that therefore such funds were not subject to garnishment.[40] The court declared that the test for determining the meaning of the term "laborer" was the kind of work done by the person in question. The matter was said to be one of determining whether the work involved mental skill, business ability, or other use of intellectual faculties, or whether it depended upon physical strength or manual labor. In other words, the criterion was whether mind or muscle predominated in the performance of the task.

36. Parkes v. Webb, 48 Ark. 293, 3 S. W. 521 (1887).

37. Griggs v. Horton, 84 Ark. 623, 104 S. W. 930 (1907), which thus limits and explains remarks made at a rehearing of Tinsley v. Craig, 54 Ark. 346, 350, 16 S. W. 570 (1891); where this distinction had not been clarified. See also Chronister Bros. & Co. v. Oswalt, 175 Ark. 337, 299 S. W. 9 (1927), where the court referred to the cultivator as a tenant throughout the opinion but decided the question of waiver in accordance with the principles announced in the *Griggs* case as applicable only where a cropper relationship exists. If such a relationship does not exist in the *Oswalt* controversy, therefore, the cases are irreconcilable.

38. Birt v. Greene & Co., 127 S. C. 70, 120 S. E. 747 (1924).

39. Ga. Civ. Code (1910) §5298.

40. Thompson v. Passmore, 9 Ga. App. 771, 72 S. E. 185 (1911).

DIVISION OF INTERESTS

What acts constitute an effective division of the interests of the landlord and the cropper in the produce? The answer to this query is sometimes rather difficult to determine. The courts are continually considering problems arising because one party has tried to take advantage of the other.

There can be no doubt that the crops may be divided and each portion set aside as the property of the landlord and cropper respectively, and that such an appropriation is effective if the intention to set aside the portions is clear.[41] For the appropriation to be lawful it is not necessary for both parties to be present at the time the crops are divided.[42] In an early North Carolina case[43] it was said that the apportionment, to be adequate, must be followed by a delivery or at least assent, the court declaring that the thing transferred was not fully ascertained until the party agreed to take the separated share. However, it may be doubted that any modern court would take such a view of the matter.

A mortgage creditor of the cropper cannot lawfully levy upon the crop until a division has been made and the title to the cropper's share transferred. If the landlord and the cropper attempt through collusion to defeat the mortgage creditor's rights by refusing to make a division, a court of equity will afford relief.[44]

A Georgia cropper carried two bales of cotton to market and directed the landlord to sell his portion. At that time the landlord could have obtained ten and five-eighths cents a pound for the cotton, but he refused to sell, and cotton fell on the market to six and three-fourths cents. The lower court, in authorizing a recovery, gave the cropper the difference between the two prices; but the appellate tribunal reversed the decision on the theory that the landowner had control of the entire crop until a division had been effected.[45]

If a cropper appropriates any portion of the crop to his own use prior to the division with the intent to steal, he may be prosecuted

---

41. Thompson v. Price, 30 Ga. App. 652, 118 S. E. 598 (1923).
42. Peoples' Bank v. Walker, 132 S. C. 254, 128 S. E. 715 (1925).
43. Frazier v. Ansley, 33 N. C. 12 (1850).
44. Fountain v. Fountain, 10 Ga. App. 758, 73 S. E. 1096 (1912).
45. Goodson v. Watson, 125 Ga. 413, 54 S. E. 84 (1906).

for larceny.[46] The indictment should allege that the right of property is in the landlord and not in the cropper.[47]

INTEREST OF THE CROPPER IN THE PRODUCE

The cropper has an "interest" in the crop, even though the title is in the landlord. An Arkansas cropper transferred a portion of the crop to a third person without the consent of the landlord, who brought an action for the conversion of the produce. The jury was instructed to find for the third person, who had been made a defendant, if the cultivator had not stolen the cotton crop or if he could be shown to have had an *interest* therein. On appeal this instruction was held to be subject to misinterpretation, for there could be no doubt that the cultivator did have an "interest" in the cotton, even though he was just an employee or cropper and not a tenant.[48] An effective transfer of this interest to the landlord may be made. Such an assignment implies a clear assertion of ownership, the antithesis of abandonment, and the landlord's acceptance implies a definite recognition of the cropper's right to his portion. To say that a transfer or sale of this kind amounted to an abandonment of the cropper's right to recompense, as contended by the landlord in one such case, would be a contradiction in terms, especially where all things essential to a valid sale were present.[49]

In Arkansas a cropper's undivided interest in the crop may be the subject matter of a mortgage.[50] The same decision has been reached in a 1928 decision from South Carolina,[51] though one judge appears to have taken an opposite view a few years earlier.[52] The latter view that the cropper's undivided interest cannot be mortgaged was also taken by the Alabama Court in a case[53] decided before the distinction between the cropper and tenancy relationships was abolished

46. State v. Sanders, 110 S. C. 487, 96 S. E. 622 (1918), State v. Saunders, 52 S. C. 580, 30 S. E. 616 (1898).
47. Betts v. State, 6 Ga. App. 773, 65 S. E. 841 (1909); State v. Jacobs, 50 La. Ann. 447, 23 So. 608 (1898).
48. Valentine v. Edwards, 112 Ark. 354, 166 S. W. 531 (1914).
49. Bank of Pageland v. Willis, 109 S. C. 338, 96 S. E. 159 (1918).
50. Beard v. State, 43 Ark. 284 (1884); Houck v. Birmingham, 230 S. W. (2d) 952 (Ark., 1950).
51. Miller v. Insurance Co., 146 S. C. 123, 143 S. E. 663 (1928).
52. Gardner v. Jarrett, 121 S. C. 338, 113 S. E. 493 (1922).
53. Carleton v. Kimbrough, 150 Ala. 618, 43 So. 817 (1907).

by statute[54] in that State. The view first stated seems to be the better one and should be followed in all future controversies.

Therefore, for a stronger reason, when the respective rights of the parties have been ascertained and adjusted and a settlement reached with the setting aside of the cropper's share, he may mortgage or dispose of it as he will, independently of the landlord's desires.[55]

The mortgagee's interest, however, is subject to the prior claim of the landlord. In a Georgia case[56] a judge had charged the jury that if the cropper had raised more than enough to satisfy the landlord's claim for rent and supplies, the mortgage which he had given to a third person would be good in respect to the surplus remaining. This instruction was held to be vague, since it did not clearly indicate that the mortgagee could claim nothing until the landlord's liens were actually satisfied. The title to the entire crop would remain in the landlord until there had been a full liquidation of the cropper's indebtedness to him.

In one instance a landlord, after giving a mortgage on a crop produced on his farm by a cropper, sold the entire yield to another person. The landlord then made a settlement with the cropper, paying him out of the proceeds of the sale and receiving due credit for all advances made by him during the year. It was shown that there had been no actual division prior to the sale. The purchaser, who had notice of the mortgage, made an attempt to show a derivation of title through the cropper to at least a portion of the crop. The court found in favor of the mortgagee, declaring that the title to the crop had never passed from the landlord to the cropper.[57]

A cultivator of the soil usually has no interest in a crop-insurance policy taken out by his landlord and therefore cannot claim benefits under its provisions.[58] However, where the cultivator has been led to believe that he is protected from loss, he will be allowed to claim the benefits of the policy.[59]

54. Ala. Code (1940) tit. 31, §23. See Chap. 2, Note 2.
55. Parkes v. Webb, 48 Ark. 293, 3 S. W. 521 (1887).
56. Fountain v. Fountain, 7 Ga. App. 361, 66 S. E. 1020 (1910).
57. Atlantic Trust Co. v. Oliver McDonald Co., 36 Ga. App. 360, 136 S. E. 824 (1927).
58. Burney v. McCall, 186 Ga. 116, 197 S. E. 238 (1938).
59. Birch v. Sallee, 150 Ky. 434, 150 S. W. 514 (1912).

ABANDONMENT OF LAND BY CROPPER

Sometimes a cropper, for various reasons, may decide to abandon the farming project which he has agreed to operate. Often he is forced by sickness to cease working the crop. The principles governing abandonment by a tenant have already been discussed in connection with the lease contract,[60] and it can no doubt be said that the law there stated is applicable where a cropper has refused to continue the work. Some additional points can be discussed here with profit.

A cropper may decide to leave and find other work, or he may stay on the land and stop the process of cultivation. In a Kentucky case where the cropper had remained on the premises, the landlord brought his action under a statute[61] dispensing with notice in proceedings against a cropper for abandonment. The court decided that the case was properly brought under this statute. It declared that another statute[62] concerning delinquent tenants, which had been interpreted to authorize an action for damages only, would have no application to croppers.[63]

Sometimes sickness forces a cropper to abandon the cultivation of the land. A Louisiana cropper who was thus afflicted turned the farm over to his son and another person, without obtaining the consent of the landlord to the change. The cropper had worked for at least a portion of the period covered by the agreement, and it was held that he might recover for his services in an action which seems to have had a quasi-contractual flavor. However, it was declared that the landlord had been justified in dismissing the sick cropper, since the latter could not choose his replacement without an agreement to that effect between the parties.[64] Furthermore, where a Georgia landlord refused to furnish supplies to the family of a cropper who had not performed even a single day's work, it was held that sickness afforded no legitimate excuse.[65] Where the landlord was under no legal obligation to furnish supplies, his refusal to give credit would not excuse abandonment, especially in an instance where supplies could have been obtained from another source.[66]

60. See Chap. 3, Notes 224 et seq.
61. Ky. Rev. Stat. (1946) §383.130.
62. Ky. Rev. Stat. (1946) §383.120.
63. Wood v. Garrison, 23 Ky. Law Rep. 295, 62 S. W. 728 (1901).
64. Jeter v. Penn, 28 La. Ann. 230 (1876).
65. Taylor v. Rainwater, 54 Ga. App. 315, 187 S. E. 704 (1936).
66. Harney v. Lewis, 19 Ga. App. 655, 91 S. E. 1052 (1917).

A Georgia cropper who had been compelled to abandon his work because of illness sought to establish a laborer's lien. He claimed that the stoppage in work had been caused by the action of the landlord in repossessing a mule, without which he could not have made a crop even if he had been able to attend to his job. The court appeared to believe that the abandonment had been caused by the cropper's illness and not by any unlawful act on the part of the landlord. As sickness was no legitimate excuse for the abandonment, the court held that there was no laborer's lien which the cropper could foreclose.[67] The opinion did not close the door entirely, however, suggesting that this might be a case for quasi-contractual relief.

AGREEMENT BY CROPPER TO TAKE SMALLER SHARE OF CROP

Sometimes a share tenant will make an agreement with a cropper which gives the tenant a larger fraction of the produce than he has contracted to turn over to the landowner. In one such case an Arkansas tenant agreed to give his landlord one-fourth of the crop, and then made a contract with another whereby the latter would receive one-half of the crop in return for the labor exerted in cultivating the land. It appeared that the tenant might easily make a handsome profit. However, other circumstances entered into the situation. The cropper claimed that he had been prevented from disposing of his interest on a falling market because the landowner's agent had notified all prospective buyers about his principal's lien on the produce, thus obstructing the cropper's efforts to get rid of his interest in the crop before the bottom dropped out of the market. The cropper therefore steadfastly refused to give up his claim against the landowner. However, the tenant had never refused to make a delivery, and hence he could not be held responsible for a failure to carry out this part of his agreement. But the court declared that if the tenant had demanded, as claimed by the cropper, that his one-fourth share of the proceeds of a proposed sale of the crop should be placed in a bank, where the money could not be reached by the landowner, and that this scheme had prevented the timely sale of the produce, then the tenant could be held responsible for any loss occasioned thereby.[68]

67. Gardner v. Smith, 39 Ga. App. 224, 146 S. E. 648 (1929).
68. Fenton v. Price, 145 Ark. 116, 223 S. W. 364 (1920).

REMEDIES OF THE CROPPER

The fact that in a cropper relationship the title to the crop is in the landlord before a division limits the remedies which the cropper may use to enforce his rights. Undoubtedly he may assert a laborer's lien on the undivided crop.[69] However, the actions which must be predicated upon more than a lien or equitable interest in property, such as detinue, replevin, trespass, or trover, cannot be successfully maintained before the respective portions of the produce have been assigned according to the terms of the cropping agreement.[70] After the crop has been divided, however, the cropper holds the title to his portion and may then maintain actions of this kind in his own name.[71]

The cropper should undoubtedly have a remedy where the landlord has converted the entire crop to his own use before a settlement. It has been held that a cropper's action sounding in contract is a proper remedy.[72] Here the measure of damages is the market price of the cropper's share at the time when a settlement is demanded, and not the highest price obtainable thereafter or the price at which the crop is actually sold.[73] It has also been held that punitive damages may be recovered in a proper case where fraud is shown.[74] Sometimes a landlord may set up a plea of set-off or recoupment based upon some wrongful act on the part of the cropper. In a case of this kind, where the plea gave no hint of any claim for damages resulting from the cultivator's neglect, the appellate court held that the lower tribunal had properly excluded evidence with respect to a possible increase in the yield which would have resulted from the proper cultivation methods.[75]

In an Alabama case[76] the landowner was a member of a cotton

---

69. Wells v. Aldridge, 75 Ga. App. 702, 44 S. E. (2d) 183 (1947).

70. Beverly v. Rhodes, 209 Ala. 300, 96 So. 205 (1923); Beck v. Crow, 204 Ala. 295, 85 So. 489 (1920); Farrow v. Wooley & Jordan, 138 Ala. 267, 36 So. 384 (1903); Jordan v. Lindsay, 132 Ala. 567, 31 So. 484 (1902); Holcombe v. Townsend, 1 Hill 399 (S. C., 1833).

71. Sivley v. Moore, 20 Ala. App. 269, 101 So. 513 (1924); Bowles v. Bowles, 101 Ga. 837, 29 S. E. 35 (1897).

72. Carswell v. Smith, 145 Ga. 588, 89 S. E. 698 (1916); Holcombe v. Townsend, 1 Hill 399 (S. C., 1833).

73. Todd v. Jackson, 24 Ga. App. 519, 101 S. E. 192 (1919); Mattison v. Glenn, 117 S. C. 404, 109 S. E. 105 (1921).

74. Sullivan v. Calhoun, 117 S. C. 137, 108 S. E. 189 (1921).

75. Farrabee v. Wade, 200 Ala. 583, 76 So. 941 (1917).

76. Hunt v. Matthews, 132 Ala. 286, 31 So. 613 (1902).

dealers' partnership which was an alleged creditor of the cropper. The landowner's share of the cotton crop had been delivered to the other partner at a public warehouse with instructions from the cropper to let it remain there until the landowner should order it to be sold. The cotton was disposed of and the proceeds were applied toward payment of the partners' alleged claim instead of to the landlord's individual claim. The cropper claimed that this could not lawfully be done without special authority on his part, and the court held that this was a correct view of the law.

When a landlord breaks his contract to furnish supplies to a cropper, the Georgia courts have said that the latter can do one of three things: If the necessary articles can be obtained elsewhere, the cropper may get the goods wherever he is able to do so, complete the work required by the agreement, and hold the landlord responsible for the damages caused by the breach. As an alternative, he may sue immediately for his special damages, including the value of his services up to that time. Again, he may wait until the end of the harvest season and sue for the full value of his share of the crop, or, rather, what his share might have been if both parties had faithfully observed the terms of the contract.[77] The cropper may elect on which basis he will attempt to enforce his rights and, when committed to one course of action, he is restricted to that method. As an additional remedy, he may foreclose his laborer's lien.[78] This right to foreclose the lien forms the basis for an effective remedy, since he would not be permitted to maintain trover or any other action for which more than an equitable interest in the property is required.[79] The contract and foreclosure remedies are concurrent, and the one does not exclude the other.[80]

Certain cases have arisen where it was necessary for the laborers to go into equity in order to obtain relief. In one instance a cropper had agreed to use his own mule and plowing implements in making and gathering crops, and the landlord had promised to pay him twenty dollars for their use. The agreement was the usual one with

77. Surrency v. O'Quinn, 45 Ga. App. 455, 165 S. E. 171 (1932); Perdue v. Cason, 22 Ga. App. 284, 96 S. E. 16 (1918).

78. Surrency v. O'Quinn, 45 Ga. App. 455, 165 S. E. 171 (1932); Garrick v. Jones, 2 Ga. App. 382, 58 S. E. 543 (1907).

79. De Loach v. Delk, 119 Ga. 884, 47 S. E. 204 (1904); Smart v. Hill, 29 Ga. App. 400, 116 S. E. 66 (1922).

80. Brown v. Coleman, 39 Ga. App. 172, 146 S. E. 512 (1929); Jennings v. Lanham, 19 Ga. App. 79, 90 S. E. 1038 (1916).

respect to the staple crops of cotton and corn, a share of both going to each party, but certain beans and peanuts were to be the property of the cropper alone. After the crops had been raised the cropper was ordered off the premises by the landlord. Most of the produce had been gathered, and the cropper alleged that he was ready and willing to harvest the rest. He claimed that the landlord was insolvent and that he was entitled to equitable relief, there being no adequate remedy at law. He petitioned the court to appoint a receiver and to issue an injunction to prevent the landlord from selling the crops. The landlord claimed that the cropper had an adequate remedy at law in the form of a proceeding for the enforcement of a laborer's lien. The court decided that there was no adequate remedy because a proceeding to enforce the lien would not compensate the cropper for the use of his mule, and it therefore ruled that equitable relief should be granted.[81]

In another case an owner of land, farmed on shares under a cropping agreement, mortgaged the crops to a corporation. The parties contracted that, as the crops were gathered, they would be delivered to the mortgagee. There was also a promise by the mortgagee to settle with the croppers for their interests in the produce after deducting the amounts which they owed the landowner for advances. The croppers had consented to this arrangement and had thereby waived their liens. Upon the refusal of the mortgagee to settle the cropper's claims in accordance with the agreement, a successful suit in equity was maintained. In permitting the croppers to sustain the suit the court declared that the mortgagee might have settled with the croppers at the market price on the day that they demanded an accounting. However, since there had been a refusal to make this settlement, the mortgagee must account to them at the price on the day of the proposed settlement. If the price had fallen after that date, the mortgagee would not be allowed to take advantage of his own wrong. On the other hand, if the market price advanced and a higher figure was obtained, the mortgagee must not only account for the value of the croppers' shares at the price obtained at the later date, but must also pay interest on the net amount from that date until payment was actually made.[82]

81. Kelley v. Moody, 176 Ga. 138, 167 S. E. 101 (1932).
82. Rainwater v. Bank of Cheraw, 114 S. C. 353, 103 S. E. 587 (1920).

REMEDIES OF THE LANDLORD

The landowner, being vested with the title to the crop where a cropper relationship exists, may maintain such actions as detinue, replevin, and trover to recover the produce or to obtain damages for its appropriation.[83] The right to maintain trover remains until there has been a final settlement of accounts, even though the crop has been actually divided.[84] In Georgia, when a cropper withholds possession of the crops without settling the account with his landlord, a possessory warrant may be sued out and is a proper method of enforcing the landlord's rights.[85] This action may be brought notwithstanding the fact that an action of trover is also maintainable, the remedies being concurrent.[86] However, before the enactment of the statute of 1922[87] declaring crops to be personalty, it was said that the landlord could not maintain a statutory possessory action until the crops were severed from the soil.[88]

A landlord may make a claim for advances made to a cropper and attach the crop by virtue of his title.[89] It is very clear that there is no landlord's lien here, especially in a case where the cropper's debt did not arise out of the farming operations and was entirely independent of them.[90] Sometimes the parties agree that the cropper's share of the crop shall not be removed until the landlord's advances are paid. In such a case it was held that a landlord who had contracted to supply his cropper had a right to retain possession of the whole crop until a full settlement of the claim, as against the cropper himself, or as against subsequent purchasers or mortgagees claiming under him. Here it is clear that the right of property will not be transferred until the agreement has been fully complied with.[91]

Sometimes a remedy is refused because the landlord has either declined to furnish supplies to the cropper or delayed the delivery of

83. Willard v. Cox, 9 Ala. App. 439, 63 So. 781 (1913); Williams v. Mitchem, 151 Ga. 227, 106 S. E. 284 (1921); Welch v. Lindsay, 27 Ga. App. 164, 107 S. E. 891 (1921); Cowart v. Dees, 7 Ga. App. 601, 67 S. E. 705 (1910).
84. Harley v. Davis, 7 Ga. App. 386, 66 S. E. 1102 (1910).
85. Courson v. Land, 54 Ga. App. 534, 188 S. E. 360 (1936); Smith v. Brinson, 21 Ga. App. 169, 94 S. E. 59 (1917).
86. Whitworth v. Carter, 39 Ga. App. 625, 147 S. E. 904 (1929).
87. Ga. Acts 1922, p. 114, later Ga. Code (1933) §85-1901.
88. Williams v. Mitchem, 151 Ga. 227, 106 S. E. 284 (1921).
89. Stewart v. Young, 212 Ala. 426, 103 So. 44 (1925).
90. Rhodes v. Verdery, 157 Ga. 162, 121 S. E. 221 (1924).
91. Appling v. Odum & Mercier, 46 Ga. 583 (1872).

promised farm implements. In Louisiana a landowner wrongfully took over a crop after an inexcusable delay in supplying his cropper with indispensable farming equipment, thereby preventing a complete harvest. Here it was held that the landowner could not recover sums which had been spent by him in making an effort to salvage what remained of the crop.[92]

A cropper is entitled to hold possession of the crop for the satisfaction of his laborer's lien and for no other purpose. Thus he has the right to retain possession until his claim is paid; but if he assumes control and holds possession of the crop by refusing to divide and declining to recognize the lawful right of the landlord to the agreed portion of the produce, the latter may maintain a possessory action such as detinue and recover his share.[93]

Sometimes a landlord will make an error with respect to the true relationship and bring his action on the theory that the cultivator is a tenant, when in reality he is a cropper. In one instance such a mistake was made, and the landlord attempted to enforce a lien against his cropper. It was held that no such action could be brought, and the landlord was denied a recovery.[94] This decision places a heavy responsibility upon the landowner, since the distinction between the two relationships is rather vague, to say the least.

An interesting situation arose when a Georgia landlord instituted a suit in equity to enjoin a cropper from continuing to occupy a farm after being discharged. The contract gave the cropper the right to market the crops as they matured. At an interlocutory hearing an injunction was granted, as prayed by the landlord, and a receiver was appointed to harvest and divide the crops remaining on the land, as prayed by the cropper. On appeal it was held that the lower court, after having enjoined the cropper from continuing to occupy the premises following his discharge, had acted properly in appointing a receiver, notwithstanding the admitted solvency of the landlord.[95]

CONCLUSION

In summing up it may be said that croppers have generally been given remedies which are very much like those of the landlord in a tenancy relationship. The cropper has a laborer's lien in most juris-

92. Pleasant v. Anderson, 36 So. (2d) 731 (La. App. 1948).
93. Crow v. Beck, 208 Ala. 444, 94 So. 580 (1922).
94. Fields v. Argo, 103 Ga. 387, 30 S. E. 29 (1898).
95. Hanson v. Fletcher, 183 Ga. 858, 190 S. E. 29 (1937).

dictions and a right to sue in equity where the lack of a sufficient title prevents him from obtaining redress at law. In theory he is in much the same position as others who have no legal title to the crops. If one presupposes a just administration of the law, there is very little to criticise here. The remedies given by the present law in most states seem to offer adequate means of preventing the machinations of unscrupulous landlords. In other words, the remedies for the most part are there, and all that is needed is a program to teach the cropper how to use them.

XXI

Peonage

AT the end of the Civil War the South was left with great numbers of freedmen who had very little idea of the responsibilities of citizenship. While some decided to remain as day laborers with their former masters, a great majority of the Negroes wandered about the countryside and into the towns. The irresponsible freedmen were prone to commit minor depredations and sometimes serious crimes.

Faced with this situation, the state legislatures, controlled for the most part by plantation owners and ex-Confederates, sought some lawful means of preventing reprehensible conduct of this kind. Thus the "Black Codes" were born. Among the provisions of these statutes were so-called apprentice laws, which gave the masters a great degree of authority over the Negro workers. There were also vagrancy provisions and other laws making the freedmen subject to the authority of the white man.

A defense of the "Black Codes" is not maintainable in the light of history, but it may be said that these statutes were the natural attempt of men who had had authority snatched from them to perpetuate it under another guise. The way of authority was the only way they knew to meet the problems confronting them.

The Maryland statute was tested in the federal courts[1] and, because it gave less protection to Negro apprentices than it did to the whites, was found to be in conflict with the Civil Rights Act of 1866, the principle of which was carried over into the Fourteenth Amendment.

One of the more immediate results of the "Black Codes" was the Thirteenth Amendment to the Federal Constitution prohibiting involuntary servitude except as a punishment for crime and giving Congress power to enforce its provisions by appropriate legislation. Faced with a system of Indian peonage which had grown up in New Mexico Territory as well as the Southern situation with respect to the Negro, Congress enacted legislation outlawing the practice

1. *In re* Turner, Fed. Cas. No. 14,247 (C. C. D. Md., 1867).

435

everywhere in the nation.[2] These laws apply no matter what racial, economic, or industrial group is sinned against. Hence they would clearly apply to tenants or croppers who are kept in a state of involuntary servitude by landowners wishing to hold them on the land. In this respect one federal court has defined "peonage" as a condition of compulsory service based upon the indebtedness of the victim, the debt being the cord by which he is tied to the person to whom he owes the obligation.[3]

The Negro and poor white tenants of the South have frequently been in a state of economic doldrums. Their lot has been notoriously hard, and except in time of war and in boom years, they have been hard put to it to make ends meet. The able ones usually turn to some other occupation, and a few become landlords themselves. It is a rare thing for a person to continue under the system and accumulate wealth and property. Once in a while a tenant will have three or four exceptionally good years in a row, but if he continues under the system, bad luck is bound to catch up with him sooner or later. Then he goes into debt to landlord or merchant, and that is the seed from which dependence and peonage often spring.

After the whites regained control of the legislative machinery of the Southern states, means were sought to make the tenants fulfill the obligations of their contracts. Some tenants would obtain money and/or supplies from the landowner and then quit the premises without completing the crop. This led to the enactment of labor contract laws making it criminal to violate contracts of this kind. These laws were of two types, one making it a criminal offense to take employment from another without giving notice of a former contract, and the other making it indictable to break the contract under which the tenant or cropper has obtained supplies without returning the advances made. Both the former[4] and the latter[5] types have been declared unconstitutional as being in conflict with the Thirteenth Amendment and federal peonage statutes. Laws of both

2. 8 U. S. C. A. §§ 56 et seq. (1926), Rev. Stat. §§1990, 1991, 5526, 5527 (1875).
3. In re Peonage Charge, 138 Fed. 686 (C. C. N. D. Fla., 1905).
4. Peonage Cases, 123 Fed. 671 (M. D. Ala., 1903); State v. Armstead, 103 Miss. 790, 60 So. 778 (1912).
5. State v. Oliva, 144 La. 51, 80 So. 195 (1918), overruling State v. Murray, 116 La. 655, 40 So. 930 (1906), a decision in line with State v. Williams, 32 S. C. 123, 10 S. E. 876 (1890), which was later repudiated by state and federal courts in Ex parte Hollman, 79 S. C. 9, 60 S. E. 19 (1908) and Ex parte Drayton, 153 Fed. 986 (D. S. C., 1907) because of conflict with the equal protection clause of the Fourteenth Amendment.

kinds have also been held to violate the Fourteenth Amendment.[6] It is immaterial that the service was begun voluntarily by contract.[7] Labor laws of this general type have been held to violate a state constitutional provision prohibiting imprisonment for debt except where there is fraud.[8] A portion of a statute of this kind penalizing a person who hires a contract breaker with knowledge of the former employment is open to the objection that it depends on other portions of the act which make the laborer criminally liable for a mere breach of contract.[9] Add the element of fraud to the requirements of the statute, however, and the objections to its validity disappear.[10]

It has been said that one who induces a person to work by threats of prosecution under a labor contract law is guilty of intimidation which amounts to peonage, if, by reason of the character of the threats, the will of the person is overcome and a continuation of the labor results.[11] The court declared that unless the fear was engendered by threats of prosecution made by the employer or landlord, the fact that the alleged victims were induced to work out their debts by fear of prosecution would not render the landowner guilty of peonage.

The failure of statutes of this type to stand the constitutional test merely set the legislators to thinking up new devices to hold the tenants to their agreements. Usually the tenants were financially unable to pay damages for breaches of contract, and it was evidently believed that the threat of a jail sentence was the most effective way to insure a full performance. Several states adopted statutes making it a criminal offense to make a labor or tenancy contract with a fraudulent intent not to carry out the agreement. Some states added a clause making the refusal of the laborer or tenant to perform the contract presumptive or prima facie evidence of fraudulent intent. The state courts of Alabama[12] and Georgia[13] held that this type of

6. See Toney v. State, 141 Ala. 120, 37 So. 332 (1904); *Ex parte* Hollman, 79 S. C. 9, 60 S. E. 19 (1908); *Ex parte* Drayton, 153 Fed. 986 (D. S. C., 1907).

7. State v. Oliva, 144 La. 51, 80 So. 195 (1918).

8. Minton v. Early, 183 N. C. 199, 111 S. E. 347 (1922); State v. Williams, 150 N. C. 802, 63 S. E. 949 (1909).

9. Minton v. Early, 183 N. C. 199, 111 S. E. 347 (1922).

10. State v. Norman, 110 N. C. 484, 14 S. E. 968 (1892).

11. U. S. v. Clement, 171 Fed. 974 (D. C. S. C., 1909).

12. Bailey v. State, 158 Ala. 18, 48 So. 498 (1908).

13. Townsend v. State, 124 Ga. 69, 52 S. E. 293 (1905). *Prima facie* clause omitted from court's discussion but an examination of the statute shows it to have been present.

statute was valid. The Alabama statute[14] and finally the Georgia act[15] as well, were challenged before the Federal Supreme Court. It was decided that, although a state may enact legislation providing that one fact may be prima facie evidence of another, there must be a rational relationship between the two. The Court declared that no such rational relationship existed in this instance and held that such statutes violated the constitutional guarantees against involuntary servitude.

It has been suggested that in deciding the Georgia case the Supreme Court may have been influenced by the fact that the Georgia law does not permit the defendant to be sworn. In the Alabama case the Court seems to have been influenced by a rule of evidence that an accused person cannot testify with respect to uncommunicated motives or intentions. This rule of evidence does not prevail in all jurisdictions, and after the Alabama case had been finally disposed of, attempts were made to uphold similar legislation in other states where no such rule was in effect. It was argued that this matter had so influenced the Supreme Court that its decision would not have been the same had there been no such evidential factor. The language of the opinion, however, is subject to no such interpretation, for the Court clearly denied the validity of the statute on constitutional grounds. The rule of evidence is merely referred to as an additional factor which led to the decision. Some courts did consider this as a differentiating feature,[16] however, and the matter was not decided until 1944, when the Supreme Court ruled that any such statute was invalid on constitutional grounds, and that these evidential matters were immaterial.[17]

The statutes of this type usually appeared in two sections, one being devoted to a description of the fraudulent crime, and the other to the presumption arising from the failure to live up to the agreement. Some jurists urged that the first section might be valid in spite of the unconstitutionality of the second. Two state courts upheld the validity of the first section, employing the doctrine that one portion of a statute which is not void in itself will not be declared invalid for the reason that other parts of the same are unconstitu-

14. Bailey v. Alabama, 219 U. S. 219, 31 Sup. Ct. 145 (1911).
15. Taylor v. Georgia, 315 U. S. 25, 62 Sup. Ct. 415 (1942).
16. See Phillips v. Bell, 84 Fla. 225, 94 So. 699 (1922); Wilson v. State, 138 Ga. 489, 75 S. E. 619 (1912).
17. Pollock v. Williams, 322 U. S. 4, 64 Sup. Ct. 792 (1944).

tional.[18] Where the sections are so tied together that the purpose of the entire statute could not be accomplished without the invalid section, there can be no separation, and the statute is void. In one instance a person was convicted under the first section when there was an abundance of evidence to sustain the charge of fraud and it was therefore unnecessary to use the presumption contained in the invalid second section. The appellate court of Florida upheld the conviction and refused to issue a writ of habeas corpus, thereby approving the theory of separability.[19] Another court refused to approve a writ of habeas corpus applied for by a defendant who had pleaded guilty to a charge of violating the first section.[20]

In a recent Supreme Court case, however, a very different conclusion was reached on this matter of separability. In this instance the defendant had pleaded guilty when charged with the offense denounced by the first section of the Florida statute. Hence it had been unnecessary to apply the prima facie provision contained in the act's second section. In arguing the case, the defendant's attorneys made the point that the Florida legislature had enacted this statute after similar laws had been declared invalid by the Supreme Court itself. The tribunal declared that in view of the persistence of the state legislature in enacting a statute which it knew to be void according to the decisions of the highest court in the land, it could not be said that the defendant's plea of guilty was not at least somewhat influenced by the threat of conviction through the use of the invalid prima facie provision of the act. The court seemed to believe that this prima facie provision, even though like provisions had been held invalid, would influence the whole procedure at the hearing to the extent that the defendant would believe a fair trial of the issue of fraud could not be had, thereby inducing his plea of guilty.[21] Mr. Justice Reed in his dissenting opinion argued that the record did not show that the defendant's plea of guilty was influenced in any way by fear of the operation of the presumption or prima facie rule. In this the Justice scores quite a point, for the presumption indulged in by the majority of the court is rather illogical, and the court in the above Alabama case had held that illogical presumptions are not to be upheld. It is extremely doubtful whether the defendant had ever

18. Phillips v. Bell, 84 Fla. 225, 94 So. 699 (1922); Latson v. Wells, 136 Ga. 681, 71 S. E. 1052 (1911).

19. Phillips v. Bell, 84 Fla. 225, 94 So. 699 (1922).

20. Latson v. Wells, 136 Ga. 681, 71 S. E. 1052 (1911).

21. Pollock v. Williams, 322 U. S. 4, 64 Sup. Ct. 792 (1944).

even heard of the prima facie provision of the statute; hence he can hardly be said to have been influenced thereby.

Statutes of this general type which do not have the presumptive or prima facie provision seem to have received the approval of the courts,[22] but there is authority to the contrary.[23]

A North Carolina act punishes any person who, with intent to defraud, obtains money by virtue of a promise to begin work, and then wilfully fails to commence or complete the work. To obtain a conviction under this statute it has been held that mere proof that the accused had received advances upon the promise to work and had broken his contract is not sufficient to establish the offense, there being no showing of fraud.[24] In this instance an amendment[25] to the original act[26] setting up a presumption similar to that contained in the Alabama statute was held to be violative of the Fourteenth Amendment under the principles announced above. Nothing is said relative to the possibility that the entire statute was rendered unconstitutional by the enactment of an invalid amendment.

With respect to the Georgia Labor Contract Law it has been held that the State must prove that there was a definite contract and that the defendant failed to perform the agreed services or failed to return money or goods advanced with interest, without good and sufficient cause, to the hirer's damage. Mere proof that the defendant had failed to carry out his contract did not mean that he had done so without cause. The court also declared that the latter element of the offense was not supplied by the hirer's statement that he knew of no good reason for the refusal of the laborer to comply with the contract. It appeared that the laborer had done enough work to offset the advances, and that the hiring landowner still owed him for this.[27] It was held in another case that a conviction was not supported by evidence that a landowner advanced money on the faith of the accused's agreement to furnish one-half of the labor and guano under a contract to farm on a fifty-fifty basis, and that the landowner declared that he knew of no good reason why the accused should not perform the services or pay the money.[28]

22. Bailey v. Alabama, 211 U. S. 452, 29 Sup. Ct. 141 (1908); Thomas v. State, 13 Ala. App. 431, 69 So. 908 (1915).

23. Goode v. Nelson, 73 Fla. 29, 74 So. 17 (1917).

24. State v. Griffin, 154 N. C. 611, 70 S. E. 292 (1911).

25. N. C. Pub. Laws 1905, c. 411.

26. N. C. Pub. Laws 1889, c. 444.

27. Banton v. State, 57 Ga. App. 173, 194 S. E. 827 (1938).

28. Adams v. State, 57 Ga. App. 802, 197 S. E. 62 (1938).

A Georgia statute[29] provided that when the relationship of employer-employee, landlord-tenant, or landlord-cropper with respect to agricultural land had been established by written or parol agreement made in the presence of witnesses, and this contract had been partly performed, it would be unlawful to hire or rent land to an employee, tenant, or cropper without first obtaining the written consent of the landowner or employer. The act provided that a landowner or employer who had been injured could decide whether the culprit should be criminally prosecuted or merely be liable in damages. The court held that this statute violated the due process guarantee of the Fourteenth Amendment, in that it delegated to an individual at his option the power to determine whether the act complained of should be a crime or merely a tort remediable in damages. It was also declared that the statute constituted an unreasonable restriction on the right to contract with respect to one's own labor and the right to employ labor as well. The statute peremptorily forbade the renting of land to the tenant or cropper of another, the relationship between the landlord and cultivator making no difference in the overall picture. The court further pointed out that the cultivator might have rented lands insufficient for his needs, and, under this act, would not be permitted to supplement his farm by renting additional land from another.[30]

According to a Louisiana statute[31] it would be unlawful for any person to go upon the premises or plantation of any citizen of the State at night or between sunset and sunrise and, without the consent of the landowner, move or assist in moving any laborer or tenant therefrom. There were certain stated exceptions in the statute. The state court held that this act was not invalid as violating the privileges and immunities clauses contained in Article IV, Section 2 of the Federal Constitution and the Fourteenth Amendment, nor was it violative of that Amendment's due process and equal protection guarantees. The defendant, who had interfered with a worker on the plantation of a citizen of the State, was not allowed to complain because the legislature, in enacting the statute, had not gone further and forbidden a similar act upon the plantation or premises of a citizen of another state. If the trespass had been committed on land belonging to a citizen of another state, there would have been no violation of the statute. The citizen of another state would have

29. Ga. Civ. Code (1910) §§3712-13.
30. Fortune v. Braswell, 139 Ga. 609, 77 S. E. 818 (1913).
31. La. Acts 1926, No. 38.

no way of compelling the Louisiana legislature to make the law applicable to the trespass on his land, and no right to demand that the statute be declared void because it was not applicable to his property.[32] This would seem to be a matter of equal protection of the laws, no question of peonage or involuntary servitude being involved here.

Certain portions of the Reconstruction legislation[33] protecting individuals from violations of their constitutional rights were brought to the fore in an attempt to protect certain Negro laborers in Arkansas from the machinations of unscrupulous men who were trying to force them to break farm labor contracts. There had been a conspiracy by certain persons to prevent the Negroes from making and carrying out these contracts. Force was employed, and the situation became very serious. The case reached the Federal Supreme Court where it was decided that the federal courts had no jurisdiction. In the opinion of the Court no right guaranteed by the Anti-slavery Amendment or other portion of the Constitution had been violated here.[34] Such a conspiracy was declared to be within the exclusive province of the state courts. In another instance, however, one[35] of the federal statutes was invoked where Negroes had been persuaded to labor on a farm by fraudulent representations that they would be paid for their efforts. Afterwards they were compelled to continue through threats of violence and brutality. The statute was held to be applicable in this situation.[36] In one case the interference was aimed at the individual's right to choose his employer, while in the other it was directed at his right not to be forced to work against his will. There is only a thin line of demarcation between the two situations.

At common law a person may recover damages from another who entices away his servant. In a South Carolina enticement suit the judge's instructions to the jury were subject to the interpretation that an employer might be held responsible for enticing away the servant of another, even though the employee had violated the contract voluntarily and the defendant's attempt to hire him had not been made until after he had left the premises. It was held on appeal

32. State v. Hunter, 164 La. 405, 114 So. 76 (1927).
33. 8 U. S. C. A. §§42-43, 18 U. S. C. A. §§51-52 (1926); Rev. Stat. §§1978-79, 5508, 5510 (1875).
34. Hodges v. United States, 203 U. S. 1, 27 Sup. Ct. 6 (1906).
35. 18 U. S. C. A. §51 (1926), Rev. Stat. §5508 (1875).
36. Smith v. United States, 157 Fed. 721 (C. C. A. 8th, 1907), *cert. denied* 208 U. S. 618, 28 Sup. Ct. 569 (1908).

that such an interpretation would countenance involuntary servitude.[37] Economic necessity would practically force the employee to continue the work, since all other prospective employers would be faced with an enticement suit if they hired him. Enticement statutes applying to renters and croppers have been enacted in most of the Southeastern states.[38] The Arkansas statute has been held not to be violative of the Thirteenth Amendment or the peonage statutes.[39]

In the South of today many tenants and croppers are tied to the land in a state of near-peonage. During depression years the situation is much worse than in a period of prosperity when jobs in industry are plentiful. Even in years of prosperity, however, there are some who are so deeply in debt that the landlords are able, if they so desire, to hold them in a state bordering on involuntary servitude. The courts seem to be disposed against anything which even savors of peonage, and it remains for the prosecuting officials, backed by an aroused public opinion, to ferret out the offenders and bring them to justice.

37. Shaw v. Fisher, 113 S. C. 287, 102 S. E. 325 (1920).
38. See Chap. 13, Note 78.
39. Johns v. Patterson, 138 Ark. 420, 211 S. W. 387 (1919).

XXII

Suggested Reforms to Alleviate Plight of Farm Tenants and to Modernize Laws Pertaining to the Landlord-Tenant Relationship

THE law concerning real property in general and the landlord-tenant relationship in particular has come down from feudal times. As the world has changed during the last two hundred years, the tenancy laws have remained more or less static. In fact there has probably been less development here than in any other important field of our jurisprudence. A possible explanation of this lack of change is that up to the beginning of the current century there was always cheap land to be had on the expanding frontiers of the New World. Any able-bodied man could "go west" and obtain virgin soil with very little capital outlay. Hence the demand for land in the earlier-settled portions of the country was not too pressing. Homestead laws were enacted with a view to inducing settlers to "pull up stakes" and go to the frontiers, where good farming land was supposed to be limitless. Enterprising young men would think twice before settling down as tenants on someone else's land when such a pot of gold awaited them at the foot of the rainbow of ambition and hope. Thus the West was settled and the last practical frontier finally reached.

Of course the tenancy system in the South, as has been shown, grew out of the destruction of the institution of slavery. Few of the freedmen, however, had the necessary training for a break with their old environment, and hence the number of Negroes going West was very small. The farmers among them became the tenants of their former masters, some even before the overthrow of the Reconstruction governments. The native whites who had no incentive or ambition to go elsewhere in an effort to better themselves became the tenants of the large landowners and formed the nucleus of the large white tenant farmer class in the Southeastern states of today.

Some of these people, white and colored, have probably the lowest living standards of any group in the country at the present time. Many volumes have been filled with descriptions of the life led by the poor tenants of Arkansas and the eastern Carolinas, the people of the Black Belt and Delta regions, the "Crackers" of Florida and Georgia. These people sometimes live in squalid huts or log cabins in a state of poverty and filth aggravated by a lack of sanitation.

The cotton and tobacco which they grow is often not even enough to satisfy the rent and to pay for the advances received from the landowners to give them subsistence through the year. Frequently interest rates are high on loans of money and sales of goods on credit. Supplymen claim that their charges must be high on such transactions because of the great risks and the frequency of default. Yet a great number of merchants make their living on just this type of transaction. In some states, as has been seen, these supplymen have the added security of a lien on the crops, while in others this type of security is limited to landlords who wish to furnish supplies to their own tenants. At times these interest charges are exorbitant, and there is a crying need for legislation such as that enacted in North Carolina[1] for the purpose of limiting the rates to be charged in transactions of this kind. Under this legislation the landlord or merchant who charges excessive interest rates is deprived of his lien.[2]

In 1915 a Texas statute[3] was enacted setting maximum rentals in share contracts. Where the tenant furnished most of the essential things except the land the maximum rental was set at one-third the value of the grain and one-fourth the value of the cotton, the customary rental which has been charged in various portions of the South for this type of farm aid. Where the landowner furnished everything but the labor the maximum rate was made one-half of the grain and cotton. Lease contracts or cropping agreements with rates exceeding these limits were to be unenforceable, and the landlords making such contracts were to be subject to a penalty of double the amount of the rental. The State Supreme Court ruled that agriculture was not so affected with the public interest as to justify price- or rate-fixing, and that the statute violated the due process guarantees of both the State and Federal Constitutions.[4]

1. See Chap. 14, Note 173.
2. N. C. Gen. Stat. (1943) §44-54.
3. Tex. Acts 1915, p. 77.
4. Culberson v. Ashford, 118 Tex. 491, 18 S. W. (2d) 585 (1929). In accord with this decision are Miller v. Branch, 233 S. W. 1032 (Tex. Civ. App., 1921); Rumbo v. Winterrowd, 228 S. W. 258 (Tex. Civ. App., 1921), which were

Soon after this decision, however, the legislature adopted another statute[5] providing that there should be no lien for rent or supplies where the stipulated rental exceeded the shares stated in the statute which had been declared invalid. This act kept the provision for double damages, but eliminated the rent-fixing features. It has never been tested in a court of last resort.

Certain dicta enunciated by the Texas intermediate appellate courts have indicated that the legislature has power to restrict the landlord's lien or even to abolish it entirely.[6] In one case a distinction is made between the rent-fixing legislation and the laws to limit liens, basing the legislative power to enact the latter on a reasonable classification argument.[7] Further, it may be doubted, when the decision of the Federal Supreme Court in the New York milk case[8] is considered with a view to the liberalization of the public interest doctrine, that the rate-fixing portions of the first Texas statute would be ruled invalid today. In the milk case the Supreme Court upheld price-fixing regulations authorized by a state statute. It was a five-to-four decision, and since that time the Court has become even more liberal in this respect.

Legislation abolishing or restricting the landlord's lien would be rather difficult to put through the legislatures of the Southeastern states today, as the landowners consider the lien to be of prime importance in securing the indebtedness of the tenant. The landlords would be afraid to give up this security device unless they could see some other method of securing themselves against loss from defaulting and dishonest tenants. There are base and careless tenants as well as avaricious and knavish landlords. However, a statute like the one in Texas would prevent the charging of excessive rents to tenants, who are in no equal bargaining position with the landowners except in times of great economic prosperity, such as those during the two great wars of the twentieth century. Some support for standardized share-rent might be found among certain liberal and forward-looking legislators.

In Kansas certain objectionable features had crept into the tenancy contracts of large corporate and individual landowners. These

---

contrary to Hawthorn v. Coates Bros., 202 S. W. 804 (Tex. Civ. App., 1918).

5. Tex. Acts 1931, c. 100, Tex. Stat. Ann. (Vernon, 1936) Art. 5222.

6. Hawthorn v. Coates Bros., 202 S. W. 804 (Tex. Civ. App., 1918); Dunbar v. Texas Irrigation Co., 195 S. W. 614 (Tex. Civ. App., 1917).

7. Miller v. Branch, 233 S. W. 1032 (Tex. Civ. App., 1921).

8. Nebbia v. New York, 291 U. S. 502, 54 Sup. Ct. 505 (1934).

agreements were often extremely burdensome and were standardized to a great extent. The leases were drawn up with identical provisions of a very harsh nature. The state legislature, disliking these highhanded efforts to make the tenants agree to unfair terms, enacted a statute[9] outlawing contracts which contained *all* these provisions. Tenants who entered under these contracts were required to pay a reasonable rent only. The statute was applicable to five-thousand-acre tracts, and anything smaller was not included within its terms. According to another provision, the landlord's lien was limited to the crops and stock raised on the premises and to sums received by the tenant for pasturage. This statute was very easy to evade, since it was not applicable to contracts which omitted a single one of the burdensome provisions. Among the clauses contained in these particlar agreements were those extending the lien to all the property of the tenant, those requiring him to pay taxes and assessments, those requiring him to make improvements and extending the lien thereto, and those prohibiting the feeding of grain stalks to his stock instead of to the landlord's animals. Another statute[10] applying to the same class of large landowners requires that compensation shall be paid to the tenant for all buildings and improvements which he has constructed on the land during the tenancy and invalidating any provisions to the contrary. It would seem that the Kansas court has given its tacit approval to the validity of this act in a case[11] arising prior to the passage of the act but not decided until afterwards. In this instance a tenant claimed that there was an implied covenant of compensation for improvements, since the landlord had made a business practice of requiring tenants to make improvements on the leased premises. The court upheld the tenant's contention and in doing so declared that the statute had only been an affirmation of the public policy of the state.

In 1937 the Oklahoma legislature enacted a statute[12] setting up the Oklahoma Farm and Landlord and Tenant Department. The functions of this Department were to establish better relationships between landlord and tenant, to make a thorough study of the tenancy problem, to prepare the way for more equitable contracts for longer periods, to work out a better understanding between the parties with a view to encouraging arbitration of disputes, and to take ad-

9. Kans. Gen. Stat. (1935) §§67-531-533.
10. Kans. Gen. Stat. (1935) §§67-501, 67-5012.
11. Berg v. Scully, 120 Kans. 637, 245 Pac. 119 (1926).
12. Okla. Laws 1937, c. 53.

vantage of the opportunities offered by farm organizations and co-operatives. This would seem to be an excellent way of attacking a problem of this nature. Particularly is this true in respect to the provisions which should go into model farm leases. A period of trial and error on a voluntary basis should precede any attempt at making such model leases compulsory—a procedure of questionable validity —or even recommendatory. This period of trial and error would no doubt serve as a testing ground for various provisions, ideas, and theories. In other words, the landlord and the tenant could be educated into an acceptance of lease provisions which would benefit both. Thus faith in the provisions might be built up and made into a lever which would compel the enactment of statutes implementing the proposed reforms.

The administrative unit published a report of its findings, reference to which will be made later. Then, in 1939, the whole setup was abolished by statute.[13] Furthermore, nothing has been done in Oklahoma to implement the program envisaged in the legislation and the report. In fact the only law referring to tenancy enacted through 1943 was an act requiring the consent of the landlord to a tenant's application for terracing land and making the former jointly liable with the latter.[14]

These state statutes are interesting in that they show that the great Southwest has awakened to the fact that the tenancy laws are outmoded and need a general overhauling. The Southeastern states would do well to follow in their neighbors' footsteps and show some interest in the establishment of a better and more truly progressive set of laws concerning farm tenancy. In fact a study of the Kentucky tenancy laws has been made with a view to liberalization and modernization. Other Southeastern states have also shown indications of an interest in the matter. The Alabama statute[15] abolishing the distinction between the tenant and the cropper is an example of this trend.

In the middle 'thirties the plight of the tenant farmer became a subject of national concern. The country was in the throes of an economic depression. President Roosevelt appointed a committee to make a report on the farm tenancy situation with a view to the betterment of conditions on rented lands all over the nation. The report

13. Okla. Laws 1939, c. 53.
14. Okla. Laws 1939, c. 35, Art. 8, §2.
15. Ala. Code (1940) tit. 31, §63.

showed that tenants were having great difficulty in advancing along the road to land ownership. Many tenants and croppers, particularly in the South, were living under conditions which were far below standards of health and efficiency set up by the medical profession. In this report it was clearly shown that the tenancy laws were inadequate and needed a general overhauling. The application of the laws to both urban and agricultural tenancies was to be deprecated in certain particular instances. A greater security of tenure for the tenant population was needed. Both the landlord and the tenant should be encouraged to improve the farms. It was pointed out that there was little incentive under the present system of laws for a tenant to make improvements of a permanent nature. The insecurity of his tenure under the prevailing one-year oral lease was such that he could not be assured of reaping any substantial advantage from his efforts, and the law with respect to improvements would not allow him to remove or be compensated for the unexhausted value of any substantial improvements he might make. This led to an exploitative attitude on the part of the tenant which is very bad for the land. Since he is not assured of a further term, he will not undertake soil-building processes, construct pens for livestock, or make other improvements of a similar nature. It is true, however, that the more ambitious and expensive projects like the construction of buildings, permanent fencing, or irrigation works, should not be undertaken without the landlord's consent.

As has been seen in the study of the Louisiana law,[16] the Civil Law differed from the common law in respect to allowing compensation for improvements. In adopting the principle of compensation, the legislatures would only be approving what has been in effect under that continental system for a long while.

The English Agricultural Holdings Act of 1923[17] classified the types of improvements. It made three classifications, one requiring the consent of the landlord before the improvement might be made, another requiring notice but not consent, and a third requiring neither notice nor consent. However, it is best to accept the view of an Illinois Commission[18] in making only two classifications, the

16. See Chap. 12, Note 12.

17. 13 & 14 Geo. V, c. 9. For a more detailed description of this legislation, see Farm Tenancy Report, 72-75; A. H. Cotton, *Regulations of Farm Landlord-Tenant Relationships*, 4 Law & Contemporary Problems 524-527 (1937).

18. Hannah and Ackerman, *Legal Aspects of Farm Tenancy in Illinois*, 268 (1940).

first two mentioned above, since it should not be too burdensome to require at least a notice to the landlord of any projected improvement, no matter how insignificant it might be. This would not include minor repairs, which could be undertaken without any notice whatsoever. Of course, any repairs of an extensive nature should be brought to the attention of the landlord, particularly if caused by unforeseeable accidents or contingencies. It seems better to make the tenant responsible only for such ordinary repairs as would be necessary to prevent waste or deterioration, and it is probable that an implied covenant to make such repairs is rooted in the law of most of the Southeastern states. Georgia is of course an exception because of her statute shifting the burden of repairs to the landlord. More extensive repairs should be apportioned according to the interests of the parties. Length of the term would probably be the most important factor in determining the interest of the lessee, although certain other factors, such as fluctuations in the value of farm property, would no doubt have an effect.

In the Kentucky report[19] the view was adopted that any compensation for improvements should be offset by provisions of a more modern character with respect to waste. It was suggested that courts hesitated to invoke the treble-damage feature of the statute in force in Kentucky and several other Southeastern states and would only enforce it where the acts complained of were malicious. Thus it is urged that this feature inherited from the early English law should be dropped and the new set-off principle adopted. This set-off of waste against improvements might benefit the landlord more than the treble damage provision, since a great many tenants own very little property from which judgments against them could be satisfied.

The Oklahoma report[20] advocated a law which would restrict the value of the improvements for which a tenant might claim compensation to a stated percentage of the rents paid during the tenancy. It suggested that the best criterion of valuation for an improvement is its value to the incoming tenant. While this would be a good general rule, it might not give a just result in instances where the incoming tenant planned a change in the type of farming or was pre-

19. *Legal Aspects of Farm Tenancy in Kentucky,* H. A. Hockley and W. D. Nicholls (1941).
20. *Legal Aspects of Landlord-Tenant Relationships in Oklahoma,* W. J. Coleman and H. A. Hockley (1940).

paring to raise a different type of crop. As a complement to this, the measure of waste or deterioration should be the decrease in the value of the farm to the incoming tenant.

The privilege of removing improvements in the form of fixtures should be limited, as is done in Illinois,[21] by making it subject to the landlord's claim for rent. Furthermore, any revision of the tenancy laws should make it clear that no remnants remain of the early English doctrine[22] that the right to remove trade fixtures does not apply to agricultural tenants. The English themselves repudiated this doctrine by statute[23] in 1851, and there is no doubt that this discrimination against the farm tenant has no basis in reason.[24]

There is an implied covenant in every farm lease that the tenant will cultivate the land in accordance with the rules of good husbandry prevailing in the neighborhood where the farm lies. This is useful in making the tenant cultivate the land in such a manner as not to injure the reversionary interest. But this covenant and the doctrine of waste are not sufficient to protect the landlord fully, and the compensation for deterioration outlined above is necessary to give him full relief against a tenant who does not have the wherewithall to settle a judgment for damages.

The landlord's lien has been criticized because it interferes with the tenant in his efforts to obtain production credit. But some special remedy is necessary for the protection of the landlord where a tenant is unreliable. A failure to pay the rent and the conversion of the crop may be very disastrous to some project which the landlord had planned. A good substitute for the landlord's lien has yet to be devised. Of course the landlord can sometimes be persuaded to waive his lien, but there is no assurance of this and no way of compelling him to do so. The lien should certainly be limited in such a manner that it has no application to property of the tenant other than the crops produced on the rented premises. The general lien, as it is known in Georgia and Kentucky at the present time, would seem to be a little harsh. Furthermore, it might be well to adopt legislation like the above-mentioned Texas and North Carolina statutes, which seek to prevent the landlords from making excessive

21. Hannah and Ackerman, *Legal Aspects of Farm Tenancy in Illinois*, 251 (1940).
22. Elwes v. Maw, 3 East 38 (1802).
23. 14 & 15 Vict., c. 25.
24. A. H. Cotton, *Regulations of Farm Landlord-Tenant Relationships*, 4 Law & Cont. Prob. 517-520 (1937).

charges for rent and advances. There are landlords who abuse their economic advantage and charge excessive rates and prices. In the case of the cash renter, moreover, the landlord's lien during certain emergencies might be limited to a lesser sum than that called for by the rental contract. A sliding scale might be adopted for rent payments under the leasing agreement. Such a plan would take care of a sudden drop in the prices of farm products. In fact a recommendation of this sort was made by President Roosevelt's Committee on Farm Tenancy.[25]

Some measure should be found for setting up an arbitration procedure, either under present general arbitration statutes or according to laws especially designed with a view to landlord-tenant disputes. In Scotland a special Land Court has been set up to handle tenancy matters. It is hardly necessary or constitutionally possible to establish special courts in the Southeastern states, but the setting up of some sort of permissive arbitration machinery would certainly be of great value in the settlement of landlord-tenant disputes. It is evident that compulsory arbitration legislation would not be constitutional under the decisions of the courts relating to the matter.[26] Arbitration would no doubt be an excellent way to handle the complicated estimates of value involved in the above proposals for giving compensation for improvements and deterioration. Provisions providing for such arbitration might very well be placed in lease contracts.

One of the chief difficulties and thorniest problems of the farm tenancy system is the great lack of security of tenure. Out of this insecurity comes a very large number of the ills which have contributed to the instability of the agricultural economy. The tenants on the Southeastern farms are very mobile, moving about from farm to farm and often staying only a year or two at any one place. This mobility allows the tenants no opportunity to form normal social and vocational contacts. Some of the families move every year, and the cost of this in money, equipment, and nervous energy must be terrific. Moving time comes right in the middle of the school year, and the children cannot possibly be expected to thrive, educationally speaking, under such circumstances. Business, social, and religious contacts also suffer, for these are things which require time

25. Farm Tenancy Report p. 18 (1937).
26. A. H. Cotton, *Regulations of Farm Landlord-Tenant Relationships,* 4 Law & Cont. Prob. 536 (1937).

to establish and cement. Often new people in a community are let alone because it is felt that they are only temporary residents. Some grievance may be fancied by the landlord or the tenant. Sometimes a tenant will accuse the landlord of being usurious or the landlord will swear that his tenant is the most shiftless fellow who ever worked on his place. Yet it all may be due to a misunderstanding which has come about as a result of uncertainty concerning an oral tenancy contract.

It is not believed, however, that the written lease is the panacea which some people believe it to be. There are many written contracts which are controversial and concerning which judges, lawyers, and arbitrators may disagree and contend with one another. Yet there is no doubt that a written lease is more certain than an oral one and is far more presentable from the standpoint of the rules of evidence. A few practical agriculturists would advocate the extension of the Statute of Frauds to include yearly tenancies within the type of oral contracts which it invalidates. One reason for this is that there are still plenty of illiterate tenants, especially in the Southeastern states, who would be put at a disadvantage by a change in the law which would compel a dependence upon others. An illiterate tenant could never be sure what kind of a contract he had entered into or just what sort of provisions the agreement contained. But the main reason why this extension of the statute is opposed is that there would be many persons who would not heed the law. They would make oral contracts anyway, whether by desire or ignorance, and there would then be many farmers holding land under void contracts, a result distinctly not to be desired.[27] Because of the high percentage of such oral tenancies which have been declared void under the statutes and yet exist as *de facto* relationships, the courts in the several states have dubbed the occupants tenants from year to year.[28] It has been suggested that a statute be enacted which would provide that, in the absence of a written contract, a certain form of lease with detailed provisions outlined in the statute would be presumed.[29] This lease form, however, would

27. A. H. Cotton, *Regulations of Farm Landlord-Tenant Relationships,* 4 Law & Cont. Prob. 528 (1937).

28. Hannah and Ackerman, *Legal Aspects of Farm Tenancy in Illinois,* 265 (1940).

29. W. J. Coleman and H. A. Hockley, *Legal Aspects of Landlord-Tenant Relationships in Oklahoma,* 16 (1940).

often make the parties subject to provisions very different from those agreed upon orally.

An educational program is needed to convince agricultural land-lords and tenants that it is much better to have their agreements in black and white. The introduction of model leases in writing would tend to bring them to the notice of the public and make their adoption less subject to opposition. In refusing to advocate a statute requiring all farm leases to be in writing it must be realized that one of the measures urged by President Roosevelt's Committee on Farm Tenancy is being opposed. In principle, of course, this reform is all right, but it is believed that as a practical matter it is as yet far too revolutionary. If such a reform is adopted, the consequences of ignoring its mandate should be outlined in the statute.[30]

With respect to that common type of farm tenancy, the tenancy from year to year, a return to the six-months notice for termination recognized by the common law is advocated. Pressure from urban dwellers has shortened this period of notice in several of the South-eastern states.[31] This is one of the situations in which it would be better to give different treatment to urban and farm tenants. Renters of farms should know at least six months in advance whether they will be permitted to remain on the leased premises another year.[32] It might be well to adopt a statute like the one enacted in Iowa[33] which provides that an agricultural lease continues from year to year unless either party gives notice as of a certain time before the end of the lease year. That statute requires a four-months notice, but this could be changed to six or any other period desired. It is thought to be much better to treat agricultural tenants who hold over as tenants from year to year rather than as tenants at will.[34] In fact the Kentucky and Oklahoma studies indicate that sentiment is growing for the abolishment of tenancies at will in agrictultural relationships of this sort.[35] In two Southeastern states, North Caro-

30. A. H. Cotton, *Regulations of Landlord-Tenant Relationships*, 4 Law & Cont. Prob. 528 (1937).

31. See Chap. 6, Notes 18-22.

32. A. H. Cotton, *Regulations of Landlord-Tenant Relationships*, 4 Law & Cont. Prob. 532-533 (1937); H. A. Hockley and W. D. Nicholls, *Legal Aspects of Farm Tenancy in Kentucky*, 257 (1941).

33. Iowa Laws 1939, c. 235.

34. W. J. Coleman and H. A. Hockley, *Legal Aspects of Landlord-Tenant Relationships in Oklahoma*, 17 (1940).

35. H. A. Hockley and W. D. Nicholls, *Legal Aspects of Farm Tenancy in Kentucky*, 257 (1941); W. J. Coleman and H. A. Hockley, *Legal Aspects of Landlord-Tenant Relationships in Oklahoma*, 17 (1940).

lina[36] and Virginia,[37] the courts have used language in respect to tenancies of uncertain duration which would seem to favor tenancies from year to year rather than tenancies at will. Hence, under this view, the tenant who holds over without objection after a one-year term has expired should become a tenant from year to year until he is ousted by the giving of the statutory notice. This would no doubt make the tenant more secure and give him a more stable status. A seeming reversal of this policy is seen in a recent South Carolina statute which abolishes tenancies from year to year.[37-a]

Long-term leases have been urged by some as a means of giving the tenant more security. However, many landlords and tenants object to such arrangements because they do not want to be tied to one another for a long term of years. The landlords are afraid that the tenants will spend the first years of the term in building up the land and then work it very hard during the later years in order to realize the greatest possible return before the termination of the lease contract. Such exploitative conduct would be likely to leave the land in far worse shape than it had been in at the beginning of the term.[38] Short-term leases with renewal clauses might answer some of these objections. In fact it has been suggested that all agricultural tenancies should be automatically renewable unless the statutory notice is given.[39] This would merely put all such tenancies in the same category as tenancies from year to year and would not greatly change the law from the way it is at present.

The proposal of President Roosevelt's Committee on Farm Tenancy that, after the first year of occupancy, payment shall be made for inconvenience or loss occasioned because of the termination of an agricultural lease without due cause[40] seems a bit drastic. Neither party would then be permitted to terminate the tenancy without making himself liable for damages, even if the notice were given. At least this is the meaning of the proposal as one commentator[41] interprets it. The constitutionality of this extremely radical proposal

36. Stedman v. McIntosh, 26 N. C. 291 (1844).
37. Elliott v. Birrell, 127 Va. 166, 102 S. E. 762 (1920).
37-a. S. C. Stat. 1946, No. 873, §13.
38. W. J. Coleman and H. A. Hockley, *Legal Aspects of Landlord-Tenant Relationships in Oklahoma*, 17-18 (1940).
39. W. J. Coleman and H. A. Hockley, *Legal Aspects of Landlord-Tenant Relationships in Oklahoma*, 18 (1940).
40. Farm Tenancy Report 18 (1937).
41. A. H. Cotton, *Regulations of Farm Landlord-Tenant Relationships*, 4 Law & Cont. Prob. 533 (1937).

can well be doubted, but a statute of this type might be sustained under the state's power to regulate the forms of land tenure.

The right of a state to regulate the duration of agricultural leases has been recognized in cases from various state tribunals,[42] and the Maryland court has approved a statute allowing tenants to redeem lands under leases exceeding fifteen years by making cash payments to the landlord.[43] Yet, since these decisions are not strictly in point and there is no adjudication by the Federal Supreme Court which approves such regulation by a state of the nation's basic resource, it is doubtful whether the above proposal would be held to be a valid exercise of the police power.

The President's Committee made a recommendation that certain housing standards should be put into effect.[44] If such a law should meet the approval of the legislators in any of the Southeastern states, the standards set would have to be extremely low, such as requirements for a water-tight roof, window panes, and chimneys. Minimum health regulations should require a sanitary toilet and an unpolluted water supply.

It is not believed that the proposal of the President's Committee concerning the differential taxation of farm lands and the exemption of small rural homesteads from taxation[45] would be of any great aid in inducing and helping tenants to become farm owners. Some states have adopted the exemption provision, and it has not had a particularly great effect in increasing home ownership. There are so many stronger forces pulling the tenant toward that goal, such as ambition and the desire for a piece of ground that he may call his very own, that this added incentive would have little if any effect.

Farmers' co-operatives should be encouraged and tenants urged to join them. Under the usual co-operative marketing agreement the producer agrees to deliver to the association all crops produced by him or for him on his farm. It has been held that such an agreement does not include and is not applicable to the share of the landowner's tenant[46] or cropper.[47] This is true notwithstanding a

42. Robertson v. Hayes, 83 Ala. 290, 2 So. 674 (1888); Lerch v. Missoula Co., 45 Mont. 314, 123 Pac. 25 (1912) Stephens v. Reynolds, 6 N. Y. 454 (1852).

43. Marburg v. Mercantile Building Co., 154 Md. 438, 140 Atl. 836 (1928); Stewart v. Gorter, 70 Md. 242, 16 Atl. 644 (1889).

44. Farm Tenancy Report 18 (1937).

45. Farm Tenancy Report 18 (1937).

46. Louisiana Farm Bureau Cotton Growers' Cooperative Ass'n v. Clark,

statute which vests possession of the crop in the hands of the land-lord until the rent and advances are paid.[48]

A Louisiana statute provided that products raised on the land of a member of a co-operative association would be conclusively presumed to belong to the landowner. Thus any crop produced on the land would be subject to a marketing agreement between the association and the landowner. In respect to crops raised by a tenant this provision[49] was held to be unconstitutional, in that it violated both the due process and equal protection guarantees of the Four-teenth Amendment and unduly invaded the right to contract. It was said that this legislation was not a legitimate exercise of the police power for the protection of the general welfare.[50] Thus a co-opera-tive association, to be assured of complete success, must obtain the membership of tenants as well as of landlords and small owners.

A few other minor reforms may be mentioned here. It has been suggested that a statute might be enacted requiring accounts to be kept of expenditures and other things pertaining to proper man-agement of the farming enterprise.[51] This practice would be very useful in any state which had adopted the above proposals concern-ing the set-off of waste and deterioration against improvements.

Some means should be found to safeguard the civil liberties of tenants, croppers, and farm laborers, especially the rights of peace-ful assembly and collective bargaining. Various episodes of violence in Arkansas and elsewhere have indicated a need for protection. Proper curbs should also be placed on vandalism among the irre-sponsible members of the tenant group and other similar practices detrimental to society as a whole.

Provision should also be made to encourage and finance research projects concerning the legal, social, economic, and technical phases of the entire problem of farm tenancy.

During the depression of the 'thirties the plight of the nation's

---

160 La. 294, 107 So. 115 (1926); Staple Cotton Cooperative Ass'n v. Hemphill, 142 Miss. 298, 107 So. 24 (1926); Tobacco Growers' Cooperative Ass'n v. Bissett, 187 N. C. 180, 121 S. E. 446 (1924).

47. Louisiana Cooperative Ass'n v. Banister, 2 La. App. 620 (1925).

48. Tobacco Growers' Cooperative Ass'n v. Bissett, 187 N. C. 180, 121 S. E. 446 (1924).

49. La. Acts 1922, No. 57, §17c.

50. Louisiana Farm Bureau Cotton Growers' Cooperative Ass'n v. Clark, 160 La. 294, 107 So. 115 (1926).

51. A. H. Cotton, *Regulations of Farm Landlord-Tenant Relationships*, 4 Law & Cont. Prob. 532 (1937); Farm Tenancy Report 18 (1937).

farmers, aggravated by drought and floods in some sections, became very serious indeed. Farm prices sank very low, and mortgages were being foreclosed on lands which were the means of livelihood for thousands of people in the rural districts.

The situation became so grave that Congress and President Roosevelt were forced to give the matter much attention. The first methods tried, the AAA with its attendant legislation such as the Bankhead Cotton Control Act, the moratorium on mortgages, and the various relief projects, under such agencies as the Civilian Conservation Corps, Federal Emergency Relief Administration, Civil Works Administration, and Public Works Administration, had no features which were pointed particularly toward the tenancy aspects of the farm problem. Nevertheless it is true that many tenants were helped through the use of funds provided by these relief agencies. But many tenants abandoned their farms and moved into the towns and cities in the hope that they might find better conditions there. Usually they found that they had not bettered themselves, and some returned to the rural areas from whence they had come.

The existing farm credit agencies, both federal and state, could not greatly help the tenant and laborer groups because these people did not usually possess adequate security according to the laws under which these institutions had been established.

Some tenants were claiming that they were not receiving their just share of the benefit payments under the AAA's crop reduction program, and many of them were being discharged and left homeless and without employment. In one Louisiana case[52] the court acceded to the proposition that, in the absence of special agreement, the tenant was entitled to a just credit for the crop reduction benefits paid by the government. To take care of this matter of fair distribution, clauses were written into the government's contracts with the landowners to assure the tenants a proper share of the payments. Under these agreements the tenants were permitted to remain on the land as long as they behaved themselves and were given certain other privileges such as wood for fuel and a plot of land for a garden.[53]

In one Arkansas case[54] a landlord under the contract with his tenant was entitled to have 35 bales of cotton delivered to him without being made responsible for the processing tax levied under the

52. Young v. Geter, 174 So. 661 (La. App., 1937).
53. C. D. Downing, *The AAA Redistributing Production*, 15-16.
54. Kinney v. Smart, 193 Ark. 1057, 104 S. W. (2d) 469 (1937).

provisions of the Bankhead Cotton Control Act.[55] The court declared that the agreement made the tenant a "standing rent tenant" and not a "managing share tenant" within the meaning of the instructions and regulations authorized by the administrative agencies set up under the act. The landowner received the tax exemption certificates and delivered as many of them to the ginner as was necessary to obtain a free ginning of the 35 bales, giving the remaining certificates to the tenant's attorney. Since the contract clearly provided that the tenant was responsible for the processing tax on the cotton, the landlord was held to be justified in so applying the certificates.

The difficulty about benefit payments was one of the grievances that led to the formation of the Southern Tenant Farmers' Union, the promoters claiming that the landowners, in spite of the contracts, were not giving the tenants a just share of the benefits, and that the contract provisions were drawn with a view to giving the landlords too much discretionary power.[56]

With a view to the betterment of conditions in agriculture, the Resettlement Administration was established with its program of relief for groups of farmers with low incomes, some so low that living standards had fallen below a proper subsistence level. The program of this agency was two-fold: Loans were made available at low interest rates for subsistence and for capital goods with which the farmers might build up their shattered economy. The other part of the plan was long-ranged in scope and involved readjustments in land use, the employment of farms of a more suitable size, progressive farming methods, the encouragement of co-operatives, soil conservation and reforestation, the retirement of land submarginal for crops, and the resettlement of displaced farmers on land fertile enough to provide a comfortable living. The rehabilitation aspect of this program had as its object the giving of effective assistance to those members of the farming community who, because of the lack of sufficient security, were not able to obtain credit from the established governmental agencies such as the Farm Credit Administration.[57]

After a thorough study of the farm tenancy problem, President

55. U. S. Stat. at Large, Vol. 48, c. 157, p. 598 (1934).
56. Howard Kester, *Revolt Among the Sharecroppers*, 29-30 (1936).
57. A good account of the Resettlement Administration and its work is available. Clarence A. Wiley, *Settlement and Unsettlement in the Resettlement Administration Program*, 4 Law & Cont. Prob. 456 (1937).

Roosevelt's committee made its report early in 1937 to the members of a new Congress who had made promises to do something about tenancy. There had been much agitation during the past few years favoring a program which would encourage tenants and other farm personnel to become owners of farm land in their own right. It seemed to be the consensus of opinion that the general agricultural situation would be aided by an increase in the numbers of farmers who owned their own small or medium-sized tracts. Of course the idea behind this program was that an owner of a farm will usually take better care of it than a mere renter. Senator John Bankhead of Alabama and Congressman Marvin Jones of Texas had been the leaders of a movement during the past few years to obtain the enactment of legislation which would make it possible for tenants to obtain credit at low interest rates and give them a better opportunity to climb the rungs of the agricultural ladder. Their efforts had come to nothing because the various supporters of such legislation could not agree upon the administrative organ or the method by which the program would be financed. The Department of Agriculture opposed any effort to set up an independent agency to run the program, and there were some who did not wish the Department to have full control. The President's committee had favored a program of purchase of land by the Government and the disposal of this land to farmers under long-term contracts of sale at liberal terms after a trial leasing arrangement. The interest rates on loans were to be low, and the terms of repayment very liberal, with provision for variable payments so as to avoid the difficulties of a financial nature that may sometimes arise, such as those caused by an unusual natural catastrophe or a depression in the prices of farm products. This plan was opposed by some on the ground that it would put the government in the land business.

As an alternative, a program of mortgage loans at low interest rates was proposed by Representative Jones and his supporters. This group was also in favor of taking the control of the program out of the hands of the Department of Agriculture and creating a new agency of an independent nature to be called the Farmers' Home Corporation. This plan was supported by the House Committee on Agriculture, whereas the proposals of the President's Committee had the backing of Senator Bankhead and a majority of the Upper House.[58] The bill which finally passed both houses and

58. A good description of the provisions in the various bills and of the

was enacted into law was quite evidently a compromise measure. It left the control of the program in the hands of the Secretary of Agriculture, setting up a Farmers' Home Corporation within the framework of the Department to implement the authorized mortgage and rehabilitation loan projects. It adopted the long-term mortgage loan procedure rather than the committee-recommended plan for purchase and resale. But the act must be described more thoroughly.

The statute[59] was known as the Bankhead-Jones Farm Tenant Act and recited three principal objectives: (1) To encourage farm home ownership by providing funds through a program of long-term mortgage loans. (2) To rehabilitate certain persons not eligible or fortunate enough to be qualified for such mortgage loans through a system of short-term loans for supplies, livestock, and/or machinery and equipment. (3) To retire lands submarginal for agricultural uses with a view to putting through a program of reforestation and land conservation and utilization. Provision was also made for administrative agencies and machinery necessary for carrying out the purposes outlined.

The rehabilitation and submarginal land purchase schemes had been put into effect at an earlier date under the Emergency Relief Acts, and the Bankhead-Jones Act merely gave these programs independent legislative authorization. Therefore the only really new feature was the provision for the low-interest mortgage loans. The Act was implemented by an appropriation of $10,000,000.00 for the first year, $25,000,000.00 for the second, and $50,000,000.00 a year thereafter. The statute provided that the appropriations must be distributed equitably "among the several States and Territories on the basis of farm population and the prevalence of tenancy, as determined by the Secretary," who must administer the program with the aid of county committees under a procedure outlined by the act itself.

The funds thus obtained from these loans were to be secured by a first mortgage or deed of trust on the farm desired by the applicant, the sum borrowed to be repaid according to an amortization schedule announced by the Secretary. The rate of interest was set at three per cent, and it was provided that the period for repayment

---

jockeying which took place is contained in an article by J. G. Maddox, *The Bankhead-Jones Farm Tenant Act*, 4 Law & Cont. Prob. 434, 451-454 (1937).

59. U. S. Stat. at Large, Vol. 50, c. 517, p. 522 (1937).

must not exceed forty years. The borrower had to pay taxes and carry insurance. The statute directed the Secretary to require whatever covenants were necessary to prevent waste. Upon the borrower's failure to carry out the terms of the contract, the Secretary could declare the whole unpaid balance of the indebtedness to be immediately due and payable. He might do the same thing if the borrower should sell, assign, or otherwise transfer any interest in the farm without obtaining the consent of his authorized agents. Another clause provided that without the consent of the Secretary, no final payment should "be accepted, or release of the Secretary's interest be made, less than five years after the making of the loan."

The purpose of these consent provisions was evidently the prevention of land speculation with the government funds provided under this program. As pointed out by one commentator,[60] a program of government purchase and resale would be far less conducive to land speculation than the program of mortgage loans adopted in this legislation. One reason for this preference is the probability that land values will tend to rise less when the government is the only new purchaser in the market than they will when several individuals are trying to obtain good land in the same neighborhood, often bidding against one another for the same plot. Furthermore, under the mortgage program a speculator who thinks real estate values will rise may obtain land with the idea of selling it at the end of five years at a profit, since after that period of time he is permitted to sell to anyone without the Secretary's consent. Such a person should not have too much trouble in obtaining a loan from some private mortgage agency to settle the debt to the government in full. Hence it is seen that the safeguards against speculation contained in the act are inadequate and clearly will not prevent or decrease this evil. Under a purchase and resale scheme, however, the contracts could be written to provide that the title should not pass to the purchaser until he had a substantial equity of a stated amount in the property. A person who wished to buy the land from the first holder could not then obtain a marketable title to the property until that condition had been met. Thus speculative buying at government risk would be discouraged. For this reason the President's Committee had recommended a program of purchase and resale after a trial lease period of not more than five years, to be terminable when the

60. J. G. Maddox, *The Bankhead-Jones Farm Tenant Act,* 4 Law & Cont. Prob. 434, 451-454 (1937).

farmer had demonstrated his worth and capacity.[61] In fact the Committee had declared that final payment should not be allowed until the stated period for payment of the indebtedness had elapsed. The farmer would be permitted to dispose of his equity provided the administrative agency was given an option to purchase the property and the right to approve the buyer.[62] The option on the farmer's equity ought to be at a figure equal to the "current appraised value," the government "sharing with him pro rata, according to the amount of debt remaining unpaid, any increase or decrease in value not attributable to wastage or improvements for which the holder is responsible." [63]

Furthermore, it may be said that the government could better supervise a program of purchase and resale after a trial lease, since a test could be made of the farmer's ability to conduct an agricultural project and he might be taught better methods of farm husbandry, thus allowing the beneficiaries to be drawn from the more needy families of the community. The mortgage loan program could not be said to offer as much opportunity for supervision as the committee-sponsored plan of purchase and resale.[64] After all, it was these needy rural families that the statute was intended to assist, and the average Southern farmer of the tenant class is certainly badly in need of supervision and help.

The purchase and resale plan is also better than the mortgage program in that it would allow the purchase and subdivision of large tracts of land and the development of large irrigation, drainage, or levee projects, whose cost would be prohibitive if undertaken by a few farmers of small means.[65] Furthermore, more efficient management could be obtained if the beneficiaries were concentrated in one locality and were not scattered, as they might be under the mortgage plan.[66]

In any future program of this kind it might be well to authorize both plans, as there are doubtless some persons for whom the mort-

61. Farm Tenancy Report 12 (1937).

62. J. G. Maddox, *The Bankhead-Jones Farm Tenant Act*, 4 Law & Cont. Prob. 434, 453 (1937).

63. Farm Tenancy Report 12 (1937).

64. J. G. Maddox, *The Bankhead-Jones Farm Tenant Act*, 4 Law & Cont. Prob. 453-454 (1937).

65. J. G. Maddox, *The Bankhead-Jones Farm Tenant Act*, 4 Law & Cont. Prob. 454 (1937).

66. J. G. Maddox, *The Bankhead-Jones Farm Tenant Act*, 4 Law & Cont. Prob. 455 (1937).

gage loan program is better suited. The advent of World War II and the consequent scarcity of farm labor has, of course, prevented the program under the Bankhead-Jones Act from being thoroughly tested. However, recurrence of the problems arising out of the much-criticized tenancy system may be expected as soon as the labor market is glutted with men wanting jobs. Of course laborers are still in demand on farms as well as elsewhere, but an unfavorable turn in economic conditions could change this situation almost overnight. When jobs are fewer in the cities and the small industrial communities, many persons who have had farm experience will want to return to the rural life. These people will create great problems of social adjustment that will try the patience and inventiveness of agricultural experts. They must be given an opportunity to earn a decent living and be made secure in a rural economy which will give both the landlord and the tenant a square deal. Laws must be passed to aid the people in reaching that goal.

Index

Date Due

MAY 21 '63			
	PRINTED	IN U. S. A.	